www.routledgesw.com

Melinda Lewis, University of Kansas, Series editor

An authentic breakthrough in social work education …

New Directions in Social Work is an innovative, integrated series of texts, web site, and interactive case studies for generalist courses in the Social Work curriculum at both undergraduate and graduate levels. Instructors will find everything they need to build a comprehensive course that allows students to meet course outcomes and prepare for effective and ethical social work practice. The New Directions series is distinguished by these unique features:

- All texts, interactive cases, and test materials are **linked to the 2022 CSWE Policy and Accreditation Standards (EPAS)**.
- **One Web portal with easy access** for instructors and students from any computer—no codes, no CDs, no restrictions. Go to www.routledgesw.com and discover.
- **The Series is flexible and can be easily adapted for use in online distance-learning courses as well as hybrid/blended and traditional format courses.**
- Each Text and the Web site can be used **individually** or as an **entire Series** to meet the needs of any social work program.

TITLES IN THE SERIES

Human Behavior in the Social Environment: Perspectives on Development and the Life Course, 6th Edition by Anissa Taun Rogers

Social Work and Social Welfare: An Invitation, 6th Edition by Marla Berg-Weger and Vithya Murugan

Social Policy for Effective Practice: A Strengths Approach, 6th Edition by Rosemary K. Chapin and Melinda Lewis

Research for Effective Social Work Practice, 4th Edition by Judy L. Krysik

The Practice of Generalist Social Work, 6th Edition by Sabrina W. Tyuse and Marla Berg-Weger

For more information about this series, please visit: www.routledgesw.com

The thread of solution-focusedness, narrative techniques, and empowering strategies used throughout this textbook for both assessment and intervention across practice with individuals, families, groups, communities, and organizations is a clever teaching and learning framework! Additionally, *The Practice of Generalist Social Work* by Tyuse and Berg-Weger is a superb resource for integrative learning, assisting students in connecting the five main areas of social work education and practice with ease (i.e. practice, research, policy, diversity, and HBSE).

Dr Raquel Warley, *Walden University*

This is an essential tool which unlocks and connects ethics, theory, the CSWE 2022 EPAS, and current research across diverse client systems while preparing students for direct practice and graduate school. This textbook is infused with up to the minute comprehensive theory and interventions through engaging and interactive case studies, which guide the emerging social worker to be prepared for micro, mezzo, and macro level practice from engagement to termination in a seamless manner.

Dr Lara Vanderhoof, *Central Christian College of Kansas*

The Practice of Generalist Social Work

In its new edition, *The Practice of Generalist Social Work* provides in-depth understanding of the knowledge, skills, values, and affective and cognitive processes needed for social work practice in the present moment. Grounded in a strengths-based perspective, chapters in the textbook discuss practice with individuals, families, groups, communities, and organizations and guide students through all phases of the change process with the aid of case studies, examples, and exercises that highlight and provide connections to real-life practice situations. Theoretical frameworks, important value and ethical considerations, and pivotal communication skills are all included in the text's comprehensive coverage of different practice settings with clients and communities.

The sixth edition is now guided by the 2022 Council on Social Work Education Educational Policy and Accreditation Standards (EPAS), with connections to renewed objectives and competencies integrated throughout, and is further updated to reflect and focus on new developments within the discipline. These include anti-racism efforts and movements to address entrenched racial inequities; the practice of cultural humility and cultural responsiveness; and attention to community-based implications of the COVID-19 pandemic. Strengthened and now fully up to date, this edition of *The Practice of Generalist Social Work* provides a sweeping, in-depth, and lively introduction to social work practice for generalist courses, and is supported by a range of fully updated resources for instructors and their students on www.routledgesw.com/.

Sabrina W. Tyuse, PhD, is Associate Professor in Social Work at Saint Louis University. Dr. Tyuse holds social work and sociology degrees at the master's and doctoral levels. Areas of research are voting rights, social welfare policy, and mental illness and the criminal justice system. She serves on the Board of Directors for Influencing Social Policy (ISP), a non-profit organization for social work educators, students, and practitioners with a passion and for policy, and Voting is Social Work (VISW), the National Social Work Voter Mobilization Campaign that works to integrate nonpartisan voter engagement into social work.

Marla Berg-Weger, PhD, LCSW, is Professor Emeritus in the School of Social Work at Saint Louis University, St. Louis, Missouri and Executive Director of the Gateway Geriatric Education Center in the School of Medicine. Dr. Berg-Weger holds social work degrees at the bachelor's, master's, and doctoral levels. Her social work practice experience includes gerontological social work practice, public social welfare services, intimate partner violence services, mental health, and health social work. Her research and writing focus on gerontological social work and social work practice. She is the co-author with Vithya Murugan, PhD, of *Social Work and Social Welfare: An Invitation* (6th edition). With Julie Birkenmaier, she co-authored the textbook, *The Practicum Companion for Social Work: Integrating Class and Field Work* (4th edition). She is Past President of the Association of Gerontology in Social Work and Managing Editor of the *Journal of Gerontological Social Work*, a fellow in the Gerontological Society of America, and Past President of the National Association of Geriatric Education.

NOTE ABOUT THIS EDITION

We would like to welcome the sixth edition publication of *The Practice of Generalist Social Work* with a note about its excellent authors, past and current. Throughout its history, this textbook has been a collaborative endeavor with great and lasting contributions made by Marty Dewees, Julie Birkenmaier, Deborah Adams, Marla Berg-Weger, and now, beginning with the sixth edition, Sabrina W. Tyuse. The sixth edition was written and revised with the full participation of both Sabrina W. Tyuse and Marla Berg-Weger. In reflection of their work together and in anticipation of future editions, a late update was made to the authorship. Sabrina W. Tyuse is now first author and Marla Berg-Weger is second.

The Practice of Generalist Social Work

Sixth Edition

Sabrina W. Tyuse and
Marla Berg-Weger

Designed cover image: Getty Images

Sixth edition published 2023
by Routledge
605 Third Avenue, New York, NY 10158

and by Routledge
4 Park Square, Milton Park, Abingdon, Oxon, OX14 4RN

Routledge is an imprint of the Taylor & Francis Group, an informa business

© 2023 Taylor & Francis

The right of Sabrina W. Tyuse and Marla Berg-Weger to be identified as authors of this work has been asserted in accordance with sections 77 and 78 of the Copyright, Designs and Patents Act 1988.

All rights reserved. No part of this book may be reprinted or reproduced or utilised in any form or by any electronic, mechanical, or other means, now known or hereafter invented, including photocopying and recording, or in any information storage or retrieval system, without permission in writing from the publishers.

Trademark notice: Product or corporate names may be trademarks or registered trademarks and are used only for identification and explanation without intent to infringe.

First edition published by McGraw-Hill College 2005
Fifth edition published by Routledge 2017

ISBN: 978-1-032-29362-2 (hbk)
ISBN: 978-1-032-29361-5 (pbk)
ISBN: 978-1-003-30126-4 (ebk)

DOI: 10.4324/9781003301264

Typeset in ITC Stone Series Std
by Apex CoVantage, LLC

Access the companion website: www.routledgesw.com. Online Resources and Instructor Material for this edition were prepared and assembled by Julie Franks, DSW, LCSW, MTS.

BRIEF CONTENTS

Preface xxiv
Acknowledgments xxxvi

CHAPTER 1   *Understanding Social Work Practice*   1

CHAPTER 2   *Applying Values and Ethics to Practice*   36

CHAPTER 3   *Communication, Interviewing, and Engagement: Relationship Skills for Practice at All Levels*   68

CHAPTER 4   *Social Work Practice With Individuals: Assessment and Planning*   99

CHAPTER 5   *Social Work Practice With Individuals: Intervention, Termination, and Evaluation*   179

CHAPTER 6   *Social Work Practice With Families: Engagement, Assessment, and Planning*   253

CHAPTER 7   *Social Work Practice With Families: Intervention, Termination, and Evaluation*   311

CHAPTER 8   *Social Work Practice With Groups: Engagement, Assessment, and Planning*   362

CHAPTER 9   *Social Work Practice With Groups: Intervention, Termination, and Evaluation*   417

CHAPTER 10   *Social Work Practice With Communities: Engagement, Assessment, and Planning*   465

CHAPTER 11   *Social Work Practice With Communities: Intervention, Termination, and Evaluation*   508

CHAPTER 12   *Social Work Practice With Organizations: Engagement, Assessment, and Planning*   539

CHAPTER 13 *Social Work Practice With Organizations: Intervention, Termination, and Evaluation* 578

References 613

Index 636

DETAILED CONTENTS

Preface   xxiv

Acknowledgments   xxxvi

CHAPTER 1   ***Understanding Social Work Practice   1***
    The Purpose of Social Work   2
    Practicing Social Work   2
    Social Work Roles   4
    Social Work Competencies   5
        Knowledge, Values, Skills, and Cognitive and Affective Processes   6
            Knowledge   6
            Importance of Self-Knowledge   7
            Values   8
            Skills   10
            Cognitive and Affective Processes   11
    Clients and Communities in Social Work Practice   11
        Practice With Individuals, Families, and Groups   12
        Community, Organizational, and Policy Practice   13
    Phases of Competent Social Work Practice   16
        Engagement   16
        Assessment and Planning   16
        Intervention   17
        Termination   18
        Evaluation   18
    Professional Tensions in Social Work   19
        Balancing Work With Individuals, Families, and Groups With Work in the
            Larger Environment   20
            Integrated Social Work Practice   21
        Social Change and Social Control   22
        Change and Acceptance   22
        Experts and Shared Power   23
        Thinking Globally and Practicing Locally   25
    Theoretical Perspectives for Social Work Practice   26
        Ecosystems Perspective   27
        Social Justice Perspective   27
        Strengths Perspective   28
        Narrative Theory   29
        Solution-Focused Approach   29

Quick Guide 1 Summary of Perspectives for Social Work Practice 29
Critical Considerations in Understanding Social Work Practice: The Grand Challenges 30
Grand Challenge: Eliminating Racism 31
Conclusion 32
Main Points 33
Exercises 34

CHAPTER 2 *Applying Values and Ethics to Practice* **36**
A Brief History of Social Work Ethics 38
Professional Codes of Ethics 39
   The NASW Code of Ethics 40
   Global Social Work Statement of Ethical Principles 42
   Limits of Ethical Codes 43
      The Role of Context 43
      Critical Thinking and Professional Judgment 45
      Diversity 47
Ethics and the Law 47
   Parallels Between Ethics and the Law 48
   Conflicts Between Ethics and the Law 48
      Duty to Report: Child Protection 48
      Duty to Report: Adult Protection 50
      Duty to Protect: Threats of Violence 50
   Conflicts in Working With Individuals, Families, Groups, Organizations, and Communities 52
   Collaboration Between Ethics and the Law 52
Identifying and Resolving Ethical Dilemmas 53
   Making a Distinction Between Value Conflicts and Ethical Dilemmas 53
   The Ethical Principles Screen 54
Quick Guide 2 Elements of the Ethical Principles Screen 54
   Other Models for Resolving Ethical Dilemmas 55
   Representative Examples of Practice Dilemmas 56
      Dual Relationships 56
      Responsibility to the Larger Society and Individual Well-Being 59
      Paternalism and Client Self-Determination 60
Critical Considerations About Values and Ethics 61
   Risk Management in a Litigious World 61
   Social, Economic, and Environmental Justice 63
Grand Challenge: Create Social Responses to a Changing Environment 63
Conclusion 64
Main Points 64
Exercises 65

CHAPTER 3 *Communication, Interviewing, and Engagement: Relationship Skills for Practice at All Levels* **68**
Listening to and Engaging With Clients and Community Members 69
Quick Guide 3 Listening to Clients and Community Members 70

Common Factors in Helping Relationships 72
    Warmth 72
    Empathy 72
    Genuineness 74
    Unconditional Positive Regard 74
    Helping Alliance 75
Communication Skills 76
    Talking With Clients and Community Members 76
    Cultural Considerations 78
Interviewing Abilities 79
    Beginning the Interview 80
    Encouraging Responses 80
    Reflection of Feelings 80
    Silence 81
    Paraphrasing 82
    Asking Clarifying Questions 83
    Summarizing 83
    Balancing Open-Ended and Closed-Ended Questions 84
Avoiding Communication Errors 86
    Jargon 86
    Leading Questions 86
    Irrelevant Questions 87
    Excessive Questioning 87
Minimizing Power Imbalances Within the Helping Alliance: Jasmine Johnson 88
Critical Considerations in Engaging and Building Relationships With Clients and Community Members 90
   Confidentiality 91
   Privacy 92
   Ongoing Evaluation 93
Grand Challenge: Close the Health Gap 93
Conclusion 94
Main Points 94
Exercises 95

CHAPTER 4 *Social Work Practice With Individuals: Assessment and Planning* 99
Assessment and Planning in Contemporary Practice 100
Where Does the Client Want to Go? 104
Implications of Theoretical Perspectives 104
   Classic Theories 105
      Psychoanalytic Theory 105
      Attachment Theory 106
      Cognitive Theory 106
Contemporary Theoretical Perspectives 107

Strengths-Based Perspective   107
Quick Guide 4 Examples of Strengths-Based Supportive Questions   108
  Narrative Theory   108
  Solution-Focused Approach   110
Evidence Matters   112
Implications of Diversity and Culture in Assessment   115
  Cultural Competence, Humility, Intersectionality, and Anti-Racist, Anti-Oppressive Practice in Culturally Responsive Assessment   117
  Anti-Racist and Anti-Oppressive Practice Behaviors   120
  Connecting With the Spiritual Aspects of the Client   121
  Global Connections   121
Quick Guide 5 My Cultural Heritage Journey   123
Skills for Assessment and Planning   123
  Strengths-Based Perspective   124
Quick Guide 6 Assessment Questions for Discovering Strengths   125
  Narrative Theory   125
  Solution-Focused Approach   128
  Developing a Shared Vision of Assessment and Planning   130
  Support for the Client's Goals and Dreams   131
    Planning and Setting Goals   132
    Contracting   133
Quick Guide 7 Sample Contract With Jasmine Johnson   134
  Honest Responding   136
    When Confrontation Is Necessary   136
    Aligning Goals With Possibilities   138
  Using Mapping Skills to Enhance the Dialogue   139
    Genograms   139
    Ecomaps   141
Skills for Assessing Resources   142
  Formal and Informal Resources   143
  Assessment When Resources Are Available or Unavailable   143
Critical Considerations About Assessment and Planning: The Agency, the Client, and the Social Worker   144
  The Agency Perspective   144
    Administrative Tasks   145
    Documentation   148
Quick Guide 8 Recommendations for Social Work Documentation   149
  The Client Perspective   151
    Involuntary, Mandated, and Nonvoluntary Clients   151
    Challenges in Working With Involuntary Clients   152
Quick Guide 9 Involuntary Clients   153
    Opportunities in Working With Involuntary Clients   154
    Violence   156
    Workplace Violence in Social Work Practice   156
    Skills for Working With Clients Who Display Anger   157
    What Agencies Can Do   157

Crisis Intervention   157
Suicide   160
The Social Worker Perspective: The Social Worker as a Whole Person   166
Painful Events   166
Personal Triggers   167
Self-Care   168
Sustaining Ethical Practice in the Face of Challenges   171
Grand Challenge: Eliminating Racism   172
Conclusion   173
Main Points   174
Exercises   175

CHAPTER 5   *Social Work Practice With Individuals: Intervention, Termination, and Evaluation*   **179**

Interventions That Support Client Strengths   180
Strengths-Based Perspectives and Interventions   181
Acting in Context   181
Capitalizing on Strengths   183
Narrative Interventions   183
Solution-Focused Interventions   184
Cognitive Behavioral-Focused Interventions   189
Environment-Focused Processes and Skills   191
Cultural Humility and Anti-Oppressive Practice   191
Providing Information   193
Refocusing and Confronting   194
Interpreting Client Behavior   195
Mapping as an Intervention Strategy   196
Social Work Roles in Social Work Practice   196
Case Manager   197
Common Components of Case Management   197
Purposes and Practice of Contemporary Case Management   198
Counselor   199
Broker   200
Brokering Functions and Context   200
Building and Maintaining Networks for Brokering   200
Making the Match in Brokering   201
Mediator   201
Finding Common Ground   201
Walking Through It   202
Educator   203
Developing Client Skills   203
Working With the Community   204
Client Advocate   204
Case Advocacy   205
Cause Advocacy   205
Legislative Advocacy   206

Thoughts About Power and Advocacy 206
Collaborator 207
Putting It All Together 209
Empowerment Practice 209
Empowerment and Roles 212
Empowerment Practice and Different Strategies 213
Quick Guide 10 The Spirit and Principles of Motivational Interviewing 214
Quick Guide 11 Skills and Strategies for Motivational Interviewing 215
Critical Considerations About Social Work Interventions With
Individuals 216
Unexpected Events in Practice 217
Therapeutic Use of Self 218
Managing Transference and Countertransference 219
Professionalism 219
Self-Care 220
Use of Technology 220
Supporting Clients' Strengths in Termination, Evaluation,
and Follow-Up 222
Endings and Termination 222
Planning the Process: Overview of the Termination 223
Negotiating the Timing of the Termination 223
Reviewing the Agreement for Work 225
Processing Successes and Shortcomings 225
Developing and Clarifying Plans for Termination and
Maintenance of Change 226
Sharing Responses to Endings 227
Respecting Cultural Humility 229
Critical Considerations About Termination and Endings 229
Formal Evaluations 231
Evaluation Priorities and Guidelines 231
Quantitative and Empirical Processes: Evidence-Based Practice 232
Single-Subject Design 233
Goal Attainment Scaling 234
Quick Guide 12 Goal Attainment Scaling 236
Other Forms of Evaluation 237
Postmodern Views of Evaluation 237
Qualitative and Reflective Processes 238
Case Studies 238
Quick Guide 13 Guiding Principles for Clinical Writing 239
Quick Guide 14 Creating a Case Summary 240
Explorations of Compatibility With Theoretical Perspectives 243
Explorations of Relationship Quality 244
Critical Considerations on Evaluation and Practice Knowledge 245
Conclusion 247
Main Points 248
Exercises 249

CHAPTER 6   *Social Work Practice With Families: Engagement, Assessment, and Planning*   253

Familiar Perspectives   255
Historical Antecedents for Social Work With Families   258
   The Family as a Functioning Unit   259
   Family as a System   260
      Change in One Component Affects All Other Components   261
      Subsystems and Boundaries   261
      Family Norms   263
Implications of Systems Theory for Generalist Practice With Families   264
      Family Structure   265
      Intergenerational Patterns   265
The Contemporary Context for Social Work With Families   266
   Grandparents Rearing Grandchildren   267
   Lesbian, Gay, Bisexual, Transgender, and Queer Couples and Families   269
      Parenthood   270
   Single-Parent Families   271
   Families of Multiple Racial, Ethnic, and Cultural Heritages   272
   Families That Include Persons With Disabilities   274
   Blended Families   277
   Immigrant and Refugee Families   279
   Summary   282
Contemporary Trends and Skills for Engagement and Assessment With Families   283
   Narrative Theory in Family Engagement and Assessment   283
      Thickening the Story   285
      Externalizing Problems   287
      Unearthing the Broader Context   287
   Solution-Focused Family Work   288
      Assessment Process   289
      Environmental Focus   291
   Constructionist and Social Justice Approaches to Family Social Work   291
      Social Justice Emphasis   292
   Generalist Practice Skills Guidelines for Family Engagement and Assessment   293
      Mapping: A Family Assessment and Planning Tool   295
Quick Guide 15 Family Mapping Options   298
      The Family Interview   298
      Planning   301
Critical Considerations About Social Work Practice With Families   301
   Self-Care   302
   Documentation   302
Quick Guide 16 Documenting a Family Assessment   303
Quick Guide 17 Documenting a Family Intervention Plan   303
Conclusion   304

Grand Challenge: Ensure Healthy Development for All Youth   304
Main Points   306
Exercises   306

CHAPTER 7   *Social Work Practice With Families: Intervention, Termination, and Evaluation*   311

Theoretical Approaches to Intervening With Families   312
- *Strengths and Empowerment Perspectives and Family Interventions*   315
- *Narrative Theory and Family Interventions*   317
- *Solution-Focused Family Interventions*   320

Trends and Skills for Intervening With Families   326
- *Reframing*   332
- *Perspectival Questions*   332
- *Family Group Conferencing*   333
- *Motivational Interviewing*   335
- *Mapping as an Intervention*   337
- *Documentation for Family Interventions*   338

Ending Work With Family Constellations   342
- *Endings With Strength and Empowerment*   344
- *Endings in Narrative-Focused Work*   345
- *Endings in Solution-Focused Work*   345
- *Evaluation of Social Work Practice With Families*   347
- *Strengths- and Resiliency-Based Family Evaluation Measures*   348

Quick Guide 18 Caregiver Well-Being Scale   350
Quick Guide 19 Walsh Family Resilience Questionnaire   351
Quick Guide 20 Strengths-Based Practices Inventory (SBPI)   352
Quick Guide 21 The Three-Item Brief Assessment of Family Functioning Scale (BAFFS)   353
    Practitioner Reflection   354

Critical Considerations About Family Intervention, Termination, Evaluation, and Follow-Up   355

Grand Challenge: Build Healthy Relationships to End Violence   356
Conclusion   357
Main Points   357
Exercises   358

CHAPTER 8   *Social Work Practice With Groups: Engagement, Assessment, and Planning*   362

Groups: The Source of Community   363
- *Implications of Global and Cultural Connections for Social Work Group Practice*   364
- *Group Orientation as a Cultural Dimension*   366
- *Historical and Contemporary Contexts for Group Work*   369

Dimensions of Social Work Practice With Groups   372
- *Types, Forms, and Functions of Groups*   373
  - Task Groups   375

Social Action or Goals Groups   376
Client Groups   376
Roles and Phases of Group Interventions   378
Group Work Logistics   382
Quick Guide 22 The Pros and Cons of Creating a Group: Questions to Consider   383
Theoretical Approaches to Engagement and Assessment With Groups   385
Systemic Perspective   385
Narrative Approach in Group Engagement and Assessment   386
Solution-Focused Approach in Group Engagement and Assessment   387
Contemporary Trends and Skills for the Beginning Phases of Group Work: Engagement and Assessment   388
Pregroup Planning   389
Client Need   391
Purpose   392
Composition, Eligibility, and Appropriateness   392
Structure   393
Content   394
Agency Context   394
Social Context   395
Pregroup Contact   395
Contacting Prospective Group Members   396
Engagement   397
Assessment and Planning   400
Critical Considerations About Group Engagement and Assessment   402
Engagement   402
Assessment and Planning   404
Documentation   409
Quick Guide 23 Social Goals and Task Group Notes Template   410
Quick Guide 24 Task Group Minutes Template   411
Grand Challenge: End Homelessness   411
Conclusion   412
Main Points   412
Exercises   413

CHAPTER 9   *Social Work Practice With Groups: Intervention, Termination, and Evaluation*   **417**
Interface: Social Justice, Diversity, and Human Rights   418
Theoretical Approaches to Intervening With Groups   420
Strengths and Empowerment Perspectives on Group Intervention   420
Narrative Theory and Group Interventions   422
Solution-Focused Group Interventions   423
Developmental Models   424
Boston Model   425

Contemporary Trends and Skills for the Middle Phase of Group Work:
   Intervention   427
  Examples of Social Work Group Interventions   429
    Motivational Interviewing Groups   429
    Intergroup Dialogue (IGD) and Social Justice   430
    Narrative-Focused Practice With Groups   430
  Social Work Skills and Strategies for Group Interventions   431
    Social Worker Roles   432
    Group Dynamics   435
    Leadership Skills   435
    Communication Skills   437
    Problem-Solving Skills   438
  Group Member Roles   441
Quick Guide 25 Group Member Roles and Potential Strategies
   to Address Them   441
Quick Guide 26 Summary of Intervention Skills for Social Work
   Group Practice   443
Contemporary Trends and Skills for the Ending Phases of Group
   Work: Termination and Evaluation   443
  Group Endings   443
    Using the Strengths and Empowerment Approach in Group
      Endings   444
    Narrative-Focused Group Endings   445
    Solution-Focused Group Endings   445
  Skills for Social Work Group Endings   446
    Ending the Relationship Between Group Members and the Social
      Worker   446
    Ending Relationships Among Group Members   448
    Ending the Group Itself   449
  Evaluating Social Work Practice With Groups   451
Quick Guide 27 Group Facilitator Self-Evaluation: Group Member
   Perspectives   453
Critical Considerations About Group Intervention, Termination, and
   Evaluation   458
Grand Challenge: Harness Technology for Social Good   458
Conclusion   459
Main Points   459
Exercises   460

CHAPTER 10   *Social Work Practice With Communities: Engagement,
   Assessment, and Planning   465*
   Community as a Context for Social Work Practice   466
     Community Practice and Generalist Practice   467
     Challenges in Community Engagement   468
   Types of Community   469
     Spatial Communities   469

  Social Communities 470
  Political Communities 471
 Functions of Communities 471
 Understanding Communities 472
  Systems Theory on Community 472
  Ecosystems Perspective on Community 473
  Power and Conflict Within Communities 474
   Theories Regarding Power and Conflict 474
  Strengths, Empowerment, and Resilience in Communities 476
 Engaging Communities 477
 Assessing Communities 478
  Community Needs Assessment 479
   Using Evidence-Based Practice in Community Social Work 479
   Community Needs Assessment Process 480
  Sources of Data for Community Needs Assessments 481
   Observation 481
   Previous Studies and Service Statistics 481
   Census Data 482
   Administrative Data 482
   Interviews With Key Informants 482
 Quick Guide 28 Guide to Key Informant Interviews 484
   Focus Groups 485
 Quick Guide 29 Guide to Focus Groups 485
   Community Forums 486
 Quick Guide 30 Guide to Community Forums 487
   Survey Data 489
 Quick Guide 31 Sample Needs Assessment Survey Questions 489
  Comprehensive Community-Based Analysis 491
  Mapped Data, Asset Mapping, and Asset Building in Community
   Practice 494
   Mapped Data 495
   Asset Building 497
 Planning 498
 Contemporary Trends in Community Practice 500
 Critical Considerations in Community Practice 503
 Grand Challenge: Financial Capability and Asset Building for All 505
 Conclusion 505
 Main Points 506
 Exercises 506

CHAPTER 11 *Social Work Practice With Communities: Intervention, Termination, and Evaluation 508*
 Theoretical Traditions and Models for Community Intervention 509
  The Planning/Policy Model 510
  The Community Capacity Development Model 511
  The Social Advocacy Model 512

Quick Guide 32 Activities to Promote Social Change   513
   Applying Community Practice Models to a Case Example   513
Quick Guide 33 Providing Testimony   514
   Blending Models   515
      Blending the Planning/Policy and Community Capacity Development Models   515
      Blending the Social Advocacy and Planning/Policy Models   516
      Blending the Social Advocacy and Community Capacity Development Models   516
Skills for Community Intervention   517
   Community Social and Economic Development   517
      Community Development Skills   518
Quick Guide 34 Elements of Effective Meetings   519
Quick Guide 35 Utilizing Robert's Rules of Order   520
Quick Guide 36 Utilizing Consensus for Decision-Making   521
      Community Development Programs   521
   Asset-Based Community Development   524
   Community Organizing and Related Skills   526
      Community Organizing Skills   528
   A Generalist Approach to Community Intervention   528
Quick Guide 37 Examples of Efforts to Promote Evidence-Based Community Practice   529
Skills for Termination, Evaluation, and Follow-Up in Community Practice   531
   Community Social Work Practice Termination   531
      Termination and Follow-Up in Community Practice   532
   Evaluation of Social Work Practice With Communities   534
Critical Considerations in Community Intervention, Termination, Evaluation, and Follow-Up   535
Grand Challenge: Reduce Extreme Economic Inequality   535
Conclusion   536
Main Points   536
Exercises   537

CHAPTER 12   *Social Work Practice With Organizations: Engagement, Assessment, and Planning*   **539**
   Understanding Organizations   540
      Organizations as Social Systems   540
      Purpose of the Organization   541
         Organizations Sanctioned by Law   542
         Organizations With Service Goals   543
         Organizations Arising From Social Movements   544
      Structures of Governance   545
         Bureaucracies   545
         Project Teams   546

        Functional Structures   547
    Internal Power Relations   547
        Traditional Authority   547
        Charismatic Authority   547
        Rational Authority   548
    Intersections Among Dimensions of Organizations   548
    Social Work Practice in Host Settings   549
        Guest Status   549
        Interprofessional Teams   550
Organizational Engagement, Assessment, and Planning   551
    Engaging the Organization   551
    Assessment of Organizations   552
    Elements of an Internal Assessment   553
        Legal Basis   553
        Mission Statement   553
        Bylaws   554
        History   554
        Administrative Structure and Management Style   554
        Structure of Programs, Services, and Activities   555
        Organizational Culture   555
        Physical Surroundings   557
        Public Relations   557
        Language   557
        Procedures   557
Quick Guide 38 Dignity Assessment and Human Services
        Guide   558
        Social Justice/Diversity Factors   559
        Personnel Policies and Procedures   560
        Resources   560
    Elements of an External Assessment   561
        Relationship With Funders and Potential Funders   561
        Serving Clients and Communities With Limited Resources   561
        Relationships With Organizations in Service Network   562
Quick Guide 39 Guide to Nonprofit Organizational Partnerships   562
        Relationships With Political Figures   564
Quick Guide 40 Nonprofit Organizational Assessment   565
Quick Guide 41 Organizational Policy Advocacy Activities   567
Organizational Engagement, Assessment, and Planning in
        Generalist Practice   569
Skills for Engagement, Assessment, and Planning With
        Organizations   569
Critical Considerations in Practice With Organizations   572
Grand Challenge: Promote Smart Decarceration   573
Conclusion   574

Main Points 574
Exercises 575

CHAPTER 13 *Social Work Practice With Organizations: Intervention, Termination, and Evaluation* 578

Approaches, Perspectives, and Models for Interventions With Organizations 579
- *Self-Learning Approaches to Organizational Change* 580
- *The Systems Model and Organizational Change* 580
- *Perspectives on Power in Organizational Change* 581

Framework for Organizational Change 582
- *Origins of Organizational Change* 583
- *Gathering Allies and Creating a Group to Work on Organizational Change* 584
- *Developing Feasible Solutions for Organizational Change* 585
  - Selecting Feasible Solutions 586
  - Structure of Change Proposals 587
- *Selecting Organizational Change Strategies* 590
  - Collaborative Strategy 590
  - Campaign Strategy 590
  - Conflict Strategy 591
- *Strategies and Skills for Interventions With Organizations* 592
  - Implementation Skills 592
  - Capacity Building 592
  - Education 593
  - Persuasion 593

Quick Guide 42 Persuasion Skills 594
  - Mass Media and Social Media Appeals 595
  - Bargaining and Negotiation 595
  - Group Actions 596
  - Ethics and Change Strategies 596

Implementing Organizational Change 599
- *Implementation Structure* 600
- *Using a Gantt Chart* 601
- *Challenges to Implementation* 602
  - Staff Member Resistance 602
  - Generality of the Change 602
  - Organizational Supports 603

Termination, Evaluation, and Follow-Up in Practice With Organizations 604
- *Evaluation of Social Work Practice With Organizations* 605
  - Types of Evaluation 605
  - Structure of Evaluation 606

Logic Model 606
  Information and Data Sources 607
  Roles in Evaluation 607
Critical Considerations on Organizational Life 608
Conclusion 609
Grand Challenge: Achieve Equal Opportunity and Justice 609
Main Points 610
Exercises 610

References 613

Index 636

PREFACE

MAJOR CHANGES TO THE SIXTH EDITION

Like the previous editions, this new edition of *The Practice of Generalist Social Work* provides detailed coverage of the knowledge, skills, values, and affective and cognitive processes needed for contemporary generalist social work practice. Using a strengths-based perspective, students are given a comprehensive overview of the major areas relevant for social work practice, including theoretical frameworks, values and ethics, expanded coverage of communication skills for all client systems and examples of their use, and extensive coverage of practice with clients and communities through all phases of the change process. *The Practice of Generalist Social Work* offers a comprehensive discussion of practice with individuals, families, groups, communities, and organizations, including the concepts of planned change, encompassing engagement, assessment, intervention, evaluation, termination, and follow-up. Students have the opportunity to learn about generalist practice through in-depth case studies, examples, and exercises integrated throughout the text. This edition provides all the material necessary for a two- or three-course sequence.

This sixth edition is guided by the 2022 EPAS and has been updated to reflect the contemporary world in which social workers practice. Included are examples of the application of theory and knowledge through case studies, highlighting realistic practice situations with individuals, families, groups, communities, and organizations. For example, chapters have case studies, which are used throughout, to refer back to to provide additional connections between content and real-life practice.

Additional values and ethics material and discussions of cultural humility and culturally responsive practice content provides additional guidance for contemporary practice. Each chapter incorporates a link to a Grand Challenge for Social Work, from the American Academy of Social Work & Social Welfare (AASWSW) (2021), which facilitates a connection between the profession and the most significant societal challenges of today. The Quick Guides within the text offer students guidance for their field experience and practice after graduation. New end-of-chapter exercises connect with the wealth of case-based information available at www.routledgesw.com and facilitate a dynamic, experiential introduction to social work for your students. The sixth edition has undergone multiple changes and updates, primarily to reflect the evolving nature of social work practice. A summary of these changes includes:

- The sixth edition includes co-author, Sabrina W. Tyuse, PhD, MSW, MA. Sabrina's experience in voting rights and teaching social policy, and human behavior and the social environment, and sociology courses provide her with expertise and insights to strengthen and enrich the book's content.

- To address the historic changes in the world in which social workers practice since the fifth edition was released, we have revised, added, and updated content in the areas of:
  - Anti-racism—efforts to eliminate racial inequities and creating opportunities for all persons in society (Kendi, 2019).
  - COVID-19 pandemic—the pandemic impacted all of us personally and professionally. We highlight areas in which the pandemic exposed and illuminated inequalities among underserved, vulnerable, and marginalized populations as well as ways in which social workers responded to the needs of clients, patients, organizations, communities, and research interests.
  - Critical Race Theory (CRT)—asserts that racism is a longstanding, dominant, pervasive, and permanent component of social structure. CRT is also a theoretical approach that investigates race and racism by tracing the roots of racism in American society (Bousseau & Martell, 2021).
  - Cultural humility—to evolve beyond cultural competence that involved cultural awareness, knowledge, and skills and to incorporate cultural humility. Cultural humility "ask us to de-center our own knowledge in favour of prioritizing the clients' [lived] experiences and urges ongoing vigilance to power imbalances and the impact of systems on both client and practitioners" (Gottlieb, 2020).
  - Culturally responsive practice—requires social workers to educate themselves about other cultures and then to take that cultural context into account when interacting with and providing services to individuals, families, groups, communities, and organizations.
  - Diversity, equity, inclusion, and belonging (DEIB)—specifically centering DEIB to elevate anti-racist and anti-oppressive practice, including a critical review of our profession's history that perpetuated discrimination and oppression: the contributions of the Black, Indigenous, and Persons of Color (BIPOC) community to the profession; and culturally responsive and anti-racist practice across all areas of the profession. Individuals must also feel that they belong and are an accepted member of society. A key element of becoming culturally competent and practicing through an anti-racist lens that is addressed is the process of unlearning the inaccurate ideas and beliefs and incomplete histories that are commonplace within US society.
  - Language—as language is evolving and we are all learning more daily, we have chosen terms that reflect commitment to respect for inclusivity, gender identity, and non-gendered language. Specific terms used in this text include: (1) Black, Indigenous, and People of Color (BIPOC), (2) Latinx (e.g., Hispanic, Latino/a), (3) LGBTQIA+

(lesbian, gay, bisexual, transgender, queer/questioning, intersexual, asexual+), and non-gendered pronouns (e.g., they/them). Updating language to reflect commitment to and respect for inclusivity, gender identity, and non-gendered identity.
    - LGBTQIA+—persons who are gay, bisexual, transgender, queer, intersex, asexual, and, non-gendered pronouns (e.g., they/them).
    - Microaggressions—commonly occurring, brief, verbal or nonverbal, behavorial, and environmental indignities that communicate derogatory attitudes or notions toward a different "other." Microaggressions may be intentional or unintentional, and perpetrators may possibly be unaware of their behavior (APA, 2017).

- The companion website includes updates of the interactive cases and adds three static cases with accompanying exercises that bring to life the theories and concepts covered in this book, readings, and classroom discussions.

The six interactive cases and the three static cases provide students with peer-reviewed, multidimensional cases that ask students to consider how they would work within individual, family, group, organizational, and community contexts, across all phases of the helping process. The most recent updates incorporate new material on the influence of the pandemic on different client groups, an emphasis on anti-racist and anti-oppressive approaches, and the exercise of critical thinking as a core requirement for social work competency.

The content in this text is supported by a range of fully updated instructor-led and student resources that are available on its companion website, www.routledgesw.com. These include the following resources:

- Updated companion readings that are linked to key concepts in each chapter, along with questions to encourage further thought and discussion.

- Six interactive fictional cases with accompanying exercises that bring to life the concepts covered in the book, readings, and classroom discussions.

- Three static fictional cases with accompanying exercises that bring to life the concepts covered in the book, readings, and classroom discussions.

- A bank of exam questions (both objective and open-ended).

- PowerPoint presentations, which can serve as a starting point for class discussions.

- Sample syllabi demonstrating how the text and website, when used together through the course, satisfy the 2022 EPAS from the Council on Social Work Education (CSWE).

- Quick Guides from the book offered online for students to print and take into the field for guidance.
- Annotated links to websites and other online resources, such as videos and podcasts, articles, and other suggested reading materials.

In sum, this new edition provides expanded resources that contain up-to-date individual, family, group, community, and organizational guidance for the beginning practitioner.

ORGANIZATION OF THE BOOK

The following paragraphs serve to briefly introduce each of the chapters included in this book with emphasis on the updated content. All chapters have updated and specific connections to 2022 CSWE EPAS and expanded end-of-chapter exercises that use online resources.

Chapter 1

Understanding Social Work Practice provides an overview of social work practice by grounding students in the purpose of social work; social work competencies; types of client groups; and the practice framework of engagement, assessment, intervention, termination, and evaluation. A discussion of the ethics that guide social work practice, licensure of social work, client populations and communities that social workers help, and tensions in social work provide students with real-world information about the profession. Students are also introduced to major theoretical perspectives for social work practice, including ecosystems, social justice, and strengths perspectives. The COVID-19 pandemic is added with discussion on the ways in which it impacted us all personally and professionally. Specifically, we highlight areas in which the pandemic exposed and illuminated inequalities among underserved, vulnerable, and marginalized populations. The role COVID-19 has had on social work practice as it relates to social service delivery via technology is also discussed. Finally, in this sixth edition, the newest Grand Challenges for Social Work, Eliminating Racism is introduced and discussed. The case presented in this chapter focuses on social work practice with a survivor of intimate partner violence.

Chapter 2

In contrast to a straightforward overview of values and ethics, **Applying Values and Ethics to Practice** provides a brief history of social work ethics and the National Association of Social Workers (NASW) *Code of Ethics* (2021a), then contrasts the *Code of Ethics* with the International Federation of Social Workers' Ethical Statement, and also discusses the limits of ethical codes. A discussion of the intersection of ethics and the law gives students information about the interplay between the two, followed by a discussion of ethical dilemmas and processes for resolving them. Extensive discussion about common practice dilemmas gives students exposure to situations that they may encounter in practice, followed by an emphasis on risk management. Expanded coverage of ethics violations and state sanctions round out the discussion. Also covered in this chapter is the way in which the pandemic-related social distancing mandates led to incorporating more digital technology-based interventions in educating social work students and service delivery, as well as the usage of social media to disseminate information. The ethical considerations related to confidentiality and ensuring client privacy when incorporating digital technology and telecommunication into social work practice and service delivery is also discussed. Throughout the chapter, a case on social workers who are expanding community-based mental health services is presented.

Chapter 3

Communication, Interviewing, and Engagement: Relationship Skills for Practice at All Levels provides students with the characteristics of core relationship qualities, as well as a description of the specific skills for talking with clients and community members, including coverage of common communication pitfalls. Engagement and relationship-building skills are covered extensively, and the common factors of effective helping approaches are reviewed. Practical questions guide students toward active listening. Students are also provided with strategies and skills for promoting social justice in helping relationships. New content in this edition includes discussion of the COVID-19 pandemic and the technologies social workers were required to use to provide services to clients, especially for low-income and rural clients who lacked broadband and computer access and/or acumen. The updated case that is woven through this chapter involves a young survivor of human trafficking.

Chapter 4

Social Work Practice With Individuals: Assessment and Planning includes an updated focus on the assessment and planning process within the global environment in which practicing social workers live. The chapter begins with a discussion of the history of assessment and moves to an overview of theoretical approaches to social work practice, both classic and contemporary (strengths, narrative, and solution-focused). The application of evidence-based practice approaches is highlighted. The need for practice knowledge and behaviors in the area of diversity within the assessment and planning phases emphasizes the need for cultural humility and competence. The chapter introduces the concepts of compassion satisfaction, intersectionality, and the cultural genogram and includes an exercise to address culture change from the student perspective. New to this chapter is content on diversity, equity, inclusion, and belonging as well as anti-racist/anti-oppressive practice; impact of the pandemic on assessment; and updated content on self-care, secondary/vicarious trauma, and compassion fatigue. The chapter concludes with a discussion of the relevant skills and practice behaviors in the assessment and planning phases of the social work intervention process, including skills needed for strengths-based, narrative, and solution-focused approaches, documentation, and self-care for the social worker. This edition offers content on synthesizing biopsychosocial-spiritual information, expectations for and effective use of supervision, and professionalism in working with clients in crisis. A discussion of the Grand Challenge for Social Work to "Eradicate Social Isolation" is brought to life with an exercise.

Chapter 5

Social Work Practice With Individuals: Intervention, Termination, and Evaluation introduces students to key areas of social work practice that will impact virtually every dimension of their professional lives. With an emphasis on theoretical perspectives, students learn to apply various intervention, termination, evaluation, and follow-up skills and behaviors. Traditional and contemporary social work roles are highlighted and discussed. Documentation and record-keeping for social work interventions is explained with accompanying examples. Interventions with individuals are also framed within an empowerment practice approach. Framed within theoretical perspectives for understanding diversity, students are offered an overview of the skills required to be a culturally responsive social work practitioner. New features in Chapter 5 include additional content on the COVID-19 pandemic, cultural humility and anti-oppressive practice, evaluating treatment outcomes, and use of technology in social work practice. A Grand Challenge for Social Work, to "Advance Long and Productive Lives," is addressed through discussion, reading, and an exercise.

Chapter 6

Social Work Practice With Families: Engagement, Assessment, and Planning begins with a history of social work practice with families, grounded within a systems framework. Theoretical perspectives, including narrative and solution-focused, are discussed within the context of the engagement, assessment, and planning phases of interventions with families, with emphasis on empowerment. Students encounter a broad range of family constellations as they read about contemporary family social work. Practice behaviors and skills are presented for achieving engagement and assessment with families and documentation strategies are included. This newest version of Chapter 6 offers a case integrated throughout the chapter and more examples relating to the engagement, assessment, and planning with families. To "Ensure Healthy Development for All Youth" is the Grand Challenge for Social Work that is the focus in this chapter.

Chapter 7

Social Work Practice With Families: Intervention, Termination, and Evaluation conceptualizes generalist social work practice interventions with families. Continuing with the theoretical perspectives discussed in Chapter 6, this chapter develops interventions with families using strengths and empowerment, narrative, and solution-focused approaches. Skills and behaviors for intervening, terminating, evaluating, following up, and documenting family-focused interventions are discussed in detail. New to this edition is updated family assessment tools, their uses, and administration. Additional examples related to intervention with families, specifically management during meetings, ethical issues, and linking contracting to intervention, are integrated throughout the chapter. The termination and evaluation of family interventions sections are expanded, particularly related to monitoring outcomes. The Grand Challenge for Social Work, "Build Healthy Relationships to End Violence," is the focus of this chapter with a reading and an exercise.

Chapter 8

Social Work Practice With Groups: Engagement, Assessment, and Planning provides students with up-to-date perspectives on social work practice with groups. The chapter opens with an overview of the role of groups within our communities and profession followed by a historical and contemporary perspective on the use of groups for change. The dimensions of group practice are presented within the framework of theoretical perspectives (i.e., narrative and solution-focused). Planning for group interventions, including the engagement and assessment of group members, is emphasized from a practice perspective along with the importance of cultural competence in the group setting. With this edition, Chapter 8 includes expanded content and examples on engagement, assessment, working with diverse populations, technology, ethical issues, documentation, and solution-focused approaches. The number of exhibits has been increased to highlight chapter content. To "End Homelessness" is the Grand Challenge for Social Work that is highlighted in this chapter.

Chapter 9

Social Work Practice With Groups: Intervention, Termination, and Evaluation emphasizes the development and implementation of interventions with various types of groups. Continuing the framing of skills and techniques within theoretical perspectives, the use of evidence-based interventions with groups is introduced using the strengths, narrative, and solution-focused frameworks. Models for group intervention are described, along with an in-depth examination of the roles, skills, and practice behaviors required for carrying out a group-level intervention. Termination, evaluation, and follow-up of group interventions are also covered. This chapter includes additional exhibits to highlight content on group interventions. A Grand Challenge for Social Work that emphasizes how to "Harness Technology for Social Good" is discussed.

Chapter 10

Social Work Practice With Communities: Engagement, Assessment, and Planning introduces students to the concept of community. The chapter defines and discusses types and functions of communities. Students learn about various theoretical perspectives, including contemporary perspectives for community practice. Engagement and assessment concepts, including community-based analysis, evidence-based practice, and community needs assessments, are extensively discussed. Examples of types of needs assessments, surveys used in needs assessments, and needs assessment summaries provide additional practice guidance. Community practice skills are thoroughly covered. This edition contains Quick Guides on running focus groups and community forums, as well as content on interprofessional engagement and community planning. New to this chapter is a discussion to reflect the role the COVID-19 pandemic has had on social work practice with marginalized communities. Also new to this chapter is a discussion of environmental justice, and the latest Supreme Court decisions affecting voting rights and women's reproductive rights.

Chapter 11

Social Work Practice With Communities: Intervention, Termination, and Evaluation builds on the engagement and assessment content of Chapter 10 to present strategies and techniques for community practice. Using the insights gained about practice at the individual, family, and group levels, this chapter expands the students' awareness of social work practice with communities through a discussion of skills for intervention, including community social and economic development, and community organizing. Examples of public and private efforts to promote evidence-based community practice assist students in applying the material. Additional guidance on advocacy efforts and asset building are presented. Students also learn the knowledge and skills needed for termination and evaluation of community practice. A chapter case focuses on an intergenerational community gardening intervention.

Chapter 12

Social Work Practice With Organizations: Engagement, Assessment, and Planning covers a challenging level of practice for beginning social workers—social work practice with organizations. Students learn a wealth of practical and theoretical aspects of organizations, including a discussion about the purpose and structure of organizations, power relations within organizations, and social work within host organizational settings. The chapter provides discussion about the dimensions of an internal assessment of organizations, including organizational culture, as well as external assessments. Content on organizational policy and nonprofit partnerships helps guide practice. Examples of organizational engagement and assessment provide students with helpful illustrations of key content. This chapter includes a more in-depth discussion of social movements such as the Black Lives Matter and Me-Too movements. Chapter 12 includes discussion of the Grand Challenge for Social Work to "Promote Smart Decarceration," to end mass incarceration in the United States. Students are required to complete assignments to determine which organizations in their community are working to achieve equal opportunity for marginalized individuals and communities. The case that weaves throughout the chapter involves a collaborative practice among social workers whose agencies are members of a state-wide coalition of shelters and intimate partner violence (IPV) prevention programs.

Chapter 13

Social Work Practice With Organizations: Intervention, Termination, and Evaluation uses the foundation built in Chapter 12 to discuss approaches, perspectives, and models for intervening with organizations. This chapter provides extensive coverage of the relationship between theoretical perspectives and organizational change, as well as a practical framework for thinking about generating change and necessary knowledge for a social work generalist in this endeavor. Content on termination and evaluation of change efforts within organizations, including a discussion about the role of the generalist practitioner in this process, helps students see their potential role in a change effort with organizations. Content about the challenges of implementing organizational change, and persuasion skills to assist in these efforts, provides direction for the practitioner. Chapter 13 includes discussion of the Grand Challenge for Social Work to "Achieve Equal Opportunity and Justice." The chapter features a case on organizational change in a school setting to establish services and support for LGBTQIA+ students.

Interactive Cases

Updated since the 5th edition, the website located at www.routledgesw.com/interactive-cases/ presents six unique, in-depth, interactive, fictional cases and the website www.routledgesw.com/static-cases/ presents three unique, in-depth, static fiction cases. These cases have dynamic characters and current, real-life situations that students can easily access from any computer. They provide a "learning by doing" format unavailable with any other text. Each of the cases use text, videos, and graphics to help students learn about engagement, assessment, intervention, evaluation, and termination at multiple levels of social work practice. The cases can be integrated into classroom instruction and/or woven into programs' online or blended instructional modalities. Instructors can have students prepare written responses to critical thinking questions, or this content can be incorporated into class discussions or online discussion boards. To complement other course assignments, students can be required to complete tasks associated with the dynamic features of the cases, such as genograms and ecomaps, or utilize practice skills to "engage" with the individuals, families, and groups in the cases. Throughout the texts and across the curriculum, these interactive cases enrich and enliven students' learning experiences.

The Sanchez Family: Systems, Strengths, and Stressors The ten individuals in this extended Latinx family have numerous strengths and are also faced with a variety of challenges. Students will have the opportunity to experience the phases of the social work intervention, grapple with ethical dilemmas, and identify strategies for addressing issues of diversity, racism, oppression, equity, and intersectionality.

Riverton: A Community Conundrum Riverton is a small Midwest community. The social worker identifies an issue that presents the community with a challenge. Students and instructors can work together to develop strategies for engaging, assessing, and intervening with the residents of the neighborhood. This case also incorporates current issues related to the unhoused and to substance use—both timely concerns that affect multiple practice domains.

Carla Washburn: Loss, Aging, and Social Support Students will get to know Carla Washburn, an older Black woman who finds herself living alone after the loss of her grandson and in considerable pain from a recent accident. In this case, students will apply their growing knowledge of gerontology, reflect on how individual life experiences shape one's values, and exercise the skills of culturally responsive practice.

RAINN: Rape Abuse and Incest National Network The RAINN Online Hotline links callers to local Rape Crisis Centers and hospitals, as well as other services. This case prompts students to think about how evolving technologies are reshaping social work practice and highlights the critical issue of sexual violence, which itself presents numerous ethical and practice dilemmas. The RAINN case also exposes students to the use of research to inform and assess practice—a crucial competency for social workers at all levels.

Hudson City: An Urban Community Affected by Disaster Hudson City has just been devastated by Hurricane Diane, a Category 4 hurricane with wind speeds of 140 miles per hour. Students will take up the role of a social worker who has been tasked with finding workable solutions to a variety of problems with diverse clients' systems. Students will learn about disaster response and how to focus on many clients at once. This case centers the demands of environmental justice, underscores the connection between the natural environment and human well-being, and situates individual practice within the context of community change.

Brickville: Families and Communities Consider Transitions Like many areas of the country, Brickville is a marginalized community faced with a development proposal that would dramatically change the community. Students will take the role of a social worker who works for a community development corporation. Students will learn about community development approaches that can be used to empower community members, while navigating ethical issues and learning to see situations from the perspectives of differently positioned stakeholders.

Static Cases

River's Family   River is a 7-year-old boy whose mother, Candace, has struggled with substance use disorder, which has contributed to concerns about River's well-being. River does not have contact with his biological father, who is an enrolled tribal member, but he has spent two summers living with his paternal grandparents on the Blackfeet Nation reservation, located several hours away. River's mother is not indigenous, and she is estranged from her own biological family. River came to the attention of the Department of Child Family Services when his first-grade teacher made a report about his frequent school absences and evidence of neglect.

Willow's Transition   Willow is a 13-year-old White, eighth grader, born male. Willow and their parents are seeking help with the transition, to access health care for the transition, and assistance with navigating the Public School system. Students and instructors can work together to develop strategies for engaging, assessing, and intervening with the healthcare and public school systems.

The Community Reacts to Mr. Richardson's Killing   This is a community in a large metropolitan area that has to grapple with the killing of a well-respected member of the community by a law enforcement officer. Students take the role of social worker who must navigate ethical dilemmas while simultaneously finding workable solutions as the community reacts to racism, oppression, power, and trauma.

This book takes full advantage of these interactive elements by including exercises that require students to use the cases and to demonstrate their emerging competencies and culturally responsive practices in this arena. To maximize the learning experience, you may want to start the course by asking your students to explore each case. The more the students are familiar with the presentation of information and the locations of the individual case files, the Case Study Tools, and the questions and tasks contained within each phase of the case, the better they will be able to integrate the text with the online practice component.

In Sum

When presented as separate issues, all of the aforementioned topics can seem overwhelming to students, particularly when they realize they have to keep at hand all their knowledge when working with clients and communities. However, all of these topics, as well as other topics that are discussed, are set in a framework that will help students think about the types of problems their clients might be likely to face at different phases in life. Students will also learn that organizing their knowledge about these areas into a theoretical context that "makes sense" to them will help them to manage the seemingly endless stream of information at their disposal. Ultimately, then, students will become more and more proficient at being culturally responsive and applying concepts to the problems facing clients and communities. Meanwhile, students can enjoy the process of learning about them.

Being an effective social worker means being able to understand the complexities of human behavior, the societies and cultures in which we live, and the interplay between them. Being an effective social worker also means having a solid grounding in various disciplines, such as psychology, sociology, and human biology. It means possessing a well-rounded education and an ability to apply this knowledge to the myriad problems and situations that students will face in the profession. This edition is intended to help students understand this complexity in the field and to help them gain the knowledge and critical thinking skills they will need to practice social work.

ACKNOWLEDGMENTS

We would like to thank the many colleagues who helped to make this book and previous editions possible. To Julie Birkenmaier we owe an extraordinary debt for her contributions to previous editions. To Alice Lieberman, and Melinda Lewis, we are grateful for your combined innovation and vision that has resulted in this series and the web-based supplements that bring the material alive. We appreciate the camaraderie and support of the authors of the other books in this series—Rosemary Chapin, Melinda Lewis, Anissa Rogers, Vithya Murugan, Judy Krysik, and Jerry Finn. A special thanks to Shannon Cooper-Sadlo for sharing her practice wisdom and exercises, as well as to graduate student assistants Olivia Gartlan, Mariah Lynn, and Adien Kupka for their assistance. We also want to thank:

Elissa Mitchell
University of Southern Indiana
Raquel Warley
Mercy College
Stacey Gandy
Arizona State University

for their reviews of the book as it was evolving. Finally, we are most appreciative to the staff of Routledge for their support and encouragement for making this book a reality. It takes a village.

CHAPTER 1

Understanding Social Work Practice

SOCIAL WORK IS A HELPING PROFESSION unlike any other. With a proud history of understanding people in the context of their social environments, the professional commitment of social workers to simultaneously helping individuals and advocating for social justice sets it apart from other professions. While this commitment can be challenging because it requires social workers to engage in multilevel practice, working for structural change while supporting individual well-being, social workers develop a deep sense of purpose and find that helping people and working for social justice has many personal and professional rewards.

Understanding Social Work Practice provides an overview of social work practice by grounding you in the purpose of social work; its competencies; types of clients; and the practice framework of engagement, assessment, intervention, termination, and evaluation. A discussion of the ethics that guide social work practice, licensure of social work, client populations and communities that social workers help, and tensions in social work provide you with real-world information about the profession. You are also introduced to major theoretical perspectives for social work practice, including ecosystems, social justice, and strengths perspectives. This chapter provides an overview of the social work profession and an initial grounding in generalist social work practice. The chapter also features the social work competencies that students must be able to demonstrate before entering the field, as well as current social challenges being addressed by the profession as a whole. We start the chapter with a case that focuses on social work practice with a survivor of intimate partner violence.

Lakeisha is a young woman from the southern United States. She came to a large city in the Midwest to see a different part of the country. Very early in her stay, she met and fell in love with Tom, a native Midwesterner. Lakeisha and Tom developed a serious relationship, and when Lakeisha discovered that she was pregnant, she moved into Tom's apartment. From then on, things did not go well for Lakeisha. Tom began to resent her interest in the coming birth, and at times, he was verbally abusive, insulting her background and what he called her "southern accent." He became physically abusive with her when they had any difference of opinion. At first, he would always apologize afterward, and things would be good between them again for a while.

> *Eventually, Tom began to shove Lakeisha into the wall, slap her, and kick at her belly when she disagreed with him. Lakeisha was disillusioned and frightened. She began to try to keep Tom calm at all times and stopped expressing her opinions about anything. The abuse continued, and when Lakeisha became urgently afraid for herself and her child, she contacted a local women's shelter. By this time, Tom's abuse and manipulation had convinced Lakeisha she was, at least partly, responsible for Tom's behavior, and that she would never find anyone else who would love her. Lakeisha was at a very low point, vigilant about protecting her health and safety during her pregnancy, and fearful for her future.*

Key Questions for Chapter 1

1. How can I understand social work practice?
2. How do social work competencies, the phases of practice, and the professional code of ethics help guide social work practice?
3. How are tensions within the field of social work best understood?
4. How can I prepare to engage, assess, plan, intervene, and terminate with clients and communities?
5. How can I work with clients, colleagues, and community members to evaluate my social work practice?
6. How do common theoretical perspectives guide social work practice?

THE PURPOSE OF SOCIAL WORK

The primary mission of social work is "to enhance human well-being and help meet the basic human needs of all people, with particular attention to the needs and empowerment of people who are vulnerable, oppressed, and living in poverty" (National Association of Social Workers [NASW], *Code of Ethics*, 2021a). Unlike other helping professionals, social workers have a person-in-environment perspective, meaning that they prize multi-system knowledge, skills, abilities, and competencies. Whether working in mental health, corrections, child welfare, aging, public policy, or any of several other practice arenas, social workers are committed to helping individuals in the context of their environments. This multi-level focus means that social workers use their knowledge, helping skills, and abilities to enhance individual and family well-being while also advocating for social, economic, and environmental justice.

PRACTICING SOCIAL WORK

Social work practice can be conceptualized in several different ways, including:

- a type of practice or range of practice settings,
- a set of activities,

- a set of roles,
- a set of competencies and practice behaviors,
- types of clients and communities,
- a profession that is licensed by states,
- a profession that is guided by a *Code of Ethics* (NASW, 2021a), and
- a multi-level focus that makes social work distinctive from other helping professions.

Undergraduate and graduate programs in generalist and advanced social work practice prepare students to work with a range of systems, from practice with individuals and families to group-level practice, community practice in the United States and around the globe, and policy practice within agencies as well as at all levels of government. Areas of specialization in social work practice programs include advanced-level work in a variety of arenas including medical and health care settings, mental and behavioral health centers, clinical practice settings, and administration of social service organizations. The range of generalist and advanced practice settings includes psychiatric facilities, schools, community organizations, family service organizations, legislatures, correctional settings, hospitals, libraries, and a host of others.

Social work practice activities are often associated with particular agencies and their functions in the community. Examples of these include:

- advocating for policy change regarding the rights of families with school-aged children who are unhoused to services from an area agency on aging,
- facilitating an empowerment group in an intimate partner violence program, such as the group that Lakeisha may join as she begins to receive services from the local women's shelter,
- mentoring students in a neighborhood school,
- developing a psychoeducational group in a mental health services agency,
- supporting families in an emergency housing shelter,
- advancing human rights in another culture by learning a new language and traveling to another part of the world to collaborate globally,
- advocating with public officials, companies, and corporations,
- working with a group of adolescents who are dealing with issues of bullying,
- fundraising from government and foundation sources to assist in the empowerment of disadvantaged neighborhoods, and
- working in a library to help patrons who are unhoused to access social welfare services.

SOCIAL WORK ROLES

Generalist social work practice emphasizes a holistic understanding of the roles of the social worker and the relationship between social workers, clients, and communities. In the helping process, the generalist social worker may take on the roles of:

- **case manager** when assisting people with assessing, arranging, and coordinating needed goods and services (case manager roles are discussed in more detail in Chapter 4),
- **counselor** while providing suggestions to assist people to reach their goals,
- **broker** when making inquiries on behalf of clients or community members and referring them to additional services,
- **mediator** when assisting two parties to mutually resolve a dispute,
- **educator** when providing relevant information to clients or communities, and
- **advocate** when working with or on behalf of clients and communities for needed resources, programs, or policies to enhance well-being and/or social justice.

These roles help clarify the nature of the interactions between social workers, clients, and community members, as well as define their respective responsibilities. Social work roles are fluid; they can change from interaction to interaction and even within interactions. Social work practice involves a wide variety of roles because social work deals with the breadth of human experience. Social work roles are discussed in more detail in Chapter 4.

SOCIAL WORK COMPETENCIES

The Council on Social Work Education's Educational Policy and Accreditation Standards (EPAS) have established nine competencies that social work students must be able to demonstrate before earning a Bachelor's in Social Work (BSW) or Master's in Social Work (MSW) degree. A competency is the "ability to integrate and apply social work knowledge, values, and skills to practice situations in a purposeful, intentional, and professional manner to promote human and community well-being" (Council on Social Work Education [CSWE], 2022, p. 7). The requirement that students demonstrate these competencies guides social work education and, therefore, social work practice. Each competency consists of four dimensions that together inform competent social work practice. These dimensions are knowledge, values, skills, and professionally appropriate cognitive and affective processes, that is feelings and responses related to value and emotion-laden behavior or beliefs (discussed in more detail in a later section of this chapter). Exhibit 1.1 lists the competencies that social workers should be able to demonstrate effectively in their work with individuals, families, groups, organizations, and communities.

EXHIBIT 1.1

Core Competencies of Social Workers

Upon program completion, social work students must be able to:

Competency 1: Demonstrate Ethical and Professional Behavior

Competency 2: Engage Anti-Racism, Diversity, Equity, and Inclusion in Practice

Competency 3: Advance Human Rights and Social, Racial, Economic, and Environmental Justice

Competency 4: Engage in Practice-informed Research and Research-informed Practice

Competency 5: Engage in Policy Practice

Competency 6: Engage with Individuals, Families, Groups, Organizations, and Communities

Competency 7: Assess Individuals, Families, Groups, Organizations, and Communities

Competency 8: Intervene with Individuals, Families, Groups, Organizations, and Communities

Competency 9: Evaluate Practice with Individuals, Families, Groups, Organizations, and Communities

Council on Social Work Education (CSWE) 2022 EPAS Core Competencies.

Knowledge, Values, Skills, and Cognitive and Affective Processes

Knowledge, values, and skills are the core of social work education and training. Along with professionally appropriate cognitive and affective processes, these dimensions of competent social work can be considered the tools that a practitioner brings to the work. These four dimensions, discussed next, reflect both personal and professional attributes of the social worker, and each is necessary for effective social work practice.

Knowledge Professional knowledge is made up of facts and research findings as well as less concrete elements such as cultural awareness and **self-knowledge**, the knowledge or understanding of one's own values, character, abilities, and biases. Practicing social workers need to have biopsychosocial knowledge; that is, they need to know facts, histories, theories, and trends about human development, policy, research, and practice. Theories of human behavior and the social environment are central to generalist social work practice. Familiarity with these theories and their applicability in context enables social workers to understand, for example, what behaviors to expect for an adolescent under stress, or the likely dynamics in an agency when the administration initiates a policy change. Specifically, social workers must have culturally relevant knowledge and be able to critically assess a theory for utility and relevance with diverse cultures.

The profession has agreed on the knowledge areas needed by social workers, and the knowledge is attainable through study, discussion, research, and related activities. Social workers should know the history of social work, the value base and ethical standards of the profession, and current structures of social policies and human service systems (CSWE, 2022). Because the social work knowledge base is always evolving, social workers continually need to update their knowledge to ensure that they are relevant and effective. Through their professional experience, social workers gain firsthand knowledge, or "practice wisdom," which helps them integrate what they learn "on the job" with knowledge from other sources, such as prior education and continuing education. Practice wisdom is the social worker's application of their "accumulation of information, assumptions, ideologies, and judgement" (Barker, 2014, p. 331) (discussed more fully in Chapter 5).

Knowledge and understanding of cultures, spiritual beliefs, and social norms are also critical to professional practice. Social workers must understand the broad ways in which the structure, norms, and values of a culture may create or enhance privilege and power for certain groups in society. This understanding can eliminate the influence of personal biases when working with diverse clients and communities (Cross, 2013; Gitterman & Knight, 2016).

Cultural competence refers to the "capacity to function effectively as a helper in the context of cultural differences" (Cross, 2013, p. 3). More recently, the concept of **cultural humility** is being widely used in social work education and practice to reflect the notion that a social worker can never be completely competent in another community's culture (Fong et al., 2019; Ortega & Duntley-Matos, 2020). The profession's goal to strive for cultural competence has continued to evolve with the inclusion of knowledge, skills, and values related to cultural humility, culturally responsive practice, intersectionality, and anti-racist and anti-oppressive practice. Approaching practice in a manner that acknowledges humility in the face of diverse clients and communities is one demonstration of competency for social workers. **Culturally responsive practice** requires social workers to recognize their own values and bias, to take the client's culture into account, to learn from the client about their experiences, and to relate respectfully to the client (Ortega & Duntley-Matos, 2020). **Anti-oppressive practice** requires social workers to understand the historical origins of structures in society, social work's role in government, White supremacy, racism, marginalization, exploitation, and violence (Detlaff et al., 2020; Hölscher & Chiumbu, 2020; Kendi, 2019),

Diversity in practice also includes the notion of spirituality. Spirituality is an integral part of many cultures and gives social work practitioners access to knowledge about important dimensions of clients and communities (Canda & Gomi, 2019). For example, recognizing a Navajo child's spiritual affirmation of harmony may help a social worker understand the child's reluctance to engage in competition in school. In some areas of practice, such as end of life, social workers use a model that combines two major areas of knowledge—a "biopsychosocial-spiritual" model to serve the needs of clients as whole persons (Hodgson et al., 2016).

Importance of Self-Knowledge In order to practice competently, social workers must have a clear understanding of themselves and their own biases. For example, do you find that you respond differently to people who are living in poverty than you do to people who are socioeconomically middle class? To become more culturally responsive, you can explore the reasons for this difference; perhaps you learned as a child that "poor people" are somehow less worthy than affluent people or that they are not hardworking. Your family and/or the wider culture may have supported these views.

To uncover your possible socioeconomic biases, consider the following questions: How does this view clash with the view that people living in poverty are resilient in the face of debilitating exploitation? How do you act on this view in your practice? Are you less empathic, energetic, or invested when you work with people living in poverty? Are you less likely to advocate or seek out resources for them? Do you have an opinion about an individual or family or community that is a "truth" in your mind, or do you treat your initial opinion as one interpretation out of the many that are possible? How would such biases interfere with your efforts to effectively partner with clients of different socioeconomic status? How would such biases interfere with your efforts to effectively partner with clients of a different race or ethnicity? How can you challenge these biases as part of your own professional preparation and growth?

Self-knowledge is also a critical component of effective practice. Social workers use supervision and regular reflection to develop and maintain a clear understanding of themselves, their values and beliefs, as well as their own biases so that these biases do not shape their practice decisions and behaviors without their knowledge. Regular reflection on their own experiences, attitudes, and feelings helps social workers gain self-knowledge about their work to help people and advocate for social justice.

Values Values are intricately tied to self-knowledge. Social work has always identified itself as a profession of values, which are strongly held beliefs about preferred conditions of life. The core social work values are (NASW, 2021a):

- service
- social justice
- dignity and worth of the person
- importance of human relationships
- integrity
- competence.

Though the National Association of Social Workers (NASW) *Code of Ethics* (2021a) clearly articulates the social work professional values, you may hear spirited discussion about how best to implement these values in practice. At times, you may even feel conflicted yourself about how to practice in a values-centered manner.

Values and ethics present many challenges to social workers. They often look different in complicated practice contexts than they do in isolation. The NASW *Code of Ethics* (NASW, 2021a) plays a significant role in sorting out complex situations in which values and ethical conflicts arise. While values guide professional thinking about behavior and judgments regarding conduct, ethics are the rules or prescriptions for behaviors that reflect those values. For example, the ethical principle that social workers should actively prevent any person from being harmed stems from the cardinal social work value that all human life is important. Conflicting ethical principles lead to dilemmas, as when the act of trying to prevent harm to a person may infringe on another person's self-determination or when preventing harm to a person may infringe on that same person's self-determination (in the case of self-harm). The NASW (2021a) developed its *Code of Ethics* to clarify the principles of ethical practice. Values provide the criteria for examining the ways in which the profession shapes itself, and for regular self-reflection on the professional rules of conduct for social

> **EXHIBIT 1.2**
>
> ***NASW* Code of Ethics**
>
> The full NASW *Code of Ethics* (2021a) is available in English at:
>
> www.socialworkers.org/About/Ethics/Code-of-Ethics/Code-of-Ethics-English
>
> The link above will also lead you to a site to order the Spanish-language version of the Code.
>
> NASW has also published a series of publications that articulate standards for social work in various practice settings (e.g., school social work) and with various populations (e.g., family caregivers of older adults). These publications provide guidance to practitioners about the basic standards which practitioners and their organizations should aspire to meet. See the listing of standards publications here:
>
> www.socialworkers.org/practice

workers. Exhibit 1.2 provides more information about the *Code of Ethics* (NASW, 2021a).

Our experiences, motivations, values, attitudes, and other factors shape our practice decisions, sometimes without us realizing it. Social workers need to continually explore how they prioritize their values and the patterns they develop in making decisions and exhibiting practice behaviors. This exploration may include recognizing idiosyncratic approaches, quick responses, and typical reactions. Are you patient and likely to stand by your clients and community members, even when things do not go well? Are you quick to assume someone is judging you or wants to bring you harm? Are you likely to blow off steam or sulk when you are rebuffed? Do you assume that you are competent to deal with any crisis? Are you inclined to address an interpersonal problem privately and quietly? Are you likely to "sound off" in a meeting? All of us have our own ways of dealing with relationships, stresses, and social interactions. However, some of our behavioral patterns can be cause for concern in professional practice (see, especially, the upcoming section on cognitive and affective processes). Social workers must recognize their own behavior patterns, understand how they impact their practice, and identify those responses that, if changed, would help them to develop a higher degree of competency and skill.

Culture profoundly influences social work practitioner biases. For example, culture may impact practitioner beliefs and attitudes about a situation in which an adolescent's choice of vocation may clash with the family's more gender-rigid ideas about suitable professions. In another example, cultural bias may influence a practitioner's belief that, in social relationships, participants are equal, and all should speak out honestly about tensions in relationships. These two examples demonstrate cultural variants that are not necessarily shared by all people. Emphasis on individual drive and ambition, nurturing professions for women, as well as equality and forthrightness have been heavily emphasized in Western cultures and may clash with other cultural beliefs. For instance, a practitioner who is an Asian American male and who is younger than a client who is a White female client may attempt to demonstrate respect to the client by speaking in terms that the client perceives to be quite formal. This may result in the client appearing to be reluctant to share details about her family life, even though she has been referred for parent support and family information is needed. Rather than labeling her "resistant" or "closed," the practitioner can recognize his own potential bias about the helping relationship. He may plan to spend more time to engage and build rapport before moving on to the assessment and planning phases of helping.

Skills The third element social workers bring to their work with clients and communities is their professional practice skills. Detailing these skills for generalist practice is the primary focus of this book. Social workers need a wide range of skills such as:

- communication skills for work with individuals,
- skills in facilitating groups, including family and client groups,
- organizing skills for community practice,
- clear and concise written and verbal skills, and
- research and public speaking skills for policy practice and other social change efforts.

Communication skills are of course important at all levels of practice; a later chapter references, for example, the written communication skills essential for effectively documenting individual practice.

Early in your social work student experience, the skills you learn and practice while you develop expertise are often focused on building relationships and rapport with individuals and families, as well as with small groups of people. With additional study and continued ongoing practitioner experience, you can develop and enhance your skill repertoire. You may, as your social work education continues, develop areas of specialization.

As an example, if you are working in a setting that offers walk-in services as you begin social work practice with individuals, you will practice the use of active listening and empathy. You will also learn how to develop short-term goals and outcomes that you and the client can agree upon. Later in your education or career, you may choose an area of specialization that requires deeper knowledge and more advanced skills in working with individuals. These may include establishing and maintaining a collaborative process with clients around longer-term treatment goals and therapeutic modalities that take the clients' needs and preferences into account.

Another central skill in social work practice is the demonstration of genuine cultural humility. As much as cultural humility reflects our social work values, as discussed previously, demonstrating such humility is also an essential practice skill. Knowledge of and curiosity about the lived experiences of individuals, families, groups, and communities is essential for culturally relevant anti-oppressive social work practice.

> *Returning to the case at the beginning of the chapter, we can see cultural humility at work as Joyce, a social worker at the women's shelter, begins to build rapport with Lakeisha. When Lakeisha is able to share her experiences of moving from the southern part of the United States to the Midwest, Joyce has the opportunity to mention that she has always wanted to know more about how people experience differences between these two different parts of the country. As Lakeisha talks about her own experiences, Joyce picks up on the parts of Lakeisha's experiences that highlight positive aspects of her life in both places, and especially in the south, to help counter the negative messages about growing up in the south that Lakeisha has been hearing from Tom. This rapport-building strategy helps Lakeisha begin to rebuild her self-esteem.*

Cognitive and Affective Processes Professionally appropriate cognitive and affective processes are the fourth and final dimension of the core competencies for social workers. Social workers use critical thinking in every interaction they have with people, whether they be individuals or families, agency colleagues, or community members. Critical thinking allows us to practice with good judgment in difficult, unpredictable, and complex situations. Further, social workers' affective reactions, such as facial expressions and body language, serve as nonverbal cues to other people and must accurately reflect what they want to express. For example, the effective use of empathy in social work practice is invaluable. Interpersonal communications often include affective demonstrations of active listening, even when the social worker is not using verbal means of following what other people are saying such as reflection or summarizing and paraphrasing. Social workers must always bring an awareness of what they are projecting through their body language and other affective processes in order to demonstrate respect in their interactions with people from diverse backgrounds.

CLIENTS AND COMMUNITIES IN SOCIAL WORK PRACTICE

Social work practice competencies apply to work with individuals, couples, families of all types, groups, communities, and organizations. These categories of social work practice often overlap, as when a social worker engages in group work within community practice or in community work to assist families. Further, continuing expansion of global awareness has resulted in more social workers practicing across international borders over the course of their professional lives or, at least, balancing their work at the local level with efforts to build their understanding of the rapid changes in social, economic, and environmental arenas across the world. Unfortunately, many global practice options were disrupted during the COVID-19 pandemic and may need to be reassessed and rebuilt. The levels of practice will be discussed in greater depth in later chapters.

Practice With Individuals, Families, and Groups

Most social workers in the United States practice with individuals, families, and/or groups. Individual casework may involve working with an adolescent struggling with sexuality issues, a parent concerned about their child's development, and an older adult facing increased care needs. Group casework can include helping group members make individual changes, helping the group as a whole make changes in communication and behavior dynamics within the group, or helping the group make changes in their larger social or physical environments. The nature of the work is heavily influenced by the agency's purpose and practice perspective, the personal characteristics of the client (individual, family, or group), and the social worker's skills and theoretical perspectives. Cultural context, social and political influences, and current community concerns also affect social workers' relationships with clients and families. Levels of practice will be discussed in greater depth in later chapters.

Within the field, social work with individuals, families, and groups is sometimes called social work practice with individuals, families, and groups (*micro practice*), while social work practice with organizations, communities, or policy practice is sometimes referred to as *macro practice*. These terms may be helpful as shorthand within social work, but they have important limitations. Not only may these terms be meaningless to those outside the field, but the reality is that most social workers in practice work with a wide array of client and community groups simultaneously and/or over the course of their careers. Further, practicing with individuals, families, and/or groups involves many different kinds of work. Hahn and Scanlon (2016) note that case management, advocacy, mediation, and prevention initiatives, in addition to counseling, are ways that many social workers practice with individuals, families, and groups. Other practice activities common in social work with individuals, families, and groups include mobilizing resources, assessing safety, facilitating and monitoring therapeutic play activities, providing information on local services and resources, helping people apply for benefits or apply for government documents (e.g., birth certificate, Social Security card, driver's license or State ID, etc.), managing shelter services, and facilitating support groups.

One common type of practice with individuals, families, and groups is *clinical social work*. In the social work context, the word *clinical* has a specific meaning. As opposed to all other types of social work practice with individuals, families, and small groups, clinical social work involves helping people resolve emotional or psychological challenges. Other terms that are used to refer to clinical practice include *counseling, therapy, behavioral health interventions*, and *mental health services*. In some settings, the term *clinical* is not used at all in favor of broader terms such as *individual* and *family services*.

Even when social workers describe their practice as clinical, they tend to use a breadth of skills and approaches to address the needs of a wide range of clients and community members. For example, clinical work can include intervening individually with an adolescent to address their self-harming behavior, facilitating a series of groups for children who have experienced the death of a parent, or assisting a family to redefine or re-evaluate the communication patterns among three generations within a family. The exercise of clinical practice skills, which are obtained at the graduate (MSW) student level, is common in many practice arenas, such as physical and mental health, substance use disorder treatment, school social work, and gerontological social work. We can further explore social work practice by returning to Lakeisha's case from the beginning of this chapter:

At the women's shelter, Lakeisha met regularly with her social worker, Joyce. These sessions helped Lakeisha and Joyce strengthen their therapeutic relationship, and, with Joyce's help, Lakeisha began to see that Tom's violence was a function not of anything that Lakeisha was doing or not doing but rather of his own background and choices. There were two key breakthroughs that happened as part of this change. First, through Joyce's use of active listening and minimal feedback, Lakeisha shared that she had faced Tom's anger and violence at random times and in unpredictable circumstances. He only became enraged and violent when they were home alone. Joyce pointed out that Tom was making the choice to avoid becoming violent in front of other people. Second, Tom had told Lakeisha repeatedly that he would not become abusive, except that Lakeisha made him so angry. Joyce asked Lakeisha if she knew of anyone else with whom Tom was often angry, and Lakeisha said that he was always angry with his boss at work. Joyce noted that Tom chose to manage his anger without violence with his boss but made a different choice when dealing with anger at home. Tom, not Lakeisha, was responsible for his abusive behavior. With Joyce's support, Lakeisha began to regain her sense of self and the feeling of independence.

Community, Organizational, and Policy Practice

Social workers have the knowledge, values, and skills to practice with individuals, families, and groups while also working on community, organizational, and policy issues to increase the well-being of clients and community members. Community practice usually involves a common locality, such as a city neighborhood, small town, or rural area. Beyond locality, however, *community* also refers to a common concern, interest, or identification. For example, you might consider yourself to be a part of a community of gay men or Jewish women or people of Irish descent. Social work practice has historical roots in community practice and aims to actively involve community members in the solutions to their self-defined concerns (Popple, 2018).

Social work practice with communities, organizations, and policy practice focuses on opportunity and change in the environments surrounding individuals and families. As noted earlier, among social workers, the term *macro practice* is often used to refer to the work of reducing or eliminating social problems at community, organizational, and policy levels. Social workers who engage in this type of professional practice attempt to achieve social change through grassroots organizing, community planning, economic development, public awareness, policy development, organizational administration, and social action.

Social work practice at the community and organizational levels also involves policy practice efforts. Policy practice is a type of social work practice in which social workers endeavor to improve social structures and institutional responses or advocate for policies (governmental regulations, agency rules, laws) that enhance the well-being of large groups of people, especially those who have been oppressed because of their race, ethnicity, class, religion, gender, sexual orientation, gender identity or expression, ability, and/or age. Policy practice focuses on ensuring that policies are responsive to the needs and rights of clients and communities.

Similarly, research is another growing area of social work practice, with social workers helping to gather and analyze data on individual or community well-being as a primary job responsibility or as part of their job. The COVID-19 pandemic's social distancing restrictions resulted in social workers having to shift not only providing social services and counseling, but also continuing and initiating research studies and data collection through the use of online video conferencing platforms and telecommunications for individuals who lacked broadband access or acumen (e.g., older adults and low-income residents and in many rural communities) (Mishna et al., 2021; Walter-McCabe, 2020). The shift also requires social workers to develop strategies to manage ethical considerations related to providing client services and conducting research as it relates to participant privacy and confidentiality (Cheung, 2022). Social work practice and technology is discussed more fully in later chapters.

Another emerging focus of practice is global social work, which may involve work across national borders or work in international aid, economic development, clean water, adequate nutrition, or human rights. On a related topic, Healy (2017) notes that social workers also have professional responsibilities to work with and on behalf of migrants and refugees, especially in the context of political conflict regarding their status in new countries. In recent years, this responsibility has taken on greater resonance as wars, religious persecutions, famines, and natural disasters have significantly increased the numbers of immigrants and refugees, worldwide (United Nations High Commissioner for Refugees, 2020; Folkwein, 2022).

Although the distinctions between types of clients and communities can be a useful way of thinking about social work, generalist practice emphasizes an integration of knowledge, values, skills, and appropriate cognitive and affective processes when working with individuals, families, groups, communities, and organizations, as well as when conducting research and working to change social policies. Regardless of the specific kind of work you do in your practice, you will want to be aware of employment, licensure, and continuing education issues. These are covered briefly in Exhibit 1.3.

EXHIBIT 1.3

Employment, Licensure, and Continuing Education in Social Work

The U.S. Department of Labor reported 708,100 social work jobs in the nation in 2021, and estimate faster growth in the field than the average of other occupations. In fact, while the labor market is admittedly volatile, social work is poised to thrive in the future; in the decade between 2021 and 2031, the employment of social workers in the United States is expected to grow by 9 percent (Bureau of Labor Statistics, U.S. Department of Labor, September 2022). These projections, however, do not take into account the economic downturn and a possible impending recession due to the effects of the COVID-19 pandemic and the war between Russia and Ukraine. Becoming a social worker is not a matter of just deciding to take a social work job or even completing a degree. As with many other helping professions, social work in the United States is licensed and regulated by each state to protect the public. All 50 states, the District of Columbia, Puerto Rico, and the Virgin Islands regulate the social work profession through licensure. Other countries that have social work licensure include England, Australia, and Canada. Licensure protects the public by establishing: (1) the qualifications that a professional must possess, (2) a means of holding professionals accountable, and (3) a system for the public to lodge complaints against incompetent or unethical practitioners and to have them investigated and adjudicated.

While they vary from state to state, requirements for licensure for social workers with BSW and MSW degrees generally include earning the relevant level of education from a CSWE-accredited social work program, demonstrating knowledge by passing an exam, providing references, and displaying evidence of good moral character. Most states use licensing examinations developed and administered by the Association of Social Work Boards (Grise-Owens et al., 2016). In many states, specialized licenses also require gaining experience under the supervision of an approved practicing social worker. For example, some states offer a clinical social work license that requires more than two years of supervised clinical experience, proof of a minimum number of hours in a clinical field placement, and/or proof of specific clinical coursework.

After licensure, many states require that licensed social workers complete ongoing professional continuing education units (CEUs) through professional training sessions or conferences that provide training on topics such as professional ethics, new and emerging issues in the field, and avoiding secondary trauma (Quinn et al., 2019). In addition, some states require additional or different credentials to work in some areas (e.g., an addictions certificate for professionals working with people who have substance use disorder). Because states have different licensing rules and regulations, social workers must be familiar with the licensure requirements for the states in which they wish to practice.

Similarly, you must stay informed about the requirements for continuing and professional education for social workers in your state. Social workers seeking CEUs have a variety of online and in-person options. Moreover, many schools of social work offer high-quality Professional Continuing Education (PCE) offerings that enhance professionals' knowledge and skills, including those delivered through a variety of modalities (synchronous/asynchronous/in-person, etc.). Finally, a listing of social work continuing education resources can be found at www.socialworkers.org/careers/continuing-education.

From NASW: www.socialworkers.org/careers/continuing-education

PHASES OF COMPETENT SOCIAL WORK PRACTICE

Social work practice, whether with individuals, families, groups, organizations, or communities, typically progresses through phases including engagement, assessment, planning, intervention, and evaluation. As noted in Exhibit 1.1, these phases are reflected in core social work competencies as articulated by CSWE (EPAS Competencies 6–9). Although the phases are described here in a linear manner, social work practice frequently loops back and forth between phases as necessary. Chapters 3 through 13 discuss these phases of social work practice more fully in the context of working with individuals, families, groups, communities, and organizations.

Engagement

In social work practice, the process of building relationships with clients and communities is called *engagement*. Successful engagement involves establishing a degree of trust and a sense that the work ahead will be helpful to clients and/or community members. Engaging individuals and families requires effective communication and relationship skills, as well as significant collaborative connections with people and institutions in their surrounding social environments. For example, imagine that you work with a young mother named Lara who has asked you to help negotiate and advocate within the school system for their child who has a disability. You carefully develop a relationship with Lara so that you understand their issues and experiences. You could engage with the school as part of Lara's surrounding social environment and learn about policies, procedures, and programs as well as any constraints, services, and challenges at the level of the school itself and/or the school district to effectively facilitate a more productive relationship between Lara and the school. However, engaging with the school and school district in this way, without Lara's step-by-step involvement, may create unnecessary barriers in your ability to engage effectively with them. Despite the extra time it may take, a better way to proceed may involve working together with Lara to learn what the school can and cannot do for their child.

Assessment and Planning

The goals of clients and communities are central to the *assessment* process and to *planning* for an intervention. Through mutual exploration of the challenges at hand, social workers, clients, and community members work together to decide how best to achieve these goals. In situations where there is disagreement about the ultimate goals, social workers can take care in building a therapeutic alliance with their clients to ensure that they share the same goal. In community practice, social workers can work with groups of community members to assist in their coming to consensus or compromise, and/or

developing a collaborative way to make group decisions. Assessment focuses on the analysis of the major purpose for the work, the strengths of clients and/or community members, the resources of the community as a whole, any potential barriers to success in achieving the goal, and aspects of the environment that may support a solution.

Planning is an integral part of the change process. Plans describe how social workers and community members will work to establish and achieve shared goals that represent positive outcomes for individuals, families, groups, organizations, or communities. Developing a plan requires the assessment and evaluation of options, resources, barriers, preferences, and agreed-upon goals, along with various methods of achieving those goals.

Intervention

The next phase, *intervention*, refers to the actions involved in implementing the plan in order to accomplish the agreed-upon goals. Generalist practice interventions vary widely, from helping low-income or marginalized community residents to lobbying city officials on the importance of tearing down abandoned and dilapidated houses in their communities, to helping a family apply for Medicaid benefits. Intervention may involve the social worker listening to and reflecting on an individual's situation, helping the individual's family members discuss that situation and each of their roles in it, and/or facilitating an opportunity to create a different, preferable situation. In many cases, both planning and intervention are collaborative processes, with the social worker and client sharing responsibility for deciding upon and carrying out the best course of action. As with other aspects of social work practice with individuals, families, or communities, the type, level, and focus of the intervention vary widely.

Termination

One aspect of intervention is ending a relationship with clients and communities, or *termination*. Social workers are committed to facilitating appropriate and effective termination. In general, the termination process includes discussing the development of the working relationship, reviewing the work and accomplishments, and planning to sustain the changes that have been achieved. At times, termination may include establishing follow-up plans. To many social workers, termination is one of the most difficult and most important aspects of the work. Those who want to focus more on the future sometimes call this stage *graduation*, especially when working with individuals, families, and groups, and "consolidation of achievements" in work with communities and organizations.

Evaluation

Although many social workers are pressed for time to complete other tasks, making the effort to *evaluate* practice helps to determine the effectiveness of various interventions. The social work *Code of Ethics* (NASW, 2021a) mandates that social workers engage in and utilize research to improve practice. CSWE accreditation guidelines require that social work educators prepare students to "engage in practice-informed research and research-informed practice." There is increasing emphasis on evidence-based practice, defined as "an educational and practice paradigm that includes a series of predetermined steps aimed at helping practitioners and agency administrators identify, select, and implement efficacious interventions for clients" (Dudley & Herman-Smith, 2020; Jenson & Howard, 2013, p. 1). Evidence-based practice involves integrating current research findings, the values and preferences of clients and communities, practitioner knowledge and expertise, and other important factors related to the situation at hand to guide social services, programs, and policies. Moreover, research used in practice will not only come from the social worker's own practice experiences; they also have a professional obligation to contribute to the research knowledge base through evaluating their own practice as well.

Research on practice may involve evaluation tools that assess the progress of a program as well as outcomes associated with the program for clients or communities. Research from scholars and the experiences of social work practitioners can be useful in effective advocacy with and on behalf of clients and communities. For example, if you want to advocate for people who are homeless by demonstrating that existing services are inadequate or not delivered effectively, you need to understand the size and scope of the unhoused population in your area as well as previous research findings about effective services for individuals and families who are homeless and at risk of being homeless. In advocacy, you can also share your own practice experiences by systematically collecting information on outcomes for individuals and families who are homeless and who transition to housing where they receive ongoing case management and other services, sometimes known as *supported housing*, and comparing that data with outcomes for those who move to an independent living situation.

There are many kinds of research and evaluation designs and methods. You will undoubtedly learn about research on social problems, social welfare policies, and social work programs in your required classes covering research content. Your research classes will introduce you to the differences between formative evaluations conducted during the time that clients and communities are working with social workers and summative evaluations conducted at the end of a social work intervention. You will also learn about the difference between quantitative research methods in which numbers and statistical analysis are used to better understand social welfare problems and social work programs and qualitative research. Qualitative research often depends on analysis of notes or transcripts from interviews, focus groups, and meetings to understand the lived experiences of clients. Prevailing trends in funding and assuring accountability in social work practice requires more research to demonstrate efficacy of our approaches in the field and to justify continued financial support for policies and programs.

Knowledge about the phases of practice are helpful in building a better understanding of the field. However, this discussion most certainly falls short of describing the full day-to-day realities of social work practice. For example, the professional connections between social workers, clients, and community members must be attended to and fostered or they will wither. Likewise, assessment occurs throughout the course of the work. Therefore, while knowing the phases of helping is necessary, flexibility in their application is important. Similarly, generalist social work requires proficiency at all levels of practice. Levels are more similar than they are different, and the reality of practice is that there is a great deal of overlap between the knowledge, values, skills, and cognitive and affective processes needed for various types of practice.

PROFESSIONAL TENSIONS IN SOCIAL WORK

Social work is a profession with a wide range of theoretical foundations, practice areas, skills, and settings. Like many professions, tensions exist among these differences. Since inception, the social work profession has faced a set of tensions, the most significant of which are those that shape the professional identity of social workers and the way in which they practice. These include:

- how to achieve an appropriate balance between the emphasis on working with individuals, families, and groups, and the need for community, organizational, and policy practice;
- the extent to which social workers should exercise social control or promote social change (social control is defined and explained and fully discussed later in this chapter);
- how social workers accept clients and communities just as they are in all of their diversity while also promoting changes that improve well-being for themselves, their families, and their communities;

- the extent to which social workers depend on their own professional, expert position or share power with clients and community members; and
- the tension in resource-constrained social work settings to address local needs while remaining informed of and concerned with vast social, economic, and environmental global changes and challenges.

The next sections address these tensions.

Balancing Work With Individuals, Families, and Groups With Work in the Larger Environment

The *Code of Ethics* (NASW, 2021a) requires social workers to engage in work that supports social, economic, and environmental justice. The perceived tension in balancing practice with individuals, families, and groups with community, organizational, and policy practice is a challenge in contemporary social work. This tension evokes a longstanding discussion within the field regarding the appropriate allocation of time and energy in helping clients adjust to, while simultaneously challenging, the current social, economic, anti-oppressive policies and environmental circumstances.

When clinical practice focuses entirely on individual issues and ignores or excludes the advocacy and power analysis work inherent in the pursuit of social justice, it comes into conflict with the *Code of Ethics* (NASW, 2021a). Further, some common clinical practice settings, such as mental health centers and substance use programs, are often part of the larger health care delivery system, which often has requirements for decontextualized pathology labels that tend to confine services to individualized treatment. This delivery system, and the related methods of billing and paying for services, sometimes discourages or diverts social workers from entering into social justice pursuits as part of their job responsibilities.

This tension between working with individuals, families, and groups or working with organizations, community, or in policy practice has historical roots. The late Harry Specht, a social work policy educator, noted that social work historically prized community and policy practice to effect changes for large groups of people in the Progressive Era (1875–1925). Following the emergence and popularization of psychotherapy in the United States (1960s), the field of social work began to emphasize therapeutic services to help people with issues related to feelings and perceptions that relate primarily to the self. Specht asserted that psychology and psychiatry, rather than social work, should deal with these issues. Significantly, Specht argued that social work had been seduced from its original mission by clinical psychotherapy, which many people characterize as a higher-status activity. Specht's last major co-written publication was tellingly called *Unfaithful Angels: How Social Work Has Abandoned Its Mission* (Specht & Courtney, 1994). Social workers who shared Specht's perspective advocated for an emphasis on the well-being of the social environment rather than emotional and psychological well-being. They also called for more social work education in community, organizational, and policy practice, a call that continues in the field today (Abramovitz et al., 2019; CSWE, 2022; Donaldson et al., 2014; Mehrotra et al., 2018; Moya et al., 2017; Rome, 2022).

Many social workers, however, are committed to the kind of work that Specht dismisses as inappropriate. These practitioners view clinical social work as providing useful methodologies for dealing with intrapersonal and interpersonal issues, and professionally appropriate tools for individual counseling, family intervention, and a host of other areas that might be called clinical or therapeutic (Higham, 2020). The critique and debate engendered by Specht today includes pushing back on both the extent of the societal and ideological differences of the earlier era (particularly regarding the acceptance of ideas regarding racial superiority) and the overlooking of ways current practitioners are working to achieve justice.

Integrated Social Work Practice The Educational Policy and Accreditation Standards (EPAS) (CSWE, 2022) for social work education underscore social work's commitment to competencies and behaviors that require competency in terms of knowledge, values, skills, and professionally appropriate cognitive and affective processes in work at all levels. Gitterman and Germain (2013) argue that social work professionals must be prepared to work with all types of clients, as situations require. The use of many methods and skills are common across all clients. Historical loyalties both to individual clients and to advocacy for entire communities are a strength of the profession. One way to reconcile the conflict between an individual focus and a focus on the social environment is to integrate the two approaches. For example, consider the way in which Joyce, the social worker who is working with Lakeisha at the women's shelter, moves into integrated practice.

> *As their work together continued, Joyce encouraged Lakeisha to attend group services with other women residents in the shelter in addition to their individual sessions at the shelter. Hearing the experiences of other women who had survived abusive relationships, Lakeisha began to see her individual experience as part of a larger pattern of the way in which society condones men's use of violence against women. By the time Lakeisha had located safe housing and had returned to work, she was regularly meeting with the women's support group in the community. Before Lakeisha left the shelter, Joyce asked her if she would be willing to volunteer from time to time with other survivors on the shelter's outreach and education team. As Joyce described it, this team of volunteers went in pairs to talk about the realities of intimate partner violence to women's groups in civic organizations and faith communities, health classes at area high schools, and continuing education events for professional groups. Lakeisha agreed to attend an upcoming volunteer orientation and training session and later became a volunteer, following several months of focusing on her own healing.*
>
> *The volunteer work that Lakeisha did from time to time for the shelter empowered her by allowing her to share her individual experience with the*

support and presence of another team member while meaningfully addressing an all too common problem in society. The social work approach that Joyce used in her work with Lakeisha is an example of integrated practice that addresses both individual issues and social justice concerns. This integrated approach allowed Lakeisha to turn an individual tragedy into a personal contribution to a better social environment for her community. Further, through her volunteer work, Lakeisha's self-esteem and self-efficacy continued to grow, and she discovered newfound public speaking skills and a strong network of friends.

Social Change and Social Control

Social workers have three major roles: connecting clients to social welfare services and providing services, structural and social change, and social control. With regard to social control, social workers promote social change efforts by advocating for policies to strengthen society, social institutions, communities, families, and social welfare services; they also exercise social control by enforcing governmental rules and policies in some areas of their practice, such as child protection, juvenile and criminal justice, and mental health. Since the social work profession's early beginnings, social workers have been involved in structural change efforts, community-building, policy advocacy, and organizing for social change. For example, social workers were leaders and advocates of the suffrage movement (1900s), the civil rights movement, the disability movement, and the gay rights movement. In addition to providing treatment and connecting clients to social welfare services and resources, social workers are also required to act as social control agents of the government, particularly in the arenas of investigating, documenting, and reporting alleged incidents of abuse and neglect of children, older adults, people with disabilities, and other vulnerable individuals (CSWE, 2022; Day & Schiele, 2013). Social workers also play a social control function when we enforce eligibility rules that keep people from the services they seek (and may arguably need). In some circumstances, this control appears to be at odds with the profession's commitment to social change. For example, reporting a parent for suspected neglect could be viewed as being at odds with encouraging the same parent to advocate for more adequate family economic support—and dedicating the social worker's professional energies to actively countering the oppressive forces in society (e.g., low-wage jobs, lack of affordable health care, etc.) that make parenting so challenging for many families. The two functions—social change and social control—are not inherently irreconcilable, but the ways in which they play out in their respective practice arenas tend to make them appear incompatible at times.

Change and Acceptance

Another tension involves how much the goal of social work is to implement change—either individual or environmental—or to help clients and communities accept difficult circumstances that seem unlikely to be totally resolvable.

For example, in the absence of a policy that guarantees long-term care for older adults and/or persons with disabilities, many people will find themselves at some point in their lives needing to care for a family member who is older and/or disabled. This work falls disproportionately on women, often wives, daughters, or daughters-in-law, who may need the support of social workers known for providing services to caregivers.

In this situation, a social worker will surely offer emotional support and bolster the caregiver's existing coping mechanisms, perhaps facilitating the identification of existing self-care opportunities and activities, or introducing new means of self-care such as meditation, yoga, or approaching friends to arrange for visits or phone calls. In addition to this work, and when the time is right for the caregiver, the social worker may begin to explore sources of respite care from other family members or agencies.

Some respite care would facilitate caregivers attending a caregiver support group where they can talk freely about both the personal toll that providing care for a loved one takes, and their sense of injustice regarding the lack of affordable, quality services for people who need such care. With others in the support group sharing similar experiences, thoughts, and feelings, the social worker who facilitates the group may help members organize for change by inviting a speaker who knows which state and federal policies need to be changed to provide for more affordable in-home care services. The caregivers may begin communicating regularly with their elected officials and encouraging their friends and family members to do the same, once they may learn, for example, that Home and Community Based Services (HCBS) under Medicaid needs to be expanded in their state.

This example illustrates that different approaches to social work practice do not have to be polarized. They can be thought of as situated on a continuum, meaning that social workers, clients, and community members may work for large-scale social change, even as they continue their efforts to improve well-being on the individual, family, and small group level. Further, working simultaneously toward these goals may have synergistic effects supporting positive changes in well-being at all levels.

Experts and Shared Power

The history and development of both educational and professional systems in the United States have a foundation in the assumption of expert knowledge. Social workers are educated and socialized in professional programs to become respected members of a profession in which others share the same or similar expertise.

As ideas of shared power have grown in social work, claims of expert power have been challenged. In shared power, individuals are considered the experts on their own lives, cultures, dreams, experiences, and goals. This perspective mandates that social work practitioners assume power and expertise only over the methods of helping in which they are trained, while individuals and community members retain the power to direct the work. For example, if you are working with and advocating for an international college student who has experienced discrimination in housing options in the local community, you may claim expertise on the advocacy process, but the student will retain control over those issues on which you focus and the goals of the advocacy. In this way, you will share power throughout the helping process.

For some people, actively working to minimize the power of the social worker and share power with clients and communities may not come easily. Social workers have spent decades trying to demonstrate the effectiveness of their interventions and have fought for professional prestige through the *expert* label. Individual social workers have spent years accruing knowledge, skills, and experiences to equip themselves to operate as respected members of the social work profession. However, social workers have come to recognize that the only expert on the experience of any particular relationship, experience of oppression, or significant life event is the person who has lived it, and social workers can honor that person's wisdom by sharing power within the professional relationship.

In the contemporary world, many voices of clients and community members have made it known that social workers who adopt the *expert* role are not entirely helpful, because that role often obscures their ownership of, or participation in, the work itself (Corley & Young, 2018; Twikirize, 2019). Social workers see firsthand how certain service systems that rely on expertise can come across as humiliating, insulting, or patronizing and thus inspire disillusionment and anger in the people they are intended to serve. For example, clinical social workers are often required to conduct parenting assessments and provide parenting skills classes to parents who have been accused of child neglect or abuse. Often the social worker is of a different race, ethnicity, and socioeconomic status than the parents/clients. The development of many contemporary social work perspectives that attempt to reduce the centrality of expertise and to substitute an enhanced commitment to partnership, or shared power, reflects this reality.

Many theoretical constructs perspectives such as the strengths-based perspective, feminist approaches, and empowerment theories that are covered throughout the book make a conscious effort to minimize the boundaries of expertise between social workers, clients, and community members. For example, anti-oppressive practice is addressed in the 2022 EPAS which highlights anti-oppressive practice competency in social work practice at the individual, family, group, organizational, community, research, and policy levels. Such perspectives help social workers view individuals as experts on their lives and the social worker as a competent helping professional who can assist people and communities in reaching goals that they have defined for themselves. One example of how minimizing the distance between social workers, clients, and communities can work is that sessions, meetings, and other interactions can take place in public places selected by the client, such as coffee shops, houses of worship, and community centers, rather than in agency offices. Minimizing the distance promotes a relationship in which the rights of clients and community members in a helping relationship of shared power is recognized.

These theoretical perspectives support and conceptualize shared power as an allocation of shared responsibility according to each participant's particular strengths. This view does not require equality of responsibility but recognizes that skill levels differ and emphasizes the worth of all contributions. Social workers are responsible for maintaining professional ethics, and individuals and community members are responsible for making changes in their lives, with social work support. For example, in a situation involving substance use, social workers may ask questions like, "How does your drinking affect your family life?" rather than making a statement such as, "You need to quit drinking." This approach discourages hierarchies in the helping relationship and encourages a sense of joint investment in both the process and the results.

Thinking Globally and Practicing Locally

Most social work settings in the United States are moderately to severely resource-constrained. Social workers often have waiting lists and see other indicators of the need for more public and private resources to support services for clients and communities in their local areas. Moreover, the United States ranks poorly on many key indicators, even compared to other parts of the developed world. Yet, the needs are often even more severe in many parts of the world, and social workers are often more aware of the tension between local and global investments of effort than the general public.

Traditionally, many people in the United States have regarded global developments as remote. The history, geography, and resource wealth of the United States have contributed to national insularity. The COVID-19 pandemic, however, has vividly illustrated the interconnections across the globe and the speed with which what happens elsewhere can affect other communities and around the globe. The list of global issues that are affecting the local social work practice context continues to grow and includes migration, public health, and climate security. Similarly, as we hear on a daily basis, US domestic and foreign policies have global ripple effects.

Globalization is a process comprised of complex economic, social, and technological processes that have resulted in the formation of a single world community to which we all belong. Globalization involves the flow of information, ideas, knowledge, technology, capital, labor, artifacts, and cultural norms and values across national borders. Social problems such as homelessness, neglect and exploitation of children, human trafficking, poverty, violence, health and aging issues, and pandemics are worldwide issues that impact all nations. Individual practitioners can incorporate globalization into their work by making a commitment to follow global events and understand the ways in which events that occur within the United States impact individuals outside our borders and vice versa. In this way, social work practice can be infused with the field's commitment to advance human rights and social, economic, anti-oppressive policies, and environmental justice at home and abroad.

THEORETICAL PERSPECTIVES FOR SOCIAL WORK PRACTICE

Social work has a history of critically assessing the usefulness of theories first developed in other disciplines. For example, theories from biology, ecology, sociology, anthropology, psychology, and economics have been adopted and adapted to the understanding of individuals, families, groups, organizations, communities, and social policies from a social work perspective. A **theory** is an explanation, supported by a body of empirical evidence, of some event or phenomenon, which provides the basis for propositions or hypotheses that allow us to test the predictive framework of the explanation. Theories have been developed to help explain a wide array of social phenomena of vital interest to social workers, who can compare and contrast their value and usefulness to practice contexts. Applying theory to practice is a skill that social workers must take seriously as they attempt to advance their practice skills (Payne & Reith-Hall, 2019). Moreover, critical thinking is key to social work competencies.

Theories can bring order and coherence to practice situations at all levels so that social workers, clients, and community members can base their work on a logical assessment of the fit between the situation at hand and the assertions of the theory. Theories about the social world evolve and adjust to accommodate new evidence that adds to or contradicts their explanations of social phenomena. When theoretical explanations are refuted by rigorous research time after time, they are discarded, although, of course, not by everyone. For example, out-of-date, erroneous, and harmful theories asserting that people have inherent differences based on race or ethnicity have been contradicted by reliable research. Other theories evolve, such as contemporary interpretations of Freud's 19th-century psychoanalytic theory.

A **perspective** is a view or lens through which to observe and interpret the social world. A perspective is generally less structured than a theory and can be based on values and beliefs about the nature of people in various social contexts. For example, if social workers believe people are generally inclined to act in their own self-interests, that perspective will guide their practice and interpretations of the situations facing clients and community members. In that way, theories and perspectives can play similar roles in shaping practice. In this book, the terms *theory* and *perspective* are sometimes used interchangeably and may also be called *theoretical perspectives*.

In social work, a perspective that underlies practice at all levels is often referred to as **person-in-environment (PIE)**, in which is stressed the importance of understanding the client and their behavior in context of their lived environment (Encyclopedia of Social Work). This perspective holds that adequately understanding individuals requires an understanding of their surrounding family, community, social, and political environments. Several theoretical perspectives that are consistent with PIE are introduced briefly here and are presented in more detail later in the book. The common thread between them is that they emphasize the interface between people and their environments.

Ecosystems Perspective

Drawing on systems theory and ecology, the **ecosystems perspective** is an often-used framework for generalist social work practice. This perspective examines the exchanges between individuals, families, groups, communities, and their environments. Systems theory is used in sociology and other disciplines to describe and understand complex activity in the social environment, while ecology seeks to explain how people adapt to and influence their environments. Taken together, these two concepts describe the functioning and adaptation of human systems in dynamic interchanges with one another and the surrounding environment. Striving to improve the fit between human needs and the surrounding environment can lead social workers to influence the social and physical environment with and on behalf of their clients and communities. Influencing the environment can include working with organizations to develop more responsive policies and programs, as well as shaping legislation, regulations, and the implementation of policies (Gitterman et al., 2021).

Social Justice Perspective

Social justice refers to the manner in which society distributes resources among its members, including material goods and social benefits, rights, and protections. In this context, rights include procedural rights that are increasingly important in protecting our most vulnerable clients and other citizens (Hammond, 2019; Simonson, 2019). While there are various ideas about how societies can achieve a socially just distribution of income, wealth, natural resources, rights, and opportunities, many social workers hold the notion that one of the roles of society is to strive for a fair distribution of resources and access to opportunities for all. From this perspective, developing or distributing social and natural resources based on political or social power rather than on social justice or human need is unacceptable (Libal & Harding, 2015).

The NASW *Code of Ethics* (2021a) requires social workers to spend significant time and effort on championing those who have been oppressed in terms of individual, group, and community rights, working toward more effective institutional responses, and shaping major social policies. Social work is, therefore, a political profession. Social workers identify individual, family, group, and community needs and seek to address areas of injustice. For example, if a social worker is working at the community level with veterans who are homeless and who are eligible for but are having trouble accessing mental and health care services, it is the social worker's responsibility to help them apply for and access US Department of Veterans Affairs program benefits.

The following discussions on the strengths, narrative, and solution-focused perspectives are more contemporary theoretical approaches that promote empowerment.

Strengths Perspective

An increasingly widespread approach in social work practice, the **strengths-based perspective**. The strengths perspective and other theoretical perspectives are more fully explained and discussed in later chapters of this text.

Saleebey (2013) identified six key principles for the strengths perspective (pp. 17–21):

1 *Every individual, group, family, and community has strengths:* Social workers must view clients as competent and possessing skills and strengths that may not be initially visible. Social workers should also explore useful resources in client families and communities.
2 *Trauma and abuse, illness, and struggle are challenging, but they may also present opportunities:* Clients not only can overcome difficult situations, but they can also learn new skills and develop positive protective factors. Individuals exposed to a variety of traumas are not always damaged beyond repair.
3 *Assume that you do not know the upper limits of clients' capacity to grow and change and take individual, group, and community aspirations seriously:* Too often, professional *experts* hinder their clients' potential for growth by viewing client-identified goals as unrealistic. Instead, social workers need to set high expectations for partnership with their clients so that the clients believe they can fully recover and that they can achieve their goals.
4 *We best serve clients by collaborating with them:* Playing the role of expert or professional with all the answers does not allow social workers to appreciate their clients' strengths and resources. The strengths perspective emphasizes collaboration between the social worker and the client.
5 *Every environment is full of resources*; Every community, regardless of how impoverished or disadvantaged, has something to offer in terms of knowledge, support, mentorship, and resources*:*
6 *Caring, caretaking, and context all matter:* The strengths perspective recognizes the importance of community, the inclusion of all members in society, and working for social justice. This principle is premised on the idea that caring for each other is a basic form of civic participation.

Although these key principles may evolve, the strengths perspective focuses on clients' personal assets along with their environmental resources rather than on their pathology and limitations. Strengths-based social work interventions center on helping clients achieve their goals, affirming and developing values and commitments, and making and finding membership in or as a community. The strengths perspective does not preclude the need to validate the suffering and pain (physical, emotional, or existential) of the client or the seriousness of the situation or distress. Rather, the strengths perspective seeks to acknowledge clients' expertise regarding their own lives and to focus on their resilience and capacities to survive and to confront seemingly overwhelming obstacles.

Narrative Theory

Social work interventions that are based on **narrative theory**, which is having a client write or tell their own story(ies) helps them make sense of the meanings they give to events in their lives. This is consistent with the notion of social construction, which suggests that people construct reality based on their experiences in the social world and that those experiences occur within the context of a particular culture, society, history, and language (Smith, 2022). Narrative theory guides practitioners to use stories to understand the lived experiences of people with whom they work. A social worker using narrative theory would take a conversational approach to unearth the cultural discourses about identity and power that have shaped the experiences of clients or community members. This approach involves helping people make sense of the meanings they attach to events in their lives. Narrative approaches view problems as separate from people and rest on the belief that people possess the qualities and skills needed to address any challenge they face in life (Madigan, 2019).

Solution-Focused Approach

In contrast to a narrative approach, a **solution-focused approach** invites clients to explore and determine the concrete change they desire in their lives and the resources and strengths they possess to make the change occur (Bolton et al., 2017; Choi, 2019; Franklin et al., 2018; Franklin et al., 2018). Using a solution-focused approach, clients identify a specific goal they believe will make their lives better and attach specific strengths to a plan to reach that goal. Often clients are asked to think about an *exception,* or a time in which the challenge did not exist, and to identify the conditions under which the challenge did not exist as indicators of potential ways to address the problem. For example, if a child is struggling to focus in school, a discussion of the exceptions to this situation, or conditions under which the child has been able to focus on schoolwork, may shed light on possible solutions. Is the child able to focus early in the school day? When seated with specific classmates or away from distractions? Every time the teacher is reading out loud?

QUICK GUIDE 1 Summary of Perspectives for Social Work Practice

Ecosystems perspective: Examines the exchanges between individuals, families, groups, and communities and their environment.

Social justice perspective: Focuses on the manner in which society distributes resources among its members, including material goods and social benefits, human rights, and protections.

Strengths perspective: Affirms and works with the strengths found in people seeking help and in their environments.

Narrative theory: Writing or telling their own stories helps people make sense of the meanings they give to events in their lives.

Solution-focused approach: Explores and identifies the concrete changes people want to make in their lives and focuses the work on using available resources and strengths to make the changes.

CRITICAL CONSIDERATIONS IN UNDERSTANDING SOCIAL WORK PRACTICE: THE GRAND CHALLENGES

Students and social work educators have often questioned the relevance of theoretical perspectives to actual practice situations. Some of the frameworks and perspectives may seem abstract or far removed from clients and communities. On the other hand, when perspectives reflect and honor the experience of people and fit the situation, they can be a critical guide to social work practice. For example, the strengths perspective may direct social workers to focus on the support networks and cleanup efforts of a struggling neighborhood, emphasizing the capabilities and strengths of the residents, rather than the abandoned housing and cars that line the streets. While applying frameworks and perspectives and integrating theory and practice can be challenging, efforts to do so are essential in professional, competent social work practice.

As a profession, social work has historically focused on the problems of society and addressed social problems such as poverty, child welfare, and mental illness. Led by the American Academy of Social Work & Social Welfare (AASWSW), the Grand Challenges for Social Work is an initiative to spur social progress on significant social problems using social work's science and knowledge base. In this way, social work can meet the challenges of individuals, families, groups, and communities in individual and coordinated efforts locally and regionally, as well as in society as a whole. The Grand Challenges are areas of focus for social work that collectively serve as an agenda for the profession by promoting individual and family well-being, a stronger social fabric, and a just society (AASWSW, 2016; Barth et al., 2022).

The Grand Challenges are:

1. *Ensure healthy development for youth:* Prevent mental, emotional, and behavioral problems in youth to help youth grow into healthy and productive adults.
2. *Close the health gap:* Use evidence-based social strategies to ensure access to health care and prevent ill health effects from discrimination, poverty, and dangerous environments.
3. *Build healthy relationships to end violence:* Use proven interventions to prevent and identify abuse among individuals, families, and communities, to help break the cycle of violence.
4. *Advance long and productive lives:* Facilitate engagement in education and productive activities throughout life to promote better health, financial security, and a vital society.
5. *Eradicate social isolation:* Promote deep social connections and community for all.
6. *End homelessness:* Develop service innovations and technologies and create policy that advances affordable housing and income security.
7. *Create social responses to a changing environment:* Forge new partnerships with communities and catalyze innovations to address the environmental challenges of climate change and urban development that affect all, but especially marginalized, communities.

8 *Harness technology for social good:* Use new technologies to more quickly address growing societal needs.
9 *Eliminate racism*: Develop a model for eliminating racism by identifying evidence and practice-based interventions that will end racism and ameliorate the negative outcomes of our history of racism.
10 *Promote smart decarceration:* Develop an evidence-based strategy to reduce the prison population and ensure a just approach to public safety.
11 *Build financial capability and assets for all:* Promote adoption of social policies that improve lifelong income and savings, expand workforce training, and expand access to financial literacy and services.
12 *Reduce extreme economic inequality:* Promote education, wages, tax benefits, and changes in labor practices.
13 *Achieve equal opportunity and justice:* Engage in practice and policy efforts to address racial and social injustices, dismantle inequality, and embrace diversity of the population.

Each chapter in this book features one of these Grand Challenges for Social Work to provide examples and ideas about the ways in which the profession of social work can provide knowledge, skills, and experience to achieve these challenges to improve social, economic, and environmental well-being for all.

GRAND CHALLENGE

Eliminating Racism

One of the most enduring and systemic problems facing American society is the historical effects of structural and institutional racism. Eliminating racism, therefore, has been identified by the American Academy of Social Work and Social Welfare Grand Challenges for Social Work initiative as one of the most challenging social problems facing our society. Eliminating racism, as discussed by Teasley and colleagues (2021) is a key social work concern.

> In this context, in 2020, the Grand Challenge to Eliminate Racism, added belatedly, was established, recognizing that the United States is built on a legacy of racism and white supremacy that has consistently and significantly affected the daily lives of millions of people. It acknowledges that today, racist policies, bias, and discriminatory practices continue to promote racial inequality in myriad ways.
>
> (Teasley et al., 2021, p. 10)

Incidents of racial injustice in 2020 gave increased urgency to the Grand Challenge to eliminate racism. Specifically, spurred by effective organizing by Black Lives Matter and other racial justice organizations, these incidents brought the brutality of racist systems and racially oppressive power to the forefront of the consciousness of many Americans, millions of whom joined protests demanding change throughout various systems of society. Moreover, as the world grappled with the COVID-19 pandemic, the United States was also forced to recognize and address the historic racism, systemic violence, and oppression experienced by Black people as evidenced by the killing of Breonna Taylor and George Floyd by law enforcement officers.

> **GRAND CHALLENGE**
>
> *Continued*
>
> The goal of this Grand Challenge call to action is to promote racial equality by identifying
>
> > empirical evidence and practices that take on discrimination in all its forms and address racism's most dangerous and negative side effects on the health and well-being of our country by joining the national efforts to build and organize antiracism policies, systems, and communities. Specifically, the Eliminate Racism Grand Challenge efforts focus on evidence and evidence-based research that cultivates innovation to improve the conditions of daily life for all impacted by racism and facilitates change at the individual, organizational, community, professional, and societal levels.
> >
> > (Teasley et al., 2021)
>
> The issue of racism permeates all facets of society, intersects with the other Grand Challenges, and has relevance to the chapters in this text. To familiarize yourself with the issues related to eliminating racism, visit the Grand Challenges website and read Working Paper No. 26, Eliminating Racism (Teasley et al., 2021) at https://grandchallengesforsocialwork.org. (See Exercise #1 for additional exploration of this Grand Challenge.)

CONCLUSION

This chapter introduced generalist social work practice at multiple levels providing five theoretical perspectives that guide social workers to empower people and communities at society's margins. Lifelong learning maintains professional growth and adherence to social work values and ethics. Social workers—and people in the general population—understand the profession in many different and overlapping ways. This is germane because social work is a broad and complex field with: (1) a wide range of practice settings; (2) required competencies and related knowledge, values, skills, and professionally appropriate cognitive and affective processes; and (3) many different types of clients and communities. Because of the complex nature of the field, self-knowledge is essential to effective social work practice at all levels.

The framework that gives social work a distinction among the helping professions is the person-in-environment perspective. This perspective holds that all practice activities are undertaken with an understanding of the interactive nature of individuals, families, groups, organizations, and communities, as well as the social norms and policies of society. An example that was woven through this chapter followed Lakeisha and her social worker, Joyce, who together worked at the individual, group, and community levels to end the violence that Lakeisha was facing at the hands of an intimate partner and to give her the opportunity to help end similar violence in the larger community. Chapter 2 delves further into the role values and ethics play in social work practice. Later chapters cover generalist practice in detail to help prepare you for entering the field with the knowledge and skills you need to help clients and communities.

MAIN POINTS

- Social work practice can be conceptualized in many different ways, including as a type of practice or range of practice settings, a type of professional activity, a set of roles, and a licensed profession. Social work is guided by a professional code of ethics.

- Each required competency in social work practice as detailed by the Council on Social Work Education (CSWE) has four dimensions: knowledge, values, skills, and cognitive and affective processes.

- Social work with individuals, families, and groups requires the same competencies and many of the same skills as social work with the community and organizations. There are more similarities between types of practice than there are differences.

- Phases of social work practice include engagement, assessment and planning, intervention, termination, and evaluation.

- Tensions that persist in social work include identifying the appropriate balance between micro and macro forms of practice, social change and social control, acceptance and change, professional expertise and shared power, and thinking globally while working locally.

- Effective social work practice requires questioning your own assumptions and understanding how they impact your work. Self-knowledge is essential to all types of social work practice.

- Theoretical perspectives play a significant role in guiding practice activities. The five perspectives or frames, presented in this book are: the ecosystem perspective, the social justice perspective, the strengths perspective, narrative theory, and the solution-focused approach.

- The ecosystems perspective provides a frame for generalist practice and examines the fit between individuals and their environment.

- The social justice perspective addresses the manner in which resources are allocated.

- The strengths perspective is a practice approach that highlights and works with individual, family, group, and community resilience and capabilities, honors people's goals and dreams, and asserts that all communities possess resources.

- Narrative theory holds that telling one's own story can help make sense of life experiences and the meaning of critical life events.

- Solution-focused approaches focus on identifying the changes that clients and communities desire and determining how to use strengths and resources to make the changes.
- The Grand Challenges serve as a collective agenda for social work's professional efforts to address society's most pressing social problems.

EXERCISES

1. To apply your learning of the Grand Challenge to eliminate racism that was discussed in this chapter, visit the Grand Challenge page at https://grandchallengesforsocialwork.org/wp-content/uploads/2021/05/Eliminate-Racism-Concept-Paper.pdf. Next go to www.routledgesw.com/static-cases and click on the "River's Family" and answer the following questions:
   a. How does the Indian Child Welfare Act (ICWA) come into play in River's case? What do you need to know about the ICWA to be effective in this work?
   b. What does culturally congruent child welfare practice look like in a case like River's? How can you, as a non-indigenous worker, engage effectively with River's family? What should a social worker understand about the history of child welfare intervention with indigenous and tribal families, to approach this case from an anti-oppressive perspective?
2. Go to www.routledgesw.com/interactive-cases/ and explore the Sanchez family interactive case study by reviewing the introduction and the tasks of each of the four phases. Click on the "Start this case" button (under the "Engage" tab) and complete Tasks #1, #2, and #3.
3. After completing Exercise #2, consider the social justice issues involved in the family's permanent resident status and the ways in which these issues are related to human rights. Respond to the following:
   a. From your knowledge of human rights and the Sanchez family, identify two human rights that apply particularly to Hector and Celia as immigrants.
   b. How might you expect that having legal permanent resident status, as opposed to having US citizenship, would impact the family?
4. Consider the consequences of different social work practice discourses and respond to the following:
   a. Describe the ways in which a social work discourse of strengths differs from a discourse of pathology when applied to the Sanchez family.
   b. Describe how a strengths-based social worker would approach the family. How would you describe the professional relationship? How would you describe the focus of the work? How could you show evidence that you have cultural humility? Be as specific as possible.
5. Go to www.routledgesw.com/interactive-cases/. Click on the Sanchez family and then under the "Engage and Discover" tab click "Case Files" to review the case file for Emila Sanchez. Click on "Mapping the Case" under "Case Study Tools." Explore Emilia's relationship with her relatives by reviewing the family genogram. Also review Emilia's Ecomap. Answer Emilia's Critical Thinking Questions.

6 Write a two-paragraph reflection journal entry to answer the question, "Why do I want to be a social worker?"
7 Reflect on three of your concerns about being an effective helper. How can those also be strengths? (For example, Concern: "I am afraid that I will become too attached to clients and community members." Strength: "I am capable of developing strong relationships.").

CHAPTER 2

Applying Values and Ethics to Practice

TO BE A SOCIAL WORKER, it is crucial for students not just to identify their own values, but also to reckon with what they may have to rethink. CONSIDER THE DEGREE TO WHICH YOU AGREE WITH the following statements related to social work practice. Your response to these statements may shed light on your personal values and the extent to which they may conflict with values held by the social work profession:

- People who choose to smoke cigarettes, chew tobacco, vape, or drink excessive amounts of alcohol are responsible for resolving and paying for their own health care since the risks of these behaviors are widely known.
- Under some conditions, physical discipline of children is acceptable.
- Children who are sexually abused should never be returned to the residence of the person who abused them.
- Social workers who agree to an agency's terms of employment do not have the right to criticize the agency's practices.
- Most people who are unhoused want to live on the streets.
- Under particular circumstances, suicide is an acceptable response for dealing with life's problems.
- Individuals who are working fulltime deserve to be free from hunger.
- Federal government mandates to pressure or compel people to be vaccinated violate individual rights.
- Perpetrators and victims of crime are equally deserving of social work services.

Social work is a value-laden profession. While social workers may not agree about all values, adherence to professional social work values is central to the practice of social work and facilitates identification as a professional social worker.

Values are strongly held beliefs, and **ethics** are rules of conduct that people follow in demonstration of those beliefs (Marson & McKinney, 2019). This chapter focuses on the way that social work values shape professional ethics—specifically, ethical codes and their application to practice, the relationship between ethics and the law, and the ways social workers manage ethical conflicts and dilemmas. The chapter starts with a brief history of social work ethics and the National Association of Social Workers (NASW) *Code of Ethics* (2021a), then contrasts the document with the International Federation of Social Workers' ethical statement. A discussion of the intersection of ethics and the law provides information about the interplay between the two and is followed by a discussion of ethical dilemmas and processes for resolving them. Extensive discussion about common practice dilemmas provides exposure to situations that you may encounter in practice, followed by an emphasis on risk management (e.g., ethical standards to guide conduct to manage liability risk and avoid professional malpractice). Coverage of ethics violations and state sanctions round out the discussion. The chapter starts with a case about social workers expanding community-based mental health services:

> *Diego works at a health clinic in a large city in Southern California that provides affordable health and mental health care services. He recently completed his BSW degree and passed the social work licensure test. Diego was older than most of the students in his social work program because he had returned to finish college after getting help for his challenges with depression and substance use.*
>
> *The clinic recently received funding from the city to establish an outreach program for people with depression, after a local study found that most people with depression in the city do not have the resources to find or pay for counseling. The clinic arranged for a two-week intensive training course for Diego's team on brief, solution-focused helping approaches and best practices for making effective referrals.*
>
> *After training, Diego and other team members began each day by taking a few comfortable, portable chairs to busy public places in the clinic's large service area. With colorful signs and brief videos on depression and its effects positioned nearby, team members handed out bottles of water and encouraged people who passed by to take a seat for a few minutes to get to know a team member, learn about the program, share experiences with or questions about depression, or sign up for services. The team found that, within a few visits to the same locations, people did begin to stop by to watch the videos or talk with the team about the program.*

Key Questions for Chapter 2

1. What does it mean to identify as a professional social worker?
2. In what ways does the NASW (2021a) *Code of Ethics* guide me in conducting myself as a professional social worker?
3. How can I apply social work ethical principles to guide my professional practice?
4. How can I apply critical thinking to inform and communicate ethical decision-making?

A BRIEF HISTORY OF SOCIAL WORK ETHICS

When social work first became a profession in 1908, some social workers were more concerned about the morals of clients and community members than about the training and conduct of individual social workers (Reamer, 2018a). In the first two decades of the 20th century, the emphasis on social reform shifted to address social problems, such as those related to health, employment, and poverty (Reamer, 2013a). In the late 1940s and early 1950s, social workers made several attempts to develop an official, written code of conduct that articulated the current, collective thinking of the profession. In 1947, the American Association of Social Workers (one of seven organizations that later joined to become the National Association of Social Workers) adopted the profession's first formal code that established guidelines and standards for ethical conduct (Reamer, 2018a). The National Association of Social Workers adopted its first formal *Code of Ethics* in 1960 (Reamer, 2013a).

The second wave of ethical development occurred in the late 1970s and early 1980s. Advances in biotechnology, such as organ and bone marrow transplants, changed the medical profession. These advances were especially influential in sensitizing social workers and other human service workers to the importance of their values and the relationship between their values and their professional decisions. New concerns about decision-making developed: Who should make certain decisions? Who should be involved in decisions? For example, who decides whether a dying relative is taken off life support? Which decisions were acceptable? Other societal changes, such as developments in computer technology, globalized ecopolitics, and growing interest in human rights, also shaped and intensified the concern for values in ethical practice (Reamer, 2013a).

It can be credibly argued that a third wave of ethical development, which had been under way for at least two decades, was further galvanized by the COVID-19 pandemic. Specifically, the COVID-19 social distancing mandates necessitated social work educators and social work practitioners to switch to and incorporate more digital technology-based interventions to educate students and to deliver services to clients, as well as usage of social media to disseminate information to the wider public (Merrill et al., 2022; Mishna et al., 2021; Walter-McCabe, 2020). As outlined by the Council on Social Work Education (CSWE), there are numerous ethical considerations related to confidentiality and ensuring client privacy when incorporating digital technology and telecommunication into social work practice and service delivery:

> With growth in the use of **communication technology** in various aspects of social work practice, social workers need to be aware of the unique challenges that may arise in relation to the maintenance of confidentiality, informed consent, professional boundaries, professional competence, record keeping, and other ethical considerations.
>
> *(NASW, 2021a, p. 4)*

Chapter 3 will more fully discuss the 2021 NASW *Code of Ethics* and ASWB et al. (2017) *Standards for Technology in Social Work Practice*, regarding the ethical use of technology in social work education and practice.

In the last several decades, social work ethics have been shaped by a growing concern with risk management. Ethical standards guide conduct to manage liability risk and avoid professional malpractice. A body of literature has arisen around risk-management strategies that protect clients and prevent ethical lapses (Reamer, 2015, 2019b; Voshel & Wesala, 2015). Over time, social work has developed standards to guide workers, prioritize ethical principles, affirm its values, and clarify social workers' responsibilities. The *Code of Ethics* (NASW, 2021a) reflects the profession's official views on appropriate conduct with clients, with one another, with organizations, and with society at large. For more detailed information about the history of the *Code of Ethics* (NASW, 2021a) go to www.socialworkers.org/About/Ethics/Code-of-Ethics/History.

PROFESSIONAL CODES OF ETHICS

The social work *Code of Ethics* (NASW, 2021a) is a comprehensive code of ethical standards and guidelines that serves to: (1) affirm social work as a legitimate profession, (2) provide guidance for practice circumstances, and (3) explicate the standards to which the public may hold the profession accountable. The *Code of Ethics* (NASW, 2021a) provides social work practitioners with a useful structure for today's increasingly complex practice situations. The *Code of Ethics* (NASW, 2021a) is the official code of social workers in the United States. Another important guide to ethical practice for social workers is the ethical statement of the International Federation of Social Workers (IFSW, 2018). This chapter reviews the *Code of Ethics* (NASW, 2021a) and the IFSW (2018) ethical statement and discusses them as tools for social work practice.

The NASW Code of Ethics

The six core values in the preamble of the *Code of Ethics* (NASW, 2021a) form the basis of the *Code*. These core values, shown in Exhibit 2.1, represent a mix of social workers' activities, skills, principles, character, and attitudes. The ethical standards cover and are organized according to the following six categories:

1. Social workers' ethical responsibilities to clients.
2. Social workers' ethical responsibilities to colleagues.
3. Social workers' ethical responsibilities in practice settings.
4. Social workers' ethical responsibilities as professionals.
5. Social workers' ethical responsibilities to the social work profession.
6. Social workers' ethical responsibilities to the broader society.

Each of these six categories of the *Code of Ethics* (NASW, 2021a) contains between two and sixteen standards, along with varying substandards, for a total of 155 standards. These standards explain appropriate conduct for social workers (see Exhibit 2.2 for a sample of the *Code of Ethics* [NASW, 2021a]). This set of guidelines is intended to explain social worker's ethical responsibilities to both their clients and to the broader society. Social workers may only deviate from these expected norms in unusual situations, such as when they come into conflict with one another.

EXHIBIT 2.1	CORE VALUES	ETHICAL PRINCIPLES
The Foundation of the Social Work Perspective	Service	Social workers' primary goal is to help people in need and to address social problems.
	Social justice	Social workers challenge social injustice.
	Dignity and worth of the person	Social workers respect the inherent dignity and worth of the person.
	Importance of human relationships	Social workers recognize the central importance of human relationships.
	Integrity	Social workers behave in a trustworthy manner.
	Competence	Social workers practice within their areas of competence and develop and enhance their professional expertise.

EXHIBIT 2.2	**6. SOCIAL WORKERS' ETHICAL RESPONSIBILITIES TO THE BROADER SOCIETY**
Sample of the NASW Code of Ethics	6.01 Social Welfare Social workers should promote the general welfare of society, from local to global levels, and the development of people, their communities, and their environments. Social workers should advocate for living conditions conducive to the fulfillment of basic human needs and should promote social, economic, political, and cultural values and institutions that are compatible with the realization of social justice.

> **EXHIBIT 2.2**
>
> *Continued*
>
> 6.02 Public Participation
> Social workers should facilitate informed participation by the public in shaping social policies and institutions.
>
> 6.03 Public Emergencies
> Social workers should provide appropriate professional services in public emergencies to the greatest extent possible.
>
> 6.04 Social and Political Action
>
> a Social workers should engage in social and political action that seeks to ensure that all people have equal access to the resources, employment, services, and opportunities they require to meet their basic human needs and to develop fully. Social workers should be aware of the impact of the political arena on practice and should advocate for changes in policy and legislation to improve social conditions in order to meet basic human needs and promote social justice.
> b Social workers should act to expand choice and opportunity for all people, with special regard for vulnerable, disadvantaged, oppressed, and exploited people and groups.
> c Social workers should promote conditions that encourage respect for cultural and social diversity within the United States and globally. Social workers should promote policies and practices that demonstrate respect for difference, support the expansion of cultural knowledge and resources, advocate for programs and institutions that demonstrate cultural competence, and promote policies that safeguard the rights of and confirm equity and social justice for all people.
> d Social workers should act to prevent and eliminate domination of, exploitation of, and discrimination against any person, group, or class on the basis of race, ethnicity, national origin, color, sex, sexual orientation, gender identity or expression, age, marital status, political belief, religion, immigration status, or mental or physical ability.
>
> *Source:* NASW, 2021a

Now, we can explore the core value of competence by returning to the case of Diego and the outreach program from the beginning of the chapter:

> *Within a few weeks, Diego and other team members had talked with many people through their outreach activities, and a number of them had shared struggles with their own or a loved one's depression. Using their active listening skills and offering genuine empathy and support, team members built rapport with people who stopped to talk. Diego and his colleagues used an encrypted messaging app on their phones when people asked to make an appointment with a clinical social worker at one of the health center locations. In rare cases, when someone indicated suicidal ideation or past suicide attempts, team members also used the messaging app to make immediate*

referrals to the clinical social worker on call who, with the client's permission, would come to the team's location to do a safety assessment and offer specialized suicide prevention services.

One of the people who had started stopping by with some frequency was a young woman named Sheryl who had talked to Diego on a few different occasions. One day, Sheryl told Diego that she had been struggling with depression for the last several weeks and that it had become so severe that she had taken an unpaid leave of absence from her part-time job. She said she knew that she needed to get help but did not have health insurance. She had realized that she kept coming by to talk to the outreach team for some support, and wasn't sure that she would be able to talk with a different social worker. She asked Diego if she could just keep talking to him to get the help she needed.

Diego faced a challenge because he wanted to help Sheryl, but he knew that social work ethics required him to practice within his area of competency (NASW, Code of Ethics, 2021a). Diego responded with both honesty and compassion. He first told Sheryl that he was honored to know that she believed he had been able to help her as they had gotten to know each another. Then he told her that there were different specializations within social work, and that he was a generalist social worker while some of his colleagues at the health clinic had advanced training and experience in helping people manage and recover from severe depression. Diego talked with Sheryl about his colleagues in a positive manner and said that his concern for her meant that he wanted her to get specialized services from the most qualified people at the clinic.

Sheryl was hesitant to have Diego set up an appointment for her with one of the clinical social workers. Diego asked her if she would feel more comfortable if he accompanied her to the first session and introduced her to his colleague. Sheryl said she appreciated his offer and would like him to come along. She stayed while Diego used the encrypted messaging app on his phone to make an appointment the following day, and then they arranged to meet at the clinic.

This example highlights the issue of integrity and competence, as well as social work agency colleagues using confidential encrypted apps to communicate (*Code of Ethics, 2021a*). Reamer (2019) describes ways in which information and communications technologies are rapidly transforming social work education and practice and notes that social workers can and should apply ethical principles to both their in-person and their remote practice. Allan Barsky, a scholar who has written extensively on social work values and ethics, discusses managing complex ethical situations in detail via a video presentation titled "Ethics and Values in Social Work: Client-Centered Processes for Managing Ethical Concerns" (Alexander Street, 2018).

Global Social Work Statement of Ethical Principles

The International Federation of Social Workers (IFSW, 2018), a worldwide professional organization of social work organizations and individuals, documents its position on ethical practice in a statement that reflects concerns that are similar, but not identical, to those articulated in the NASW (2021a) *Code of Ethics*. The IFSW approved a *Global Social Work Statement of Ethical Principles* in 2018. The statement begins with a definition of social work:

> Social work is a practice-based profession and an academic discipline that facilitates social change and development, social cohesion, and the empowerment and liberation of people. Principles of social justice, human rights, collective responsibility and respect for diversities are central to social work. Underpinned by theories of social work, social sciences, humanities and indigenous knowledge, social work engages people and structures to address life challenges and enhance well-being.
>
> (IFSW, 2018, p. 1)

The IFSW assumes that member organizations, including NASW, adhere to the standards in the *Statement of Ethical Principles* (IFSW, 2018). A comparison of the *Code of Ethics* (NASW, 2021a) and the *Statement of Principles* (IFSW, 2018) reveals that they both contain essentially the same principles but have different emphases for US and international ethical practice. For example, the IFSW *Global Social Work Statement of Ethical Principles* (IFSW, 2018) has a decided emphasis on human rights and social justice. These emphases are demonstrated in the first three principles in the statement in Exhibit 2.3.

Limits of Ethical Codes

Although ethical codes such as the NASW *Code of Ethics* (2021a) and the IFSW *Global Social Work Statement of Ethical Principles* (2018) offer helpful guidance to social work practitioners, following ethical codes in all situations can be difficult for a number of reasons:

- ethical code language is comprised of statements that are general, while each practice situation is specific,
- different social workers may interpret ethical codes in different ways, none of which are strictly inaccurate, and
- creative or innovative ways to help clients or communities may put social workers in the position of unintentionally challenging ethical codes.

Other challenges in applying ethical codes involve diversity among and between social workers, clients, and communities; situations in which two ethical codes come into conflict; and the environmental context of particular social work interventions.

The Role of Context Social workers make ethical decisions within a practice context, and that context may shape the decision-making process in subtle ways. For example, if, without realizing it, a social worker attributes negative

EXHIBIT 2.3

Sample of the IFSW Global Social Work Statement of Ethical Principles

Principles

1 Recognition of the Inherent Dignity of Humanity

Social workers recognize and respect the inherent dignity and worth of all human beings in attitude, word, and deed. We respect all persons, but we challenge beliefs and actions of those persons who devalue or stigmatize themselves or other persons.

2 Promoting Human Rights

Social workers embrace and promote the fundamental and inalienable rights of all human beings. Social work is based on respect for the inherent worth and dignity of all people and the individual and social/civil rights that follow from this. Social workers often work with people to find an appropriate balance between competing human rights.

3 Promoting Social Justice

Social workers have a responsibility to engage people in achieving social justice, in relation to society generally, and in relation to the people with whom they work. This means:

3.1 Challenging Discrimination and Institutional Oppression

Social workers promote social justice in relation to society generally and to the people with whom they work.

Social workers challenge discrimination, which includes but is not limited to age, capacity, civil status, class, culture, ethnicity, gender, gender identity, language, nationality (or lack thereof), opinions, other physical characteristics, physical or mental abilities, political beliefs, poverty, race, relationship status, religion, sex, sexual orientation, socioeconomic status, spiritual beliefs, or family structure.

3.2 Respect for Diversity

Social workers work toward strengthening inclusive communities that respect the ethnic and cultural diversity of societies, taking account of individual, family, group, and community differences.

3.3 Access to Equitable Resources

Social workers advocate and work toward access and the equitable distribution of resources and wealth.

3.4 Challenging Unjust Policies and Practices

Social workers work to bring to the attention of their employers, policymakers, politicians, and the public situations in which policies and resources are inadequate or in which policies and practices are oppressive, unfair, or harmful. In doing so, social workers must not be penalized.

Social workers must be aware of situations that might threaten their own safety and security, and they must make judicious choices in such circumstances. Social workers are not compelled to act when it would put themselves at risk.

3.5 Building Solidarity

Social workers actively work in communities and with their colleagues, within and outside of the profession, to build networks of solidarity to work toward transformational change and inclusive and responsible societies.

Source: IFSW, 2018, pp. 1–5.

qualities to David, a client, because of missed appointments, the social worker may believe that David does not want services, is unable to take full advantage of scarce resources, or does not deserve these resources. If the social worker is in a position to choose which clients have access to a limited service, they may disqualify David without further reflection. On the one hand, it may appear that the social worker is using good judgment in seeking to maximize the effectiveness of the scarce service. On the other hand, the decision reflects a decision-making process that is not transparent and that is influenced by one possibly inaccurate interpretation of David's behavior and could also be inconsistent with social justice. For example, if the social worker took into account that David missed appointments because he lacked reliable transportation, had an unstable home life, or had a child with medical needs, the decision-making process may have resulted in a different outcome.

Judgments such as these, which may be based on inaccurate or incomplete information, present an ethical question relating to the professional discretion and impartial judgment that ethical codes require. This example demonstrates that ethical codes provide decontextualized guidance. Social workers following ethical codes must still exercise judgment based on the specific circumstances of each situation.

Another component of the practice context has to do with the importance of **self-knowledge,** knowledge or understanding of one's own values, character, abilities, and biases. Social workers must maintain a high level of self-knowledge in order to consistently analyze how their own values shape their thoughts, beliefs, and perspectives as they attempt to assure that they make ethical practice decisions. Dolgoff et al. (2012) detail various ways in which social workers resolve ethical questions and the many unique circumstances and complex situations in practice that contribute to making ethical decisions. Ethical decision-making often benefits from consultation with knowledgeable colleagues (Reamer, 2018b). In some settings, social workers find it helpful to initiate an in-depth conversation with their colleagues regarding their thinking, the implications of varying choices, and an analysis of their values. In other settings, committees review cases with ethical questions and the group makes a decision.

Critical Thinking and Professional Judgment The rigid interpretation of ethical rules can also lead social workers to oversimplification in their practice decisions. Social workers may rely solely on the *Code of Ethics* (NASW, 2021a) rather than using their own critical thinking and professional judgment. Using critical thinking to inform professional judgment is a valuable component of social work practice that sometimes requires the social worker to take risks (Strom-Gottfried, 2008, 2015). There is rarely one correct answer to an ethical dilemma. Social workers must have tolerance for ambiguity and must determine how to apply ethical principles in practice (Dolgoff et al., 2012).

The following case vignette illustrates this idea:

A white school social worker named Cora, in strict adherence to the ethical principle of practicing only within her area of competency (Code, Standard 4.01a), at first declined to see a young Black student from a family struggling with poverty, with limited income, who was using substances on a daily basis. Cora felt competent to work with adolescents with developmental issues, but she was not educated to treat those struggling with substance use issues, so she decided it would be unethical to work with the student. The student needed assistance, was ready to work on the problem, and had no other obvious or realistic options for services in her rural community. The student's substance use issue was intertwined with other challenges related to growing up in difficult circumstances, and developmental issues were involved.

When the student asked her to reconsider, Cora decided to discuss the matter with a colleague. The colleague reminded Cora that she had skills and experience that would directly benefit the student. For example, she knew about adolescent development, had strong relationship skills with adolescents, and was committed to a hopeful, resilience-based perspective. Cora's colleague also advised that she might find a resource in her former supervisor, who was a certified addiction counselor. Cora contacted her former supervisor, who recommended available training and the supervision of a clinical social worker who specialized in recovery services for adolescents.

Substance use in school populations is a common and potentially life-changing issue for youth. Cora was able to negotiate with the school administration for time and reimbursement to obtain training that would allow her to better serve her clients and the school population in general. Because Cora was willing to explore options in response to important needs, her client(s) were likely to receive competent services from an experienced worker who sought both training and supervision. There is some risk in Cora's assumption of the role of providing services to a student with substance use issues; however, getting consultation and supervision in order to provide services is more closely aligned with social work's values than denying help to the student.

Strict and nonreflective adherence to a standard code can help preserve the current social order, which may be in direct conflict with the profession's commitment to confront social injustice and oppression (MacDonald, 2016). Since the student's family in the example was limited financially and belonged to an ethnic population that experienced oppression, the student would likely face more barriers to receiving needed services than students in families without these characteristics. The student's access to needed resources would be constricted, a situation of social injustice. Cora's commitment to responding to the student's need and providing services embodies social work's obligation to confront injustices.

While Cora made a decision using the *Code of Ethics* (NASW, 2021a), colleague advice, and critical thinking, not everyone will agree that her solution was the best one. For example, advocates for diversity empowerment might view Cora's effort as perpetuating social injustice because the situation could involve people of color receiving substandard services from a worker without the appropriate credentials. While there may be different, well-informed opinions about the best course of action in a situation, a too-narrow interpretation of the *Code of Ethics* (NASW, 2021a) that precludes critical thinking and creativity should be avoided. Practitioners are encouraged to consider the *Code of Ethics* in the context of their unique practice situations and to talk to colleagues to fully explore issues. This decision-making process contributes to the ongoing development of the profession's larger ethical stance.

Diversity Another concern about the rigid use of ethical codes is the possible impact on marginalized populations. Universal codes meant to apply to everyone in all situations can fail to address the contexts of individual social workers, clients, and community members, or fail to recognize differences among people and cultures. For example, the ethical mandate for confidentiality, which refers to the social worker's obligation to keep information about the people with whom they work from becoming public in any way, is often regarded as absolutely critical in maintaining a professional relationship. However, universally applying confidentiality as an ethical mandate may present an obstacle in cultures less individualistic than some of those in the United States. For example, in some cultures, the larger community may be both the reference point and a rich source of resources that often help individuals and families. In such communities, maintaining confidentiality can be experienced as secretive, alienating, divisive, and harmful.

With these examples of the importance of context, critical thinking, and affirming diversity in resolving ethical challenges, it is worth noting that the NASW (2021a) *Code of Ethics* provides a valuable guide for the social work profession, especially in the United States. The *Code* (NASW, 2021a) articulates expectations and provides overall guidance about conduct so that social workers have clear expectations and can identify points of departure from the norms. The *Code* (NASW, 2021a) is value-based and is consistent with social work history. While it has limitations, it is framed in consideration of experiences outside of the mainstream. There is a growing commitment to critically considering our history *as a profession*, as well as growing recognition of some of the differing perspectives on that history. As such, the *Code of Ethics* (NASW, 2021a) addresses growing concerns for recognition and affirmation of diverse peoples worldwide. Codes are evolving documents that reflect the consensus of the profession at the time of adoption, a consensus that can change as contexts change. Social workers are encouraged to be involved in professional dialogue about the *Code of Ethics* (2021a) through professional organizations and to contribute to its evolution.

ETHICS AND THE LAW

International, federal, state, and local laws have a significant impact on social work practice, and their constant changes create a complex, sometimes bewildering climate in which to practice (Strom-Gottfried, 2015). Ethics and the law are related and sometimes overlap, yet there are clear distinctions between the two. The following discussion highlights parallels and distinctions between social work ethics and the law, as well as the potential for, and benefit of, collaboration between social workers and lawyers.

Social worker doing health and mental health outreach in a community.

Parallels Between Ethics and the Law

Many parallels exist between social work ethics and the laws that impact practitioners. For example, social workers who breach confidentiality may be accused of violating the *Code of Ethics* (NASW, 2021a). In many states, client or community members could initiate a complaint with the state licensing board that a social worker has violated the *Code of Ethics* (NASW, 2021a). State social work licensing boards can impose sanctions or require various forms of corrective action, such as license suspension or revocation (Nobel, 2022; Reamer, 2015). NASW can also sanction social workers through an ethics committee process and can impose a range of penalties such as suspension from NASW, mandated supervision or consultation, censure, publishing the names of those sanctioned in organizational outlets, and others disciplinary actions (Reamer, 2013b). While NASW's process is professional rather than legal, sanctions can still harm a social worker's career because being investigated for an ethics violation will potentially damage one's professional credibility and future.

Conflicts Between Ethics and the Law

Social workers may experience practice situations in which there is an overt conflict between ethical practice and the law. This section considers two legal duties: the duty to report and the duty to protect. Both of these legal mandates support ethical practice in most contexts but can create conflicts on occasion as well. The following practice scenarios demonstrate the difficulties inherent in situations when the duty to report and the duty to protect are in conflict.

Duty to Report: Child Protection Social workers operating in the arena of child protection frequently find themselves in a contentious environment. Like many types of helping professionals, social workers have a legal duty to report their suspicions of child abuse or neglect to child protection authorities or law enforcement. Yet, children and youth who have experienced abuse have reported a desire for more confidentiality in the handling of their cases (Matthew et al., 2019).

A common sequence of events leading to a report of suspected child abuse or neglect begins with children telling a school nurse, teacher, administrator, or school social worker that they have been abused or neglected. Alternatively, an adult in the school may suspect child maltreatment (e.g., abuse or neglect) based on physical signs. In either situation, the professional reports these allegations to the proper authorities. A child protective services worker then investigates the charges, often interviewing the parents/guardians as well as the child and determines whether the charges are substantiated, and further action is required.

People making such referrals may be convinced that the child is being abused or neglected, but they may also suspect that the abuse or neglect is going to be difficult to substantiate. In such cases, reporting abuse might place children at much greater risk, because the parents/guardians may learn about the reports and become angry, possibly taking their anger out on the children. Many social workers find it helpful to get to know local child protective service agency workers and to build trust with them over time so that it is more likely that investigations can be undertaken with the social worker's involvement to help decrease risk to the child.

A similar situation may occur if the social worker is cynical about the adequacy, timeliness, or effectiveness of the response of child protective service agencies. For example, a social worker who must wait an unreasonably long time for a response from a child protective services agency due to inadequate department staffing may be reluctant to report again. Keeping in mind that public child protective agencies are routinely underfunded and therefore understaffed can help social workers in such situations overcome such reluctance to report. Social workers in such situations can also use their practice experiences in reporting to advocate for more adequate public resources for child protective services and can organize for better public–private child welfare initiatives and collaborations in their communities.

Social workers may encounter other practice situations in which compliance with the law appears to create more harm than good. For example, consider a social worker who is working with a pregnant 16-year-old client to discuss her options. In a discussion with the client, the social worker discovers that the teen knows that the father of the baby is her long-time boyfriend, and that he is 19 years old. In the state where the social worker practices, the boyfriend is an adult and the client is a child, meaning that the pregnancy represents a status offense and that the client, a minor, has technically been sexually assaulted. Since the client claims that the sexual activity was consensual, reporting may not assist her. Reporting will possibly alienate the baby's father, who might otherwise participate in thinking through the options and be supportive of his girlfriend's decision. It may also distance the client from the social worker, precisely when she needs more support. However, it is important for the social worker to remember that even a relatively small difference in age at this stage of development can be associated with relatively large differences in interpersonal power. In complex cases, social workers will want to seek consultation from peers, supervisors, and child protection workers to help assure an ethical and legal resolution of duty to report challenges.

Duty to Report: Adult Protection Social workers may experience similar challenges between the law and ethical duties in situations involving suspected abuse of older adults or adults with intellectual and developmental disabilities. All states have reporting laws designed to protect older adults and adults with intellectual and developmental disabilities from abuse, neglect, and exploitation. However, each state has its own definition of reportable acts and its own designations of who is responsible for reporting and what entity is responsible for accepting and investigating the report (Barsky, 2019). An additional consideration emerges with recent research on the rights of vulnerable adults in need of care to have a voice in discussions about their welfare (Lindsey, 2019). Specifically, the augment is to use special measures to make the giving of testimony less stressful by alleviating their anxiety by having their testimony take place via an online platform. Another measure may be to give the older adult a walk-through or a tour of the courtroom where the testimony will take place.

An example of the complexity of such cases can be seen in the following example. A social worker may encounter evidence that her client, Betty, who is an older adult with dementia, was financially exploited by her daughter at least once. The daughter handles Betty's bills, and the social worker encountered evidence that the daughter sometimes paid her own bills with Betty's money. The social worker may wonder whether it is worth reporting financial exploitation if it only happens sometimes as far as she knows. The social worker also knows that Betty relies on her daughter for many other tasks that enable her to maintain independent living. Reporting could put this vital relationship at risk as well as risk Betty's ability to remain in her own home.

While situations such as Betty's challenge social workers, resolving what appears to be a conflict between the legal duty to report and the ethical responsibility to best serve one's client is not impossible. Social workers who routinely work with older adults and adults with intellectual and developmental disabilities are often closely involved with the adult protective services agency in their area and may know the social work staff in that agency rather well. In Betty's case, her social worker can work with Betty's daughter to support her non-financial efforts to allow Betty to remain in her own home as long as possible, while helping her arrange for another family member or friend to handle or oversee paying Betty's bills. Findings from an adult protective services investigation, done with full knowledge of the social worker's efforts, may help provide resources and other kinds of support to ensure in-home care without financial exploitation in the future.

Duty to Protect: Threats of Violence In a comprehensive discussion of malpractice risks for social workers, Reamer (2020b) covers what has been called our "duty to warn" people from imminent threats of violence. A limit to the ethical standard of confidentiality, this responsibility emerged from a court case resulting from a tragic situation. In 1969, Tatiana Tarasoff, a young student at the University of California at Berkeley, had a casual dating relationship with a graduate student from India. He apparently did not understand US dating customs and, consequently, was despondent that Tatiana was simultaneously dating several men. Depressed, he went to a psychologist at the University Health Service and told the psychologist that he intended to kill Tatiana. The psychologist wrote a letter to the campus police and asked that the graduate student be detained in a psychiatric hospital. The police interviewed the young man but did not feel there was evidence to prove that he was dangerous. The police required him to promise that he would not contact Tatiana. When Tatiana returned from a summer visit abroad, the man stalked and, ultimately, killed her (Buckner & Firestone, 2000).

Tatiana's family sued the campus police, the University Health Services, and the Regents of the University of California for failing to warn them that their daughter's life was in danger. The trial court dismissed the case because although there was precedence for notifying the victim, there was no precedence for warning a third party (which, in this situation, would have been Tatiana's parents. Moreover, Tatiana was also not warned). The appeals court supported the dismissal, and an appeal was taken to the California Supreme Court, which overturned the dismissal, citing the therapist's responsibility to warn people who have been threatened as Tatiana had been. This case, *Tarasoff I* of 1974, is often called the "Duty to Warn" decision.

This ruling opened the way for the family to sue the police and the therapist. A massive outcry from members of both police and treatment-related groups led the California Supreme Court to hear the case again. The 1976 court decision, *Tarasoff II*, stressed that, when clients pose serious danger of violence to others, therapists must "use reasonable care to protect intended victims against such danger." The court's position was that therapists might have to take any of several steps to ensure the safety of people threatened by their clients, and the emphasis was on the "duty to protect" rather than the warning emphasized in *Tarasoff I*. Although the Tarasoff decisions were based on the work of a clinical psychologist, social workers and other human service professionals are subject to the same legal precedents in most states.

Social workers must now carefully consider any threats of violence they learn about in the course of practice. For example, if a client with a history of violence threatens to hurt his girlfriend after her discharge from a hospital, the social worker is obligated to assess the seriousness of the threat. Additionally, social workers must protect themselves and their employers against legal charges. A situation of this type is complex, and social workers must respond with several considerations in mind, including their employer's policies, the legal obligation of "duty to protect," and the NASW (2021a) *Code of Ethics*. In the case of the *Tarasoff* decisions, the courts, not the ethics board of the profession, defined the parameters of responsibility. Moreover, social workers have an obligation to inform clients of the limits and exceptions to confidentiality. Specifically, there are at least three areas in which social workers may be required to break confidentiality: as mandated reporters, social workers are legally required to report cases of child abuse, neglect, or exploitation; social workers are required to report abuse, neglect, or exploitation of older adults and persons with disabilities; and social workers have a duty to report if an individual threatens to harm themselves or others.

Conflicts in Working With Individuals, Families, Groups, Organizations, and Communities

While the previous scenarios have involved social work with individuals and families, practice situations at various client system levels can involve the legal system. US society has become increasingly litigious, and social workers may encounter practice situations with legal questions in policy practice, research, and community practice, as well as practice with individuals and families (Barsky, 2019). For example, a social worker may encounter ethical challenges at the policy level if a new law requires adoption workers to provide the "adoption triad" (i.e., birth parents, adoptive parents, and adopted children) with access to all information about the adoption. If a birth mother was guaranteed confidentiality at the time of the adoption, she, along with her social worker, may be distraught by this sudden breach of the document that she signed, which she considered a binding legal agreement that would be in effect permanently.

Collaboration Between Ethics and the Law

In the United States, the law drives much of the complex social welfare system, as well as the structures for shaping income and benefits distribution. In the most desirable scenarios, the law and the social work professions work together to empower people whose legal and social rights are frequently violated. For example, collaborations occur in legal clinics for people who are immigrants and refugees and in family law and social work partnerships. Joint efforts between the professions of social work and the law, based on common goals, can benefit a great number of people, with each profession enhancing and enriching the work of the other. In addition, Masters in Social Work students may also pursue a dual degree in Law. A dual degree allows for a broader understanding of how the psychological and social perspectives interact with environmental factors when representing and advocating for vulnerable populations (e.g., children, families, women, older adults, incarcerated individuals, the homeless, and people with disabilities). Moreover, a social worker with legal skills will be better prepared to advocate more effectively for clients within the complex legal system. Dual degree graduates often choose careers in social justice, are often employed with the court systems as negotiators or mediators, or work with nonprofit organizations, such as policy think-tanks and advocacy groups.

Social workers may be faced with maintaining a city zoning ordinance against a group home for persons leaving prison, an establishment that they believe is critically needed in the community. One social worker may be working with a citizen-led "**smart decarceration**" group (a comprehensive reform approach that could lead to socially just criminal justice system reform) (Pettus-Davis & Epperson, 2015) in the community that wants to change the ordinance, while another social worker may be working with a neighborhood association that has voted to work to maintain the ordinance. Social workers working at the community level can thus experience ethical challenges in supporting community initiatives.

The law also places pressure on all of the helping professions to hold one another accountable within their professions. The law protects the public from the possibility that helping professionals can collude to cover up or obscure unethical conduct within their profession. Although the incidence of covering up unethical behavior is relatively low, all professionals may be tempted to minimize the seriousness of any offense raised. In recent decades, child maltreatment allegations and convictions involving religious leaders and the abuse of persons with intellectual and developmental disabilities who reside in state-operated facilities have served as tragic reminders of the potential dangers the unethical behavior of people in the helping professions poses to vulnerable populations.

IDENTIFYING AND RESOLVING ETHICAL DILEMMAS

The complex context of real client and community situations can make it difficult to identify appropriate ethical decisions. This section addresses the distinction between ethical conflicts and dilemmas, introduces various models for resolving ethical dilemmas, and presents some examples of common ethical dilemmas in social work practice.

Making a Distinction Between Value Conflicts and Ethical Dilemmas

Value conflicts occur when an individual's personal values clash with those of another person or social system. In contrast, ethical dilemmas occur when a social worker must choose between two or more relevant, but contradictory, ethical directives. An ethical dilemma exists when there is no clear single response that satisfies all ethical directives in a situation (Dolgoff et al., 2012). For example, school social workers are not allowed to give money to students who have food insecurity issues, but are instead required to link students and their families, to the appropriate services and resources (e.g., SNAP benefits, food pantries). The dilemma is that this is problematic when a hungry student is sitting in your office.

Many practice situations involve clashes of values that are not ethical dilemmas. For example, a social worker may learn that a married client is having an affair outside of their marriage. While the social worker may not agree with the client's choices, the situation does not meet the criteria for an ethical dilemma because it does not create an issue for the social worker who is obligated to keep client confidentiality. Another example would be when a number of different community members ask a social worker to help another person who is experiencing a family crisis, but the person has not sought services. In this instance, the social worker could suggest the community member have the person contact the agency to set up an appointment to discuss their issues or situation. In these circumstances, a social worker who would tell the spouse of a client that the client is having an affair would be violating the *Code of Ethics*. Social workers must grapple with their ethical and legal mandates, consult with colleagues and supervisors, increase their commitment to self-knowledge and self-awareness, and analyze the unique circumstances in the case at hand to arrive at a decision.

The Ethical Principles Screen

A useful tool in considering ethical priorities is what Dolgoff and colleagues (2012) call "the Ethical Principles Screen." In this context, a screen is a practice tool that can assist social workers in the decision-making process by highlighting the relative significance of often-competing ethical mandates. Reflecting on the principles highlighted in this tool can help social workers understand the likely results of particular decisions. The elements in the screen, listed in Quick Guide 2, are rank ordered so that Principle 1 has the highest priority and Principle 7 has the lowest.

QUICK GUIDE 2   Elements of the Ethical Principles Screen

- Principle 1: *Protection of life:* This principle refers to guarding against death, starvation, violence, neglect, and any other event or phenomenon that endangers a person's life.
- Principle 2: *Social justice:* This principle reflects a commitment to equal and fair access to services and basic treatment.
- Principle 3: *Self-determination, autonomy, and freedom:* This principle affirms the notion of self-determination and supports people's right to make free choices regarding their lives.
- Principle 4: *Least harm:* This principle supports the idea of protecting people from harm; when harm seems likely in any event, it asserts that people have the right to experience the least amount possible.
- Principle 5: *Quality of life:* This principle confirms that people, families, and communities all have the right to define and pursue the quality of life they desire.
- Principle 6: *Privacy and confidentiality:* This principle supports the right of people to be protected from having their personal information made public. Maintaining confidentiality means the social worker must not share client circumstances, struggles, or decisions without the client's explicit (generally written and signed) permission. Information revealing any identifying characteristics (such as name and physical description) must also be kept confidential.
- Principle 7: *Truthfulness and full disclosure:* This principle directs social workers to tell clients the full truth of any information pertaining to them and explain whatever is needed to ensure understanding.

Source: Dolgoff et al., 2012

The following scenario demonstrates the use of the Ethical Principles Screen (Dolgoff et al., 2012):

A social worker believes that a child on her caseload is at risk because his father regularly spanks him as a form of punishment. This case clearly reflects Principle 1 regarding threats of bodily harm. A competing concern with reporting is the necessary violation of confidentiality and, if not well explained and understood, the continuing trust of the child. Thus, the case also involves Principle 6. To resolve the dilemma, the social worker identifies the ethical principles involved: the protection of life versus confidentiality. The social worker then ranks the priority of these principles using the ethical principles tool. In this situation, the life of the child is a more urgent and compelling guiding principle than the desire to maintain confidentiality.

While not all social workers would agree with the way in which ethical principles are prioritized in this situation, the tool provides help for social workers who need to make ethical choices and decisions. Even so, the principles address very broad concepts that are subject to interpretation, and the evaluation of their relative importance in unique practice situations often requires critical consideration.

Other Models for Resolving Ethical Dilemmas

Social work scholars have developed other models for resolving ethical dilemmas. These models provide a series of steps that reflect professional values and guide social workers in enhancing the quality of their decisions regarding ethical dilemmas.

Strom-Gottfried (2015) proposes a model which adds several options for addressing ethical dilemmas, including researching the literature, relevant laws, and policies; consulting formally with established committees; obtaining supervision; and consulting peers. Strom-Gottfried suggests consideration of the following components of the options being considered in resolving ethical dilemmas:

- the "worst case scenario" of each option;
- the principles of least harm, justice, and fairness;
- the setting of practice and ethical implications of each option;
- the process involved in implementing each option; and
- identified power relationships that may be affected by each possible decision.

Used in conjunction with other decision-making resources and tools, considering each of these components will likely inform the resolution of ethical dilemmas.

Reamer (2018b) proposes a set of guidelines to use with any model. It guides social workers to follow several steps to optimize their ethical decision-making:

1. Identify the ethical issues, including the social work values, principles, and duties that conflict.
2. Identify the individuals, groups, organizations, and/or communities that are likely to be affected by the decision.
3. Tentatively identify all possible courses of action and the participants involved in each, along with the possible benefits and risks for each.
4. Thoroughly examine the reasons in favor of and opposed to each possible course of action.
5. Consult with colleagues and appropriate experts (i.e., professional colleagues, supervisors, agency administrators, and attorneys).
6. Make the decision and document the decision-making process.
7. Monitor and evaluate the decision.

Both Reamer's and Strom-Gottfried's approaches help analyze the issues involved in any particular dilemma. Like codes of ethics, neither of their models can produce infallible results, and critical thinking is needed in applying models to specific social work contexts. In sum, there is not one right-or-only model. What is most important is that you have a process or protocol that you follow that will help guide your decision-making.

Representative Examples of Practice Dilemmas

Of the many potential dilemmas that emerge in social work practice, three types are especially common: dual relationships, responsibilities to the larger society and individual well-being, and struggles between paternalism and client self-determination.

Dual Relationships Relationships between social workers and clients that exist prior to the professional relationship can create conflicts of interest and unhelpful dynamics. Such relationships, outside the helping context, are referred to as **dual relationships**. The NASW (2021a) cautions social workers against initiating or participating in dual relationships. The risk to confidentiality in dual relationships is heightened, as is the potential for client harm (which is higher-order as described previously), as is the potential for power dynamics to emerge as a barrier to effective social work practice. We can further explore the issue of dual relationships in social work practice by revisiting the case from the beginning of this chapter involving Diego and the mental health outreach team:

> One day while Diego and the outreach team members were working in a park near Diego's neighborhood, Vivian, a woman who lived in Diego's building, stopped by to say hello to him. Previously, Diego and Vivian had become friendly by occasionally borrowing small tools and other household items from each other. Recently, Vivian had generously lent Diego a few dollars for

breakfast one morning when they unexpectedly met in the café down the street and he realized he had forgotten his wallet.

As Diego and Vivian began to talk in the park, Vivian revealed that she had struggled with depression on and off throughout her adult life. Diego asked if she had ever thought of getting help for her depression, and Vivian said that she felt awkward talking about it with someone she didn't know. Diego's first thought was to offer to talk with Vivian himself because he wanted to be a good neighbor. But he realized that his professional ethics regarding dual relationships guided him to help Vivian access services, if she decided to do so, with someone else.

Diego told Vivian that he was glad that she told him about her depression, and that he knew it was sometimes difficult for friends to confide in each other. He also said that he hoped she knew that she could always talk with him about anything when she needed a friend. Vivian smiled and said that she appreciated having his friendship and support and offered that she would not want to jeopardize their friendship by taking advantage of his professional training by trying to get help with her depression from him.

Diego felt relieved that Vivian understood professional boundaries without him having to explain that he could not begin a dual relationship with her. Before they ended the conversation, Diego gently turned the conversation to the other outreach team members who were working with him that day. He told Vivian that he trusted them because of their listening abilities, compassion, commitment to confidentiality, and belief in letting people decide the kind of help they wanted and the timing of pursuing that help. He encouraged Vivian to stop by anytime if she decided that she wanted him to introduce her to any of his colleagues.

This example demonstrates a situation in which a dual relationship represents a conflict between personal values and professional responsibilities. Diego wanted to be a good neighbor to Vivian and valued his friendship with her. However, his professional responsibilities to avoid initiating or participating in a dual personal–professional relationship caused him to place Vivian's long-term well-being ahead of the temporary positive feeling he might have experienced in offering to provide services himself.

Sometimes dual relationships only become public in extreme circumstances, such as when social workers have sexual relationships with clients or community members with whom they work. Sexual relationships, although an egregious professional violation, are clearly unethical because ethical guidelines clearly prohibit such relationships. Therefore, social workers can be reported for ethical violations to their state licensure boards, NASW, and potentially to the legal system.

Nonsexual dual relationships can also increase the risk of exploitation or other types of potential harm. Reamer (2018b) classifies dual relationships as unethical when they:

- interfere with the social worker exercising professional discretion and the social worker exercising impartial judgment;

- exploit clients, colleagues, or third parties to further the social worker's personal interests; or

- harm clients, colleagues, or third parties in some other manner.

In many cases, dual relationships highlight conflicts between social workers' personal values and their professional ethics. For example, consider the situation of Lara, a new social worker:

Lara works in a local community center with young adults who have been arrested and assigned to diversion programs. A diversion program allows some arrested individuals to be given the opportunity to participate in a treatment program as an alternative to serving time in jail or prison, to address the underlying reasons for the behavior that led to law enforcement contact. Her responsibility is to support their integration into the community's youth employment program that the center sponsors. Lara finds her work interesting and rewarding, and she particularly enjoys working with one client, Joe, who is progressing in the program. Lara's 20-year-old sister recently called her to tell her about her new boyfriend. As her sister described her boyfriend, Lara realized that he was her client, Joe.

Lara values both her job and her family relationships. She enjoys her job and does not want to consider resignation. She also values her work with Joe. Lara also wants to continue participating in her family gatherings, which are likely to include her sister's new boyfriend. Because of the ethical mandate regarding confidentiality in the Code of Ethics (NASW, 2021a), Lara is not free to tell her family that she works with Joe or to reveal anything about his situation.

In this example, the dual relationship Lara has with Joe has the potential to affect her professional discretion and impartial judgment. For example, if Lara discovers personal information about Joe that suggests he may not be a good partner for her sister, Lara may experience difficulty conducting herself in a professional manner. On the other hand, Lara may develop positive regard for Joe, given his new role in her sister's life, and her professional judgment may be affected by these feelings.

How could she be certain that her decisions regarding work hours, stipend amounts, job assignments, and regular evaluations of Joe as a participant in the youth employment program were not being shaped by her knowledge of her sister's relationship with him? How could Joe know that he was being treated in a fair and honest manner in the program? Lara will need to evaluate the risk of exploiting Joe rather than empowering him if she were to continue working with him. Lara might also consider the likelihood of increasing Joe's vulnerability through her knowledge of his past struggles.

It is likely that Lara will be at risk of clouding the professional relationship by working with Joe while he is dating her sister. Although her dual relationship with Joe is naturally occurring in this example, the dual relationship is not empowering for Joe and has the potential to decrease, rather than increase, his well-being. Lara needs to talk with Joe and meet with her supervisor to develop an ethical way for Joe to continue in the program while avoiding a dual relationship.

In rare situations, social workers may need to carefully consider how to handle dual relationships that cannot be avoided. For example, in rural areas, dual relationships may be very difficult to avoid, given a relatively small number of professional service providers (Reamer, 2018c). In a rural area, clients may work for or with a member of a social worker's family, share the same faith community as the social worker, or belong to the same civic organization as the social worker. Such practice realities require self-awareness and clear communication between the social worker, clients, and community members to establish clear boundaries, an expectation of strict confidentiality, and other safeguards against common problems inherent in dual relationships.

With technological and communications advances, dual relationships are likely to emerge more frequently, even beyond small communities. The widespread use of social media, for example, requires that social workers be more vigilant in their efforts to avoid dual relationships, including online relationships in which people can be near or far geographically and often do not share identifying information.

Responsibility to the Larger Society and Individual Well-Being Relationships that involve maltreatment of a child or vulnerable adult or intimate partner violence were once considered private family issues outside the jurisdiction of the law or of any public sector interest. Through the legal and social welfare systems, the larger society has wrestled with the question of whether certain events are private matters or public issues that impact society. While social workers often tend to value the private experience of families in the effort to recognize and acknowledge people's perspectives on their own experiences, social workers are also sometimes obligated to intervene within the family environment. The dilemma in this situation arises when the social worker values both the family's right to privacy and the potential benefit to the community of making the family issues public in order to prevent violence or help others in the same situation.

For example, social workers might struggle with their obligation to encourage a survivor of rape to report the incident to the police (Dombo, 2011). Survivors may be reluctant to pursue legal recourse for many reasons. These include: (1) wanting to heal and to avoid dredging up the past through legal proceedings; (2) fear of rejection if their experiences are made public; and (3) fear of re-traumatization if authorities imply that the survivor is the guilty party. For these and other reasons, rape is often underreported. Many social workers encourage reporting, so the crime is logged, and appropriate resources can be devoted to the issue for the individual involved, and others who may be in the same situation in the future. Reporting may also increase the possibility that jurisdictions will devote additional resources and attention to the prevention of sexual assault. The benefit to society of reporting the crime must be balanced with the experiences and wishes of individuals who have been raped. Attempting to influence a person to report an experience of rape to authorities may jeopardize the individual's mental and physical well-being but ensuring the client they will be supported by you (or others), should they opt to file a report, can communicate that they are not alone in this process.

Striking a balance between promoting the public's general welfare and honoring the wishes of individuals is challenging in practice and requires the application of critical thinking and practice experience. When making decisions between a responsibility to the larger society and a responsibility to individual clients, social workers must consider the following questions: Which issues are public, and which are clearly private? Is violence against people an individual event or a violation of a larger social order as well? Does violence affect the entire community? Does a social worker have the right to raise a public issue if the discussion increases an individual's distress?

Paternalism and Client Self-Determination Long a cornerstone of social work, self-determination is the right of individuals to make choices and exercise control over their lives. In the NASW (2021a) *Code of Ethics*, self-determination is listed immediately after the general commitment to clients and communities, indicating its ethical importance for social work professionals.

Paternalism occurs when social workers believe they have a better understanding than the client or community of what is in their best interests. Reamer (2018b) identifies three forms of paternalism:

(1) withholding information from clients or community members "for their own good";
(2) deliberately lying to clients or community members; and
(3) intervening to prevent certain behaviors or actions by controlling their movements, in cases such as involuntary commitment, when not necessary for safety.

A social worker who provides too much assistance to clients and communities can decrease the development of their own problem-solving skills. For example, social workers who do tasks for clients who should and can do them for themselves such as making phone calls to set up appointments for services or resources, or social workers who give too many suggestions or who interact in a controlling manner are also taking paternalistic approaches.

Questions about the rights and responsibilities social workers have to interfere in the lives of their clients and community situations have been debated since the profession began. In some situations, involving abuse, neglect, and exploitation, the law dictates social workers' rights and responsibilities. However, social workers are sometimes asked to make an ethical decision concerning self-determination without a clear-cut guide, such as intervening with a client who is disorderly or a community group that is not adhering to social norms in public. Other examples include whether a client should be forced to conform to mainstream standards of cleanliness in a residential setting or whether a social worker must facilitate the involuntary hospitalization of a person with a mental illness who is not able to adequately attend to their self-care. In such cases, someone must make a judgment about the standards of "adequate." Consider the social worker who struggles with the question of whether to intervene with clients who are eating in an unhealthy manner that exacerbates an existing health condition. Situations in which social workers question whether to intervene involve social control and social change and raise broader issues about the degree to which US society tolerates eccentricities or even mere differences. Social workers must make decisions about the balance between responsible caretaking and excessive interference with client self-determination.

A subtler variation of this dilemma occurs when the social worker urges clients to engage in an activity that the worker values. Reamer (2018b) has called this "pseudopaternalism" because the paternalistic interference does not arise out of professional values but from personal self-interest, even if the social worker has good intentions. For example, most social workers would agree that it is consistent with the profession's values to encourage a young person to achieve the highest level of education possible. At the same time, most social workers also personally value education. If a social worker encourages adolescents with great academic potential to achieve scholastically beyond the goals of the adolescent and their families, the social worker could be acting paternalistically if the clients are not interested in such achievement and would rather attend job training at a vocational school or plan only to seek employment after high school. Social workers could be imposing their dreams and goals on their clients. In contrast, accepting the adolescent's limited view of life may not be upholding the social worker's commitment to promote an individual's well-being. In another example, a social worker could encourage a community to enact a community-wide recycling program when the community is not interested in recycling. The social worker could again be imposing personal values about environmentalism on the community. The issue of client self-determination versus paternalism occurs frequently in social work practice; social workers must be constantly aware of this dilemma and make decisions based on critical thinking and self-awareness.

CRITICAL CONSIDERATIONS ABOUT VALUES AND ETHICS

Many issues concerning ethics and values are complicated by context and are difficult to resolve in actual practice situations. Social workers must consider values and ethics thoughtfully throughout their careers. The following sections consider ethical social work practice in terms of (1) risk management and (2) other large concerns in the social and political environments.

Risk Management in a Litigious World

Some situations require social workers to be concrete and decisive about their actions. As noted earlier, US society is increasingly litigious, particularly in the helping professions. State regulating bodies obligate licensed social workers to uphold the NASW (2021a) *Code of Ethics*, even if practitioners question certain aspects and/or challenge the *Code* to encourage change. Though litigation in social work is relatively uncommon, social workers do face costs of lawsuits charging malpractice or negligence, and the related risks of censure. The profession holds social workers accountable for upholding the *Code of Ethics* (NASW, 2021a) through the NASW ethics complaints process. The courts and state licensing boards also hold social workers accountable for their professional actions. Social workers are sometimes indicted on criminal charges about ethical misconduct such as allegations of fraudulent billing (Reamer, 2020c).

In a national study of the actions of 44 states and the District of Columbia regulatory boards against certified and licensed social workers, Boland-Prom et al. (2015) and Gricus (2019) found that the most frequent violations were license-related problems, dual relationships, crimes, problems with basic practice (e.g., record keeping, informed consent, and confidentiality), professional practice while impaired (e.g., alcohol, drugs, mental illness), and practices below specific standards of care. Regulatory boards typically revoked licenses or required the license to be surrendered followed by suspensions, sanctioned social workers with letters of warning, or issued another admonishments.

Areas that pose key risks for social work also include:

- client rights,
- use of digital and electronic technology, social media, using personal mobile phones to communicate with clients or colleagues about clients,
- documentation,
- defamation of character,
- record storage and retention of protected client data on a company server on in the "cloud,"
- supervision and consultation,
- client referral,
- fraud,
- termination of services, and
- practitioner impairment and misconduct.

(Reamer, 2018d, 2015)

When wrestling with decisions that have an ethical component, social workers are encouraged to take advantage of the knowledge and experiences of other competent and concerned social workers through supervision. Strategic thinking and planning with another professional, particularly one with more experience in identifying critical aspects of the practice situation, can be an invaluable decision-making aid. Further, receiving input on practice through regular social work supervision can assist in the prevention of inadvertent ethical violations.

Social work practice occurs within a context of reflective, contextual practice, in which values are explored and rules about them are challenged as needed. Social workers must practice in ways that honor the NASW (2021a)

Code of Ethics, follow legal mandates and especially adhere to the duty to report and the duty to protect, and maintain a personal and professional obligation to engage in critical thinking when values come into conflict and ethical dilemmas emerge in work to help clients and communities.

Social, Economic, and Environmental Justice

Current professional ethical inquiries tend to focus on ethics enforcement and risk management (Reamer, 2020c). Rather than large and serious issues, such as poverty, racism, or environmental degradation, the *Code of Ethics* (NASW, 2021a) and most ethical inquiries focus on the conduct of individual practitioners. Social workers, however, can explore other dimensions to enrich the professional discourse about ethical practice. Two examples are the emerging focus on environmental justice (Erickson, 2018) and anti-racism in social

---

EXHIBIT 2.4

Grand Challenge

Create Social Responses to a Changing Environment

One of the most pressing challenges for today's society, particularly in marginalized communities, is environmental change. Identified by the American Academy of Social Work and Social Welfare Grand Challenges for Social Work initiative as one of the most challenging social problems facing our society, the impact of environmental factors is discussed by Kemp and Palinkas (2016) as a key social work concern.

Due to climate change and increasing urbanization, the world is facing such environmental challenges as prolonged drought, pollution, rising sea levels, and natural disasters. These challenges threaten human health and well-being because of their destabilizing effects on communities, and they particularly negatively impact people with low income or social status. The vulnerable are affected through disrupted employment and income instability, food and housing insecurity, and ecological degradation in their communities.

Social work is well-positioned to strategize and implement interventions to prevent and address the human and social dimensions of environmental challenges. Social work can be involved in disaster preparedness and responses, and those dislocated can be provided with resources and support. Social workers can also work at the macro level to increase the capacity of local communities to prevent and respond to local needs, as well as advocate to change policy so that further attention is given to the human and social aspects of environmental challenges.

Social workers are required in the *Code of Ethics* to give "attention to environmental forces that create, contribute to, and address problems in living" (NASW, 2021a, preamble, para. 1, p. 1). Social work's person-in-environment perspective requires attention to the human and social implications of increasing social and economic inequality, increased population density, and inadequate infrastructure and services. To familiarize yourself with the issues related to environmental changes, visit the Grand Challenges website, http://grandchallengesforsocialwork.org, and read Working Paper No. 5, Strengthening the Social Response to the Human Impacts of Environmental Change (Kemp & Palinkas, 2016).

work practice (Pittman et al., 2022). Social workers interested in expanding the notion of ethical practice might examine the degree to which their practice is consistent with nonviolence, closing racial income and wealth gaps, prioritizing the needs of the disadvantaged, anti-racism, and environmental justice.

CONCLUSION

This chapter has examined values and ethics that guide and govern social work practice. As social workers gain skills in ethical decision-making, they are increasingly able to recognize ethical dilemmas and make ethical decisions. Although social workers strengthen the profession through active questioning of ethical standards and codes, they must also understand the continuing need for widely shared acceptance of and support for professional ethics, public concern about ethical violations, and the need for critical thinking about societal expectations. Social workers encounter complex practice situations regularly as they help individuals, families, groups, organizations, and communities. Professional and ethical decision-making in such situations requires knowledge of social work values and ethics, the commitment to self-awareness and self-knowledge, comfort with some degree of ambiguity in cases involving competing values and ethical standards, the ability to weigh and balance differing priorities on a case-by-case basis, and a willingness to consult with colleagues and supervisors in resolving ethical dilemmas in practice.

MAIN POINTS

- Ethical codes are useful in providing standards of professional conduct, but they may also be limited in some cases when social workers are dealing with complex cases and competing ethical standards. Can be reviewed at https://www.socialworkers.org/About/Ethics/Code-of-Ethics/Code-of-Ethics-English and www.nabsw.org/page/CodeofEthics.

- Social workers have an ethical responsibility to gain and maintain a high level of self-awareness, knowledge of current ethical codes and standards, and practice experience in resolving ethical challenges and dilemmas.

- Social work ethics and the law do not always coincide, although they have parallels and offer the potential for interdisciplinary collaboration, especially between social workers and attorneys.

- Value conflicts occur when an individual's personal values clash with those of another person or social system. In contrast, ethical dilemmas occur when a social worker must choose between two or more relevant, but contradictory, ethical directives.

- Social workers need to develop sophistication in professional ethics and risk-management practices to help them avoid ethical violations.

- While social work ethics are most often discussed in the context of practice with individuals, families, and groups, there is a growing commitment in the profession to apply values and ethics to larger social systems including organizations, communities, and societies.

EXERCISES

1 To apply your learning of the Grand Challenges for Social Work—Strengthening the Social Response to the Human Impacts of Environmental Change, visit the Grand Challenge website at http://grandchallengesforsocialwork.org and read Working Paper No. 5. To appreciate the ethical issues that environmental challenges can pose for social workers, review the Hudson City case at www.routledgesw.com/interactive-cases/. After reading Working Paper No. 5 and reviewing the Hudson City case, respond to the following questions:
   a Which of the environmental challenges identified in Grand Challenges Working Paper No. 5 are present in the Hudson City case information?
   b What is your assessment of Hudson City's problems related to these challenges?
   c Select one of Hudson City's challenges. Use the tools on the book's website to develop an assessment and intervention plan for working with your selected Hudson City challenge.
2 Go to www.routledgesw.com/interactive-cases/ and select the Sanchez family case. Review the client histories of Celia and Hector Sanchez. Imagine that you are a social worker employed by Our Lady of Guadalupe Church, where the Sanchez family are parishioners. You have noticed that, when Celia comes to pick up commodities, she talks about the desperation of her family. When asked about Supplemental Nutrition Assistance Program (SNAP) benefits (also known as Food Stamps), she replies that her husband will not allow her to enroll in the program. She thinks it would be a good idea and is considering enrolling despite her husband's wishes, if she can think of a way to do it. You have helped other families access the program, even when one member does not wish to enroll. Should you encourage Celia to use your assistance to enroll? What social work values are involved in this situation? Is it an ethical dilemma? How might you resolve the situation? What might be the implications? Please discuss your responses with classmates.
3 Go to www.routledgesw.com/interactive-cases/ and go to the Riverton case. Under the "Engage" tab, answer Critical Thinking Question #1.
4 Go to www.routledgesw.com/interactive-cases/ and become familiar with the RAINN case. Under the "Engage" tab, answer Critical Thinking Question #2.
5 You are a social worker in a psychiatric hospital setting. While most patients are discharged from the hospital setting after only a few days, some patients are covered by insurance plans or court mandates that allow for longer stays. However, the hospital mandates that patients be discharged as soon as possible, and discharge planning begins when patients are admitted.

Your client, Bea, was admitted for psychiatric symptoms and is terrified to leave the hospital after a stay of more than two weeks. Your responsibility is to locate long-term housing and outpatient mental health care for her. As you meet with her one morning, you find her tearfully pleading that she be allowed to stay longer, as she does not feel able to live independently. You are not sure that she is ready either, although the medical staff state that she is ready for discharge. You feel caught between the demands of your organization and the wishes of Bea. Respond, in writing, to the following questions:

a What three primary values does Bea's situation highlight?
b Is this an ethical dilemma? Justify your answer.
c In what section of the NASW (2021a) *Code of Ethics* would you look for guidance?
d Apply one strategy for resolving ethical dilemmas that is discussed in this chapter to Bea's situation.
e How will you go about resolving this situation?
f Compare your response with other students. Do different strategies lead to different resolutions?

6 Read the following scenarios then consider the following questions and answer any three scenarios:

Scenario A: In a public setting over lunch, one of your co-workers begins speaking disparagingly about a client who they find challenging. The co-worker does not use the client's full name.

Scenario B: You are new to the area in which you have taken a job. Your new client, a hairdresser, offers to cut your hair.

Scenario C: A colleague is applying to be a foster parent and has asked you to be a reference. You, however, know that she is a hoarder and believe that her home situation is not fit for a child.

Scenario D: You are working with a teenage girl in a youth shelter. She reveals to you that she was raped by her neighbor, who is involved with gangs and drugs. She reports that she told her father, and they agreed not to press charges due to fear of retaliation.

Scenario E: One of your clients reports symptoms of a mental illness to you. They report that they wander around the neighborhood at night in the winter without appropriate clothing, hear voices, and refuse to take their medication or go to the hospital. You are concerned about their safety.

Scenario F: You are working with a family in a family preservation program. In the home, the teenage daughter is violent toward her mother. During an altercation, the mother leaves a mark on her daughter as she attempts to protect herself from a physical attack by her daughter.

Scenario G: You are leaving the agency for another position. On your last day, a client brings you a goodbye gift and asks if you will still call her.

Scenario H: You receive an emergency call from your client. He reports to you that his boss just fired him. He states, "I am not going to let him get away with this. He is going to be sorry. He has not seen the last of me." You know that this client has access to firearms and a history of assault.

Scenario I: You receive a call from the spouse of your client. He wants to discuss his spouse's case with you. The spouse's chart does not contain a release of information.

Scenario J: A client's insurance benefits have ended, but you feel they need continued care.

    a What is the ethical issue?
    b What are the values of the client system?
    c Are they in conflict with your values? Societal values?
    d What strategy would you use to resolve the situation?
    e What would you do?

Compare and contrast your answers with those of classmates.

7 In a journal entry, reflect on a time when you faced a situation that challenged your personal values. What did you do? Why? How did you decide what to do? What were the results of your decision? If you could relive the situation, would you handle it differently?

CHAPTER 3

Communication, Interviewing, and Engagement: Relationship Skills for Practice at All Levels

THE ABILITY TO CREATE RELATIONSHIPS is at the very heart of social work practice. The idea of building relationships is part of what attracts many people to social work in the first place, and it can be an abiding component that sustains a social worker's commitment. Social work scholars and practitioners have long recognized relationships as a crucial element of the profession's work with clients and communities. Relationship building, or engagement, is the first step in the professional helping process and leads to the other steps of assessment, intervention, and evaluation.

When you think of relationships, you may first think of the one-to-one partnerships that characterize much of social work practice. These relationships, however, rarely stand alone. They are usually intertwined with other relationships those clients have with members of the community, such as teachers, doctors, therapists, case managers, religious leaders, friends, family, and anyone else helping clients reach their goals. Relationships are as critical in practice with families, groups, organizations, and communities as they are in interventions with individuals.

Given this multi-system emphasis, we often use language regarding clients and community members in this book. In generalist practice, some social workers are comfortable with using the term *client* regardless of whether they are working with individuals, families, groups, organizations, or communities. In other words, you will hear the term *clients* used to describe social work practice at any system level. Other social workers avoid defining colleagues or community members as clients when they are doing organizational, community, or policy practice. From this perspective, people we work with at any level of practice should not be labeled based on the role they play in relationships to us and the services we provide. To honor both traditions in the field, you will notice that we frequently use the term *client and community members* in this book.

This chapter explores aspects of **engagement**—the process of building relationships across levels of practice and practice settings—and its critical role in the overall success of social work practice. The first section examines the importance of listening to clients and community members as you first begin to help. It introduces communication and interviewing skills and approaches that can help people share information, thoughts, and feelings with you. These skills also help you enlist the assistance of others who may play important roles in the success of clients and communities. We start the chapter with a case that is woven throughout this chapter, which involves a youth survivor of human trafficking.

> *Ashley is a new client at a residential program for survivors of child trafficking. Her social worker is Marilyn, who is preparing to meet her for the first time. From the intake information that Marilyn's colleague gathered when Ashley was dropped off by the police the previous evening, Marilyn knows that Ashley is 15 years old and was lured into prostitution by Michael, a family friend and neighbor. She listed a local home address and her mother's phone number in case of emergency. This is unusual, given that so many of the girls who are in residence have not lived with or been in touch with their parents for some time. As Marilyn plans for her first individual meeting with Ashley, she thinks of the challenges she may face as she works to engage and build rapport given the trauma Ashley has survived.*

Key Questions for Chapter 3

1. How can I prepare to engage and build rapport with clients and community members?
2. What interpersonal and communication skills do I need to work with clients and community members?
3. What communication mistakes can I avoid?
4. How do I use a social justice and human rights perspective when working with clients and community members?

LISTENING TO AND ENGAGING WITH CLIENTS AND COMMUNITY MEMBERS

Regardless of your agency's focus or your theoretical perspective, the most important moments of a social work relationship often occur at the beginning, when you listen to and begin to build rapport with clients or members of the community to learn their situations and perspectives. The length and type of listening you do will vary depending on the needs of the clients and/or community members with whom you are working, as well as the agency and practice setting. For example, some agencies expect social workers to complete a comprehensive psychosocial history detailing a client's whole life as soon as possible. This approach seems to focus more on the past than on the present. Quick Guide 3 provides questions that align well with a social work perspective for your consideration as you begin listening to clients and community members.

QUICK GUIDE 3	Listening to Clients and Community Members

The following questions can help guide the engagement process. As you listen to clients and community members, ask yourself the following questions:

- Why did the client or community member come here today?
- How do people describe the situation that brings them to your agency or organization, and what meaning does that situation have for them?
- What might life look like when the client's or community's situation improves?
- What strengths, talents, and resources can you identify at the client and/or community level?
- Do clients and community members have expectations of me?
- What do these clients or community members hope to gain from working with me?
- What can we accomplish together?

You may find yourself in a practice setting that requires a lengthy and detailed intake process through which you collect comprehensive historical, psychological, and social information before listening to clients or community members. In this situation, you may be able to use your listening and other communication skills to suggest changing agency policies and procedures over time toward more of a "listening first" approach with more engaging questions about current life circumstances like those in Quick Guide 3. These initial considerations are helpful in establishing the respect and connections that lead to a successful working relationship. Strive to demonstrate genuine curiosity in your questioning and to show interest in all of your interactions. When you seek to understand the client's situation and perspective with an open mind, you are less likely to ask questions that are not relevant to the current situation or seem designed to confirm what you already think. It is easier to hear people share their stories and perspectives if you avoid drawing conclusions mid-conversation based on prior information or experience. The ability to listen carefully is a critical social work skill because you want to understand client and community situations according to client and community experience, rather than your own expectations.

In most cases, people respond in a positive way to our efforts to establish rapport and to demonstrate our interest in listening to them. However, some first meetings with clients and community members are more difficult. As social workers we routinely use both verbal and nonverbal communication skills in our early engagement efforts. Focusing on communicating your genuine desire to "listen first" often helps to set the stage for a productive helping relationship.

Example

Lucas is a social worker at the Juvenile Justice Center. His work as a Diversion Specialist involves working with adolescents and teens who have had their first punitive experience with law enforcement. As Lucas prepares to meet a new client, he makes sure that he has cleared his computer screen and turned off his phone so that he can attend to welcoming and attending exclusively to his client.

Xavier enters the room, and Lucas offers his hand for a handshake, makes eye contact, smiles, and greets him. Xavier ignores his hand, does not make eye contact, sits down in a chair, and crosses his arms.

Lucas calmly sits down and takes a couple of quiet, long, deep breaths. After a period of silence, Lucas begins to reestablish eye contact and speaks softly to Xavier.

Lucas: *I'm glad to meet you, and hope we can work together to help you through this difficult time. Can you tell me why you are here at the Center?*

Xavier: *No reply.*

Lucas: *I understand that you don't want to talk right now, but when you get more comfortable being here with me, I hope you can share some of your recent experiences. I'm good at listening to people's thoughts and feelings, too.*

After several minutes of silence, Xavier uncrosses his arms and begins to talk.

Relationship and listening skills are essential to work with clients, client family members, community members, and staff. For example, suppose you have forged a connection with a client after listening to their situation and perspective, conveying professional warmth and acceptance, demonstrating confidence and hope, and working with them to set tasks and goals. One of those tasks is to help the client locate and secure housing that better suits their needs, and in completing this task, you encounter a reluctant landlord. In this type of situation, you might perceive the scenario only in the client's terms—that is, you might be inclined to criticize the landlord for being reluctant to rent to your client. For this reason, in your initial contacts with the landlord, you should use the same relationship approach and listening skills that you used with your client. Avoid stereotyping the landlord and instead enter the conversation with an open mind. Do not assume that your past experience with landlords means you know about the rental business. Being open-minded may enable you to hear the landlord's assessment of the current situation and even a solution that you might not have thought about on your own. Approaching the landlord as an adversary will make it more difficult to be persuasive on behalf of your client. Trying to understand the difficulties the landlord faces maintaining rental properties in a profitable manner will help form an alliance with the landlord, and a solution to the situation may be more possible than approaching the landlord with a closed mind.

Another example of the importance of developing effective relationships with everyone involved in a complex case comes from continuing to learn about Marilyn's work with Ashley, the case discussed at the beginning of this chapter. In Marilyn's experience, residents at the center rarely have supportive family members in the area, particularly if they have been trafficked from other parts of the country or other countries altogether. After beginning to build some rapport with Ashley, Marilyn proceeds in a slow and careful manner emphasizing that she wants to understand the situation from Ashley's perspective. By approaching the helping relationship in this way, Marilyn may eventually learn about unique aspects of Ashley's situation. But if she works from the basis of her own preconceived notions about Ashley's family relationships, she may miss the chance to hear Ashley tell her story in a way that accurately reveals both the crimes she has survived and the potential support that she may have from her family. The social worker's role is to listen first, with an open mind, and to be prepared to communicate and engage with all parties that may be able to help.

Common Factors in Helping Relationships

Common factors in helping relationships have been found to explain more improvement for clients than the specific type of therapy the counselor is using. In fact, there is a large and compelling area of scholarship in the helping professions on common factors in counseling with classic works by Asay and Lambert (1999), Hubble et al. (2010) and Rosenzweig (1936). Similarly, in a seminal work that still applies to social work practice, psychologist Carl Rogers (1957) wrote of common aspects of the therapeutic relationship that are central to effective helping. These common factors include the ability of the helping professional to express warmth and acceptance, demonstrate empathy, show genuine interest in helping resolve the problem at hand, express unconditional positive regard for those needing assistance, and form an interpersonal alliance with people that involves shared goals and expectations that circumstances can and will improve. In recent studies, common factors continue to emerge as central to helping relationships, such as marriage counseling (Luguet & Muro, 2018), working with adult clients who have symptoms of depression (Gellis & Kenaley, 2022), and counseling services for a multitude of other problems in living (Fluckiger et al., 2018).

Warmth Social workers demonstrate warmth when they express sincere interest in clients and members of the community. Examples of warmth include compassionate facial expressions, a soothing tone of voice, and appropriate pacing of verbal interactions. Social workers also exhibit warmth when they extend courtesies, such as making sure people are physically comfortable, offering them a beverage, making eye contact, and using well-timed, appropriate humor (Shebib, 2019). In your work, consider ethnic and cultural considerations about the expression of warmth and adjust the amount of warmth you demonstrate to coincide with the comfort level of those with whom you are talking. Warmth is similar across groups but there are some things that one must consider with certain populations. For example, women from some cultures and religions do not touch or show familiarity or are friendly with men who are not their husband.

Empathy A vital component of all helping relationships, empathy is the "act of perceiving, understanding, experiencing, and responding to the emotional state and ideas of another person" (Barker, 2014, p. 139). Social workers must develop a capacity for working with feelings, even intense feelings, without displaying inappropriate emotions, changing the subject, offering quick solutions, or moving the dialogue to an intellectual level. Suspending judgment by controlling personal biases, assumptions, and reactions is a first step toward adopting an empathetic attitude. Sympathy involves understanding an issue from your own perspective, whereas empathy involves putting yourself in the other person's situation. Moreover, "Social empathy is the ability to understand people by perceiving or experiencing their life situations and as a result gain insight" (Segal, 2020, p. 76). Clients do not need our sympathy. A practitioner who is empathetic is willing to learn about the emotional world of another without actually experiencing that person's feelings.

To demonstrate empathy, social workers identify the feelings a client is expressing and communicate their understanding of those feelings to the client. Empathic communications help clients identify and label their feelings and process feelings that might seem overwhelming. When you hear about losses experienced by clients and community members, it is often difficult to know what to say. It can be helpful to remember that the most genuine response is often the most helpful.

> **Example**
> Client: *My son died in a fire last week.*
>
> Social Worker: *Oh, I am so sorry for your loss. (A short period of silence) Losing a child should not happen to any parent. And an unexpected and tragic loss like yours can result in a kind of shock on top of all of the other feelings and reactions.*

Empathy is important in all professional relationships, not just those involving clients. For example, if a social worker learns of a death in the family of a client, colleague, or community member, rather than making assumptions about how the person feels, an empathetic social worker tries to understand the person's experience of and feelings about the loss.

> **Example**
> Social worker: *I'm sorry to hear about the death of your brother.*
>
> Other person: *Yes . . . well, it is a loss. But my brother and I had not been close for a number of years.*
>
> Social worker: *I see . . . and that can complicate some people's grief.*
>
> Other person: *You can say that again! We just drifted apart after I got married, because he let it be known that he didn't believe in same-sex marriage and I was so mad.*
>
> Social worker: *It sounds like you were angry about your brother's views on the rights of same-sex couples to marry, especially since you and your partner were making that commitment to one another.*
>
> Other person: *Exactly! I was angry . . . and also hurt that he couldn't be supportive of us.*

From this example, you can also see that when responding with empathy, it is helpful to reflect feelings back to people in your own words, so they know you are listening and understanding.

Genuineness Genuineness, the quality of being honest and sincere, is essential to the development of an effective working relationship. Social workers who are genuine provide information that is timely, helpful, and accurate, and communicate in a way that is honest and open. When you are genuine, you avoid pretense, acknowledge your limitations, and provide only sincere reassurances (Barker, 2014). Being authentic and reliable encourages trust, which is the core of a helping relationship.

Unconditional Positive Regard Each human being is a person "of worth whose rights and dignity are to be respected without reservation" (Barker, 2014, p. 391). As such, social workers must approach clients with unconditional positive regard and nonjudgmental acceptance regardless of whether they approve of the actions of those with whom they interact.

In the examples provided earlier in the chapter, you can see many instances of social workers demonstrating warmth, expressing empathy, and being genuine as they communicate with clients and community members. For example, as Marilyn's relationship with Ashley develops, there will undoubtedly be many instances for Marilyn to express unconditional positive regard.

> **Example**
>
> Ashley: *Why is everyone here so nice to me? I mean, it doesn't feel real after what I did. I was so stupid!*
>
> Marilyn: *I think everyone is nice to you because they know you deserve all the care and concern you can get, after surviving Michael and his crimes against you.*
>
> Ashley: *Well . . . other girls here are definitely victims of crime because they have been brought here against their will from all across the country . . . even other countries! I went along with Michael's plan at first, and started staying with him when he suggested it.*
>
> Marilyn: *In my experience here—and I've worked here for some time now—I see that sex trafficking happens to girls in all kinds of ways. Some is international, but some happens in our country, and even in our own neighborhoods. You probably wouldn't call any of the other girls here "stupid" but they have all experienced some sort of desperate situation like your financial challenges at home, and most of them put their trust in someone who they later realized they couldn't trust at all.*
>
> Ashley: *(after a bit of silence) Yeah, I guess we have more in common than I saw at first. Everyone here has probably made mistakes, but mistakes don't have to stay with you forever.*
>
> Marilyn: *Yes, that's another thing you all have in common. You all had the courage to find a way to get out of terrible situations, even though it was scary.*

Warmth, empathy, genuineness, and unconditional positive regard are necessary to the formation of a positive relationship, or what is sometimes called a therapeutic or helping alliance.

Helping Alliance   When the common factors described previously are present in a helping relationship, and both the social worker and the client or community member are conscious of the collaborative possibilities of the relationship, they can form an alliance. Such helping alliances, or bonds between social workers and clients or community members, are thought to make an important contribution to positive client and community outcomes. Fluckiger and colleagues (2018) note some key components of such alliances:

- Belief that a professional helper can provide needed assistance in the context of a warm and supportive relationship.

- Conscious decision-making to form a collaborative helping relationship in which both (or all) parties share goals for their work together.

- Agreement on the specific steps that need to be taken to reach those goals, and who will be responsible for taking which steps.

McClintock and colleagues (2017) suggest collecting ongoing feedback about common factors from both professional helpers and those they are helping. The feedback should include information about the bond between the social worker and the client and collecting such feedback may have the potential to improve the helping process itself (McClintock et al., 2017).

There are other ways to improve your collaborative relationships with clients and community members as well. Sometimes, social workers are in the position to give people the choice of day, time, and even location to meet. Unless your agency or organization prohibits it, you may be able to offer to meet in a community location rather than an office setting. Some people and small groups may need to meet at a community center or a playground, because they have small children, lack transportation, or are simply more comfortable in community settings. As always, you must think about safety, for your clients and yourself, first. Practicing in community settings rather than in an office sometimes requires working in teams, for example.

Incorporating recreational or fun activities can also help people engage and feel comfortable. Some people struggle with sharing aspects of themselves in a face-to-face office setting and may be more comfortable in another setting or while engaged in another activity. For this reason, playing basketball with an adolescent, walking in a park with a client struggling with mental health issues, or playing a board game with a group of children, for example, can create an environment that feels less intense for some people than a meeting in an office. Further, as the use of communications technology increases in social work practice, you may find that it is easier to engage some people through a video chat than in person. In some cases, the use of such technologies makes it possible to deliver social work services to people who would not have been able to access them before. During the COVID-19 pandemic, various technologies were utilized (e.g., telephone, text, video counselling, and/or avatars) to provide health care and social services. For example, child protection social work has been performed using virtual platforms (Pink et al., 2022). One social work team utilized telephones to conduct surveys with low-income older adults who lacked internet access to determine their level of loneliness and social isolation (Rorai & Perry, 2020).

Your work may also provide natural opportunities to accompany people to various places in the community, which will give you the chance to engage with them outside of an office setting. You will undoubtedly find other ways to use common factors to build strong, helping alliances with clients and communities as your social work career develops.

Communication Skills

Communication is complex, and communication skills are important to professional practice. This section addresses approaches and skills that can be effective in purposeful communication with clients and community members. These include both nonverbal and verbal communication skills that facilitate professional relationships. This section emphasizes skills that facilitate talking with clients and community members followed by a discussion on social work interviewing skills.

Talking With Clients and Community Members When you convey interest in communication with clients and community members to promote the exploration of challenges and strengths, you are attentive to the client. Attending involves verbal and nonverbal efforts designed to demonstrate that you are fully engaged with and paying close attention to the person or people with whom you are talking (Barker, 2014). For example, you can show you are paying attention and engaged with the client's comments by nodding or even smiling, when appropriate, at a comment.

To have a professional conversation in the best interest of the client, ensure that any potential needs or distractions you may have do not interfere with your ability to listen. In preparing to talk with and listen to clients and community members, many social workers make sure they have water available for themselves and others, freshen up as needed, turn off their cellphones, and take a few deep breaths. Attending also requires that you fully disengage from interactions with others before beginning to meet and that you mentally prepare yourself to avoid reacting, either verbally or nonverbally, in a way that conveys judgment or impatience.

The same attending skills apply in community practice as well. For example, when you speak with a group of people in a community setting, it is important to attend closely to each question and comment from participants without letting your eyes wander around the room, checking the clock for the time, or glancing at your cellphone.

If meeting outside of the office, social workers must exercise flexibility because they have less control over the environment in which the interaction takes place. In settings outside of an agency or organization, such as in community centers and other public locations, social workers must ensure and maintain privacy/confidentiality, professional verbal and nonverbal communication, and must work diligently to minimize distractions.

Certain nonverbal behaviors can help facilitate dialogue, while others detract from appropriately directed communication. Exhibit 3.1 lists general nonverbal behavior guidelines; you will need to adjust your nonverbal behaviors to match the comfort levels of those with whom you are talking. In most cases, you will want to sit relatively close without encroaching upon personal space. Try to minimize any height differentials, perhaps by sitting on a low chair positioned to empower others to control the amount of eye contact to their comfort level. This is especially important when you are talking with children and youth, or people in hospitals or other facilities who need to remain in bed while you talk. Again, here you should use your verbals and nonverbals (Exhibit 3.1) by making eye contact, smiling and nodding, when appropriate, to keep the client engaged and to help them feel comfortable to continue the discussion.

The degree of eye contact you maintain with clients and community members may be highly variable. In most cases, you will make strong intermittent contact to indicate interest and connection. For people from almost any culture, eye contact that is too constant and intense may be uncomfortable; to some, even minimal amounts may seem intrusive. Individualizing your eye contact to maintain the comfort of those you are talking with is an important practice skill.

Another nonverbal aspect of professional interaction is your appearance. In general, the clothing you wear will be guided by the policies of your agency. Some agencies ask their staff members to dress in modest business attire, while others require "business casual" (i.e., professional but less formal than traditional business wear). Some agencies and organizations ask social workers to more or less "match" the style of dress typical of clients and community members, which may be informal. Clothing that is relatively modest in nature helps ensure that the discussion focuses on the client or community rather than on the social worker. In general, aim to communicate respect for those you are working with and for the nature of your work together. For example,

---

EXHIBIT 3.1

Nonverbal Behavior Guidelines

Nonverbal guidelines that may be helpful in talking with all clients and community members can include:

- Turn toward the person or people with whom you are talking.
- Sit with an open body position, without crossing your arms and legs.
- Lean slightly toward the client or community member.
- Smile and nod your head as appropriate to provide positive reinforcement.
- Use responsive facial expressions.
- Maintain eye contact, within the other person's comfort level and cultural norms.
- Speak in a warm, pleasant tone.
- Offer brief, encouraging comments.
- Avoid the presence of large objects and heavy furniture between people who are talking with one another.

in most practice contexts, it would not be appropriate to wear jeans to accompany someone to a courtroom appearance or to use informal language with the judge. Conversely, you might dress more informally while engaging in community organizing or community outreach.

Cultural Considerations Cultural humility "asks us to de-center our own knowledge in favour of prioritizing the clients' [lived] experiences and urges ongoing vigilance to power imbalances and the impact of systems on both client and practitioners" (Gottlieb, 2020, p. 463). Social workers who practice with cultural humility use verbal and nonverbal behaviors consistent with the cultural expectations and personal comfort levels of their clients and community members (NASW, 2021a). You must use your cultural humility to modify nonverbal guidelines as necessary. For example, people from different cultures may have different comfort levels in terms of how close they sit or stand when conversing. Social workers learn to take cues from those they are helping to guide them in maintaining culturally appropriate personal space. Further, people from different cultural backgrounds require social workers who have learned all they can about the norms and communication patterns in those cultures before their first meeting. This is an important part of becoming a culturally responsive social worker, as is developing a genuine sense of humility in approaching people from other cultures.

Preparation to talk with clients and community members should include consideration of elements of culture—both yours and theirs—to which you need to attend. Social workers have prized being competent across cultures since the beginnings of the profession, and more recently have recognized that a person cannot ever be completely competent in a culture different from their own. We are instead most prepared for professional helping when we approach clients and communities with cultural humility (Richmond et al.,

2018; Sue et al., 2019). As we discussed in Chapter 1, *cultural humility* refers to having a deep understanding that helping professionals do not know all there is to know about clients and communities who come from different backgrounds and cultures. Social workers who are culturally humble approach clients and community members willing to be open to and learn about daily life, traditions, and how cultural considerations shape their strengths and challenges.

Suggestions from your supervisor and other experienced social workers, peer consultation, and a general assessment of the community and agency cultures in which you work will be helpful in developing cultural humility. Weigh whether your dress, posture, and language are appropriate to the people with whom you are working and the setting in which that work takes place. Continually be aware of the relevant customs and contexts and strive to match nonverbal behaviors of the person or group with whom you are talking.

In an effort to communicate respectfully and effectively with people from all ethnic, cultural, and linguistic backgrounds, social workers have a responsibility to provide services in the chosen language of the person or community. Fulfilling this obligation may require the use of qualified language interpreters or translators. Interpreters work in two languages in the moment to make sure that people who are talking together understand one another. Translators work with written documents, making sure that the language of the person who wrote the documents can be understood by the person needing to read it.

Interpreters generally must be proficient in both English and the client's chosen language and must have undergone orientation and training. This includes certified or registered sign language interpreters. It is your responsibility to ensure that, at a minimum, interpreters maintain confidentiality, are properly trained in the ethics of interpreting in a helping situation, and understand the terms and concepts specific to agency programs. Therefore, the use of family members (particularly children) or neighbors as interpreters is problematic and should be avoided whenever possible. You may need to prepare for work with specific populations by learning at least the basics of their languages and cultural customs and by completing training about how to work with professional interpreters who have cultural humility (NASW, 2021a).

Interviewing Abilities

In addition to the basic communication abilities discussed previously, social workers use more specific interviewing skills to help clients and community members share information about their current situations and goals in seeking professional assistance. In this section, we discuss skills for beginning your work with clients or community members, and then cover other interviewing skills, including the use of encouragement and silence, paraphrasing, asking clarifying questions, balancing closed-ended and open-ended questions, and summarizing. This section also includes information on how to avoid common mistakes in interviewing.

Beginning the Interview Your role as a social worker is to hear other people's situations and perspectives in the way in which they want to tell their stories, without making assumptions and filling in gaps yourself. You want to open the interview in a way that invites people with whom you are talking to convey their purposes in communicating with you and to express goals for the helping relationship. Beginning an interview may involve waiting a brief time after you make welcoming introductions to allow people an opportunity to begin. If they do not take that cue, you can invite them with such phrases as "Please tell me what brings you here today" or "Where would you like to begin?" Beginning a session like this helps you get to know people and can put them at ease.

Encouraging Responses Encouraging follow-up responses gives people immediate feedback that you have heard and understood their message. This immediate feedback is designed to encourage people to keep talking and sharing information about their current situations and what they are looking for by seeking assistance. At the same time, you are demonstrating attentiveness through short verbal statements and questions such as "Go on," "I see," and "Can you tell me more?" (Barker, 2014). Such comments should provide only enough of a response to encourage the client or community member to continue speaking. A more complete response may interrupt the direction of the conversation and distract the speaker from fully sharing the current situation or perspective.

Similar responses can be used in community practice as well. For example, imagine that you are facilitating a community-wide listening session about a proposal to raise the sales tax to help close the rural digital divide by boosting access to affordable broadband in a rural disadvantaged community. Two perspectives have been shared so far, both offering support for the proposal, and then a long silence ensues. You first encourage other comments by remaining silent yourself for a few moments. But when no one else speaks, you may need to provide an encouraging response to the group. You may do this by briefly reviewing the two perspectives that have been shared and asking the group for affirmation that you summarized the comments correctly. This approach often elicits clarifying comments or the sharing of other perspectives. At some point during the listening session, you may need to offer encouragement for someone to "play the role of devil's advocate" in order to give encouragement for someone to speak up for consideration of a perspective that is less supportive of the school district's proposal. Overall, your goal is to speak as little as possible yourself, while briefly encouraging the expression of diverse opinions.

Reflection of Feelings At times, merely reflecting feelings of the person with whom you are working is enough to help continue and deepen the conversation. For this reason, it is important that you can identify and are comfortable talking about a wide range of emotions. To be prepared to reflect feelings appropriately, you want to have a "mental list" of synonyms for various emotional states so that your reflections do not sound as though you are simply repeating or parroting the person who is sharing with you. For example, if you are working with a client or a community member who says they are "mad" because of their situation, you can be ready to reflect their anger without using the same words that they have used. Remember that people express emotions both verbally and nonverbally, so you will need to be prepared to reflect feelings expressed in both ways.

> **Example**
> Social Worker: *You mentioned that your daughter was angry with you the other morning, and you had a fight before she left for school. What was the argument about?*
> Client: *Well, I think we . . . (lapses into silence for a minute). (The client begins to cry.)*
> Social Worker: *(After a few minutes) This argument really upset you.*

Another use of reflection of feelings is to make sure that you are on the right track in the way that you have identified the emotions of the other person correctly. Because of the complexities of the lives of the people we help, social workers need to have ways to be certain they are understanding as conversations unfold.

Silence   As you talk with a client or community member, allow for moments of silence. Silence can be interpreted in many ways, and some people feel more comfortable with silence than others. Exhibit 3.2 describes the possible meanings of silence in interviews.

During moments of silence, you can remain attentive through eye contact; your nonverbal focus on the person with whom you are talking (i.e., avoid shifting your body, checking your watch or phone, or other means of communicating discomfort); and minimizing external and internal distraction. You can encourage silence during the interview to allow for self-reflection and to slow the pace of the conversation. Silence can also lead people to answer their own questions and to discover their own next steps toward a resolution (Shebib, 2019). At times, you may wish to break a silence to discern its meaning or to shift to another topic. For example, you could say, "I notice that you have been silent for several minutes. If you are comfortable talking about it, I hope you can share what you are thinking about or feeling."

The situation or context determines the appropriate length of silence in a helping session. If, for example, you are working with a client who is giving extensive thought to a question you have asked, a long silence may be appropriate. Long silences may be less appropriate in situations like school settings when you believe a student would rather miss class in favor of being in your office for a longer period of time. Ultimately, professional judgment must be the guide to interpreting and responding to silence.

> **EXHIBIT 3.2**
>
> *Meanings of Silence*
>
> Silence can mean many things. Six of the most common meanings are listed here:
>
> 1. *The person is thinking:* Some people need more time than others to gather and organize their thoughts. Allowing time for this helps people feel empowered and worthy of your patience.
> 2. *The person is confused:* Your questions may be unclear, or the person with whom you are meeting may be unsure what you expect. If you suspect this may be the case, ask whether the person is confused and would like you to repeat your question or explanation.
> 3. *The person is experiencing uncomfortable thoughts and/or feelings:* Silence gives people time to process pain or anxiety and to consider proceeding further in the discussion. If you think the client is silent because of powerful emotions, you may wish to provide empathy. A statement such as "I sense that your daughter's life choices have provoked some strong feelings" provides support and conveys understanding.
> 4. *The person is working to develop trust with you:* Silence provides people with a sense of dignity and control over their lives, a way to avoid rejection, and a way to maintain control over the conversation. To move the relationship toward more openness, you could proceed slowly with a discussion of less personal matters, or you might choose to raise the issue of trust directly.
> 5. *The person simply tends to be quiet:* You might use open-ended questions to encourage the person to share. When the time is right, you may want to initiate a discussion in a supportive manner about their silence in terms of how it may affect your working relationship. You may also consider using other helping methods to elicit sharing, as some people are more expressive when combining an activity with a discussion, when journaling, or when expressing themselves through the arts.
> 6. *The person has achieved closure:* If you think this may explain the silence, you can ask after a moment if there is anything else to discuss at the moment.

Paraphrasing When you express an idea of the relevant points of a statement made by a client or a community member in your own words, you are paraphrasing. When you paraphrase, people are assured that you heard and understood them accurately. Paraphrasing can also help people clarify their own thoughts (Barker, 2014). After paraphrasing, you can invite the person to whom you are talking to correct you if you are mistaken. An invitation to correct can communicate both that you care enough about them to want to accurately understand their situation and perspective and that you recognize that you may have the wrong understanding of the specific issues at hand. When you paraphrase, do so without judgment, without adding meaning or changing the meaning of the statement, and without attempting to solve any issues (Shebib, 2019).

> **Example**
>
> Client: I don't really get what is going on. I mean, I put food on the table, keep a roof over our heads, and try to keep her going to school. I don't understand what her problem is!
>
> Social Worker: You are working really hard to provide for her and cannot understand what your daughter is talking about.
>
> Client: Yeah! She is skipping school, running off, and now I am in trouble!
>
> Social Worker: In other words, she is not grateful for everything you are doing for her. In fact, others are acting as though you are at fault in some way.

To avoid monotony, social workers can use a variety of lead-ins for paraphrasing, such as:

> As I understand it . . . .
> It sounds a little like . . . .
> As I hear it . . . .
> The picture I am seeing as you talk is . . . .

Asking Clarifying Questions Clarifying is closely related to paraphrasing, but when clarifying, the social worker directly asks for additional information or feedback to illuminate a point. Clarification helps you to understand the uniqueness of the messages other people are making rather than generalizing or framing the messages in ways that match your own perceptions. Clarifying also increases the accuracy of your assessment while communicating a respect for the complexity of each person's situation. Clarifying could be used at the end of a paraphrase. For example, you might say, "What I understand you to be saying is . . . Is that right?" Clarification may be needed at any point in the interview, especially to clarify each other's intent, interpretations, and meanings. For example, crying can indicate joy but can also be a sign of regret, loss, or confusion.

> **Example**
>
> Client: *The last time my husband had to "work late" he didn't come home until just before sunrise. I think he is having an affair . . . or something. (eyes fill with tears)*
>
> Social Worker: *It seems like the thought of your husband being unfaithful is very upsetting. Is that right?*
>
> Client: *(after some hesitation) You know what? I think I'm crying because I'm relieved to have finally said it out loud. It took me a long time to come here, and I haven't had anyone to confide in until now.*

Summarizing Summarizing, or providing a concise statement of main points, can help to establish organization for the entirety of your work with a client or a community member as well as to frame a particular interaction or series of interactions. A summary is a way of confirming your understanding of the person's message thus far and checking the validity of your assumptions. A summary can also provide closure and consensus, either after a segment of the interview is complete or at the conclusion of the helping session. In situations in which the issues evoke significant emotion, or in which the work is directed at some complex task, summing up the interaction can demonstrate manageability and hopefulness. Summing up can provide a snapshot of the topics discussed, which can help to clarify the future direction of the session. Summarizing can also help focus a conversation that wanders off topic.

Balancing Open-Ended and Closed-Ended Questions Open-ended questions are designed to elicit extensive answers and to encourage people to share their experiences and perceptions in the manner most comfortable to them and in the way that makes the most sense to them (Barker, 2014). You can use open-ended questions to allow clients and community members the freedom to choose whether to respond as well as to provide flexibility in the type of response.

> Examples of Open-Ended Questions
> Client: *My brother and I always fight after school.*
> Social Worker: *What are your fights like?*
> Community Member: *We are trying to push the drug dealers out of our community.*
> Social Worker: *How do the drug dealers affect the neighborhood?*

On the other hand, there are times when you need precise information about a specific topic. These moments in a helping session require closed-ended questions to encourage the person with whom you are talking to provide factual information in a concise manner.

> Examples of Closed-Ended Questions
> Client: *I have not eaten in quite a while.*
> Social Worker: *How many days has it been since you have eaten?*
> Community Member: *We had a community organizer working on health care in this neighborhood a while back.*
> Social Worker: *How many years did the organizer work in the neighborhood?*

Closed-ended questions help social workers glean specifics about behaviors or events, such as their frequency, duration, and intensity. This type of question can be answered "yes" or "no" or with a numerical answer. While such questions do not encourage clients to open up and share, they are useful in situations in which you need information about the current status of a situation or when dangerous conduct or some imminent threat of harm must be dealt with directly to ensure safety. For example, you would seek concrete information if someone is expressing the intent to hurt themselves or others and you need to know if they have a real plan to engage in the dangerous behavior and the means to carry out the plan (Shebib, 2019).

One of the most important skills in interviewing clients and community members is mixing open-ended and closed-ended questions to help people feel less pressured as your conversation continues. Balancing these two types of questions can also help to avoid monotony in the wording and pacing of the helping session.

To exemplify some of the communications and interviewing skills and abilities discussed here, we return to the chapter opening case in which a social worker, Marilyn, is working with a 15-year-old human trafficking survivor named Ashley.

> Marilyn: *Girls get help here for a lot of different problems. Can you tell me why you are staying here at the Center?*
>
> Ashley: *There was a raid, and I decided just to tell the police that I was 15 instead of lying like Michael told me to. I needed to get away from him, but now I can't go home.*
>
> Marilyn: *I'm so glad you had the courage to tell the police that you are only 15. Can you explain a bit more about who Michael is and why he told you to lie about your age?*
>
> Ashley: *Michael lives in the same neighborhood as my family and used to give me and my sister candy and little toys sometimes. (Her eyes fill with tears, and she pauses.)*
>
> Marilyn: *I see . . .*
>
> Ashley: *I thought he was nice, but he isn't nice to me anymore. He tricked me into thinking that he could help me earn money for my family when my Mom got sick and lost her job.*
>
> Marilyn: *I'm so sorry that happened to you! Can you explain how he tricked you?*
>
> Ashley: *Well . . . first he was really nice to me and bought me clothes when I told him we were broke. The clothes were beautiful, but more for going to clubs than to school. I still thanked him and all, but I made a point to let him know that I wanted to stay in school. He said that I needed a nighttime job, and that he thought he could help me get one if I was a good dancer. I was a little scared at first, but he promised I would only be dancing. I shouldn't have believed him . . .*
>
> Marilyn: *It's starting to sound to me like it may not help to blame yourself. What happened next?*
>
> Ashley: *The first night he took me to the club, I came home with almost $200 and I thought I could make that much money each time I went with him. He said I was a great dancer and that he would be glad to help me anytime I wanted to do it again. After a while we thought it would be easier if I just went to his place after school until it was time to go out. Some nights when the tips were low, Michael offered to "make up the difference" and would just give me money from his own pocket. The only thing he made me do at first was to tell people that I was 20, if anybody asked.*

Marilyn: *So, he gained your trust.*

Ashley: *Yeah . . . but it didn't stay that way. Pretty soon he said that he had done all this for me and my family, and now he needed something from me. Before I knew it, he was setting me up with "dates"—always older guys who wanted sex for money. When I said I didn't want to do it anymore, Michael hit me and said I owed him all this money. He said I could quit anytime, but I would have to pay him back first. And if I didn't . . . well, he told me to remember that he knew where my family lived.*

Marilyn: *Is that why you said that you can't go home?*

Ashley: *Yes. I mean, I know my Mom is worried, but I don't want to tell her all of this when she is sick and trying to get better. And I am really worried, too. What if Michael tries to hurt my Mom or my sister to get back at me?*

Marilyn: *Well, if you would like to, maybe we can make a safety plan and then find a way to talk with your Mom together.*

Avoiding Communication Errors

When interacting with clients and community members, social workers should be wary of communication errors. This section describes some of the more common communication errors that occur in social work practice.

Jargon Social workers, like most professionals, have their own jargon, or verbal shortcuts, to describe their activities, which others may not understand. Jargon can include abbreviations like DJO ("Deputy Juvenile Officer"), distinctive words ("intake process," "ecomap"), and routines ("level one"). Keep your communication with clients and community members as free from jargon as possible (Shebib, 2019).

Examples of Jargon
Social Worker: *After the intake process, you will be on level one for a week. Then your DJO will assess you and decide whether you can go to level two or you need to go back to court.*

Instead, Try
Social Worker: *After I've gathered all of the needed information from you, we'll move you in to your room, and I can tell you all of the rules that you'll need to follow for the first few weeks. After your Deputy Juvenile Officer (sometimes called the DJO) has met with you, we can decide together whether you will have the same rules after that, or if we can change them.*

Leading Questions How you ask questions can shape the responses. Leading questions can encourage people to answer in a certain way. People who have a need to be liked and/or those who are compliant are especially vulnerable to leading questions (Shebib, 2019).

Examples of Leading Questions
Social Worker: *Given all that you have tried in the past, don't you think it is time to call the police to get the drug dealers out of the neighborhood?*

Client: *Well, I guess so.*

Social Worker: *Do you want to call now to report what you have seen?*

Irrelevant Questions   To avoid asking irrelevant questions, which are questions that do not relate to the topic at hand, it is important to have a clear idea of the purpose of the conversation or interview. While you might be curious about details of situations or perceptions, consider whether the information is relevant before asking a question.

Examples of Irrelevant Questions
Client: *My boyfriend broke up with me for the second time this week. He already asked my friend out!*

Social Worker: *How did he tell you that he wanted to break up?*

Client: *My mother wants me to wear clothes that are so out of style and boring. I don't want to wear her stupid clothes!*

Social Worker: *Exactly what type of clothes does she want you to wear?*

Excessive Questioning   While questions are an essential part of communications and interviewing, the asking of questions also puts the social worker in control of the conversation, which does not lead to empowerment of the client or community member. When talking with people, mixing different types of questions with empathic communication, silence, summarizing, and other approaches discussed previously may help with relationship building. When you must ask many questions, it may be helpful to check in and take periodic breaks to convey respect and recognition that the questioning may be taxing (Shebib, 2019).

Example of Check-in
Social Worker: *I have asked a lot of questions of you today. How are you doing so far?*

Related to excessive questioning, social workers should avoid asking about two things at the same time which is also known as asking "double-barreled questions." For example, asking the client the following question: "Do you think it was your neighbor who reported you for neglect and did she do so because you are a single mother?" Likewise, confusion and miscommunication can occur when we ask more than one question without waiting for answers or responses.

In minimizing the number of questions, and especially closed-ended and double-barreled questions, social workers attempt to share control of the conversation and thereby empower the clients and community members with whom they are talking. Balancing the amount of interpersonal power between participants in a conversation, including sessions between a social worker and a client working within a helping alliance, is a skill that can help us in our work with families, groups, organizations, and communities, as well as with individuals. We will cover power issues in social work practice at each of these levels in future chapters. For the moment, we focus on further developing communication, interviewing, and engagement skills and abilities with an in-depth example of minimizing power imbalances in a one-on-one helping relationship.

Minimizing Power Imbalances Within the Helping Alliance: Jasmine Johnson

Social workers have been granted permission, by the state, to "force marginalized, deviant, and vulnerable clients to conform" (Dolgoff et al., 2012, p. 75). This "power" leads to issues in helping alliances between social workers and those with whom they work. The following vignette provides an example of how a social worker can work with an individual client in a way that addresses such issues directly. This vignette is about a client named Jasmine Johnson and the social worker, Marian, who is a White woman without children and who is younger than Jasmine.

> *In your work at a family support agency, Jasmine Johnson is a Black woman and a mother who comes to you with a concern about parenting. Her teenage son is behaving poorly both at home and, increasingly, at school, and Jasmine is unsure how to deal with him. He often does not seem to respect her authority and ignores her attempts to discipline him. She says that he talks back and is occasionally disrespectful to her. He ignores the limits she sets and does not obey school-night curfews or help with any household chores. Jasmine struggles to support him financially and his father has passed away. Her job pays poorly, carries little status, and she is unable to afford any recreational activities for or with her son. Overall, Jasmine struggles with low self-esteem.*

At first glance, Jasmine's challenges may appear to be strictly personal. Jasmine knows that she does not feel good about herself or her situation, and she assumes she needs to improve in some way. You might assume that she needs to address her self-esteem issues, or you might even conclude that she is depressed and needs medical attention. It is likely, though, that power, or lack of it, plays an important role in her experience. Jasmine has to play many interpersonal roles (i.e., single mother, widow, worker, and friend) and is part of a racial group that has experienced pervasive and persistent oppression in the United States for more than 400 years. You can examine these external conditions and stressors with the goal of helping Jasmine claim more personal power (Marsiglia et al., 2021; Sellon & Lassman, 2022). Although she may have interpreted her experiences as signs of her own deficiencies, she has also exhibited remarkable resilience in dealing with disadvantages and oppression. She has managed to survive in trying circumstances that have had far-reaching repercussions in her life. Recognizing the conditions and circumstances in which her life is embedded can be empowering. A skilled social worker can help empower Jasmine by purposefully articulating these circumstances.

This does not mean that Jasmine's own sense of her problem is erroneous. Rather, one of the social worker's goals is to validate the client's experience and to recognize the meaning she makes of it. Jasmine may not recognize how her experience on the negative side of the power differential has fed into her feelings of inadequacy. That realization can open many doors. For example, Jasmine may begin to separate her feelings of inadequacy from her sense of identity and start to view her experiences as a function of her social location. This new perspective might inspire her to some action, such as joining an informal support group for single Black mothers. This group shares stories and experiences, exchanges informal child care from time to time, and coordinates grocery shopping. Adopting a different outlook and receiving encouragement from a social worker also might inspire Jasmine to eventually become active in organized efforts to change policies regarding child support or benefits for single working parents. The possibilities for Jasmine's roles and activities are endless, and these types of activities may affirm Jasmine's experiences even as they are instrumental in changing the quality of life for her and possibly for others.

It may seem to Jasmine that there are few areas in which her social worker's life bears any resemblance to her own. As long as the profession sustains the concept of the social worker as expert, there will be a felt power differential between social workers and clients based on their distinct roles in the social worker–client relationship. There are also likely to be additional differences between client and social worker related to gender, age, race, socioeconomic status, and other dimensions of diversity. These differences, if perceived as problems, can complicate the engagement process, as clients may not think that they can relate to the social worker.

Suppose Jasmine's case is assigned to a social work student. Jasmine may find it challenging to think of social work students or less experienced workers in general as a genuine source of help to her. Students may come from a different cultural or ethnic background, and they may not have partners or children. They may also seem to her to be so privileged by their race and education that she thinks that they cannot relate to her experiences. Yet, social workers are supposed to be knowledgeable, and, as such, they have some level of power that she may not recognize or, conversely, notice and resent or admire. In most cases, these differences in social worker and client roles or attributes are, at the core, about power and power differences. It is necessary, then, to discuss these issues openly if they impede the work. Simply raising them can open up the relationship and facilitate client engagement and a genuine effort to balance power within the helping alliance.

For example, in the early stages of the relationship, a social worker might ask Jasmine if she has any hesitation about their working together. The social worker might acknowledge that their past and present life experiences differ and might ask that Jasmine tell her about her background and current life situation so that the social worker can better understand and help her. Asking clients to share this type of information, and giving clients the opportunity to talk about any qualms they may have about working together gives clients the opportunity to talk about differences and the impact they may have on the relationship. Using this approach is also consistent with a sense of cultural humility on the part of the social worker.

Situations that involve power differentials are sometimes awkward or even embarrassing. You may understand that the client sees you as having power simply because of your role as a helping person, an employee, or a student. At the same time, you may wonder about the extent to which you can help someone like Jasmine, an exasperated parent who might be of a different race and socioeconomic class, when you might not even be a parent yourself. You may feel some hesitation at working with an oppressed client when you have enjoyed considerable privilege. Thus, power in social worker–client relationships can be quite complex.

When concerns about power in the social work relationship arise, you might hope that they will pass or that clients will just trust that you know what you're doing in spite of these differences. Once you or your client identify a difference as problematic, however, the issue will not simply go away. You and your client should confront it directly through open acknowledgment and exploration.

One way to proceed in such a situation is to start by addressing power differentials as they emerge from your conversations, and acknowledging your own privilege as a natural part of the discussion. In the previous vignette, it would be important to demonstrate your cultural humility in your conversations with Jasmine when she discusses life experiences related to her age, race, income challenges, or parenting. To do so, you might say:

> *When you mentioned not being able to afford recreational activities with your son, it was clear to me that I know very little about what teenage boys like to do when they have some free time. Can you tell me what your son likes to do, or when you last did something together that he enjoys?*

In this way, the people you are working with have the opportunity to be the expert in terms of their own day-to-day life. You also pave the way for ongoing honesty by addressing, and working to balance, the power differentials in the helping relationship openly and directly.

CRITICAL CONSIDERATIONS IN ENGAGING AND BUILDING RELATIONSHIPS WITH CLIENTS AND COMMUNITY MEMBERS

While engaging and building relationships with clients and community members, social workers strive to be transparent or explicit about the many ways that forming a helping alliance can work to their advantage. To establish meaningful and trusting relationships, it is important to be clear about the help you can provide as well as the parameters or boundaries of your role as a social worker. For example, while you may want to be fully accessible to a community group working to have the city demolish abandoned and dilapidated housing, you probably want to avoid having members of the group call you day and night for guidance, advice, and resources. At the individual level of practice, clients will appreciate your attention to confidentiality, including an honest discussion regarding the limits of confidentiality for social workers like yourself. Confidentiality, as well as privacy and ongoing evaluation of the helping relationship, are critical considerations in communication, engagement, and relationship building in social work and are covered in this section.

Confidentiality

Confidentiality is important to your engagement with clients and community members, and it is also important to address the limits of confidentiality as you begin to form a professional relationship. There are at least three areas in which social workers may be required to break confidentiality:

1 As mandated reporters, social workers are legally required to report cases of child abuse, neglect, or exploitation as are many helping professionals.
2 Most states also mandate that social workers report the abuse, neglect, or exploitation of older adults and persons with disabilities.
3 Social workers in many states have a duty to report if people threaten to harm themselves or others.

Legal ramifications regarding these reporting requirements may vary somewhat by state or locality; however, social workers must report incidents of abuse, neglect, or exploitation of which they become aware and take steps to ensure the safety of all parties involved.

Depending on the work setting, the mandate to break confidentiality may appear to be a significant obstacle to establishing trusting relationships. For example, you may be concerned that community members will not share information with you if they know that you are obligated to inform authorities in certain situations. Although this concern is legitimate, to represent yourself fairly, you must communicate your responsibilities early in the work. Further, informing people of the limits of confidentiality may affect the relationship in unexpected ways. For example, many people recognize when they need help from authorities as is shown in the following case.

> *Kim, is a social worker who has a client who struggles with substance use disorder and has a difficult time keeping track of her five children, for whom she is the only parent. During a session, the client confided in Kim that she felt sure she was grossly neglecting her younger children and that she often struck the oldest child "hard" when he "mouthed off" to her. She told Kim that she had decided to reveal this information because Kim was a mandated reporter and she knew Kim would be able to get help. Kim was supportive of*

> her client, noting that her decision to reveal the information showed a tremendous amount of courage and maturity, and that it was the most caring thing a parent in her situation could do. She suggested that the client stay in the office while Kim called the hotline so that she would know exactly what and how Kim was reporting to child protective services.

Social workers must be honest about their roles, and their boundaries, and should not assume that an adversarial relationship will evolve simply because of mandated reporter obligations. Most people who are getting help from social workers have good intentions and want to build a better life. Even in the worst circumstances, you still have significant opportunities to build helping relationships. For example, in the case of child abuse or neglect, you can address the obstacles to successful parenting, maintain a genuine relationship in which you support your client's parenting competence rather than searching for deficits, and build the foundation for further work. The imminent safety of a child is always the priority, and this strategy is useful for work in cases, like the one in which Kim is helping, where reporting is required; you will also be in a situation to immediately begin helping a parent create a safe home for her child.

Privacy

Privacy is related to, but different from, confidentiality in important ways. Both can lead to challenging issues for social workers. In certain circumstances, caring behaviors can be interpreted in different ways by different people. Actions that some people interpret as caring may seem invasive to others, while still other people may view the same actions as indicating that the social worker wants to become a friend. This is one reason that it is important to discuss your role and the nature of the helping relationship, including privacy issues, as early as possible in your work with a client or community. Similarly, when you are working with a small group, it is a good idea to discuss informed consent, the Health Insurance Portability and Accountability Act (HIPAA) rules, confidentiality of what is discussed in the group and privacy, or the personal information that will and will not be shared with the group. Straightforward discussions of social worker involvement and agreed-upon privacy parameters help prevent situations in which participants feel disappointed or even betrayed.

As a practitioner in your particular role and setting, you might consider the extent of privacy to which the people with whom you are working are entitled. For example, in a residential or correctional setting, what personal information does a social worker need to know about a client? If your work involves closely monitoring a group of patients, how do you balance their privacy with your duty to know what is going on within the group? Regardless of your agency's purpose, ensuring that people are afforded as much privacy as possible will take work on your part, including the regular examination and discussion with colleagues of policies and procedures for opportunities to provide more client privacy, when possible.

Ongoing Evaluation

Just as the engagement process is a precursor to assessment, planning, intervention, and termination, each of these social work processes helps to shape ongoing evaluation at each stage of the helping relationship. As a social worker, you invest your energy and skills to establish a solid initial connection with a client or community that will grow as your work together progresses. It is important as the work advances to evaluate the effectiveness of your efforts in an ongoing manner. Ongoing evaluation involves both your impressions of how the helping relationship is going and the impressions of those people with whom you are working. Does your work together need to change in any way to make the alliance stronger and more effective in achieving goals?

When services come to an end after termination and follow-up, agencies may provide a formal tool for client and community feedback. At that time, evaluation of services will include questions for clients and community members about outcomes related to the provision of social work services. However, it is also helpful during service delivery to ask people how they feel about the work so far. For example, you might ask individual clients whether they are comfortable talking about the issues you have discussed. Other examples of questions that may be helpful in ongoing evaluation include the

---

EXHIBIT 3.3

Grand Challenge

Close the Health Gap

The COVID-19 pandemic brought into sharp relief health disparities in the United States which is another of the most pressing challenges for today's society, according to the American Academy of Social Work (2016), which identified it as one of the Social Welfare Grand Challenges for Social Work.

Vast health disparities exist by race, ethnicity, gender, age, disability status, geography, sexual and gender identity, and socioeconomic status. In recent decades, the general population in the United States has been dying at younger ages than the general populations in peer nations. Yet population health also has a social dimension; populations that experience high rates of social, racial, and economic exclusion also experience higher rates of poor health and premature mortality. Addressing the social, political, and economic dimensions of health is needed to secure sustainable, population-based health advances. Also needed are research and practice collaboration between disciplines to examine the social, political, and economic determinants of good health.

Social work's role in providing leadership on health equity is rooted in its historical social justice mission and commitment to serve disenfranchised populations. Social work has been involved in public health and the health care field for most of its history as a profession, including advocating for conditions that promote good health and increasing access to services.

To familiarize yourself with the issues related to health equity and social work's role, visit the Grand Challenges website and read Working Paper No. 19, *Health Equity: Eradicating Health Inequalities for Future Generations* (Walters et al., 2016).

following: Is the process of meeting with you similar to, or different from, what they thought it would be? If it is different, how do they feel about it? How comfortable are they with the fact that you are of different racial or ethnic backgrounds? What can you do to be more supportive, clearer, or more helpful? For group work, you might ask for feedback about your role as facilitator. At the community level, seeking feedback from individuals and colleagues in the community as well as from committees can elicit important suggestions. This type of ongoing evaluation is less focused on outcomes and more focused on the process of helping. Evaluation will be discussed in later chapters on individual, family, groups, and community and organization interventions.

CONCLUSION

Now that you have explored the importance of various aspects of engagement and relationship building in social work practice, you are one step closer to using communication skills and interviewing abilities in your work with clients and communities. Although you are not likely to address all the issues presented in any one interaction with a client or a community member, you have the framework to go beyond initial connections to engage in an ongoing, dynamic helping relationship. If you ask for feedback along the way, you will find that a positive working relationship is established and is shaped by the nature of your shared activities and experiences.

At first, you may feel that thinking about and trying to use these skills interferes with your spontaneity and/or responsiveness. However, as you practice and use these skills, they will feel much more natural to you and you will cultivate your own style. Engagement is a process that occurs not only in the beginning, but throughout your work with clients and communities. As the work progresses, you will continue to notice how communication skills, interviewing abilities, and engagement with clients and communities continues to help through the assessment, planning, and implementation of the work. In particular, the next step, assessment, builds on the relationship foundation that you create during the engagement phase.

MAIN POINTS

- The first and probably most important activity for social workers in the engagement process is carefully listening to the situations and perspectives of the clients or community members with whom they are communicating. This requires you to skillfully initiate a purposeful conversation that nurtures the helping relationship.

- Social workers use common factors in helping relationships, including warmth, empathy, genuineness, and unconditional positive regard, along with excellent interviewing skills, to establish strong alliances with clients and communities.

- Explicitly discussing the purpose and direction of the work together enhances the trust between social workers, clients, and community members.

- Respecting the strengths and resilience of people is critical in establishing relationships, and such respect must be demonstrated throughout the work.

- Social workers should discuss issues of confidentiality and privacy openly and directly with clients and community members.

- Social workers should evaluate their work, including the helping relationship, at all stages beginning with engagement.

EXERCISES

1. To apply learning about health equity discussed in Grand Challenges Working Paper No. 19, *Health Equality, Eradicating Health Inequalities for Future Generations*, review the Riverton case at www.routledgesw.com/interactive-cases/ and respond to the following items:
    a. Imagine that you are a social worker engaging a client in a health setting. The client is experiencing health problems related to asthma made worse by pollution created by the heavy industry located in her low-income community. How might health inequity considerations emerge during the engagement process?
    b. What environmental factors could cause health inequity for Riverton residents as compared to residents of other communities?
    c. The director of the local health clinic would like to reduce health inequity in Riverton by increasing health services. Formulate a response that addresses prevention versus remediation and describes the limits of health services toward decreasing health equity.

2. Log onto www.routledgesw.com/static-cases/. Review Case 1: Willow's Transition. Answer the following questions.
    a. What would be your first steps in building rapport with Willow? With Laura? With Rob? Who else do you need to build relationships with in order to work effectively with this family?

3. Go to www.routledgesw.com/interactive-cases/. Select the Sanchez case and under the "Engage and Discover" and "Introduction" tabs, review the Engagement phase and its tasks. With classmates, discuss the needs of the Sanchez family.

4. Review the Client History, Client Concerns, and Goals for the Client for Alejandro Sanchez. Next, click on "Explore the Town" to review the neighborhood, Alejandro's Critical Thinking Questions, and his Interaction Matrix. Consider the following scenario: *Alejandro is one of your clients. He presents as pleasant and respectful but melancholy. He says he is "unhappy" and seems to carry an existential sadness related to his family. He notes in the first interview that his father Hector was also 19 when he came to this country as an undocumented worker.*

Pair with a classmate and role-play for 5 to 10 minutes the first meeting between Alejandro and you. In the session, attempt to engage Alejandro and begin an assessment. The classmate who is playing the role of Alejandro should prepare by reviewing Alejandro's concerns and goals as well as his strengths. Have other classmates observe and consult during the role-play. Afterward, the class can debrief by considering the following questions:

a Which attending skills did the social worker use? Which did they not use?

b Did the social worker employ empathic responses? What were they? In what ways was the use of empathy challenging?

c Was the social worker able to validate Alejandro's feelings of unhappiness, identify his strengths, and verbally share those strengths with Alejandro? Can the class think of other strengths the social worker did not mention? How can a social worker emphasize a client's strengths when the client is not receptive to hearing them?

d What was the experience of the student who played the role of Alejandro? Did the student, in character, feel that the social worker demonstrated specific listening skills? Which skills?

e What elements of Alejandro's experiences reflect social justice and human rights concerns?

5 Go to www.routledgesw.com/interactive-cases/ and, under the Sanchez family case, watch the videotaped interview with Emilia and the social worker. While watching the interview, note where in the interview each of the following skills is demonstrated:

a Open-ended question
b Closed-ended question
c Paraphrasing
d Attending
e Nonverbal communication
f Clarifying
g Summarizing

What are the strengths of the interview and what could the social worker do differently?

6 Go to www.routledgesw.com/interactive-cases/ and become familiar with the Riverton case file (under the "Assess" tab). Using the questions in Quick Guide 3, consider the following scenario: A client arrives for her first appointment with you at the Alvadora Community Mental Health Center and she is clearly intoxicated. In a one- to two-page paper, state which of the questions might be most significant and your rationale. Would you use some of the questions to guide your interaction? Why or why not?

7 You are a social worker in a neighborhood community mental health center. You are awaiting the arrival of a new client, Jasmine Johnson (discussed in this chapter), who lives near the center. After you introduce yourself and she relaxes somewhat, she states, "My life is a mess; nothing I ever do is right; sometimes I think I can't go on." Indicate how you would respond to her statement using each of the following

relationship-building and interviewing skills. Give a very brief verbal (one sentence or less, if possible) or behavioral example (if appropriate).
   a   Attending
   b   Responding nonverbally
   c   Responding with minimal verbalization
   d   Paraphrasing
   e   Clarifying

   What other skills do you think would be helpful in this situation?

8 For the following role-playing exercises, create groups of three students so that one is the client, one is the social worker, and one is an observer.
   a   Set a stopwatch for 3 minutes. The social worker may not speak during the 3 minutes. During this time, the client tells the social worker a peculiar story, something that does not ring true or seems odd. The social worker conveys nonverbally that they hear the client. At the end of the 3 minutes, the observer provides feedback to the social worker, and the social worker and client share their perspective on the process. Each student should have the opportunity to play each role.
   b   Set a stopwatch for 3 minutes. The client tells the social worker about a serious concern in their life. The social worker reacts in each of the following ways:
       1 Disinterested
       2 Inappropriate affect (forced smile, blank stare)
       3 Distracting behaviors (e.g., foot tapping, excessive gesturing, fidgeting, head nodding, checking watch)

   After 3 minutes, the client provides feedback regarding the process. Next, the observer provides feedback to the social worker, and the social worker and client share their perspectives on the process. Each student should have the opportunity to play each role.

9 Review the following case to prepare for role-playing: Gina is your 16-year-old female client at a local teen drop-in center. Gina is usually talkative and outgoing with staff and other participants. Today, you notice that Gina is sitting in the corner alone, and she looks as though she has been crying. When you approach Gina and inquire about her day, she wipes her eyes and says in a quiet voice, "I can't do this anymore. My parents are always fighting, and I just can't take it. I am not going back there." For the role-play, create groups of three students so that one is the client, one is the social worker, and one is an observer. Using the case described here, the client begins the interview. The observer will tell the social worker whenever they become aware of the social worker using the following:
   a   Excessive questions
   b   Closed-ended questions
   c   Jargon
   d   Leading questions
   e   Irrelevant questions

10 For this exercise, the instructor provides flashcards with various interviewing skills. For the role-play, create groups of three students so that

one is the client, one is the social worker, and one is an observer. Use the case of Gina provided in Exercise #8. During the interaction between Gina and the social worker, the observer randomly presents a card with a skill listed on it to the social worker, who must demonstrate the skill in the interaction. Each student has the opportunity to play each role. After a 10- to 15-minute role-play, discuss the degree to which the social workers used the skills appropriately.

11. For this exercise, the instructor provides flashcards with various interviewing skills. For the role-play, create groups of three students so that one is the client, one is the social worker, and one is an observer. Use the case of Gina provided in Exercise #8. During the interaction between Gina and the social worker, the observer selects the card that corresponds with each skill the social worker is using and creates a pile. At the end of the 10- to 15-minute role-play, compare the pile of cards that state the skills that were used to the pile of cards that state the skills that were not used. Discuss how the skills were used and whether any other skills may have been used appropriately during the interaction. Each student should have the opportunity to play each role.

CHAPTER 4

Social Work Practice With Individuals: Assessment and Planning

ASSESSMENT IS THE MEANING-MAKING PROCESS that helps social workers prioritize relevant factors in a client case and determine appropriate action. Assessment is a key social work practice skill that involves collecting information about clients to determine their strengths and challenges (Jordan & Franklin, 2013). In the context of social work, **planning** refers to the process of preparing for carrying out an intervention and involves arranging and scheduling the choice of activities that are generated from the assessment process. Acknowledging the complexity of the situation while also focusing with enough specificity to intervene in a helpful way can be challenging. The social worker's assessment and planning processes, therefore, attempt to identify and gain insight into the client's situation to strive to accomplish the client's desired goals.

In her classic 1993 work *Assessment in Social Work Practice*, Carol Meyer notes that there are many dimensions to the assessment process. The following case scenario illustrates the multiple dimensions of the assessment and planning process for a woman named Briana, including the perspectives and boundaries that apply.

> *Briana is an 18-year-old mother of a 6-month-old son who receives Temporary Assistance to Needy Families (TANF) and lives alone in one room. She dropped out of school when she became pregnant, her family and the father of the baby have abandoned her, and her only social contact is a neighbor who works during the day. One afternoon, Briana, lonesome and depressed, went out for an hour and left the baby alone. The baby fell off the bed and cut his head on an object, seriously injuring himself. When Briana returned home, she took him to the hospital, where the physician in the emergency department, suspecting child abuse (maybe neglect?), made a report to child protective services. The baby was admitted to the hospital for observation and placed in emergency foster care with the plan being reunification with Briana.*
>
> *Adapted from Carol Meyer (1993, p. 22)*

Social workers bring their own experiences and beliefs to the assessment process. Consider your own conceptual boundaries and *unconscious (implicit) biases* (i.e., stereotypes or myths about a group); as you read about Briana, what comes to mind? Do you see her as an unfit mother? As a lonely young woman? What are the major issues you see? What do you want to know more about? Where would an assessment begin? Are you concerned about child abuse/neglect, Briana's depression, a single teen mother with economic needs who lacks social support? Which of these concerns do you center, in your assessment and then planning, for intervening alongside Briana?

The assessment and planning processes begin at the start of the social worker–client relationship when you as the social worker listen to the client's story and consider its meaning. Putting a client's story into the context of the values of social justice and human rights frames the social worker's understanding. Regarding Briana's situation, by carefully listening to and engaging with her, you will gain insight into how she views her life and her goals and the ways in which she hopes you might help her achieve those goals. As a social worker, you may have reservations about the obstacles that seem to block Briana from achieving her goals, about your agency's policies and restrictions, larger governmental policies such as TANF's rules, or even about the legal system, including standards for determining child treatment. Thinking through these issues, including Briana's strengths and the resources on which she can draw, is the heart of the assessment and planning process.

This chapter builds on the previous chapter on engagement and considers two facets of the change process: assessment and planning. The phases of assessment and planning guide the implementation of the intervention, termination, evaluation, and follow-up phases of work. We begin with an introduction to assessment and planning in contemporary practice.

Key Questions for Chapter 4

1. What information, knowledge, and skills to I need to prepare for assessment and planning with individual clients?
2. What evidence-based theoretical perspectives will I use to guide my assessment and planning with individual clients?
3. What potential ethical dilemmas do I anticipate with an individual?
4. How can I ensure that I engage in appropriate professional and personal **self-care** activities?

ASSESSMENT AND PLANNING IN CONTEMPORARY PRACTICE

Since Richmond (1917) published her pioneering work, *Social Diagnosis*, assessment has been a critical component of social work practice. Social workers still consider assessment to be central to practice as it guides the focus of the social work intervention, although the process has evolved over time

Source: Pikul Noorod/Shutterstock

to include strengths and capacities and the client's own definition of needs and goals. Concern has been raised that standard assessment-related language implies social workers have the power to define the client's situation and bring their own initial assumptions about the situation. Social workers must guard against the tendency to insert their own frame, but commit to anti-oppressive practice, including an orientation to collaborative and empowerment assessment and planning. Current practice should view the client as the expert on their life, not the social worker.

In Briana's situation, she has been reported for possible child abuse and/or neglect and does not seek your services voluntarily. Initially, as the social worker, you will likely bring your own initial assumptions about the situation but, as you begin to work together, you can work with Briana to collaboratively frame the issues and determine the course of the planning and intervention processes. The assessment of the client's situation should be framed by the client's perception of events, attitudes, and potential outcomes. Your role as a social worker is to gather and organize information and collaboratively interpret its meaning and implications with your client. A look at how the profession arrived at the word *assessment* may provide some perspective on this debate.

Since Mary Richmond introduced the term *diagnosis* into social work practice, the concept has been a part of the profession's history. However, diagnosis now connotes a medicalized understanding of disease, dysfunction, symptoms, and the authority associated with the person who makes the diagnosis. As the concept of diagnosis is not rooted in a strengths-based perspective, social workers may find it limiting to use a diagnostic term as it conveys presumed pathology.

Instead, contemporary social workers have adopted the term *assessment* to represent a more complete understanding of the client's context, one that focuses on strengths and resources as well as areas of challenge. Today, assessment is considered a collaborative process by which clients can partner with a professional to make informed decisions about the work they can do together. Client resources include the environment in which the client lives as well as the history, culture, and traditions embedded in the client's life experience. Treating assessment as an act of client-focused discovery emphasizes client definitions of the situation, including the parameters of the work, over professional definitions. This process can be a source of empowerment for clients.

A strengths-based systemic perspective invites social workers to examine the whole person, whose many dimensions can never be fully recognized in targeted assessments or diagnoses. Social workers stress the importance of dialogue as a way of gaining a more complete perspective on client situations, considering their significance, hearing clients' goals, and understanding the ways in which clients believe they can achieve these goals.

Consider the complexities of assessment in a situation like Briana's. In addition to her family relationships, her own development and goals for the future, her involvement with child protective services may mandate that she participate in services. Working with a client who may be reluctant or resistant requires ongoing sensitivity and establishing rapport and building trust may take longer to accomplish.

While theoretical approaches, models, and instruments for assessment can vary considerably, common features of social work assessments typically include (Jordan & Franklin, 2021):

1) Emphasis on people and their social environments
2) Use of evidence-based assessment tools and protocols
3) Embrace of a strengths- and resiliency-based perspective
4) Utilization of a transtheoretical or eclectic (e.g., more than one theory) framework and knowledge from other disciplines
5) De-emphasis of long history taking to maintain the focus on current concerns
6) Use of a task-centered approach to organize planning and goal-setting with a future focus
7) Collection of similar information, including definitions, strengths, specific goals, intervention planning and solution-building, and outcome monitoring
8) Client-centered foci on collaborative working relationships

When you and your client develop a shared vision and specify the goals, means, and end points for the work, you have the components of a solid, detailed plan. *Planning* is an interactive process between the social worker and the client that uses rational, incremental decision-making to choose and develop objectives, alternatives, action steps, and evaluative strategies (Barker, 2014).

The key components that influence the concrete plan for work include:

- setting and prioritizing goals,
- identifying methods for reaching goals,
- developing a clear understanding of worker and client responsibilities,
- establishing time frames,
- recognizing indicators that the original plan is not working and the flexibility to develop an alternative plan as necessary,
- identifying resources, and
- identifying an end for the work.

Incorporating these elements into a plan can enhance the client's understanding of the actions that will evolve from the assessment process. The issues illuminated by both the client and the social worker during the assessment process provide a framework for the development of the intervention plan using the identified concerns, priorities, and available and needed resources. The client and social worker negotiate these components as an ongoing feature of the work, and this constitutes the mutually developed plan that can change over time.

You have likely already observed that the COVID-19 pandemic impacted every aspect of the social work profession. Among other effects, it exposed a number of inequities in the health and social services, particularly related to access to care and services, especially technology. For most social workers and clients, each phase of the social work intervention underwent change in terms of delivery format, needs, and outcomes. To maintain continuity in service delivery, social workers nimbly shifted assessment and planning from in-person to online/phone where they responded to client concerns and goals that focused on both COVID-19- and non-COVID-19-related issues. These transitions often required social workers to provide, adapt, and create strategies for clients to gain access to services and to modify previous assessment and planning tools and processes, including helping clients gain technology literacy. As with any crisis, assessment and planning phases provided opportunities for social workers to model for the client the capacity to be resilient and creative while maintaining goal-focused work (Miller, 2020).

In sum, while assessment and planning may appear to occur simultaneously, they are, in fact, two distinct functions within the social work intervention. Assessment emphasizes the construction of the client's "story" (i.e., their history, current concerns, goals, and existing and needed resources) while planning is a collaboration between the social worker and the client to translate the information gathered during the assessment into a viable plan for implementation during the intervention.

WHERE DOES THE CLIENT WANT TO GO?

Many assessment processes begin with detailed social histories. These detailed histories have advantages and disadvantages. On the positive side, asking clients to talk about their life events can reveal important information, such as their resilience in the face of childhood trauma, that might not otherwise be apparent but that is important to fully understand the client's situation. On the negative side, a social history that includes lengthy and detailed questioning can seem intrusive, irrelevant, or even judgmental to a client who, for example, only came to talk about a child care allowance so she can attend a class. Such an approach is inconsistent with the way social workers want to be approached themselves. In thinking about the helping process from the client's perspective, how might you feel when asked for so much information? Such histories may also seem to emphasize previous difficulties or situations that the client would prefer to leave in the past. Finally, the histories may seem disconnected from whatever sense of urgency the client brings to the first interaction.

> *For example, Briana may find an extensive history-taking process invasive and beside the point when she is being investigated by child protective services and may be interested only in getting her baby back. At the same time, such a process could reveal aspects of Briana's life that might assist you in helping her achieve her goals using more or better-placed supports. The major requirement in this assessment process is that the social worker uses effective communication and relationship-building skills (as discussed in Chapter 3) to make the client feel supported and respected. By providing Briana with information regarding why certain questions are important and by maintaining a flexible and patient approach, you can help Briana feel more understood and respected when giving information.*

Such action ensures the social worker will collect only information that is relevant to the situation and that advances the client's interests. Whether the history is lengthy or brief, it is critical that the work start with you inquiring about the client's goals for the service. The most detailed social history is of little use if it—and not the goals of the client—becomes the driving force of the work.

IMPLICATIONS OF THEORETICAL PERSPECTIVES

Despite efforts to minimize prejudices and personal/implicit biases about the client's situation, assessments are not neutral gatherings of facts. The questions you ask and the information you gather are important for an effective intervention. For every area on which you choose to focus, there are others you exclude. For example, if you focus on Briana's relationship with her baby because you see her case as one of "mother and child," rather than considering her experience as a child herself, you choose to explore one area over another that could influence the work you and Briana do together. Likewise, if you stress one factor of her history (for example, teen pregnancy) but not another factor (for example, being a survivor of child abuse), those choices will affect the nature of the work.

In both scenarios, you take a specific approach based on your judgment about what is relevant and important. This judgment is usually influenced by your personal attributes, such as who you are, what you believe about the nature of people, and where you work, and by the type of information you believe helps make a story understandable. Of critical importance is the need to maintain professionalism in all social work encounters, as negative displays of emotion can be perceived as oppressive and can detrimentally impact your work with clients. Specifically, in maintaining your professionalism, you should adhere to social values and ethics, including not displaying anger, frustration, a blaming attitude, or sympathy.

The theoretical perspectives to which you subscribe as well as your assumptions will also influence what you consider useful, as will the context and function of the agency. All these components shape the kinds of questions you ask and, therefore, the information you receive. Framed as it is by your perspectives, the client's assumptions, and your own interpretation of a situation, the assessment process is never unbiased.

Classic Theories

The theoretical perspectives you adopt influence the assessment and planning processes, the client–social worker relationship, and the work that the client and you do together. Throughout the history of social work, three classic theories have influenced assessments: psychoanalytic theory, attachment theory, and cognitive theory. All theories are predicated on assumptions that impact the way the social worker perceives, relates to, and works with clients. Every social worker will have tendencies toward certain theories in certain situations. We are all guided by theories, formal or not. No one theory is "truth." You may use a combination of theories to frame the approach you select for working with each client. The theoretical perspectives to which you subscribe as well as your assumptions will also influence what you consider useful, as will the context and function of the agency.

Psychoanalytic Theory Based primarily on the writings of Austrian physician Sigmund Freud, psychoanalytic theory maintains that the unconscious is at the root of human behavior. Freud identified three structures that interact to determine human behavior: the id, ego, and superego. Each structure has a distinct function. The id is the repository of unconscious drives such as sex and aggression. In contrast, the ego is the managerial, rational part of the personality, which mediates between drives and perceived obligations. Finally, the superego serves as judge and conscience.

A social worker who believes that inner, unconscious motives and explanations determine the client's choices would orient an assessment toward interpreting the client's unconscious wishes or desire for rewards and gratification.

For example, if Briana repeatedly describes herself as a "loser," your assessment could be directed toward discovering the unconscious rewards and gratification Briana receives from presenting herself as a perpetual failure. In actuality, Briana may not be perpetually failing at all, but she may be receiving gratification by allowing others to see her as a failure. Perhaps she needs people to tell her that she is successful and to be reassured that she has competence and self-worth. These rewards may include more attention from previously disinterested parents or protection from the high expectations of others. If Briana labels herself a failure, then perhaps people will not ask too much of her. If she does succeed, people will be pleasantly surprised, thus eliminating the pressure she feels.

The first models of assessment were rooted in psychoanalytic theory, but as psychoanalytic theory gave way during the 20th century to evidence-based models, assessment approaches followed suit (Jordan & Franklin, 2013), including attachment- and cognitive-based approaches and, later, such approaches as strengths-based perspective, narrative, and solution-focused as discussed here.

Attachment Theory Attachment theory, originally proposed by US psychologist John Bowlby (1982), holds that very early bonding occurs between a mother and an infant and subsequently plays a critical role in the child's future capacity to provide and sustain attachment opportunities for their children. Most of this bonding activity occurs within the first two years of life and creates the foundation for the health of all the child's future relationships.

A social worker who uses attachment theory would focus on Briana's relationships with her early caregivers and the way in which these relationships may have contributed to her current struggles. To assess the attachment between Briana and her child, you might observe Briana and her child during visitations to identify behavior patterns that both the child and Briana demonstrate when a stranger enters the scene. In stressing these relationships of parental bonding during the assessment, a social worker who uses attachment theory would de-emphasize Briana's other relationships.

Cognitive Theory The cognitive approach is grounded in the assumption that people are thinking beings and, if they change their thinking, their emotions will also change (Beck, 2011). It further posits that one's feelings influence both specific behaviors and general approaches to life. An assessment informed by the cognitive approach would focus on Briana's self-perception through questions about mood and thoughts, the ways in which these influence her behavior, and how she would like to change them. For example, because Briana felt depressed, lonely, abandoned, or hopeless, she used poor judgment in leaving her baby. A social work intervention based on cognitive theory may involve helping Briana appreciate her assets, which in turn would help her feel better about herself and lead her to make safer choices for her baby.

Contemporary Theoretical Perspectives

Like the classic theories, the worldview inherent in each contemporary theoretical approach influences assessment practice behaviors. We now turn our attention to major contemporary theoretical perspectives and to their implications for assessment approaches and skills. Strengths-based, narrative theory, and solution-focused approaches all emphasize client empowerment and the mobilization of client strengths and resources, yet they also each have their own unique methods and strategies (Smith, 2022). Some practitioners elect to combine these approaches with one another and with other approaches (e.g., cognitive behavioral interventions), but to combine approaches, a practitioner needs skills, knowledge, and competence in the areas being combined.

Strengths-Based Perspective Growing out of a movement that shifted away from identifying clients' deficits, a strengths-based assessment focuses not on a history of client failures but instead concentrates on successes, resources, and goals for the future and examines the potential for the environment to nurture and support client strengths. In fact, the entire focus of the assessment should be focused on abilities and assets within the client themselves and their environment (Kim & Bolton, 2019). Strengths-based champion Dennis Saleebey (2013, pp. 109–111) proposed two elements for strengths-based assessments:

1 *The social worker meets the client in the struggle:* It is critical for the social worker to identify positive dimensions of a client's personality, skills, or accomplishments while validating client experiences and feelings in terms of their negative dimensions (e.g., grief, terror, sorrow, or discouragement). Starting where the client is and listening to the client's concerns, painful though they may be, can help the client identify evidence of potential strengths on which you can work together to develop a strengths-based intervention.
2 *The social worker stimulates the discourse and narratives of resilience and strength:* A narrative approach can be helpful in reframing the work around the client's strengths. This reframing is dependent on the social worker supplying the words to help articulate the client's strengths, affirming those strengths, and emphasizing possibilities. Supportive questioning (i.e., questions that emphasize a positive aspect of the situation or a recollection of past successes) can focus the discussion on client strengths. Even in the face of repeated, entrenched stories of trouble and pain, you can help clients recognize their capacities for survival and learn the language of strengths to uncover a seed of hope. Quick Guide 4 provides examples of supportive questions in various situations.

QUICK GUIDE 4 Examples of Strengths-Based Supportive Questions

CLIENT SITUATION	POSSIBLE SUPPORTIVE QUESTIONS
Middle-aged man who was recently laid off from his job and fears he will not be able to find new employment	"How did you approach your last successful job search?" "What were your greatest assets in your last position, and how can you include those in your presentation to prospective employers (i.e., what can you bring to their organization)?"
Single mother with four young children who is feeling overwhelmed with her life	"What do you see as your greatest strength as a mother?" "When do you feel the most successful as a parent?"
15-year-old teenager who is stressed by daily arguments with their mother	"Can you recall times when you and your mother had fun together? What are those times?"
75-year-old who is experiencing depression	"How have you handled other challenges in your life?"
33-year-old combat veteran who is having difficulty adjusting to civilian life	"What were your best assets as a soldier? How might those transfer to this new chapter of your life?"
Middle-aged person struggling with the decision to seek long-term residential care for their mother, who is suffering from dementia. They feel that placing their mother would be a betrayal of the deathbed promise made to the father to always keep mother with them.	"How has your family traditionally handled difficult decisions? How might other family members be able to provide support for you in making these hard decisions?"

A strengths-based assessment should go beyond simply just gathering information and content for planning and intervention (Simmons et al., 2022). Exhibit 4.1 provides guidance for conducting a strengths-based assessment.

A strengths-based assessment process helps clients identify their own strengths, use the resources in their environment, and tell their story about the current challenge. Integrating the client's strengths as a key component of the assessment helps guide the process of finding solutions (Hall et al., 2019). The approach recognizes and articulates the power relationships in clients' lives. Consider how you might engage Briana in identifying her strengths and help her view those strengths as resources that may be mobilized in the current situation.

Narrative Theory Recall from Chapter 1 that narrative theory, drawing on postmodern thought, focuses on the client's story as the central component in the work. Social workers using this approach are primarily interested in

> EXHIBIT 4.1
>
> *The Strengths-Based Perspective in Assessment*
>
> - Identify strengths that can promote change.
> - Identify those areas/resources that are positive (i.e., current strengths) and the client's positive goals.
> - Ask questions that will elicit how strengths and positive goals can be used in an intervention focused on change even in the context of past failures (e.g., "In what perceived failures or barriers can you search for strengths and growth opportunities?" (p. 107).
> - Strengths-based screening can aid in identifying areas with the fewest strengths for supporting and helping the client cope—these insights can be used to guide the plan for change.
> - Promote client choice in the engagement and assessment process to encourage the sharing of relevant and high-quality information.
> - Assessments should be comprehensive in their inclusion of the client's strengths and resources.
>
> *Source:* Simmons et al., 2022

discovering client stories and in helping them to "re-author" those stories if they wish. In this context, a plot (i.e., understanding of oneself) and subsequent narrative (i.e., meaning one gives to one's life) are the focus for change so that new narratives can be created that embody strength and resilience (Hall, 2016).

Narrative theory is consistent with the mission and values of the social work profession as it: (1) conceptualizes people within the context of their environments; (2) promotes social justice by confronting unjust policies; (3) fosters helpful social worker–client relationships; and (4) develops a collaborative process that serves to empower clients to use their strengths (Hall, 2022). Narrative practitioners subscribe to a person-centered approach that embraces the essentials of respectful listening, avoidance of labels, fostering empowerment, and emphasizing social justice (Smith, 2022).

Narrative practitioners are interested in helping the client to broaden or "thicken" their story. For example, consider the case of Lakeisha, a 25-year-old woman whom you met in Chapter 1. Lakeisha developed a negative self-story response to her experience of intimate partner violence. Before, her self-story was that of a strong and competent young woman, but with the experience, it slowly began to erode, reflecting her increasing doubt and finally dejection as she adopted the persona of an unworthy human being. It became a "thin" story in that it lacked complexity; it reflected only her self-rejection. Lakeisha's perception of herself as unworthy focuses on one dimension of her person (i.e., self-rejection) while ignoring her strengths, life lessons, and capabilities.

In addition to trying to build a more in-depth story, the social worker recognizes the importance of the broader social context of the client's life. In one sense, Lakeisha's story is about her and her partner. In a broader sense, however, it is also about a pervasive social problem that results in the deaths of thousands of women every year. The social work intervention aims to help Lakeisha rewrite her thin story of feeling unvalued into one that more accurately reflects her talents, competence, and worth as a human being. This is the goal of assessment: to discover the alternative story the client wishes to author and to guide the development of a person-centered intervention to identify tasks and activities that will enable the client to tap into their talents, worth, and competencies.

> *In Briana's situation, the social worker using a narrative approach would first want to hear Briana's story. How does she fill the day? What is it like to be a mother to her baby? When are the best times? When did her loneliness first interfere with her life? When is she able to conquer it? Who would say she is a good mother? To assess if Briana's self-perception or story has "thinned," you might ask her to describe herself before she became a mother.*

Though narrative theory differs from many more classic theoretical perspectives, it is similar in that the story is the emphasis of the assessment process. In a narrative approach, the person seeking assistance is the primary driver of the assessment, although the social worker contributes ideas as well. A narrative approach aligns with the strengths perspective as it assumes that people are the experts on their lives and that they have multiple talents, values, beliefs, and skills for improving their lives. We will look more closely at the applicability of narrative approaches in interventions with families and groups in Chapters 6–9.

Solution-Focused Approach Like a narrative approach, a solution-focused intervention builds on a strengths perspective that emphasizes successes, supports resilience, and encourages the client to reflect on ways in which they accomplished success and resiliency when facing challenges (Metcalf, 2017). Developed in the 1980s by Berg, de Shazer, and colleagues, the solution-focused approach is a future-focused, goal-directed intervention that is widely used in the helping professions to address a range of challenges and in diverse settings (de Shazer et al., 2021). The tenets of this therapeutic approach include (de Shazer et al., 2021):

- *If it isn't broken, don't fix it:* If there is no problem, consider the role that an intervention can play.
- *If it works, do more of it*: By identifying what worked in the past, the client is able to repeat this success and the solution further evolves.
- *If it's not working, do something different:* No matter how good a solution might seem, if it does not work it is not a solution.
- *Small steps can lead to big changes:* When a small change has been made, it will lead to a series of further changes, which in turn lead to

others, gradually resulting in a much larger systemic change without major disruption.

- *The solution is not necessarily directly related to the problem:* Solutions are developed by first eliciting a description of what will be different when the problem is resolved.

- *The language for solution development is different from that needed to describe a problem:* The language of solutions is usually more positive, hopeful, and future-focused, and suggests the transience of problems.

- *No problems happen all the time; there are always exceptions that can be utilized:* People always display exceptions to their problems, even small ones, and these exceptions can be utilized to make small changes.

- *The future is both created and negotiable:* The future is a hopeful place, where people are the architects of their own destiny.

(pp. 1–3)

Three primary assumptions and principles guide practitioners using this approach: (1) language is the mechanism by which clients and social workers understand the meanings of the client's life and actions; (2) because clients are the experts on their own lives, they have the resources and answers that will guide their solutions; and (3) clients, not professionals, function as the "knowers" within the intervention process and are therefore in the best position to create their meaning-making solutions (Lee et al., 2022). Diagnoses and client history are de-emphasized to send the message that you perceive the clients as being competent people seeking change but who are immobilized by a problem-saturated story (Metcalf, 2017).

In the assessment stage, clients work with the social worker in stages, using a series of questions, to develop solutions to issues. While the social worker poses these questions, their content is rooted in the story the client shared during the assessment phase. The social worker asks questions to fill in historical gaps, identify previous successes and solutions, and explore the client's perceptions for outcomes. Stages of solution-building include: (1) description of the problem; (2) development of well-formed goals; (3) exploring with the client "exceptions to their experiences" questions (i.e., questions aimed at identifying instances in which the problem did not exist); (4) provision of end-of-session feedback; and (5) evaluation of client progress (De Jong & Berg, 2013, pp. 17–18). The social worker asks questions aimed at eliciting the client's self-evaluation of the meaning of their life events and an exploration of future possibilities that the client can pursue.

Returning to Briana, you may ask how she views her current situation, life before motherhood and the current situation, and her goals for resolving the current challenges (e.g., depression, need for parenting support, and/or involvement of the child welfare system). This series of questions will help you both gain insight into the understanding and meaning she has attached to her life.

Although similar in their strengths-based orientation, client-centered empowerment approach, and commitment to collaboration, narrative and solution-focused approaches are not the same. Proponents of the narrative approach emphasize the importance of "not knowing" (i.e., not being the expert on the client's life) and listening for unique outcomes to the client's presenting concerns, whereas solution-focused adherents delve into the possibility of "exception" questions (Smith, 2022). In pursuing information regarding "exceptions," the social worker can ask the client to describe their life before the crisis or situation that brought them in contact with the social worker. Information regarding coping skills the client has used successfully in the past can provide insight into possibilities for a successful intervention for the client's current difficulty.

Evidence Matters

Although theory guides and informs the development of social work practice knowledge, values, and competence, evidence also helps social work practitioners determine the appropriate skills, competencies, and behaviors to apply to the social work intervention. Evidence helps to refine theories and lend credence to their validity, while contextualizing their application in practice. The Council on Social Work Education (CSWE) Educational Policy and Accreditation Standards (2022) calls for social workers to engage in practice-informed research and research-informed practice.

Evidence-based practice (EBP) helps practitioners "systematically integrate evidence about the efficacy of interventions in clinical decision-making" (Jenson & Howard, 2013). In evidence-based practice, social workers systematically determine, use, and assess interventions based on the consideration and integration of research findings; clinical expertise; client preferences, values, and presenting issues; and the values and circumstances that will best serve the client (Thyer, 2021).

It is important to emphasize that using EBP approaches does not eliminate the need for social workers to engage in critical thinking by centering the client's experiences in decision-making. For example, there are promising practices that are not yet evidence-based and EBP approaches that have not been shown to be effective with all populations and communities. Referred to as **evidence-informed practices (EIPs)**, these methods have had some empirical study and show promising results (Dodd & Savage, 2016, p. 3). These approaches can incorporate theory, practice wisdom, critical reflection, client values and choices, and intersubjectivity (i.e., knowledge gained through practice interchanges) (Dodd & Savage, 2016, p. 7). As the evidence supports both the design of the practice and its delivery, it is important to implement evidence-based and evidence-informed practices with fidelity.

As noted by Chodnody and Teater (2018): "Evidence alone is not enough to warrant the use of a particular practice" (p. 1245). Appropriate evidence can be developed through multiple methods, including empirically supported treatments (ESTs), empirically supported interventions (ESIs), and research-supported treatments (RSTs) (Drisko & Grady, 2018, p. 270); therefore, social workers should be knowledgeable about the origins of the evidence they use.

Because social workers are ethically bound to consider client values and preferences in assessing and planning for interventions, using evidence is a process that begins by providing clients with treatment options (Chodnody & Teater, 2018). Three factors guide the social worker in synthesizing the evidence to be applied: best available research; the social work practitioner's knowledge and expertise; and the client's wishes, values, and circumstances (Chodnody & Teater, 2018, p. 1237). In determining if an intervention is evidence-based, Slayter (2021b) suggests synthesizing and comparing four areas of the literature—intervention(s) tested, populations studied, assessment/measurement tools used, and results/outcomes—to identify themes and trends in measures and results that help you determine if the intervention has sufficient evidence to meet EBP criteria.

Building on the foundation of evidence-based medicine (Straus et al., 2019), Thyer (2021) presents a five-step evidence-based practice process: (1) translating practice issues and potential interventions into answerable questions; (2) locating evidence to answer the questions; (3) critically appraising the evidence to determine validity, impact, and applicability; (4) integrating evidence into practice knowledge and the client's unique values and circumstances; and (5) evaluating the effectiveness and efficiency of using evidence to guide and improve the practice intervention (p. 694).

Although the assumed focus of an EBP approach is on informing the intervention, assessment and planning should include evidence-based tools and protocols that are relevant for the client's situation and should be psychometrically validated through research; encompass client diversity, characteristics, contextual issues, and co-occurring conditions (e.g., health and/or mental health challenges); and be appropriate for your setting (Jordan & Franklin, 2021).

To collaborate with the client, a viable and effective intervention plan, with an evidence-based foundation for gathering and processing information, helps ensure a successful outcome. Drawing from available evidence on assessment and planning, multiple factors influence the way in which assessment is conceptualized, including (Grady & Drisko, 2014):

1 *The social worker's role:* If the social worker's task is only to gather information but not develop a plan or implement the intervention, the assessment will differ from one that involves an ongoing relationship. For example, a social worker's role may be to conduct an intake assessment and compile the information assigned to another worker for planning and implementing an intervention plan.
2 *Agency/organizational factors:* While agencies rely on assessments to guide and support service delivery, social workers need to have insight into the factors that influence the assessment/planning process, including agency mission and purpose, services provided, the social worker's role, client needs, and agency culture about assessment. For example, you should

investigate whether mandates are structured assessments with little room for including the client and social worker's perspectives and, if so, how you can practice effectively within this context.

3 *Client availability and capacity:* A variety of issues may impact the client's willingness and ability to fully engage in the assessment process, including cognitive capacity, mental illness, cultural norms, values related to receiving help, and power dynamics between worker and client, including those related to the client's experience of intersectional identities and potential complications of a client's involuntary status.

4 *Assessment format and structure*: The inclusion of well-accepted social work frameworks such as strengths and person-in-environment perspectives, the format (e.g., one session versus multiple sessions), and structure (e.g., individual versus couple or family) all serve to shape the approach and outcome of the assessment.

Utilizing the EBP process and the influencing factors described here, how would you apply this process to work with Briana? Consider the following (Jenson & Howard, 2013):

1 Convert practice information into questions about background information, effectiveness of intervention, or policy:
   - Information: As Briana is single parenting without sufficient financial or social support, her child's safety was jeopardized when he was left alone.
   - Question: What are the risk factors most associated with parental neglect?
   - Information: Briana wants to be a good parent.
   - Question: How can social workers help teen parents, like Briana, at risk of child neglect?
   - Information: Briana appears to be experiencing depressive symptoms, which may be related to postpartum depression.
   - Questions: What assessment tools are most appropriate to assess for depression in new mothers? What tools consider the extent to which Briana's age is the determinant factor? What are the most effective intervention strategies to lower depressive symptoms in new parents?
2 Locate evidence to answer the questions.
   - Conduct a search of research and literature on child development, child maltreatment, parenting, and assessment of and intervention with depression.
   - Consult with one or more social work practitioners who possess knowledge and expertise in the areas of interest and ask for their opinions of best practices in the areas.
3 Appraise evidence.
   - Assess the quality of the best available evidence, including the appropriateness of the research design for the question, source of research sponsorship, similarity of the research subjects to your client, and other factors, including the evolving nature of scientific and psychological knowledge.
   - Using the evidence compiled from your literature review, your judgment, practitioners' discussion and experience, and the client's goals and social context, develop a plan for assessment and intervention.

4 Apply evidence to practice decisions.
   - Implement the assessment and intervention plan.
   - Determine if the intervention is appropriate for your client's situation.
5 Evaluate the process of using evidence to guide practice intervention.
   - At each step in the change process, evaluate the efficacy of the assessment and intervention process. Questions to consider:
     - With input from the client, was the assessment accurate?
     - Guided by the agreed-upon goals, was the intervention effective?
     - Was the information compiled from the literature and practitioner helpful?
     - Did ethical questions emerge? How were those resolved?
     - What would you have done differently? Why?

Evidence-based practice approaches are an evolving area that can be used to guide practitioners to information regarding assessment, intervention, and evaluative strategies and other key resources needed for effective work with a client. An increasing number of social workers are accessing evidence to inform and guide their practice, due in part to the requirements from private (non-governmental) and public (governmental) funders that will only support evidence-based practices. To be prepared for contemporary practice, social work students must develop knowledge and skills in research design, measurement, statistical analysis, limitations, and application (Drisko & Grady, 2018).

The clinical judgment and skills required for competent and ethical social work practice also play an important role in effective interventions. Each client circumstance is unique, and each situation must be assessed individually. Such an approach allows practitioners to account for the complexities of client situations when implementing interventions.

IMPLICATIONS OF DIVERSITY AND CULTURE IN ASSESSMENT

Diversity and culture have a significant impact on assessment. The social work profession is a cultural institution and is therefore affected by the same pressures and forces that influence other aspects of our society. Shifting patterns of diverse populations in US society require social workers to develop appropriate competencies for effective practice within different cultures. The NASW *Code of Ethics* (2021) compels social workers to emphasize social justice, commitment to respect for diversity and inclusions and an obligation to those oppressed by other systems.

Consider these diversity, equity, inclusion, and belonging (DEIB)-related questions as they may impact your work with Briana:

1 *What is Briana's background, including race, ethnicity, family background, religious/spiritual beliefs, and education?*
2 *How might Briana's experiences related to aspects of diversity and intersectionality impact her experience with parenting?*

3 How does your background impact your knowledge of Briana's ethnic, racial, and cultural backgrounds?
4 What information do you need to work with Briana in a culturally competent and humble way?
5 What culturally congruent practice behaviors will be appropriate for working with Briana?

The social worker who uses a strengths-based and/or narrative or solution-focused approach must be committed to affirming individuals' strengths and respecting their culture. Critical to the assessment and planning processes is ensuring that every client encounter is viewed through the perspective of the client's **biopsychosocial-spiritual (BPSS)** and cultural lenses. Gathering and analyzing the information provided by the client through such a multifaceted lens can ensure that you view the client as a "whole" person within the context of the physical, psychological, social, and spiritual environments in which they live. Each area of the BPSS includes the following elements (Grady & Dombo, 2016):

- *Biological/Physical:* bodily elements, diagnoses, health concerns, genetic predispositions, prescribed physical characteristics (gender identity and race), abilities and disabilities, and timing (i.e., aging process)

- *Psychological:* gender, sexuality, personal experiences, significant others, habits/behaviors, relational patterns, language, and personal history

- *Social:* roles, culture, values, economic elements, race and ethnicity, community connections, stereotypes, physical spaces, access to services, historical events, political situation, institutions, legal status, and national origin

- *Spiritual:* spiritual beliefs, organized religion, values, and meaning-making

(p. 51)

During the assessment process, the BPSS helps the social worker to: (1) explore multiple areas of the client's life that may be both strengths and needs; (2) gather, organize, synthesize, and summarize the information; and (3) use the information to inform the planning and intervention processes (Grady & O'Toole, 2022). Not only does this holistic ("whole person") approach to assessment and planning enable you to help create a person-centered plan and intervention, but it also provides a broader and deeper understanding of the client's history, physical and emotional status, beliefs, and life—all critical to the assessment and planning process. For example, if you learn that Briana's family are members of a conservative, fundamentalist faith community that does not support pre-marital sex or birth control and values loyalty to the church and family above all, you can gain insight into her choices. While some may be uncomfortable asking about religious and spiritual beliefs, learning from the client about their history can provide insight into actions, resources, and changes over time (Grady & Dombo, 2016). The social worker must also acknowledge the implications of such a commitment for the assessment and planning processes, particularly in the areas of (1) cultural competence, humility, and intersectionality, (2) connecting with the spiritual aspects of the client, and (3) making global connections.

Cultural Competence, Humility, Intersectionality, and Anti-Racist, Anti-Oppressive Practice in Culturally Responsive Assessment

A social worker who embraces a systemic, strengths-based perspective includes meaningful components of the client's culture in the assessment process (NASW, 2015). As highlighted in Chapter 1, the goal of the social work profession to strive for cultural competence has continued to evolve with the inclusion of knowledge, skills, and values related to cultural humility, intersectionality, and anti-racist and anti-oppressive practice.

Being a culturally responsive social worker requires that social workers are aware of their limitations and respect and respond to the unique, culturally defined needs of others. As you have learned, assessment involves discovering what is important to the client, and that includes those cultural influences that shape the client's values, how those influences have affected the client's experience, the intersections and impact of being a member of multiple groups, and how the client's perspectives differ from that of the social worker. Clearly, the social worker's ability to demonstrate cultural humility and anti-racist and anti-oppressive values and practices requires that they understand their own personal cultural influences, including power and privilege, examine how those influences affect their work, and understand the role culture plays in all our lives. In determining if the client's concerns relate to race, ethnicity, or cultural experiences, Oluo (2018) provides these rules to consider:

1) It is about race if the BIPOC client(s) think(s) it is about race.
2) It is about race if the client is or has been disproportionately or differently affected.

Cultural humility broadly refers to a commitment to self-evaluation and self-critique to reduce the imbalances of power that inherently exist within the professional–client relationship (Tervalon & Murray-Garcia, 1998, p. 117). From a practice perspective, having cultural humility within the context of the social work intervention enables the social worker to function in the role as a learner and allows the client to serve as the expert on their life. Gottlieb (2020) offers three principles of culturally humble social work practice:

1) *Commit ourselves to an ongoing process of compassionate self-awareness and inquiry, supported by a community of trusted and cognitively-diverse colleagues—*

in the context of assessment, we can acknowledge that our initial reactions to a client are from our own life experiences and exploring and confronting our own biases to separate them from our responses to clients.
2) *Be open and teachable: strive to see cultures as our clients see them, rather than as we have come to know or define them*—within the assessment process, we commit to listening to the client's perspective and story so that we can join with them to develop plans and solutions.
3) *Always bear in mind the social structures that have helped shape reality as our clients experience it*—critical to the assessment stage of work is the need to view the client's story and perspective through the lens of their lived experience as it relates to the impact of various systems with which they interact during their lives.

(pp. 12–14)

As a social worker, demonstrating cultural humility means being open to seeing the person's life through their lens and recognizing that every client's experience is unique, they are the expert on their life, and that your role is to facilitate the change process with them (Sanchez, 2020). Acknowledging that you cannot know everything about the client's cultural heritage and traditions might involve saying to the client: "I am committed to learning more as we work together, but I have not had much experience with your culture. I hope you will tell me more about it." Such a statement signifies your commitment to forging an open and collaborative relationship with the client but be careful to ensure that the client is not responsible for being your cultural guide.

Approaching social work practice with a perspective on intersectionality recognizes the multiple aspects of diversity that influence the client's life including, but not limited to, age, caste, class, color, culture, disability and ability, ethnicity, gender, gender identity and expression, generational status, immigration, legal status, marital status, political ideology, race, nationality, religion/spirituality, sex, sexual orientation, and tribal sovereign status (CSWE, 2022). Intersectionality is an important paradigm to incorporate into working at all levels of social work practice, including assessment and planning processes with individuals, families, and groups. Taking an inclusive and culturally responsive approach enables the social worker and the client to holistically consider the many and varied aspects and identities associated with the client's life, thus embracing the person-in-environment perspective with a commitment to social justice. In reflecting on the concept she developed, attorney and activist Kimberlé Crenshaw says, "Intersectionality is a lens through which you can see where power comes and collides, where it interlocks and intersects. It's not simply that there's a race problem here, a gender problem here, and a class or LBGTQIA+ problem there" (Columbia Law School, 2017).

An effective assessment and planning process depends on the social worker's level of cultural responsiveness, use of multicultural assessment tools and strategies, cultural humility, and commitment to intersectionality. Intersectionality is not additive, but instead, with each dimension of identity influencing others, there is a unique manifestation and experience of the specific social location. You cannot simply assess the ways in which your client's intersectionality is different or similar from your own; you must recognize the way in which your own cultural beliefs and experiences impact the client relationship and accept that you cannot be an expert on the client's cultural experience. Consider these reflective questions you can ask yourself during the assessment phase (Sellon & Lassman, 2022):

1) How could my personal values be skewing the questions that I am asking?
2) Am I helping the person so that they can get a better understanding of their situation or am I defining their situation for them because it is easier for me to understand?
3) What is the person's understanding of oppression and the role it plays in their life?
4) What resources do they believe they need? What resources do they have access to and what additional resources need to be located?
5) What strengths does the person possess that they can build on?

(p. 307)

Gilbert and Olcón (2021) note that assessment tools are not often validated on BIPOC populations, therefore encompassing an inherent bias which results in social workers relying on generalizations and stereotypes as the assessment and intervention are completed. To ensure you create a comprehensive picture of the client and their situation, consider using multiple types of assessment tools and approaches. Strategies offered by Gilbert and Olcón (2021) to conduct culturally responsive assessments include:

1) Use tests that have been revised for the population you are assessing and/or newly created ethnic-specific tools.
2) Include assessment of culture and ethnic identity, acculturation, and acculturative stress as moderators of the standardized tests.
3) Incorporate thematic apperception-type testing (i.e., tests depicting visual content have been validated and can be effective, particularly with children and adolescents).
4) Adding qualitative approaches to assessment strategies, to include client records, thoughts, beliefs, feelings, and life history.

Your understanding of the issues the client brings, and the role the client's culture plays in those issues, impacts how you perceive the presenting "problem" and the extent to which you recognize and champion strengths. For example, your client describes communicating with the spirit of his deceased father. You might wonder if he is demonstrating psychosis or hallucinations, unless you ask the client about his beliefs so you can develop a clear understanding that this kind of spiritual communication is part of his Latinx cultural celebration of the Dia de los Muertos (i.e., Day of the Dead), which encourages reaching out and encouraging the spirit of the deceased to be present for a moment to hear the prayers and love of the family for them.

Anti-Racist and Anti-Oppressive Practice Behaviors

Developing the skills necessary to conduct a culturally responsive assessment and plan, including the ability to ascertain, through talking to the client, the meaning of their culture, language, cultural norms, and behaviors, takes time and effort and is an ongoing part of the social work intervention. It requires the social worker to see these attributes as strengths on which to build a culturally meaningful a mutually agreed-upon plan and intervention (CSWE, 2022). Engaging in anti-racist practice requires holding ourselves accountable and open to change, particularly in "unlearning" the biases we bring to our practice through reading, observing, listening, studying, and retaining new information (Oluo, 2018).

A social worker who adopts a strengths-based, culturally responsive model of assessment and planning begins the relationship by initiating friendly yet purposeful conversations. The goal of the assessment phase is to explore the client's sense of self and, together, develop a common understanding which requires the social worker to listen to how the client defines and discusses intersectionality and the role of oppression in their lives (Sellon & Lassman, 2022). Rather than focusing on long social histories, you may consider some aspect of the client's cultural frame that they find puzzling or particularly interesting and ask about it using a "global question." For example, consider the situation you encounter as you work with Emilia Sanchez (refer to www.routledgesw.com/interactive-cases/ for information), a 24-year-old Latina with a history of substance use and the mother of a 4-year-old, Joey. Joey has lived with his grandparents for most of his four years and, while he knows that Emilia is his mother, he sees Hector and Celia as his parents. Emilia has just learned that Hector and Celia are going to take legal action to officially adopt Joey. She is furious and has come to you for help to prevent the adoption from going forward.

As a culturally responsive practitioner, you inquire about Emilia's cultural background and work to understand the impact it has on her beliefs and situation. As she answers your questions, you remain attuned to the language she uses, and you inquire about **cover terms**, expressions, and phrases that seem to carry more meaning than the literal meaning the words would suggest. For instance, your client might respond to the question about what her family thinks with a comment like, "I will never be the person they want me to be." In this case, the cover term is "person they want me to be," because it seems to have an ethnic or familial cultural relevance to how she understands her position and role within the family.

Should clients be excluded from ownership of the assessment and planning process, two negative consequences can occur. First, important information that only the person experiencing the context can provide may be dismissed or ignored. Second, for many clients, exclusion contributes to the internalization of oppression; clients come to believe that they have no right or capacity to participate. The **internalization of oppression**—the process by which individuals come to believe and accept external judgments that devalue their sense of self—is one of the most sinister aspects of the oppression and domination dynamic (Van Soest, 2013), and one that clearly undermines the principles and commitments of human rights.

Although extensive cultural-responsive interviewing could seem removed from the main issue and even distracting or exploitative, understanding the impact of the client's culture and lived experiences can contribute to the success of the work. It is particularly important to identify early on those cultural-related areas that have the potential to become assets or barriers in the working relationship. A commitment to practicing with an anti-racist and anti-oppressive perspective enables the social worker to recognize the impact of their own biases, privilege, and values as well as those of societal interactions to forge a collaboration with the client (CSWE, 2022). For example, given what you have discovered about Emilia, you know not to begin by suggesting a family conference with her parents.

Connecting With the Spiritual Aspects of the Client

The social work profession is committed to serve all clients, specifically those experiencing oppression, which includes gaining more in-depth understanding of the client's spiritual beliefs, practices, and experience to determine how to incorporate this information into the intervention to address the current situation (Hodge, 2022). There are challenges in defining and measuring spirituality as it is individualized and complex; measurement strategies have been developed, including: (1) standardized scales which may not fully capture the multi-faceted nature of spirituality; (2) semi-structured and qualitative questions (e.g., "Do you consider yourself a spiritual or religious person?"); and (3) spirituality-specific tools (e.g., spiritual history, spiritual lifemap, spiritual genogram and ecomap) (Hodge, 2022; Stewart, 2022).

Insofar as this change process might be a spiritual quest, it can encourage people to find the most sustaining areas of their lives. People find such areas of meaning in many places, including religious practices, outdoor activities, and in social connections like volunteering in a hospice. The social worker and client can incorporate these areas of meaning into both the assessment and action stages of the work.

> *For example, after inquiring about Briana's religion and spirituality experiences and practices and learning that she has not been involved with her church since she left her parents' home, you may inquire if she would like to reconnect with a faith community, which might reduce her sense of isolation. Facilitating a client's connection with their spiritual side can be a lasting and significant contribution of the social work intervention.*

Global Connections

In the United States, foreign-born immigrants make up 13.7 percent of the population, the highest percent since the early 20th century, and these numbers are growing (Budiman, 2020). Social workers may work with individuals who have come to live in the United States as nonimmigrants (e.g., visitors, students, and temporary workers); those who are asylees, documented and undocumented immigrants, and refugees who fled political or religious persecution. The context of these individuals' lives may be changed depending on the extent to which they have been targets of political hostility and legal and political attack. It is therefore essential that social workers develop competence in internationally focused practice.

At the individual practice level, social workers can work with international migrants in a number of areas, especially health, including assessment of health beliefs and treatment expectation, case management, and health education; culturally and linguistically appropriate psychosocial treatment; mental health, including case management, crisis intervention; culturally and linguistically appropriate and evidence-based individual, marital, and family therapy; ethnic identity and acculturation intervention; reminiscence therapy; language education; economic well-being, including job search and training/retraining assistance, coaching, and mentoring; interethnic relations; child care; and conflict resolution (Potocky & Naseh, 2019). Social workers may also work with individuals in foreign countries in such areas as relief and disaster interventions and working with immigrants and refugees (Healy, 2016).

Whether you work with clients in your country of origin/residence or abroad, you can build on your cultural competence and humility to individualize your approach for each client. When working with immigrants, a strengths-based approach is particularly appropriate. Because permanently leaving one's country of origin takes courage and coping skills, these clients can draw on considerable strengths.

Working cross-culturally in domestic and international areas can be a learning experience for you and your client. To begin your journey toward becoming a culturally responsive and humble practitioner, you can start the process by developing critical reflectivity about your own experiences, positions, and perceptions about others through a lens of power, inequality, and oppression (Nadan, 2017). Quick Guide 5 offers suggestions for beginning your cultural heritage journey, values, and beliefs. After exploring your own cultural identities, you can begin to gain knowledge and develop skills to work with an international client. Learn as much as possible about your client's heritage and avoid making assumptions about the client's culture, particularly in terms of beliefs, knowledge of you and your professional value system, language proficiency, or openness to working with a helping professional.

Not presuming to understand the client's life experience or goals is important in work with any client, and it is critical with a client who has relocated to a new country. Some clients may have fled their country of origin to escape trauma or torture, and some may have experienced trauma during relocation or challenges adjusting to the new culture and environment. Some clients may have concerns regarding their legal status in their new country. A client who is unfamiliar with the customs, language, legal issues, or the role of helping professionals in the United States may have difficulty building the rapport

> ### QUICK GUIDE 5 My Cultural Heritage Journey
>
> The cultural heritage journeys of both clients and social workers impact their perspectives on life and work. Consider the following:
>
> - Where do my family's roots begin?
> - If my family immigrated to the United States, did they migrate voluntarily and how long has each of my parents been living here?
> - If I am in an adoptive family, what do I know about my biological family's cultural heritage?
> - What traditions has my family passed down through the generations? Have there been obstacles to passing along those traditions? Have those traditions been celebrated or denigrated in media, political discourse, or my community?
> - Do my family's traditions relate to religion or spirituality, holidays, rituals, and/or significant events for the family?
> - What values surrounding ethics, wealth, religion and spirituality, race, ethnicity, health, education, sexual orientation, and body image have I learned from my family?
> - Have I challenged any of my family traditions or values?
> - Has my family had experiences that challenge their traditions and values? If so, how have I responded?
> - What significant life experiences have shaped my view of the world and specifically of people who are different from me?
> - How will my cultural heritage impact my social work practice?
> - Would I like to change or add to my traditions? How might I start?

and trust crucial to a successful social work relationship. In these situations, strategies for developing a trusting working relationship may include:

1) outlining your role, boundaries, and limitations as a social worker.
2) asking questions about the client's culture, country of origin, traditions, and beliefs being mindful not to be overly intrusive. Ask only those questions that are relevant for the service being provided.
3) sharing information about the culture of the agency and community, particularly as it relates to the provision of social and or health services.
4) creating an environment in which the client feels comfortable asking for clarifications on any issue. You may communicate with this client through an interpreter, which places a third person into the relationship. Working with an interpreter requires you to clarify your respective roles, the style of interpretation, and how confidentiality will be maintained.

SKILLS FOR ASSESSMENT AND PLANNING

During the assessment and planning phases of the social work intervention, the social work skills used help the social worker and the client work together to form a shared vision for what the client hopes to achieve and how they will work together to reach that goal. In developing this vision, social workers help clients articulate the kinds of changes they want to make. Social workers ask questions that affirm the client's ability to make changes to improve their life. Building on the foundations of strengths, narrative, and solution-focused perspectives, skills for assessing and planning with individual clients emphasize a collaborative, client-focused approach. While each of the approaches is unique, there are common elements. For example, engagement and rapport-building skills figure prominently in each approach.

An essential skill to use as a first step in the assessment and planning process is to create an environment in which the client feels comfortable and can develop a sense of trust that will enable the relationship to move forward with openness and honesty. Building trust varies depending on the setting and format of the service being provided. For example, if you staff a crisis hotline, the entire intervention may occur in less than one hour without benefit of a face-to-face encounter, so you must establish trust with the client in the first few minutes. In this instance, you can state at the beginning how you can be helpful, that you are there to listen and offer options and resources, then allow the client to share their story without interruptions. Social work practice during the COVID-19 pandemic often required social workers to work with clients in new ways (e.g., telehealth) so establishing trust was key to being able to support clients in crisis. Setting the parameters of the service and following through are helpful in building trust. In face-to-face and virtual encounters with multiple opportunities to meet, the same guidelines can be followed, but you have the benefit of seeing nonverbal communications and having more time.

Strengths-Based Perspective

During the engagement, assessment, and planning phases, a social worker committed to the strengths-based approach fosters a climate in which both the social worker and the client recognize the strengths the client brings to the intervention and identify those resources that can be mobilized and those that can evolve. When completing collaborative assessment and planning (i.e., goal-setting) within a strengths-based framework, it is important to invite the client to identify goals as this practice will promote information gathering and enable the client to let the social worker know how they might support the client through the intervention (Simmons et al., 2022). While all the goals may not be achieved, it is possible that small achievements can help to reduce barriers and can be generalized across other goal areas (Simmons et al., 2022). During this phase, the social worker can support the client by using the client's language to establish rapport, help them define problems, goals, ways of being helped, and prioritize the client's perspectives on the problem and potential solutions (Jordan & Franklin, 2021). In the beginning with your help, the client can prioritize the goals that are of most immediate or greatest importance. As those goals are achieved or reframed, other goals on the list can be addressed.

Saleebey (2013) provides a group of questions designed to elicit information that focuses on identifying client strengths that may be factored into planning. Quick Guide 6 contains eight such types of questions.

QUICK GUIDE 6	Assessment Questions for Discovering Strengths

SURVIVAL QUESTIONS

How have you managed to survive thus far, given all the challenges you have faced? What have you learned about yourself and your world during your struggles?

SUPPORT QUESTIONS

Who are the special people on whom you can depend? What do they respond to in you that helps you to feel supported?

EXCEPTION QUESTIONS

When things were going well in your life, what was different?
What parts of your world and your being would you like to recapture?

POSSIBILITY QUESTIONS

What are your hopes, visions, and aspirations? How can I help you achieve those goals?

ESTEEM QUESTIONS

When people say good things about you, what are they likely to say? When was it that you began to believe that you might achieve some of the things you want in life?

PERSPECTIVE QUESTIONS

What is your perspective on your current situation? How would you describe your current situation to others?

CHANGE QUESTIONS

What thoughts do you have about ways your situation could change? What strategies have worked well for you in the past? How can I help?

MEANING QUESTIONS

What beliefs do you hold above all others? What gives you a sense of purpose? What are the origins of your beliefs?

Source: Adapted from Saleebey, 2013, pp. 107–108

Narrative Theory

The skills used when social workers elicit and interpret client perceptions differentiate narrative approaches from other empowerment approaches, although the building of new "stories" can be like the strengths-based emphasis on envisioning possibilities. Narrative practitioners first help clients "deconstruct" their stories. In other words, the social worker helps the client examine the way in which they have organized their life stories, which is then reviewed with the purpose of looking for new "truths" (i.e., new stories) (Smith, 2022). The practitioner and client work together to expand upon and externalize perceptions and meanings of the client's words by re-envisioning the way the client's life is organized and lived. This expansion can help the client to "reconstruct" those stories to develop a broader, more effective approach to functioning (Smith, 2022).

Narrative social work practice may be viewed as a four-stage approach encompassing: (1) exploring with the client problems, meanings, and interactions related to their experiences; (2) raising questions that enable examination of the meaning of the presenting problem/issue; (3) constructing a new story by identifying exceptions to the previously created story; and (4) sharing the new and empowering stories with others (Hall, 2016).

After listening to the client's perceptions of their current realities, the social worker helps the client through the following process:

1. "Externalize" the problem by refocusing on the outcome rather than on the root cause and by de-emphasizing *problem-saturated stories* (self-perceptions in which problems dominate the client's life).
2. Discover "exceptions" (i.e., those instances in which the problem or concern did not exist for the client), which is also one type of strengths-based inquiry.
3. "Re-author" or reconstruct a new reality through mapping of the domain of the issue or problem (i.e., reviewing an issue or problem from a past, present, and possible future perspective to enable the client to prepare for a desired change).
4. "Reinforce" the change by involving others who have been or are currently in the client's life who have an understanding or insights about the change situation and/or by sharing/complementing the client's planned or actual change experience to identify unique outcomes and encourage a continuation of the same behaviors.

(Smith, 2022)

Throughout the assessment and planning process, the social worker poses questions that aid the client in reaching their desired new reality. For example, consider the case of a client, Charlie, a 35-year-old man who is struggling in his relationship with his husband, Alex, to whom he has been married for one year. The couple had been together for two years prior to marrying and felt they knew each other well before making the commitment to marry. In the past year, Charlie has begun to realize that he and Alex did not discuss in depth their individual life goals as he now feels that they have different life goals, particularly in terms of having children, pursuing their careers, purchasing a home, and saving money. While these are his goals, he is coming to realize that his spouse does not share them at least at this point in their lives. Here are some questions a narrative-focused social worker may pose to Charlie:

- *Deconstruction questions* refocus on an outcome.
  Social Worker: *Charlie, you have shared your concerns about you and your husband, Alex, having different priorities for your lives. What goals and priorities did you have in common when you got married? Which of those do you continue to share?*

- *Opening space questions* create the possibility for unique outcomes the client may not have considered.
  Social Worker: *Charlie, is there a possibility that you and your husband do want the same things in life but are not on the same schedule for achieving those goals? Is there a possibility that he appears to be resistive to your goals for other reasons? If that were the case, what could those reasons be?*

- *Preference questions* translate unique outcomes into preferred experiences.
  Social Worker: *If you learned that Alex did share some or all your life goals but does not feel capable of making plans now, how would your perspective change?*

- *Story development questions* create a new reality (or story) based on a client's preferred experiences.
  Social Worker: *Charlie, if you and Alex could create a new life plan/set of goals, what could that new reality look like? What are the strengths of your relationship that you can build on? Where are the possibilities for negotiation and compromise?*

- *Meaning questions* provide an opportunity for the client to replace negative perceptions with positive interpretations based on the strengths identified in story development.
  Social Worker: *In thinking about a new reality with Alex, how could the negative perceptions that you had at the beginning of our discussion be replaced with more positive perceptions of your life together?*

- *Extending the story into the future* empowers client to see themselves in future situations. This phase may involve bringing others into the process to support the client as they embark on a new reality.
  Social Worker: *You have envisioned a new reality for your life with Alex—what does that life look like in one year? Five years? Who else needs to be a part of this conversation?*

With an emphasis on deconstructing and re-envisioning one's life, a narrative approach can be an empowering experience for the client as the approach promotes building on their strengths and supports by reframing negative perceptions as their preferred outcomes.

Solution-Focused Approach

Using strategies like those in a narrative-focused assessment and planning process, solution-focused assessment focuses on possible *solutions* as opposed to *problems* (De Jong & Berg, 2013). A solution-focused approach is compatible with social work values with its emphasis on a systemic and strengths-based perspective, client's right to self-determination, and uses across settings and problem issues (Corcoran, 2022a). Corcoran (2022a) provides this overview of the approach:

- Clients' right to self-determination enables the social worker and client to identify strengths which can be "amplified" so that the client can determine their own solutions.
- The future orientation (i.e., "when the problem is no longer a problem") de-emphasizes the significance of the past and the origins of the problem.
- Using "exceptions" to create solutions can lead to greater success than changing existing problem behaviors (i.e., placing emphasis on a time when the situation has improved instead of focusing on the client changing a specific behavior).
- Identifying exceptions can lead to exploring existing strengths and resources and enlarging resources through the use of questions focused on positive change (i.e., "when things are better, what will be happening?").
- When clients perceive themselves as capable, they can feel more empowered to work toward future positive behaviors.

(p. 349)

Like other empowerment approaches, a solution-focused approach incorporates a series of questions to elicit client perception, strengths, resources, and, ultimately, a solution. To initiate the engagement and assessment process, the social worker can first develop a collaborative relationship with the client by ensuring the client feels heard and validated and asking, for instance, "how are you hoping I can help you?" (Nichols & Davis, 2020, p. 178). This question invites clients to share their story and provide insight into their reasons for seeking help. Utilizing the social work skill of starting where the client is at, the social worker continues the assessment process, asking the client to share their concerns, and then works with the client to set goals.

Let us return to the case of Charlie and Alex, the married couple struggling with their respective life goals, from the discussion on narrative approaches in the context of a solution-focused approach. As you can see in the following examples, assessment can be considered a part of the intervention process itself (Jordan & Franklin, 2021). Providing an opportunity for the client to share their story and verbalize concerns can enable the client to gain perspective on the situation, including seeing potential solutions. Solution-focused question types include the following (de Shazer et al., 2021; Lee et al., 2022, p. 595; Nichols & Davis, 2020):

- *Problem description questions* engage the client in an evaluation of the "doing, thinking, and feeling" as these areas relate to the issue that brought them to you. Such questions enable the client to assess the situation, associated feelings and actions, and potential solutions.
  Social Worker: *Charlie, you have shared your concerns about you and your husband, Alex, having different priorities for your lives. What have you done about your feelings? What are your thoughts about your situation? What emotions do you experience when you think about your marriage?*

- *Miracle questions* ask the client to "describe a vision of the future in which the problem or concern no longer exists." Miracle questions promote creativity and hopefulness as well as client self-determination and participation in planning for concrete and achievable change.
  Social Worker: *Imagine your future if your concerns about shared life goals are no longer a problem. What does that future life look like?*

- *Exception questions* allow the client and social worker to identify existing assets and resources that may point to strategies the client and social worker can use in the situation.
  Social Worker: *In describing your relationship history with Alex, you indicated that you once shared the goals of marriage, children, buying a house, and saving for your future. What convinced you at that time that you could build a life together based on these shared goals? What was happening at that time in your life? Their life?*

- *Scaling questions* ask the client to "consider your situation on a continuum from worst (1) to best (10). How would you scale it?" Quantifying issues enables the client and social worker to frame goals, provide feedback, monitor progress, change course, and evaluate outcomes.
  Social Worker: *Using a scale where 1 is your relationship with Alex at its worst and 10 is your relationship with Alex at its best, what numeric score would you assign right now? For your relationship to be where you would like it to be, what number would it need to be at? Based on the value that you have given your current relationship, what change do you believe must take place for you to be happy with your marriage?*

As described in this section, solution-focused approaches can help clients evaluate their current situations and envision a time from the past and in the future in which the present concerns would not exist. Being able to quantify their evaluations of the situation can serve as a springboard for creating an action plan for change. Using resource-oriented questions that emphasize resources and strengths (e.g., relational, coping, and exception-finding questions) and are linked to the client's desired outcomes can serve to bolster the client's sense of hope and **subjective well-being** (i.e., individual's self-perception of their current overall satisfaction with their life) (Joubert & Guse, 2021).

Developing a Shared Vision of Assessment and Planning

Preferred reality refers to the client's goal for a changed, improved circumstance. It reflects a postmodern assumption (i.e., clients are the experts about their lives and situations) and narrative assumption that different realities can exist for the client (i.e., they are not limited to only one perception about their lives).

Our discussion of the assessment and planning process has emphasized the way in which the social worker engages in a dialogue with the client about the client's history (including cultural experiences and intersectionality), goals, and dreams. In that process, the social worker collaborates with the client to develop a picture of what could be. It is sometimes difficult for clients to see beyond the obstacles they face. Clients living at society's margins where they have experienced discrimination and oppression may be accustomed to seeing their dreams defeated. It is the social worker's job to help clients see that their lives can be different, that other realities exist, and that clients can work toward the reality that they desire.

For a social worker, maintaining and expressing a hopeful perspective can be a challenge. When you hear painful stories, it can be natural to feel disheartened. For example, hearing about generations of violence or oppression can be discouraging and can result in the social worker experiencing compassion fatigue (will be discussed later in this chapter). The concept of preferred realities benefits both the social worker and the client because the idea that the client's reality can be different helps both develop a hopeful view of the client's situation.

Working toward a preferred reality does not necessarily require replacing poverty with wealth or vicious violence with complete harmony. These are meaningful, long-range dreams, but they will appear elusive and unrealistic in many contexts. The strengths perspective does not require denying the existence of real—even devastating—problems and pain, but just a refusal to let that be the whole "story." If the client seeks a goal that may initially seem unrealistic, it is not for the social worker to dissuade the client, but to encourage them to identify small, achievable steps that will move the client toward the goal. The starting point in any work should be the client's vision for change—not the social worker's vision. Both clients and social workers can have visions that may involve only small changes in the situation or may be drawn to more ambitious transformations. The social worker's role is to ensure that neither they nor the client are overwhelmed by the goals.

Support for the Client's Goals and Dreams

Consider once again the case of Jasmine Johnson, the single mother you met in Chapter 3. Recall that Jasmine is concerned because she sometimes hits her son when he speaks disrespectfully to her. Jasmine may ask you to help her find another way to respond to him. This request might seem like a relatively concrete goal for behavior change, but it also represents a vision of a preferred reality. Realizing this goal would result in a different mother–son relationship, which could have many positive consequences. Right now, Jasmine is asking for help modifying her behavioral response. Her goal might be simply to avoid child protection charges or to reduce the likelihood that her son will respond violently. Therefore, you might work with her to explore her long-term goals. For example, Jasmine might want to establish a more satisfying emotional connection with her son. She may not have allowed herself to emphasize feelings in her interpersonal experiences, she may never have had the time to think that way, or she may be stressed by other difficult relationships, financial pressures, health concerns, and/or being isolated during the pandemic. Any of these factors may alter her ability to respond to her son in the way she would ideally like. Perhaps she has never known anyone who articulated such a goal. It is important to explore Jasmine's view of the situation without imposing your own meanings.

Based on the goals Jasmine articulates, and because you both agree that it is appropriate that you contribute to her work toward those goals, you develop a shared vision of a future in which Jasmine has learned other ways to respond to her son. As you work together toward achieving this vision, other, more encompassing dreams about her relationship with her son might evolve. Your role in this strengths-based assessment and planning strategy is to support Jasmine's dreams, always affirming her potential to achieve them. To help

Jasmine turn her dreams into reality, you both need to specify her goals and articulate a plan for your collaboration.

Planning and Setting Goals A thorough assessment is key to effective and, ultimately, successful goal-setting and planning processes. Planning for the intervention includes using information gathered during the assessment to make decisions with the client, specify the client's concerns, plan for the intervention, and to continue to monitor those concerns as the intervention is implemented (Jordan & Franklin, 2021).

Setting goals gives the work a clear purpose and helps clients recognize the difference between current concerns and the long view of the vision. One straightforward approach to setting goals when working with clients is to apply the SMART format, an acronym that encompasses goals that are *Specific, Measurable, Achievable, Relevant, and Time-bound* (Substance Abuse and Mental Health Services Administration [SAMSHA], 2017). First developed by Doran (1981) for use in management, this approach guides goals that are: **S**pecific in terms of the work to be done; **M**easurable to enable monitoring of progress; **A**chievable within client's realities; **R**elevant for the culture and desired outcomes; and **T**ime-bound to clearly articulate the completion (SAMHSA, 2017).

Using the SMART format to assess the goals with the client once they are established and depending on the client's wishes and needs, goals may take on multiple forms. Consider the following varieties of goals in the context of your work with Jasmine (Garvin, 2015):

1 Goals can be *discrete* (a single outcome) as well as *continuous* (part of an ongoing plan).
   In Jasmine's case, a discrete goal might be for her to respond differently when her son speaks to her in a disrespectful way, while a continuous goal might be to improve her relationship with her son.
2 Goals that are *framed within different aspects of the client system* (individual, family, group, or community).
   In Jasmine's case, earning greater respect from her son and others (e.g., family and co-workers) would be this sort of goal.
3 Goals that are related to *various behaviors and behavior changes*.
   In Jasmine's case, a desire to get a new job or change her interactions with her son in hopes of eliciting more respect would be her behavioral goals.
4 Goals that are *dependent on the individual client or that require the involvement of others* (e.g., couple or family).
   In Jasmine's case, as an incremental goal, she could invite her son to participate in family meetings with the social worker.

(pp. 561–562)

There are a variety of ways to measure Jasmine's progress toward her goal of responding differently when her son is disrespectful to her. For example, does Jasmine want to "feel better" about their conversations? Initially, does she want to halve the number of times she responds to him physically? Long term, does she want to eliminate those episodes altogether? Does she want him to report that their relationship has improved as evidenced by fewer conflicts? An appropriate measure reflects Jasmine's priorities. By setting priorities, Jasmine and the social worker determine the outcomes that are most critical within a particular time frame. For instance, what if Jasmine's son is well behaved two times and then rude once, which provokes Jasmine to hit him? Do his two instances of positive behavior matter in terms of the goal? Is the goal to change Jasmine's behavior or to change her son's behavior?

Establishing goals and measuring progress toward achieving them can be complicated. Nevertheless, it is worth the effort to clarify how each party defines the goal of the work and how each one will know when the goal is achieved. Unless you agree on an end, Jasmine may believe you will work with her on her situation until some undefined time when she feels it is "fixed." To avoid misunderstandings, make sure you have an agreement regarding this issue and have considered the agency parameters that may influence the timelines. Setting goals helps both client and social worker evaluate the degree to which their communication is clear, their expectations match, and they are making progress. Agencies and organizations also need to understand the purpose and goals of the work, often in concrete, measurable terms. Chapter 5 will discuss this topic as a function of formal evaluation.

Contracting In contracting, the client and social worker reach an agreement about priorities and determine who will do what and when. Developing a clear, measurable, and achievable contract with the client emphasizes the client's role in the planning and intervention and recognizes their right to self-determination (Rothman, 2015). Contracts vary greatly depending on practice setting, and they can be formal or informal. The planning document can serve as a formal contract, which is generally a written document signed by both parties. In contrast, an informal contract may be simply a verbal agreement.

In crafting a contract, the social worker and client should agree on details, including goals, individual roles, ways to change the plan, how progress will be monitored, frequency of interaction, and the degree to which each goal needs to be met. Whatever the nature of the contract, it is important that both social worker and client understand the desired outcomes for the intervention. While the assessment and planning components of the intervention can change, the social worker and client need clearly stated goals and a clear path to achieving those goals to avoid frustration or even putting the success of the intervention at risk. Quick Guide 7 provides an example of a contract you might find helpful in your work with Jasmine Johnson.

Even the most careful approaches cannot account for every obstacle that might arise. Many clients face limitations, which may include emotional, cognitive, or physical challenges that make it almost impossible for them to participate fully in assessment, planning, goal-setting, and contracting. Although social workers should never minimize these obstacles, they need to work directly with the client to the greatest extent possible, bearing in mind that many clients who have experienced lifelong challenges have never been

QUICK GUIDE 7   Sample Contract With Jasmine Johnson

Client Name: _Jasmine Johnson_

Client Description of Issues to be Addressed:

Relationship with my son

Deal with my anger toward my son when he is disrespectful to me

Goals and Tasks:

Goal	Client Tasks/ Timeline	Social Worker Tasks/ Timeline	Three-Month Follow-Up
1. Improve my relationship with my son	Begin attending weekly family therapy with my son as soon as an appointment can be made.	Within one week, refer Jasmine and her son to a family therapist and communicate regularly with the therapist regarding progress (with Jasmine's informed consent).	Social worker made referral and has had three contacts with the therapist. Jasmine and her son are attending therapy regularly.
2. Learn better strategies for disciplining my son, particularly when I am angry	Participate in weekly parents of teens class and support group (next group begins the first of next month).	Within one week, refer Jasmine to parenting class and support group and communicate regularly with the group facilitator regarding progress (with Jasmine's informed consent).	Social worker made referral and has had one contact with the therapist. Jasmine is attending class/support group regularly and finding it very helpful.
3. Get Devon's father to pay child support more consistently (an additional goal identified as the assessment process evolved)	As soon as possible, contact Legal Services Child Support Enforcement office to inquire if they can help.	Within one week, provide Jasmine with Legal Services contact information and eligibility requirements.	With information provided by social worker, Jasmine has made an appointment at Legal Services.

Date Contract will be reviewed: _We will review the contract monthly for the next 3 months_

I agree with the above stated goals, to complete the contracted tasks, and to participate in a review and evaluation of the contract on the specified date.

Jasmine   _Julie_
Client   Social Worker

_____   _____
Date   Date

Source: Adapted from Berg-Weger & Murugan, 2022

considered full participants in service provision planning. Although these clients can make substantial contributions, they may be hesitant or even afraid to participate. Those who have experienced racial, ethnic, and/or gender identity oppression may have difficulty trusting the mutual assessment and planning process.

In their zeal to develop a plan, address issues, mobilize resources, and establish a contract, social workers may sometimes forget that certain elements of the work are not as visible or as easy to categorize as others. For example, clients' emotional responses to a recent loss may have significant influence on their ability to develop and plan for change. Social workers must be attuned to and consider the impact of issues that may be "unseen." By the time social workers have listened to clients' stories and collaborated to identify clients' preferred realities, they will probably have heard and felt a lot of emotional content related to clients' experiences. However, they may not recognize the power a client's complicated feelings about change can generate. In recalling Briana's stated goal of regaining custody of her son, it would be important to recognize that she may feel both motivated and frightened and be uncertain if she can make the changes necessary for a reunification plan to be successful.

Whole family systems can be organized around one member's situation or needs. Consider the family in which one member is addicted to alcohol. In some families, everyone knows how to respond if Dad is drunk and has passed out on the couch. John, the eldest son, may be the one to carry him to bed; everyone else might ignore Dad, step around him, and pretend his drinking does not happen. Mom takes this opportunity to make decisions about the family finances that Dad once made. The social worker must be aware that, although Mom has come to an agency to get help with Dad's addiction because it is destroying his health, their marriage, and their family life, there is a cost to change. Mom may feel uniquely competent to make major decisions she never made before, or John may take pride in being able to endure the chaos and even feeling, at times, like the "man of the house." If Dad successfully changes his relationship with alcohol, Mom may have regrets because she may feel she will be forced to give up the larger role that she felt obligated to assume (and in which she began to thrive) when Dad was drinking. Similarly, John may lose his place as competent caretaker, and all members of the family will need to learn to relate to Dad and to each other differently. Renegotiating family roles can have emotional consequences.

A change in one part of the client system has the potential to change the entire system. Any change a client seeks is embedded in a social context and therefore can generate a powerful emotional response. This response may take the form of reluctance to engage in ongoing collaboration or hesitation when making progress on specific goals. In such cases, consider engaging in a dialogue with the client that goes beyond the specifics of goal-setting and contracting to explore the meaning of the change itself in terms of emotional and logistical outcomes as well as the impact of the change on roles, functioning, and patterns.

Honest Responding

Up to this point, you have learned how social workers and clients can identify and work toward a preferred reality. This discussion has emphasized the importance of establishing a shared vision that reflects the client's goals and dreams. However, you might find yourself in a situation in which, after hearing a client's story, you are inclined to challenge their priorities. For example, if your client's overall goal is to continue selling drugs and avoid being arrested again for selling illegal drugs, you might want to contest that goal as a purpose for the social work intervention. You might instead encourage the client to abstain from selling drugs or to separate from a drug-using peer group. Conflicts over goals raise difficult questions for social workers. For example, do you have the right to disagree with a client's priorities? Are you inappropriately pushing your values? Does agency policy prohibit you from disagreeing with the client's goals? At the same time, how can you engage enthusiastically to achieve a goal you cannot support and one that violates social work professional values?

In these situations, the following questions may be helpful:

- Are you able to maintain objectivity about client goals?
- Do client goals align with your personal and professional priorities, values, or cultural practices?
- How might the client's culture and lived experiences that may include abuse, trauma, discrimination, and oppression, influence their goal-setting?
- What are your legal, ethical, and professional commitments in this situation?
- Does forcing a client to confront an issue they do not want to prioritize violate an ethical principle or, conversely, is guiding a client to grapple with issues they are avoiding at the heart of effective social work practice?
- Do you think the client's goals are unrealistic, not extensive enough, or may be one step on a journey to substantive change?
- What is the value of working toward a client's goal that you think may be ill-advised?

Although there are no easy solutions when client and social worker do not agree on appropriate goals, you can respond honestly if you "own" your own biases (e.g., you do not agree with the client's prioritization of their goals), one of which may be a greater belief in the client's potential than the client seems to possess.

When Confrontation Is Necessary In some situations of acute goal conflict, the social worker directly confronts the client. Consider again Jasmine Johnson. Jasmine has requested your help to change the way she responds when her son, Devon, talks to her. You learn from Jasmine's description of their interactions that she may be physically abusing him. How does this revelation ethically and/or legally affect the assessment and planning process? You may be convinced that you must call the child protection agency to investigate the allegations, and those authorities may in turn temporarily separate Jasmine from her son. If this occurs before you can begin to work with her on a different way of relating to him, you may decide that you must postpone that work until after you have established and achieved a new, short-term goal to carry out your professional and legal commitments. The assessment then moves to an intermediate plateau in which you address a dangerous, or potentially dangerous, situation that requires a more immediate (and ethical) response. At the outset of the relationship, you will need to be honest with Jasmine about your understanding of the situation and what you see as your ethical obligations (e.g., limits of confidentiality); that is, you will need to confront her with the immediacy of reaching your short-term goal and the necessity of temporarily delaying her long-range goals. Exhibit 4.2 provides examples of practice skills that may be helpful when you must face a similar dilemma.

In this scenario, any decision that might lead to a separation between Jasmine and her son does not necessarily disregard her preferred reality of getting along with him better. Ideally, this temporary separation will improve her chances of working on her original goal after the crisis is past. It will be critical in your work with Jasmine to show that you support her dream, even though you must initiate another intervention first. Your honest dialogue with her will reassure her that you share her vision, that you want to help her work toward it, and that you can be trusted to tell the truth.

EXHIBIT 4.2

Responding With Honesty

In an early meeting with Jasmine Johnson, the social worker learns that Jasmine routinely punishes her son physically when he treats her in a way that she considers disrespectful. The following is an example of the conversation the social worker is legally and ethically obligated to have with the client. In the conversation, the social worker balances honesty about her legal obligation with an expressed desire to keep working together:

Social Worker: *Jasmine, it is my understanding that when you feel Devon is being disrespectful to you, you hit him. If that is correct, I want to state that before we can talk about other ways to handle your situation, I would like to talk about the issue of using physical punishment. We must be certain that the form of punishment you are using does not constitute physical abuse as defined in the state's child maltreatment statute. I want to make sure that you know that if I have reason to believe that you are physically abusing him, state law and my social work ethical code require that I report that concern to Child Protection Services.*

EXHIBIT 4.2

Continued

> Once a report is made, the agency will send a social worker to investigate. If the report is substantiated or found to be true, the agency will decide whether they want to recommend that the court remove Devon from your care and place him in foster care. They could also decide, because you and I are already working together, not to pursue removal but to instead monitor the situation and get regular reports from me. If they find no support for the allegations, no case will be opened. I want to be very certain that you and I are both clear and comfortable with all this information and the possible outcomes. As we discussed before we began working together, while your confidentiality is important to me, confidentiality is not absolute. When I have information about the safety of you or someone else, I have an obligation to take necessary action to prevent harm. I will want to talk with Devon about those times when the two of you are having trouble. Using the information I have from the both of you, I will decide about making a report.
>
> I understand that you may be angry with me for even raising these issues and angrier still if I do feel I should make a report, but I want to remind you that I am legally and ethically obligated to ensure the safety of children. I hope that we can continue to work together, but I understand if you don't feel you will be able to continue working with me.
>
> Jasmine: Yes, I just get so mad and he won't listen to me when I tell him he can't talk to me like that. I would never hurt him, though. I just slap him, just to get him to stop mouthing off to me. I haven't left any bruises or anything.
>
> Social Worker: I want to thank you for your honesty. Having a complete picture of the relationship you have with him and the way in which you use discipline can help me to help you find alternative strategies for responding to his behaviors.
>
> Jasmine: I know you just got to do what you got to do. I don't think you will find that I have been abusing him, so go ahead and talk with him. If he says I have been, then we'll just deal with that.

Aligning Goals With Possibilities While clients may need assistance clarifying and articulating their goals, you are not in the position to determine whether the goals are realistic or to define the upper limits of the individual's capacity for growth and change. If social workers are to "hold high our expectations of clients and make allegiance with their hopes, vision, and values" (Saleebey, 2013, p. 19), you should not simply disregard a person's dream as unrealistic but focus on determining steps to achieve their goals.

For example, if you are a high school social worker and your client states they want to be a physician, together you can consider what level of education they will need, what it might cost, and how long it might take. You should not use this kind of step-by-step discussion to discourage them but rather to provide information. You may then help them consider smaller goals that could serve as stepping-stones to a larger aspiration. Breaking down goals into workable and achievable sub goals, or procedural goals, can help clients clarify the practical side of their dreams and how far they want to take them. In the high school example, you might consider telling your client the following:

> *Let's put together a plan for you to achieve your goal of becoming a physician. The plan might include gathering information on the educational requirements for medical school and the obligations for completing a residency. Once we know the requirements, we can create a plan that includes strategies for each step you will need to take to reach each phase of the goal—what you can do while you are still in high school, the major and experiences you may want to consider for college, and what you can do to make yourself a strong candidate for medical school. What do you think about this idea for a plan?*

Using Mapping Skills to Enhance the Dialogue

Your interpretation of the client's story influences the assessment and planning processes. Human stories often have many layers and can be difficult to grasp. Frequently, a visual can make the information more accessible and organized. In mapping, complex phenomena are represented visually so that they can be absorbed perceptually rather than linguistically. Let's examine three fundamental types of mapping: genograms and ecomaps.

Genograms Technically a family tree, the **genogram** usually represents at least three generations and indicates various aspects of the relationships of the individuals included. Exhibit 4.3 presents a sampling of the conventions for indicating these relationships and Exhibit 4.4 is a genogram for the Sanchez family interactive case (see www.routledgesw.com/cases). A genogram can portray a broad range of issues and family patterns, such as strained and stable relationships that can affect individual and family functioning.

Using a genogram to review an individual's family history can add important information to the individual assessment, which may inform your work with a client. Your client can label the genogram to indicate such elements as life accomplishments, substance use and addiction issues, financial situations, and health issues. For example, identifying an intergenerational pattern of addiction that exists within a family may provide insight to a client struggling with a gambling addiction. Exploring a family's past and present can serve to shed light on patterns but also trigger emotional responses to experiences with abuse, discrimination, and oppression. Should the exploration create distress, you can pause the exercise to discuss and possibly re-visit in the future.

EXHIBIT 4.3

Genogram Symbols

People in a genogram are represented by the following symbols:

- Biological sex:
  Males = ▫ (occasionally represented by the medical symbol ♂)
  Females = ○ (occasionally represented by the medical symbol ♀)
  *Non-binary = ◇ (Not included in the original genogram concept)
- Unborn children are triangles (Δ)
- ✗ through a person symbol indicates death (usually accompanied by age or year of death)

Relationships are represented by the following symbols:

- Jagged line = hostile relationship ~~~~
- Strong, solid black line = strong, positive relationship _____
- Slanting vertical lines = separation or divorce (on line that depicts marriage or partnership) //
- Circle enclosing people indicates household
- Perforated line indicates a conflicted relationship with possible estrangement _____

EXHIBIT 4.4

Sanchez Family Genogram

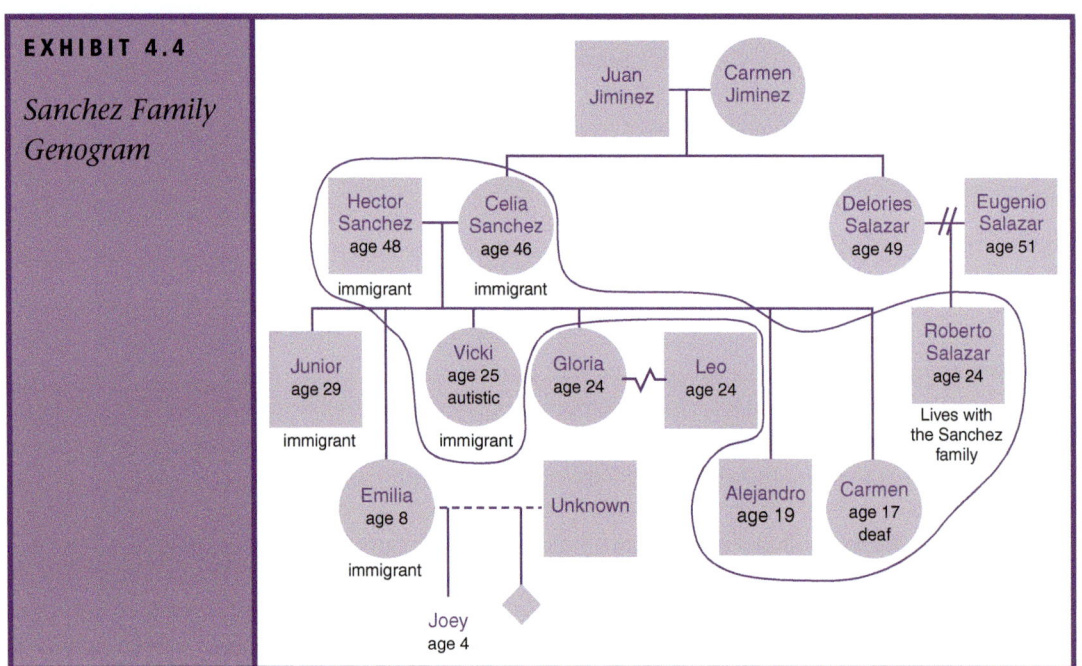

Importantly, patterns can indicate family strengths as well as struggles (e.g., educational achievements or career choices and longevity).

Genograms should be introduced carefully and with sensitivity. For some people, the visual nature of a genogram may trigger more intense emotions (e.g., a sense of loss or regret) than mere words would. For example, a client reviewing a genogram may become so distraught at the memory of a relative's suicide that they may abruptly leave a meeting with the social worker.

Like other assess care, genograms are frozen in time; that is, they represent relationships in the moment of the map's creation. They represent one person's perception, and they may seem deterministic, especially when they exhibit individual and family patterns. For example, if a multigenerational exploration reveals that all or nearly all young male members on one side of a family have had major substance use problems, a client may be tempted to see such a pattern as inevitable. When discussing the genogram, the social worker can provide assurance that a family pattern does not doom the client to repeat family members' past behaviors and decisions. Rather, a family history provides context and can help you and your client locate the most effective intervention points.

Ecomaps   An **ecomap** is a diagram of the client's world that illustrates the client's levels of connection to such institutions as schools, religious centers or spiritual practices, the workplace, extended family, friends, and recreation. An ecomap helps clients make sense of their experience by showing them how their day-to-day world looks and the resources and strengths that exist within that world. Ecomaps can also focus on a particular aspect of the client's life. For example, a social worker involved with children with special health needs can use an ecomap of medical and social supports to help shape the intervention. Some ecomaps include a miniature genogram. Specifically, to clearly depict the relationships of those who co-reside in the same household, an ecomap "insert" may be included in the center circle of the larger ecomap.

Like all mapping techniques, the ecomap may enable clients to explore patterns of everyday living not initially accessible to them in verbal form. For example, a client may complain about feeling lonely and estranged from the community. An ecomap could reveal that they have few supports in the community—no satisfying work life, only one friend, no spiritual connections, and no outlet for recreation. Such a diagram would suggest that you expand your dialogue with the client into these areas. Here, as always, it is important not to interpret and draw conclusions directly from the map without exploring the meaning of the indicators with the client.

Consider the Sanchez family ecomap depicted in Exhibit 4.5 (refer to the Sanchez family case at www.routledgesw.com/interactive-cases/ for more information). Can you identify strengths, resources, and areas for potential intervention? Note the stressful relationship described in the case between Celia and Emilia and that Celia perceives that the relationship is not a reciprocal one (i.e., Celia feels she devotes more energy to the relationship than she receives from it). You can invite Celia to share with you the reasons for her perception, her emotional response to the relationship, and the implications of her feelings for her relationships with Emilia and with others in the family.

Social workers occasionally use a sequence of ecomaps to evaluate the effectiveness and progress, or lack thereof, of the work. For example, if a client experiencing loneliness wants to expand their social world but fears that

EXHIBIT 4.5

Sanchez Family Ecomap

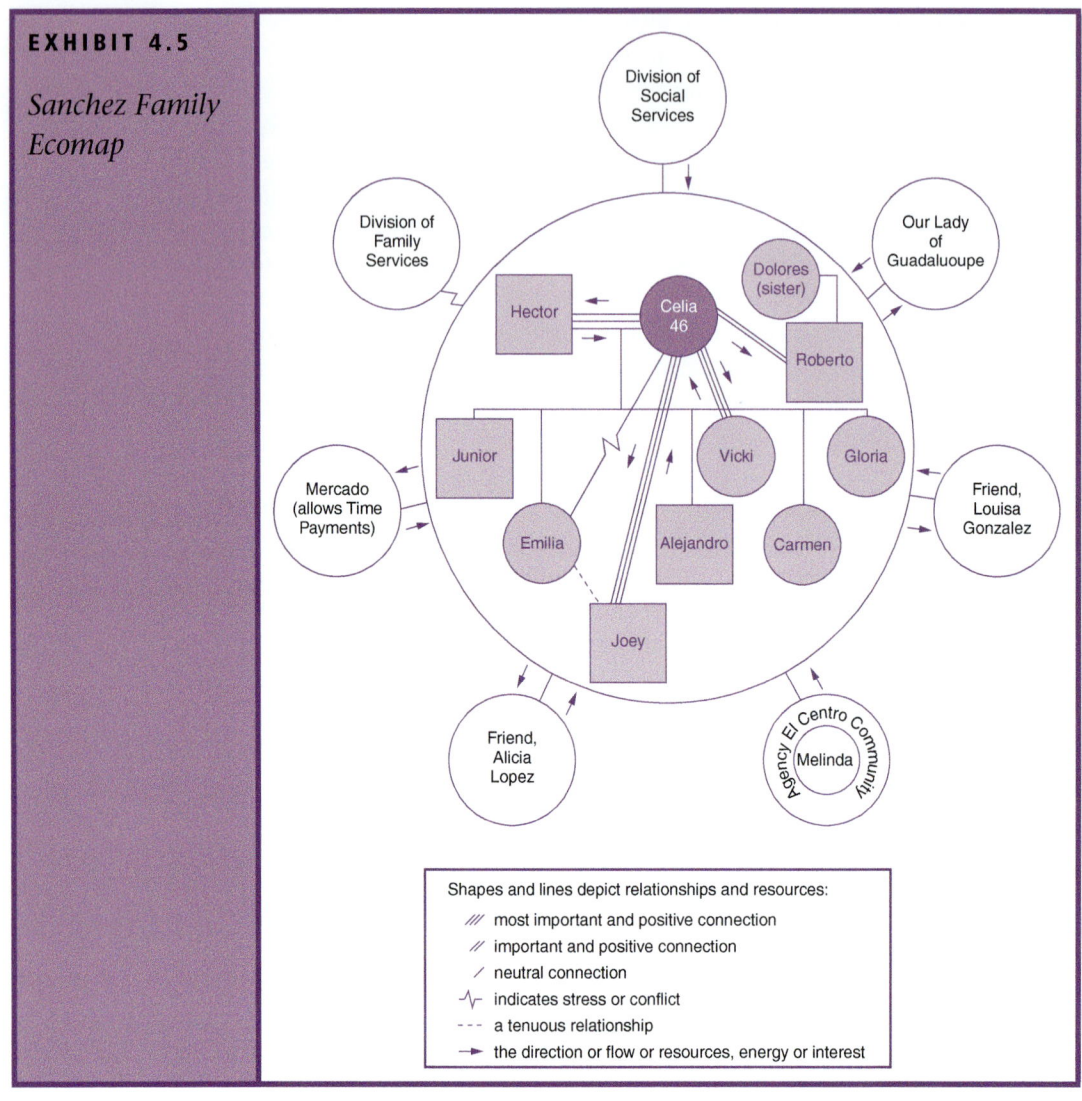

prospect, you might work with them to develop safe connections that you could indicate on subsequent ecomaps.

The importance of mapping as a part of the assessment and planning phases of work cannot be underestimated; therefore, developing skills for collecting and organizing client-related information through mapping is crucial for all social workers. Numerous strategies for mapping client information exist; selecting the format and strategy that is the best fit with your setting, client population, and services should be your guide.

SKILLS FOR ASSESSING RESOURCES

Even the most skilled workers can rarely provide all the assistance a client needs. Social workers should familiarize themselves with resources available in the larger environment. There are qualities to consider when assessing resources that may be useful in reaching client goals, from their type and source to their availability.

Formal and Informal Resources

Structured opportunities for assistance, which usually take the form of services, are **formal resources**. Training in parent education, financial assistance, caregiver respite, and support groups for children in schools are examples of services that are helpful to clients. These resources may be available within your organization (internal) or offered by another organization (external).

Not all resources are formal. **Informal resources** may be the worker or client's creativity, or naturally occurring social networks, like faith groups, neighbors, friends, or families. Informal, internal, or community-based assets can be mobilized to better serve clients. Within the practice context, natural helping networks, such as individuals, groups, families, and communities, can be the most important. These resources may endure long after formal resources cease to be involved with a client. For example, many children benefit from regular contact with an older child who befriends them, understands their concerns, or supports their abilities. An older adult may benefit from creating peer networks through volunteer work. It is not always necessary to hire someone, and the individual providing support need not be a professional. Some of the most meaningful relationships emerge from informal contexts of community life.

Assessment When Resources Are Available or Unavailable

Your familiarity with formal/informal and internal/external resources is an enormous benefit to your clients. Simply locating resources is not adequate. You also need to know enough about the client and the resources available to estimate the likelihood of a successful interaction between them.

> *Consider Briana's concern about fulfilling the expectations from child protective services to regain custody of her son. As the social worker, you agree that support would help your client become the effective parent she wants to be. You might explore the availability of formal and informal resources. For example, you could investigate informal parent support resources such as childcare cooperatives, family, and friends as well as formal parent support programs/support groups, parenting classes, or home visit programs such as Parents as Teachers. Gathering and sharing information with Briana about these resources, discussing the logistics of participating (locations, times, eligibility), and gaining insight into her comfort level are within the scope of the social worker's role.*

Unfortunately, social workers cannot always locate necessary resources. At some point in your social work career, you will probably seek help for a client and find that it does not exist. You have at least three options when adequate resources are not available: You can advocate for improved formal resources, policies, or programs (e.g., updated adult day centers), you can work with the client to leverage informal resources they may not have considered, or you can create resources where none exist. For example, you might assist single parents in a housing complex to organize a network of child care.

As you complete the assessment and planning process, unmet needs may be identified which you need not simply accept. For example, an uncooperative agency does not respond appropriately to clients or that a housing project has no child care facilities. Social workers can identify and develop resources but must also be realistic and careful not to promise more than they can deliver. With clients who may be accustomed to broken promises, social workers foster trust when they are honest about possibilities.

Few experiences are more positive or powerful than a successful social action based in client–social worker advocacy. Even if the results are somewhat less than hoped for, the process itself can be empowering for both social worker and client. Consider your work with a client living in an apartment building that is in dire need of maintenance and repairs. Through the assessment and planning process, you work with your client to organize a group of tenants to advocate with the landlord to address their concerns. While the social action occurs in the intervention phase, this points to the importance of assessment and planning throughout the client relationship. Assessment and planning drive the intervention stage of the work and, therefore, must also address the action inherent in it.

CRITICAL CONSIDERATIONS ABOUT ASSESSMENT AND PLANNING: THE AGENCY, THE CLIENT, AND THE SOCIAL WORKER

The following discussion addresses a range of issues you will likely encounter as a social worker from agency, client, and professional perspectives. These insights can equip you with the knowledge and skills to respond competently and ethically in your social work practice.

The Agency Perspective

From the agency perspective, during the assessment and planning phases, the social worker needs to openly discuss work methods, schedules, the length of the work, documentation, and agency resources with the client. For example, it is essential to provide the client with information regarding your schedule, appropriate ways to contact you, the information and format in which you will document your interactions and the client's access to those records, and agency resources available to them. Social workers should inform clients about their work processes from the beginning to avoid confusion or frustration as the relationship evolves, including ethical obligations to the employing agency and client and the potential for conflict that can develop between these two mandates.

Administrative Tasks   With the increasing emphasis on brief, effective, and accountable (i.e., measurable, evaluated, and documented) treatment for individuals, families, and groups, managed care organizations and the Affordable Care Act influence assessment and planning by placing time limits for completion and client access to information (NASW, 2021b).

Assessment tools can be used as a strategy for monitoring problems and progress toward the desired outcomes as needed (Jordan & Franklin, 2021). A note of caution regarding the use of standardized tools in the assessment process: although standardized measures provide helpful data on which to build a plan, they are not designed to "start where the client is," which is the cornerstone of the social work intervention. However, quantitative, standardized measures can complement narrative information provided by the client to create a fuller picture of the client situation (Jordan & Franklin, 2021). Assessment tools should be used in partnership with the client and both of you agree about the role that assessment results play in the overall process.

Quantitative assessment can be completed using a variety of tools and strategies, including (Jordan & Franklin, 2021):

1) Client self-report or self-monitoring of activities or behaviors
2) Self-anchored rating scales (e.g., "1" indicates low; "10" indicates high)
3) Questionnaires
4) Direct behavioral observation conducted by someone other than the client
5) Role-playing specific behaviors
6) Psychophysiological measures that use technology or medical devices to assess function or behaviors
7) Goal-attainment scaling to monitor ongoing progress toward goals
8) Standardized instruments
9) Projective measures that can have multiple responses (e.g., learning a new skill)

Using standardized, rapid assessment tools can help practitioners complete assessments quickly while maintaining optimal accuracy. In the current service delivery environment, your agency may opt to use a rapid assessment process. Fortunately, there are numerous, validated rapid assessment instruments to choose from. Of critical importance for the social worker is to confirm that the instruments address the language and cultural needs of the individual client and have been shown to be appropriate for that population (Killian & Springer, 2022).

Exhibit 4.6 provides an example of a psychometrically validated rapid assessment for memory and cognitive function, the Rapid Cognitive Screen (RCS) (Malmstrom & Morley, 2013). The RCS is a shortened version of the Saint Louis University Mental Status Exam (Tariq et al., 2006). Although not a diagnostic instrument, the RCS may be administered by a professional in less than 5 minutes and identifies potential impairment in memory and cognitive function that can then be further assessed.

EXHIBIT 4.6

Rapid Assessment Tool

Rapid Cognitive Screen (RCS)

Name _____ Age _____

Is the patient alert? _____ Level of education _____

1 **Please remember these five objects. I will ask you what they are later.** [Read each object to patient using approximately 1 second intervals.]

Apple Pen Tie House Car

Please repeat the objects for me. [If patient does not repeat all 5 objects correctly, repeat until all objects are recalled correctly or up to a maximum of 2 times.]

2 [Give patient pencil and the blank sheet with clock face.]
This is a clock face. Please put in the hour markers and the time at ten minutes to eleven o'clock.

/2 (points) Hour markers correct

/2 (points) Time correct [When scoring, give full credit for all 12 numbers. If the patient puts only ticks on the circle, prompt them once to put numbers next to those ticks for full credit. Do not repeat the time. When scoring the correct time, make sure that the minute hand points at the 10 and the hour hand points at the 11.]

3 **What were the five objects I asked you to remember?**

/1 (point) Apple

/1 (point) Pen

/1 (point) Tie

/1 (point) House

/1 (point) Car

4 I'm **going to tell you a story. Please listen carefully because afterwards, I'm going to ask you about it.**

Jill was a very successful stockbroker. She made a lot of money on the stock market. She then met Jack, a devastatingly handsome man. She married him and had three children. They lived in Chicago. She then stopped work and stayed at home to bring up her children. When they were teenagers, she went back to work. She and Jack lived happily ever after.

What state did she live in?

/1 (point) Illinois

[Do not repeat the story but do make sure the patient is paying attention the first time you read it to them. Do not prompt or give hints. The answer of "Chicago" as the state she lives in gets no credit, but you may prompt them once by repeating the question when "Chicago" is given as the answer.]

	EXHIBIT 4.6
SCORING 8–10 .... Normal 6–7 .... Mild Cognitive Impairment 0–5 .... Dementia _____Total Score [0–10 points] _____ _____ _____ CLINICIAN'S SIGNATURE DATE TIME *Source:* Malmstrom & Morley, 2013	*Continued*

To have confidence in the efficacy of a standardized assessment tool, social workers need to see psychometric and clinical evidence that it is valid for use with the target population. Utilizing any assessment tool on a population for which it has not been shown to be effective can produce misleading outcomes. Evidence-based practice enhances the potential effectiveness of the intervention.

It is also important to inform the client about other formalities related to administrative tasks and financial coverage, duration, type, and nature of intervention. For example, if you are required to submit monthly reports to a judicial court, you should discuss this with your client. Even when clients are not happy about the requirement, they are likely to respect you for discussing it from the outset of the relationship.

Increasingly, community agencies mandate diagnosis as part of the assessment and planning process. Many institutions now demand a *DSM* diagnosis (from the American Psychological Association's *Diagnostic and Statistical Manual of Mental Disorders*) to bill for third-party payment (payment from an insurer). Complying with this mandate can be uncomfortable for social workers who believe strongly in helping clients identify and use their own strengths. Formulating a psychiatric diagnosis requires a focus on deficiencies and can create a stigma. For example, a school social worker providing support to a teenager struggling with loneliness who is being diagnosed with "depression" so that services can be reimbursed.

Only professionals with appropriate training are qualified to make or use diagnoses as they inevitably categorize clients. Some may find the process tolerable if it facilitates service provision. Still others may find the use of diagnoses helpful because they enable social workers to use evidence-based practice to provide the best service to clients and to collaborate with non-social work colleagues who also use the *DSM*. Clients may find having a diagnosis as helpful—your role is to collaborate with the clients in this process.

All social workers are ethically obliged to inform their clients when a diagnosis is required to access services. Clients can then decide whether they want to participate in that exchange. For some clients and social workers, the diagnostic process may be worthwhile if it enables the client to receive services and possibly medication, whereas for others, the benefits do not outweigh the costs. If Briana were to describe symptoms of depression to you, consider questions you can ask to determine if she is experiencing depression and actions that you can take to facilitate treatment provided by other professionals or you.

Documentation Social workers record encounters in virtually every setting, but the requirements and formats for each encounter are typically setting-specific. Social workers need to be able to create a variety of documents aimed at diverse audiences to serve a range of purposes. In work with individuals, social workers complete intake/psychosocial assessments, treatment plans, case notes, case studies, and reports to external organizations (e.g., schools and court systems). Communication to these audiences occurs in a variety of formats (e.g., memos, letters, and reports). Social work documentation begins with the first encounter and continues through each phase of the planned change experience.

Although documentation processes differ based on the setting and services provided, the purposes for record-keeping can generally be placed into four categories: (1) opening a case, (2) monitoring progress toward goals, (3) reporting significant events, and (4) closing the case (Weisman & Zornado, 2013, p. 11). Regardless of the documentation format, recording information in each phase of the intervention is critical for accountability (need for services, decision-making, evaluation, outcomes, and compliance), supervision, and administrative purposes; practice enhancements; reimbursement; and planning (Kagle, 2013) as well as legal liability, continuity of care (specifically for case transfer), and coordination of interprofessional teams (Weisman & Zornado, 2018). NASW has called on the profession to ensure that social workers comply with legal, ethical, and technology-related requirements to protect client information, while also promoting transparency and access for clients (NASW, 2021–2023a). The *Code of Ethics* (NASW, 2021a) addresses documentation standards in Social Workers' Ethical Responsibilities in Practice Settings Section 3.04—Client Records:

1 Social workers should take reasonable steps to ensure that documentation in records is accurate and reflects the services provided.
2 Social workers should include sufficient and timely documentation in records to facilitate the delivery of services and to ensure continuity of services in the future.
3 Social workers' documentation should protect clients' privacy to the extent that is possible and appropriate and should include only information that is directly relevant to the delivery of services.
4 Social workers should store records following the termination of services to ensure reasonable future access. Records should be maintained for the number of years required by relevant laws, agency policies, and contracts.

While agencies' preferred documentation methods vary, some basic components are common. Case-related writing is primarily descriptive, brief but comprehensive, organized, objective, and readable (Weisman & Zornado, 2018, p. 70). Reamer (2020b) offers suggestions for content to be included in the social work record (see Quick Guide 8).

An opening summary portion of the documentation covers the engagement phase of your intervention, including the client's eligibility to receive services. As all agencies have criteria for determining client eligibility, social workers must be familiar with the criteria and communicate requirements to potential clients. Even within one agency, individual programs can have different eligibility criteria, eligibility standards can change, and not all members of a family may meet criteria; therefore, maintaining knowledge and open communication with clients is essential.

The assessment and planning portions of the client record typically include information related to the client's demographic characteristics and social worker observations. This may be an appropriate place to record perceptions of strengths, resources, needs, cultural factors, and risks related to services that may be delivered. While formats are agency- or program-dependent, certain elements of social work recording are common across the profession. Most agencies have structured formats for documenting the assessment and planning process to include client encounters or meetings, the intake or eligibility interview, the social history, and the treatment/intervention plan. Exhibit 4.7 lists the types of information to include in a client assessment; Exhibit 4.8 provides an example of information associated with the planning phase to include in an intervention plan (Jordan & Franklin, 2021).

QUICK GUIDE 8 Recommendations for Social Work Documentation

- Social history; reason(s) for requesting services, assessment, goals, intervention plan and progress, termination (with reason), and evaluation summary, and timeframe (number and duration).
- Informed consent procedures and signed consent forms for release of information and treatment.
- Listing and method of contacts made with third parties (e.g., family members, acquaintances, and other professionals), including a brief description of the contacts or consultations and any important events surrounding them.
- Brief description of all decisions made and interventions provided during the course of services.
- Summary of critical incidents (e.g., suicide attempts, threats made by the client toward third parties, child abuse, and family crises) and the social worker's response.
- Guidance provided to client (e.g., referrals and consultation suggestions).
- Summary of all client contacts, including type, dates, and times of the contacts and any failed or cancelled appointments.
- Summaries of previous or current psychological, psychiatric, or medical evaluations relevant to this intervention.
- Reasons for termination and final assessment.
- Copies of all relevant documents (e.g., signed consent forms, correspondence, fee agreements/payments, and court documents).

Source: Reamer, 2020b, pp. 11–12 (including items from Reamer, 2001, 2015)

EXHIBIT 4.7 *Checklist for Brief Assessment Demographic Data*	• Identifying Information: name, address, phone number(s), date of birth, members living in the home (and relationship), occupation, income, gender/gender identity, race/ethnicity, religious/spiritual affiliation • Brief description of the presenting problem • Nature of presenting problem(s), including specific, discrete concerns and priorities • Client relationships with family, work, school, or peers • Context and social support networks, including agencies and client's environmental context • Assessment measures administered with results • Strengths and resources within client and environment • Assessment summary and treatment recommendations, including baseline and social worker impressions *Source:* Jordan & Franklin, 2021

EXHIBIT 4.8 *Information to Include in a Treatment/ Intervention Plan*	**Intervention/Treatment Plan** In collaboration with the client, a treatment plan is developed and may include: • Assessment summary • Problem identification • Goal(s) as mutually agreed upon with client • Assessment process and methods • Objective(s) and strategies to measure progress • Intervention(s) selected • Timeframe for intervention • Evaluation *Source:* Adapted from Jordan & Franklin, 2021, pp. 39–40

A second form of documenting practice that social workers find helpful is referred to as **narrative recording**. Narrative recording is a description of the interaction that occurred, typically written in sentence form (Sidell, 2015). The reader should be able to gain a clear sense of the issues discussed, plans agreed upon, client perceptions, and social worker observations and assessments.

As it is the official record of the social work intervention, social workers must pay attention to the accuracy and professionalism of their documentation. Specifically, any documentation should first and foremost be an accurate representation of the social worker's observations and assessment of the client as well as professionally written. The document should be clear, concise, specific, factual, grammatically correct, and written in an active (versus passive) voice and should include no unnecessary or biased information, acronyms, or slang/jargon. Social workers should write their documentation with the assumption that every record could ultimately be subpoenaed for inclusion in a court case; therefore, you should view each word as important and meaningful. Clients should be informed of their right to view their documentation, any limitations to this right, and ways in which the helping and documentation processes may be affected. The 21st Century Cures Act now requires individuals to have immediate access to their health information without charge. Social workers working in mental health settings are required to share meeting start/stop times; modalities and frequencies of services provided; clinical test results; and a summary of diagnosis, functional status, treatment plan, symptoms, prognosis, and progress to date (NASW, 2021b).

As technology has evolved, many organizations have transitioned to full electronic record-keeping. Electronic records are intended to improve the quality and efficiency of service delivery through "real-time" documentation, access by multiple providers and by clients, decreased cost of staff time for documentation, and faster sharing of information (Sidell, 2015). While documenting in an electronic record is commonplace, it is critical for social workers to ensure they are familiar with the ethical obligations and implications of electronic record-keeping and are adequately trained as mistakes in record-keeping can be costly to the organization and the client. Professionals relying on cloud-based storage of electronic records are ethically and legally obligated to ensure client confidentiality. The future of documentation will focus on adaptation and use of evolving technologies to further expand information and its access; however, social workers must anticipate and address the ethical implications of each new technological advance for the profession, the employer, and most importantly, the clients (Reamer, 2020a).

The Client Perspective

Some client situations present unique challenges in the assessment phase of work. Involuntary, mandated, and nonvoluntary clients; violent situations, including suicidal clients; and crisis interventions all require specialized practice skills.

Involuntary, Mandated, and Nonvoluntary Clients When you first considered social work practice, you may have assumed that clients would come to you because they wanted your services. The principles of self-determination and working toward a preferred reality seem the opposite of coercion, and some social workers question the appropriateness of working with clients who are required to participate in services. Yet, because of the tension between some social workers' potentially conflictual roles as both agents of social control and change, a portion of social work clients (in some settings, all clients) are involuntary.

Involuntary has several meanings. In some sense, most clients are involuntary in that they are receiving services in response to a crisis (e.g., loss, illness, life change). The distinction between voluntary and involuntary is not always clear-cut, but the profession generally accepts characterizing clients, including mandated and nonvoluntary clients, as involuntary if they have been compelled to receive services (Barker, 2014). Typically, an authority (e.g., legal system, employer, etc.) requires **mandated clients** to receive services to achieve a desired outcome, such as reuniting with their children, escaping criminal charges, or avoiding institutionalization. Such mandates occur most often in systems of care that are heavily shaped and sanctioned by the law, such as child protection, mental health, and criminal justice. **Nonvoluntary** clients are not formally or legally obliged to participate in services but are pressured into receiving them. For example, an employer may "strongly encourage" an employee with substance use issues to seek help, or a parent may "take" an adolescent to family counseling. In these situations, the client is in some way persuaded that they need to get services in order, for example, to keep the peace, remain married, or stay employed.

Patterns of engagement with involuntary clients vary and may be unpredictable. Anti-oppressive practice includes accepting as valid clients' reluctance to engage. Some mandated clients may become convinced that they can benefit from genuine involvement and will work for change. Others may simply go through the motions, sometimes just to satisfy someone else. The notion of involuntary clients presents both challenges and opportunities.

Challenges in Working With Involuntary Clients For many social workers, including both students and seasoned practitioners, the idea of working with a client who does not want to be there is uncomfortable, if not daunting. In some cases, this discomfort relates to the social worker's responsibility to interface with the mandating agency, which may seem restrictive or overly authoritarian. In others, social workers might dislike the involuntary client's behavior (for example, the client's engagement in child abuse, criminal activity, or substance use). In still others, social workers may be unsure how to build a relationship with an involuntary client. These are understandable concerns, but social workers committed to anti-oppressive practice should not assume that involuntary clients will not engage in or benefit from services.

For a first visit with an involuntary client, prepare yourself to interact with a client who may be angry, hostile, and/or fearful. If the client assaults you with spiteful remarks at the beginning of a meeting, you may feel surprised and hurt; it is helpful to be aware of how you may react and to consider ahead of time how best to respond. In a hostile encounter, strive to remain calm and nonreactive. Clients who are emotionally agitated or distressed may seek to shock or outrage the social worker. A professional response to a client's outbursts can defuse a potentially volatile situation.

While clients who are not voluntarily seeking your services may not initially engage with you, services can be delivered as the assessment and planning processes are being completed; that is, a mutually agreed upon contract may come later in the intervention (Jordan & Franklin, 2021). While this may seem to be an overwhelming challenge, it can help you refrain from taking angry remarks personally, because the client has no expectations of you and/or makes few demands on you. Another way to prepare for resentment and negativity is to place yourself in the client's position by remembering times you have felt coerced, invisible, unrecognized, or ignored. This will help you to empathize with and better understand the client's disinclination to trust anyone, including you.

Of course, not all clients will present this level of antagonism. Some may maintain a complacent or controlled demeanor, attempting to prevent you from "touching" them in any significant emotional way. Some may see meeting with you as an opportunity to think about making changes. Resist the temptation to assume the client is uncooperative before you start the work or see their reluctance as an immutable obstacle to effective collaboration. As in any client situation, the most helpful approach is to actively listen. Learn how the client sees the situation. Ask the client how things could be different, respect the client's view of reality without judging or challenging, and assume the client has both strengths and competence despite the current predicament. Find out what is important to the client and how they want things to change. This is often an excellent time to ask questions that probe for the client's perspective, because the client's answers can reveal parts of their identity beyond the involuntary situation. For example, the client is not merely an offender or a parent involved in a child welfare investigation. If an adolescent who is using substances feels like a "loser" and worthless, you might ask, "What would your best friend say is your greatest strength?" or "What would your favorite teacher say you're good at?" (De Jong & Berg, 2013). For more on approaches that may be useful with involuntary clients, see Quick Guide 9.

In most cases, you will have some externally imposed pattern for delivering mandated services. This may be a set number of sessions (such as 12), conclusion of a period of confinement, or a curriculum to follow. Explaining

QUICK GUIDE 9   Involuntary Clients

GUIDELINES FOR INTERVIEWING INVOLUNTARY CLIENTS

- Assume you will be interviewing someone who probably will start out not wanting anything you might have to offer.
- Assume the client has good reason to think and act as they do.
- Suspend your judgment and recognize their cautious, protective posture.
- Listen for who and what is important to the client, including when the client is angry and critical.
- When clients are openly angry or critical, ask what the person or agency who offended them could have done differently to be more useful to them.
- Be sure to ask for the client's perception of what is in their best interest; that is, ask what the client might want.
- Listen for and reflect the client's use of language.
- Ask questions about the client's relationships with others to bring in the client's context.
- Respectfully provide information about any nonnegotiable requirements and immediately ask for the client's perceptions regarding these.
- Always stay "not knowing" (i.e., the social worker's focus is on the client's frame of reference, not their own).

Source: De Jong & Berg, 2013, p. 184

this structure can help encourage the engagement, assessment, and planning processes. One of the ways you can assist your client is to give them as much control as possible by emphasizing any choices (e.g., you are able to meet once or twice/week, on Tuesdays and/or Fridays) and by being transparent about requirements (e.g., the court requires you to notify authorities if the client misses a session). Be sensitive to the fact that mandated clients often feel as if control and choice have been taken away from them. Provide all the information you can about contingencies as a gesture of respectful recognition and acknowledge that you are aware that the client does have choices (e.g., to work with you or not work with you), even if the client does not recognize those choices.

Despite your best efforts to engage your client, mandated or not, you may find yourself having to take a position that is contrary to the client's wishes but may be in the best interests of the client's health, legal status, or safety. This may be especially the case in work with children and vulnerable older adults, the latter being covered by state adult protective services statutes. This position can become difficult when you have been trying to respect the client's situation and work with their goals and wishes. For example, do not decide prematurely that Briana is not ready to have her son back in her custody or that your older adult client cannot live alone safely in the community. You want to keep working toward the goals of the client to arrive at a point at which their preferred reality can be realized.

There will be times when you may have to take a conscience-driven stand that may seem to work against the client's wishes. For example, if, because of advancing dementia, an older adult is no longer able to maintain the activities of daily living, including cooking and bathing, they may not be able to continue living alone in their home. You may recommend that the court seek care for your client in a residential setting. The client may be upset about your recommendation and feel you are not supporting them. In this situation, make the client(s) aware of your intentions before any court hearing or another meeting. Avoid any surprises that would further violate your client's trust. For example, initiating an honest dialogue (e.g., "This is the way I see it") conveys respect even if the client does not agree with your assessment.

> *Another way to help Briana understand the perspective of others is to ask perspectival questions, such as "What do you think the judge might think about the time when you left the baby alone?" (De Jong & Berg, 2013). In Briana's situation, communicating the process, your role, and possible timeline for achieving the goal of reunification with her son can aid her in perceiving you as being supportive and trusted and enable her to feel control over her actions.*

Opportunities in Working With Involuntary Clients Although involuntary situations are not ideal, such interactions present the opportunity to engage people who might never undertake change without being forced to seek services. Work with involuntary clients gives social workers the opportunity to practice their most cherished social work skills. Listening to and respecting clients' perceptions, assuming clients can grow, and believing that their situation is workable enables you to engage them in ways that can potentially transform their lives. In working with Briana, for instance, listening to her in a respectful, non-judgmental, and strengths-based manner talk about her childhood, pregnancy, and challenges related to single parenting at a young age can help her to gain perspective on her situation and begin to see her strengths, and possibilities.

Developing skills when working with involuntary clients can prepare you for effective work with those who may not be required to work with you, but who may have some dimensions of resistance. Consider the following situation. The court judges a man to be a perpetrator of intimate partner violence, but because he has a substantial history as a client of mental health services and has just been discharged from a psychiatric facility, your supervisor asks you to meet with him individually. Normally your agency works with men in groups, but your supervisor has determined that this client would not respond well to the potential confrontation of a group. He is painfully embarrassed at being singled out as inappropriate for a group process, angry that he feels he is being treated like a "common criminal," and exceedingly hostile about meeting with you.

Using a basic approach of respect, a willingness to hear him out, and a position of wanting to understand his life, you connect with him after several sessions. He then confides that he has never had the opportunity to talk about the challenging issues in his family and that before your work together, he felt humiliated and stigmatized about receiving mental health services. By the end of the 12 mandated sessions, he wants to engage in further work, and he has come to believe that he can change his violent behaviors by responding differently to stress. This is an example of the way clients may respond to an affirming approach that recognizes their strengths even when they are not initially involved in making treatment decisions.

Any kind of non-voluntary service involves coercive power. Regardless of the relationship or work that transpires, you may have considerable influence in determining events and actions that will occur in your client's life (e.g., removal of a child, probation, parole, or mandated treatment). In these situations, recognize the power you have, be as comfortable with it as possible, articulate your understanding of the power to your client, and elicit the client's understanding. Transparency about power creates a rich opportunity to demonstrate your genuineness and trustworthiness to clients and to discuss power and what it means to your client. It allows you to balance your potentially conflicting roles as agent of social control and advocate for your client.

Focusing on power with all clients, but especially with involuntary clients, provides a context for discussing client goals and strategies. A client's goal might be as simple as getting authorities "off my back," or it may involve more complex efforts to change a system that they experience as oppressive.

> *For example, in trying to regain custody of her son, Briana may have to see you, get a job, and find a new home, all without support from others, or might want to join with others in an empowerment-focused approach to influence the system to help her meet her mandates.*

Violence Social workers frequently work with the effects of a violent culture and are not immune from direct exposure to violent threats in the workplace. The escalation of violence in our lives has become an insidious component of contemporary experience and should be addressed on personal, agency, and policy levels. The following discussion focuses on raising your awareness about your personal safety.

Workplace Violence in Social Work Practice Although it can be common to think of violent acts as discrete, chance occurrences, there is often a difficult-to-deny connection between violence and many historical, political, and cultural influences that reflect a cycle of escalation. In addition to being aware of strategies that can be implemented to eliminate the root causes of violence, social workers must be prepared to respond to violence should it occur in any practice setting. Violence in any setting breeds destructive attitudes and relationships. School bullying, interracial taunting, and sexual harassment are just a few pervasive examples of interpersonal persecution that may affect social work clients and practitioners. These situations escalate into physical violence on an interpersonal or social level in the form of isolated attacks, school murders, or racially motivated attacks. The availability of guns is an influence that impacts the lives of social workers and clients.

The latest update to the NASW *Guidelines for Social Work Safety in the Workplace* (2013a) states that "social workers have the right to work in safe environments and to advocate for safe working conditions" (p. 7). When social workers observe the growing inequality in the United States and consider the political components that seem to spur people to hate one another, it often prompts them to renew their efforts to work for a just society. Building on the profession's systemic perspective, social workers can examine and advocate for anti-racist economic policies, including welfare reform that does not punish people of color or maintain poverty. Social workers can also use a systems lens to analyze, for example, legal approaches to limiting the availability of weapons, their commitment to antiviolence principles, and their positions on war. These issues affect people in local communities and in every society across the globe. The universal nature of these issues reminds us that social justice is a fundamental component of social work at all levels, and that our focus on social justice is one of the distinctive components of our practice.

Social workers are not immune from being the objects of violence themselves (NASW, 2013a). Shier and colleagues (2018) offer that workplace violence is a complex construct that can lead to worker stress, burnout, and resignations with staff in in-patient and community-based mental health settings being at higher risk. To support worker well-being, organizations need policies and training to help workers identify antecedents to violence and address their own well-being (Shier et al., 2018).

While violence can occur in any situation or setting and with any population, the following list includes potential safety risks and strategies to consider client and/or family history of violence or the agency's history of response to workplace violence (e.g., existing policies for assessment, planning, and orientation/training) (Anderson, 2018). In a meeting with client and/or family, assess the demeanor of those present, including pets you may not have previously encountered as well as the presence of weapons (Anderson, 2018).

Skills for Working With Clients Who Display Anger   As a social worker in a context of potential violence, you can take precautions based on common sense and effective communication. Consider the strategies in Exhibit 4.9. Empathy may be the single most useful tool for working with a client who is angry or hostile. Empathic responses to clients (e.g., actively listening while maintaining emotional and physical objectivity and distance) demonstrate that you recognize they are upset, would like to understand the reasons for their distress, and want to assist them. Trusting your instincts is also critical in potentially volatile situations. If you begin to feel a situation is becoming unsafe, communicate your feelings to the client, let them know you will end the meeting if the behavior continues, and be willing to follow through with that statement or seek help if needed (Grady & Dombo, 2016).

What Agencies Can Do   In situations of potential violence, agencies need to assume some of the responsibility to avert danger. Employers can recognize and validate the hazards to which workers are exposed so that workers will feel supported and will report their experiences openly. The American Federation of Government Employees (2016) calls for more laws, policies, standards, and training that will address workplace violence prevention in all organizations. Policies for preventing and handling incidents should be clear and worker-focused. Opportunities for reflecting on incidents and safety concerns and group consultation should be frequent and responsive. Preparation for workers entering possibly dangerous situations and debriefing for those who have experienced aggressive or violent clients should be standard practice and should not require that the worker initiate a formal request. Agencies committed to anti-racist and anti-oppressive practice prioritize development and implementation of policies and protocols that keep workers and clients safe, including a management team to address violence, and should offer training on physical safety and verbal de-escalation procedures that meet worker and client needs and interests. Staffing ratios and other investment by organizations can help keep workers and clients safe, while budgetary cuts can place workers at risk.

Crisis Intervention   All social workers must develop competencies for responding to the range of crises they will encounter in their practice. While a life crisis may be the trigger that brings the client to the social worker, each client experiences a crisis in their own way and can potentially experience growth as a result of the crisis. Crises occur when an intense, stressful event

EXHIBIT 4.9

What Social Workers Can Do in the Context of Violence

- While home visits can be a part of each phase of the social work intervention, always inform your client of the time you expect to make a home visit. Keep to that schedule as closely as possible. This is respectful, and you are more likely to be safe if your appearance does not take anyone by surprise.
- Consult with others (especially a supervisor) before entering a situation you think may be dangerous. If your client has a history of violence and is highly stressed or is known to have firearms or other weapons, do not make a home visit or an office visit after hours without talking it over with others who may have more experience and can consult with you about your decision.
- When you leave the office to make home visits, always inform someone about your schedule. Check in by phone in all situations.
- Pay attention to your surroundings. If you are on a home visit and before you enter the home you hear fighting or crying inside the residence, reassess the timing of your visit and plan to return at another time. If there is activity that seems suspicious and/or is not what you expected, avoid confrontation.
- Do not put yourself in a position to be physically trapped in the home of a potentially violent client. Keep a clear path to the door, so you can leave quickly if necessary.
- Connect with local law enforcement if you work in a dangerous neighborhood or a rural area. Alert them of your plans when circumstances warrant and to the extent that confidentiality permits. In the current context of police involvement escalating situations, it is important to know when police should accompany you, and do not hesitate to ask them when appropriate.
- Do not challenge an angry client with rebuttals or consequences. A calm, kind, and reflective presentation can encourage de-escalation.
- If you sense that something is wrong and you are at risk, even if you cannot tell exactly what it is, leave. There is time for analysis later, and if you overreacted, you can explore that in a safe environment, including triggers and unconscious (implicit) biases.
- Report incidents of any kind to your supervisor or use an agency-designated process if there is one. This helps you work through your own reactions and skills and facilitates the agency's effective response to its workers.
- Recognize your own tension. Be alert for feelings of defensiveness and prepare yourself to avoid returning angry or hostile comments.
- Acknowledge the client's strengths as you listen and include them in your responses when they can be heard as genuine (rather than patronizing).
- Focus on positive and current alternatives that are realistic and available to the client.
- Avoid moralizing or lecturing, no matter how destructive you think the client's conduct has been.
- When necessary, focus on keeping your own control rather than on the client's anger.

disrupts a person's life in a way that they cannot resolve using everyday coping mechanisms; when a client perceives a precipitating event to be emotionally meaningful or threatening; or when a client experiences fear, tension, confusion, and/or subjective discomfort following a period of disequilibrium (Yeager & Roberts, 2015, p. 12).

Regardless of the origins of the crisis (e.g., forces over which the client has no control or the result of a poor life choice), the trauma a client feels can be devastating. The social worker's ability to quickly and accurately conduct an assessment and develop an achievable plan can support and empower the client in response to the crisis. While crisis situations provide the opportunity for the client to grow and change, we must remember that we are likely engaging them at a time and in a space (emotional and physical) at which they are the most vulnerable. It is incumbent on the social worker to have a repertoire of practice skills that can help the client view the crisis experience as an opportunity to strengthen their coping skills and even quality of life. You may be the first to assess client safety, basic needs, available supports, trauma-related experiences, and emotions, and goals—gathering this information can move the discussion forward into planning and steps to achieve goals (Goelitz, 2021). You can approach assessment through a trauma-informed care lens which recognizes the impact of the client's past or current trauma (Briar-Lawson & Naccarato, 2021).

Social workers can benefit from having an evidence-based model, informed by theory, for responding to crises. Two models that lend themselves particularly well to assessing and intervening in crisis situations are Roberts' seven-stage model of crisis (Roberts, 2013; Yeager & Roberts, 2015) and the solution-focused approach. Roberts' model emphasizes the importance of assessment in an effective intervention plan (Roberts, 2013; Yeager & Roberts, 2015). Specifically, initiating a rapid and timely assessment of and plan for responding to the client's crisis is a critical first step. In reviewing the seven stages of crisis intervention presented here, note the prominent roles assessment and planning play in the professional's response, both in the initial steps and throughout the intervention (Eaton-Shull, 2022, pp. 245–246; Yeager & Roberts, 2015):

1. Plan and conduct a crisis assessment including lethality, danger to self or others, and immediate psychosocial needs.
2. Rapidly establish rapport and the therapeutic relationship by genuine, empathetic expression of concern.
3. Identify issues pertinent to the client and any cause related to the client's crisis contact.
4. Use active listening skills to deal with feelings and emotions.
5. During the planning process, generate and explore alternatives by identifying the strengths of the client as well as coping mechanisms the client has used successfully in the past, both of which can contribute to desired outcomes.
6. Formulate the action plan.
7. Establish a follow-up plan and agreement.

Through its emphasis on strengths, solutions, the present and the future (as opposed to the past), and short-term intervention, the solution-focused approach is a viable option to consider using when assessing and intervening in crisis situations. Utilizing "miracle or dream" questions can help the person in crisis to consider previously not considered possible solutions (Goelitz, 2021).

Suicide All situations related to suicide—whether a client is threatening or has attempted to intentionally take their life, a family is coping with the suicide of a loved one, or a client experiencing depression is at risk for suicide—present the social worker with an individual or a group in crisis. As with any client crisis, social workers are ethically bound to identify and assess clients who may be at risk for suicide and develop and implement plans to prevent suicide attempts. While advocating for the client's right to self-determination is a social work value, preserving life takes priority in the case of threatened or attempted suicide as well as risk of harm to others (Freedenthal, 2013). In the practice context, this means that the social worker intervenes when a client has threatened suicide to prevent the client from acting on the threat by contacting authorities or negotiating a no-suicide contract.

The key to effectiveness is rapid and timely assessment and planning. An important first step in preventing a suicide attempt is to directly ask the person if they are considering suicide (Praetorius, 2021). As a student approaching professional social work practice, you may have concerns about discussing suicide with a client. While some people believe that discussing suicide or self-injury with clients can increase the risk, the evidence about suicide intervention is not consistent with this belief. In asking direct questions about suicidal ideation or self-injury, avoid vagueness and possibly incomplete responses (Praetorius, 2021). In a suicide risk assessment, the social worker asks the client questions focused on any thoughts they may be having about death and suicide. The social worker then inquires if the client has developed a plan, a time frame, and/or a means for carrying out the suicide. The social worker then assesses the lethality of the client's plan. Indicators of serious intent can include: previous attempts; access to the means of suicide they state will be used; if, after hearing the plan, you determine it is well-formulated; and/or the client talks about giving away personal possessions. Other areas for inquiry should include (Praetorius, 2021):

1) Do you have social supports who can help you cope? If so, how often are you in touch with this person(s)?
2) Have you lost a loved one to suicide? If so, who was the person, when did the loss occur, and how did you respond?
3) Have you recently experienced the end of a relationship (e.g., divorce, breakup, moving away)?
4) Have you had a recent and significant health event? If so, have your activities of daily living (e.g., eating, sleeping, work, hygiene, etc.) changed?
5) Are your basic needs being met (e.g., food, clothing, safe housing)?
6) Have you experienced trauma in your past (e.g., abuse or neglect during childhood, intimate partner violence, or sexual victimization)?

Exhibit 4.10 provides examples of a brief and more detailed suicide risk assessment that you may find helpful in assessing a client's risk for suicide. Upon completion of the assessment, the social worker determines the client's level of risk to attempt suicide and takes action, which can include negotiating a no-suicide contract or facilitating hospitalization.

When assessing the potential for suicidal ideation in individuals in vulnerable populations (e.g., veterans, LGBTQIA+ youth, and persons subjected to bullying), the social worker needs a specialized set of skills to assess and plan competently and sensitively. Considerations for assessing vulnerable populations and planning for action include the following:

- In assessing suicide risk, recognize that the client is likely to have experienced short-term trauma (veterans) or long-term trauma (LGBTQIA+ youth); you want to talk about risk without contributing to the trauma already experienced.

- When possible and safe (i.e., there is no immediate concern for client safety), allow the client to determine the pace of the assessment and recognize that the client may or may not want to talk during the first meeting.

- Acknowledge that you may have limited time to intervene.

EXHIBIT 4.10

Suicide Risk Assessments

Suicide Risk Assessment: Columbia-Suicide Severity Rating Scale (CSSR-S)

Ask the First Two Questions

1) **In the past month, have you wished you were dead or wished you could go to sleep and not wake up?**
2) **In the past month, have you had any actual thoughts of killing yourself?**
   If YES to 2, answer questions 3, 4, 5 and 6
   If NO to 2, go directly to question 6
3) **In the past month, have you thought about how you might do this?**
4) **Have you had any intention of acting on these thoughts of killing yourself, as opposed to you have the thoughts but you definitely would not act on them?** (High Risk)
5) **Have you started to work out or worked out the details of how to kill yourself? Did you intend to carry out this plan?** (High Risk)
   Always Ask Question 6 for both lifetime and past 3 months:
6) **Have you done anything, started to do anything, or prepared to do anything to end your life?** (e.g., collected pills, obtained a gun, gave away valuables, wrote a will or suicide note, held a gun but changed your mind, cut yourself, tried to hang yourself, etc.) (High risk)

Source: The Columbia Lighthouse Project (n.d.)—for detailed information, visit https://cssrs.columbia.edu/

EXHIBIT 4.10

Continued

CRISIS WORKER _____ DATE _____ TIME _____

Life Crisis Services, St. Louis *Suicide Risk Assessment*
Caller Name _____ Phone# _____

1. Are you thinking of suicide?   2. Have you thought about   3. Have you ever
   (If yes go immediately to   suicide in the last two months?   attempted suicide?
   assessment)

   Y   N   Y   N   Y   N

RISK FACTORS	RISK LEVELS	LOW	MEDIUM	HIGH	IMMED HIGH

INTENT: *expressed intent to die; availability of means to and opportunity for attempt; specificity of plan; and preparations for attempt.*

Attempt in Progress	no	no	no	yes
Plan to hurt self/other	unclear	some plan	well thought out	
– time frame	in the future	>24hrs.	<24hrs	0–12hrs
– method	unclear	some plan	well thought out	
– location	unplanned	unsure	known	
Preparatory steps taken	none	some	many	
(giving items away, goodbyes, etc.)				
Expressed Intent to die	1	2	3	4

(on a scale of 1–4, with 1 being low and 4
high, when you think about killing yourself,   **Details of method:** _____
how much do you really want to die?)   _____

DESIRE: *no reason for living, wish to die, wish not to carry on, desire for a suicide attempt*

Wants to hurt self/others	no	sometimes	most of the time	now
Hopelessness	none	sometimes	most of the time	always
Helplessness	none	sometimes	most of the time	always
Perceived burden	none	sometimes	most of the time	always
Feeling intolerably alone	not at all	sometimes	most of the time	always
Feeling trapped, no escape	not at all	sometimes	most of the time	always
Psychological pain	1	2	3	4

(on a scale of 1–4, how much hurt, anguish or misery are you feeling right now?)

CAPABILITY: *a sense of fearlessness to make an attempt; a sense of competence to make an attempt*

Means available	have to get	close access	have with	used
History of attempts	none	one	2–3 times	>3
Exposure to suicide	no	know someone	close relative/friend	
Hx of violence to others	none	occasionally	frequently	
Alcohol/drug use/abuse	none	average use	excessive use/abuse	yes
Currently intoxicated/impaired				
Recent dramatic mood swings	none	within last month	within last week	daily
Increased anxiety	none	monthly	weekly	daily
Decreased sleep	none	monthly	weekly	daily
Out of touch with reality	not at all	occasionally	frequently	now
Recent acts/threats of aggression	none	some	many	daily

> **EXHIBIT 4.10**
>
> *Continued*
>
> **BUFFERS/CONNECTEDNESS:** *how many connectors to meaningful components of life are present?*
>
> | Immediate support present | available now | possibly available quickly | not possible |
> |---|---|---|---|
> | Other social supports | available now | available occasionally | no support |
> | Future plans goals | concrete plans | some plans | no plans |
> | Purpose in life | strong purpose | some purpose | no purpose |
> | Ambivalence about death | much | a little | none |
> | Beliefs about suicide | against belief system | belief system ambiguous | no belief system |
> | Rapport with Crisis Worker | very engaged | somewhat engaged | not at all engaged |
>
> We've been talking for a while now . . . can I ask you about how you're feeling now? On a scale from 1–4, how likely are you to kill yourself?
>
> | | 1 | 2 | 3 | 4 |
> |---|---|---|---|---|
> | **ENDING RISK** | low | medium | high | Imm-high |
>
> ____follow-up scheduled ____Pager called ____traced call ____Police called
>
> *Source:* Life Crisis Services, n.d.

- In beginning to engage in the planning process, ask about and reinforce coping strategies that the client feels have helped them in the past.

- Use applicable general information and whatever the client shares to come to an overall understanding of your client's experience, but do not make assumptions or presume to know their individual experience, even if you have gone through something similar.

- Do not be overly directive as your client may connect receiving instructions with their traumatic experience. Specifically, do not say "you need to relax"; instead ask about any anxiety the client may be experiencing.

- Encourage the client to be in control as the crisis that brought on suicidal thoughts has likely robbed them of the sense of control.

- Do not minimize the crisis or offer positive prediction—you cannot know the client's experience or its outcomes.

- While some clients may find it helpful to share with others who have similar experiences or similar family situations, other clients may not feel comfortable in a group environment, so do not force the issue.

- For effective planning, be knowledgeable about services and resources available to clients by familiarizing yourself in advance with evidence-based intervention practices and best practices for intervening with vulnerable groups.

- Above all else, maintain a nonjudgmental status.

Exhibit 4.11 provides a sample dialogue between a social worker and a youth who expresses suicidal thoughts.

EXHIBIT 4.11

Suicide Risk Assessment With Vulnerable Populations: A Dialogue With Sam

You are a social worker in a multiservice not-for-profit agency that serves at-risk youth. Your organization provides crisis intervention, emergency shelter, transitional and independent living, mobile outreach, educational and employment programs, and individual and family treatment. You are conducting an initial intake interview and assessment the morning after Sam arrived at the emergency shelter. Follow along with the interview below to learn more about assessing a client who is particularly vulnerable:

Social Worker	*Sam, it's good to meet you. What brings you to our shelter?*
Sam	*My parents kicked me out a couple of weeks ago. I've been staying with different people, just sleeping on their couches.*
Social Worker	*How are you feeling today?*
Sam	*Okay.*
Social Worker	*Do you want to talk about your parents kicking you out of the house?*
Sam	*They don't like my lifestyle, so they wanted me out of their house.*
Social Worker	*What is it about your lifestyle that you think they don't like?*
Sam	*They found something and flipped out.*
Social Worker	*What did they find?*
Sam	*Well, actually, they saw an email between me and my boyfriend.*
Social Worker	*What was it about the email they had a problem with?*
Sam	*It's that I have a boyfriend. Turns out they didn't know I was gay.*
Social Worker	*Sounds like they didn't take it well?*
Sam	*You could say that . . . .*
Social Worker	*How are you coping?*
Sam	*So, my boyfriend breaks up with me because my parents called their parents, and now their parents won't let them see me anymore. They say I'm a bad influence. I'm just done. If my parents don't want me and my boyfriend doesn't want me, and I don't have anywhere to go, then I'm just outta here.*
Social Worker	*When you say you're done, what do you mean?*
Sam	*I mean . . . what's the point?*
Social Worker	*Again, let me ask what you mean.*
Sam	*What's the point of living if I don't have a place to stay and nobody cares what happens to me?*
Social Worker	*This is so much loss to deal with, Sam. I'm sorry you have been going through so much. I am particularly concerned about your mention of "point of living." Are you saying you would think of ending your life?*
Sam	*Yeah, I guess that's what I'm saying. I don't have anything to live for, do I?*
Social Worker	*Have you thought how you would do that?*

Sam	*Yeah, I guess I have. There's a lot of times lately that I've sat at the Metro stop and thought how easy it would be to just step in front of that train. It would just end all the pain, you know, for everybody.*	**EXHIBIT 4.11** *Continued*
Social Worker	*Do you have a time frame for when you thought you might do that?*	
Sam	*No, just been thinking about it sometimes.*	
Social Worker	*What's keeping you from doing it?*	
Sam	*My friend saw this flyer at the Metro stop about you guys and said I should call. So, I did. I don't know what you can do to help though.*	
Social Worker	*That was a good idea. I'm glad this friend helped you to connect to us. That took courage for you to call. I'm glad that you came in. Let's talk about how we can help you to deal with some of these feelings you have without you hurting yourself.*	
Sam	*{Silence .... they begin to cry}.*	
Social Worker	*I see this is emotional for you. Can you share what's going on?*	
Sam	*I don't really want to die. It just seems like it's the easiest choice.*	
Social Worker	*Let's talk about things that would help you to be able to not follow through with this plan and some resources that help you cope with what you're dealing with. Would that be okay?*	
Sam	*Maybe.*	
Social Worker	*Let's talk about an agreement that includes some alternatives for when you are feeling bad.*	
Sam	*Like what?*	
Social Worker	*We can both come up with ideas, write them down, and even sign them ... just like a contract.*	
Sam	*What kind of things?*	
Social Worker	*For instance, what makes you feel good?*	
Sam	*Listening to my music.*	
Social Worker	*What is it about the music that makes you feel better?*	
Sam	*I just connect with it.*	
Social Worker	*How about if you agree that when you are feeling bad, you will listen to your favorite group?*	
Sam	*I guess maybe I could agree to that.*	
Social Worker	*What else do you do that makes you feel good?*	
Sam	*Getting high.*	

At this point, the social worker offers Sam shelter until a permanent housing plan can be developed. They agree to meet in a few days. Sam also agrees to talk with a shelter staff member if they begin to have feelings of harming themself. The social worker and the client go on to discuss healthy and unhealthy coping strategies and the long-term consequences of each. Eventually, they agree on a list of alternatives to suicide, which they write down. Each signs the contract, they make copies, and they agree to revisit the contract within the week.

It is critical that the social worker have knowledge of agency and legal procedures to immediately and appropriately respond to suicidal ideations, threats, or attempts. Mobilizing an emergency response is imperative. Responses may include negotiating a contract in which the client agrees not to attempt suicide, involving members of the client's support network or community, facilitating the prescription of antidepressant medication (as appropriate), and/or seeking hospitalization for the client. Regardless of your response, a thorough and immediate assessment is critical for your client.

The Social Worker Perspective: The Social Worker as a Whole Person

Just as it is necessary to be attuned to safety issues, social workers must be sensitive to their own physical and emotional health. As you have seen, challenges in social work practice may result in the social worker experiencing negative emotional and physical responses to their work situations. Working with clients who experience discrimination and oppression and trying to help with inadequate resources, engaging involuntary clients who may challenge your capacities, confronting a violent culture and avoiding its direct expression against you, coping with the bureaucratic tensions of policies regarding service provision—these may seem to confound and certainly challenge your best intentions in the practice of social work (Wagaman et al., 2015). When added to the pressures of feeling a lack of sufficient personal and institutional power and adhering to organizational policies and practices (discussed in Chapters 10 and 11), social workers can experience frustration and alienation. **Secondary or vicarious trauma** can occur when helping professionals react to the pain clients are experiencing, while **burnout** is a chronic, stressful response to the work. When both secondary trauma and burnout occur, the social worker may experience **compassion fatigue**, which is characterized by feelings of apathy, anxiety, depression, and hopelessness (Barker, 2014, p. 83).

Painful Events Although most of social work practice deals with struggles clients experience, most practitioners at one time or another encounter a particularly jolting event that shakes their confidence and makes them question their capacity or commitment. This event is often a crisis—for example, a client suicide, a murder, an extreme case of child abuse or neglect, an annihilating fire, a pandemic or natural disaster, financial malfeasance in the agency, an ethical crisis/conflict with an employer, or a colleague who is negligent. Such events can take a generally well-balanced human being off guard. Social workers who are usually able to cope without considerable difficulty may be reluctant to recognize or acknowledge when they have an untenable reaction. Ignoring the signs of secondary or vicarious trauma can be dangerous for a social worker's stability and resilience. Social workers need to allow themselves to be human; the experience of overload, rather than showing that a social worker is deficient, can reflect the traits of a caring person.

When situations such as these occur whether they are isolated events or ongoing events such as the COVID-19 pandemic, the social worker should seek as much support as possible. Time away from work, debriefing sessions, peer or supervisory support, or a shift in responsibility may be indicated. Supervisors should always assure social workers that these responses are appropriate to the situation; that is, the responses should be **normalized**. With appropriate supports and adequate time, most workers will come to terms with such situations and return to their practice as committed as they were before.

Personal Triggers In a related scenario, the social worker may have some unresolved personal issues that affect their capacity to carry out the agency's work. For example, a social worker who experienced abuse or trauma as a child may harbor a great deal of rage. While anger may be understandable and normal, it can be problematic if the social worker over-identifies and becomes emotional in an encounter with a client suspected of child abuse. In such cases, the agency is likely to address the issue administratively or with corrective action. Here, the social worker can engage in a process (i.e., therapy or education) to change their behavior. An extreme reaction can be a difficult experience for someone who is committed to the profession and has the capacity to make a solid contribution. The intensity of the trigger situation can lead a social worker to self-assess as inadequate and not suited to the profession. However, appropriate consultation with a professional (e.g., supervisor, mentor, or mental health practitioner) can help many social workers who experience an intense reaction to work through the emotional aspects of that reaction to reconcile the personal and the professional. All helping professionals can be triggered, so this phenomenon can be somewhat normalized. While no professional can claim perfect balance, social workers are obligated to identify and respond to those triggers that may impact their own personal and professional well-being. It is important to recognize that people of different identities bring different experiences to the work and the profession has an obligation to support diverse professionals in successful practice.

A concern that arises for social workers, particularly in the early stages of their careers, is over-empathizing with a client and developing feelings of sympathy, which they fear can take an emotional toll and ultimately become compassion fatigue. Cuartero and Campos-Vidal (2019) contend that being overly compassionate about a client's situation can cause social workers to lose sight of themselves and compromise their well-being. Having the ability to regulate one's emotions, a supportive work environment, and a well-established self-care plan can aid the social worker in finding a balance when relating to clients.

While all social workers are at risk for compassion fatigue, most social workers experience **compassion satisfaction**, which encompasses positive outcomes of working with clients (Gottfried & Bride, 2018). Not surprisingly, social workers who are aware of stressors and engage in self-care activities two-three times/week, particularly when they feel overwhelmed, experience lower levels of compassion fatigue and report higher levels of compassion satisfaction, suggesting that finding balance and gratification from one's work mediates the negative effects of the stressors (Cuartero & Campos-Vidal, 2019). Compassion satisfaction among social workers is linked to working in organizations that promote emotional intelligence, allow greater autonomy in decision-making, and create a supportive work environment that encourages work-life balance (Bae et al., 2020).

Self-Care To increase the likelihood of a rewarding professional social work career, students and practitioners are well served by committing themselves early in their careers to a self-care routine. While the effects of secondary or vicarious trauma and compassion fatigue can impact one's personal and professional life, protective factors can promote resilience even when working in intense practice situations.

While challenging to define, self-care should not be simplistic (i.e., a single activity), a product (i.e., a spa day), or an "extra" responsibility added to your schedule, but it should be holistic and include multiple domains, including (Grise-Owens & Miller, 2022):

- physical—movement, sleep, and/or dietary focus
- social—connections to people, nature, and positive activities
- spiritual—engaging in meaning-making activities
- psychological—mental health, recreation, and/or creative activities
- professional/academic—mentoring and professional development
- practical—structured to become part of your daily routine

At the professional level, self-care can include peer (emotional and case management) sharing and incorporating humor and mindfulness into your work (Cuartero & Campos-Vidal, 2019). Organizationally, administrators can facilitate a range of initiatives to support employees, including job sharing, working in teams, professional development/training to promote skill mastery, advocating for fair salaries and work hours, supporting younger workers at higher risk for negative outcomes, and integrating self-care accountability in supervisions and evaluations (Caringi et al., 2017; Miller et al., 2018).

The social work profession has identified self-care as a necessity and an ethical obligation. For the first time, the 2021(a) NASW *Code of Ethics* includes self-care in two sections:

Purpose: #5—The Code socializes practitioners new to the field to social work's mission, values, ethical principles, and ethical standards, and encourages all social workers to engage in *self-care*, ongoing education, and other activities to ensure their commitment to those same core features of the profession.

Principles: Social workers behave in a trustworthy manner. Social workers are continually aware of the profession's mission, values, ethical principles, and ethical standards and practice in a manner consistent with them. *Social workers should take measures to care for themselves professionally and personally.* Social workers act honestly and responsibly and promote ethical practices on the part of the organizations with which they are affiliated.

While challenging to define, operationalize, and maintain an effective self-care routine, the plan should encompass personal relationships, physical health, and professional development while being guided by both evidence and practice wisdom (Miller et al., 2018). Establishing a regular self-care plan can improve your well-being, work environment, and work processes (Cuartero & Campos-Vidal, 2019). Self-care has never been more important than during the COVID-19 pandemic. A study of MSW students reported that those who increased self-care practices, maintained structure and routine, and prioritized academic productivity experienced a greater sense of normalcy and less stress (Hargons et al., 2021). See Exhibit 4.12 for self-care strategies offered by social workers for social workers.

Just as social workers emphasize the whole client in context, we need to think of ourselves as whole people, too. This means that we are not *just* social workers. Like clients, we are children, partners, cyclists, amateur politicians, musicians, parents, and artists. We are successful in some roles and need to improve in others. We may connect well with involuntary clients and yet steer away from children or older adults. We may be stimulated by institutional

EXHIBIT 4.12

Self-Care Strategies for Social Workers

- *Learn to use yourself as a resource*: Knowing your own responses, biases, and limits in various processes of your work is a first step in self-care. Appreciating your strengths and accepting your vulnerabilities will help you make solid practice connections with clients and avoid expecting too much of yourself, which frequently leads to feeling disheartened. In the face of extensive client need, you may expect to save the world and inspire clients to love you while you do it. When you know that about yourself, you can laugh at your own grandiosity, let go of the need for all clients to like you, and continue to strive for competent practice and positive outcomes.

Strategies:
- Use reflection to get to know yourself and areas you will and will not compromise.
- Identify your priorities.
- Acknowledge that your self-care practices are unique to you.
- Routinely conduct your own self-assessment regarding your vision for your future (e.g., where do I want to be, what is needed to get there, and what are the barriers).
- *Understand shared power*: Within a model of planned change that includes engagement, assessment, intervention, termination, and evaluation, the strengths perspective assumes that clients can control their lives and do not need you to do it for them. Recognizing that you are not responsible for your clients' lives can be a component of your self-care plan.

EXHIBIT 4.12

(Continued)

- There is no need to be all-knowing and all-delivering—expectations can be burdensome and harmful to clients and professionals.
- You cannot assume responsibility for the behaviors of your clients and others. You are responsible for yourself—taking care of yourself can enhance your capacity to deliver effective services.
- Concentrate on client strengths and their capacity to achieve their own goals, and when you stress social justice and human rights in ways the client can relate to, you are more likely to see joint successes which can bolster your commitment.
- *Focus on practical goals*: By committing to making self-care a lifestyle, you can plan, prioritize, and implement practices that will help you to be accountable, intentional, and consistent in your self-care.

Strategies:
- Schedule self-care but keep it simple and take small steps—routine habits can have significant impact.
- Practice self-compassion, forgive yourself for mistakes, and give yourself grace.
- Learn to say "no" without apologizing.
- Be open to change as it is inevitable.
- Strive to increase your awareness of risks and consequences of compassion fatigue.
- *Find your own support systems:* Social workers understand how important support is for clients but may underestimate its value in their own lives. Support, inside and outside the workplace, is critical. Developing a group of peers at work can be helpful and enjoyable. Such a collective can function as a peer support network, or it can be a strictly social group. Both friends outside of work and family are also critical. Spiritual support, whether a formal religious affiliation or a more informal spiritual connection, can help put the occasional but inevitable disappointments and frustrations of the work into a perspective that helps keep you from feeling overwhelmed.

Strategies:
- Ask for help.
- Prioritize making healthy connections.
- Prioritize boundaries and respect them.

Sources: Gazda, 2021; Grise-Owens, 2021, 2022; Holmes, 2021; McKenzie, 2021; Wolkenstein, 2021

settings or find them hopelessly oppressive. We may be passionate about working to change urban agency policies, or we may thrive in rural locations where the sole agency has no walls and policy is an on-the-go venture.

Social workers may be subject to restrictions related to social justice themselves. Their identities are privileged in some contexts and devalued in others, such as in the case of not being supported when experiencing secondary trauma. When you see yourself as a whole human, belonging in a context, you will be more likely to engage in your work with enthusiasm and vigor.

Sustaining Ethical Practice in the Face of Challenges *The Code of Ethics* (NASW, 2021a) requires social workers to care for themselves and to practice ethically despite setbacks; to keep growing in response to new ideas, perceptions, and experiences; and to maintain a vision of what ethical social work practice can be and how they can contribute. The struggles social workers face can sometimes obscure ethical aspects of practice. Social workers need to keep the ethical considerations of omission as much in mind as those of commission. For example, not working for active reform of harmful systems (omission) is as neglectful as committing an outright violation of the *Code of Ethics* (NASW, 2021a). If workers increasingly withdraw, defending themselves against the challenges of dehumanizing contexts, they can slowly lose the spirit of ethical practice without even realizing it. As an example, resigning oneself to funding cuts or practices that do not promote diversity, equity, inclusion, and belonging is counter to our ethical principles so we must be vigilant to ensure our silence does not convey acceptance.

One of the most effective ways for social workers to improve their practice and reduce the risk for work-related stress and turnover in their positions is to have the benefit of regular opportunities to discuss their work with clients with other professionals (Cuartero & Campos-Vidal, 2019). The supervisory relationship is one such opportunity to improve your practice. Through discussion of direct practice, professional impact (e.g., interprofessional practice), job management, and continued learning, social workers can improve their knowledge and skills (Shulman, 2020). In fact, social workers report that a trusting supervisory relationship provides benefits in the areas of critical reflection, opportunity to discuss needs, social work values, ethics, and systems change while promoting creativity and knowledge development (Egan et al., 2017). As the social worker, you can contribute to that relationship by being an initiator of and collaborator in the process. The term *supervision* may evoke a hierarchy. Literally interpreted as "watching from above," it suggests an authoritarian relationship in which one member judges and corrects the other. Fortunately, social work supervision is not limited to that configuration, despite the inevitable evaluative nature of the term. In social work, supervision is not a passive relationship but, rather, interactive, collaborative, and dynamic.

Supervision in all its forms—individual, group, ad hoc, formal case, and peer—has the potential to contribute a great deal to sustaining ethical practice in challenging contexts. Hearing others' beliefs about the issues involved in a challenging practice situation, for example, can expand your thinking and help you work through the values and ethics of situations in which you feel immobilized or perplexed. Social workers often engage in team meetings or group supervision sessions in which cases are presented for review and feedback. Effective, collaborative supervision can provide technical support in that it has the potential to increase and improve your practice responses but should also provide emotional support, reducing isolation and increasing hopefulness. Supervisees should expect that supervisors will serve as mentors/models who share and demonstrate knowledge and skills, creating a safe and supportive environment for exploration, testing theories and techniques, and self-reflection and critical thinking (Ketner et al., 2017). Supervision can be both supportive and challenging as supervisors guide supervisees through the complexities of professional practice and socialization (Dill, 2017). See Exhibit 4.13 for tips on effectively engaging in supervision. Beginning with the field education experience, supervision is an opportunity to integrate classroom experiences into practice.

EXHIBIT 4.13 *Tips for Using Supervision Effectively*	• Be prepared for each session by reviewing your work and identifying the issues you want to discuss. A productive supervisory session is one in which the supervisee takes the initiatives and does most of the talking. • Demonstrate a genuine eagerness about learning and expanding your knowledge and experience base in practice. • Take responsibility for your work, your thinking, and your reactions. • As much as possible, trust in the supervisory relationship so that you do not need to cover up mistakes or deny any struggles you have with the work. • Be willing to take thoughtful risks. • Understand the parameters of your work and the expectations your agency/supervisor has of you. • Respect the difference between the focus of supervision (how an issue affects your work) and the focus of psychotherapy for yourself (how an issue affects your emotional life) which you may choose to seek at times throughout your career. • Remain open and non-defensive if/when your supervisor suggests you do things differently while utilizing critical thinking to evaluate supervisor recommendations and evaluations. • Demonstrate a respectful and professional approach to relationships with all colleagues, including your supervisor. • Incorporate self-care into supervisory and evaluation discussions to ensure that you will be accountable for your self-care.
GRAND CHALLENGE *Eliminating Racism*	Identified by the American Academy of Social Work and Social Welfare Grand Challenges for Social Work Initiative as one of the most challenging social problems facing our society, social isolation is an issue that affects the physical and mental health of persons of all ages, as noted by Lubben and colleagues, authors of Grand Challenge Working Paper No. 7, *Social Isolation Presents a Grand Challenge for Social Work* (2015) (Lubben et al., 2015, p. 1): Solid epidemiological evidence links social isolation to health. Both the World Health Organization and the U.S. National Institutes of Health have affirmed the importance of addressing social isolation which was significantly exacerbated during the COVID-19 pandemic among all age groups, but particularly for older adults. Prior to the COVID-19 pandemic, The American Association of Retired Persons (AARP) adopted reduction of social isolation as one of its

> **GRAND CHALLENGE**
>
> *Continued*

top five new initiatives. Working in tandem with other key professions, social work possesses the unique expertise to greatly reduce the risk and consequences of social isolation by strengthening social ties among all populations. Loneliness and social isolation should routinely be included in the assessment process for those clients at-risk (e.g., older adults and persons with chronic illnesses and disabilities).

Created in response to an urgent need for change, the challenge to eradicate social isolation in our society calls upon the social work profession to collaborate within and outside the profession to conduct research and work with individuals, professionals, and organizations. The goal of this call to action is to develop and test interventions for individuals at risk for or experiencing social isolation in their communities (Lubben et al., 2015). In a comment in *NASW News* (Laurio, 2016, p. 9), one of the authors of this Grand Challenge, Johnson, states that social workers are uniquely positioned because our training has us looking at patients holistically. . . . Our training has taught us to look deeper, more broadly, at a person's situation. Social workers look at social health, mental health, and physical health as a complete picture.

The issue of social isolation has relevance in this chapter, which is focused on assessment and planning, as many clients who seek services from social workers are at risk for or may be experiencing isolation due to physical or functional impairment, limited financial resources, mental illness, or lack of social connections and support. To familiarize yourself with the issues related to social isolation in children, youth, and older adults, visit the Grand Challenges website and read Working Paper No. 7, *Social Isolation Presents a Grand Challenge for Social Work* (Lubben et al., 2015) at http://grandchallengesforsocialwork.org. To learn about the progress on achieving this Grand Challenge, review the "Eradicating Social Isolation" by Brown and colleagues (2022). (See Exercise #1 for additional exploration of this Grand Challenge.)

CONCLUSION

This chapter has addressed a range of practice issues and skills related to assessment and planning along with challenging issues in social work practice today. Clearly, the assessment and planning processes involve a broad combination of efforts and tools. There are hundreds of instruments social workers can use in these phases of the helping process, depending on the practice setting, type of client served, and range of issues. Your agency will use a few selected instruments consistent with the mission and focus of the agency's services or funders' directives.

Social work assessment and planning are integrated activities that arise out of an effective engagement with the client and progress into the action-oriented intervention phase of the work. The tone and focus of the assessment and planning processes should be consistent with having an eye toward strengths and a commitment to empowerment, particularly in the early phases of the work. Assessment and planning continue throughout the practice process, sometimes shifting the work depending on changes that occur within the client's life situation.

MAIN POINTS

- Building on the engagement process, assessment involves culturally responsive dialogue to discover the goals and aspirations of the client, while planning emphasizes the collaborative development of action steps aimed at achieving the client's goals.

- The theoretical perspective the social worker uses has significant implications for the assessment, planning, and intervention processes. This chapter discussed six theoretical frameworks: psychoanalytic, attachment, cognitive, strengths-based, narrative, and solution-focused.

- Ideally, the social worker develops a shared vision with the client by respecting and honestly responding to the client's preferred reality.

- Mapping is a useful addition to verbal assessment and planning. Three types of maps many social workers use are genograms and ecomaps.

- Assessment and planning evaluate the types of resources, both formal and informal, that the client and the client's environment can bring to bear.

- When the assessment and planning processes identify the need for resources that are not present, adequate, or available to clients, social workers must respond creatively and appropriately. In some cases, social action can be used to create needed resources.

- Assessment and planning move from a shared vision to the specific details of the intervention. Internalized oppression and the emotional impact of change can influence the entire assessment process and the client's capacity to participate in planning.

- Social workers are ethically bound to be clear and honest with clients about specific agency constraints and requirements that will influence the client's experience of the work.

- Social workers can meet the challenges of working with involuntary, mandated, or nonvoluntary clients if they adequately frame these challenges and approach these clients with basic respect and a willingness to listen.

- Violence influences the work of the social work practitioner and can affect their personal safety. Social workers can engage in social justice–oriented practice to try to minimize societal violence, and they and their agencies can develop skills and policies to deal with situations of potential violence associated with clients.

- Secondary or vicarious trauma, burnout, and compassion fatigue may arise out of painful events and personal triggers and can be mitigated through appropriate agency and social worker response.

- Regular and ongoing self-care is consistent with ethical practice, and it can carry you through difficult moments. As in your work with clients, think of yourself as a person, with strengths, vulnerabilities, and a need for your own support systems.

- Effective supervision is a useful interactive relationship for negotiating difficult practice contexts, exploring and testing theories and skills, and processing emotional responses.

EXERCISES

1 To integrate the issues of social isolation into social work practice, review the case of Carla Washburn at www.routledgesw.com/interactive-cases/ and respond to the following items:
   a Which of the social isolation risk factors identified in Grand Challenge Working Paper No. 7 are present in the information on Carla Washburn?
   b On what information are you basing this assessment? What tools might help you with this assessment? How can you partner with Carla in the assessment process?
   c To help you develop an assessment and plan for working with Carla, view the two videos located at www.bc.edu/centers/ioa/videos/social-isolation.html. Incorporating the information provided in the videos into your assessment of Carla, create a plan for intervening with her.

2 Go to www.routledgesw.com/interactive-cases/ and review the case file for Emilia Sanchez (in Engage and Discover), including the genogram and ecomap of the family for both its content and form. Click on Assess the Situation and view the tasks you will need to complete. To prepare for this exercise, also review the Biopsychosocial Perspectives.

   Using Emilia as the anchor family member, develop two genograms. The first should reflect her relationships prior to age 14 and the second should be an "update" to her current age of 24. Include as much information as possible while ensuring that the drawing is informative and clear. After completing the first genogram and before completing the second, develop an ecomap that represents your interpretation of the systems and networks supporting Emilia's "change" (her involvement in substance use) that might have led to her estrangement from her family.

   Partner with another student and exchange the three tools. Are they similar? In what respects do they differ? What information is particularly helpful? What facets of Emilia's life are most effectively represented in a social mapping format? Which ones are the most challenging?

3 Go to www.routledgesw.com/cases and review Emilia's video vignette. After viewing the vignette, complete the following exercise. Emilia Sanchez has come to you for help because she has decided she must

conquer her substance use disorder. Emilia's long history of substance use, her family's distress regarding the out-of-wedlock birth of her son Joey, and the following abortion of another child resulted in her feeling discouraged. She doubts her ability to make a place for herself in the family again and to make the changes she wants to make. Using the strengths perspective, the social worker can identify and assess Emilia's strengths. Respond to the following:

   a What was the most challenging aspect of identifying the strengths of someone who has had the number of challenges Emilia has experienced?
   b How do you as the social worker encourage Emilia to recognize her strengths?
   c Identify the strengths the social worker in the vignette points out.

4 Go to www.routledgesw.com/interactive- cases/ and review the case of Carla Washburn. Begin by reviewing the case information in the Engage and Discover Section. Click on Assess the Client Situation and review the Introduction section, including the goals. Complete Tasks #1, #2, and #3.

5 Go to www.routledgesw.com/interactive-cases/ and review the case of Hudson City. Address each of the following areas:
   a Click on Engage and Discover. Select Case Files and review Community Background and Your Concerns.
   b Continuing with the engagement phase, click on Critical Thinking Questions and respond to each question.
   c Moving to the assessment and planning phases, click on Assess the Situation. Select Biopsychosocial Perspectives. Review the biological, psychological, social, and spiritual lenses and respond to the questions related to each area.

6 Go to www.routledgesw.com/interactive-cases/ and review the case of Hudson City. Two professional issues are relevant to the social worker in this case: dual relationship and self-care due to compassion fatigue. After reviewing the case materials, conduct a literature search regarding one or both issues and develop practice strategies that are appropriate for your future as a social worker.

7 Go to www.routledgesw.com/interactive-cases/ and review the Brickville case. Address each of the following areas:
   a Click on Engage and Discover and complete the Tasks for this section with specific emphasis on strategies for engaging Virginia and other key persons in her life.
   b In the Assess the Situation section, review the ecomap centered on Virginia Stone and her family. Identify all relevant linkages Virginia has within her family and community, the character of those relationships, and strengths and areas for changes.
   c Return to Engage and Discover, review View the Town and develop a list of Virginia's needs on the individual, family, group, and community levels.

8 Go to www.routledgesw.com and review Downloadable Case #1: Willow's Transition. After reviewing the information, develop responses to Questions #1, 3, 4, and 5.

9 To begin the process of developing engagement, assessment, and planning practice skills, complete the following role-playing exercise. Begin by partnering with two other students.

Using Confrontation: Engage in brief reenactments of the following scenarios with each student assuming the role of the social worker, the client, or the observer. Use the engagement and assessment behaviors highlighted in this chapter to role-play the beginning phases of work with clients in these situations. Upon completion of the role-play, each member of the triad will provide balanced feedback regarding the others' demonstration of skills. Select from the following list of potential client scenarios:

a Client sporadically attends scheduled meetings/sessions.
b Client reports that when she was angry with her 10-year-old son at the mall she spanked him in public.
c Client is having difficulty obtaining employment. You recognize that the client's style of dress and hygiene may be a concern for employers.
d Client continues to use language that you find offensive (e.g., abusive, racist, or explicit).
e Your colleague is not completing tasks and you are experiencing negative consequences.

Upon completion of the role-play activity, reflect with your group (or in writing) on situations in which you have been involved that resulted in a confrontation between you and another person. If you cannot recall such a situation, remember a situation in which a confrontation may have been warranted but did not occur. Imagine in that situation that you were confronted by a caring individual in your life. What was your reaction to being confronted? How did you receive feedback? How do you give feedback? How comfortable are you confronting others? What were the benefits to being confronted?

10 Review and discuss with other students the following situations. Evaluate your level of comfort in them. What makes you comfortable or uncomfortable? Be specific. Upon completion of the discussion, brainstorm with other students strategies for maintaining your safety.

a Conducting a home visit that involves risks to your safety
b Working after dark at your agency
c Driving a client to an appointment
d Working with individuals with mental illness
e Working with individuals with substance use issues
f Having an initial meeting with a client who is unknown to you
g Working with a client with a criminal record

11 Returning to the scenario at the beginning of this chapter that involved Briana and her baby, develop a plan for conducting the assessment and planning phases of the social work intervention using one of the theoretical frameworks discussed in this chapter with attention paid to the biopsychosocial-spiritual, cultural, and mapping information that would enhance the assessment and planning process. Select one of the assessment tools described in this chapter or identify another validated tool

from the literature to gather information to be used in the planning of the intervention. This activity may be completed as an in-class role-play or discussion with other students or as a written exercise.

12 Exploring your own cultural heritage is an important part of becoming a culturally competent professional. Select one of the following options to gain insights into your journey:

   a Quick Guide 5 provides questions to consider regarding the cultural heritage journey each of us takes. Consider the following:
   - If my family immigrated to the United States, how long has each of my parents been living here?
   - If I am in an adoptive family, what do I know about my biological family's cultural heritage?
   - What traditions has my family passed down through the generations? Have there been obstacles to passing along those traditions? Have those traditions been celebrated or denigrated in media, political discourse, or my community?
   - Do my family's traditions relate to religion or spirituality, holidays, rituals, and/or significant events?
   - What values surrounding ethics, wealth, religion and spirituality, race, ethnicity, health, education, sexual orientation, and body image have I learned from my family?
   - Have I challenged any of my family traditions or values?
   - Has my family had experiences that challenge their traditions and values? If so, how have I responded?
   - What significant life experiences have shaped my view of the world and specifically of people who are different from me?
   - How will my cultural heritage impact my social work practice?
   - Would I like to change or add to my traditions? How might I start?

   Upon completion of your examination of your cultural heritage, turn your focus toward assessing your own cultural lens from a practice perspective. Specific attention can be devoted to the influence of your cultural heritage on your knowledge, awareness, and interactions with persons and groups different from yourself.

   b To create your own cultural genogram, go to the National Center for Cultural Competence (n.d.) at https://nccc.georgetown.edu. Using the instructions provided, develop your own cultural genogram. Upon completion of your cultural genogram, reflect in writing about new or confirmed insights, yourself as a cultural being, and the connections between your insights and the influences of your cultural heritage.

   (Warde, 2012)

CHAPTER 5

Social Work Practice With Individuals: Intervention, Termination, and Evaluation

INTERVENTION, termination, evaluation, and follow-up are all components of the planned change process, which also includes engagement, assessment, and planning. To be effective and meaningful for the client, the assessment, the intervention plan, the intervention itself, and the evaluation and follow-up must all connect to one another. They must address the problems/issues presented by the client and lead to desired outcomes. For example, a client seeks services at your agency for an eating disorder but is hesitant to address issues related to their current eating practices. While you must start where the client is, respect their right to self-determination, and follow the client's wishes regarding discussion of specific areas of their life, you can point out that bringing current behaviors and practices into the intervention can be a helpful part of the intervention. By providing the client with the information but not directing the intervention, you enable the client to choose whether to delve into either of those issues.

The **context** of the social work intervention plays a crucial role in shaping the meaning clients and social workers attach to the experience. The choices and capacities of individuals, the systems in which they are embedded, and the accessibility of existing and potential resources make up the social work practice context. Whether you work with someone recently diagnosed with a chronic illness, an adult child experiencing the stress of caring for an aging parent, or an immigrant seeking US citizenship, your actions will affect and be affected by the context of the work. This chapter explores the impact of context on all aspects of practice with individuals. The chapter also examines generalist practice competencies and behaviors that support client strengths within their environments, as well as the variety of social work roles and methods that support client–worker relationships, including strengths-based, narrative, solution-focused, and cognitive behavioral approaches. As with other chapters, this chapter includes case examples to help you integrate the strengths-based approach with environmental justice, social justice, human rights, and social construction perspectives. The chapter ends with a discussion of the termination, evaluation, and follow-up of the planned change intervention, focusing on strengths-based strategies to celebrate and help the client maintain accomplished goals. First, we will start by looking at a case that we will revisit throughout the chapter:

> *Maria is a middle-aged, single Latinx woman who experiences serious mental illness and co-occurring substance use disorder. She has lived with family her entire life, most recently with her sister. Her sister died three months ago, and Maria has been staying with a brother and his family. Both Maria and her brother agree that this cannot be a permanent arrangement as her brother and his spouse are caring for their three young grandchildren. Maria wants to live in her own apartment. While she has a history of employment, she has not consistently been employed due to multiple hospitalizations related to her diagnosis of bipolar disorder. Her family has always been supportive of her but sometimes she feels they have been overly protective of her. She is both eager to live on her own and anxious about her ability to meet the demands of everyday independent living, self-sufficiency, and maintaining her sobriety.*

Key Questions for Chapter 5

1. How can I prepare to intervene with and empower individual clients?
2. How can I use the strengths-based perspective to guide the development of intervention, termination, evaluation, and follow-up strategies with individuals?
3. What social work roles enable me to effectively intervene, terminate, evaluate, and follow up with individuals? What roles will enable me to effectively work with Maria?
4. How do I determine which evaluation tool(s) are appropriate for interventions with individual clients?

INTERVENTIONS THAT SUPPORT CLIENT STRENGTHS

Each individual client's unique circumstances and what they define as the most pressing issue will determine the starting point of your work. The goal of all social work interventions is to empower clients to make changes to enhance the quality of their lives and their ability to function within their environments. Within the social work profession, there is increased awareness of the need for approaches that emphasize strengths, resilience, spirituality, and culturally relevant interventions that encompass race, ethnicity, gender, sexual identity and orientation, and political factors (Briar-Lawson & Naccarato, 2021). There are several approaches and frameworks that can incorporate these components and be used to inform and guide the interventions. While not all evidence-based frameworks can be highlighted here, we will discuss four intervention frameworks that are commonly used within the social work profession to guide and inform interventions, including strengths-based, narrative, solution-focused, and cognitive behavioral approaches.

Strengths-Based Perspectives and Interventions

The strengths-based perspective focuses on identifying, expanding, and sustaining the client's resilience and assets. A worker using a strengths-based method will not only seek out and identify client strengths in the assessment (see Chapter 4) but will also support and maximize those strengths throughout the working relationship. For many practitioners, this effort is the major focus of the work.

Social work scholar Dennis Saleebey (2013, pp. 109–111) identifies four elements of the strengths-based approach that apply to the practice context and the action of intervention. In this approach, the social worker:

- *Identifies hints and suggestions of strengths even in the struggle:* As the client relates their current situation, which often focuses on challenges and stresses, the social worker can "listen" for the client's inherent strengths.

- *Stimulates the discourse and narratives of resilience and strength:* Most of us have difficulty recognizing our positive attributes. In addition to recognizing strengths, the role of the strengths-based social worker is to affirm any positives the client identifies, suggest the possibilities that exist for the client, and facilitate assessments and interventions that are grounded in the client's strengths and resilience.

- *Works with the client to develop goals grounded in strengths:* The strengths the client and social worker collaborate to identify are part of the context for the work. These competencies can be the focus of the assessment and intervention process and can guide the development of goals.

- *Works with the client to move toward normalizing, validating, and capitalizing on strengths:* A strengths-based assessment results in an intervention that brings together articulated strengths and resources, normalizes them, and puts them into action.

A strengths-based intervention process builds on the engagement and assessment phase of work in which strengths and resources were identified. The social worker should prioritize the integration of those strengths and resources so that both social worker and client can monitor progress toward the positive changes and goals which moves the client closer to the goal of termination (Simmons et al., 2022).

Acting in Context Regardless of the theoretical approach guiding the social work intervention, the social worker's activity centers on helping clients use the strengths and resources that they already know and those they are beginning to recognize and to link them with their goals and dreams. That kind of effort might lead, for example, to the social worker supporting clients who desire more independence or to become more assertive. Inherent within the strengths perspective is a commitment to social justice by including all members of the community and society (Kim & Bolton, 2019). The client's capacities are identified within the context of the systems in which they are embedded and the client's ability to access/mobilize existing and potential resources.

Returning to your client, Maria, she has located an apartment to rent but is anxious about negotiating a lease. In working with Maria, you can help her identify her strengths and resources related to the goal of negotiating a lease that may include gathering information such as her credit history, previous success with negotiations, and existing resources (e.g., employment, letters of reference, etc.). You can encourage Maria to recognize her capacity to understand the business-focused details of renting and to negotiate for those items she feels are important and fair. For example, if she is willing to paint the living room walls, in return she can ask the landlord to provide the paint and reduce her rent for one month. This may require Maria to stretch beyond her comfort zone to initiate change, but it also gives her the opportunity to act on her own behalf. If the venture is successful, the client adds another competency to her growing list. If the effort is unsuccessful, she can use the experience to reflect on the areas in which she wants to direct her energies to make changes. She may decide to work on becoming a better negotiator or decide to seek out someone in her social network who has this competency to be her advocate in the next situation. Also consider the role that contextual factors (i.e., discrimination) may play in constraining her potential for success and the way in which you can help Maria to anticipate and address previous experiences with discrimination in employment and social situations, for example.

Capitalizing on Strengths Focusing on strengths allows the social worker and client to work together to recognize the client's success in establishing and stabilizing the client's competencies.

> *In Maria's case, a strength on which Maria can build is her willingness to invest her energy toward a fair rental agreement. Following your strategizing with Maria, she has found a new apartment she likes. She works with the landlord to arrive at an arrangement whereby she paints the apartment in return for a reduction in rent. She has built on her strength of willingness to invest the energy needed to negotiate and gained competency in negotiation. As her social worker you would then affirm the skills Maria demonstrated in her negotiation with her landlord, encourage her to generalize those skills into other arenas (i.e., employment and personal and work relationships), and support her ability to generate new skills. You can also help Maria recognize that she is building useful relationships in the community. For example, when she has established a positive rental history, her landlord could become a resource if she needs a reference for a job or wants to find a larger apartment.*

Thus, a social worker's education, advocacy, and support efforts can enable clients to develop a network that links their accomplishments to their broader life goals. By framing the task as a normative life event—in this case, of securing housing—the social worker not only demonstrates the client's capacities, but also reinforces the availability of community resources (i.e., the landlord) and establishes that disengagement, or ending the work, is appropriate once the goal has been achieved. The ultimate normalization is the client's continued development and the recognition that they can manage the everyday tasks of living.

Narrative Interventions

Building on the deconstruction of client perceptions that the social worker and client completed together during the assessment process (discussed in Chapter 4), a **narrative intervention** remains focused on the client, their strengths, and the meaning assigned by the client and social worker to current and future realities. In a narrative intervention, the social worker's questions are key. As opposed to eliciting information and interpretation of the meanings shared by the client, questioning that occurs during the intervention stage is aimed at helping the client move toward implementing changes to reach their goals.

Once the client and social worker have deconstructed the original concern or issue in the assessment phase and conceived a plan, the social worker continues to question the client in a way that helps the client shift from the view that they *are* the problem to the view that they have a relationship *with* the problem that is affecting them (Nichols, 2020). During the intervention, the social worker continues to help clients view themselves from a position of strength and to work toward a different understanding of the situation that separates the person from their situation. By exploring past events and questioning the meaning attached to those events, clients' views of the problem can be expanded such that the problem story can be exchanged for one of redefinition and strength (Hall, 2016).

Be cognizant of the need to listen to the way in which the clients describe their concerns and life experiences, specifically related to the language used, as their experiences. Clients' experiences and perceptions are influenced by their cultural experiences and message which can become their realities (Smith, 2022). The narrative intervention can aid in reconstructing the negative stories. Upon achieving success with the intervention, using this strategy, clients can celebrate and share their new perceptions of their relationship with the problem with people who are important to them.

As with most interventions, the path from beginning to end may not be linear; rather, it may feel more circular in nature. Helping the client separate the person from the problem can help the client to focus on solutions. To maintain a person-centered focus on the intervention when using a narrative approach, both the client and social worker can periodically return to the problem as identified by the client and reconstruct it considering new insights. Consider the earlier example of the client who seeks help with an eating disorder; it is important to not only expand the client's perception of the issues that will be the focus of your work together (i.e., anxiety about weight) and connect goals (i.e., changing eating patterns) to the intervention, but also to help the client develop strengths-based, person-centered, and measurable goals. In this scenario, measurable goals are those that are clearly stated, incremental, tangible, and focused on the client and their strengths. For example, a goal for this client might be to build on the desire to become healthy by starting with a daily food journal in which they document their food intake and graduate to the introduction of new foods, adding one at a time.

Solution-Focused Interventions

Solution-focused interventions are designed to achieve client goals in a relatively brief, time-limited manner. Specifically, solution-focused interventions aim to facilitate change by helping clients co-construct new perceptions and meanings for challenging events in their lives (Franklin et al., 2016). As you recall from Chapter 4, in solution-focused assessment and planning, the client engages in a self-evaluative process (evaluative questions) to learn how they view the situation. The client also envisions times when the problem did not exist (exception questions) and will not exist (miracle questions). These questions provide insight into strategies for resolving the problem using the client's strengths and resources.

Unique to the solution-focused approach is the lack of distinction that is made between the assessment and intervention phases. Specifically, the series of questions that are used to identify the past concerns and solutions become the basis for the change process (Jordan & Franklin, 2021). In the intervention phase, the answers to these questions continue to be important reminders of the goal and connections to the client's past and future life. Research suggests that the solutions-focused approach is most effective when a combination of techniques is the focus of the work, including strengths, resources, future orientation, and a co-construction of meaning (Franklin et al., 2016). de Shazer and colleagues (2021) suggest the use of such techniques as:

- Demonstrating a positive and collegial solution-focused stance
- Looking for previous solutions used successfully by the client
- Asking questions as opposed to offering directives or interpretations of the client's statements
- Asking questions that are future-oriented and not focused on the client's past experiences
- Providing compliments to the client for successes and changes
- Offering the client gentle reminders to do more of what is working.

Prompting clients to regularly assign a numeric value to an issue, experience, or behavior—that is, asking scaling questions—is a client-centered strategy that can empower clients to engage in self-evaluation and mutual feedback (i.e., both client and social worker provide feedback to each other) (Lee et al., 2022). This exercise is one you return to throughout the intervention to monitor progress toward goals. For example, if the client rated the situation as a "4" in July, what rating might the client assign in September? Is that second rating an indication that the intervention is moving in the desired direction, does it suggest that a shift in the plan is needed, or are factors external to the social work intervention influencing the rating?

Acknowledging small, concrete gains can be an effective motivator for both the client and social worker. Developing measurable goals with regular client check-ins to monitor progress and connection to the goals (or lack of progress and disconnect with the goals) helps empower clients and inspires confidence that change can, in fact, be achieved. Exhibit 5.1 provides examples of scaling questions and strategies for monitoring scaling questions over the course of the social work intervention.

With its emphasis on concrete results, a solution-focused intervention can be impactful and empowering for the client. The social worker implementing this intervention assumes a collaborative stance with the client to support the client in identifying and exploring their desired future and subsequently the solutions to achieve that future (de Shazer et al., 2021). When using this approach, by itself or in concert with another intervention model, the social worker attends to maintaining the client's motivation and focus on solutions and change while reinforcing respect for and confidence in the client's capacity to reach the desired outcome (Lee et al., 2022).

EXHIBIT 5.1

Integrating Scaling Questions Into a Social Work Intervention: Virginia Stone

Virginia Stone of the Brickville neighborhood (www.routledgesw.com/interactive-cases/) has identified several stressors in her life. Scaling questions can help Virginia identify and prioritize areas of concern and strength. They can be infused into the intervention process to frame goals and to track and empower Virginia's progress toward achieving those goals.

During engagement and assessment work, Virginia felt particularly stressed about the potential loss of her family's home. The following dialogue provides examples of how a social worker could use scaling over the course of several sessions:

Session #1: Engagement/Assessment Phase

Social Worker: *Virginia, on a scale of 1 to 10, with 1 being the lowest and 10 being the highest, how would you rate your stress today regarding your housing situation?*

Virginia: *I would say my stress level is a 10. I am so worried that we're not going to be able to prove the house belongs to my Grandma Stella. Then we won't even be able to sell it to that developer if he does move in here and take over.*

The social worker and Virginia worked together to develop a goal to reduce her stress. To achieve this goal, they determined that they would take action to obtain proof of Virginia's family ownership of the house. They mapped out strategies, which the social worker documented both in Virginia's case file and in the client contract.

Session #3: Intervention Phase

Social Worker: *Virginia, since we last reviewed your progress toward your goal, you visited Legal Services to ask for help locating a deed to determine ownership of the house. They told you that they believe you have a strong case. Using the same 1–10 scale, how would you rate your stress today related to this issue?*

Virginia: *I am feeling better about things today. I would have to say I'm at a 5 right now. It seems there is a chance we will be able to prove Grandma Stella was the rightful owner and that ownership passed to my mom when Grandma died. I'm still worried, though, that something will go wrong.*

The social worker asked Virginia to consider other actions she could take while she waited on the outcome of the legal investigation. Virginia acknowledged that there was little she could do but wait. Once she realized that much was out of her control, she acknowledged that she was feeling better about not being able to act now. The social worker documented the events and Virginia's perception of her current stress level.

> **Session #8: Intervention Phase (Three Weeks Later)**
>
> **Virginia:** *I heard from Legal Services, and they were able to find proof that Grandma Stella is the rightful owner of the house! I can't tell you how much better I feel about this thing.*
>
> **Social Worker:** *Using that 1 to 10 scale we have used before, where would you rate your stress level on the housing issue today?*
>
> **Virginia:** *On this one issue, I would say I'm at a 6 today. I'm still worried about losing the house to that developer fellow, but at least now I know that if we do have to sell out, we will hopefully get paid enough that we can find another place for all of us to live.*
>
> Once Virginia and her social worker were able to diffuse the effects of this stressor, they were able to turn their full attention to addressing other goals. While clients can pose scaling questions to themselves, when a social worker instigates this exercise with clients, it may help them to realize improvements even before the social worker can acknowledge the change, which can foster a sense of client empowerment. Though Virginia was working toward other goals, this stressor dampened her motivation to fully engage in working on her less tangible issues of caregiver stress and unresolved grief. At the point she made progress on the home ownership question, this enabled her to increase her resolve and she felt empowered to tackle other issues.

EXHIBIT 5.1

Continued

Van Hook (2019) offers the following guidance for a solution-focused intervention approach:

- Maintain a future-oriented focus to support the client in imagining how their life might be different than it currently is.
- As a result of re-imagining their life, the solutions identified through the questions may not be a direct result of the presenting problem.
- When the client continues to use the same unsuccessful strategies to address their problem, the negative perspectives can be a barrier to change.
- People want to change.
- The social worker should not enter into the client relationship with pre-existing ideas and expectations.
- Shifting from problem-focused to solution-focused language can be a powerful intervention.
- Priorities and goals are established by the client, not the social worker.

Returning to the earlier example of your client who is experiencing an eating disorder, solutions-focused strategies that may prove particularly helpful in this scenario include the use of miracle and scaling questions. You can query the client to envision a time when their eating patterns were not unhealthy and how their life might be if they returned to healthy eating patterns. In establishing measurable and achievable goals, you can also use scaling questions which can help to establish both a baseline and incremental goals that can be monitored and regularly linked back to clients' goals.

Building on the use of questions that were key to the assessment and planning process, consider in the following scenario related to a client's alcohol use the ways in which questions are an integral part of the SFBT intervention when used to initiate and monitor progress (adapted from Zhang & Franklin, 2022; Steenbarger, 2018):

(Future-oriented) Goal Formulation Questions can be revisited throughout the intervention to assess relevance:
- What will your days be like when you are no longer drinking?
- What would have to be different for you to not drink daily?

Miracle Questions enable the client to think outside of constraints to a more positive future:
- What would your life be like if you were able to reach your goal of being sober for one year?
- What do you need to accomplish the goal of becoming sober for one year, and how can I help you?

Exception-finding Questions come from the client's experience of recalling what it was like when the problem did not exist:
- What was your life like when you were not drinking?
- What is it like for your family when you are not drinking?

Scaling Questions use a numeric scale to rate past, present, and future status and serve to highlight progress that serves to reinforce strengths and/or identify coping skills and inner resources:
- On a scale of 1 to 10, how motivated were you to not drink when we began meeting? Where do you need to be to continue your sobriety? What do you need to do to get from 5 to 8?

Coping Questions can be helpful when the client is discouraged and is invited to identify previous accomplishments:
- When you feel like drinking again, what do you do to stop yourself?
- You were drinking daily—what did you do to change that?
- How will you know when things are better? What will you be doing, who will you be with, and how will you be feeling, thinking, and acting?

What's Better Questions serve to illuminate progress toward goals:
- What is better in your life since we last met?
- How is your life better since you stopped drinking?

For clients who are motivated but see their problem originating from outside of themselves, work can be completed during the meeting with the social worker as well as between meetings in the form of "experiments" or homework assignments. These strategies can be used from the first session and include: (1) pre-session change (i.e., "what changes have you noticed occurring in the period since you made this appointment and coming here today?") and (2) ask the client to engage in an activity/behavior that is familiar and is already moving them toward a desired goal; or (3) ask the client to develop their own homework assignment that is familiar to them and linked to their goals and solutions (de Shazer et al., 2021). Activities/behaviors that are familiar or designed by the client will be linked to the goals and enable greater investment by the client (de Shazer et al., 2021). An activity may involve observing actions and behaviors they want to see continue. For your client experiencing an eating disorder, they might choose to continue to join their family for dinner each evening, an activity they engaged in last with less anxiety than in previous attempts.

To encourage the client in identifying an activity, the social worker might say, "What activity might you try this week that would be new for you and bring you one step closer to your goal?" For example, a teen whose goal is for their parents to treat them like an adult instead of a child is frustrated because they feel their parents are punitive and too restrictive and are not allowing them to grow up. They may be asked to note behaviors their parents do that they view as positive and would like to see continue. The social worker could encourage the client not to attempt wholesale change, which might be too difficult, but rather to think about an incremental step. It is important for the social worker to recognize the client as the expert on their life and to listen to the language the client uses to describe their situation and experiences (Kondrat & Miller, 2020). This approach by the social worker leads to the development of strategies and solutions. Activities and developments should be reviewed at each meeting with the client and will likely have one of three outcomes (de Shazer et al., 2021): (1) things got better; (2) things stayed the same; or (3) things got worse (p. 7). Depending on the response, the social worker may compliment and explore how success occurred or was maintained but not dwell on a lack of success and instead discuss even small changes that were achieved.

A solution-focused approach can be used in concert with other intervention strategies and in multiple settings. Payne (2020) notes that the solution-focused approach is linked to the social work priorities of building alliances, establishing aims and actions, embracing critical practice (i.e., disruption of social assumptions), and promoting client rights; therefore, making it consistent with psychotherapeutic social work and feminist ideas (p. 301). Building on the basic solution-focused tenet of "if something is working, do more of it," clients and social workers can incorporate aspects of solution-focused work with other interventions, including couple and family therapy and substance use disorder treatment (de Shazer et al., 2021).

Cognitive Behavioral-Focused Interventions

Considered to be one of the most common and well-researched modalities for intervening with clients experiencing a range of mental and physical health challenges, cognitive behavioral therapy (CBT) is another approach used by many social workers. CBT is based on the premise that thoughts drive one's feelings and actions and that changing one's thoughts can lead to changes in one's behaviors (National Association of Cognitive-Behavioral Therapists [NACBT], n.d.). CBT has been extensively researched, and the evidence suggests that this approach is effective with children and adults experiencing a wide array of relationship and mental and physical health issues, including depression, anxiety, bipolar disorder, social phobia, obsessive-compulsive disorder, post-traumatic stress disorder, schizophrenia, substance use disorders, eating disorders, chronic pain, sleep disorders, habit disorders, caregiver stress, couples treatment, smoking cessation, weight loss, and child behavioral management (NACBT, n.d.). CBT techniques are also effective strategies for working individually or in groups with those who have experienced trauma to learn relaxation and coping skills (Goelitz, 2021) and addictions such as internet gambling to replace escape-oriented coping with improved self-efficacy (Anthony et al., 2020).

The primary components of CBT include the following (NACBT, n.d.):

- *Brief and time-limited format:* Meetings with the client are limited to a specific number, with the client often continuing to work on behavioral change following the formal relationship.

- *Collaborative relationship:* The social worker and client work together to identify and implement goals. The social worker's role is to listen, teach, and support, while the client focuses on expression and learning.

- *Structure, direction, and education:* The social worker facilitates the change process by teaching the client specific techniques during the session. The social worker also works with the client to identify homework (e.g., activities, behaviors) the client completes between sessions that emphasizes learning and unlearning behaviors; this work is then discussed at the next meeting.

A hallmark of CBT is the structure. Each session is guided by a mutually agreed-upon agenda that includes such key elements as: (1) evaluation of client's mood using a symptom scale; (2) agenda setting; (3) bridging from previous meeting (review of the action plan/homework; (4) prioritizing the day's agenda; (5) addressing agenda items and skills teaching; (6) creating a new action plan; and (7) summarizing and providing feedback (Beck & Hindman, 2018). CBT includes a range of strategies, including (but not limited to) (Beck & Hindman, 2018):

- Problem-solving to identify and evaluate client's thinking followed by brainstorming options and choices

- Giving credit to the client for achieving successes

- Using activity monitoring and thought records which are tasks the client can complete between meetings to document thoughts, beliefs, and behaviors
- Weighing the advantages and disadvantages of change

When identifying frameworks and strategies to incorporate into your practice, it is important to consider the congruence of your selections with the social work profession. With a goal to collaborate with clients to change thoughts, beliefs, and behaviors to gain a sense of self-determination, control and self-efficacy, CBT approaches are consistent with social work values and can be further expanded to embody anti-oppressive principles as well so the client may address their experiences with social injustices and inequities (Ghelani et al., 2021). While the delivery of CBT requires advanced training and experience, generalist social workers can incorporate aspects of behavioral-oriented strategies into their interventions and can identify those clients who may benefit from working with a CBT-trained clinician. CBT techniques can be used during the initial phase of the intervention to collaboratively create individualized plans to not only to help the client to change maladaptive thinking but to build a positive, trusting relationship with the client (LeCroy, 2022). As the focus of change is directly related to client behaviors, CBT is a logical choice for working with a client experiencing an eating disorder, for example. Collaborative strategies can be explored, planned, and rehearsed during the client–social worker meeting. Homework can be assigned that relates to eating behaviors and food-related interactions with others. Then, reflections on progress (or lack of progress) can be facilitated at future meetings.

Environment-Focused Processes and Skills

Regardless of the model used, when used effectively, many social work practice skills and behaviors can affirm client strengths and support clients' important roles in the work. Social workers can also apply the skills and behaviors previously discussed to supporting clients' effective use of environmental supports. What follows is a discussion of behaviors that social workers can use with individuals.

Cultural Humility and Anti-Oppressive Practice As discussed in Chapters 3 and 4, a client's cultural background is a potential source of strength. As you strive to become a culturally humble and competent social work practitioner, you can build your skills around the following concepts (Gottlieb, 2020):

1 Commit yourself to an ongoing process of compassionate self-awareness and inquiry supported by trusted and diverse colleagues.
2 Be open and teachable (i.e., strive to view cultures through the client's lens).

3 Consider the power and privilege of social systems and the way in which they shape your client's realities and experiences.
4 Be aware of the real and perceived power that you possess, and what your client perceives, and work to balance it within your relationship.

Within the social, cultural, political, and historical context, these concepts can inform the way you view both your client and you. They can also serve as reminders that a client-centered assessment and intervention are more accurately viewed within the context of the client's biopsychosocial-spiritual-sexual lens and should be connected to clients' perception of their situations, strengths, and goals. The social worker should also take into consideration the role that intersectionality may play in the client's life and the social worker's own ability to understand the client's journey. Identifying with multiple groups (e.g., being transgender and a woman of color) will influence the client's worldview and realities.

Make use of those traditions or aspects of your client's culture that nourish and give meaning to life. For example, many cultures demonstrate great respect for authority and the wisdom of older adults. When you work with clients from such cultures and backgrounds, support those values; they are assets you and your client can incorporate into the intervention phase of your work. Although you should always confer with your clients regarding your actions, when conducting a client-centered intervention that includes clear and measurable goals, remain especially sensitized to how your approach "fits" your client's culturally influenced sense of propriety. Could it be potentially challenging for a client who is from a culture that has high respect for authority and older adults to be encouraged by friends to participate in a rent strike aimed at a prominent elder statesman who owns a property? While such an intervention strategy may be clear and measurable, the option may be so incongruent with the client's cultural beliefs and practices that the strategy may be unsuccessful and result in the client feeling disillusioned with the prospect of change.

Having confirmed the importance of recognizing and supporting client strengths and cultural influences in the intervention process, we focus now on identifying and intensifying the strengths of clients' environments. This dual emphasis on person and environment is consistent with the social justice traditions of the social work profession. Social workers often direct their efforts toward making clients' environments more responsive to client needs. In this approach, the focus of the intervention looks to institutions and policies outside of the client, rather than viewing the client's difficulties as a symptom of individual pathology. The process assumes that clients possess the capacity to identify their difficulties and to participate in the work necessary to alleviate them. Consider these reflective questions relevant to the intervention phase of your work (Sellon & Lassman, 2022):

Intervention Questions

1) Does the client feel as though they were involved in developing the intervention?

2) Has the intervention been shown to be effective with marginalized groups?
3) Does this intervention help to empower the client?
4) What oppressive systems or contexts may make it difficult to carry out the intervention?
5) Are there groups or social movements that could help to empower the client? (p. 308)

Providing Information Clients often want, need, and ask for information about their environment, which may be their most valuable resource. You may worry that you will unintentionally overinfluence decisions, be too directive, or create dependency. For example, if your client is returning to college and tells you they want to major in social work because they feel you have helped them, you may be concerned that you had undue influence on the client. While such concerns are legitimate, they also can be managed by remembering that your role is not to advise or "fix" the situation for the client—you are a collaborator with the client to identify strategies for change. Information in our society is clearly linked to power, and when we provide information to clients, we empower them. The challenge arises when clients confuse information with advice or when the information provided is strongly biased. You can never have all the information related to a situation, but you can offer what you know as a simple proposition, framed by the limits of your knowledge.

Consider the situation of the older refugee. She is concerned about the impact previous experiences of violence may have on her younger female family members and does not want this information shared within their social networks. You have been working with her daughter and granddaughters, and she has asked you to share with her the information you have learned about them and to direct them not to discuss their experiences of violence with anyone. While you are sensitive to her concerns, you are ethically bound not to share information about other clients without their consent unless there is threat of harm to oneself or others. Moreover, your commitment to practicing social work in an ethical manner would not allow you to direct any client's beliefs or behaviors.

Let clients know that you have no expectations about what they will do with information they obtain through your work together. It is not your prerogative to place restrictions on what clients do with the information you provide. For example, suppose you work in a child welfare organization and are helping a young couple learn more effective methods to care for their 3-year-old son who has been diagnosed as being on the autism spectrum. You want to compile resources you think would be helpful to the parents. You believe that respite services would help the parents develop trust in a caregiver outside the family. You provide them with the names of several agencies that provide these services. When they do not follow up on this information, you may become frustrated. In this case, the client chose not to act on the information you provided, which is well within their rights of self-determination. The parents maybe are unable to follow up, disagree with your assessment of resources needed, or were expecting different help from you. This example illustrates the problematic nature of attaching expectations to the information you provide. When you provide information, make your suggestions transparent and let clients know that they are free to accept or reject that agenda without ramifications on your professional relationship.

Refocusing and Confronting Often clients are coping with more than one challenge and may struggle to maintain their focus on goal(s). When life circumstances draw the client's focus away from the plan, you can help them to refocus by bringing them back to the heart of the work. Refocusing can take several forms, including referring to the original purpose of the work, as well as recognizing clients' beliefs, plans, and/or behavior.

When clients begin to move away from the agreed-upon focus of the work, a simple reference to that agreement is sometimes all that is necessary. It may be an indication that the goals and planning should be reviewed for possible changes. Occasionally the client (or social worker) will become distracted by other compelling issues. Although such diversion is understandable and can, sometimes, be helpful, you are responsible for using your time with the client productively. If you are working with a client who has lost focus or commitment on your agreed-upon goals, you might suggest that you revisit those goals to determine whether you are both still engaged in the plan. If together you feel your original goals are no longer realistic, propose revising the original plan. For example, if the goal was for the client to return to school, but the client was offered a promotion that will require travel, the two of you may need to re-evaluate whether returning to school at this time is feasible or if this goal should be revisited in the future.

In other situations, the client may not carry out the agreed-upon plan or contract because they do not embrace it as a priority, they find it uncomfortable, or they are unable to implement it. For example, suppose your client, Jayden, established a plan to seek counseling because they had been sexually abused and are experiencing painful memories. Initiating contact with a helping professional required Jayden to break family and cultural rules forbidding the discussion of such subjects with an outsider. Jayden found the effort to initiate this counseling more difficult than they had imagined. In this situation, rather than refocusing Jayden, you might instead confront them gently, saying, for example, "Help me to understand your concerns about discussing your painful memories with an outsider." Jayden may simply need more informal support and acknowledgment from you to manage the unanticipated struggle. This development might also signal that the plan is not working for Jayden and is not likely to lead to the desired outcome. In situations like these, return to the goals of the work to determine whether they continue to flow from the presenting issues, review the client's experience, and make changes as necessary. It is important to approach the speed of change at the pace comfortable to the client, however slowly, rather than try to move more quickly than the client can manage.

Significantly, clients often perceive gentle recognition of their behavior as helpful and supportive. A client may perceive a social worker contrasting the client's actions with the client's stated goal as a sign of respect because the social worker's effort affirms the client's capacity to meet commitments. For example, you may say to a client: "Your goal was to obtain employment, but you did not apply for any jobs this week. Please help me understand how your actions will help you reach your goal." Preventing the client from experiencing this type of confrontation as hostile or argumentative requires that you handle the interaction with sensitivity, recognizing that this response on your part can prove challenging. In most cases, social workers try refocusing before confrontation. Instead, you might say, "Your goal was to obtain employment, but you were unable to apply for jobs this week. Are you able to identify any barriers that prevented you from applying that we could address today?" When a social worker uses confrontation selectively and sensitively, however, they can convey hope and respect to a client.

In some situations, a digression from the intended focus of the work is warranted. You will be called upon to exercise your professional judgment to recognize when a digression warrants a new focus. For example, if Jayden came to your office with an eviction notice in their hand and asked you to help them with this, you might place the original focus of your work on hold until they could resolve their housing crisis.

Interpreting Client Behavior When the social worker makes sense of the client's behavior in ways the client may not perceive or acknowledge in the hopes of inspiring the client to consider their situation in a new or different way, the social worker is interpreting that behavior. From a social constructionist view, accurately interpreting can be one of the most challenging practice skills to master.

The meanings you and your client ascribe their behavior may differ. There still may be a place for offering your interpretation but be careful to test it out with clients and acknowledge that your interpretation of the situation is only one possibility. For example, consider the following conversation with Jayden.

> Social Worker: *It seems to me that you do not feel ready to take on the kind of work likely to be involved in this type of counseling. Is that correct?*
>
> Jayden: *I don't know what you're talking about.*
>
> Social Worker: *Each time we try to discuss your painful memories, you change the subject. I think we might best use our time right now talking about other aspects of your life. When you feel more comfortable with me, we can revisit your memories. How does this sound to you?*

Although many of us have benefited from learning how others construe our behaviors, having others interpret our experience can also be frustrating and alienating. This is particularly true when their interpretation seems judgmental or "expert," that is, as if someone else possesses the secret to understanding our behavior. Jayden may also perceive that you are giving up on them or judging them for their inability to disclose their feelings. Interpreting is a widely applicable process, but one that should be used only in an established trusting relationship with the client. Further, you should always ask the client to evaluate the accuracy of your interpretations.

Mapping as an Intervention Strategy   Recall from the discussion in Chapter 4 that incorporating the client's family and community system is an important aspect of the assessment phase of the intervention. Just as mapping the client's family constellation and current living arrangement and relationships can be a useful assessment strategy, visual depictions of the client's environment can be helpful in the intervention itself. As you know, the genogram gives the client insights into their family history, behavior patterns, and a wide array of issues, including physical and mental health, substance use, relationship patterns, and estrangements. Ecomaps, on the other hand, visually depict the client's current life situation, including relationships, resources, assets, and challenges.

During assessment, planning, and intervention, you can incorporate the information you gathered using genograms and ecomaps into the client's goals and action steps for facilitating behavior and life changes. For example, consider the client who has experienced violence in their relationships and who, while completing their genogram, identifies a multigenerational pattern of intimate partner violence directed toward the women in their family. Identifying this pattern of abuse can help them understand the nature of their previous relationships and select strategies they can use to engage in healthier relationships. Later, you can use the genogram to help the client determine whether they have successfully broken the pattern.

In the assessment phase, the ecomap helps the client identify strengths, the directionality of energy and benefits (i.e., where, and how much energy the client is devoting to the areas of their life and what and how this energy compares to the benefits received), and areas for change. Later, during plan development and implementation, the ecomap can enable the client to envision their life after the intervention is implemented. This new perspective on the client's current life can help them devise specific behavior and life changes. Previously unrecognized resources are mobilized, unhealthy behaviors are addressed, and dysfunctional relationships are targeted for change. The ecomap thus becomes a "work in progress" and serves as a mechanism for monitoring progress, determining a time frame for the work and termination, evaluating outcomes, and following up.

SOCIAL WORK ROLES IN SOCIAL WORK PRACTICE

In thinking about the preceding descriptions of selected social work skills and behaviors, consider the specific roles workers assume during the intervention process in support of client strengths:

- Case manager
- Counselor

- Broker
- Mediator
- Educator
- Client advocate
- Collaborator

The following discussion focuses on the assumptions that underlie these roles and the ways the roles are actualized in social work practice.

Case Manager

Case management is "a procedure to plan, seek, and monitor services, resources, and supports from different social agencies to enhance client strengths and well-being in helping them achieve their goals" (Barker, 2014, p. 56). Clients with multiple challenges and needs particularly benefit from case management. For example, a client with a serious mental health challenge, a back injury, and a housing issue may need medication, a referral to vocational rehabilitation, and a referral to a housing resource. Because of this client's multiple needs, they may be an appropriate candidate for case management.

Case managers coordinate services and are responsible for monitoring how well services meet client needs by holding providers accountable, ensuring client participation, and collaborating with others to raise awareness of unmet needs. A case manager may also collaborate with others to advocate for and build needed resources in a community. Case managers work in a variety of settings, including aging services; behavioral health; substance use disorder and addiction treatment; child, youth, and family services; corrections; disabilities programs; educational settings; employee assistance; health care; housing; immigrant and refugee services; income support programs; military and veterans services; and tribal programs (NASW, 2013b). Case managers provide services in the areas of discharge planning, connecting with community resources, prevention, advocacy, planning, assessment, and ongoing monitoring of client needs and well-being (Hall et al., 2019). The client's situation and needs can impact case manager involvement. For example, a case manager working with a client experiencing a substance use disorder who also is involved with the justice system and has physical health challenges may need to be more intensively engaged in goal setting, monitoring, referrals, and advocacy than with a client experiencing fewer challenges (Zweban & West, 2020).

Common Components of Case Management A planned case management process includes these steps (Roberts-DeGennaro, 2013):

1 Ensuring eligible clients are informed of available services at your organization.

2. Assessing a client's needs and strengths.
3. Developing a plan for intervention.
4. Identifying and designing an appropriate network of services.
5. Creating a written contract that includes achievable and measurable goals, time limits, agreed-upon actions, and consequences of failure to fulfill the contract (if any consequences exist).
6. Implementing the plan.
7. Monitoring the plan to determine progress or a need to re-evaluate the contract.
8. Evaluating the outcomes of the intervention.
9. Terminating the case management relationship.
10. Following up, as appropriate (and based on agency policy and practice) on the client after termination to determine if the client has maintained the desired change or would benefit from additional support.

The case manager may also serve as an informal, personal support/contact person. Because therapy is an advanced-level intervention, the social worker is bound by the *Code of Ethics* (NASW, 2021a) to possess an appropriate degree and training to deliver this service. This does not mean the social worker provides therapy, just that all clients can benefit from having people on whom they can call when they need a supportive ally. In contrast to brokers, who may match a client to a single service, case managers take responsibility for assessing, monitoring, and evaluating the coordination of all services a client requires and providing follow-up services, as needed. This role may also involve client advocacy to ensure clients receive services sought from other agencies or that needed services are developed.

Purposes and Practice of Contemporary Case Management For decades, the profession has used the term *case management* to describe this overall coordinating function. Contemporary case management has two primary—and often conflicting—purposes: to improve the quality of care while at the same time controlling its costs. While case management was originally conceived to address the integration of system-level services, it has become a functional and cost-effective practice approach in many types of work, including family preservation, school social work, and substance use disorder treatment, corrections, and health care delivery systems (e.g., operationalization of services and policy).

NASW has developed *Standards for Social Work Case Management* (NASW, 2013b), which are intended to support case managers in competently and efficiently serving their clients by:

- strengthening the developmental, problem-solving, and coping capacities of clients.

- enhancing clients' ability to interact with and participate in their communities, with respect for each client's values and goals.

- linking people with systems that provide them with resources, services, and opportunities.

- increasing the scope and capacity of service delivery systems.
- creating and promoting the effective and humane operation of service systems; and
- contributing to the development and improvement of social policy. (p. 17)

Case management can be delivered within the context of a strengths-based perspective and enables the social worker to emphasize strengths, goals, collaboration with the client, resilience, and solutions. Such an approach can reduce the client's need for services while increasing their satisfaction with their lives (Hall et al., 2019).

Returning to the case scenario of Maria, consider the ways in which a case manager might help her as she faces the challenges of transitioning to independent living and self-sufficiency. The case manager can work with Maria to obtain housing and employment and manage her mental health treatment and medications. Once these goals have been achieved, the case manager can continue to support Maria in maintaining her function and independence.

Counselor

The helping professions use the term **counselor** in a variety of ways. Within the social work profession, counseling is typically a specialized clinical social work skill performed by graduate-level social workers who have advanced clinical training and are working in health, mental health, and family services. In this context, a counselor serves individuals, families, groups, and communities, providing suggestions, alternatives, and information and helping to articulate client goals (Barker, 2014). In the helping professions, a counselor also describes volunteers and professionals or paraprofessionals who work in group settings (e.g., camps and residential settings).

While the counseling role can include an array of activities, the social worker functioning as a counselor typically works with clients on a specific issue or concern. The counselor uses different approaches and strategies based on their expertise and training and on the needs of clients but should always maintain a client-centered perspective viewed through a biopsychosocial-spiritual-sexual lens. Regardless of the different theoretical approaches used by the practitioner working in a counseling setting, viewing the client and their environment from a holistic, comprehensive frame will guide the development and implementation of an effective intervention.

The social work counselor or clinician working with Maria, for example, may see her in individual and/or group therapy and focus treatment on identifying and addressing the symptoms related to her bipolar disorder and substance use history and helping her develop coping and interpersonal skills to enhance her quality of life.

Broker

Social workers often act as **brokers**, linking clients to a needed service or resource, sometimes within the case manager role. Needs may range from instrumental assistance (e.g., food, clothing, and shelter) to services such as counseling, support groups, and advocacy. Consider the functions and context of brokering as the processes of building the necessary networks and of matching clients to services.

Brokering Functions and Context   Social work functions of brokering include:

- assessing client needs and available resources,
- matching the client with appropriate services and initiating referrals,
- linking or networking services, and
- sharing information with the client and/or with the referring agency.

The brokering role can also entail modifying resources and creating new resources where none exist. For example, a school social worker may work with staff at a local faith organization to start an after-school tutoring program when they notice that students at their elementary school are struggling academically and not completing homework. These activities can strengthen the client's environment, or context, while supporting their strengths.

Today, brokering may be viewed as simplistic due to the availability of information online. For example, if your client requests assistance locating used children's furniture, you simply "refer" them to the appropriate agency by providing agency contact information or website. Brokering requires familiarity and relationship building with resources. In rural areas, where the service system may be much less comprehensive, with fewer choices, knowing and maintaining effective relationships with available resources is critical. Oftentimes, social workers will provide a "warm handoff" to a resource by having a joint meeting to introduce the client to the resource person or agency.

Building and Maintaining Networks for Brokering   To develop a brokering network, you must make contacts with providers in other agencies and organizations, discover who will help your clients most effectively, and become familiar with program eligibility criteria and service elements. To broker effectively, you also need to establish stable working relationships with people, organizations, and systems that will help your clients. To provide referrals that best fit the intended service, you may develop relationships with network resources in which you each use the other's services. Building and maintaining a network requires reciprocity and open, regular mutual communication.

To build a network, you need knowledge of the formal and informal aspects of a resource. For example, it is helpful to understand the formal aspects of a resource, such as the mission statement of a community hospice program, population and geographic areas served, eligibility requirements, payment information, and philosophical approaches. It is also helpful to be aware of informal aspects of resources, such as new staff and program offerings, changes in program emphasis, and news and happenings related to a resource. For example, it could be helpful to know that a program has received a large grant for an additional building or that the board of an affiliated organization has approved funding to hire a development director. Your attention to, and continuous connections with, both the formal and informal aspects of the networks you maintain will enrich your understanding of and the ability of your clients to access and use your community's resources. Staff turnover rates can be high in many of these roles; therefore, social workers will need to invest in continual revisiting of these networks.

Making the Match in Brokering   Developing and maintaining a resource network (or "service system linkage") nearly always requires you to use the skills you learned about in Chapter 3 in connecting with clients—that is, building rapport and trust. Following up on your referrals is important, both to determine whether a client benefits from the service and to determine whether the provider perceives your referral and the client to be appropriate for the organization. How well a client matches a service is important, not just from the perspective of the client, but also from that of the service provider. When you take the time and care to learn about an effective and successful referral, you establish trust with these providers, who will respect your competence and skills. When you develop a genuine understanding of, and appreciation for, the work that others do, you are likely to develop an appreciation for how well "the system" is responsive to your clients. For example, instead of handing a list of apartments to Maria, you may refer her to a specific landlord with whom other clients have had positive experiences. You may follow up with her to learn more about her experiences with a particular landlord, so that you can update and refine your understanding of the rental market and your landlord network. The potential success for brokering may be dependent on the type and amount of information you provide to the client.

Mediator

Mediation has both a formal and informal function in the delivery of human services. Mediation as a professional practice has its own identity and is often associated more with the legal system and public policy than it is with social work practice. Some social workers complete specialized training to become mediators in such areas as divorce or restorative justice. Most social workers, regardless of whether they have specialized training, engage in some informal aspects of mediation fairly frequently. **Mediators**, as outsiders to a dispute, try to: (1) establish common ground between disputing parties, (2) help them understand each other's point of view, and (3) demonstrate that each party has an interest in the relationship's stability beyond the current differences.

Finding Common Ground   Locating points of agreement during a dispute is a common social work practice skill. Suppose you work in a youth agency and see Jamal, a 16-year-old transgender male who has run away from home.

From your conversation, you understand that he is distraught over the relationship between his mother and her new live-in boyfriend. He is upset and scared and is not certain about the ramifications of being on his own. He dislikes his mother's boyfriend and objects to the harassment he endures from the boyfriend due to his transition from female to male, and the curfew and other rules the boyfriend imposes which seem overly punitive. Jamal misses his mother's companionship the way it was before the boyfriend entered the scene. His mother has been supportive of his transition. Although there has been no physical abuse, Jamal does not feel safe at home. You ask for his permission to schedule a meeting with his mother, her boyfriend, and Jamal to explore the issues among them. He reluctantly agrees. When his mother enters the youth center, she seems exasperated with her son, but she is also relieved to see him. She begins to cry and hugs him. Her boyfriend remains quiet, but when he catches Jamal's eye, he smiles at the boy just slightly.

Walking Through It One mediation process you might try with Jamal's family could involve the following:

- Represent yourself warmly and genuinely as someone who wants to help resolve the issue without taking sides. Convey to the family that you trust the mediation process and will walk through that journey with them. You might let the family members know that you are there to listen, explore options, and facilitate but not to direct or advise.

- Attempt to establish common ground. In this case, Jamal's present well-being is the immediate point of common interest. Jamal is not prepared to support himself physically, financially, or emotionally (or legally in most places). He is scared and concerned about his future. At the same time, he is vocal about his freedom, does not want to be bound by all the rules his mother's new boyfriend has imposed, and is understandably committed to being treated with full human rights. His mother cares for him and wants him to be safe. Her boyfriend wants a peaceful household and says he likes Jamal well enough, although he says he cannot relate well to his "lifestyle choices" which is how he perceives being transgender.

- Help Jamal, his mother, and her boyfriend understand and appreciate one another's points of view. Assume that Jamal's mother and her boyfriend may have different perspectives and acknowledge all points of view. Facilitate their direct dialogue with one another. The skill of looking at the situation from diverse perspectives will be beneficial to this interaction. You might open a dialogue aimed at establishing a process in which each person is willing to listen to the others' points of view in the following way:

    I would like each of you to be able to share your perspective on this situation. For each of you to be able to hear what the others are saying, it is important that we establish some ground rules for the discussion. For instance, I would like to ask that we each remain silent until the other person is finished speaking. If we have questions or thoughts to share, those should wait until the person has completed their statements. I will try to summarize what I hear each of you say so that you can confirm or modify our understanding.

- Establish with Jamal, his mother, and her boyfriend that it is in all their interests to work together so that they can come to a resolution regarding Jamal's living arrangements and his general safety.

- Help all parties recognize that each will benefit from an ongoing positive relationship in which they can settle differences that go beyond the current dispute. Jamal's future, including the quality of the relationship between Jamal's mother and her boyfriend, may depend on their ability to work together. These are the abiding points of common interest.

This scenario represents just one way in which this situation might play out. You might try other avenues to find common ground and identify solutions. You will notice that this process does not imply any *particular* solution. Jamal, his mother, and her boyfriend might agree that Jamal should return home, live with another family member, try to survive on his own on a trial basis, or other possibilities. The major point is that the relationship between Jamal and his mother (and her boyfriend) is collaborative and that each has a stake in working out a solution that affirms their mutual benefit.

Educator

In many ways, social workers function as educators. While the mission and scope of practice settings will determine the nature and level of such activity, some form of education is common in most social work settings. On an interpersonal and concrete level, social workers serve as **educators** who provide information to an individual. You may teach clients about a range of topics; for example, you might teach them how to complete an application, inform them of new programs, or educate them about the maximum allowable percentage of income they may have to pay to rent in public housing. Much of the direct service aspect of acting as educator relates to helping clients to access resources and to make behavioral changes they want to make. Being a competent educator requires the social worker to maintain up-to-date knowledge of the information they impart. With your client Maria, you may provide information on the local rental market, negotiating with a landlord, developing a budget, and managing medications and appointments.

Developing Client Skills When practicing with individuals, you, as the social worker, can help clients develop the skills they need to participate in the intervention and reach their goals. The client's motivation for this kind of change needs to be generated from their vision of change, rather than from your opinions about needed improvements. You can help clients understand the steps they need to take to accomplish that change through providing them with information they can use to develop change or through teaching them new skills by providing information, modeling, and practicing with the client.

For example, if your client wants to be more assertive in the workplace, you might demonstrate a more assertive (but respectful) stance in a relevant interchange, and/or role-play or otherwise help the client practice the new behavior. You can help older adult clients learn to organize their medications to increase their compliance with a health provider's directives. You can teach parents strategies for using positive feedback to support their children. You can model clear communication and help your client participate more effectively in problem resolution. For example, if you work with an adolescent who is frequently suspended from school because of angry outbursts, you can work with the client on appropriate ways to communicate. You might accompany the client and their parents to a meeting with the school principal. You can help the client process the session, evaluate what went well and areas for change, and support the ability to negotiate these relationships with further practice. To support the client's goal of competence in these situations, you may then role-play the next meeting so that the client will be ready to attend on their own.

When you use skills with clients, you **model** (e.g., demonstrate) behaviors that they may use on their own in their relationships. The goal is to foster in the client a sense of strength—a change in clients' thinking about themselves and a greater integration of self and skills into the environment.

Working With the Community Social workers frequently work with the community using the roles of educator, mediator, and advocate (explained next). For example, social workers educate large groups about issues that affect clients. In some instances, social workers engage in these efforts to prevent the development of or respond to a problem. For instance, you may present a session on ways to support racial and ethnic diversity and inclusion in the classroom to a group of teachers. You may testify in a legislative hearing regarding the cultural needs of refugee children, or you may respond to a community group's concerns about a new group home in their neighborhood that will house discharged clients with histories of psychiatric problems.

Client Advocate

Taking on the role of **advocate** in social work practice means seeking to secure rights, striving to obtain resources, working to modify existing policies or practices, and/or promoting new policies that will benefit clients. Advocating for and with clients is a foundational aspect of the social work profession. Social workers often advocate formally on behalf of the political or civil rights of clients. They also frequently advocate in informal, everyday situations when a client is treated disrespectfully or denied needed services. You may find that you can advocate on Maria's behalf when her landlord has not responded to her request to have her air conditioning repaired.

Many social workers distinguish between case (i.e., client) advocacy, that is, advocacy on behalf of an individual client or a single group of clients, and cause (i.e., class) advocacy, which the social worker initiates on behalf of a category of clients. Legislative advocacy is a specialized version of cause advocacy that addresses some aspect of the law or regulations.

Case Advocacy Social workers usually practice case advocacy at an agency or organizational level. For example, if your client is denied Supplemental Nutrition Assistance Program (SNAP) benefits to which they are entitled, you can advocate with the state organization that oversees implementation of SNAP services. To be an effective advocate for your client, you will need to know SNAP eligibility requirements; agency appeal policies, regulations, and power structures; and contextual variables such as how SNAP fits into the overall organization. While the desired point of entry is that of least contest and unnecessary resistance, this may not always be the most effective strategy for effective advocacy. Therefore, you can address the situation with the worker who originally denied the SNAP application and use the agency grievance process before taking other measures like involving powerful outside parties, calling the media, or organizing a protest.

Cause Advocacy More political than case advocacy, cause advocacy involves both larger numbers of people and, by definition, a cause or issue that affects them all, either because it imposes obstacles to attaining resources or because it directly deprives people of these resources. Cause advocacy can involve speaking for a group of people (not necessarily your clients and who may not be empowered to directly participate in forming the goals or the preferred methods of the advocacy effort) or equipping a group to speak for themselves and helping them navigate the system with which they are advocating.

Cause advocacy is particularly effective when you partner with other concerned organizations in a coalition, and it can spur change that positively affects many people. It is also helpful when an issue is clear and when the proposed solution will address the power imbalances that sustain injustice. For example, if your community has no adequate facilities for after-school child care, concerned agencies, places of worship, businesses, or other institutions may join to advocate for the development of such a facility. If you require funding from local public sources, your coalition of interested partners (who are well organized and empowered) will be able to advocate for child care facilities. As in case advocacy, your coalition will need complete information on the proposed change; for instance, to understand how many children the facility will serve, what those children need, how much the service is likely to cost, how likely children and their families are to participate, how you will go about getting the issue onto a funder's agenda, and how the proposed facility will benefit all stakeholders. They will also need advocacy skills.

Legislative Advocacy This form of cause advocacy is devoted to adding, changing, or eliminating legislation to benefit a large group of clients. For example, when a social worker advocates to lower the legal alcohol limit for driving a motorized vehicle from 0.08 blood alcohol content to 0.06, they engage in legislative advocacy designed to benefit a large cross-section of people—drivers and passengers.

There are many scenarios in which a large group of people would benefit from a change in legislation because nearly all policies have limitations that may present obstacles to your clients. Access to controversial resources such as family planning and abortion clinics is likely to be more constrained (e.g., by age limits or pregnancy duration) than less disputed services like food pantries.

Legislative advocacy usually requires intensive, cooperative work with one or several organizations. Initiating or collaborating in legislative advocacy is within the purview of social work practitioners at all levels of practice. It requires considerable knowledge, insight, and organization, but with careful preparation and diligence, it can produce desired results.

Thoughts About Power and Advocacy Social work advocacy frequently involves trying to make changes so resources are allocated in ways consistent with social justice; therefore, it is helpful to recall the assumptions about power that guide social work. In general, advocates recognize that those who have power do not readily relinquish that power. Power is not equally distributed, involves conflict, and is required to bring about substantial change. These points may seem harsh if you have not considered power and advocacy within such a context before. Familiarity with these concepts can prepare you to enter a political arena and can help you understand the social locations of those who are oppressed.

Case and cause advocacy are important to social work practice and strategizing about advocacy can be helpful. Exhibit 5.2 provides cautions and strategies for advocacy.

> **EXHIBIT 5.2**
>
> *Strategies Regarding Advocacy*
>
> - Consistent with our obligations to obtain clients' consent to participate, when clients are directly involved, ensure that they genuinely support your advocacy efforts, that they are, to the greatest extent possible, positioned in the center of the work in roles they choose, and that they understand the possible repercussions.
> - Be prepared with relevant knowledge (e.g., eligibility requirements, entitlement limitations, number of people in each category, history of advocacy on this topic, or legislative process).
> - Be clear and specific about your goals; a complaint about a policy is unlikely to produce change if you do not present a solution.
> - Begin with simple persuasion efforts; first assume that there is good intent, or an oversight and others will want to do the right/best thing in the situation.
> - Understand when persuasion is not working with the targeted audience, and you must progress to another approach that may involve activating other constituencies and/or approaching from other angles.
> - Assess that more intense effort prior to action: Can you be successful in making change? Can you be successful even if you do not win the policy change (e.g., more visibility, more engagement, and/or new capacity)? Are your clients still supportive? Do collaborative partners agree on the next step? Do all parties support the means as well as the ends?
> - Use carefully cultivated social work skills, including listening, empathy, clarifying, and negotiating.
> - Use collaboration to find common ground.
> - Seek supervision and consultation to process your experience.

Collaborator

Collaboration is an inherent part of the daily fulfillment of the social work mission for most social workers. In addition to using collaboration skills with clients to develop plans for change, social workers engage in collaborative relationships with other professions in different ways. For example, social workers work interprofessionally with health, social service, and legal providers to deliver client services, develop programs and policies, advocate, and research. *Interdisciplinary practice* (also referred to as *interprofessional practice* or *interprofessional collaboration, collaborative practice,* and *partnered practice*) involves professionals from different disciplines integrating their professional knowledge to work together, in a single intervention, toward a common goal. For example, professionals from different disciplines may engage in multidisciplinary practice where each provides services to an individual but not discuss the client as a group or share information in the client record. An interprofessional practice approach involves regular communication and coordination of services. For example, an interprofessional team of social workers, public health workers, and law enforcement can collaborate on a plan for helping a client address hoarding and safety issues in their home.

Social workers often work in host settings in which the primary mission is not the provision of social work services. These include health care facilities and programs, educational institutions, law enforcement or legal systems, military programs, libraries, and even financial institutions. Social workers collaborate interprofessionally in virtually every setting in which they are employed, and it is essential that social workers working in host settings understand the philosophies, professional cultures, imperatives, and language of those settings and other professions. Interprofessional collaborations, while often effective, can be complex and, sometimes, frustrating working relationships. Social workers may encounter difficulty communicating with other professionals who have their own professional "jargon"; perceived hierarchy of professional influence; and conflicting opinions on approach, roles, implementation, and outcomes related to the work.

Social workers can use their training in collaboration and negotiation with clients to prepare for becoming effective professional collaborators and to initiate partnerships that emphasize that others are committed to positive outcomes for the client. To be an effective interprofessional practitioner, social workers must be open to collaborating and communicating with other professionals, respectful of all professions involved, and striving for a trusting and safe culture (Konrad, 2020).

Social workers' knowledge and skills position us well to collaborate interprofessionally as our training prepares us to competently engage in problem-solving, conflict resolutions, mutual respect, and empathy (Konrad, 2020). Upon gaining familiarity with your collaborators' professional training, language, ethics, and culture, you can seek out common ground on which to build a professional collaboration. Strategies for enhancing your interprofessional practice competence include (Bathgate, 2016):

1. familiarizing yourself with the duties (and ethical standards/philosophies) of other professionals with whom you work.
2. recognizing and respecting the philosophy and orientation of other professions and framing your activities and documentation accordingly, avoiding social work-specific language and details not relevant to the situation.
3. maintaining a focus on being flexible, accommodating, supportive, and empowering versus an emphasis on problem-solving; and
4. appreciating and celebrating the progress and successes (no matter how small) achieved by the client and team.

There is considerable overlap among the roles described in this discussion. For example, in your role as a social work case manager in the foster care unit of your agency, you have identified that your clients and their foster families have several unmet needs. You then determine that educating the legislature regarding the needs of foster children may pave the way for a future advocacy effort. Because this blending and overlapping of roles (i.e., case manager, educator, and advocate) is common, it is important for your and the client's benefit that everything is clear. If roles are not realistically or clearly communicated, the client, social worker, and even other interested parties can become frustrated and unable to participate fully in the intervention process. While education and advocacy are often interlinked, it is important to be clear about when you are advocating for a client and when you are educating about the client.

PUTTING IT ALL TOGETHER

Thus far, this chapter has explored various aspects of social work practice in action, including interventions that support clients' strengths and their environments and the practice activities associated with social work roles. The chapter now turns to empowerment practice as a model for examining the possible points of integration for social work roles within the context of a client-centered, strengths-based practice approach.

Empowerment Practice

The social work profession has long been committed to empowering clients, but our collective understanding of empowerment and how to catalyze it is evolving. One of the early scholars of empowerment practice, Simon (1990), asserted that, in its purest sense, empowerment cannot be given to someone else because empowerment is not one person's to give to another. Empowerment resides within the individual, and the social worker can only encourage or perhaps release empowerment. Ultimately, change comes from clients themselves. Empowerment practices suggest that (Ortega & Rodriguez-Jenkins, 2021):

- Social workers are not the experts on client's lives; clients are the experts and the architects of the change they seek.
- Power is personal, social, and structural. The process of empowerment typically strives through transformation, interaction, and relationships to change a situation that has created bias and/or inequities.
- The social work role is to develop meaningful relationship to generate the transfer of knowledge and engage in problem-solving with the client.

Empowerment-focused social work connects a client's strengths, environment, and capacity for empowering action. This connection supports intervention in multiple interconnected settings and recognizes the importance of the client's sense of self. As a departure from the traditional problem-solving approach that emphasizes identifying the problem and its causes, an empowerment-focused model of social work practice can enable the client to focus on future-oriented solutions, rather than becoming discouraged and feeling victimized by their situation (De Jong & Berg, 2013). Exhibit 5.3 provides an illustrative case example of an appropriate and sensitive empowerment approach.

EXHIBIT 5.3

Thomas's Story

This story begins in a rural New England community in the 1980s. Thomas, a man of color, was born with cerebral palsy, a neurological disorder. His parents had little idea how to deal with his severe physical limitations and had three other children to rear as well. His parents cared about him and did what they could to learn ways to support him and his abilities. He received the standard medical care of the time and was sent to school with his age group, being integrated into class with his age-peers.

Early on, it was evident that Thomas's physical challenges interfered with the demonstration of his aptitude for schoolwork. He was intellectually capable and did exceedingly well in the subjects in which teachers supported him. His family did not understand, however, the ways in which Thomas's physical impairments affected his socialization or how he experienced his life or the intersectionality of being a person of color who also had a physical disability. Although Thomas had only a few friends, he attempted for several years to maintain a positive outlook, even developing an excellent sense of humor. Nevertheless, he continued to feel excluded by peers and adults alike.

COLLIDING WITH THE WORLD

Over time, Thomas became hostile with teachers because he had to prove himself repeatedly every time he entered a new grade or school. Each teacher and school administrator he encountered initially assumed he was unable to do grade-level work. One teacher questioned his very presence in the regular classroom. His pastor advised that he seek supported employment through a public vocational program. Everyone seemed to think he was unable to do, know, or even feel anything. His medical treatment included the excruciating requirement, promoted in those days, that he walks in physical therapy. No one noted or responded to Thomas's pain.

EXHIBIT 5.3

Continued

When Thomas was an adolescent, his parents sent him to a therapist to explore the reasons for his intense anger. To Thomas, this was yet another insult. His therapist told him he needed to "get the chip off his shoulder" and tend to his schoolwork as his parents did not have funds to pay for him to attend college—he would have to earn scholarships if he wanted to do more than sit in the living room until he got matched to a job he did not want.

MEETING MAURA

When Thomas needed a new wheelchair, his parents could not pay the required deductible, so he was directed by his physician to a social worker for assistance. That social worker, Maura, who worked in the primary care office of Thomas's physician, first spent time getting to know him and hearing what he had to say about the wheelchair. She helped him get funding for his new chair and continued to ask about his overall experience. He began to talk about his options regarding school, his family, his anger, and his growing sense of estrangement from the world.

Maura listened with an openness and reflexivity that showed Thomas she believed he was the expert on his experience. She heard his story, took him seriously, and helped him look at what his disability meant to him by asking him to talk, not only about his physical pain, but also about the exclusion he experienced. She helped him appreciate his resilience in the face of all he had been through. She respected his perception of his experience and did not challenge it. She asked him to articulate how he wanted his life to be different and affirmed his strong capacities. She encouraged him to reflect how he might address his goals. As time passed, Maura helped Thomas secure vocational rehabilitation funding for college and validated his by-then strong commitment to working in human services on disability issues. She also met with Thomas's family to help them understand his choices and the impact these choices would have on the family.

CHANGING DIRECTION

Thomas earned a master's degree and is in a career in which he can advocate for people with disabilities. He is a full participant in his community and in the surrounding context of his family, friends, and culture. He is still angry sometimes, but he is not fearful or alone.

Reading this (almost all) true story, you can see how Maura implemented the empowerment focus: She helped liberate Thomas's "potent self" and encouraged his interpersonal connections. She supported his understanding of his environment and the intersectionality of being a person of color and a person with a physical disability. She helped connect him to a direction in which he could address the more political aspects of his experience. Consider now the connections between Thomas's experiences and other social work perspectives:

Social justice: Maura worked diligently to expand Thomas's access to benefits, helping him find funding for education. She did not accept the status quo in which those with private resources are privileged and those without are not. To complete this role as advocate for social justice, Maura works toward reallocating educational funding for all people, not just for Thomas.

EXHIBIT 5.3

Continued

Human rights: The fact that Thomas is a person with a disability cannot be considered as a rationale for discrimination in education. Article 26 of the United Nations Universal Declaration of Human Rights states that his disability must not preclude the "full development of [his] personality" through education. The 1990 Americans with Disabilities Act also addresses issues related to access for persons with disabilities. Recognizing Thomas' human rights, Maura recognized Thomas as a person who has needs, abilities, and the right to fulfill his life as he chooses.

Strengths perspective: Maura recognized Thomas's considerable strengths, validated them, and encouraged linking the full expression of his strengths to his goals. She saw him as a whole human being with many talents to offer, not as a "victim of cerebral palsy."

Critical social construction: Maura viewed Thomas's disability as a social construction resulting from the prevailing collective meaning ascribed to it. She questioned the limitations that construction imposed, and she believed Thomas could do what he set out to do. Maura accepted that there are multiple realities and honored his experience of exclusion and oppression. Because his experience developed within the context of his social location, on which he is the expert, she made no attempt to "correct" his understanding. Her effort focused on changing his future experience so that it is more consistent with how he wants to arrange his life.

Empowerment and Roles

The concept of empowerment is applicable to each role a social worker assumes when intervening with a client. The social worker can use empowerment concepts to carry out the tasks associated with being a case manager, counselor, broker, mediator, educator, client advocate, and collaborator. Even in crises or tragedies that impact entire communities, regions, country, or globe, the social worker, working at any level of practice and using any of the strategies discussed in this chapter, can approach interventions with an empowerment perspective in mind. If you work with individuals who have experienced violence, a natural disaster, a pandemic, or other community-wide crisis, your role can be not only to meet their immediate needs by establishing measurable and attainable goals, but also to help empower them to survive, advocate for themselves or others, or change systems. As Kohli and colleagues (2010) write: "We should appreciate the strengths of individuals that help them to survive in the worst of situations and use their strengths to empower them" (p. 266). Consider the resilience and fortitude of a client who has survived a significant life event such as having contracted COVID-19 and begin the intervention at that point of strength.

A social worker can play a strong role in empowering the client to engage in self-advocacy by building on the strengths of the client and the client's self-efficacy. Activities that promote self-advocacy and empowerment include helping clients prepare, providing education and support, and accompanying them during the advocacy process.

Empowerment Practice and Different Strategies

Social workers need a repertoire of strategies to initiate and facilitate a strengths-based intervention that empowers clients. While the narrative approach does not provide specific therapeutic skills, a social worker using the narrative approach can help empower clients to construct, deconstruct, and finally reconstruct the conceptualizations (i.e., stories) that have defined their lives. The social worker's role is to help clients determine if they wish to change their perceptions by challenging and broadening their thinking about their lives. Consistent with the values of social work, this externalization of the client's concerns can strengthen the client's self-perception and promote collaboration with the social worker, enabling the client and social worker to share expertise in understanding the issues (Hall, 2016).

One such empowerment-focused strategy that social workers can use to help clients reconceive how they view their lives is **motivational interviewing (MI)**. Initially developed in the 1980s for practice with clients with addictions and/or mandated for services, MI builds on the client's strengths and right to self-determination to implement a client-directed plan for change (Miller & Rollnick, 2013). Building on the client's motivation to change, MI is transtheoretical (i.e., can be implemented across approaches) (Payne, 2020). MI has been used to intervene with a wide range of client concerns and issues, including eating disorders, medication, and treatment compliance, health and risk behaviors, and gambling, as well as being adapted successfully across diverse populations and cultures (Teater, 2020). MI can also enhance client participation in the engagement and intervention processes, particularly at the beginning of the intervention process when the client may be ambivalent about change (Teater, 2020).

Motivational interviewing is an evidence-based, person-centered "conversational journey" in which the social worker uses compassion, acceptance, and collaboration to guide clients through the change process by identifying and evoking strengths and resources (Paris & Martino, 2017, p. 71). With an emphasis on client self-determination, dignity, and worth and use of empathy and evidence-based practices, MI is consistent with social work values and ethics (Salisbury et al., 2022). To demonstrate, this strategy emphasizes a client-centered, collaborative partnership that uses such skills as listening to the client's narrative, empathizing with the client's story, and sharing responsibility for change (Salisbury et al., 2022). As the expert on their lives, clients are responsible for articulating their story and developing motivation to initiate life changes. While MI can be an effective strategy for working with behavioral change, it can also be applied in situations in which clients struggle to identify, accept, and adjust to a life event, and clarify feelings about an experience. As preparation for embarking on a change process, MI can also serve as a strategy to empower clients to begin treatment. For instance, MI is a helpful strategy for working with individuals who want to change an unhealthy behavior and they feel ambivalent and fearful about making the change. Using MI, the social worker can support the client in improving their confidence about making the change and that they are ready to make the change (Teater, 2020).

The founders of MI, Miller and Rollnick (2013) conceptualized four interrelated components underlying the perspective or "spirit" of MI: partnership, acceptance, compassion, and evocation. Quick Guides 10 and 11 detail these components, the principles of MI, and skills and strategies for integrating motivational interviewing into practice. They review change talk, evoking change, and the four processes of MI, known as OARS—Open questions, Affirmation, Reflection, and Summary. Chapter 7 will discuss how social workers can use MI with families.

In keeping with the emphasis on a strengths-based, person-centered framework, planning the intervention (i.e., change plan) involves the client

---

QUICK GUIDE 10   The Spirit and Principles of Motivational Interviewing

Motivational Interviewing Embraces the Following Concepts

1. *Partnership:* The client is an active partner in the social work relationship who brings expertise about themselves, their history, circumstances, and prior change efforts.

Acceptance: A component of the social worker–client partnership involves four areas of acceptance of the client by the social worker, including:

- *Absolute worth*—we all must be viewed as having value, but in MI, the client is respected as having value *and* the potential to grow beyond where they are, even in those situations in which their behaviors may not be perceived as having value.
- *Autonomy*—essentially the client's right to self-determination; the client has the power to make decisions about their lives and the changes they wish to pursue.
- *Accurate empathy*—the social worker's ability and willingness to view the client's world as the client views it, but not to get entrenched in it so that the helping relationship is compromised.
- *Affirmation*—ongoing commitment to identifying the client's strengths and resources.

Compassion: The social worker conveys compassion by demonstrating a caring approach as well as the willingness to work on behalf of the client to help them achieve their goals.

Evocation: With an emphasis on the client being the expert on their lives, the social worker elicits the client's expert views about themselves, including the reasons for change and strategies to achieve the change.

The principles upon which motivational interviewing is built stem from this spirit. They emphasize the social worker's ability to:

1. *Express empathy* to enhance client rapport and comfort and to decrease client resistance.
2. *Develop discrepancy* to help the client see any gaps between their value system and current behaviors.
3. *Avoid arguing with the client.*
4. *Roll with client resistance* to convey to the client that the social worker respects their apparent resistance to change and views it as normal.
5. *Support client self-efficacy* to promote the client's confidence in their ability to change behavior.

Source: Miller & Rollnick, 2013, pp. 14–21; Rosengren, 2018.

> ## QUICK GUIDE 11   Skills and Strategies for Motivational Interviewing
>
> - *Change Talk* occurs when clients make statements that encourage them to make a change in their lives (e.g., "I would like to quit smoking"). Change talk contrasts with *Sustain Talk*, statements that favor maintaining the status quo (p. 7).
> - *Evoking Change Talk* is a type of talk in which a social worker, using a person-centered approach aimed at initiating a desired change, elicits clients' wisdom and experience, including their ambivalence about change.
> - *OARS* is a mnemonic device that encompasses the four core skills social workers use to facilitate the four processes of motivational interviewing (pp. 32–34):
>   - *Open Questions* involves questions such as "How are you feeling about your goal to stop smoking?" to engage the client in expanded, reflective discussion about potential change.
>   - *Affirmation* is when the social worker makes positive statements regarding the client's intentions, strengths, efforts, resources, and courage related to the proposed change. For example, the social worker may say to the client striving to stop smoking: "I admire your commitment to living a healthier life. You are a good role model for your children."
>   - *Reflective Listening* explores the client's previous statements, clarifying and deepening their meaning. The social worker might say, "It seems you are able to maintain your smoking cessation plan well, but you struggle in times of stress, like when you lost your mother."
>   - *Summarizing* briefly recaps previous reflections, preparing the social worker and client to transition to the next phase of work. Summaries bring together the most important aspects of the conversation and aid in both the planning of the change process and the evaluation of change that has occurred. The social worker might summarize discussions with the client working on smoking cessation as follows: "We have talked about your past efforts to stop smoking, the strategies you feel worked and did not work, and your commitment to being successful this time. We have also explored the triggers that make it more challenging for you to stick to your plan. We have brainstormed some strategies you can use when you feel particularly stressed and want to revert to smoking."

making a commitment to change, activation, and taking steps along with a plan for routine follow-up on progress to determine if re-focusing is needed (Salisbury et al., 2022). To determine whether MI is an appropriate intervention strategy for a particular client, consider the following (Miller & Rollnick, 2013, p. 25):

1. Are you and your client discussing change? MI is an appropriate strategy for virtually any type of change effort but particularly helpful in working with clients who are reluctant to engage in a change effort (e.g., addiction).
2. Should you initiate a conversation about change? The client may initially present to you not asking for help with change (does not see the need and/or thinks others are forcing the change), and MI techniques can help the client to view the change issues from a broader perspective.

3 Will client changes influence client outcomes? MI strategies can be used to help clients connect their own behaviors with desired outcomes.
4 Is the client ambivalent about change? MI techniques have long been used in working with clients who are uncertain or resistant to making changes in their lives.

With similarities to the social work helping process (i.e., engagement, assessment and planning, intervention, and termination/evaluation), the process of implementing an intervention using MI encompasses four overlapping components (Paris & Martino, 2017; Salisbury et al., 2022):

- *Engaging:* building rapport to promote a mutual understanding of the client's concern and identifying the client's motivation for change.
- *Focusing:* choosing a direction for motivational enhancement, providing normative feedback, and guiding but not directing.
- *Evoking:* eliciting client's motivation and commitments for change.
- *Planning:* collaborating with the client to formulate a specific change plan.

The role of the social worker is to focus on the client and their desire to make a change. Specifically, social workers engage in MI when they listen and reflect, affirming those behaviors/activities that the client is doing well, identifying change talk, drawing out the client's motivation, wisdom, and strengths; and resisting the "righting reflex" (i.e., advice-giving, confronting, or arguing) (Miller & Rollnick, 2013, p. 324). A technique for exploring change talk is to ask the client to rate on a 1–10 scale the importance of the change, their confidence in making the change, and their readiness to make the change—discussing the feelings behind the numeric ratings are a part of the intervention process (Salisbury et al., 2022). This technique highlights the client's readiness for change and the fact that the change itself is within the client's control (Teater, 2020). As with any social work intervention, the social worker's role is not to: (1) ask too many questions as that can promote passivity; (2) appear to be the expert on the client's life and situation; (3) focus the intervention and change process before the relationship is established as it can lead to a power struggle later if the client is not committed; (4) labelling (i.e., diagnosing) as it can be stigmatizing; (5) blaming the client as that can create defensiveness; and (6) chatting with the client as it can cause distractions and dissatisfaction (Paris & Martino, 2017).

CRITICAL CONSIDERATIONS ABOUT SOCIAL WORK INTERVENTIONS WITH INDIVIDUALS

A critical component for social workers implementing the intervention phase of the planned change effort is to maintain a focus on professional behaviors and issues. In addition to gaining skills in selecting and applying theoretical frameworks and executing appropriate strategies and techniques, social workers must attend to an array of professional issues that can influence their work with clients. Regardless of the theoretical approach used in the intervention, several areas are critical to the well-being of the client and social worker, including unexpected events that can and will occur in practice, therapeutic use of self, managing transference and countertransference, professionalism, self-care, and effective use of technology. While your attention to these areas of practice begins during your social work education, you will continue to develop in each throughout your career.

Unexpected Events in Practice

If you practice effective engagement, carefully assess both the client and the environment, and plan consistent methods for acting on behalf of your clients, you might be seduced into thinking that the work will always go smoothly. This is a mistake.

In the practice world, not everything goes as planned. Because social work is so immersed in the lives of clients, social workers have limited control over their work with clients and must accept (or at least tolerate) the up-and-down nature of the work. In the world of practice, people experience illness, have accidents, change their minds, lose their jobs, become disheartened, and move. On the positive side, people also get promoted, find their strengths, find their voices, get jobs, read inspiring books, discover new friends, and develop insights. These factors and many more have the potential to interrupt, postpone, redirect, or even terminate your work together.

In some cases—for example, if a client becomes discouraged or simply loses interest—you will want to inquire about how your words or actions might have contributed to these developments. In many cases, your responsibility will be to acknowledge, honor, and explore the meaning the client ascribes to the new situation and to reconfigure your work when indicated. It will be helpful for you to *expect the unexpected*. Flexibility is one of the most critical of all social work attributes. Consider the volatile couple whom you have been helping to work toward as amicable a divorce as possible. The divorce is granted, and they come to you for help in reconciling—most likely a development you did not anticipate!

Just as you have consistently evaluated the progress of your work with your client and others involved throughout the engagement and assessment processes, you will want to periodically evaluate the direction of the intervention as well, particularly if the client has experienced substantial changes or unexpected events. Due to inertia and a tendency to continue going in one direction, it can be difficult to divert from the plan you carefully crafted, even when it no longer fits the client's situation and/or needs well. It is a good idea to check in with the client frequently during the intervention process. In that way, you can ensure that you always provide a relevant service that can become important should the client encounter a crisis.

The social worker's ability to intervene effectively in crises is contingent upon a timely response and accurate assessment. Goelitz (2021) provides guidance for the social worker intervening with clients during times of crisis, including:

1 Tune in to your own experience with crisis.
2 Recognize that crises create a loss of equilibrium caused by a stressor or trauma which trigger a sense of being out of control and helpless.
3 Facilitating the client's safety and access to resources can be a first step to restoring balance in the client's life.
4 Interventions should include:
   a an individualized, person-in-environment approach that focuses on the client's expressed needs (including safety and basic needs, stressors, coping strategies, support systems, and goals).
   b establishing connections that determine the focus of the intervention.
   c creating a safe environment for the intervention to occur.
   d processing emotions that relate to the crisis.
   e planning for support of coping strategies and steps toward goals.
   f implement steps to achieve the goals, including referrals, advocacy, and organization.
   g following up to determine client's status related to the crisis. (p. 203)

Crisis intervention can also involve the social worker and client collaborating to devise a viable plan to address the root causes of the crisis. The plan should emphasize concrete action strategies and include clear, agreed-upon steps for follow-up and maintenance.

Therapeutic Use of Self

Generally, the term "use of self" refers to the knowledge, skills, values, and personal characteristics (i.e., personality, ego, and self-concept) that social workers bring to the social work intervention at all levels of practice (Kaushik, 2017). Bringing yourself to the social work relationship is at the core of your efforts to enhance the well-being of the client. It is critical that you must know yourself to know others, so self-examination and reflection are part of your lifelong professional development (Kaushik, 2017).

"Use of self" in the social worker–client relationship occurs when the practitioner shares information about their own life with the hope that the client can relate the professional's experience to their own. For example, a social worker who has struggled with addiction themselves may reference that in their initial work with a client striving for recovery, so that the client has a foundation for believing the social worker can understand some of the challenges of sobriety. The practice is controversial as some consider that it is a violation of professional–client boundaries, suggesting that the two can relate on a social (versus professional) level or, at least, centering the professional in a way many find indefensible. Others view the time spent on the professional's life experiences as potentially distracting the worker and client from the intended work, which is to focus on the client.

Despite the concerns noted here, it is not uncommon for social workers to share personal information with clients. The social worker is ethically obligated to determine if self-disclosure is related to the client's current situation and if sharing personal experiences will be helpful in building a trusting and collaborative relationship (Kwon, 2017). As in all practice decisions, the focus must remain on clients' needs and interests. To determine if self-disclosing personal information with a client is appropriate, consider these guidelines (Israeli, 2017):

1. Self-disclosure should be kept to a minimum and only within self-imposed guidelines that include sharing, not impulsively, but with deliberation and forethought.
2. Sharing should always be appropriate to the context of the client's situation.
3. The rationale for self-disclosure should be clear and aimed at strengthening the client–worker relationship or promoting client disclosure of information.
4. Following the worker's self-disclosure, the focus should return quickly to the client (p. 72).

Inserting your own experiences into the relationship you have built with your client can be a powerful and meaningful experience for both you and your client. It can also be inappropriate and unhelpful, particularly if it takes the focus away from the client.

Managing Transference and Countertransference

When a client has a strong reaction to the social worker (typically negative in nature), the client may associate the social worker's behavior with an experience from their past. This phenomenon is known as **transference** (Barker, 2014, p. 434). Conversely, when a social worker consciously or unconsciously experiences an emotional reaction (i.e., feelings, wishes, or defensiveness) to a client, this response is defined as **countertransference** (Barker, 2014, p. 98). As a professional or a client, identifying with the other can help in establishing rapport and trust; however, over-identifying can be disruptive to the intervention and can be potentially damaging for the client, the worker, and/or their ability to engage in an effective intervention together. All client relationships should be monitored for the emergence of either of these reactions. Should you determine that either the client or you are experiencing transference or countertransference, consult with colleagues and/or your supervisor to identify an appropriate strategy for responding, which can include raising the issue with the client or referring the client to another practitioner if the situation has become unhealthy for one or both of you.

Professionalism

Maintaining professional standards and behavior is paramount to being a competent, ethical, and effective practitioner. It is part of the lifelong learning and professional development process for social workers. As noted in the 2022 CSWE *Educational Policy and Accreditation Standards*, social workers:

- Make ethical decisions by applying the standards of the National Association of Social Workers *Code of Ethics* (2021a), relevant laws and regulations, models for ethical decision-making, ethical conduct of research, and additional codes of ethics within the profession as appropriate to the context.

- Demonstrate professional behavior; appearance; and oral, written, and electronic communication.

- Manage personal and professional value conflicts and affective reactions.

- Use technology ethically and appropriately to facilitate practice outcomes.

- Use supervision and consultation to guide professional judgment and behavior (pp. 4–5).

Being a professional social worker means that you possess and demonstrate competence in applying the knowledge, skills, and values of the profession (Senger & Wiest, 2022). Within these constructs, professionalism means ensuring that you identify yourself as a social worker, act in an ethical manner with and on behalf of your client, maintain appropriate boundaries with the client, and commit to further your knowledge and skills through lifelong learning and professional development. Professionalism encompasses a commitment to anti-oppressive practice. A critical component of professionalism is to seek knowledge, skills, and values to practice with cultural and linguistic competence in working with individuals, families, groups, communities, and organizations (NASW, 2021–2023b).

Self-Care

Related directly to your ability to demonstrate professionalism is your ability to care for yourself, particularly during the phase of work in which the client and you implement the agreed-upon intervention, as this can be a stressful and challenging time. During this phase, goals and intervention plans may have to be re-negotiated, clients may question their ability to move forward, or your work may have to cease due to an unforeseen crisis. As highlighted in Chapter 4, self-care is essential to your ability to function as a competent social work professional. While effective self-care routines are unique to the individual, certain aspects of professional/personal self-care are common for social workers. These include regular and frequent monitoring of your own stress levels; ongoing use of supervision, consultation, and mentoring; diligence in adhering to your personal health and well-being regimens; and realistic expectations of your client and yourself. Social workers can benefit from practicing the same principles they promote in their work with clients.

Use of Technology

Technology is integral to the practice of social work. Professionals document client encounters and case notes in electronic formats, routinely communicate with clients and co-workers using texts and electronic messaging and deliver services through videoconferencing, avatar-based programs, and other technologies. Technology use now includes the use of social media, mobile apps, gamification, artificial intelligence, wearables, and virtual reality; social workers are not only adopters but also helping to create these applications (Griffin, 2022). While technology is well integrated into our professional lives and became an especially critical tool for delivering services during the COVID-19 pandemic, we must be cognizant of the rapid developments of the technology, the ethical and legal implications associated with its use, and the controversy that surrounds its use.

As noted in Chapter 3, the 2021 NASW *Code of Ethics* and 2017 NASW, ASWB, CSWE, & CSWA *Standards for Technology in Social Work Practice* address the ethical use of technology in the areas of disseminating information, delivering services, and communicating with clients, colleagues, and the public. The 2021 revisions to the NASW *Code of Ethics* expanded language related to the use of technology in the profession. Specifically, social workers are ethically obligated to eliminate clients' barriers to access technology; assess cultural, environmental, economic, mental and physical ability, and linguistic issues that impact client's use of technology to receive services; and become more proactive in anticipating the impact of technology on organizations and clients, future technological advances, and related policies (Cummings, 2021). Ensure that you are well versed in the profession's standards, your organization's policies and practices, and boundaries with clients. Issues of particular concern during the intervention phase of work includes client privacy and confidentiality, worker knowledge and skills in using technology, and client access to their own as well as your information (Reamer, 2018a).

A new format for service delivery is the use of texting instead of or as an adjunct to phone or in-person sessions. While texting provides privacy, flexibility, and greater access to services, communicating via text with clients requires the social worker to be trained in the use of this strategy to gain skills for asking/answering questions clearly, concisely, and without emphasis (Nesmith, 2018). For example, texting has been used to complete assessment and evaluation tools, education and support services, and initial crisis interventions.

The COVID-19 pandemic created a need for health and social service providers to pivot rapidly from in-person service delivery to virtual or telehealth delivery. Pre-pandemic, telehealth accounted for <1 percent of outpatient care; this number soared to 40 percent of visits for mental health and substance abuse treatment (Lo et al., 2022). Changes in regulations and reimbursements facilitated this rapid practice shift and may result in more permanent alternatives to traditional delivery of services. While most physical health visits have returned to in-person, mental health and substance use disorder telehealth visits remain at 36 percent with most frequent users being clients in rural areas, younger adults, and females (Lo et al., 2022). Virtual service delivery is likely here to stay, thereby obligating the social work profession to ensure that we are competently and ethically trained to deliver services in these formats. Social workers must continue to address the social justice aspect of access, need for evidence to support technology-mediated interventions, and need for regulation of online services (Sage & Singer, 2022).

SUPPORTING CLIENTS' STRENGTHS IN TERMINATION, EVALUATION, AND FOLLOW-UP

Clients may demonstrate both positive and negative feelings about the termination process. They may view termination with a sense of accomplishment, ambivalence, sadness, and/or as a loss (possibly one of many) in their lives (Fortune, 2015). Even when all participants in a relationship agree that it is time to move on, termination can be a wrenching process, often punctuated with doubts about whether the social worker has given or done enough, or wishing, in some vague way, to start over. This is a common experience that you have probably had yourself, perhaps when you left home, changed jobs, or ended a significant relationship. Endings tend to raise ambivalence: On the one hand, they may be sad, while on the other hand, they represent a kind of freedom to make a fresh start, gain new experiences, and be who you want to be.

The ends of relationships between social workers and clients often reflect these tensions. Some clients and social workers are tempted to minimize the significance of these endings; they may simply choose to "slip away." Others tend to take scrupulous notes with contact information and schedules and agree to stay in touch with the social worker. A word of caution is warranted here regarding the mode of communication chosen for maintaining contact with a client following termination. While it may be appropriate for a client to phone or email, be familiar with agency policy regarding texting and/or connecting on social media. Many people develop patterns about how they deal with endings; these usually serve to mitigate the loss one inevitably experiences at the end of any significant relationship. Just as with the earlier phases of the social work intervention, supporting client strengths is important during the final stages of your work together.

The remainder of this chapter addresses the process of ending a professional relationship with clients and the ways in which the social worker and client can continue to build on the strengths that the client brought to the relationship and developed during the intervention. It explores strategies for evaluating the practice intervention on multiple levels. Terminations that occur at the family, group, organization, or community level are unique; we will explore them in later chapters. Our discussion in this chapter emphasizes general termination and evaluation issues relevant to social work relationships with individual clients.

ENDINGS AND TERMINATION

Endings can represent a metaphorical death. It is important to recognize your responses to that, and to respect your clients' responses to it, to say goodbye to clients in an effective, positive, and professional way. Endings should be discussed openly at the outset of the social worker–client relationship and incorporated throughout the entirety of the intervention, guided by the mutually agreed-upon goals and work together.

Endings occur in social work practice in numerous ways depending on your identities and those of your client (e.g., age, gender, ethnicity, socioeconomic status, cultural experience, etc.). The social location of the work, its purpose, the agency, the perspective used, and the organizational pressures surrounding the work also have an impact on the way in which the social worker–client relationship ends. Whatever the nature of the social worker, the client, and the intervention, planning is important to bring healthy closure to the relationship.

Planning the Process: Overview of the Termination

The following termination tasks are common to a range of relationships and are consistent with ethical social work practice:

- In collaboration with the client and agency practices, negotiate the timing of the termination.
- Review the agreement for the work.
- Process successes and shortcomings.
- Develop and clarify plans for termination and maintenance of change.
- Share responses to ending.
- Practice cultural humility.

These tasks do not apply to all social work relationships, and their order need not be rigid, particularly as you strive to practice with cultural humility. Your theoretical orientation and the specifics of the practice situation (e.g., your knowledge of the client and agency policy and practice) will guide when and in what order you complete these termination tasks.

Negotiating the Timing of the Termination Because termination is a goal that social workers and clients establish at the beginning of the relationship, it should not only guide the intervention but remain a focus for discussion as you progress through the intervention. In some circumstances, you and your client can specify the number of sessions at the start of the relationship and determine the closing date during your first meeting. The same is often true of mandated arrangements or managed care situations in which the agency must adhere to prearranged stipulations regarding the length of the service provided. The prearranged guidelines are, of course, artificial proclamations that the work is done, and they are all externally imposed. Predetermined boundaries do not always coincide with the ideal timing for termination, which occurs when the social worker and client have achieved the mutually formulated goals. In some cases, clients may request additional sessions (as in task-centered models), and social workers may petition for an extended number of sessions (as in managed care).

Determining whether goals have been reached may not be apparent. Consider a client who has recently shared with their family that they are gay but is struggling with sharing this with teachers and classmates. Even when you and the client state goals in precise behavioral terms (for example, "The client will contact the school social worker to ask for support in having conversations with others"), there is no guarantee that the intervention will realize those goals. For example, your client may have unsuccessfully attempted to contact the school social worker, or they may have made contact but were unable to clearly articulate their message; in this case, achieving the stated goal did not address the real issue. If the true goal of talking with others about their sexual orientation has not been met, it is your responsibility to make a reasoned judgment that the client no longer needs your services. You and your client may not agree on the exact moment when that occurs, and in many cases, the two of you will need to negotiate the timing of and criteria for ending the professional relationship, remembering that you are each subject to your own interpretations of the situation.

There are at least three areas to consider when you negotiate the termination of a social work relationship. First, as a social worker, you are obligated to provide the client with full information about the possible nature and timing of termination from the beginning. In many circumstances, you will not have control over the timing, but in others, you can at least anticipate, if not change, the conditions. For example, a state contract or managed care restrictions may determine an end date that you think is inappropriate. In such a situation, you can prepare the client for the possibility that your appeal for more time/sessions may be denied. You may encounter similar complications if your agency is about to eliminate services or programs, your position is threatened, or you know you are leaving your position on a particular date.

Second, just as you have ongoing discussions with your client about goals, contracts, and progress, you should also discuss termination throughout your relationship. It is important to maintain dialogue with your client to determine whether your work together is helping and to consider what else might need to happen for the client to know they have met the goals. Even when the agency or your intervention plan determines the end point, ongoing discussion about termination can and should be integral to the work.

The final issue involves predetermined endings. When you and your client both know from the outset how many times you will meet, you can regularly check in with the client to reinforce your shared understanding of the point at which the work will be completed. Some clients may assume that you can or will extend the number of sessions at your discretion, and others might expect that, if they behave/perform well (especially in mandated sessions), you will "dismiss" them early. Always be as clear as possible about any limits imposed on you for the work and be as open as possible to discussing what those limits mean for your client. Even when both sides clearly understand the end date, either may still experience difficult relationship-ending dynamics.

Reviewing the Agreement for Work In the process of finishing your work together, you and your client should review your prearranged formal or informal agreement for the work. You may want to renegotiate the understanding each of you has about the agreement, as it may have changed in view of your completed work, circumstances in your lives, or changes in the agency.

Processing Successes and Shortcomings Throughout the work, you and your client should discuss and process those aspects of the work that are going well, those that miss the mark, and any approaches that are clearly heading in the wrong direction; this type of assessment should not be reserved for your last meeting. Nevertheless, a culminating summary of successes and areas for continued work provides valuable perspective on the experience as a whole and insight into the client's view of the work. In fact, you may consider framing a termination as a "graduation," as the term imparts a sense of achievement for which the client may feel pride and satisfaction. Sometimes, for example, you or your client may find that, in retrospect, you now associate with personal growth an experience that seemed difficult at the time.

At this point in the social work relationship, it is not uncommon for clients to indicate that they have not made as much progress as they want to make, or you believe they have. Clients may point to various criteria to demonstrate their shortcomings. They may feel that ending the work at this point represents a sort of abandonment and may raise the possibility that it would be premature and possibly harmful to terminate services. On the other hand, some clients may express these doubts to convey a lack of confidence in their ability or readiness to make their way independently. One effective way to address such dynamics is to be transparent about the process and to engage the client in a detailed discussion of the issues throughout the relationship. Whether you offer to continue to work with a client or not is a matter of your professional judgment, your supervisor's judgment, and other agency or funding constraints. Funding-related terminations that occur prior to the actual achievement of client goals can create potential ethical dilemmas but social workers are obligated to provide support and/or referrals for clients in these situations.

Some clients, anticipating the end of the working relationship, will threaten to leave the relationship early. This "I'll fire you before you fire me" response, sometimes called *flight*, may minimize a client's sense of abandonment. In a case like this, make every effort to engage the client in the process for at least one more session/meeting in which you can address the end of the relationship and strive for closure. While the idea of urging a client to meet one final time may seem counter to taking your cues from the client, a positive ending process sometimes results in the most personal growth for clients who pointedly (and physically) avoid the ending steps in the work.

Some clients may identify shortcomings in your work. When you ask for ideas about those aspects of the intervention that did not unfold as you or the client had hoped or expected, you must be truly open to receiving a critical answer. An account of your shortcomings or those of the process itself may surprise you, especially if the client has not expressed any dissatisfaction along the way. Although it can be difficult to hear critical comments, you can choose to learn from them and remain open to the message your client is attempting to impart to you.

> Recall the example of Maria, the client who struggled to locate housing. Perhaps at the time she found challenging your suggestion that she was ready to meet with the landlord on her own. As your work together progressed, however, she may have come to see your suggestion as a useful push that helped her recognize her strengths. From an empowerment perspective, your client's success suggests her ability to act on her own needs. She no longer views herself as a victim but instead sees herself as someone who has defied power imbalances to successfully reach her goals.

Developing and Clarifying Plans for Termination and Maintenance of Change Sometimes the work is clearly finished, and the client is ready to move ahead without further assistance. Other times, you may determine that the best course of action is to refer a client to a different type of service or to transfer a client to another social worker, either in your agency or in a different agency. Suppose that, throughout your practicum, you have worked with a client named Riley. As the month of May and your graduation nears, you realize that Riley is not likely to complete the work they had hoped to before you leave your position. In negotiation with Riley, you will need to reassess their progress, where they want to go, and through what arrangement they are mostly likely to continue their work effectively. You can help them clarify their options and assess their own needs at termination. Unless the evaluation indicates that the work is substantially complete, most organizations have mechanisms in place to transition clients to other workers. After you terminate your working relationship, it is possible that Riley will receive no further services. They may experience this independence as a setback, or it may promote their growth. Even if there is no plan for the client to transition to another worker, it is important to provide the client with information on the process for contacting the agency to discuss concerns and possibly even requesting a resumption of services.

When you decide to refer a client to another agency, you assume the role of broker. Fulfill this responsibility with great care; regardless of your experience, your skill level, or the success of your work with the client, your inappropriate or ill-conceived referral can undo client gains. Supervisory meetings are a helpful time to discuss the ethical implications of referring clients, particularly those you may not feel competent to help. Referring a client because you do not want to work with them or do not agree with them is inconsistent with our profession's ethical commitments to clients.

A client who is ready to end services needs a plan to maintain gains and/or continue growth without your support. Some clients may find it difficult outside the client–worker relationship to maintain changes without some way to reinforce them. You can help clients consider strategies for addressing future stresses or events. You can also encourage clients to identify a support network within their community before ending the work or direct clients to other community resources. Suppose that you and Riley identify formal (e.g., agencies) and informal (e.g., individuals) resources that will be available following the termination of your relationship. At termination, most clients will return to or continue to live in the environment in which their struggles arose. Having a strategy to cope with those environments can be critical to their ability to maintain gains; therefore, you might suggest that, once your work together is terminated, Riley can "rehearse" a response to potential situations that may arise.

Sharing Responses to Endings Identifying and articulating feelings about termination may be the most sensitive dimension of ending the work. You will need to anticipate, to the extent that you can, the ways in which your client may respond to termination and those issues that will require attention. Many clients have endured a series of difficult endings in their lives. For example, clients may have endured painful breakups or loss from death of those close to them, or they may have been removed from abusive homes, been abandoned by others, or witnessed violence that resulted in death or separation. Clients living in poverty and with social exclusion may have experienced turbulence in their living situation and abrupt disconnection from others, such as with the experience of eviction. If ending well turns out to be the most positive aspect of your work together, that, in and of itself, will be work well done, as it could provide your client with a model of a healthy ending to a relationship. Clients will often thank you for helping them through a difficult time in their lives. Should clients express gratitude for your helping them, you can remind them that they are the ones who did the actual work—your role was to support them in the change process.

Social workers, too, may have experienced chaotic, sometimes traumatic, disruptions. In termination, many social workers struggle as much as or more than clients. Many new social workers are surprised to realize how attached they have become to a client and find themselves unprepared to respond appropriately with objective emotional distance. Reactions may include self-critique, possible regret, and a range of other confusing emotions. These understandable reactions are issues to discuss in supervision. To facilitate a professional approach, the social worker should keep in mind that the purpose of the relationship is to promote the client's—and not the social worker's—well-being.

When you discuss feelings about termination, let your clients know about your own ambivalence: express your own sadness about ending the relationship, that you have enjoyed knowing them, and that you are confident they will meet their own needs effectively in the future. It is generally inappropriate to express feelings of loss so acute that clients feel they must help you cope, just as it is inappropriate to continue the relationship beyond whatever follow-up arrangements you might make without initiating a new process. Utilizing colleagues and/or supervisors to process your feelings about terminations can be an important part of your professional development and self-care. As a new social worker, seeking out the opportunity to debrief your emotional responses with an experienced colleague allows you to process and manage your emotions about the client, your work, and the termination process.

Exhibit 5.4 depicts two distinct termination-related exchanges between Virginia Stone and her social worker as they move toward ending their working relationship.

Over the course of a career, many client situations challenge these guidelines for termination. Some situations may have the potential to become dual relationships when both a professional and personal relationship exist. For example, a social worker working in a rural community would be in a dual relationship if they work with the client in a social work capacity and purchase real estate from the client. They may also be members of the same

---

EXHIBIT 5.4

The Dialogue of Termination

These two examples of an exchange between Virginia Stone (www.routledgesw.com/interactive-cases/) and her social worker demonstrate the power of an effective termination process.

Virginia and her social worker have been working on several challenging issues, including housing, caregiving, grief, and loss. Due to the number and intensity of the issues, their relationship has spanned more than a year. There are many ways to handle terminations. Which of these two examples would you choose?

Termination Option #1	Termination Option #2
Social Worker: *Virginia, as we discussed the last time we met, today will be our final meeting. I want to take this opportunity to review our progress.*	Social Worker: *Virginia, I think today should be our final meeting. You will recall that we discussed at our first meeting that we would end our work at some point. I feel we are at that point now. What do you think of this idea?*
Virginia: *I've been thinking a lot about this since last time and I feel good about things.*	
Social Worker: *Let's look at each of the items in the contract we developed early in our time together.*	Virginia: *What do you mean? I didn't know we had to stop. Did I do something wrong?*
Before we get started looking over the list, I want to let you know that I have enjoyed working with you and seeing you make such positive changes in your life. I will miss our meetings. I also want you to know that you can feel free to contact me if any further needs arise in the future. Please phone me if you would like to talk or schedule an appointment.	Social Worker: *No, you haven't done anything wrong. I'm sorry this feels abrupt to you. I just decided that we have accomplished as much as we are probably going to. Let's do a quick recap. I think that will help you see what I mean. If you still have concerns about ending our work right now, we can talk about possible options we might pursue.*

religious organization or have children in the same school. The boundaries in such situations are less than clear. In situations like these in which no simple rule is adequate, the social worker can seek dialogue with supervisors and peers to resolve issues.

When dual relationships are unavoidable, it is always the social worker's responsibility to avoid other harm to the client. Consult the NASW *Code of Ethics* (2021a) in any situation in which you are uncertain about the ethical implications of a relationship. Technology has expanded options for service delivery in these situations. For example, the social worker could refer the client to a social worker in another community who could work with the client via videoconferencing, texting, or phone.

Respecting Cultural Humility As in all aspects of the work, the social worker must incorporate cultural diversity into the termination process to ensure that it is culturally appropriate for the client (Fortune, 2015). For example, if a client lives in a culture with tightly woven informal ties, the client may view the formal aspects of ending the work and cutting off the relationship as a reflection of your annoyance or rejection. The social worker should address from the outset of the intervention that the goal is for the client to achieve their goals and the relationship to end.

Some clients may have difficulty speaking about their emotions because their cultural orientation encourages a restrained and private approach to sentiment. In such cases, it may be productive to emphasize how the client's being part of a community can help to consolidate their gains. It is equally important to discuss anticipated challenges and responses for those clients who may not live in a supportive community. In some situations, a client may bring you a gift, a gesture that may represent a more comfortable way to express feelings, reflect celebration, and offer a suitable token of closure. In others, you may prefer to maintain a more formal, business-like relationship. Note that your ability to accept gifts, no matter how small, is dependent on the policy of your organization and the ethical need to avoid any dual relationship with the potential to harm the client. As you plan for termination, consider these reflective questions about the experience (Sellon & Lassman, 2022):

1) How well did the intervention work for the client?
2) Does the intervention perpetuate the inclusion of privileged groups or exclusion of oppressed groups?
3) What knowledge and skills did they gain?
4) What knowledge and skills did I gain?
5) How well did I check my own biases? Where did I struggle? (p. 308)

CRITICAL CONSIDERATIONS ABOUT TERMINATION AND ENDINGS

The termination processes discussed thus far assume conditions in which the ending is planned. When, as often happens, endings are unplanned and not under your control, your role is to negotiate the unexpected. Sometimes, clients leave the relationship before you expect. Clients may terminate a relationship early because of a life-changing event or because they do not feel the relationship has been fully established or productive. For example, if clients are not clear about expectations or do not share the social worker's understanding of the purpose of the work, they may feel that the meetings lack focus and direction. Social workers may identify outcome goals that clients may not find relevant (even when clients "agree" to them). If clients are unclear about the end point of the work, they may not remain engaged in the process. In such cases, the work may continue, but the client may grow discouraged.

There are multiple reasons clients might prematurely end the work, all of which present the social worker with dilemmas regarding the appropriate response and its meaning to the client. If the reason for the premature ending is a result of the client withdrawing, the most useful strategy is to make low-pressure contact, if possible, and to encourage the client to return to the work, if only to end it in a more purposeful way. This approach conveys respect for the integrity of the work while leaving the client able to determine whether the work will resume. You can use this contact to explore the dynamics of the relationship, which may provide important information to inform your future work.

In institutional settings, your work with clients may be prematurely terminated when the client is transferred to another unit or service. In this case, you may want to petition your supervisor for a single meeting to reconnect with your client, if only briefly, to review the work and acknowledge the shift in care/services. Although institutions tend to organize themselves in terms that meet the staff's, rather than clients', needs, make an effort to prioritize the latter whenever you can. When you have made every reasonable effort and your client does not respond, respect the manner of ending they have chosen. At that point, it is the client's choice, and by humbly understanding the limits of your influence on the client, you respect their self-determination.

At least once in your career, it is likely that you will terminate a client relationship before the work is completed, when you leave an organization. When the social work relationship ending is worker-initiated, the social worker should make every effort to ensure that the client does not perceive abandonment if they are still in need of your help (NASW, 2021a). In these situations, it is important to notify the client as soon as possible and protect their confidentiality (NASW, 2021a).

While following up with clients can be an important part of the termination process for clients and social workers as it provides information regarding client status, progress, and sustainability of change, it may or may not be an option for social workers. Agency policy and the client's situation will determine whether having contact with the client after termination is appropriate; therefore, during the termination process, you should clearly communicate your ability and intentions regarding follow-up to the client.

FORMAL EVALUATIONS

Many practitioners feel anxious at the mention of the need to evaluate their practice. However, with evaluation tied to client outcomes, funding, and your own professional development, most social workers come to appreciate the importance of evaluating practice. Evaluation can provide feedback regarding goal achievement, the utility of a particular method, and the client's experience of the work. Evaluation can be broadly focused, behaviorally directed, and process-oriented. The evaluation process can also reflect on individual progress, group development, and changes in power structures. In short, evaluation is a useful tool for practitioner development, not a threat. Like the assessment and intervention processes, evaluation should center on the client's goals and changes that occur during the intervention (Thyer, 2021).

Evaluation Priorities and Guidelines

While the NASW *Code of Ethics* (2021a) charges social workers to monitor and evaluate practice interventions, the profession has long debated which evaluative strategies are relevant to and most appropriate for social work practice. As we discussed in Chapter 4, many scholars maintain that social work practice should be informed by empirical, evidenced-based practice. Consistent with social work approaches such as systems theory, person-in-environment, and the strengths perspective, evaluating practice aids in determining the effectiveness of the social work intervention (Friedman & Olivera, 2022). Evaluative tools can measure clients served, specific goals identified and achieved, functionality, diagnoses, and impact of the intervention for short, intermediate, and long-term timeframes (Friedman & Olivera, 2022).

Though social work ethics mandates that the provision of service obligations take precedence over data collection and evaluation, evaluative strategies are an important component of effective practice. It can serve to empower both the client and the social worker as you reflect together on progress. Imagine how empowering it can be for a client to realize they now have experience of successfully overcoming a years-long challenge or developing coping strategies for an unexpected life change. In addition to evaluation being important to the client and the social worker, the evaluation of practice has become an important component of agencies' ability to secure and maintain funding for services. Virtually all public and private funding entities require service providers to evaluate practice interventions and outcomes using standardized and multiple forms of data collection. Dudley (2020) offers a three-stage approach to evaluation that includes (Dudley, 2020):

1 Planning—prior to completing the evaluation, the social worker characterizes the client and their needs, and with the client plans the intervention and outline the outcomes to be achieved.
2 Implementation—evaluations can be completed throughout the intervention phase to monitor progress.

3 Outcomes—following the completion of the intervention, the social worker and client can engage in an evaluation to determine if the desired outcomes were achieved.

While evaluation processes and tools differ by field of practice and setting, there are similarities that apply to across evaluations. Dudley (2020) offers that all evaluations should:

1 Serve as a source of accountability to the client and organization.
2 Use scientific research methods.
3 Be open to stakeholders.
4 Address contextual issues within the agency and the environment.
5 Abide by a profession-specific ethical code.
6 Engage critical thinking (p. 11).

As you plan for monitoring your client's progress toward the mutually agreed-upon goals and evaluating your work together, it is critical that the evaluation accurately captures the client's experience as well as provides insight into the viability of the intervention. The following questions can serve to guide the evaluative process (Dudley, 2020):

1 Is the intervention effective in helping clients?
2 Does the intervention efficiently use all available resources?
3 Is the intervention being implemented at a high level of quality?
4 Is there evidence of substantial effort by staff members and others in implementing the intervention to maintain the fidelity of the intervention?
5 Is the intervention sufficiently relevant to the needs of the clients and the social problems confronting them? (p. 10)

The following sections present two major methods of evaluation: empirical design processes and reflective assessment. These two methods serve complementary purposes. Together, they contribute to evidence-based practice while validating the contemplative, postmodern social worker's inclination to critique traditional implementation and evaluation processes through focused critical reflection.

Quantitative and Empirical Processes: Evidence-Based Practice

As a core component of a social work practice intervention, quantitative and empirical evaluation processes have two approaches in common: single-subject design and goal attainment scaling. Regardless of the evaluation method you use, the process should include practical, reliable, inexpensive, and valid outcome measures that are administered at minimum two separate times (Thyer, 2021, p. 390).

Single-Subject Design Single-subject designs can be used with any theoretically guided intervention. A single-subject design (SSD) evaluation involves collecting client-specific data over a specified period of time (Thyer, 2021). Individualized to the identified goals established during the assessment and planning process, an SSD evaluation includes these components (Thyer, 2021):

1 Identify the behavior/activity to be addressed during the intervention.
2 Use evidence-based assessment tools at specified points in time (minimum of two times and ideally three times)—baseline (before the intervention begins), during the intervention (mid-way), and after the completion of the intervention.
3 Analyze the data and create a visual depiction of change on a chart or graph.

Flexible and generally easy to use, SSD provides a strategy for measuring sensitive changes before, during, and after the intervention (Thyer, 2021). Usually, the social worker and client measure an action, feeling, or behavior multiple times over the course of their work together.

> *Returning to the case of Maria, she shared with you that once she is settled in her new apartment, she would like to start a walking program to get exercise and familiarize herself with her new community. The two of you could use an SSD approach to chart and monitor her progress. The visual depiction of her activity could serve as the basis for discussion, revising the intervention plan, and evaluating Maria's progress.*

Conversely, you could use one intervention with a series of clients. Consider that you are working with a group of clients who want to stop smoking. Utilizing an SSD approach in which you track the clients individually and compile the results may help you to identify those strategies that are more effective than others, possible time frames for interventions, and events that trigger relapses.

To administer this design effectively, the client and social worker meet over a period to allow for repeated measurements. The social worker and client first agree on the behavior, attitude, or belief they will measure and how they will measure it. As in developing any intervention plans, the behavior or behaviors selected should be client-centered and reflect the client's goals of the work. SSD evaluations do not focus on concerns identified by the social worker (e.g., how often the client arrives on time) but on the client's goals.

Consistent with the person-in-environment framework, you can collect data through direct observation, reports from the clients and/or family, friend, or caregiver, and/or objective assessments (Thyer, 2021). You can measure the frequency (number) of occurrences or use a standardized measurement tool that yields a numerical result (e.g., number of occurrences or intensity scaling). You and the client should establish a relatively consistent schedule for taking measurements throughout the course of the evaluation. For example, if you want to monitor the number of new social contacts your client initiates, consider the accumulated frequency of contacts over a standard period (e.g., every two weeks).

In most cases, the phases of your evaluation will include a baseline, which is the rate at which or number of times the behavior occurred before the client came to you (for example, the number of social contacts per day); intervention (strategies to promote smoking cessation, including behavioral and/or pharmaceutical); maintenance, or the period of stabilizing client gains (tallying smoke-free days or instances of relapse); and follow-up (checking-in period). All these measures, once completed, can be charted to depict a visual pattern. If you and your client cannot establish a baseline because your client needs immediate intervention, you can still plot improvements as they occur during the intervention (for example, at one-week or one-month intervals).

If you can establish a baseline prior to the intervention, your measurements can show the differences before, during, and after the intervention. This suggests that the improvement is a result of your work together as it assumes that, without your intervention, the baseline measurement would remain unchanged. As assumptions regarding causation of change are inherently embedded in evaluation processes, social workers can critically test those assumptions by selecting designs that can control for threats to validity of the findings. It is important to consider the potential influences of other factors in the client's life that may also contribute to the observed changes. In the example of smoking cessation, it is possible that the client could stop smoking without your intervention. However, conducting and reflecting on an SSD evaluation can nonetheless aid the client in gaining insight into the process of behavior change. If the intervention is interrupted (e.g., one of you goes on vacation), reducing the frequency of your client's positive actions, you can see if improvement resumes when your work starts again. If it does, that strengthens the connection between your work and your client's improvement, resulting in lasting changes. However, such interruptions may not be in the client's best interests, and you should never disrupt the course of the work simply to demonstrate its success. Exhibit 5.5 provides an example of an SSD graph.

Goal Attainment Scaling Suitable for use in a variety of settings, goal attainment scaling (GAS) is a standardized framework that social workers can customize to fit individual client-initiated goals. This approach examines the extent to which the client's goals were met during the intervention (Dudley, 2020). GAS is a helpful tool for ongoing assessment and monitoring as it can measure different levels of progress, typically from most positive to least positive (Zhang & Franklin, 2021). Using a five-point scale indicating least to most favorable outcomes, the social worker and client complete the scale together to review progress/success for at least two or more of the client's goals and plan for the future (Dudley, 2020). The following depicts the scaling process (Dudley, 2020, p. 241):

−2 Most unfavorable outcome thought likely
−1 Less success than expected

EXHIBIT 5.5

Simple Single-Subject Design

This graph is an example of the single-subject design model. From the graph you can see that, in the baseline period before the work began, the client initiated three, then two, and then no new social contacts at two-week intervals. During the weeks of service, those numbers increased from two to seven, with a setback at week eight. After the work ended, the client initiated seven, then five, then six, and then seven new contacts. This shows improvement from the baseline period.

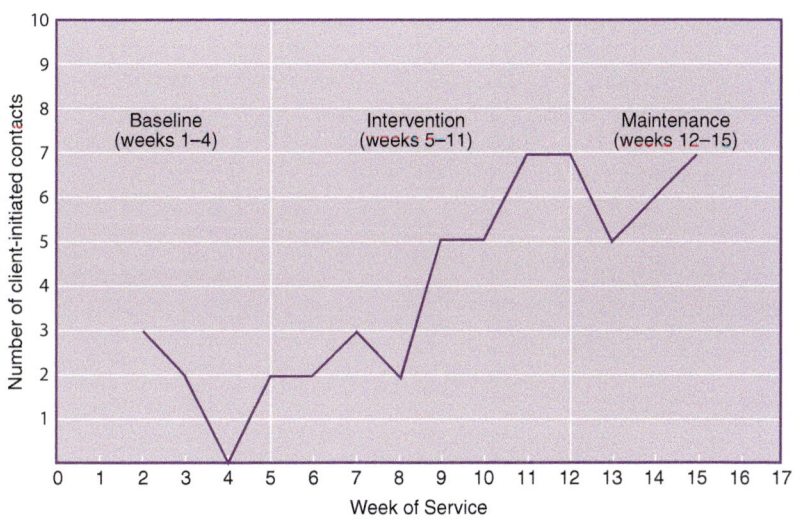

0 Expected level of success
+1 More success than expected
+2 Most favorable outcome (unlikely but still plausible)

Using this model, the social worker and client describe in a few words the client's condition or status for each goal before the intervention (the baseline). These descriptions serve as behavioral anchors to set, monitor, and measure goals, so they must be clear and not overlapping (Lewis et al., 2017). They indicate what the baseline or deteriorated condition or status might look like at the lowest point (−2). Finally, the social worker and client describe the best possible scenario (+2), a very good scenario (+1), and an expected scenario (0). For example, if your client's goals include attending parenting classes as part of a plan to regain custody of their children, you may agree to use the status descriptions in the chart in Quick Guide 12. The chart also provides status descriptions for two additional goals: attending GED (general educational development) classes and maintaining a clean apartment.

Following this process, you and the client can measure goal achievement more precisely by assigning a relative weight to each goal, reflecting its importance in the individual case situation, although use caution, as all goals have equal significance. As you can see in Quick Guide 12, based on this client's ultimate objective, the individual weight is 75 for attending parenting classes, 15 for maintaining a clean apartment, and 10 for attending GED classes, for a

QUICK GUIDE 12 Goal Attainment Scaling

Client:

Key: ✓ = Beginning level   x = Ending level

Attainment Grade	Task 1: Attend parenting classes	Task 2: Attend GED classes	Task 3: Keep apartment clean
−2 Least expected success	✓ No attendance at parenting classes	No attendance at GED classes	✓ No satisfactory ratings for cleanliness
−1 Less than expected success	Attend less than 50% of the time	✓ Attend less than 40% of the time	Receive satisfactory ratings less than 60% of the time
0 Expected level of success	Attend 50%–75% of the time	Attend 40%–60% of the time	Receive satisfactory ratings 60%–80% of the time
+1 More than expected success	x Attend 76%–95% of the time	Attend 61%–85% of the time	Receive satisfactory ratings 81%–95% of the time
+2 Most expected success	Attend 96%–100% of the time	x Attend 86%–100% of the time	x Receive satisfactory ratings 96%–100% of the time

Summary	Task 1	Task 2	Task 3	Total
Percent of goal	75%	10%	15%	100%
Change in score	3	3	4	
Total score	84	11	30	125
Possible total score	112	15	30	157
Percent of goal attained	75%	75%	100%	79%

total of 100. To track a client's progress, place a check mark in the cell that best describes the client's status at the start of the social work relationship (baseline) and an X in the cell that best describes the client's status at the end of that relationship (outcome). Then calculate the weighted change score by subtracting the start score from the end score and multiplying the difference by the weight.

Next, compute the percentage of possible change for each scaled goal. To calculate this percentage, determine the highest possible mark on the scale and divide it into the actual weighted change score. Finally, calculate an overall score by adding all the possible scores for all the goals and dividing that number into the sum of the actual weighted change scores. Although this procedure may seem daunting and overly empirical, it becomes intuitive with practice. You may want to gain familiarity with this evaluative strategy by using a change that you have experienced personally (e.g., a grade you were trying to achieve in a class).

Originally developed for use with individual clients, GAS is well suited to a range of social work interventions, including child and adult mental health and work with families and organizations. GAS can also be applied into specific intervention methods (e.g., motivational interviewing) (Lewis et al., 2017).

Other Forms of Evaluation   There are other quantitative measurement scales and other methods of attaining evaluative data that are not always quantitative (empirically based) but may be qualitative (narratively based). The latter include instruments such as client satisfaction scales or client evaluations of the agency, the social worker, or both. Although these tools are often considered highly subjective and not particularly rigorous, they frequently provide the social worker and agency with valuable information about the client's experience. While they may yield subjective perceptions of the social worker or agency, they may not yield specific outcome-based information about the client's experience with change.

Postmodern Views of Evaluation   In the world of managed care and increasing calls for evidence-based accountability, effective social workers must understand how to document, evaluate, and account for the usefulness of their efforts. To make an informed choice from among many evaluative methods, you should know the shortcomings and criticisms of each. Critics charge that many evaluative models exclude the richer, nuanced contributions of the less quantifiable aspects of client situations (e.g., those aspects related to the social worker–client relationship), as well as qualitative research, and that they overshadow ethnographic forms of evaluation that explore cultural phenomena and ultimately question the assumptions of the everyday world.

Practitioners who use quantitative evaluation methods recognize they are based on expectation, researcher bias, and a political agenda that some social workers find unhelpful. As an anti-oppressive practitioner, be aware of the potential oppressiveness of an evaluation process, particularly in terms of the purpose it serves (i.e., does it benefit the worker and agency while it does not serve the client's interest?). Even when workers must demonstrate the value of their work through empirical evaluations to accommodate their organizations and/or funders, they cannot afford to de-emphasize the possible vulnerabilities and opportunities for error in the evaluations themselves. It may be in these situations that social workers are most unlikely to feel that evaluation is helpful. In this case, it is helpful for social workers to possess a form of bilingualism—that is, you will need to speak the language of institutional demands while remaining alert to and keeping up with critiques of those demands. For example, it is important to separate the outcomes of the client intervention from the client's feelings about the agency. In this case, the client may have achieved the established goals but have negative feedback about the agency or even you. The opposite can also occur—clients do not accomplish the desired goals but feel they had a positive experience with the agency and/or you. Evaluations must therefore be framed as an evaluation of the intervention and the worker, not of the client. Evaluations must incorporate clients' perspectives and priorities, even if or when those are not aligned with the emphases improved by the accountability structures.

Social workers who find these empirical methods mechanical or lacking in substance may want to examine their work on other levels. Although support for quantitative evidence-based practice is strong and becoming the standard in the profession, social workers are not restricted to these evaluative strategies. Social workers can also reflect on their practice, as discussed next.

Qualitative and Reflective Processes

We now turn our attention to other strategies for evaluating social work practice, including case studies, explorations of compatibility with theoretical perspectives, and assessments of relationship quality. These methods are not meant to compete with empirical processes but, rather, can be combined with them to create a well-rounded evaluation.

With any of these methods, many questions about the client's experience and outcomes could be asked; we suggest some here. Whichever method you choose, you should focus your inquiry on a specific set of outcomes. If you want to gain an additional perspective on a case, consider engaging your supervisor as a second reader in a case study (discussed next) or your peers in a group conversation to explore issues. With this information, you can reflect on and expand your options for intervention and evaluation. Examining specific issues can also help focus ongoing staff meetings and professional development activities. Available technology can also enrich the data you gather about your practice. Meetings can be audio or video-recorded, which allows you to review and reflect on the content later.

Case Studies Like single-system designs, case studies involve intensive analysis of one individual, group, or family and depend on accurate, careful, and detailed record-keeping. A case study typically spans the course of the work. The case study is compiled only after the full planned change effort has been completed and you have ample information to evaluate progress and outcomes. Case studies do not generate empirical data from planned comparisons. Instead, they give an account of the client's situation while working with you. The case study is a helpful tool in assessing different areas of the intervention as well as one specific area that merits deeper examination (e.g., impact of an abusive childhood on your client's adult functioning) (Ballan & Freyer, 2021). While space prohibits the presentation of a complete case study here, we encourage you to review the interactive cases for the

Sanchez and Stone families or for Carla Washburn, which are available at www.routledgesw.com/interactive-cases/. As you review the cases and complete the interactive assignments, you can document your reactions and plans.

You can use a case study for reflection. For example, in reviewing the initial contact, you might ask if your sensitivity matched the client's need for validation, consider other ways you could have articulated your purpose, or reflect on how your work might have progressed had you taken another tack. Perhaps you thought you expressed agency requirements clearly, but looking back on the records, you can see where your language may have been confusing. How might the work have gone differently if those requirements had been clear to the client? There are many potentially helpful ways you can reflect on the work. A record of your observations, what you thought about the work, and what the client said can provide material for later analysis. When you review your experiences and those of your client using case studies, you often come to appreciate how you have grown as a professional.

The analysis and interpretation of the case notes is key to the case study evaluative process. Ballan and Freyer (2021) offer these guidelines: (1) read the case notes with a goal of gaining insight; (2) begin to interpret the case notes to identify themes and patterns; and (3) complete a cycle of immersion to continue to gain insights for use in your work with clients.

To compile a case study, social workers must have excellent communication and documentation skills. The documentation guidelines discussed in Chapter 4 are essential throughout the intervention, termination, and evaluation phases to ensure both client and social worker have well-organized, articulate social work records. Quick Guide 13 provides guiding principles for clinically focused practice writing, and Quick Guide 14 presents a sample case summary. With the integration of standardized forms and electronic records, case summaries may be created using an online form, but the data gathered and compiled continues to include key items of information related to the client's situation, including the identified need for services, assessment and planning, actions taken, and termination and evaluation notes. Ensure that the online tools protect the client's information.

QUICK GUIDE 13 Guiding Principles for Clinical Writing

- Social work values and ethics should guide your writing. Your commitment to clients' self-determination, strengths, empowerment, and cultural competence must be ever present as you write about clients in any form of documentation, including case records, case studies, letters, emails, and court reports.
- In keeping with your commitment to ethical practice, use words that do not label, denigrate, depersonalize, stereotype, or marginalize clients (e.g., never use words like "abusive parent," or "welfare mother"). Refer to your client using their preferred pronouns.

QUICK GUIDE 13 Continued

- Extend the strengths perspective into your documentation, using strengths-focused language to give "voice" to the client's narrative story (e.g., "In sharing her experiences of surviving a sexual assault, Mary focused on the coping strategies she used to regain her sense of safety and security.").
- Maintain person-centered practice standards to emphasize the client's rights to confidentiality and self-determination. Operationally, respectful writing only includes information that is relevant to the current situation. If you believe collateral sources can benefit from additional information, consider an alternative form of communication (e.g., case conference, telephone contact, etc.) and secure a detailed signed release from the client.
- Understand and follow agency and state requirements regarding what client information you may communicate, including health or disability status and compliance with the Health Insurance Portability and Accountability Act (HIPAA).
- Keep in mind those individuals and groups who may have access to the documents you create, including clients and their families, co-workers, court systems, or even media outlets, and ensure that your writing is fact-based, and that any opinion-based content is clearly labeled as such.

Source: Adapted from Sormanti, 2012, pp. 129–131

Resources to Support Practice-Related Writing
American Psychological Association. (2019). *Publication Manual of the American Psychological Association* (7th ed). Washington, DC: American Psychological Association.
Green, W., & Simon, B. L. (2012). *The Columbia Guide to Social Work Writing*. New York: Columbia University Press.
Purdue Online Writing Lab (OWL). https://owl.english.purdue.edu/owl/section/2/10/
Weisman, D., & Zornado, J. L. (2018). *Professional Writing for Social Work Practice* (2nd ed.). New York: Springer Publishing Company.

QUICK GUIDE 14 Creating a Case Summary

Effective and accurate documentation is essential for social work practice. While formats and content are agency-specific, the following example provides an abbreviated presentation of a typical case summary. For this example, let us return to Jasmine Johnson, a client discussed in Chapters 3 and 4.

Opening Summary
Jasmine is a 33-year-old BIPOC woman and a single parent to a 14-year-old son, Devon. Jasmine requested services to help her improve her relationship with her son and to find better strategies for disciplining him. She admits to having hit him when she believed he was being disrespectful to her but denies any current or past abuse or neglect.

Assessment
Family history: Jasmine was married at age 18 and gave birth to Devon when she was 19 years old. She and Devon's father divorced two years ago when Devon, then 12, was

starting middle school. Jasmine was awarded sole custody of her son and monthly child support, but the payments are sporadic. To save money, Jasmine and Devon moved out of their home and now live in a one-bedroom apartment across town where Devon sleeps on the foldout couch in the living room. The move required Devon to attend a new school.

Employment and financial situation: Jasmine has worked in the housekeeping department of a large hospital for the past 11 years. The hospital provides comprehensive benefits (e.g., health insurance, retirement, and educational support), but her salary is low, and she struggles to pay all her bills each month.

Social support and resources: Jasmine did not have any family living in the community where she moved with her then-husband for his job. Her ex-husband remains in the area but has remarried and is expecting a new child. He seems to have little time for Devon but does see him occasionally, usually when Jasmine contacts him and asks him to see his son.

Jasmine's supports in the community now include a close-knit group of co-workers, a neighbor, and members of her church. Her co-workers provide emotional support and often invite the Johnsons for holidays. The neighbor frequently "cooks too much food" and brings dishes over for Jasmine and Devon. Her church friends have provided spiritual support, which Jasmine finds comforting.

Jasmine and Devon have received support through the church's Christmas adopt-a-family program, the youth programs, and the food and clothing pantry. Devon is eligible for the breakfast and lunch program at his school.

Prioritized concerns: Jasmine's primary concern is her relationship with her son. While she wishes that he did not speak disrespectfully to her or violate the rules she has established, she recognizes that he is a teenage boy and that the divorce, the move to a smaller apartment and a new school, and the lack of support from and contact with his father has turned his life upside down. She wants to improve her relationship with Devon and find alternative ways to establish and maintain acceptable boundaries for his behavior.

Strengths and areas of challenge: Jasmine possesses a number of strengths, including: (1) the desire to be a good parent and not use physical discipline; (2) a history of consistent employment that provides benefits; (3) an active support system; (4) a willingness to seek help for relationship challenges and to use community resources; and (5) the resilience to overcome adversity.

Areas of challenge for Jasmine include: (1) a history of physically striking Devon and a lack of knowledge about other parenting strategies; (2) low self-esteem—Jasmine assumes her son's disrespect for her is her fault because she divorced his father and took Devon away from him, moved Devon to a new area and school, and never has enough money to provide Devon with anything beyond the necessities; and (3) stress related to her income, including sporadic child support payments from her ex-husband.

QUICK GUIDE 14 Continued

Intervention plan: With monthly reviews, Jasmine and her social worker jointly developed a three-month contract:

Goal	Client Tasks/Timeline	Social Worker Tasks/Timeline	Follow-Up	Termination
Improve my relationship with my son	Begin attending weekly family therapy with my son as soon as I can get an appointment.	Refer Jasmine and her son to a family therapist and communicate regularly with the therapist regarding their progress (with Jasmine's informed consent).	At 3 months, Jasmine and Devon are attending family therapy.	At 6 months, the social worker recommends the case be closed as goals have been met.
Learn better strategies for disciplining my son, particularly when I am angry	Participate in weekly parents of teens class and support group (next group begins the first of next month).	Refer Jasmine to parenting class and support group and communicate regularly with the group facilitator regarding progress (with Jasmine's informed consent).	At 3 months, Jasmine is a regular member of the class/support group.	At 6 months, social worker recommends case be closed as goals have been met.
Get Devon's father to pay child support more consistently	As soon as possible, contact Legal Services Child Support Enforcement office to inquire if they can help.	Provide Jasmine with Legal Services contact information and eligibility requirements.	At 3 months, Jasmine has made an appointment with Legal Services.	At 6 months, social worker recommends case be closed. While goal has not been fully met, action is under way.

Intervention (Including Service Options and Purpose, Goals, and Plans of Service)

Goal #1: Jasmine and Devon were scheduled for eight sessions with the family therapist. Although Devon has sometimes refused to go with his mother, he attended six of the eight sessions and agrees to "keep trying it for a while." The therapist reports to the social worker that she believes the Johnsons are making small strides toward improving their relationship. As suspected, Devon is extremely angry with his mother and does not understand why his living and family arrangements had to change. Jasmine refuses to disclose to Devon that his father's drinking and infidelities are the reason for the divorce. Early on, there was an episode at home of physical contact in which Jasmine slapped Devon for calling her a name.

Goal #2: Jasmine has been regularly attending the Single Parents of Teens classes and support group. Not only has she found the information provided very helpful, but she has also found a new group of friends who share her experiences, empathize with her, and offer helpful suggestions.

Goal #3: Jasmine was slow in contacting Legal Services, but once she got an appointment and completed the application, she met with an attorney and social worker. The attorney sent a letter to her ex-husband regarding his delinquent payments. He has yet to respond. Should he not respond, she will have to return to court and request enforcement.

Closing Summary
During the six months that Jasmine has been collaborating with the social worker, she has initiated work on each of the three goals outlined in the contract. Positive changes have been slowly occurring in her relationship with Devon. There have been no episodes of physical contact in five months. While Devon still sometimes violates curfew and speaks disrespectfully to his mother, he no longer does so as frequently.

Shortly after the implementation of the intervention, the social worker learned that someone called a child abuse hotline to allege that Jasmine had abused Devon. Upon further investigation, the social worker learned that Devon himself made the call months earlier after a particularly emotional confrontation with Jasmine. The report was unsubstantiated.

The social worker is recommending closure of this case as substantial progress is being made on all goals. Jasmine and the social worker will discuss termination and evaluation. Should Jasmine feel she needs additional services, she will be invited to request that her case be reopened.

Sample Case/Progress/Interim Notes (Brief Excerpts From the Case Record)
October 1: Jasmine Johnson came to the agency seeking help with her 14-year-old son. She believes he is "out of control," and she is worried that she will become abusive. She has physically struck him when he has violated her rules or spoken disrespectfully to her. She feels she is at her "wit's end." Intake assessment forms completed. Social worker asked Jasmine to bring Devon to the next meeting so his perspective could be included.

November 28: Jasmine and Devon have attended two family therapy sessions. Devon was a reluctant participant but did agree to attend with his mother. Jasmine reports that he said very little in the first meeting but opened up more in the second session. Her fears are confirmed—he is very angry with her. Jasmine has attended two Single Parents of Teens classes and support group meetings. She reports that she is getting a lot out of the sessions, particularly in terms of tips for ways to interact with Devon. She has not yet contacted the Legal Services office.

Explorations of Compatibility With Theoretical Perspectives Another way to evaluate your work is to explore how well the intervention strategies adhere to the theoretical perspectives you embrace. This approach is especially helpful when those perspectives challenge you and stretch your thinking.

In this text, social work practice has been placed within four frameworks thus far: social justice, human rights, the strengths perspective, and critical social construction. These theoretical frameworks represent multiple perspectives, each of which suggests a set of broad criteria for evaluating the work you have completed. For example, do you consistently recognize your clients' strengths, or do you tend to be pulled into a pathology orientation? Are you alert to social justice concerns related to the structures and systems that may impact your client? Can you truly remain open to the multiple realities that critical social construction emphasizes?

These considerations also apply to more specific practice perspectives, such as feminist or narrative lenses. If, for example, you adopt a feminist theory that stresses the importance of power analysis, is your work consistent with that type of analysis? Do you return to a more traditional perspective regarding the issues that your client brings, emphasizing her reluctance to leave an abusive relationship or her lack of self-esteem? Can you keep an analytical structure of gender relations at the forefront of the work? Which aspects of feminist theory do you carry out well, and which can you better integrate into your work?

If your framework is narrative, are you open to the complexity of the client's story? Do you recognize your client as expert, or are you tempted to believe you know better? Which aspects of the theoretical perspective are you having trouble fulfilling? Which seem to come naturally? These considerations, of course, do not yield empirical data. Rather, they can help you decide to what degree you can work within the constraints of particular perspectives and identify ways in which you want to develop skills and grow intellectually. The process of posing such challenging questions can be evaluative in and of itself and is an important routine to establish early in your career. Reflection on these areas can be illuminating and help to shape and refine your theoretical practice stances.

Explorations of Relationship Quality The nature of the relationship you develop with your client offers another opportunity for exploration. Is the relationship consistent with your purpose of the work? Was the intervention client-centered and connected to the client's stated needs and goals? Did you or your client have difficulty establishing openness? What can you learn from the client's struggle? What can you learn from your own struggle?

This investigation might highlight your own idiosyncrasies and biases. For example, do you respond more easily to people who are most like you? Do you wonder if you encouraged the client's dependence on you? Do you struggle to maintain useful boundaries between you and your client? Are you comfortable with the amount of self-disclosure you engage in? Do you have trouble being positive about some kinds of clients?

What are the implications of culture and ethnicity on the quality of the relationship and effectiveness of the intervention? While each worker–client relationship is unique and encompasses multiple and complex components, social workers can, to optimize the quality of the relationship, strive to practice using anti-racist and anti-oppressive approaches. As you evolve and grow as an anti-oppressive practitioner, you can add the following skills to your practice:

1 unlearn those biases of which you are both aware and unaware (Oluo, 2018);
2 ask yourself how you engage in oppressive actions, specifically do you attempt to speak for any group or population, tense up when clients discuss

their experiences with oppression, or are you unwilling to identify racism and oppression statements in the moment (Aguilar et al., 2021); and
3 commit to learning about racist history and the ways in which it impacts your client's life; how to listen, acknowledge your privilege (Slayter, 2021a).

Some questions that arise from this kind of self-examination may point to more general issues: What is the ideal relationship between client and worker? What does it look like? Is it different in different settings? Should it evolve over the course of a social worker's career? Is it likely that all your client relationships will fall into this ideal range? How does the ideal relationship interface with the client's goal attainment?

CRITICAL CONSIDERATIONS ON EVALUATION AND PRACTICE KNOWLEDGE

As the discussion on intervention, termination, and evaluation comes to a close, consider the distinctiveness of the social work profession and its greater purposes. Social justice, human rights, strengths, and the value of multiple realities all inform social workers, who in their work combine a practical orientation and a strong sense of caring and compassion. Context and compassion are always difficult to measure, and if you are pressured to assign numerical indicators, you may miss some of your most important contributions. Recall the term "practice wisdom," introduced in Chapter 1. Practice wisdom is the social worker's application of their "accumulation of information, assumptions, ideologies, and judgments" (Barker, 2014, p. 331). Practice wisdom is a process that encompasses tacit knowledge, critical reflections, and "intersubjectivity" (i.e., knowledge that emerges during practice) (Dodd & Savage, 2016). While it evolves throughout one's career, practice wisdom is a component of evidence-informed practice—a model that integrates theory, practice wisdom, and consideration of client values, choices, culture, and contextual factors (Dodd & Savage, 2016). Practice wisdom does not replace evidence-based practice but, instead, serves to enhance and promote its application. Through the lens of the person-in-environment and strengths perspectives, social workers develop practice wisdom for working with individuals, families, groups, communities, and organizations.

As an empowering practice that involves real people and real misery as well as real joys, social workers will ask other questions about the effectiveness of their practice, including:

- Who benefits from this work? If the goals of social work relate to empowering clients, how can clients realize those goals? If a client demonstrates improved capacity to manage a household budget, for example, does that affect her experience of poverty? Is the change identified and challenged? Will she quietly and skillfully manage on close to nothing (and is this progress?), or will the benefit go beyond, to others like her, and to challenge the structure that supports poverty?

- Whose values are most salient? Social work values are at the heart of the work. Do they dominate the client relationship? How do social workers negotiate differing values? This is one of social work's most challenging dilemmas.

- What changes have occurred in the societal power structure? Have social workers helped to raise consciousness about oppression and the internalization of it? Have clients joined with others to respond to oppressive imbalances in our society's structural arrangements?

These questions lead us back to the beginning of our exploration of social work practice and to a recognition that social work often has a dual function—we are committed to social change as well as social control and maintenance. As a social worker, you will likely find satisfaction in connecting with clients. You may initially struggle to identify the theoretical framework that best guides your work and will find it challenging to meet the demands of the client's preferred realities. You will experience frustrations and successes in each of these areas, answer many questions, and come up with many more. You will determine how to respond to this in ways that are consistent with your values, your social work ethics, your sense of social justice and human rights, and your respect for different views and experiences.

Your own story as a social work practitioner will be embedded in the hundreds of stories of your individual clients, groups, and families; the organizations and communities you serve; and in the story of global change. Your choices are legion, and your opportunities, enormous. In the end, these will return to the story of the profession. You, as a member of the next generation of social workers, will author the next chapter of social work practice.

GRAND CHALLENGE

Advance Long and Productive Lives Learning Through a Case Example With Carla Washburn

One of the Grand Challenges for Social Work identified by the American Academy of Social Work and Social Welfare is the goal of helping older adults live long and productive lives and remain socially engaged. The authors of Grand Challenge Working Paper No. 8, *Increasing Productive Engagement in Later Life* (Morrow-Howell et al., 2015, p. 1), frame the challenge as follows:

Economic security and health care, especially long-term care of older adults, are two challenges that have received the most attention. These two issues are clearly grand challenges, and most discussions about population aging have focused on these issues because of their complexity and importance. Another grand challenge comes as a response to these demands of population aging: increasing the productive engagement of older adults. This social development response seeks to shape social policies and programs to optimally engage the growing human capital of the aging population; to facilitate paid and unpaid work longer into the life course to offset the demands of population aging; and to ensure the inclusion of all segments of the older adult population, especially among those who are more likely to be excluded (e.g., by race, ethnicity, disability).

GRAND CHALLENGE

Continued

With advances in public health care, environmental safety, and lifestyle, longevity is increasing around the world, particularly in developed countries like the United States. For the first time in history, older adults are routinely living decades after they have retired. This Grand Challenge draws attention to the issue of productive aging and engagement for older adults and calls for society, in general, and social workers, in particular, to facilitate changes that will provide support and opportunities for older adults to continue making contributions to society. Changes are needed to change ageist attitudes, societal structures, and policies that will facilitate such shifts as: (1) employment policies that will enable an individual's work life to be extended should they choose; (2) educational institutions that offer learning and training opportunities for older adults; (3) increased volunteer opportunities; and (4) increased support for older adults who served as caregivers and strategies to reduce caregiver burden (Morrow-Howell et al., 2015).

The social work role in advancing long and productive lives relates to this chapter with its focus on intervention, termination, evaluation, and follow-up as social workers can identify and develop and mobilize resources to support older adults who want to be productively engaged. This Grand Challenge relates specifically to the case of Carla Washburn (www.routledgesw.com/cases) as Carla is an older adult who has experienced multiple losses and is struggling to engage with others in her life. Guided by the principles of choice, opportunity, and inclusion, Morrow-Howell and colleagues (2015, p. 4) suggest that social workers are well positioned to:

- create ample opportunities for engaging those who choose participation,
- eliminate barriers to engagement,
- support transitions between caregiving and other forms of productive engagement to prevent caregivers being negatively impacted, and
- restructure social arrangements that exclude older adults from employment and social activities.

To familiarize yourself with the issues related to advancing long and productive lives, visit the Grand Challenges website and read Working Paper No. 8, *Increasing Productive Engagement in Later Life* (Morrow-Howell et al., 2015) at https://grandchallengesforsocialwork.org. To learn about the progress on achieving this Grand Challenge, review the "Advancing Long and Productive Lives" by Gonzales and colleagues (2022). (See Exercise #1 for additional exploration of this Grand Challenge.)

CONCLUSION

In this chapter, we have explored social work intervention, termination, evaluation, and follow-up actions with individuals. The practice setting, theoretical perspectives, and social worker and client perception of roles influence your work to support clients' strengths and their environments. The overall fit of intervention activities with your beliefs about people creates a sound backdrop for expanding your work in other areas. The next chapters integrate and extend these same processes to families, groups, organizations, and communities. They consolidate the principles and skills in this first part of the book and apply them across system levels.

In the paradoxical way that some things constantly change while they remain the same, so endings and evaluations continue and evolve. We will all experience new ways of practicing social work in the future. Some of you will work in complex settings that integrate the public and private sectors. Some will choose relatively radical forms of practice in which you will challenge what you see as unjust historical and professional legacies. Others will continue to practice using largely the same models learned in social work training. All these dimensions of practice will have implications for beginning and ending the social work relationship, for implementing and evaluating the work, and for grappling with the obstacles that get in the way of the client's vision for their life. There are no magic formulas for anticipating all the implications of change for social work. Your flexibility, integrity, and creativity, as well as your caring for people who struggle, will be your own best guides for your future practice.

MAIN POINTS

- The intervention starts with the issue(s) the client perceives to be most pressing. The context of the client's situation and the actions you mutually agreed upon in the assessment and planning phase define the issue.

- Evidence-based and evidence-informed approaches are used to guide social work interventions with individuals. Three are highlighted in this chapter: strengths-based, narrative, and solution-focused approaches.

- Social workers act in context to normalize and capitalize on clients' strengths. Social workers respond to feelings, determine their meaning, and celebrate diversity.

- To support clients' environments, social workers are accountable to the client. They follow the demands of the client task; maximize the potential supports in the client's environments; identify, reinforce, and/or increase the client's repertoire of strategic behaviors; and apply these principles to themselves.

- Examining traditional social work roles and their assumptions within the context of contemporary practice provides another perspective on the roles of case manager, counselor, broker, mediator, educator, client advocate, and collaborator.

- Exploring a case situation through an empowerment lens puts the work in context and demonstrates its fit with the perspectives emphasized in this book.

- Professionalism within the social work profession is a lifelong commitment to such practices as abiding by the profession's ethical standards, using self-disclosure only when relevant to the client's situation, and maintaining your own well-being through self-care.

- The planned ending process includes several components that can benefit and empower clients by consolidating the gains of the work and the relationship. Social worker and client must share a clear understanding of the timing of the ending, the original agreement, the successes and failures of the work, and their responses to termination.

- Unplanned endings pose a special challenge to both social workers and clients. Social workers can attempt to reconnect with clients to end the work on a different note, but they may have to acknowledge the limits of their influence and should always honor client self-determination.

- Social work practice increasingly requires quantitative and empirical evaluation processes. Single-subject design and goal attainment scaling are two evaluation options.

- Qualitative and reflective practices are another important method for evaluation and professional growth. They relate to philosophical commitments, theoretical perspectives, and relationship building.

EXERCISES

1 To apply your learning of the Grand Challenge for Social Work—Advancing Long and Productive Lives—visit the Grand Challenges website and read Working Paper No. 8, *Increasing Productive Engagement in Later Life* (Morrow-Howell et al., 2015) at: https://grandchallengesforsocialwork.org/. To gain insight into strategies for empowering older adults to optimize their engagement and productivity in later life, we will consider the case of Carla Washburn at www.routledgesw.com/interactive-cases/. After reading Working Paper No. 8 and reviewing the Washburn case, respond to the following questions:
   a Based on the definition of productive engagement and utilizing the information provided about Carla Washburn, assess her level of productive engagement, specifically addressing those areas of her life you would deem provide her with gratification.
   b Building on the assessment you have developed, identify potential activities in which Mrs. Washburn might get involved. Resources that may be helpful include the community map and the sampling of innovations described in Working Paper No. 8.
   c Develop a plan for intervention, termination, and evaluation with Mrs. Washburn that is focused on optimizing her productive engagement.

2. Go to www.routledgesw.com/interactive-cases/, review the video vignette with Emilia Sanchez, and respond to the following questions:
   a. What strengths does Emilia possess?
   b. What thoughts and/or feelings do you have after watching the video that, if you were to verbalize them, would not reflect a strengths-based approach?
   c. As the social worker, what are your next steps with Emilia? How would you practice cultural responsiveness and humility in your work with her?
   d. With a group in or outside of class, develop a strengths-based intervention plan for Emilia.
3. Go to www.routledgesw.com/interactive-cases/ and click on Brickville. Focus on Virginia Stone as your primary client. Review Engage and Discover and Assess the Situation sections. Click on Intervention and Create a Plan. Complete each of the tasks identified as you plan to work primarily with Virginia. Upon completion of the tasks, consider the four components of the social work intervention—engagement, assessment and planning, intervention, and termination and evaluation—and develop an intervention and case summary using the sample in Quick Guide 14.
4. Go to www.routledgesw.com/interactive-cases/ and click on RAINN. After reviewing the information, click on Engage and Discover, review the two client scenarios (Sarah and Alan), and respond to the three questions listed below the scenarios. In addition, develop a list of skills you would need to develop to work competently with a survivor of sexual assault.
5. Go to www.routledgesw.com/static-cases/ and review Downloadable Case #2: Mr. Richardson's Killing. After reviewing the information, develop responses to Questions #1–3 and #10.
6. The admissions unit of a psychiatric care facility where you work issues a one-page daily report summarizing all the patient admissions, discharges, visits, legal proceedings, and other activities for the preceding 24-hour period. This summary is meant to convey useful information for all staff, and social workers view the summary as helpful for monitoring client status. One of the categories on the form, "body count," is a tally of the number of patients/residents in the hospital at midnight. A social worker from a local community mental health agency visits a client in the hospital and hears reference to this sheet. The social worker is horrified by the use of "body count," a phrase you have become accustomed to seeing in the reports. Answer the following questions based on this scenario and be prepared to discuss your answers in class or to submit your written response.
   a. What is the issue here? Why does it matter? Be as specific as you can.
   b. How would you address this issue? Would the way you address the issue be consistent with your view of a social worker's role?
   c. Develop a plan that includes at least three steps you might take. Compare your plan with those of other students.

7   Tamika is a 35-year-old woman of color living in a rural community. She is seeking treatment after her release from a 21-day residential drug/alcohol treatment facility. The public child welfare agency refers her to your agency. Because Tamika was convicted of driving under the influence with her 8-year-old son, Jaryn, in the car, and because of her continuing substance use, the court places Jaryn in Tamika's mother's physical custody. Tamika has a 20-year history of drug and alcohol use, and she has been diagnosed with bipolar disorder. The staff psychiatrist at the residential treatment facility recently wrote her a prescription for the disorder. It is a new medication and is not covered by her insurance. She has been noncompliant with medication in the past due to the side effects, expense, and her drug/alcohol use. She has had brief periods of sobriety but often relapses after a few weeks. This is the longest she has been sober since the birth of her son eight years ago.

Tamika has never been married and has a difficult relationship with her family of origin. Because of Tamika's behavioral challenges, her mother placed her in foster care at the age of eight. Tamika reports that her mother was physically and emotionally abusive to her and often would leave her with various relatives to go out with boyfriends. Tamika's father is not involved. She has few friends and little contact with her mother. She is angry that her mother has custody of her son. Tamika has been involved with her son's father sporadically for the past nine years. Currently, she names him as a source of support.

Tamika is not currently employed but receives public assistance in the form of Medicaid, disability assistance, and SNAP (food stamps). She lives with her boyfriend but would like to have her own apartment. She has her high school diploma and is interested in continuing her education.

Partner with other students and complete the following exercises:
a Using narrative interventions, reconstruct this case from a strengths-based perspective.
b What roles would you play to help Tamika?
c Construct a strengths-based, solution-focused intervention plan.
d Share your findings with the class and compare your plans.

8   Reflect on a time in your life when you contemplated making a change. What did you do? Were your actions successful? What factors led to the success? If your actions were not successful, what was missing?

This exercise is provided by Shannon Cooper-Sadlo, PhD, LCSW, Associate Clinical Professor, School of Social Work, Saint Louis University.

9   Identify an area or behavior in your life that you would like to change (e.g., texting while driving, exercising, budgeting money, or time management). For one week, chart your journey in a journal and note those factors that are helping you to change and those that are a negative influence on your change efforts. At the end of the week, reflect on your progress or lack thereof. Consider your feelings before the change, during the change, and about the results.

10 Write your own life story from a strengths-based perspective, noting an area or time in your life in which you felt ambivalence about a change you wanted or needed to make. Using Motivational Interviewing skills, reflect on strategies you might apply in addressing your ambivalence about the change process.

CHAPTER 6

Social Work Practice With Families: Engagement, Assessment, and Planning

FAMILY IS THE FIRST AND MOST BASIC small group one can experience during a lifetime. For many people, it can also be the most challenging. Family is also probably the most powerful group in shaping who we become. The family provides intergenerational care from "cradle to grave." However, many families require help in meeting those needs. Often, this assistance is provided by a social worker (Briar-Lawson & Naccarato, 2021). For some, family means home, safety, and acceptance, but even the most secure family environments can be shaken when crises or tragedy strike. For others, family means violence, danger, or neglect. Some people may feel important and cherished with family, whereas others may feel never quite good enough. Some may feel swallowed up in their family's dysfunction, while others derive much of their positive identity from association with their families. People within the same family may long for love and acceptance, while others appear to bask in unconditional support. Most of us experience a mix of these feelings. Family is a complicated enterprise, and many of us find it both joyful and troubled—even simultaneously. Every society has family arrangements, but they may look different within social contexts. Virtually all members of society have experienced family, and most have ideas or dreams of the qualities that an ideal family could or should possess.

In this chapter, we will explore the concept of family—its definition, meaning, and place within contemporary social contexts—and the process of engagement and assessment with families from a biopsychosocial-spiritual-sexual perspective. We will also look at theoretical perspectives for working with diverse family structures as well as the dynamics, skills, and tools for working with a range of families. This chapter will also guide you through strategies for understanding the impact family issues can have on you and your clients. We start this chapter with a case that we will revisit throughout the chapter:

> The Patel family lives in Hudson City (www.routledgesw.com/interactive-cases/) and is one of the many families displaced by Hurricane Diane, which

swept through the community a few weeks earlier. The members of the Patel family include:

- *Hemant and Sheetal—both in their late forties, they emigrated to the United States from India 15 years ago. They own and operate a family restaurant in their neighborhood.*
- *Rakesh, Kamal, and Aarti, the Patels' three children. The oldest son, Rakesh, is 18 and in his first semester at the University of the Northeast. He lives at home and commutes to school. The younger son, Kamal, is a 16-year-old high school junior. The Patels' daughter, Aarti, is 12 and in seventh grade.*
- *Bharat and Asha, Mr. Patel's parents, came from India to live with their son and his family when the restaurant opened ten years ago. They are both in their early seventies and help part-time in the restaurant. Bharat had cardiac bypass surgery last year; Asha suffers from hypertension. Bharat and Asha were forced to leave behind their medications when they fled from the storm.*

All members of the Patel family work full- or part-time in the restaurant. The Patels' restaurant and home sustained major damage in the storm. While the restaurant and house can be rehabilitated, repairs to the extensive damage may take months to complete. The Patels are staying with friends in a nearby community, but they feel they must quickly make other arrangements to avoid imposing on their friends' hospitality. As the entire family derives its income from the restaurant, money is a concern. The family are not certain how they will keep up with their financial obligations. While everyone in the family is devastated at their losses, Hemant and Sheetal are especially worried about their parents' health and their children's education. They know that disruptions are particularly difficult for these more vulnerable members of their family.

Key Questions for Chapter 6

1. What competencies do I need to engage with and assess families? For example, what specific cultural competency knowledge and skills do I need to have in working with the Patel family?
2. What social work skills enable me to effectively engage with and assess families?
3. How can I use evidence to perform research-informed practice, and how can I use practice-informed research to guide engagement and assessment with families?
4. How do my perspectives on and experiences with my present family and/or family of origin impact my engagement with and assessment of client families?

FAMILIAR PERSPECTIVES

The family life course has become longer and more complex due to increased diversity and fluidity of individuals, relationships, and structures within the family system (Briar-Lawson & Naccarato, 2021). Enormous and rapid changes in social norms and rules in most Western countries have led many to contend that the "traditional" family is a thing of the past. With changes in longevity, increasing economic inequalities, and more types of living and relationship arrangements, social workers must always consider an individual within the context of their family, including culture, inclusiveness, and responsiveness (Briar-Lawson & Naccarato, 2021).

In contrast to the traditional view of a "nuclear" family, a contemporary view of family is one in which members "assume certain obligations for each other and generally (but not necessarily) share common residences" (Barker, 2014, p. 155). This inclusive perspective on the family embraces parents who are divorced, separated, or unmarried; grandparents rearing grandchildren; gay, lesbian, bisexual, transgender, or queer families; and adoptive, multigenerational (e.g., three or even four generations co-residing, like the Patel family), and fostering families, along with couples who have no children, and families caring for older adult members. "Found" or chosen families often share responsibilities for one another and children but are not biologically related. To engage in effective assessment, planning, and intervention, social workers must be aware of and have competence in working with diverse family structures as described here (Briar-Lawson & Naccarato, 2021). The purpose of the family, regardless of the form, structure, or composition, is to help individual members grow and develop and to create and sustain a connected family unit over the life course (Paris & DeVoe, 2013).

Regardless of the family constellation or structure, we must also be cognizant of the role that culture plays in the family system, specifically intersectionality and experiences with discrimination and oppression. We must also recognize that other aspects of identity influence family membership and culture (e.g., race, ethnicity, and country of origin, as in the case of the Patel family). For example, to be inclusive and avoid assumptions and confusion, social workers should ask clients to describe their family unit and the construction of its relational systems (McCauley & PettyJohn, 2020). Given the changing nature of the family and the fluidity of membership in some families, it is important to ask each member of the family, "Who do you consider to be part of your family?" A follow-up question may then be, "Of these people, who is biologically and/or legally related to you?" For instance, a client's "aunt" may not be a legal or biological family member, but the client may consider her family. Knowing biological links can be important in situations in which health/medical information or history is relevant. Having clarity regarding legal relationships can impact financial responsibility, legal decision-making, and child custody. Through questioning, you can gain insight into who the family's connections are—is it biological and/or chosen family and natural mentors—which is particularly important for families who are marginalized (McCauley & PettyJohn, 2020).

Some people live together as couples, with and without any permanent commitment, including marriage or other legal arrangements. Unpartnered women choose to become parents without suffering the social stigma they would have experienced only a few generations earlier. Parents who are lesbian, gay, bisexual, transgender, and queer (LGBTQIA+), who in earlier generations had to conceal their sexual and gender identities to protect their children from ostracization and themselves from reprobation, are joyfully marrying and parenting biological, foster, and adopted children. In the past, LGBTQIA+ individuals were not even given the option to foster or adopt children; however, LGBTQIA+ adoption and fostering are not accepted in all areas of the country, as evidenced by legal cases being filed.

While the widespread belief for several decades has been that at least half of all marriages in the United States end in divorce, a shift in that trend has occurred, resulting in a decreasing divorce rate that is now 2.3/1000 population (Centers for Disease Control & Prevention [CDC], 2021). Also on the decline is the marriage rate (5.1/1000 population (CDC, 2021). A variety of reasons are offered for this decline in divorce, including later marriage, birth control, couples living together before marriage, changing gender roles (resulting from the feminist movement), level of education (fewer divorces among college-educated couples), and fewer marriages, or in the case of the millennial generation, staying married (Wood, 2018).

Despite a declining divorce rate, certain issues surrounding the contemporary family create concerns for social workers and impact service delivery. One area of concern continues to be the number of children living in single-parent-headed households with incomes below the poverty level. Due to the declining marriage and divorce rates, single-parent families are on the rise. Of the 14 percent of all US children living in poverty, 68 percent live in single-parent households (Children's Defense Fund [CDF], 2021). As poverty diverges by race, children of color and/or Latinx children are more likely to live in poverty (CDF, 2021). Social workers who work with single mothers must be aware of the higher poverty rate for these families.

A second area of concern for social workers is the persistence of poverty for children born to teen mothers. The number of births to teen mothers in all racial and ethnic groups continues to decline (56/1000 women 15–44) (Martin et al., 2021). Social workers working with teen parents recognize that teen births are associated with unplanned pregnancies, legacies of perpetuated poverty, increased family violence, and health and mental health issues, and with a sense that two generations—the child and the child's child—have sacrificed much of their potential. Thus, teen mothers often have a range of challenges to reaching their dreams for adulthood.

There are many ways to look at the concept of family. In keeping with this book's consideration of multiple realities, we will explore the experiences of an array of family constellations to expose popular misconceptions about the family and to develop a balanced perspective. Consider Exhibit 6.1, which describes the experience of family for people who have been marginalized.

EXHIBIT 6.1

Family: Views From the Margins

- At times in history, families considered children commodities that enhanced the economic status of their fathers, who owned them and who often equated their value to the amount of work they did. Childhood as a time to be nourished and cherished is a relatively new and narrowly prescribed phenomenon of Western culture and some nations in the East. While not yet ratified by the United States, the United Nations instrument "The Rights of the Child" reflects the need to recognize that children around the world are imperiled and that they should be considered as genuine people and not possessions.
- Historically, conceptions of the family often restricted women's role to caretakers. Many women throughout history have, like children, been viewed as property to be exploited. Men, too, have historically been pressured to fit into tightly prescribed roles that may not be compatible with their identities or goals. For persons of color and those living in poverty, their realities were often more narrowly focused on survival.
- While longevity has increased, in the past, infant and childhood mortality was high, and some parents died by their early forties. Such circumstances produced a crisis for surviving children and those family members responsible for the children, who were sometimes placed with distant relatives, with community members, or in orphanage care. The idealistic notion of earlier times ignores realities of disease, early death, and other forms of danger that shaped the overall experience of family.
- The family is the primary force for the socializing and nurturing of children and caring for disabled and older adult members.
- Rigid definitions of family that focus on biological and legal ties and heterosexual partners or adoptions have always marginalized and scapegoated significant numbers of people. Many people have meaningful and productive relationships though their families do not fit such rigid definitions.

> **EXHIBIT 6.1**
>
> *Continued*
>
> - More contemporary notions of family have liberated people of all genders and gender identities and in all family structures to pursue roles related to caregiving for children, those with disabilities, and older adults, economic provision, management, personal development, and health care in ways that do not deny their individual aspirations and talents.
> - While many families have greater biological control over the number and timing of pregnancies and can plan family composition in a way that is consistent with their financial capacities and other demands (e.g., one partner is in school or committed to the care of a parent), there are those who continue to have limited access to contraception and other reproductive health services.

HISTORICAL ANTECEDENTS FOR SOCIAL WORK WITH FAMILIES

As families have evolved, social workers have continued to work to strengthen families in such settings as community mental health centers, youth agencies, hospitals, schools, and child welfare organizations where they help families address a range of issues, including addictions, divorce, grief, health crises, and legal issues. Collins and colleagues (2013) encourage social work students interested in working with families to seek answers to the following questions as they prepare for practice:

- What is the purpose of family social work?
- How does family social work differ from family therapy?
- How can I work effectively with families who are different from my own?
- What are my roles as a family social worker?
- How will I know what factors contribute to the family's difficulties?
- How should I work with an entire family?
- How will I know what questions to ask family members? What do I say to the family?
- How do I engage all family members, particularly if some seem resistant or uncommunicative or seem to feel blamed or overpowered by another member?
- What should I do if family members become angry with one another and/or me?
- What do I need to know to help families change? What new knowledge will help the families begin to change (e.g., parenting, financial capability, or physical and mental health care)?
- What skills will I need when there are young children? What about older children?

- What can I do to protect individual family members when the rest of the family is attacking or blaming?
- How do I help families that are paralyzed by a crisis to rise above it and solve their problems?
- What do I need to know about when working with families of different ethnic or racial backgrounds or sexual orientation?
- What skills do I need to help the family prioritize their needs and goals? What skills do I need for each of the phases of work with families? (pp. 1–2)

Why is there such a concern for the maintenance of the family? What does our culture expect the family to do, and how do we think the family should work? Although there are many possible responses to these questions, we examine two perspectives that have special relevance for social workers today: the family as a functioning unit and the family as a system.

The Family as a Functioning Unit

One way to think about the importance of the family is to explore what our society requires of families. Our society typically expects families to fulfill such functions as:

- providing material and economic necessities for family members' sustenance and growth.
- offering members emotional security, respect, safety, and a place for "appropriate" sexual expression.
- providing a haven for privacy and rest.
- assisting, protecting, and advocating for members who are vulnerable or who have special needs.
- providing support for members' meaningful connection with and contribution to community life.
- facilitating the transmission of cultural and/or religious heritage.
- providing a socially and legally recognized identity.
- creating an environment in which to nurture and socialize children.

The responsibilities reflected here emphasize not only the functional roles of individual family members and their needs and identities, but also family members' connection to their culture, communities, and to the overall societal environment. Rather than seeking individual or family dysfunction, the exploration of these tasks in various areas of family life tends to highlight strengths as well as areas for improvement. In that respect, this set of functions serves as a useful guide for assessing and cultivating critique of these societal expectations and the degree to which they accommodate individual and family goals.

> *Returning to the Patel family's situation, the parents' worries as they are unable to fulfill their familial obligations of providing shelter, safety, economic security, and a sense of stability are consistent with the idea that families provide material and economic necessities for one another and protection for those members who are vulnerable. While the Patels' situation is likely temporary, consider the level of anxiety one might have if the situation were chronic, as is the case for many families.*

Despite the societal mandate for family to serve a critical function in meeting members' needs, some may have difficulty fulfilling the mandate, and thus they may require the involvement of a helping professional. Taking into consideration the type and level of need, you can focus the social work engagement, assessment, planning, intervention, termination, evaluation, and follow-up processes within a conceptual framework that encompasses both the context of those persons with whom you work (i.e., family/community, couple/dyad, and individual) and the orientation (e.g., theoretical approach) of the intervention you choose with the family.

Incorporating the complexities of the family system into the intervention, you can gain insight into the way the family functions, its members' needs, and the most effective strategies for helping them reach their goals.

> *In working with the Patel family during the disaster-related crisis, your work will focus on the entire family, but possibly on different members/clusters at different points, depending on their prioritized needs. Engaging with the family to identify immediate, short-term, and long-range needs and goals will involve helping them to articulate and mobilize their strengths, resources, and strategies for re-stabilizing the family. While their life may not look exactly as it had before, you can help them use resilience to build a new life.*

Family as a System

As discussed throughout this book, social work uses a systemic framework to focus on interactions among people and between people and their environment. Whether you are working with an individual, a family, group, or community, systems theory (also referred to as a perspective or framework) posits that a system involves a series of highly organized components that depend on each other in an orderly way. The social work profession applies systems theory to each level of practice—individuals, families, groups, organization, and community—and remains a guiding influence on many views of structural arrangements, particularly the family. Three elements of systems theory are especially important:

- Change in one component affects all other components
- Subsystems and boundaries
- Family norms

Change in One Component Affects All Other Components Possibly the most powerful systems theory concept for social workers is that change in one part of the system affects all other parts of the system. Social workers, therefore, seek to learn about every aspect of a client's environment, including family functioning. For example, when you explore why a child is having angry outbursts in school, it is useful to know that the child's father has just been sent to prison. Similarly, a client's fragile mental health is likely to suffer when they learn that their mother is experiencing intimate partner violence. Social workers often find such connections intuitive and useful, but guard against assuming a situation will automatically produce a certain response. In systems theory, one set of actions can predict multiple sets of reactions. For example, children may become more attentive to their mother or work harder in school in response to their father's incarceration. Responses to a situation can differ across families and within the same family. Consider, for example, a family in which the primary wage earner becomes unemployed. Whereas one adolescent child may seek employment to help the family, another may demonstrate anger or experience depression.

Subsystems and Boundaries Components of a system that have interacting parts, known as *subsystems*, provide a mechanism for organizing relationships and planning ways to engage with them. In systems theory, the individual is a subsystem of the family, the family is a subsystem of the community, and the community is a subsystem of the culture. A family may be a subsystem of more than one larger system (e.g., a faith community), or of differing systems, so avoid making unqualified judgments regarding the place an individual or group occupies within the system. For example, in a blended family, some

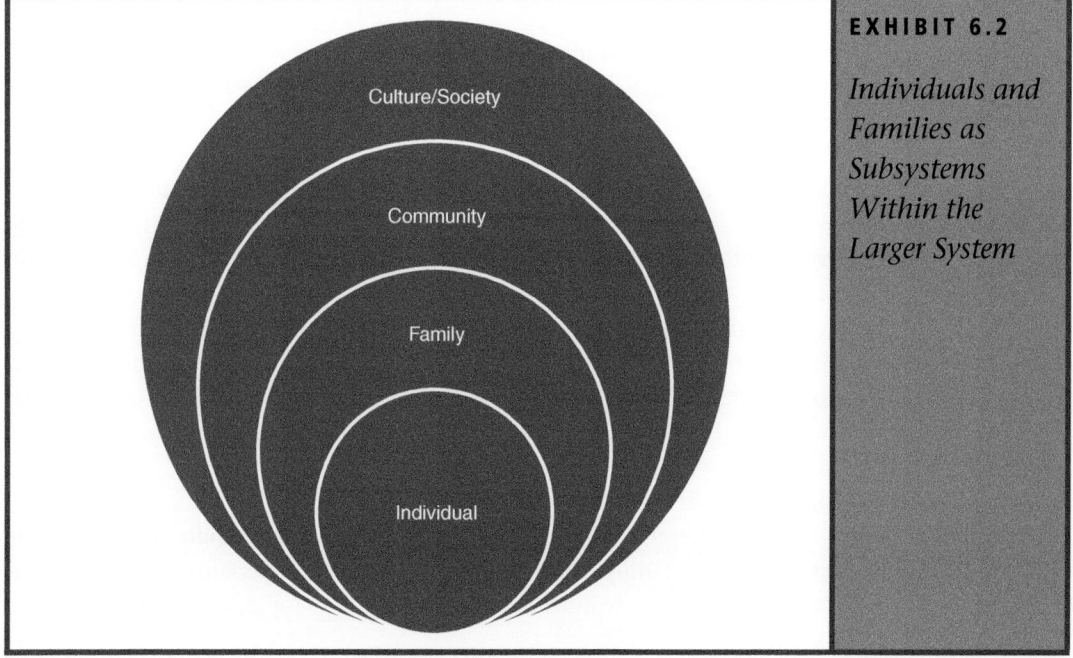

EXHIBIT 6.2

Individuals and Families as Subsystems Within the Larger System

members may consider themselves part of the family and community from the previous marriage in addition to being members of the new, blended family and community. Social workers can support and facilitate healthy transition relationships for this type of client system. Exhibit 6.2 illustrates the components of a family system.

In thinking about the concept of family, social workers often distinguish between the subsystem of the parents and the subsystem of the children. The types of **boundaries** or limits that separate the subsystems a family constructs reflect the relationship between these subsystems in that family. If children are included in most family decisions, these boundaries are *permeable boundaries*, meaning that information and interchange goes easily across them. In families in which parents have little or no decision-making authority, the boundaries are so permeable as to be almost nonexistent. These are called *diffuse boundaries*.

Appropriate boundaries between the subsystems of parents and children may vary considerably depending on culture, era, background, parents' need/approaches, and/or the boundaries within which the parents themselves were reared. In a family experiencing financial strain, addiction or mental illness of one of the parents, or limited English proficiency of the parents, the boundaries may become altered (i.e., fluid) because the children, out of perceived necessity, assume more roles consistent with those of the parent. While you may consider a mother whose preteen daughter is her primary confidante as lacking appropriate boundaries, other families may view this as acceptable. Boundaries may change over time, even within the same family, as circumstances and needs change. Can you cite examples of boundaries in your own family that are similar to or different from those of your friends or other extended family members? What functions do these diverse boundary arrangements serve? Consider the way in which your experiences with your own family might relate to families with whom you will work.

Some family boundaries may be so diffuse that they result in enmeshment, which suggests that family members are too close, have few distinctions in role or authority, and enjoy little autonomy or independence (Nichols & Davis, 2020). For example, consider a family in which the adult children share virtually every life experience with their mother and seldom make decisions without consulting one another and her. In an enmeshed family, one member's routine life experience, such as a job change or change in relationship status, creates strong reactions in other family members.

On the other hand, in a disengaged family, boundaries between family members are overly rigid. In this situation, subsystems are so unconnected that the family has little sense of identity, and parents are apt to relinquish much of their caretaking role as they and their children pursue their own separate interests. In a disengaged family, members may barely acknowledge significant life events, such as holidays, job changes, or divorce.

When you read about or work with youth/young adults who have little or no effective family connections and who have experienced school or legal problems, you may wonder about the boundaries (or lack of boundaries) their parents established and how their parents perceived their roles. Boundaries often need to change when parents age and require their children's contributions (and that failure to make these shifts can affect the family system negatively). Systems theory can help you understand the misplacement or laxness of parental boundaries when children experience challenges. In such cases, professionals will work with the family to restore clear and appropriate boundaries between children (including adult children) and parents that support parent caretaking, authority, or influence. When, for example, a judge requires the parents of an adolescent who has been arrested to undergo family management training or requires them to supervise a child's curfew restrictions, that judge is acting in a manner consistent with family systems theory.

Family Norms Most families establish family norms, or rules of conduct, related to boundaries and subsystems. Family norms can be deeply ingrained, even if no one in the family has ever articulated those norms to themselves or one another; indeed, they are often held as sacrosanct and not negotiable. For example, the family may be one in which it is well known that members do not display emotions, but this issue is never discussed. The degree of the implicit and embedded aspects of norms can make them difficult to address and challenge, so much so that while everyone in the family understands what behavior is allowable, family members may not even realize that rules exist.

For example, all members of a family may understand that no one will enter into a dispute at the dinner table, that everyone will attend religious services, or that all the children will go out of state to college. Some of these rules apply to everyday boundaries and may simplify everyday interactions (for example, if a door is closed, one is not to enter without knocking). Other rules may signal secrets that are taboo or too difficult to talk about or that perpetuate unjust or oppressive situations, such as all the female children knowing not to find themselves in the same room alone with Grandpa or the understanding that no one asks Mom how she got a bruise on her face.

When applying a systems analysis to family norms, a social worker may recognize that interrupting the family's patterns of behavior or relationship by breaking a rule is, in fact, both feasible and desirable. For example, a social worker may point out that no one ever mentions the bruises on Mom's face. This disclosure could lead the mother to talk about the violence she experiences, which might initiate the empowerment process. While this disclosure may not immediately decrease the violence, it can be the start of the process. On the other hand, this disclosure might render the mother and children vulnerable to violence; therefore, the social worker must be mindful to have safety resources in place for the mother and children. Family norms in such cases are often powerful and should be carefully evaluated to avoid putting any family member at risk. Even when safety is not at risk, breaking of family norms must be done carefully as it could imperil the social worker's ability to build common cause with the family, thus interfering with the work.

IMPLICATIONS OF SYSTEMS THEORY FOR GENERALIST PRACTICE WITH FAMILIES

Norms, subsystems, and boundaries create *family structure* and *intergenerational patterns*, two dimensions reflected in family systems theories that have influenced generalist social work practice with families. In many respects, these dimensions represent a classic approach to conceptualizing the family, and they have influenced how social service policies and agencies respond to families. You may discover that these ideas have shaped your thinking, too.

The following concepts for social work assessment and intervention with families grew out of systems theory (Rasheed & Rasheed, 2013) and provide a useful basis for considering family structure and intergenerational patterns:

1 Family is considered within a "context" comprised of multiple systems.
2 Rooted in the basic systemic foundation, the family is more than the sum of its parts, which function together as a unique system.
3 A change within one part of the family system creates change in the entire system and affects the family's ability to find balance or achieve stability.
4 A systemic-focused assessment and intervention provide a view of the family as a complex system (because these are two separate processes).
5 A systems perspective views behaviors as a product of the multifaceted system and not as the result of one individual or action; behaviors should be viewed as circular (versus linear) and having multiple causations.
6 A systems perspective that promotes a strengths-based approach frames the family assessment within the context of the environment and allows for building on family resilience and cohesiveness and incorporating the family's biological, psychological, life cycle, cultural, spiritual, and historical environments.
7 A systems perspective views individual family members within the context of their family system as well as within the different domains of diversity and larger societal systems.
8 The legal, social, and economic biases and discrimination that affect families with members considered to be cultural, racial, ethnic, religious, or sexual minorities may impact family function.
9 Viewing the family as a unique system within the larger community allows practitioners to more objectively focus the assessment on issues that present challenges to the entire system to guide prioritization and intervention planning (p. 6)

As you continue reading the following discussion about family structure and intergenerational patterns, consider the Patel family. While the three-generation Patel family itself is a system, the members form subsystems (e.g., married couples and siblings) and the family unit is a part of larger systems, including their community, faith institution, and friends/neighbors.

Family Structure The relationship among the generations of a family, especially between the subsystems of children and parents, is the family structure. One of the early scholars in defining models for family interventions, Salvador Minuchin (1974), posited that boundaries between children and parents should be clear and that, because they carry out appropriate caretaking functions, parents should be in charge of major decisions. Often, it is the blurring of the boundaries between these two subsystems that causes family difficulties.

Intergenerational Patterns The identification of a family's belief systems that are passed from generation to generation—*multi- or intergenerational patterns*—can be an important outcome of the assessment process as they can provide context for the current family situation (Edwards et al., 2020). For example, if your adult client is so connected to her mother that she experiences significant anxiety when they are separated and therefore cannot work outside the home, she is likely to establish that same kind of relationship with her own children when they are born. The anxiety that any effort to be separate from her mother generates makes it difficult for your client to think clearly and to parent her own children. In this way, she becomes dysfunctional, tending to be dominated by her feelings, and she inadvertently passes that pattern on to the next generation. Over-emphasis on feelings in a family sometimes results in frequent emotional uproar, violence, feuds, and a struggle accomplishing basic family functions.

Problematic, emotional patterns and the resulting behavioral consequences (such as violence and substance use disorder) can appear to be transmitted from generation to generation. Social workers seek to eradicate such thinking and cycles, bolster families' strengths, and support an appropriate level of autonomy in family members. Many social and educational programs are designed to break patterns of economic dependence, addictions, and to build up healthy bonds between family members.

Family systems theory, like any other theory, does not explain all situations. For example, using a systems perspective to relate crime, addiction, or school violence among youth to the families involved, regardless of evidence, may be misleading. Sometimes children engage in illegal or violent behavior even when they have caring, supportive, and engaged parents who are doing the best they can and some children thrive well even when their families are struggling. Therefore, be careful not to blame or scapegoat any person or family simply because it fits with a possible systemic interpretation of the situation. Rather, it is important to view the behavior within an even wider systems theory lens of the broader aspects of poverty, disenfranchisement, challenging school situations (e.g., bullying), or racism or the intersectionality of multiple issues. Placing blame on the parents/family removes the responsibility of addressing larger societal problems that may contribute to the problem behavior which ensures that these patterns will be perpetuated, including among families not even formed yet.

While systems perspectives can support logical approaches to assessment and have a general cultural appeal, they do not constitute a "magic," one-stop answer for conceptualizing, assessing, or working with families. They may even perpetuate incomplete or potentially harmful assessments of families' experiences. As you continue your social work education and develop your approach to practicing social work with families, you will be exposed to a wide array of philosophical and theoretical frameworks. You are professionally obligated to consider all options and to determine the evidence-based approaches that are most consistent with social work values and ethics and are appropriate for the families you serve.

> Let us return to the Patel family—can you now describe their family structure? Can you identify intergenerational patterns that exist within the family? How would you use this information as you assess and plan with the members of this family?

THE CONTEMPORARY CONTEXT FOR SOCIAL WORK WITH FAMILIES

The following sections briefly identify several types of family constellations that have not historically been considered traditional but that are a vital part of the contemporary family landscape and are viewed as they are and not as our culture has portrayed them. Then, you will consider specific strategies for working with them. Family constellations include:

- grandparents rearing grandchildren.
- lesbian, gay, bisexual, transgender, and queer families.
- single-parent families.
- families of multiple racial and ethnic heritages.
- families that include persons with disabilities.
- blended families (families formed by a blending of separate families through marriage, partnering, or non-kinship relationships).
- families that have relocated to the country through immigration or refugee status.

Beyond these types of families, other current configurations include adoptive families, foster families, multigenerational families, and, of course, many combinations of these types. In the coming generations, the social work profession will need to expect and remain open to ever-evolving forms of family. This area of sociocultural change provides social workers with the opportunity to serve clients across all levels of society in a culturally competent and humble manner.

Grandparents Rearing Grandchildren

In many past societies, grandparents played a significant and ongoing role in the nurturing and socialization of children. Some cultural groups today, typically those that are less mobile or those with strong ethnic identifications, have maintained those patterns consistent with their cultural and instrumental needs. In the Patel family, for example, the grandparents are an integral part of the family. They immigrated to the United States to be with their son and his family, live in the same house, and work in the same business where they have daily contact with their grandchildren, thus having a significant role in their lives. Yet societal changes in the post-industrialized and increasingly digital 21st century have tended to obscure such extended family organization patterns.

However, the number of children living in homes headed by one or more grandparents is on the rise. Approximately 2 percent of children under 18 years of age live with only their grandparents (Anderson et al., 2022). Grandparents become primary caregivers for their grandchildren for a variety of reasons, including family violence, addiction, physical and mental health issues, and/or the incarceration of adult children. In some cases, grandparents are sought out by child protection agencies that see biological relatives as preferable to, and more available than, unrelated foster parents.

Much more is involved in assuming primary caregiving responsibilities than simply being physically and financially "able." Many custodial grandparents have reached a point in their lives when they can pursue their own interests and the dreams they put on hold while they worked and reared families, or they may still be engaged in the workforce on a full- or part-time basis. Others may find it exhausting to keep up with young children, particularly those who have experienced trauma in dysfunctional situations and have multiple needs, demands, and activities (such as health/mental health appointments and co-curricular activities). Some grandparents take on the unexpected role joyfully, while others are enormously burdened with other caregiving responsibilities (e.g., spouse/partner, parents/parents-in-law, other family members) and sometimes guilt-ridden because of their own children's inabilities to parent (which they may blame on themselves). In any event, many parenting grandparents, even if they are eager to care for their grandchildren, need significant support from social, educational, and health care agencies, and policy support to meet their financial and other needs.

Social workers working with grandparents can use generalist practice skills and perspectives. Generalist practitioners are trained to recognize the need for and offer several types of support as they sensitize themselves to the complexities of the emotional and instrumental stresses (e.g., physical and financial care needs) grandparents experience. Grandparents who care full-time for their grandchildren may find the role emotionally, physically, and financially stressful (Marsiglia et al., 2021). Within the assessment and planning phase of work, social workers can build on the coping abilities and skills that grandparents have used in responding to life experiences, including discrimination and oppression (Marsiglia et al., 2021). Gathering specific information about the grandparent–grandchild situation is key to the assessment, planning, and intervention phases of work, including questions about: (1) the caregiving arrangement (i.e., formal or informal); (2) parents' involvement with the grandparent and child; (3) mental and physical health problems; (4) grandchild's academic performance (if applicable) and social relationship; (5) history of trauma; and (6) participation in other services (Dolbin-MacNab, 2020).

Interventions with grandparents have been shown to have positive impact on grandparents' and grandchildren's well-being in such areas as social support, parenting skills, and behavioral concerns (Chan et al., 2019). To support grandparents, interventions that focus on education, support, and resources for their grandchildren are critical (Dunn & Wamsley, 2018). Dunn and Wamsley (2018) recommend content should address grandparent concerns related to parenting a new generation of children, providing care at a point in their lives where health and retirement are priorities, and addressing the potentially complex issues related to family relationships, parental concerns, legal issues, and trauma. In addition to support in navigating services, this group can also benefit from social workers ensuring resources are available and provided. Some of these families faced significant challenges during the pandemic when schools and child care facilities were closed and grandparents' own health was threatened.

In some situations, birth parents recovering from substance use disorders or other challenges have visiting privileges or partial child caregiving responsibilities on a preliminary or trial basis. These arrangements can cause tension between grandparents and parents. These and other conflicts may indicate the need for additional assistance from social workers. Interventions should emphasize the children's and family's well-being, including a focus on the children, grandparents, other family members, and service providers, particularly in the areas of personal growth (i.e., strengths-based empowerment, coping, and capabilities) (Hayslip et al., 2017). Despite the multiple challenges present in such situations, assessment and intervention can focus on both the child(ren) (e.g., improve behaviors) as well as the grandparents (e.g., provide support), but should go beyond providing information and involve others who are significant partners (e.g., school systems, community resources) (Xu et al., 2022).

Lesbian, Gay, Bisexual, Transgender, and Queer Couples and Families

Social workers work with LGBTQIA+ clients as individuals, couples, and larger families. The following discussion highlights current characteristics and issues related to social work practice with LGBTQIA+ families. There are approximately 980,000 same-sex couple households in the United States of which 58 percent are spouses and 42 percent are unmarried couples with female same-sex couples outnumbering male couples (Walker & Taylor, 2021). Census data is not collected regarding couples and families who have a member who is bisexual, transgender, or queer.

With the 2015 landmark Supreme Court ruling making same-sex marriage legal in all states in the United Sates (Supreme Court of the United States, 2015), same-sex couples achieved marriage equality. However, LGBTQIA+ couples continue to face discrimination from some members and organizations within society. A poll commissioned by the LGBTQIA+ acceptance advocacy organization GLAAD notes that, while an overwhelming number of Americans support federal protection in such areas as housing, access to businesses and public restrooms, employment benefits, and military service, there are still 27 states that offer no non-discrimination protections (GLAAD, 2020). Levels of discomfort with situations involving members of the LBGTQIA+ community continue to be reported by one-fourth to one-third of those surveyed in such areas as attending places of worship, learning that a family member, teacher, or physician is LGBTQIA+, and an increased number of discrimination reports were made (GLAAD, 2020). While the stigma associated with LGBTQIA+ couples and families is on the decline, these groups will likely continue to struggle for recognition of their legal standing and commitment within the greater societal culture. For example, some states are engaged in efforts to investigate parents for child maltreatment who pursue gender-affirming care for transgender children and restricting LGBTQIA+ parents' adoption rights.

In all family interventions, social workers need culturally responsive and specific, competent, and humble knowledge, skills, and values, but attention to these areas is particularly important when working with sexual and gender diverse families. Experiencing stress daily can impact relationships as well as physical and mental health (NASEM, 2020). Therefore, social workers working with LGBTQIA+ families can provide support by collaborating with them to identify and implement strategies for coping with the stress that accompanies discrimination in societal acceptance, treatment of their children, and accessing services. Evidence suggests that having supportive family relationships, parental acceptance, and supportive school personnel can strengthen the well-being of sexual and gender diverse children and youth (NASEM, 2020).

Social workers can also help LGBTQIA+ families address the discrimination they face by exploring the impact of the discrimination, homophobia, and stigma on the individual members as well as the family itself and issues of intersectionality that may be experienced (Prendergast & MacPhee, 2018). Our ethical obligations require us to advocate for sexual and gender diverse children and families at all levels of practice.

Parenthood While not all LGBTQIA+ individuals and couples have children, those that do can approach parenthood, like all parents do, in ways that work for their relationship and situation. They may have children from previous relationships, adopt, or have a child by birth. Currently, 28 states and Washington DC prohibit discrimination based on sexual orientation or gender identity for fostering or adoption, while 5 prohibit discrimination based on sexual orientation only and 17 states provide no protections (Movement Advancement Project [MAP], 2022). Court cases debating these families' parenting rights introduce uncertainty in their lives.

Research continues to demonstrate that children reared by LGBTQIA+ parents suffer no detrimental emotional, psychosocial, or behavioral effects. Social workers practicing from a strengths-based and anti-oppressive perspective reject even the premise of such research, which seems to presume that parental sexual orientation could be a source of children's challenges. An extensive review of research noted that "sexual orientation is not a significant determinant of parenting ability or child development and "family processes and family stability are more important determinants among children and youth in these families than parental sexual orientation" (NASEM, 2020, p. 218).

As prospective parents, LGBTQIA+ persons and couples can still face obstacles in the foster care or adoption processes. They may still experience institutionalized stigma, even from social workers or agencies that restrict social workers' ability to practice equitably with LGBTQIA+ people seeking to adopt/parent. In both policy and practice, social workers should support the efforts of all persons seeking parenthood who, through the assessment process, are deemed capable of providing a loving and supportive environment for a child. Social workers can de-emphasize the search for dysfunction and pathology as they give expression to the strengths and resilience of the parents (Goldberg & Allen, 2013). Social workers can also recognize the effects of lingering cultural discrimination directed against the LGBTQIA+ community regarding the strengths and viability of such people as parents.

When working with LGBTQIA+ youth and families, social workers can commit to increase their knowledge and skills so they may create affirming and safe spaces for successful work together (Kaasbøll et al., 2022). Building on the resiliency potential of the family, social workers can help families identify their strengths and protective factors, including emotional support, communication, flexibility, and meaning-making (Prendergast & MacPhee, 2018). Of critical importance during the helping relationship is to avoid basing your assessment and interactions on a heteronormative standard; that is, the belief that heterosexuality is the norm and, in the case of families, the two parents are heterosexual and married.

Social workers must examine their own attitudes and values about the LGBTQIA+ community (Dessel & Rodenborg, 2017). Social workers should acknowledge that LGBTQIA+ parents face many of the same challenges all parents encounter (e.g., parental roles, discipline philosophy, and expectations of children, lack of legal protections if not married, insufficient community supports, etc.).

Single-Parent Families

Being reared in a single-parent family is more common than ever; currently, 11 million children in the United States live in a household headed by a single parent, most headed by their mother (U.S. Census Bureau, 2021b). Society and, at times, some social service providers, have historically viewed single parenthood as a risk that leads to insecure, delinquent, and otherwise dysfunctional households. While the data suggest that families headed by a single parent do have unique challenges, such generalized assumptions are unwarranted.

It is important to recognize the specific challenges when working with single-parent families. For example, when working with single-parent families, it is helpful to know that generally, if the household head is female, these families report lower levels of income than two-parent families or male-headed households (Shrider et al., 2021). Children who reside with single fathers do not experience poverty at the same rate as children living with single mothers. Fathers tend to come to single parenting later than single mothers and often do not experience the financial disadvantages that single mothers do, in large part due to gender advantage in hiring.

There are unique challenges in single parenting and in the way that such parenting impacts both the social work relationship and parenting functions. Four major issues that frequently arise for single parent families are (1) a lack of resources to cope with stress, financial obligations, or other responsibility; (2) unresolved family-of-origin issues, often brought on by the single parent's need for assistance from their parents; (3) unresolved divorce or relationship issues, such as anger, grief, or loneliness; and (4) an overburdened older child. An older child who is not yet an adult may be pressed into providing excessive household chores or care for another family member. While such an arrangement may be deemed necessary, there are risks for the older child when clear and healthy boundaries are not maintained.

Families headed by single parents are at greater risk than two-parent families for challenges for themselves and their children. In addition to economic challenges and potential stigma, growing up in a single-parent household can result in academic and behavioral problems (Lee et al., 2020). Multiple factors can, at times, be categorized as both risks and protective factors, including employment, having multiple roles and responsibilities, adaptability, family leadership, and extended family support (Van Hook, 2019). The social worker can work with the family to build on their existing strengths to optimize their ability to be resilient (Lee et al., 2020).

While social workers work with children, parents, and combinations of children with one or both parents, focusing engagement, assessment, planning, intervention, termination, and evaluation and follow-up on the family itself, social work practice with single-parent families can use the family's strengths to create and mobilize and stabilize coping skills. When working primarily with the child(ren) and/or parent(s), the intervention may be delivered individually or within a group context but should embrace a systemic approach that can address such issues as the impact of the divorce/separation, single- and co-parenting strategies, and, most importantly, ensuring that the best interests of the children is prioritized (Huff & Hartenstein, 2020). Social workers' roles can be as varied as the needs of the family, but often include (Lee et al., 2020; Van Hook, 2019):

1 shifting from a deficit perspective to emphasizing strengths and resiliency.
2 using a strengths perspective to help families build collaborative alliances with resources outside the family (e.g., school professionals and/or neighbors).
3 serving as a linkage or liaison between the family and existing and potential support systems.
4 integrating a multi-systemic approach that enables the family to engage in decision-making within and outside the family system.
5 providing and/or connecting families to education and support resources.

This knowledge and these values are consistent with a strengths-based, empowering approach that recognizes both internal and external factors and supports single parents in their ongoing efforts to provide security and nurturance for their children. Such knowledge and these values can enhance the social worker's efforts to engage and assess the family system by conveying a sense of care and concern for individual members, identifying and building on the strengths of each member and the unit, and emphasizing their self-efficacy.

Families of Multiple Racial, Ethnic, and Cultural Heritages

The number of interracial, interethnic, and intercultural marriages continues to increase with nearly half of US adults offering their support (Parker et al.,

2019). Shifting immigration patterns in the United States, globalization, and the breakdown of ethnic barriers all influence the numbers of racially and ethnically mixed families.

While many in our society value the contributions of other cultures and challenge the notions associated with racial and ethnic privilege, many gains have yet to be made for families whose members include multiple racial, ethnic, and/or cultural groups. While challenges for couples and families may arise in such areas as beliefs and practices of home, family, gendered roles and expectations, language, communication styles, and relationships among members, the social worker should not assume that all problems are related to racial, ethnic, or cultural differences (Singh et al., 2020). Social workers can address the areas for change and growth by developing awareness, knowledge, and skills to work with multiracial/multiethnic families with a focus on intersectionality and an appreciation for the layered experiences in their lives (Stokes et al., 2021).

Becoming aware of societal histories of oppression and your personal histories of oppression is a critical step toward becoming a culturally responsive (and humble) practitioner (Marsiglia et al., 2021). Flexibility, shared goals, and a commitment to explore and address challenges are critical elements in work across culturally and ethnically diverse families and communities. As with all other aspects of individual and family assessment and intervention, a family should not be defined solely in terms of its group characteristics (e.g., race, ethnicity, or culture) but should be assessed with a lens on the individuals who are members of the family (Van Hook, 2019).

As you engage in assessment, planning, and intervention with a multiracial, multiethnic, or multicultural family, being able to listen to their description of their family, relationships, and perspectives on experiences related to race and ethnicity can be a starting point for your understanding of their situation when there are different identities within the family. Social workers unfamiliar with multiracial/multiethnic families should be cautious not to apply their own cultural beliefs and values when completing the assessment process, but to be open to learning about this family's journey (Olcoń, 2019).

Assessment can be strengthened by exploring the perceptions of the actual problem and determining if it is connected to cultural differences, as well as by use of culturally specific tools that capture cultural assumptions, beliefs, perceptions of inclusion, patterns, relationships, emotions, and perspectives of others about the family (see Singh et al., 2020, for discussion of specific tools). Exhibit 6.3 provides guidance for engaging, assessing, and planning with families using a culturally responsive approach. Building on the assessment and planning phases, the intervention may focus on: (1) internal—perceptions family members identify within the context of a multicultural family and (2) external—how others perceive the family challenges facing the family (Singh et al., 2020). With their emphasis on identifying strengths, resilience, and positive lived experiences, approaches found to be effective with multicultural families include narrative, solution-focused, and strengths-based intervention models (Singh et al., 2020).

EXHIBIT 6.3

Engaging With Diverse Families: Racial and Ethnic Diversity

Remain open and nonjudgmental to alternative lifestyles.	Clearly communicate to the family that you know there are many different ways of living and doing things. Cite examples and initiate conversation into an area so that the family will feel comfortable talking to you about their family and life situations.
Disclose patterns and ways of doing things in your family and culture and ask the family to describe how things are handled in their families and cultures.	A comparison conversation may facilitate information exchange and mutual understanding. Ask, "how do you do that in your family?" or "What does this mean in your culture(s)?"
Ask for and accept feedback from the family about your demonstrated cultural knowledge and sensitivity.	Tell the family what you are thinking and ask them to comment on whether your thoughts and beliefs are accurate from their viewpoint.

Source: Zhang et al., 2021, p. 271

Families That Include Persons With Disabilities

Social workers work with families in which one or more members have physical, developmental, intellectual, cognitive, and/or psychological disabilities. The number of children identified as having cognitive challenges continues to increase with the highest rates being indigenous and tribal children (Young, 2021). Increases may be an artifact of improved identification and reporting and not necessarily an increase in the number of persons with a disability.

Family-centered care is an empowerment-focused philosophy of care that creates a partnership between the family and professionals (Institute for Healthcare Improvement [IHI], 2022). Family-centered care emphasizes (IHI, 2022):

- developing care pathways (i.e., sequencing of plans to promote access) that are co-designed and co-produced with individuals and families.

- ensuring that care preferences are understood and honored, including at the end of life.

- collaborating with partners on programs designed to improve engagement, shared decision-making, and compassionate, empathic care.

- working with partners to ensure that communities are supported to stay healthy and to provide care for their loved ones closer to home. (para. 4)

Family-centered care is a strengths-based approach that focuses on the family to ensure they have voice in decision-making and emphasizes change through positive helping relationships (Lietz & Geiger, 2017). This strengths-based approach is a promising method for working with families in many arenas, especially with those who have disabilities. When children have serious learning, and/or health challenges, such as neuro-developmental delays, interprofessional teaming, in which professionals from different disciplines work together toward the client's goals, is a valuable response.

Social workers can play a key role on such teams to help address the needs of children with disabilities across the lifespan. With our commitment to a strengths-based, person-in-environment perspective, we can document the family's lived experience with disability and facilitate the inclusion of the family into the intervention (Millington & Madden, 2018). The focus of work with families in which a member has a disability is to ensure that the intervention be client-controlled and that everyone is heard (Millington & Madden, 2018). Based on the family's needs, family-centered practice can focus on relationship building (creating trust and respect) and capacity building (creation of new strengths) (Dunst & Espe-Sherwindt, 2016).

Many agencies employ family-centered social workers to help adults with developmental disabilities learn job skills. These social workers intervene with individuals with disabilities, their families, and their broader support networks, to help during this crucial time of transition to new employment prospects. As another example, when a child with serious disabilities is born, family members usually must reorganize both their everyday lives and their long-term plans. One parent may have to stop working to facilitate the services the child needs. Siblings are affected, family interactions are affected, and parents often struggle with the emotional ramifications and physical consequences of demands of coordinating with multiple providers. Social workers can offer support and help with expanding parents' ability to identify resources. In addition, many families struggle to access services to which they are entitled and therefore may need social work advocacy to negotiate a complex system.

Societal views that emphasize deficits may challenge social workers working with families that include individuals with disabilities. In response, social workers and disability scholars have proposed the following set of beliefs to serve as a foundation for working with such families (Mackelprang et al., 2016):

- Persons with disabilities are capable, have potential, and are important members of society.

- Devaluation and a lack of resources, not individual pathology, are the primary obstacles facing persons with disabilities and their families.

- Disability, like race and gender, is a social construct, and intervention with people with disabilities is political in nature.

- There are cultures and histories within the disability communities that professionals should be aware of to facilitate the empowerment of persons with disabilities.
- There is a joy and vitality to be found in disability.
- Persons with disabilities have the right to self-determination and the right to guide professionals' involvement in their lives. (p. xvii)

Social workers have the opportunity and ethical responsibility to empower clients to embrace this belief system first as individuals and then as a profession. The recent shift toward integrating a strengths-based perspective into working with persons with disabilities provides social workers with an opportunity to develop and provide services that promote the client's self-determination (Wehmeyer, 2020). Evidence suggests that having the right to self-determination is linked to improved quality of life and life satisfaction (Wehmeyer, 2020). When individuals and organizations within our society do not embrace a strengths-based perspective, the social worker may need to become an advocate for people with disabilities.

A diversity model that views societal attitudes, structures, policies, and institutions as responsible for imposing limitations on persons with disabilities is most appropriate for work with individuals with disabilities. Person-first language (e.g., person with a disability) is currently in use in some segments of society as well as "identity-first language" (e.g., "autistic teen") but professionals should be mindful that language should focus on the needs, autonomy, and rights (including the right to self-determination) of the individual (Botha et al., 2021). Social workers may need to advocate for disability to be seen as a dimension of diversity in society, which implies that social workers need to engage in public dialogue about advocacy, structural principles, and the skills to work for social justice.

There is a growing need for social workers who have competencies in working with families in which a member has a disability. Social workers must first reflect on their own awareness, competence, and knowledge about persons with disabilities and the challenges they may face (Sue et al., 2016). In working with persons with disabilities and their families, social workers can serve in multiple roles, including education and employment advocacy, empowering persons with disabilities and their families in self-advocacy, facilitating linkages with and use of resources and technology, and promoting self-determination (Sue et al., 2016). Specifically, we can collaborate with the family and the person with a disability to de-emphasize any pathology associated with the disability and close the gap between where the family is and where they want to be (Millington & Madden, 2018). It is important to ask the family members, including siblings, what roles they would like to have in the assessment and intervention processes.

Lastly, consider that the family may be faced with multiple, and sometimes contradictory, demands for attention and resources. For example, a family may have more than one member with a disability, a member with a disability along with financial difficulties, and a child with a disability and another child with a substance use issue. An increasingly common situation involving multiple challenges is the family in which aging parent(s) have children in need. Such situations can create a crisis for the family as well as the social worker in terms of prioritizing needs and goals and allocating limited resources. In each of these examples, the family experiences multiple stressors and may feel incapable of making decisions. The social worker's role may be to focus a part of the intervention on prioritizing the needs of all family members.

Blended Families

A blended family is considered one in which separate families come together through marriage or other circumstances (Barker, 2014). Blended families include kinship and non-kinship groups including domestic partner relationships, civil unions, and nonrelated families who co-reside in the same household who assume traditional family roles (Barker, 2014). Approximately 16 percent of children in the United States live as part of a blended family and this number is increasing (Chertoff, 2018).

While most blended families come together without specifically seeking the services of a helping professional, some families value a social worker's contribution as they blend into the new family constellation. Blended families often face challenges in creating the new family unit, including: (1) increased complexity or roles and expectations; (2) loss, loyalty, conflicts, and lack of control; and (3) lack of social support (Brimhall, 2020). These challenges place the members of the family at risk for experiencing vulnerabilities and inequities in relationships, psychological strains, and physical health challenges (Adler-Baeder & Higginbotham, 2020).

Intervening with a blended family can address the issues noted previously to help the family develop stability by focusing on three areas (Brimhall, 2020):

1. Psychoeducation to address realistic expectations, validate feelings of being overwhelmed, and create a balanced view of co-parenting.
2. Interpersonal work with sub-sets of the families to strengthen the relationships among members, including non-custodial parents and other siblings, and to help family members communicate regarding myths and misunderstandings related to blended families.
3. Work with individual members of the families to address past experiences with families, relationships, and oppression and intersectionality.

Families can benefit from discussion of practical strategies to address challenges, particularly in the areas of blending family traditions, helping children adjust by having routines, addressing sibling rivalry by clearly communicating expectations and providing individual space for each child, negotiating parents' discipline styles by prioritizing civility, respect, and clarity of expectations, and having realistic expectations for children based on their ages (Chertoff, 2018).

Social workers working with blended families should be aware of the families' histories and sensitive to the dynamics that may occur when two families merge into one. Incorporating information about family blending is a critical component of the engagement, assessment, planning, and intervention processes. Family members may not be aware of or able to articulate the challenges they are experiencing regarding the "merger" of the family units. Social workers who are attuned to the issues that can occur when families blend can identify the reason the family is struggling.

Work with a blended family begins with recognition of the family members' goals and expectations for the blending of two families. Inviting each member to articulate their "best hopes" for the creation of the new family enables each voice to be heard. For example, parents may hope to be able to adapt and be involved, while children may hope for more time with their biological parent (Metcalf, 2017). Within the engagement and assessment processes, the social worker can help the family identify and discuss individual and family strengths, the roles of individual members, and boundaries between members of the families coming together. It is important to view each member of the newly created family unit within the context of both systems (i.e., the original family and new family) in which they exist.

Competence in working with blended families requires knowledge of family development and transitions. For example, children's close relationships with biological and stepparents create less transition-related stress, while children with close relationships with non-resident biological parents experience increased stress due to the "loyalty bind" they feel toward that parent (Jensen et al., 2017). Helping the family address members' transitions, stress, and feelings of loyalty can positively impact children's well-being (Jensen et al., 2017). You may need to involve noncustodial parents and extended families to help families negotiate new and different family roles, boundaries, relationships, and traditions. The social worker can also engage with and assess blended families by helping them identify their expectations for the forming of this new family. From the work of Gibson (2013), the following questions for one type of blended family, the stepfamily, may be helpful to this process:

1. What does it mean to be family? Who influenced these beliefs? How have your beliefs of family influenced your blended/step family?
2. As each person responds, the other members may be asked: What was it about what they said that made you believe them? Is there anything that was said that does not fit with your individual values now?
3. Are your beliefs about stepfamilies influenced by any outside sources like friends or media? In what way?
4. If a child has been open to new roles in the blended family, the family may be asked: What benefits have transpired from you being open to your different view of family roles?
5. What positive influences do you think you have brought to your stepparent's life? How do you think your stepparent feels about the influence you have had on them?
6. Do you have friends at school or work who are part of a stepfamily? What do you think that family is doing well together? How do they do that? (pp. 798–799)

Immigrant and Refugee Families

Social work practice with families in contemporary society requires global competency. If you practice social work with families in the United States, you will likely encounter families who have arrived as immigrants or refugees. If you are a social worker outside the United States, you will need extensive knowledge of international issues. While working with families abroad or domestically requires different knowledge regarding immigration, legal and governmental issues, cultures, and customs, the same practice skill set is common to all family social work practice regardless of setting or location. You should be prepared for working with families who are new to their country, and with those who are "stuck" in countries for many years and wish to be elsewhere (back in their home country or as an immigrant to their country of choice). In the current political climate, new challenges have arisen, including the risk of separation and the greater likelihood that these families experience harassment and discrimination. Social workers need to gain understanding of the political and policy issues, resources, and the families' experiences.

To become competent in thinking and working internationally, learn as much as possible about the family or families with whom you will work. Before you meet the client(s), expose yourself to information about their relocation history and experience and their home culture, language, customs and traditions, spiritual practices, and community. Although reading about your client's country of origin and culture can be helpful, seek out others who can provide you with firsthand personal or professional experiences and guidance.

Understanding the political context and shifting legal framework related to your clients' experiences is critical.

While some characteristics may be common to groups of people who share a country of origin, culture, or traditions, social workers should view each person within a family and the family itself as an individual. Remember also that the client family can be your best source of information and insight. You may find as many similarities between a family from the United States and a family from Ghana as between two families from Ghana. Emphasize a stance of cultural humility and allow yourself to learn from them and learn about them as a unique family. Learning about the lives of the families with whom you work is an ongoing process that can unfold as you build rapport and trust. As with all clients, it is important to explore these families' perceptions and beliefs about working with a helping professional.

While much of the social work practice knowledge and skills you learn is applicable to all families, certain competencies are unique to working with a family that has relocated from its country of origin. First, it is critical to understand the cultural norms of your client family related to the definition of family. As with any family, you need to have a clear understanding of who is considered a member of the family, how family members relate to one another, the meaning of those relationships, and any traditions that may exist within the family unit. For example, does the word "family" describe the nuclear unit or the larger, extended family? Are persons who are not biologically or legally linked considered part of the family? What rules and tasks guide family members in their daily lives and in making major life decisions such as marriage, parenting, residential arrangements, education, careers, religion/spirituality, and financial priorities?

> *In the case of the Patel family, you may meet your clients during a crisis or disaster-related time in their lives. With the Patel family, the emphasis must be on their immediate needs, so you will have to rely on the information that is shared in that context and on your observations.*

Regardless of the family's origins, you can use a strengths-based approach to complete your assessment and intervention planning. While you can use a strengths-based approach with families of any ethnic, cultural, or heritage background, identifying strengths can be particularly helpful when considered within the cultural context of the family with whom you are working, as these family dynamics can have different meanings when viewed within the cultural background of the client.

Building on family strengths can be a particularly helpful strategy as families adjust to their new country and environment. Parents, for example, may struggle with getting their children to adopt the customs, language, and dress of their family's culture, or older adults may find it challenging to live in a world that is unfamiliar to them. When a family experiences a crisis or tragedy, as in the case of the Patel family, they may find that usual coping and support systems are not available in their new country. Using the family's strengths can empower family members to find their place within their new home while maintaining their connections to their heritage. You can help to make global connections between the world from which the family has come and the one they have entered by affirming the family's ability to rely on one another in times of need despite the challenges they face adjusting to life in their new country.

Working with a family new to the country can involve a multi-faceted assessment and planning process as they may have a complex array of needs. As you work with immigrant or refugee families, your assessment and planning processes may include the following best practice areas (Potocky & Naseh, 2019):

Health

- Assessment of health beliefs and treatment expectations
- Health education and counseling
- Culturally and linguistically appropriate psychosocial treatment

Mental Health

- Case management
- Supportive counseling
- Information and skills training
- Crisis intervention
- Culturally and linguistically appropriate and evidence-based therapies

Family Dynamics

- Couple and family therapy
- Ethnic identity and acculturation interventions
- Reminiscence therapy

Language and Education

- Referral, case advocacy, and follow-up
- Supportive counseling
- Psychosocial interventions

Economic Well-Being

- Job search assistance, coaching, and mentoring
- Self-employment assistance

- Vocational education and career counseling
- Professional recertification
- Child care

Interethnic Relations

- Structured interethnic contact
- Conflict resolution

Summary

In summary, while the preceding discussions focused on family situations and circumstances, in the real world of social work practice, individuals and families may present multiple concerns and dilemmas that include a combination of financial, relationship, and physical and mental health challenges. For example, a grandparent rearing an adolescent grandson may be facing a custody battle with the child's biological parent; a couple with a child born with a disability may also be grappling with a grandparent's cognitive impairment; a blended family may be coping with employment layoffs and foreclosure proceedings on their home.

The social worker's role with families facing multiple challenges is to approach each as a unique system with individualized strengths and needs. Listening to each member of a family unit enables the social worker to gain insight into each individual's perceptions, relationship dynamics, and possibilities within the collective family system. Social workers who are competent in working with families have developed a repertoire of behaviors that include family-focused knowledge, skills, and values. Social workers can focus on organizing problem-solving into short- and longer-term goals and promoting a supportive and nurturing environment. Of importance is the need to gain insight into the family's patterns of behaviors to understand the health and functional status of the whole family as well as sub-sets within the family, specifically assessing communication styles, rules and myths, decision-making, problem-solving, and negotiation (Zhang et al., 2021). For example, a family may face an internal challenge—substance use by one of the members—and/or they may face an external challenge—the family's inability to qualify for subsidized housing. While social workers may need to use different strategies to address internal versus external issues, they can benefit by understanding the patterns used by the family to navigate challenges. As in work with individual clients, in working with a family, you may serve a number of roles (e.g., broker, advocate, counselor, or educator). The remainder of this chapter will highlight behaviors within these roles that are needed to work effectively with families.

CONTEMPORARY TRENDS AND SKILLS FOR ENGAGEMENT AND ASSESSMENT WITH FAMILIES

As with social work practice with individuals, social workers working with families often utilize multiple theories to guide the intervention (Payne, 2020). Throughout your career, you will develop the approach most consistent with your philosophical and practice perspectives and the expectations of your agency. With social work's grounding in a systems orientation, most social workers employ a systemic approach but often incorporate theories and specialized techniques into the intervention. Particularly relevant are solutions-focused and narrative approaches as they emphasize family strengths and future-focused perspectives (versus problems) (Payne, 2020). Regardless of the theoretical approach(es) you use, your goals in social work practice with families should be collaborative, culturally responsive, and grounded in the idea that the family is the client system. Moreover, every assessment should embrace a biopsychosocial-spiritual-sexual perspective and include exploration of ethnicity, race, socioeconomic status, gender, and sexual identity and expression (Edwards et al., 2020). Also remember the importance of inquiring about the impact of all relevant cultural factors on the family's ability to engage in the intervention process, including but not limited to past experiences with receiving services, access/barriers to services, language, child care, transportation, and literacy (Edwards et al., 2020). The following discussion highlights theoretical approaches to engagement, assessment, and planning.

Narrative Theory in Family Engagement and Assessment

As discussed throughout this book, narrative theory is based on a postmodern, constructionist perspective that enables clients to make sense of their lives through "stories"—that is, through the client's perception of an individual or a situation. With its roots in working with indigenous individuals and families who had experienced oppression, the focus is to build a client–worker relationship that can empower families to work toward their preferred stories (Anderson, 2016).

> *In the case of the Patel family, for example, it will be important over time for you to encourage the family members to share their stories with you about their immigration to the United States, adjusting to a new culture, and establishing their business, and their feelings about living through the hurricane.*

Family interpretations of events can differ from supporting the ongoing narrative that most members believe to refuting the narrative to a combination of the two. Families use the stories to organize their subsequent experiences. When experiences do not fit their chosen narratives, families often dismiss those experiences as not representative of the real family. The language families use to interpret and describe various family stories is significant

> **EXHIBIT 6.4**
>
> *Tenets of a Narrative Family Intervention*

1. Language (i.e., word choice) helps determine how families assign meaning to life events and provides the context for change.
2. Stories, much like language, help families give meaning to their life events.
3. The stories each family member creates shape subsequent life events, and family members may recall life events differently. It is important to acknowledge all stories, as multiple realities can and do exist simultaneously.
4. Social context, specifically culture, influences values, social roles, gender relationships, and concepts of justice, which, in turn, serve to define the stories family members create.
5. Stories are not necessarily based in fact; they may instead be the result of family members' perceptions of life experiences, which may not include strengths and positive alternatives.
6. Stories can encompass possibilities for growth and healing.
7. Families are not the problem; families experience problems.

Source: Adapted from Van Hook, 2019, pp. 250–251

and shapes how they view the experience. For example, one family may frame one member's alcohol addiction as an "occasional problem."

Exhibit 6.4 outlines the tenets on which a narrative family assessment and intervention is based. The following examples explore the ideas central to a narrative approach.

As opposed to seeking a diagnosis, conducting an assessment from the narrative perspective involves helping family members tell their family and individual stories, which you can then use to inform the intervention. Using a narrative approach intertwines the assessment and intervention processes as you invite each member of the family to share their stories and concerns and begin to separate themselves from the current problem for the purpose of re-authoring their individual and/or collective family story (Suddeath et al., 2017). The goal of a narrative approach is to help the family alter their interpretation of themselves and their current situation to one that is more liberating. The role of the professional is to serve as a co-editor and collaborator with the family in creating new meanings (Van Hook, 2019).

Consider the family who seeks out a social worker out of concern for the daughter Liza, who is 6 years old and the youngest child and only girl in a single-parent, male-headed household in a rural community. The father and siblings cast Liza in the role of family "misfit." They describe her behavior as oppositional and say that she is clumsy, speaks disrespectfully, and is disruptive. The family uses any incident involving Liza (e.g., forgetting her pencil or knocking over her milk) as just another piece of evidence supporting her misfit status. When Liza's first-grade teacher reports that Liza is exceptionally well liked, by both her peers and teachers, and that she is bright and fun, Liza's father is incredulous. He suspects the teacher has her confused with another student or that Liza must be faking at school. From his perspective, the *real* Liza, as everyone knows, is oppositional, clumsy, disrespectful, and disruptive.

The story that Liza tells about herself is different from her family's story about her that emphasizes their negative perceptions of her. Each individual story carries the power to perpetuate and expand the family story, which in turn will influence the way Liza, as the major character, plays her role. If her family persist in maintaining their original negatively focused perception of Liza and are not able to view her in a more positive, strengths-based light, she is likely to respond over time by becoming increasingly rude, failing, or developing truly disruptive conduct. On the other hand, if her family re-authors their perceptions and recognizes exceptions to their ideas about Liza, her story may unfold quite differently. Everyone has multiple stories, but some have more power, relevance, and a wider audience than others. Liza's alternative story (told by her teacher) has the potential to influence her future in positive and significant ways. While Liza's current teacher sees Liza's strengths, it is important to note that a change in teacher and family members' stories about their children can influence how others view the child.

Thickening the Story The narrative framework has many components. This chapter focuses on the concepts most relevant to generalist social work practice with families during the engagement, assessment, and planning stages of work. To begin, the social worker collaboratively engages with the family in externalizing conversations that help them to separate the negative narratives and belief systems they bring to the intervention (Van Hook, 2019). This attempt to create a more complex story may achieve the larger goal of instilling hope that the client can make positive changes. Liza's story is a good example of a negatively focused account. In the account, she has no redeeming virtues. An alternate reality version of Liza's story reveals her likable personality, talents, and ability to connect with people despite, or in addition to, any behaviors that are oppositional, clumsy, disrespectful, and disruptive.

Our second example comes from the Smith family, who emphasize the importance of race, family structure, and the value of reframing the story. The Smiths have experienced considerable child-rearing challenges. One child has been taken into state custody for behavioral concerns, and now child protection workers are investigating to determine whether they should remove another child for safety reasons. The mother disparagingly claims, in defeat and sarcastic resignation, that the Smiths are "just one of those families." Child welfare workers may likewise view them as "just one of those families" because various Smith children have been in custody for three generations (as was Ms. Smith).

Rather than assessing the narrowly defined dysfunction of this family, the narrative social worker would search for exceptions to this story to enrich it and make it more complex. Rather than maintaining a focus on problem-solving, narrative social workers view the family systemically to understand the impact of the cultural and contextual ecological systems, particularly as they relate to the family's stories (Suddeath et al., 2017). For example, the social worker can ask about Ms. Smith's ability to keep a family together for 10 years in the face of poverty, to overcome a major childhood health challenge, or to survive homelessness. As part of the engagement and assessment process, the social worker can ask questions of the family that will help to identify the family's risk factors and negative belief systems (Van Hook, 2019). The social worker's aim is to expand the narrow failure story so that the family can see its successes and potential, which in turn can support re-authoring the story to reflect the way the family would like it to be. The family then can shape its future to fit the new story. Such a narrative approach offers the potential for hope through development of the family's resilience and positive attributes.

A narrative approach can provide an opportunity to highlight the fact that a family's resilience can be a powerful aspect of the social work intervention. A resilience perspective enables the family and you to address risks of the belief system that perpetuates negative patterns while also supporting protective factors by changing negative family beliefs to those that embody hope, self-efficacy, and coherence and more positive family interactions (Van Hook, 2019). Some families need help identifying their areas of strength and resiliency. You can conceptualize resiliency as the family's ability to "absorb the shock of problems and discover strategies to solve them while finding ways to meet the needs of family members and the family unit" (Van Hook, 2019, p. 15). Be aware that a family's perspective on resiliency may be culturally influenced. For example, some families may view resilience as a family characteristic while others see it as an individual quality (Marsiglia et al., 2021).

Social workers can help families by incorporating the family's stories into the assessment and planning phases of work. Combining tenets of narrative and solution-focused approaches, Metcalf (2017) suggests these guidelines for the family intervention:

- Families are systems whose interactions result in certain behaviors; therefore, a change in interactions will result in new behaviors.
- Gathering the best hopes from every family member can provide direction, or goals, for a conversation.
- Inviting the family to describe the problem externally can release them from blame so they may join the others to build a preferred future.
- Acknowledging the effect of the problem on the family system can provide motivation to the family members to stand up to the problem and reclaim the desired family story.
- Discovering exceptions in family life and among family members provides encouragement and strategies to use once again.
- Scaling problems from 1 to 10, with 10 meaning the family is in control and 1 meaning the problem is in control, provides a way to measure distress and success.
- Writing a new chapter as a family, where each family member has a chance to describe their wishes, encourages each member to alter their narrative. (p. 157)

While the social worker's role is to help the family "co-edit" their problem-saturated stories into those of hope and possibilities, they must first reflect on their own personal narratives and professional authority to ensure the family and the work are not negatively influenced (Van Hook, 2019). The social worker can strive to empower the family to operationalize their capacities for resilience specifically by:

- incorporating a sense of hopefulness and purpose into the meaning families assign to situations (e.g., pointing out ways in which the family can show support for the family member who has just completed a substance use disorder treatment, and the importance of that support).

- supporting organizational structures that provide effective leadership and a balance of flexibility and stability to help build family resilience by streamlining access and service delivery.

- promoting clear, empathic, and supportive communication patterns among family members.

- emphasizing existing positive family relationships.

- promoting family members' problem-solving abilities.

- to the extent possible, enhancing the social support system and community and economic resources accessible to the family. (Van Hook, 2019, p. 30)

Externalizing Problems Within the narrative approach, the notion that problems are considered outside of the family is known as *externalization*. The problem is separate from the individual or family, enabling them to create an alternative story (Hall, 2022). Narrative social workers try to identify and help the family to name the issue that is creating their difficulties. By objectifying or personifying it, family members can develop a relationship with the challenge, rather than be consumed by it. Ultimately, then, they may control it.

For example, if a family feels overwhelmed by the demands of rearing a child with disabilities, the social worker may externalize their resulting concerns. To do this, the social worker asks about the feelings of being overwhelmed, helps family members label their feelings, and supports all those times when the family takes control over the concern. By separating the issue from the family's identity, the worker and the family can explore ways to defeat their concerns or at least keep them at bay.

Unearthing the Broader Context One of narrative theory's most relevant contributions to generalist social work practice is a consistent emphasis on the political context of the family. Social workers are highly sensitized to the danger of reinforcing the oppressive dimensions of a dominant pattern (such as racism and discrimination) in society. For example, consider 6-year-old Damion who is Black, and who appears to be having a fearful reaction about going to school.

Damion's reaction seems extreme for the situation. The social worker will not want to externalize the reaction prematurely as Damion being afraid of school itself if in fact Damion is being taunted and bullied because of his race. Using narrative theory, the social worker seeks to identify any political factors that affect the situation with the client and family and, through a partnership with the client, family, and advocacy coalitions, to address those factors that negatively impact the challenge at hand. In the case of Damion, it is important for the social worker to elicit the client's and his family's perception of the climate at his school that may promote an environment in which Damion does not feel safe. The social worker can work with Damion and his family to develop an externalized version of the story and to incorporate the school into the situation. Helping Damion, his parents, and school personnel (who may be contributing to the problem) to articulate a detailed description of the classroom environment and Damion's specific interactions with his peers begins the externalization of his reluctance to go to school. Externalizing the situation beyond Damion himself allows the group to identify strategies to address his fears.

Solution-Focused Family Work

Like many contemporary family models, solution-focused practice de-emphasizes history and underlying pathology by refraining from speculating on problem formation or labelling (Nichols & Davis, 2020). Solution-focused practice involves using brief interventions that focus on specific problems within the context of particular environmental variables. Therefore, solution-focused family work can be used with a range of life situations and groups. A solution-focused engagement, assessment, and planning process emphasizes the "presence of something positive, rather than the absence of something negative" (Van Hook, 2019, p. 228).

Solution-focused family social work can be effective with families in the following ways (Corcoran, 2022a):

1 Questions help each member gain insight into the impact of their behavior on others.
2 Blaming is redirected to requests for positive behaviors.
3 Family reflections on nonproblem times in their lives helps them to recall others more positively, thus, leading to a positive change in behaviors and interactions.
4 Relationships that are relevant to the change process are illuminated (e.g., coping questions identify resources, individuals reflect on their impact on others, and children are actively engaged and contributing members of the process). (p. 355)

Solution-focused social workers usually emphasize a cognitive approach and support a collaborative stance with clients. Accordingly, solution-focused social workers believe that individuals want to change. Early in his work, one of the founders of solution-focused therapy, Steve de Shazer (1984), declared resistance "dead" and in turn redefined clients' balking at practitioner directives as

> **EXHIBIT 6.5**
>
> *Tenets of Solution-Focused Family Interventions*
>
> 1. Emphasize the future and ways it will differ from the past.
> 2. Solutions may be unrelated to the problem's history; therefore, understanding the past may not aid in developing future-focused solutions.
> 3. Negativity and pessimism can overshadow family members' abilities to see positive alternatives to their ways of relating to one another.
> 4. People want to change. Perceived resistance can be a trigger for the social worker to identify different strategies for intervening.
> 5. Because the social worker can influence family members, the practitioner should focus on empowering the family to understand their problems and possible solutions.
> 6. Social workers can encourage family members to switch from using problem-oriented language to using solution-oriented language to discuss their issues.
> 7. Family members determine those areas of focus that are important to them and, as a result, which are most appropriate to formulate goals for the intervention.
>
> *Source:* Adapted from Van Hook, 2019, pp. 226–227.

their way of educating the social worker about the help they need. Exhibit 6.5 lists the seven tenets of solution-focused family interventions.

Solution-focused social workers emphasize the future and its possibilities, in which solutions can be implemented within the specification of clear, concrete, modest, and achievable goals. Solution-focused work has become an important contemporary model as it generally aspires to short-term, specific, and direct results, thus avoiding costly, protracted professional relationships. While efficiency is important, the intervention should be guided by the needs of the family. Long used in community-based programs, solution-focused interventions have shown promise in addressing couple, family, and relationship problems, treatment of sexual abuse, substance use disorders, and mental health problems, as well as in educational and business settings (de Shazer et al., 2021).

Assessment Process The assessment process begins with a series of questions to elicit the perceptions of each member. As this approach includes ongoing questions, the assessment process is unlike a traditional assessment process that is a standard set of questions that inform the planning and interventions. The social worker then uses the family's perceptions to co-edit their stories by deconstructing them to create a plan for change (Van Hook, 2019). With families, questions can focus on relationships among all members, even those who are not present. The following presents strategies for assessment using a solution-focused approach, including questions that relate to the solution-focused assessment, planning, and intervention (de Shazer et al., 2021):

- *Create a positive collegial solution-focused stance*: Convey that you are there as a collaborator and acknowledge they are the experts on their lives. In engaging with the Patel family, you can ask them to introduce themselves and tell you a little about themselves.

- *Pre-session change:* Ask the family to describe any changes that have occurred since they decided to talk with you.

  For example, you might also ask the Patel family "How can I be helpful to you today?" or "What would need to happen today to make this a really useful session?"

- *Solution-focused goal formulation:* Questions are asked of each member that are aimed at establishing goals which should be small in scope and framed in terms of a solution.

  In working with the Patels, you can ask each member of the family to respond to: "What will be different if the problem is resolved?"

- *"Miracle" questions:* Family members are each asked to think how life would be different if their current situation were improved.

  The Patels are each asked: "What would it be like to wake up tomorrow to learn that a miracle happened, and your biggest worries were eliminated?"

- *Scaling questions:* As with working with individual clients, scaling questions in family work involve asking each person to quantify (using a 0–10 scale) their perception of the challenges when the appointment was made, in the current moment, and after the miracle has occurred.

  Pose this question to each member of the Patel family: "On a 1–10 scale with 1 being no change and 10 being a major change, please tell me how you are feeling about your family's situation since you knew you were coming to see me, now that you are here, and how you think you want to feel after we have successfully addressed your concerns."

- *Constructing solutions and exceptions:* Questions that help to identify exceptions to problems enable the family to recall times when they successfully handled a situation.

  In the Patels' situation, there is no one person responsible for the hurricane; however, there may be feelings among the family about the responses of individual members. You might ask each person to share a memory of another challenging time in their lives when the outcome was positive and follow up by asking how they achieved that success. Alternatively, you could ask: "If this exception were to occur more often, would your goal be reached?

- *Coping questions:* Building on the exceptions discussion, asking coping questions will refocus the assessment to develop more concrete solution plans based on their past experiences.

  You might ask the Patel family to reflect on how they have responded to adversity in the past and inquire if those strategies may be helpful in their current situation through such questions as "How have you managed to prevent it from getting worse?" or "This sounds hard—how are you managing to cope with this to the degree that you are?" (pp. 5–10)

In applying the strategies listed here, specific solution-focused questions that may be asked in a family assessment include (Nichols & Davis, 2020):

- What needs to happen as a result of coming here, so that afterward you will look back and be honestly able to say that it was a good idea?

- Often in our experience, we have found that in between scheduling an appointment and coming in, something happens that contributes to making a problem better. Did anything happen to improve the problem for which you decided to come here today?

- What do you think needs to happen so that your daughter will be a little easier to live with?

- Following family stating a desired outcome: "What would your daughter say about how you are different with her then?" (pp. 177–178)

Like narrative proponents, solution-focused social workers concentrate on identifying and bolstering a family's successes. As early as the assessment and planning process, the conversation begins to shift from problem-talk to solutions-talk (Van Hook, 2019). When solution-focused social workers ask families to remember when their efforts worked, even when it may seem their successes have been small and infrequent, they are directing their attention to those exceptions and exploring the contextual factors that made the exception possible. Focusing on future success, the family's vision is translated into them determining their goals and using their own skills, even if the skills have to be recovered or expanded (Van Hook, 2019).

Environmental Focus   Using an ecological orientation, solution-based social work looks to the community as resource and seeks to understand problems in terms of their relationship to the surrounding context. For example, consider the client who left her young children alone in the house with the result that they have been placed in foster care. As part of the assessment process, the social worker will view the client within the context of the environment in which the client grew up and currently lives and the client's experiences of gender, racial, and/or ethnic discrimination, poverty, unmet mental health challenges, or violence. This context can help explain the client's current inability to care for her children. The intervention may then focus on education, mobilizing resources, and developing a support system for the client.

Constructionist and Social Justice Approaches to Family Social Work

The contemporary approaches described in this chapter are complementary. They share some constructionist notions as reflected in the client-defined meanings of family, the lack of rigid ideas of normalized family development, and the collaborative partnerships built with clients. Critical social construction (also referred to as constructivism) embraces the belief that "knowledge is created, acquired, and processed" and unique to each individual's perception, thus resulting in all knowledge being relative (Barker, 2014, p. 90). Both narrative and solution-focused approaches are grounded within a constructivist foundation based on the importance of individuals being able to voice their perceptions of their lives and relationships and their meaning. The approaches presented in this book are grounded in theories that center client and family experiences, which, in turn, advance social justice. In that respect, the approaches are more alike than they are different, and each makes a positive contribution to social work practice.

Whether one is utilizing a strengths-based, narrative, solution-focused, or other approach, social work interventions with families that are rooted in a social constructionist perspective enable social workers to help families tell their stories and acknowledge the meaning of those stories for them. During the assessment and planning phase of the intervention, the social worker using a constructivist approach invites the family to provide the social worker with multiple critical perspectives, each with its own implications for practice. A social construction perspective is grounded in the idea that social experiences and relationships influence the way in which we live our lives as individuals and families (Payne, 2020).

Using a critical constructionist emphasis, the strengths and solutions-oriented interventions bring a future focus in which problems are resolved using the family's strengths and self-created solutions (Payne, 2020). Payne (2020) offers guidance for a social constructionist approach, including:

- Elicit clients' experiences and understanding of their lives and the work with you.

- Use techniques to maintain the clients' forward-thinking, positive outcomes.

- Identify personal strengths, positive exceptions to behavior patterns which can be amplified to create strengths.

- Look for clients' own solutions through examination of successes.

- Develop forward-moving tasks to reach desired goals. (pp. 311–312)

Social Justice Emphasis Constructionist theorists call for consideration of both external and internal dimensions of social justice. From an external perspective, social workers direct their attention to ensuring that all families are granted the rights and privileges of society. Diverse or marginalized families, whether they differ because of their race, ethnicity, sexual orientation, socioeconomic class, or any other factor, should be guaranteed equal access to institutional benefits, opportunities, and culturally responsive services and professionals. When they are not, the social worker is called upon to intervene in whatever ways are applicable, including legal advocacy, legislative advocacy, public education, or other forms of social action.

From an internal perspective, the social worker looks within the family itself to ensure justice for all family members. The social worker challenges overt and specific oppressive behaviors, such as intimate partner violence and child abuse, but also looks at family structure, gender dynamics, and roles. Critical constructionist social workers address external influences that have clear internal ramifications by educating and advocating for more just family practices and policies. This perspective reflects the continuous and energetic efforts of the social work profession to develop practice models that confront unjust dimensions of contemporary society.

Generalist Practice Skills Guidelines for Family Engagement and Assessment

While models may differ, the following list includes the family-oriented engagement and assessment behaviors common to most models:

- During the meeting, ensure the family is as physically comfortable as possible.
- Work to facilitate a respectful tone throughout the meeting.
- Use verbal and nonverbal behaviors that transmit positive regard or warmth, support, and respect.
- Engage with and hear from each member of the family, inviting each to share their perception of the family's purpose, strengths, areas for concern, and reason for seeking services.
- Agree upon the expectations, focus, and goals of the work.
- Recognize your own biases around family forms and norms and seek to avoid demonstrating them.
- Observe the family's communication and interrelationship patterns.
- Inquire about, observe, and discuss the role and emotional function each family member serves within the family, particularly within the context of intergenerational relationships.

With all the models discussed here, the engagement and assessment processes should be focused and thorough. In the engagement process, it is key that the social worker "join" with the client. In joining, the social worker greets each family member, attempts to place each person at ease, and starts to develop an alliance with the family members to build trust and rapport (Van Hook, 2019). An established, trusting relationship is critical for moving forward into the assessment and planning phases of the helping process. Family systems are complex and may be embedded within multiple social networks; therefore, the culturally grounded social worker must view the client system as the entire family *and* recognize the role the family plays for the individual members and their social network (Marsiglia et al., 2021).

While the engagement phase of work provides the basis for ongoing work with the family, it is important to recognize that not all family members may be positive about working with a social worker. Some may be ambivalent about change altogether (Van Hook, 2019). You can take this opportunity to acknowledge these feelings and review your collaborative approach, issues of confidentiality, and the timeframe for your work together. The goals of the engagement phase of work are two-fold: (1) develop a **therapeutic alliance** with the family in which you join with the family to work toward mutually agreed-upon goals and (2) create a climate and structure for the intervention in which you clearly communicate the process, roles, and guidelines for services (Van Hook, 2019).

The practice setting typically determines family assessment processes. If you are in a setting where you use a formalized assessment protocol with standardized measures, your role is to clarify for the family the purpose and organization of the measures to allay any potential anxiety and frustration. Specifically, you can clarify the timing, place, participants, purpose, format of the standardized assessment measure(s), the meaning of the score(s), and the way in which the information will be shared and used (Corcoran, 2022b). While agency protocol may provide a structure for completing the assessment, content areas a social worker can address include the following (Van Hook, 2019, p. 67):

- *Risk factors:* What are the sources of distress in the lives of family members? What aspects within the family and their extended world contribute to these sources of distress?

- *Appraisal:* How do family members view these issues?

- *Additive factors:* Are there additional factors that contribute to this distress?

- *Protective factors:* What resources for coping and support do family members, the family as a whole, and their external world possess?

- *Access to resources:* How can family members use these resources?

- *Strengthening of resources:* How can these resources be enhanced?

- *Barriers to resources:* What barriers prevent family members from using these resources?

Family assessment encompasses an array of assessment tools and strategies. While assessment information may be gathered using formal standardized measures, visual devices (e.g., mapping tools such as genograms and ecomaps), interviews, observation, information from collateral sources, and/or the social worker's knowledge of the family, it imperative that the process be experienced as a collaboration between the worker and the family (Van Hook, 2019). Regardless of the process or protocol you use for assessing the family, consider the possibility of incorporating a pre- and post-intervention measurement. If a formalized assessment format is used, pre- and post-intervention scores can be compared and used to determine progress toward goals. If the assessment process is informal, a pre- and post-intervention comparison can nonetheless allow the family and you to reflect on the work that can be completed. The following discussion highlights the use of mapping with families.

Mapping: A Family Assessment and Planning Tool Competent family-focused assessment and planning requires mapping skills. Chapter 4 discussed the use of genograms and ecomaps in work with individuals. These tools also are compatible with most models of social work practice with families. For example, you might ask everyone in the family to participate in the genogram, or you might have each member make their own map of the family's relational patterns (see Exhibit 6.6). Whether you use an ecomap, genogram, or another mapping activity, the information gathered can provide insight into the family's current situation, stressors, and relationships within and outside the family (Van Hook, 2019).

Genograms are particularly illuminating assessment tools for family social work because, in visually depicting family structure and patterns, they can

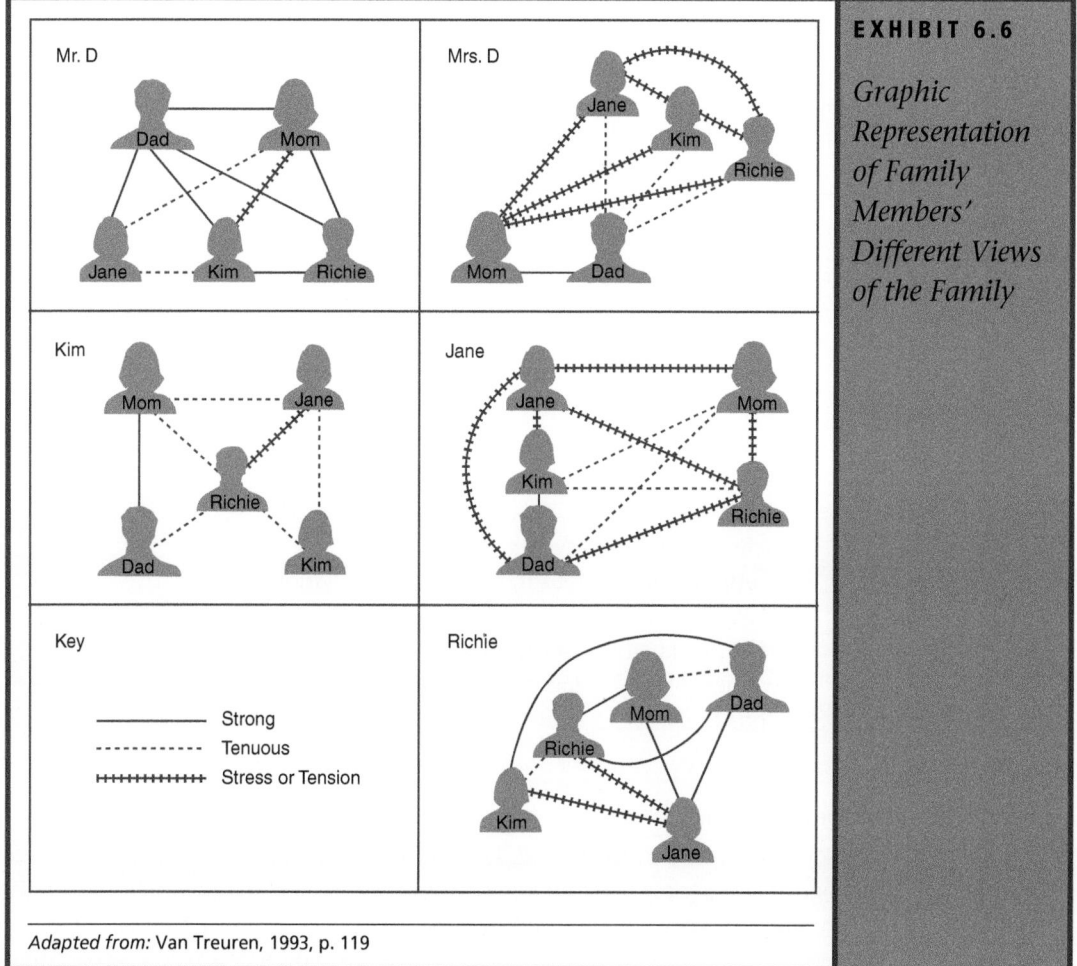

EXHIBIT 6.6

Graphic Representation of Family Members' Different Views of the Family

Adapted from: Van Treuren, 1993, p. 119

serve as an "information net" in which data and insights are captured within the larger, intergenerational context. For example, a genogram may enable you to view the presenting problem within the larger context of the family's issues, or it may facilitate an understanding of the immediate household within the context of the extended family and community. The genogram will provide a visual depiction of multi-generational family relationships, and noteworthy events that can shed light on current and past connections and patterns across the generations (Congress, 2022).

Genograms have been adapted to capture culturally focused family information. Building on the foundation of the genogram, a cultural genogram incorporates the perspective of the client on areas of culture that impact the family's experience. Culture can encompass, but is not limited to, race, ethnicity, sexual orientation, social and political influences and oppression, socioeconomic status, and religious and spiritual influences. Two types of cultural genograms particularly relevant for work with multicultural families will be discussed here:

1 *Culturegram*—developed originally by Berlin and Cannon (2013) for use with intercultural families, the culturegram is a diagram drawn by each individual around a culturally specific theme relevant to their family situation and used to engage the family members in discussion (Singh et al., 2020). Each member draws a circle and includes information on cultural/ethnic heritage and identity and beliefs they learned from their families of origin with a notation regarding the belief's relevance in their current family constellation then discusses it with other members of the family to compare and contrast knowledge and understanding (Singh et al., 2020).
2 *Culturagram*—Targeted specifically for use in engaging and assessing families who have immigrated to a new country, the culturagram can empower clients from their own cultural perspectives. The resulting map illustrates content from inquiries relating to the specifics of the family's experience, centered around ten topics (Congress, 2022):
    - Reason(s) for relocation
    - Length of time in the community
    - Language(s) spoken at home and in the community
    - Health beliefs
    - Trauma and crisis events
    - Cultural and religious traditions and affiliations
    - Experiences with oppression, discrimination, bias, and racism
    - Values related to education and work
    - Values related to family, including structure, power, myths, and rules (pp. 73–77)

Exhibit 6.7 is an example of a culturagram and the areas for discussion that generated it. The culturagram is a visual and interactive tool that helps social workers and families understand the family's internal experiences, recognize differences between and within families, see ways in which the family has been successful, and, importantly, pinpoint areas for potential intervention (Congress, 2015). This tool can contribute to the assessment and planning process by increasing understanding of the social worker and family about the family's immigration and current life experiences (Congress, 2022).

A culturagram would be a helpful strategy for learning more about the Patel family. Using the culturagram as a framework, you can engage in conversation with the Patels to learn about their experience with immigration, culture, language, faith, values about family, education, and work, and special events in the family's life. Of particular significance for their current situation could be their reflections on past crises and the impact on the family and the way in which they responded. Not only can this provide helpful assessment information, but it can also lead to discussion related to coping strategies and plans for responding to the current situation.

Ecomaps and other variations that demonstrate relationship patterns can liberate some families from what seems like endless talking. Many people enjoy developing ecomaps and examining the final product. You can use ecomaps in a visual service evaluation when the goal is to expand or alter community connections. For example, you may identify opportunities to engage in more recreational pursuits, or you may focus specifically on improving the relationship between the school and the family of a child with disabilities. Other mapping techniques can prove helpful in social work practice with families. The use of maps is limited only by the imagination and potential expectations of the employing agency. Quick Guide 15 describes other mapping options.

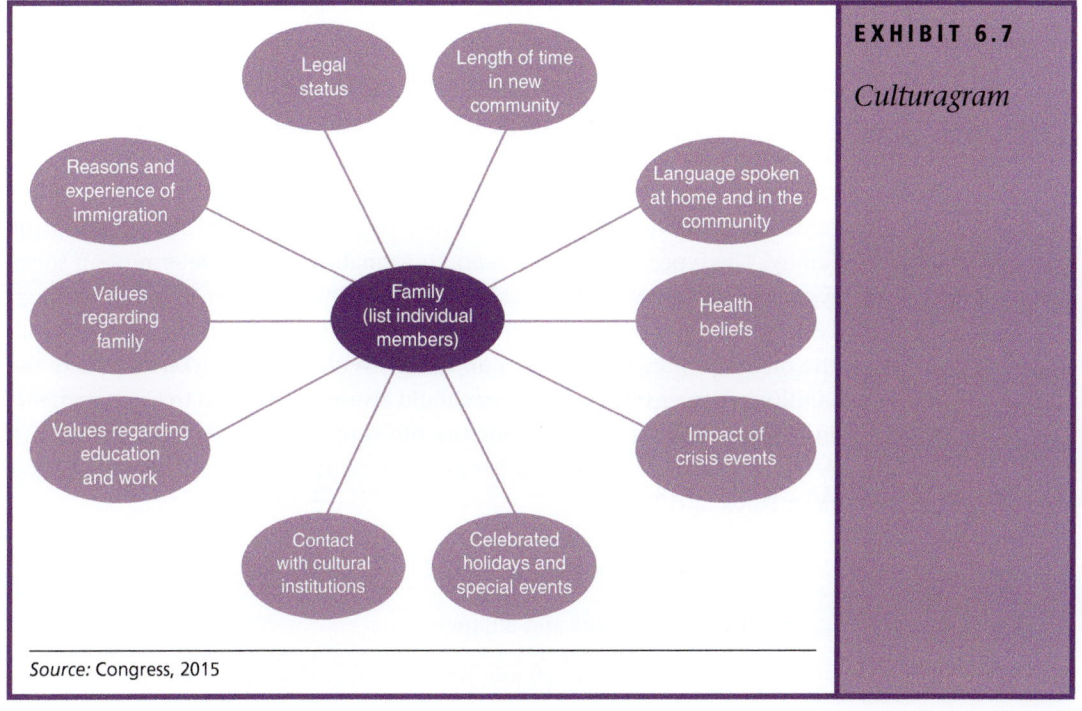

EXHIBIT 6.7

Culturagram

Source: Congress, 2015

> ### QUICK GUIDE 15 Family Mapping Options
>
> The family's needs and circumstances can guide the selection of the type of mapping used for assessment. Other formats include:
>
> - Physical map—more literal maps of physical arrangements, such as floor plans in housing situations, illustrate challenges in daily living or disparities in economic circumstances. For example, a map that shows five children's cots in a tiny bedroom or a stepchild sleeping on a couch demonstrates a person-in-environment reality that may be difficult to comprehend fully through verbal means.
> - Family map—a visual family depiction that combines concepts and symbols from the ecomap and genogram by integrating interpersonal relationships within the family hierarchy, including family dynamics such as disengagement, emotional estrangements, and enmeshment (DeMaria et al., 2017, p. 63). Mapping out the family's intergenerational patterns as well as the dynamics creates a richer, more in-depth basis for the social worker to encourage the family to share their stories, which can lead to planning the intervention. Merging these two assessment tools provides the social worker with a mechanism to learn about the family's emotional and behavioral strengths and needs (DeMaria et al., 2017).
> - Family timeline—creating a timeline of the family's expected (e.g., births, deaths, marriages, etc.) and unexpected (losses, crises, disasters, etc.) events enables a family to document their developmental and transitional events/milestones and reflect on the impact (DeMaria et al., 2017). The social worker can help the family delve into exploring members' life cycle stages and current and past challenges. A timeline can be a free-standing assessment tool but can also be used to complement information shared by the family in other assessment tools. A timeline can help the worker and family organize information on recent and cumulative stressful events, patterns of behaviors, potential resources, networks, and relationships that may be repaired (Walsh, 2016b).

The Family Interview The family interview is the core of the assessment and planning processes. The goal-setting, intervention, and evaluation and follow-up processes are all guided by the information gathered from family members. It is essential to ensure that each family member is given ample (and safe) opportunity to provide their perspective on the issues facing the family. The type of intervention and information needed determines if social workers will interview families as a unit, individually, or in sub-groupings. Issues (e.g., roles or illnesses) involving the entire family warrant having all the members present (Zhang et al., 2021). While social workers facilitate the family assessment interview, they should also actively listen to the statements individual members make, observing the verbal and nonverbal interactions. A typical interview guide for a family assessment includes the following items (Van Hook, 2019):

- Verbal and nonverbal messages.

- Observed patterns and alliances.

- Practitioner use of self and response to family members.

- Current stressors: onset, context, impact on the family, and additive factors that have made the situation more stressful.
- Family appraisal of the situation: attributions of responsibility, view of impact, appropriate ways to address the situation.
- Potential resources available to the family: coping strategies, belief systems (self-efficacy, mastery, and hope), family trust and loyalty, and spirituality/faith.
- Family organizational patterns: cohesion, leadership, communication, flexibility of family roles, and humor.
- Community context: resources and definitions of the situation and coping.
- Levels of family functioning: basic needs, family structure and organization, boundaries, and intimacy and its meaning. (p. 75)

Depending on the approach you use, family situation, and information presented during the interview, you may ask other types of questions as well. For example, you may inquire about past and current adversities and the ways in which the family copes with crisis and challenges. Family assessments may involve interviews with all or some family members. Techniques used for posing questions during a family assessment interview can include (Jordan & Franklin, 2021; Zhang et al., 2021):

1. *Circular questions* are aimed at eliciting observations about the exchanges and operations of the family from various members of the family (e.g., asking a child to comment about a parent).
2. *Conversational questions* are posed in a non-threatening way to put the family at ease (e.g., asking each member of the family to share a favorite vacation memory).
3. *Hypothesizing questions* are used when the social worker asks what the family members think about a possible issue (e.g., asking family members if they think there might be tension during the times when they are all together).
4. *Tracking problems, solutions, and exceptions* (e.g., asking the family to discuss if they have observed patterns of behaviors/interactions over a period of time).
5. *Pre-intervention change assessment* (e.g., asking the family if anything changed prior to their appointment with you).
6. *Observations* of verbal and non-verbal communication among the family members.

In addition to interviewing the family, standardized tools designed for use with families can help you gain insight into the individual members' perceptions of the family. Such understanding can be helpful as you move into the planning process. While there are numerous validated family assessment

EXHIBIT 6.8

Family Member Well-Being (FMWB)

For each of the eight statements below, please note that the words at each end of the 0–10 scale describe opposite feelings. Please fill in the response along the bar which seems closest to how you have generally felt during the past month.

1. How concerned or worried about your health have you been?

| Not concerned at all | 1 | 2 | 3 | 4 | 5 | 6 | 7 | 8 | 9 | Very Concerned |

2. How relaxed or tense have you been?

| Very Relaxed | 1 | 2 | 3 | 4 | 5 | 6 | 7 | 8 | 9 | Very Tense |

3. How much energy, pep, vitality have you felt?

| No energy at all Listless | 1 | 2 | 3 | 4 | 5 | 6 | 7 | 8 | 9 | Very Energetic Dynamic |

4. How depressed or cheerful have you been?

| Very Depressed | 1 | 2 | 3 | 4 | 5 | 6 | 7 | 8 | 9 | Very Cheerful |

5. How afraid have you been?

| Not Afraid | 1 | 2 | 3 | 4 | 5 | 6 | 7 | 8 | 9 | Very Afraid |

6. How angry have you been?

| Not Angry at all | 1 | 2 | 3 | 4 | 5 | 6 | 7 | 8 | 9 | Very Angry |

7. How sad have you been?

| Not Sad at all | 1 | 2 | 3 | 4 | 5 | 6 | 7 | 8 | 9 | Very Sad |

8. How concerned or worried about the health of another family member have you been?

| Not Concerned at all | 1 | 2 | 3 | 4 | 5 | 6 | 7 | 8 | 9 | Very Concerned |

Source: McCubbin et al., 2012 (as presented in Fischer et al., 2020).

scales available, one brief tool that can be administered with multiple members of a family unit is presented in Exhibit 6.8. The Family Member Well-Being (FMWB) scale is designed to assess family member adjustment in the areas of health, tension, energy, cheerfulness, fear, anger, sadness, and general concerns (Fischer et al., 2020).

Planning After you have gathered assessment information from the family, the planning phase of work can begin. Assessments and interventions are not clearly distinct processes as they are interactive, circular, and ongoing throughout the work (Jordan & Franklin, 2021). As with individuals, intervention planning with families is a collaborative process, albeit a potentially more complex one as all members must have the opportunity to provide input and contribute to the final plan. While the family's goals guide the planning of the intervention, the social worker can reflect the following questions to gain clarity (Van Hook, 2019):

- What is amenable to change and can make a difference?
- What are the relevant risk factors that can be addressed?
- What supports and/or resources do family members need?
- Does the family have sufficient coping skills (e.g., parenting)?
- How do family perceptions influence their experience with the problem and potential solutions?
- What are the protective factors that can be supported or need to be enhanced? (p. 97)

A family-focused plan should be a mutually agreed-upon contract among the family members and between the family and you. Items essential to the development of a clearly articulated and documented plan include measurable goals, objectives, outcomes, evidence-based intervention strategies, timeline for the work, termination, and evaluation and follow-up plans (Jordan & Franklin, 2021).

CRITICAL CONSIDERATIONS ABOUT SOCIAL WORK PRACTICE WITH FAMILIES

Families are a powerful ingredient in our lives. They have inspired fierce loyalties, lethal conflicts, abject miseries, and quiet pleasures throughout all of history and continue to do so today. Whether you view your own family as supportive, toxic, or something in between, coming to peace with your feelings can enhance your work with other families. It is difficult to assess and intervene with others' family situations if they trigger feelings because of their similarity to or difference from your own. Your family concerns need not be clearly understood or even fully resolved, but your feelings and concerns about your own family situation should not intrude on or influence your work in ways you do not recognize. If they do, your supervisor may need to become involved. You will benefit from sharing with your supervisor any struggles which you have experienced with your own family, especially if you see families in your practice.

Self-Care

At some point in your work with families, you will likely experience situations in which your feelings are difficult to manage. Egregious abuse exists in some families, and although contemporary theoretical perspectives can help you temper your responses and recognize that individuals and families do the best they can, the litany of injuries or aggressions emerging in court reports, police accounts, or living room conversations can bring on powerful emotions in the most seasoned and balanced social worker. Fortunately, you can use supervision, agency supports, peer connections, and personal strategies to cope with such reactions. Many social workers see professional therapists to process their own family issues to avoid the influence of their family challenges on their professional practice. The most encouraging truth for social workers is that most families with whom we work inspire the greatest admiration for their resiliency, spirit, resourcefulness, and agency amid potentially demoralizing circumstances. Finding a balance can enable you to maintain your own resilience in helping families.

Documentation

It is important for social workers practicing with families to keep accurate and comprehensive documentation. Family-related interventions requiring documentation can include child welfare situations (i.e., child protective services and foster care, adoptions, and early interventions). While agencies will have a standardized process for family-related documentation, practitioners working with families may have to initiate additional documentation for family members with substance use disorders, disabilities, health concerns, relationship challenges, or residential placements. In all situations, social workers should include only relevant information, consistent with a strengths-based framework that represents the perspectives of all family members.

Documentation is essential for both individuals and families, but more complex with families. Chapters 4 and 5 covered the components of basic documentation and provided documentation guidelines. While these same guidelines apply to documenting family interventions, it is important to consider the "group" aspect of family work. Recording the assessment and intervention phases of social work practice with families requires social workers to include all participating family members and to give voice to and provide perspective on individual contributions. Quick Guides 16 and 17 provide guidelines specific to documenting a family assessment.

QUICK GUIDE 16 Documenting a Family Assessment

Family Information (Include all Members Participating in the Assessment and Intervention)
- Generally, describe the family constellation and the assessment process, including number of interviews with dates and persons present

Presenting Problem
- Presenting need(s) or concern(s)
- *Living situation:* e.g., members of household and level of self-reported stability
- *Timeline:* Relevant information related to the current situation

Individual Family Member Information
- Individual family member information, including:
    - Names, birthdates, and relationship to others
    - Contact information
    - Educational/employment history of each member
    - Substance use/addiction history
    - Physical and emotional health concerns and treatment
    - Legal status or concerns
    - Financial/employment circumstances (employment status, satisfaction, financial stability, areas of concern or change)

Family Background and History
- Timeline of relevant events in the family's history (e.g., marriage, moves, deaths, etc.)

Social Support and Current Living Arrangements
- Community strengths
- Social network, support systems, and resources/services being used

Results of Assessment Measures, as Applicable

Summary and/or Recommendations
- Summarize strengths and areas of need
- Family goal(s) for intervention
- Summary of social worker's observations and impressions
- Plan for next steps

Source: Adapted from Zhang et al., 2021

QUICK GUIDE 17 Documenting a Family Intervention Plan

Intervention Plan
- Preliminary assessment as the circumstances and needs may change as the family participates in the intervention
- Preliminary plan for intervention and plan for change (to be developed at first visit), including:
    - What will each family member do differently?
    - How does each family member view themselves accomplishing changes?
    - What support and services does the family need to accomplish the plan for change?
    - Who will provide support and services?
    - Who will arrange for support and services?

> QUICK GUIDE 17   Continued

- Interventions and plans for emergency/safety needs
- Needs, including date, identified need, status (needs that are actively needed, not urgently needed, can be deferred to a later time, or referred to other resources), and reason for deferral or referral
- Strengths
- Facilitating factors for intervention
- Limitations
- Barriers to intervention
- Other care providers/referrals and purpose, including plan for service coordination
- Plan for involvement of individual family members, extended family members, significant others, and friends
- Planned frequency and duration of intervention
- Review and termination criteria/plan

Source: Adapted from St. Anthony's Hospital and Missouri Department of Social Services

CONCLUSION

Social workers can both support and challenge the contemporary family. Because social workers engage with the family and its struggles, a goal for the profession is to develop relevant models for working with families that recognize their strengths, agency, and resilience. Further, social workers need to educate about and advocate for shifts in the structural and political arrangements that impede families in their efforts to provide support and nurturing for their members. Social workers strive to create environments that validate and support families of all kinds but must have understanding of how families evolve.

Returning for a final time to the Patel family, consider what you now know about engaging, assessing, and planning with a family experiencing the aftermath of a disaster. Developing a list of the questions and areas you would like to explore with the family can be helpful to your own planning process.

GRAND CHALLENGE

Ensure Healthy Development for All Youth

The American Academy of Social Work and Social Welfare Grand Challenges for Social Work Initiative identifies one area the profession should address as ensuring healthy development for all youth. The authors of Grand Challenge Working Paper No. 10, *Unleashing the Power of Prevention* (Hawkins et al., 2015, p. 3) provide the following basis for considering the prevention aspects of this challenge:

Every day, across America, behavioral health problems in childhood and adolescence from anxiety to violence take a heavy toll on millions of lives. For decades, the approach to these problems has been to treat them only after they have been identified—at a high and ongoing cost to young people, families, entire communities, and our nation. . . . The challenge now is to mobilize across disciplines and communities to unleash the power of prevention on a

> **GRAND CHALLENGE**
>
> *Continued*
>
> nationwide scale. We propose a Grand Challenge that will advance the policies, programs, funding, and workforce preparation needed to promote behavioral health and prevent behavioral health problems among all young people—including those at greatest disadvantage of risk, from birth through age 24.
>
> Research has provided ample evidence of the significant and negative impact of behavioral health problems on individuals, in particular children and adolescents and their families. The social work profession is challenged to focus on the development and mobilization of services and programs to identify and prevent such behavioral health concerns as anxiety; depression; autism; alcohol, tobacco, and other drug use; risky driving; aggressive and delinquent behavior; delinquent behavior; adolescent violence; self-inflicted injury; risky sexual behavior; and dropping out of school. Using evidence to guide interprofessional intervention planning, actionable goals (based on Hawkins et al., 2015, pp. 14–15) include the following:
>
> - Increase public awareness of preventive interventions to promote healthy behaviors.
> - Spend 10 percent of all public funds spent on youth to support effective prevention programs.
> - Implement community-assessment and capacity-building tools to assess and prioritize risk and protective factors.
> - Establish and implement criteria for preventive interventions.
> - Increase infrastructure to supply preventive interventions.
> - Monitor and increase access of children, youth, and young adults to effective preventive interventions.
> - Prepare practitioners in health and human service professions for new roles in promotion and prevention.
>
> As we have discussed, families play a critical role in supporting the health development of youth. To familiarize yourself with the issues related to ensuring healthy development of youth, visit the Grand Challenges website, and read Working Paper No. 10, *Unleashing the Power of Prevention* (Hawkins et al., 2015) at http://grandchallengesforsocialwork.org. To learn about the progress on achieving this Grand Challenge, review the "Ensuring Health Development for Youth" by Shapiro and colleagues (2022). (See Exercise #1 for additional exploration of this Grand Challenge.)

As the structure and meaning of family itself continues to change, it is important to be aware of and to maintain your personal capacity to honor how others conceptualize the family. As a form of "group," the family has resonance for many social workers and serves as a grounding point for understanding human collectives. With that dimension in mind, the next chapter will explore the intervention, termination, and evaluation and follow-up phases of work with families.

MAIN POINTS

- Historical antecedents for involvement with families, including family function and systems theories, shape the way social workers engage with and assess families.

- Although a "traditional" notion of the family still exists, families have diverged from these stereotypical forms throughout history. Today, social workers recognize and work with many forms of family, including grandparents raising grandchildren; LGBTQIA+ families; single-parent families; families of multiple racial and ethnic heritage; families with members who have disabilities; blended families; and families who have immigrated from their home country, among others. Many families will experience intersectionality through their membership in multiple groups.

- Several contemporary theoretical perspectives have emerged for working with families that are consistent with a critical social construction perspective, the strengths-based framework, and social justice orientations, including narrative and solution-focused approaches.

- Your practice setting will guide much of your work with families, but the skills and behaviors you have learned for engaging and assessing individuals and groups from a biopsychosocial-spiritual-sexual perspective will apply to your work with families. Specific family-oriented skills and behaviors you will use include engaging the whole family, reframing, and recognizing your own biases around family forms.

- Mapping tools can be helpful in assessing and evaluating work with families and can also help empower families to change.

EXERCISES

1 To apply your learning of the Grand Challenge for Social Work—Ensuring healthy development for all youth—highlighted in this chapter, visit the Grand Challenges website and read Working Paper No. 10, *Unleashing the Power of Prevention* (Hawkins et al., 2015) at: http://grandchallengesforsocialwork.org. To examine issues within a prevention context, consider the Sanchez family at www.routledgesw.com/interactive-cases/. After reading Working Paper No. 10 and reviewing the Sanchez case, respond to the following questions:
   a Identify the children of Celia and Hector who are at risk for or are experiencing one or more of the behavioral health issues discussed in the Working Paper. Create an assessment of each of the children and the issue(s) they are experiencing. Consider where each of the individual members is in their own cultural identities.

b Building on the assessment you have developed, discuss ways in which each of these areas may be approached from a prevention perspective.
c Consider resources in your community that could be mobilized (or developed if none currently exist) to serve as prevention strategies for each area identified in this exercise.

2 Go to www.routledgesw.com/interactive-cases/ and review the case file for Roberto Salazar. As the undocumented nephew of Hector and Celia Sanchez, Roberto has consistently earned an income but has also experienced several health challenges. He is currently living with the Sanchez family due to an injury that prevents him from working. He has a number of skills, but his injury and inability to work has him feeling defeated.

Despite Hector's unwillingness to accept governmental support and with considerable reluctance, he agreed to apply for public housing support and the family was approved two years ago. He accepted so his family would have better and safer housing. You are the social worker charged with monitoring the status of Hector and Celia's Section 8 housing voucher. While Hector and Celia generally manage their rent payments, they are having difficulty meeting the payment schedule due to extra expenditures they incur supporting Roberto. Your agency is responsible for controlling Section 8–related expenses and complying with federal regulations. Your supervisor prioritizes the compliance aspect of the program.

On your visit to the Sanchez home, Hector assures you that—even though he knows the property owner can evict him and his family for violating regulations regarding occupancy—Roberto is family, and of course, he and Celia will house and feed him. He remembers his own loneliness when he came to the United States and how his uncle helped him. He has no doubt that he can assist Roberto by providing temporary housing and support. Hector explains to you that it is important for immigrants to stick together and support one another, especially family. You are feeling some pressure from the agency to report and help resolve the issue of Roberto's unacceptable presence in the Sanchez home. You are concerned that your supervisor will look unfavorably on you if you allow Roberto to continue to live in the house and may even have to evict them pending new regulations. Respond to the following questions:

a How might a family focus differ from an individual focus in this situation?
b How will you respond to Hector? Your supervisor?
c How might cultural heritage factor into this situation? Compare your responses to those of your peers. Brainstorm in class regarding strategies to approach this situation.

3 Go to www.routledgesw.com/interactive-cases/ and review the case files for Carla Washburn and her family. Create a genogram of her family. Explore connections between Mrs. Washburn and her family members and ways in which those connections impact her relationships within the family. Address the following:
a What are the strengths of the family?
b What family, community, and/or societal issues have impacted the family?

c How have those issues impacted the various family relationships?
d If you were a social worker working with this family, what issues do you think should take precedence?

4 Go to www.routledgesw.com/interactive-cases/ and click on Engage and Discover to review the case files for Brickville for the Stone family. Review the genogram (in Assess the Situation) for the Stone family and analyze the information provided by responding to the following questions:
- What additional information would be helpful to include in the genogram?
- What patterns emerge as you review the Stones' genogram? In addition to general patterns, comment on potential themes in the areas of:
    - boundaries between family members
    - intergenerational family relationships and patterns
    - single parenting
    - grandparents rearing grandchildren
- What strengths and areas of challenge are evident?
- What information does the genogram yield that suggests priorities for planning a social work intervention?

5 Go to www.routledgesw.com/static-cases/ and review Downloadable Case #3: River's Family. After reviewing the information, develop responses to Questions #1–4.

6 You are a social worker on an interprofessional team that works with children who are on the autism spectrum and their families. Three-year-old Casey is referred to your team. She is the light of her father's life—lively, energetic, and bright-eyed. In the last year, Casey has become quiet, preferring to play alone, and is less interested in the special outings that her father (Jason) loves to share. After a series of anxious appointments with the pediatrician, Casey was referred to a specialist in developmental pediatrics. Many observations and checklists later, Casey was diagnosed on the autism spectrum. Parents, Catherine and Jason, were devastated. At age two, brother, Sammy, was unaware.

Over a period of a month, Catherine began to adjust to the diagnosis. She connected with a supportive group of parents with children on the autism spectrum and read all she could about autism. She also spent considerable time with Casey, playing and coaxing her to interact with her. Jason, however, was notably uninterested in Catherine's activities. He began to refuse to go to Casey's doctor's appointments. During one argumentative dinner with Catherine, he stated that he did not believe the diagnosis; he thought Casey was fine, that they were just going through a stage, and he accused Catherine of "selling out" her own daughter. Casey's pediatrician referred the couple to the interprofessional team. Catherine engaged in the process enthusiastically, if painfully. Jason attended the assessment and seemed sullen, participating very little. The team concurs that the family would benefit from your "support work" around the diagnosis. Catherine and Jason agree to meet with you. As you prepare for the initial meeting, you speculate this might be your only chance to engage Jason, Catherine, and Casey.

Respond to the following questions and then compare your responses with those of your peers.

a   What is your assessment of this family? Identify a theoretical perspective that is most applicable to working with them. How does your choice of perspective influence your approach? Be specific.

b   Generate a list of three questions or issues you think are important to address in your first meeting.

c   How might you attempt to engage the family, especially Jason? As you compare responses with your peers, what perspective (different from your own) was most intriguing to you?

7   Go to www.routledgesw.com/static-cases/ and review Downloadable Case #3: River's Family. Develop a plan for the assessment and planning phase of the social work intervention with River's family from two separate approaches: solution-focused and narrative.

8   This chapter mentions a range of family structures about which social workers must have knowledge and skills for competent practice. Select one of the families discussed in this chapter and conduct a search of the evidence-based practice approaches social workers currently use with the family you have selected. Prepare a brief summary of the knowledge and skills needed for effective practice with this family.

9   Create a genogram of your family of origin. Explore the connections within the family and the ways in which those connections impact the relationships within the family, particularly your relationships. Address the following:
- What are the strengths of your family?
- What are the issues your family has faced?
- How have those issues impacted the various relationships?
- Who has the most/least "power" in the family? What are the sources of this power? How have these power dynamics changed over time?
- If you were the social worker working with your family, what issues would take precedence?
- What have you learned about your family from this exercise?

10   Family Assessment Movie Review: to integrate an understanding of family systems dynamics by analyzing a fictional family:

a   Select one movie to review that portrays family members in relationship with each other and in transaction with their environments (your instructor may provide a list or approve your choice).

b   Select a *research* article (published within the past five years) that studies an aspect of family.

c   View the movie and write a description of your analysis of the family relationship dynamics viewed in the movie. Include discussion of the following: family rules (spoken and unspoken), boundaries, rituals, power, communication patterns and problem-solving skills, family secrets, roles, family strengths, the family's transactions with the environment, and the manner in which these transactions seemingly influenced the family and the environment. Use quotes and scenes from the movie to support your analysis.

d Briefly discuss the research article (including information on the research question, sample, methods of data collection, and findings) and compare and contrast the findings to your assessment of the family (i.e., is the experience your family exhibits similar to what research says you should expect to find?). Support your assertions.
e Include in your critique the manner in which the family dynamics were presented in the movie, including the movie's realism, bias, and family strengths and areas for growth.

This exercise is provided by Ruth T. Weinzettle, Ph.D., LCSW-BACS, Professor of Social Work, Northwestern State University of Louisiana.

CHAPTER 7

Social Work Practice With Families: Intervention, Termination, and Evaluation

SOCIAL WORKERS HAVE A LONGSTANDING HISTORY OF intervening in family situations and crises. While social workers have always worked with families in some way, the formalization of the role occurred with the publication of Mary Richmond's landmark 1917, book, *Social Diagnosis*, in which she documents the need for and role of casework services with families (Briar-Lawson & Naccarato, 2021). The following decades saw a shift to the individualistic, psychoanalytic approach but family social work began to re-emerge in the 1960s and has flourished since with recent developments being the introduction of evidence-based practice, culturally congruent practice models, and methods to address the impact of childhood trauma (Briar-Lawson & Naccarato, 2021). For example, working with a family that has experienced trauma may include providing education about survivor experiences and symptoms using strategies that emphasize flexibility, increasing esteem and connections, periodic assessment of risk factors, and enlisting the help of other professionals (Goelitz, 2021). Contemporary social workers now work with these and other families using diverse assessment and intervention models that evolved from the previous century of work.

Building on the previously conducted assessment that focused on the family's strengths and self-determined needs, the intervention process is an opportunity to collaborate with the family to facilitate growth and change. The goal of the family intervention is to help families develop ways of coping that *depend* on the problem (Becvar & Becvar, 2018, p. 71). The family intervention is influenced by a variety of factors, both internal (e.g., relationships within and outside the family) and external (community, political, policy, and environmental context). This chapter will highlight theoretical frameworks and skills and behaviors for social work practice interventions with families that include the processes of termination, evaluation, and follow-up. We start with a case that we will revisit throughout the chapter:

The Murray family is a multigeneration family living together in the same house. Robert, a 55-year-old high school teacher, and Sharon, a 50-year-old occupational therapist, have been married 27 years and have three children. Their daughter Elle, a 25-year-old, unemployed licensed practical nurse (LPN), recently returned to her parents' home with her two children (ages 4 and 2) following a divorce. Robert and Sharon's son Stephen, 21, lives at home, works part-time as a camp counselor, and attends a local university. Their youngest daughter, Samantha, is 16 and a high school junior. Not long ago, Robert's mother Edna, who is 76, moved into the house after a car accident. Edna has Alzheimer's disease, which is progressively worsening, and the accident was attributed to her inability to focus on driving due to her cognitive impairment. When Edna and Elle and her children arrived, Stephen and Samantha had to give up their bedrooms. The family created a makeshift bedroom for Samantha in the basement, and Stephen sleeps on the foldout couch in the den. The Murray family comes to your agency when Samantha is arrested for driving under the influence of alcohol and is subsequently suspended from school. It is immediately evident that this is a family in crisis in several additional areas: Edna's illness and increasing need for care, Elle's adjustment to divorce and single parenting, displacement, and lack of privacy for Stephen and Samantha, and the stress Robert and Sharon experience supporting the family.

Key Questions for Chapter 7

1. What competencies do I need to intervene with families? As we follow the Murray family throughout this chapter, consider the competencies you will need for intervening with a family presenting such a scenario.
2. In thinking about the Murray family, what social work skills and behaviors enable me to effectively intervene with families?
3. How can I engage in research-informed practice and practice-informed research to guide the processes of intervention, termination, and evaluation with families?
4. What potential ethical dilemmas might I expect to encounter in intervening with families?

THEORETICAL APPROACHES TO INTERVENING WITH FAMILIES

Like interventions with individuals, interventions with families are planned change processes in which the social worker and client work together to implement steps to reach goals they establish in the assessment and planning process. An array of theoretical frameworks provides the basis of approaches to social work practice with families, including (Briar-Lawson & Naccarato, 2021):

> behavioral and cognitive behavioral, ecological, empowerment, systems/family systems, stress and coping, resiliency, feminist, multicultural, crisis, communications, intersectionality, developmental social control, social learning, trauma informed, psychoeducational family counseling, structural family therapy, solution-focused therapy, and narrative family therapy. (p. 4)

When you are well-grounded in theoretical approaches for working with families, you can select the approach(es) and techniques best suited to your practice philosophy and to the needs of the client family.

To best serve the families with whom they work, practitioners often combine or integrate various theoretical models and approaches (Franklin et al., 2022b). As discussed in Chapter 6, Metcalf's (2017) blending of narrative and solution-focused approaches encourages families to create new descriptions (or presentations) of their stories so that more possibilities can be explored, while the solution-focused approach provides opportunities for the implementation of the new presentations. This approach enables families to address the problem by discovering exceptions, using scaling to measure progress, and pursue their new story.

As a practitioner, you will recognize that there is no one ideal theoretical approach or technique that is appropriate or effective for all families; rather, common across the range of approaches include such factors as building therapeutic alliances, demonstrating empathy, consensus, collaborating, positive regard, and affirmation, family mastery, and congruence and genuineness (Franklin et al., 2022b, pp. 623–624). Social workers must also gain insight into the definition and structure of the family within the context of the family's culture. Recognizing the links between families and their interconnected family and social networks is key to the intervention process (Marsiglia et al., 2021). However, like all social work interventions, the family intervention models that are most effective typically share certain elements, including education, opportunities to practice and model new behaviors and skills (particularly in communication and problem-solving), and multifaceted intervention plans (Franklin et al., 2022b). As an ethical and culturally responsive social work practitioner, you are responsible for undergoing the training necessary to use the evidence on available family models and to select the approach or combination of approaches that you believe will be most effective for your client family.

Exhibit 7.1 highlights principles of family-focused social work based on conceptual frameworks rooted in systems, family lifecycle theory, cultural and social diversity theory, and strengths-based and empowerment theory. The principles provide the basis for social workers to draw from a range of practice models to meet the needs of each family. As Exhibit 7.1 shows, the process of developing a family intervention involves viewing the family as a system in itself and within the environment, one that has strengths and complexities.

The following discussion explores theoretical approaches that use the strengths and empowerment, narrative, and solution-focused perspectives. In keeping with the overall approach of this book, the theoretical perspectives presented align with critical frameworks. Systems theories help the practitioner view and frame the family within the context of their environment, while postmodern constructs help the social worker view the family within the context of the family's interpretation of the meaning of the presenting issues as provided by the family themselves. We will also explore how to help families grow and change by aiding them in identifying and building on

> **EXHIBIT 7.1**
>
> *Principles of Social Work Practice With Families*
>
> 1. Family social work practice is guided by viewing the "family as context" in which the family is seen as a social environment with multiple systems.
> 2. The family unit is more than a sum of its individual parts because they receive input from its members as well as the external environment (e.g., extended family, friends, and organizations).
> 3. Change impacts all family members, resulting in the family's ability or inability to balance between change and stability.
> 4. Viewing the family systemically enables problems to be prioritized, thus providing direction for the intervention to address complex family needs.
> 5. To capture complexity, family challenges are better viewed as circular (i.e., they have interacting origins) rather than singular in nature.
> 6. To build on the family's strengths and resilience, their problems can be perceived within the context of transactions with biological, psychological, life cycle, cultural, and historical environments.
> 7. Families from different cultural, racial, ethnic, and religious groups must be viewed within the context of their cultural and larger environments and should be asked about experiences with legal, social, and economic biases and discrimination that can impact family functioning.
>
> *Source:* Rasheed & Rasheed, 2013, p. 6

strengths, reconstructing their life experiences, and developing new realities. While the approaches highlighted here are primarily used in clinical family therapy, the concepts have therapeutic applications for all areas of family social work.

Before beginning our discussion of family social work approaches, consider how you will approach the intervention through the lens of anti-oppressive practice. First, commit yourself to honoring the family's narratives by listening to their stories as a starting point. Reinforce cultural links by listening to the stories and identifying the meanings and messages, which can then be explored within the context of how dominant narratives affect the family (Marsiglia et al., 2021). Introduced in Chapter 5 for practice with individuals, the following questions are relevant for work with families (Sellon & Lassman, 2022):

1. Does the client system feel as though they were involved in developing the intervention?
2. Has the intervention been shown to be effective with marginalized groups?
3. Does this intervention help to empower the client system?
4. What oppressive systems or contexts may make it difficult to carry out the intervention?
5. Are there groups or service movements that could help to empower the client system? (p. 308)

Strengths and Empowerment Perspectives and Family Interventions

An intervention in the strengths-based tradition strives not only to enhance the family's assets but to empower the family to develop coping and resiliency strategies. A strengths perspective views challenges as opportunities and possibilities (Saleebey, 2013). An intervention grounded in a strengths perspective builds capacity and assets and focuses on solutions (Briar-Lawson & Naccarato, 2021). For example, an intervention that emanates from the traditional deficit-based perspective views the family as the source of its own problems (e.g., poor parenting or dysfunctional relationships). A strengths-based intervention identifies the family's assets and capacities (e.g., the parents are committed to placing value on being together as a family, and the family has remained together in the face of adversity) and focuses on solutions (e.g., the family is willing to work on the challenges that brought them to a social worker).

In the face of the complexities families encounter in society, practitioners may be tempted, when developing an intervention plan, to focus on problems rather than strengths. Exploring the actions family members can take that build from their strengths can alter the family's perspective of themselves. Gaining insight into interacting in a new way with one another and with the environment can be an empowering experience for the family.

For example, consider the Murray family who initially present with multiple and complex challenges. In your initial intervention, focus should be on those challenges to which the family members ascribe the most meaning—which may be the crowded home, Edna's cognitive impairment, Elle's need for support, and Samantha's current legal and school issues. You can then work with the family to identify the strengths and resiliency (from previous experiences of coping with challenges) that they possess so that they may use those strengths to help resolve current challenges. For example, the family's strengths may include their dedication to caring for one another and remaining connected to one another even through times of adversity.

Grounded in a commitment to build on family strengths, empowerment-oriented practice has applicability for intervening with families. Having evolved over the past several decades, empowerment-oriented interventions can be utilized at all levels of social work practice with the aim being to shift the power for the purpose of changing biases and inequalities that exist within the family context (Ortega & Rodriguez-JenKins, 2021). They can be applied to work with families with various challenges. For example, the family resilience approach is grounded in empowering families through collaboration and building on the family's resources (Walsh, 2022). Consider the family facing potential foreclosure on their home as a result of lost income due to pandemic-related layoffs. With the support of extended family, the family is able to obtain financial support to prevent the foreclosure, develop a plan for repayment, and obtain new employment which ultimately strengthens the family.

To build capacity with the Murray family, you may consider sharing information on appropriate resources to support the family in caring for Edna and addressing Samantha's current challenges, building on their past successes in responding to crises, ensuring that each member's voice is heard, and being flexible when priorities change.

Empowerment-driven interventions are helpful for families in crisis—especially those who have experienced a history of crises—and can aid the social worker in helping the family create solutions. The empowerment perspective is built on the premise that crises, disruptions, and adversity impact the entire family *and* that family processes influence the whole family's ability to be resilient (Walsh, 2022). In essence, family members have the skills and resources they need to be resilient and adaptive in the face of adversity but may need help in identifying and mobilizing those skills and resources.

For example, the Murray family have survived previous losses (e.g., Edna's husband) and crisis (e.g., Elle's divorce) and have shown resilience in their response. They can again be empowered to respond in a positive, healthy manner.

An empowerment approach begins with the social worker gaining awareness of their own experiences of being oppressed or being a member of an oppressor group, then listening to the family's stories to learn about their history and experience with oppression and how the family understands it (Lee & Hudson, 2017). Such a process can heighten the family's awareness of oppression and their perspective on how it may impact their current functioning.

An important aspect of family social work is to build on and strengthen the family's capacity for resilience. A resilience framework encompasses these components (Walsh, 2022):

1 Family belief systems support resiliency through helping families make meaning of adverse experiences, sustain a hopeful, positive outlook, and use transcendent or spiritual values and purpose to achieve change.
2 Resilience can be promoted if the family's organizational structure includes flexibility, adaptability, connectedness through mutual support and teamwork, and support of extended family and social and community resources.
3 Communication processes can bolster a family's resiliency through clearly relaying information, sharing positive and painful emotions, and collaborating in solving problems and proactively planning for future challenges. (p. 260)

To bring to life the concepts discussed here, return to the Murray family. Using strengths-, empowerment-, and resilience-based perspectives, how can you support this family through this challenging period in their lives? First, consider the family's strengths, resources, and positive adaptations. To begin, Robert and Sharon have a longstanding marriage and are both employed. They have opened their home to their daughter, her children, and Robert's mother, and they are willing to provide care and support for these family members. The family can be a resource for itself, but it is important to ascertain from each member their perception of the issues and any factors they consider barriers to resolving the issues. Samantha, for example, may view her grandmother as the problem, as Edna has taken her room and her parents' time and resources. This has led Samantha to argue constantly with her parents and to spend as much time away from home as possible.

Helping the family articulate their needs in a culturally responsive, respectful way is the next step in creating alternatives with the family. For example, providing the family with information and resources related to Alzheimer's disease may help them better understand Edna's behavior and needs. Building on discussions related to experiences with oppression, positive adaptation, and risk factors and challenges related to resilience, you can enlist ideas from each family member about ways they can help and can offer suggestions for accessing resources outside the family.

Collaborating with the family to access and mobilize resources can serve as a model for their future and healthier adaptation and functioning. Examples of collaborating with the family include:

1. *Capitalizing on Elle's professional expertise as an LPN, the family can apply for a family caregiver program in which one member can be paid to care for an older adult. Elle can contribute to the family financially, care for her grandmother and her children, and work toward rebuilding her life.*
2. *Co-investigating with Stephen ways he can use his experience as a camp counselor to apply for a live-in resident assistant position on campus can provide him with space and privacy.*
3. *Samantha's substance use and arrest has effectively gotten her parents' attention. Guiding the family to consider the various responses and treatment options can enable them to make choices together and learn from one another to co-create a new way of being a family. While you may guide the family members toward resources, you would encourage family members to handle as many of the logistics of accessing resources as possible.*

Narrative Theory and Family Interventions

Like strengths and empowerment approaches, a narrative approach to intervening with families incorporates strengths, views the family as experts on the family unit, and emphasizes collaboration between the social worker and the family. Using a narrative approach, in hearing each family member's perceptions of the family and the problems that brought them to a social worker, family members give meaning to the problem and discover alternatives to that meaning that will help improve the family's interactions (Smith, 2022).

The narrative approach to working with families uses respectful listening to assess the problems confronting the family. The social worker and the family reflect upon and deconstruct the family's perceptions and then challenge perceived truths to reconstruct those perceptions. The reconstruction process facilitates collaboration between family members and the social worker in which they create an intervention plan that enables the family to arrive at meaningful and viable outcomes. For example, you are working with the Taylor-Crofts, a same-sex couple who are divorcing, and their 11- and 13-year-old children who are struggling to adapt to the change. You begin by encouraging each family member to voice their perceptions and concerns and then move to helping them, as a family, deconstruct the story, and, finally, move into a reconstruction in which each member offers a potential outcome that the family evaluates for its meaning and viability. Through a collaborative process, the family agree on a new story in which the children (1) have more input into the visitation arrangement and (2) spend equal time with each of their parents.

Implementation and evaluation of a narrative-based intervention represents the culmination of the family–social worker partnership. Much of the worker's role is in what they do not do—specifically, the worker does not initiate the intervention for the family, assume the problem serves a purpose or function, or make presumptions about the family (Smith, 2022). After respectfully listening to the family's story, the social worker's role is to help the family members to externalize the problem from themselves, re-construct a story, and "wonder" with the family about their beliefs and times when the problem did not dominate their lives (Smith, 2022). For example, narrative practice may be a helpful strategy for working with a family in which one of the children has an intellectual disability. Caring for a child with a disability can overwhelm a family; a narrative approach enables the family to explore destructive thoughts and assumptions related to the disability and helps them to make meaning of the diagnosis and disability (Ramisch, 2020).

A narrative approach provides the social worker with a variety of strategies to optimize the family's strengths to expand their perceptions of themselves and of their problems and to create a new vision. Within the discovery process, the family can envision a future in which the current problem persists or one in which they take action to alter or resolve the problem. Clients who collaborate with a social worker who hears their stories become empowered to create alternative views of their situations (Suddeath et al., 2017).

To empower clients for change using the narrative approach requires a variety of strategies and questioning formats. As a co-editor of the family's stories, the social worker's role in intervention includes such techniques as (Van Hook, 2019, pp. 252–259):

- *Listening to the family tell their problem:* Each family member shares their concerns.

- *Externalizing the problem:* Collaborate with the family to help them separate the problem from the person(s). You and the family can then form a team to tackle the problem, rather than targeting one or more of the individuals who make up the family as the source of the problem.

- *Mapping the problem:* Using relative influence questions (e.g., "How does the problem affect you/your family?"), looking for patterns from the past can help the family understand ways the problems were sustained and the impact the problems had on individual members and the family. Mapping strategies can include:
  - Searching for a unique outcome, identifying a time when the family overcame a problem.
  - Asking spectator questions to help the family consider how others outside the family view them and their current situation and functional capacity. For example, "How would your extended family members describe the way you have coped with your current stressors?"
  - *Collapsing time questions* to encourage the family to consider the current and future situation over an extended period (e.g., "How does your stress now compare to your stress one year ago? One year from now?"). The past and present are both important aspects of evolving the way the family views the problem to a newly constructed story (e.g., "Can you describe a time from the past when your siblings and you worked together to support your parents?" and "If your siblings were to help you care for your parents in the future, what would that look like to you?").
  - *Predicting setbacks*, which can help the family recognize and accept that they may find it difficult to give up on problem-saturated stories and experience setbacks. Anticipating such a possibility may lessen the potential impact of a setback. Asking questions about possible setbacks can prepare them for that occurrence should it happen.
  - *Re-authoring the family's story* to emphasize a perception in which the members have been able to overcome adversity (also known as asking significance questions). For example, "What does it say about your family that you were able to cope with the current stressful situation and stay together?"
  - *Identifying cultural messages* that support problem-saturated stories—that is, examining how previously received cultural messages have influenced the family's ability to interact with one another and to handle life's responsibilities.
- *Creating ways to reinforce the new narrative:* Encourage family members to identify strategies and individuals who can help them maintain the changes they have made. For example, provide a written communication to the family to encourage progress.

Additional mapping questions can help the family develop mutual understanding of how problem-saturated stories impact them in areas of home, school, self-perception, family and friends, spirituality, hopes, and possibilities (e.g., "What influences in your lives have made it easier for the [problem] to get between you? How has it affected you?"). This mapping tactic can be following by "sparkling moments questions" in which you ask the family if they were able to decrease the intensity or frequency of the problem (e.g., "What does it mean to you and about your relationships that you were able to keep the [problem] from butting in?" [Hall, 2022, pp. 319–320]).

A social worker using a narrative approach to frame the Murray family crisis would listen to each member share their views on the family situation. As you can imagine, each family member is likely to perceive the situation differently. Robert and Sharon may share that they do their best to provide for all family members and feel betrayed by Samantha's arrest. Samantha may believe her parents have given more to other members, particularly to her grandmother, than they have to her. Edna may feel that, because she struggles with cognitive impairment, she is a burden to her family and powerless to change the situation. Elle may express guilt for being unable to support her children and herself. Stephen may feel pressured to hold down a job, maintain his grades, and continue with his plans to move out of the house, so that he not further upset his parents.

At this point, identify the strengths each person brings to the situation. The goal is to help the family reach a consensus regarding their desired outcomes; however, there may be differences of opinions that must be addressed. Only then can you work with the family to deconstruct and reconstruct their perceptions by externalizing the problems (i.e., focusing the family on the issue, not a person). Should the family, for example, choose to focus on stabilizing the situation regarding Edna's care, you can externalize Edna's behaviors (i.e., the vehicle accident) as being, because of her cognitive impairment, outside her control. You can then help the family to envision their lives if they take no steps to improve their perceptions of Edna's situation and then to envision their lives when they understand the disease, coping strategies, care and respite options, and ways to enjoy their remaining time with Edna. While reconstructing a story of Alzheimer's disease will not alter the course of the disease, challenging the family's problem-saturated perceptions can enhance quality of life for Edna and her family. The family can view Edna as an honored family member, not as a burden, while also acknowledging the changes needed to care for her.

Solution-Focused Family Interventions

Like other postmodern family-focused interventions, solution-focused family interventions emphasize strengths and empowerment, client self-determination, and client–social worker collaboration to mobilize assets and resources to construct new realities. As discussed, solution-focused interventions differ from other approaches using a series of questions posed in a step-by-step manner that are aimed at the family identifying alternatives to problem-solving that leads to a sense of hope (Van Hook, 2019).

Family solution-focused interventions emphasize relationships and explore client skills, strengths, and competence in a way that is consistent with many postmodern approaches. This orientation embodies a collaborative relationship with the social worker and family that emphasizes positivity and respect as a strategy to building on past success (de Shazer et al., 2021). A foundational premise in social work assessment, planning, and intervention is to consider the client within the context of their environment; therefore, the social worker is encouraged to look for solutions in environmental, structural supports rather than for pathology in internal dynamics. Social workers do not disregard individual responsibility for behaviors such as those that occur in the family (e.g., abuse of a family member or substance use). Instead, the social worker and family focus on: (1) recalling times when the issue did not exist; (2) identifying small steps of progress; and (3) looking at how the family achieved progress (Van Hook, 2019). For instance, family violence, including intimate partner/family violence, and gender-based violence (e.g., sexual assault of a family member or child sexual abuse) within a family context requires evidence-based intervention that enables all members of the family to be involved and be given a voice to heal from the experience (Barth et al., 2022). When a family experiences stress and does not make use of internal (e.g., internal coping strategies) or external (e.g., social, health, mental health, or financial assistance services) resources (e.g., internal coping strategies) or external resources (e.g., social, health, mental health, or financial aid services), it can benefit from professional support to deal with that stress.

Employing a solution-focused intervention encourages the family to adopt a hopeful, strengths-based, and future-oriented view of their lives. The social worker's role in facilitating interventions is to encourage and mobilize the family to think and talk about solutions (versus problems). Families must focus on establishing and achieving a series of modest solutions using existing and expanded coping strategies in a concrete behavioral way, which often means the solutions already exist within the family's skills and experiences (but must be remobilized) (Van Hook, 2019).

Recall from Chapter 6 that social workers use a series of questions in the assessment and planning of solution-focused interventions to guide the plan for change. The questions are used throughout the intervention process to elicit new information and perspectives and to monitor progress. Not only does solution-focused practice identify strengths and competencies on which to build, it can emphasize a resilience-based focus as well. Resilience is enhanced by solution-focused interventions as they: (1) address belief systems that do not envision that the family is capable of positive change and (2) support protective risk factors by changing those negative beliefs into hopeful ones that enable the family to see possibilities to promote affection, communicate effectively, and utilize social support (Van Hook, 2019). To review, you can capitalize on the family's strengths and resilience by asking (Bolton et al., 2017):

1 Exception questions ("Can you remember a time when you did not feel stress?")—these questions can lead to ways in which the members can

understand the past, themselves, relationships, and their world, which can then be used in future situations.

2. Miracle/best hopes questions ("What would your life be like if you were not feeling such pressures?")—engaging family members into considering a future without the problems can help to shift their self-perception from one of incapability to capability, thus creating a protective factor for the future.

3. Coping/scaling questions (Coping: "You are being asked to carry a heavy load right now, how are you able to do that?"; Scaling: "On a scale of 0–10 with 0 being the worst your stress has been and 10 the best you can imagine, how would you rate your stress today?")—asking the family to describe and quantify their coping encourages them to draw on their resources and protective factors for use in their current and future situations and strengthen resilience.

4. Relationship **(perspectival) questions** ("What do you think your son thinks about your relationship?")—eliciting perspectives of others, particularly those present at the time, can be a useful strategy and support for change.

While the family's identified needs, goals, strengths, and resources should drive the intervention process, the social worker can be most helpful by developing a repertoire of skills and strategies to aid the family in achieving their mutually determined goals. Exhibit 7.2 lists six tasks for implementing a solution-focused approach. Once the plan is underway, the social worker uses "what's better?" questions to monitor members' progress and identify outcomes. A review of the solutions and exceptions that surfaced in response to the

---

EXHIBIT 7.2

Solution-Focused Social Worker Tasks

- Through your questions to the family about their goals, potential solutions, and patterns of behavior, you take on the role of "not knowing" and recognize the family members as experts on the family.
- Help the family shift from their focus on the problem that brought them to see you to a focus on solutions. The goal is that this shift in conversation produces solutions.
- Maintain your focus on helping the family to identify and accomplish small, achievable goals. Success with small goals can prompt additional positive changes, thus shifting the family's focus on problems.
- Encourage the family by acknowledging empathy and understanding of their current situation. Your future-focused orientation helps the family to envision a time when the problems are resolved.
- Individualize the intervention to the family, their situation, and the time the intervention occurs. Families need to be heard and validated in their current situation and context so that they can move on to consider and engage in finding solutions.

Source: Van Hook, 2019, pp. 229–230.

scaling questions the social worker asked in the assessment phase can highlight changes as they are made and help to address potential resistance and setbacks (Nichols & Davis, 2020). For example, the social worker might ask family members to rate on a scale from 1 to 10 how they felt about an issue when they first came to see the social worker and to compare those ratings with how they currently rate their feelings on the same issue. The social worker can also use scaling questions to anticipate future feelings and behaviors (e.g., "On a scale from 1 to 10, how confident are you that you will be able to sustain this change?").

While the Riverton case (www.routledgesw.com/interactive-cases/) initially appears to focus on a neighborhood and a community, each community is comprised of individuals and families. In your role as the social worker who has just moved into the Riverton community, consider your new neighbors, the Williamson family (not described in the interactive case file). Jocelyn is a 48-year-old single mother who lives with her two children, 18-year-old Tori and 17-year-old Jamal, and her mother, 77-year-old Nina. After years of living with her husband's alcoholism (making excuses for him to his employers, family, and friends and serving often as the sole wage earner for the family), Jocelyn divorced her husband because of his unwillingness to seek treatment. She is worried about Jamal because she knows he regularly drinks and uses marijuana, and she is concerned about his current and potential future substance use. She has come to your agency to ask for your help with Jamal. Considering the alcohol and drug issues in the neighborhood, she feels powerless to handle the situation alone. Nina owns the house, and she cannot afford to move out of the neighborhood because Jocelyn is unable to work full-time due to her responsibility to care for her mother and her desire to be with her children as much as possible.

The case of the Williamson family provides examples of additional techniques for completing solution-focused interventions, which include the following (Corcoran, 2022a, p. 350; Koop, 2009, pp. 158–160; Nichols & Davis, 2020, pp. 178–183; Van Hook, 2019):

1 Introduce outcomes and termination from the outset of the intervention by discussing goals, exception finding, and identifying when progress occurs by asking "Jocelyn, what needs to happen so that you won't need to come back to see me?"
2 Provide positive feedback (compliments) as often as possible to emphasize strengths and strategies that have been successful. Compliments may be:
   a *Direct:* "Jocelyn, you are to be commended for the concern you show for your family."
   b *Indirect:* "Jocelyn, what things have you tried to address your son's substance use?"
   c *Self-compliments:* "Jocelyn (and Jamal), I'd like you to identify something in your lives that you feel good about."
3 Focus attention on family members' relationships with one another. Questions such as "Jocelyn, how is your relationship different when you actively listen to Jamal when he speaks?" can help the family concentrate on changing their relationships.

4 Throughout the intervention phase, maintain a positive, future-oriented emphasis on "who, what, when, where, and how" questions. For example, "Jamal, what do you think would make your life more fulfilling?"
5 Redirect blaming and accusations to encouraging family members to ask for positive behaviors by asking: "Jamal, how would you like your mother to interact with you instead of accusing you of drinking and getting high?"
6 Once the family has identified goals, shift the focus to a range of behavioral tasks in which the family can engage, including:
   - *Doing more of what works:* Encourage the family to use any effective interactions and strategies they have identified to communicate what they want to continue. For instance, "Jocelyn, Tori, Jamal, and Nina, it is clear you all care about one another but have difficulty expressing your feelings. I would like to ask each of you what things have the other three done that send the message that they care about you?"
   - *Miracle questions:* Asking the family to consider a time when the problem no longer exists promotes a future-focused orientation and the willingness to take small steps toward reaching that point in time. For example, ask each member of the Williamson family what that would look like and how would it be different. Pairing miracle questions with exception (a time when the problem did not exist) and scaling (rating the problem severity on a 1–10 scale) questions can help the family to re-conceptualize the problem so they can see possibilities for change.
   - *Doing something different:* Introduce the idea of trying new strategies for relating to one another or to approach other aspects of the family's challenges. Consider a question such as "What do you each think it would be like if you were to commit to having a meal together several times a week?"
   - *Going slowly:* Promote a slow, incremental approach to change. Building on the previous question, "Is it possible to start by having three meals together next week?"
   - *Doing the opposite:* Encourage family members to engage in behaviors and interactions that are the opposite of what they currently do. For example, "Jamal, what would happen if you did not leave the house when you feel like your mother is giving you a hard time about your friends?"
   - *Predicting tasks:* Help the family predict outcomes and identify patterns that occur when they experience change. For instance, consider saying to the Williamson family:

   We have talked about making some big changes in the way you interact with one another. Building on your family's strengths, I think we have established some achievable goals, including a commitment from each of you that you will agree to share a meal together three times a week. I would like you to think about your family's past experiences with change and how you have responded. What are some examples of positive responses to change and negative responses to change? It is possible that you will not always be able

to achieve the goal of having a meal together three times a week. Thinking to the past, how would you have responded? If it happens now, you should not feel you have failed. We can talk about ways to address the challenges that come up.

7. Find, amplify, and measure progress to monitor signs of positive movement toward goals. For example, you might say, "You have all done a good job at keeping your commitment to have dinner together three times a week. What has that been like?"

8. Take a break within an interaction for you and the family to provide feedback to one another. The social worker must authentically invite and truly hear all feedback—positive and negative. For example, "Let's take a brief break, during which time we will reflect on the work we have done here today."

9. At the end of the meeting, recap the work the family has accomplished and provide suggestions for future work (i.e., "homework" that focuses on observing successes, engaging in new tasks, and predicting desired changes). Tasks can be divided into three categories:

    a. *Formula:* General tasks in which the family members consider what they might do differently. With the Williamson family, you might compliment them on the work they have done and suggest they increase the number of meals they share from three to five.

    b. *Perception:* Observational tasks in which the family note the differences in one another's behaviors. For example, "Next time we meet, I'd like each of you to share your thoughts on any differences you observe in yourself or your family."

    c. *Behavioral:* Tasks in which family members take action and interact differently with one another. For example, "Jocelyn, I would like to encourage you to identify something you believe that Jamal is doing well that you would like him to keep doing."

Continuing to explore additional strategies for the implementation of the solutions-focused intervention, let us consider miracle questions as they apply to our chapter case:

During the assessment and planning phase of your work with the Murray family, you would have asked each of the members their perceptions of life in their household. Imagine how Robert and Sharon might respond to a miracle (or "best hope") question such as: "What would your lives be like if you were not experiencing your current stresses?" Perhaps, they will talk about having imagined a near "empty-nest" household with their two older children living on their own and Samantha about to head off to college. In response to the "miracle" question, Samantha might express the desire that she not face legal issues related to her arrest, or be suspended from school, and that her grandmother no longer live with the family. Elle's "miracle" might include employment, a supportive partner, and a home of her own. Stephen's miracle may involve his own apartment. Edna may wish desperately to have her memories back and to return to independent living.

> *The use of miracle questions can illuminate individual member's perspectives and potentially pave the way to developing mutually agreed-upon goals that can begin to address individual and family "best hopes." Given the diverse goals family members may express, helping the Murray family connect with a realistic set of goals may be complicated. Highlighting the fact that the family members care for one another can foster goodwill and establish common ground on which the members can agree (de Shazer et al., 2021). Reminding the Murray family of their commitment to and concern for one another can be a regular part of the intervention. Imagine that the agreed-upon goal is to find a solution to their overcrowded housing situation. Your role can be to work with the family to develop concrete and achievable short- and long-term solutions, to check in regularly with "what's better?" questions, and to terminate the professional relationship when you and the family agree the goals have been achieved.*

Your social work values and ethical standards provide the foundation on which you develop interventions in your work with families, regardless of the theoretical approach that guides your work. For example, the client's right to self-determination, their strengths, and their diversity should be honored as top priorities. As the social worker, you should not interject proposed solutions until the family has had the opportunity to be heard. The following discussion emphasizes the behaviors that will enable you to become a competent and ethical social work practitioner working with families.

TRENDS AND SKILLS FOR INTERVENING WITH FAMILIES

Families are groups of individuals, and, as such, they benefit from the careful use of the same practice approaches and skills that assist individuals and groups that are consistent with contemporary societal and family trends and challenges. Work with families requires simultaneous work with the individuals who make up the family and the family itself—as a unit. As with all domains of practice, interventions with families are likely to vary according to practice setting and agency mission. Because the social work profession has always functioned within the context of the larger and ever-changing society, social work practice with families must use evidence to respond to the evolving structure of families and service delivery systems. For example, if you are a member of the intake unit of a public agency child protection team, your intervention with the family will differ from that of your colleague who works in a nonprofit mental health agency or family preservation program. The theoretical lens through which you work will also influence the way you intervene with family members. In any situation, your intervention begins with an invitation to the family to tell their story, but your agency mission and purpose and your own theoretical preferences influence the intervention approaches you take.

Social work practice interventions with families share many similarities with individually focused interventions. Recall the Chapter 5 discussion on social worker roles in work with individuals (e.g., case manager, counselor, broker, mediator, educator, client advocate, and collaborator). Each of these roles applies to work with families, particularly considering the setting in which the intervention may occur. For example, the social worker working with a family in a child welfare setting may engage in all these roles but may also emphasize case management and brokering activities to reunify the family. In a health care setting, the social worker may emphasize education and self-advocacy. As with social work interventions with individuals, it is important to use a biopsychosocial-spiritual-sexual lens in viewing the family, to recognize relationship dynamics, and to consider all family members' perspectives and the strengths-based intervention goals that will optimize family functioning.

While your theoretical framework and techniques may vary throughout your work with families, it is important to maintain a perspective that views the family systemically. The family itself is a system with subsystems as well as a subsystem within the larger environmental system; therefore, interventions should be implemented with the awareness that they will impact the system. Becvar and Becvar (2018) offer general principles for working with the family system, including: (1) families seek help with the goal of change but individuals may not want to change themselves, and therefore your focus can be on participation of all in the intervention; (2) as long as the family continues to interact with the identified problem, the problem will persist, so talking about the future (and not what the family does not want to be) can diminish the focus on the problem; (3) help the family view themselves as an interdependent unit as opposed to a group of independent individuals; (4) families and professionals can both idealize family relationships, so it is important to discuss realistic expectations for family functioning; and (5) the intervention may involve educational activities to promote new learning for the family. Your role in the family intervention is to listen with curiosity to the family's stories, not for the purposes of ongoing diagnosing, but so you may validate the story of their lives (Becvar & Becvar, 2018). See Exhibit 7.3 for a comprehensive list of systems-oriented interventions strategies and skills.

EXHIBIT 7.3

Systems-Oriented Family Intervention Strategies

1. Redefine family to include anyone close to the problem or helpful with a solution.
2. Recruit supportive others to participate in the intervention.
3. Offer parity for each person to be able to voice their thoughts on the problems and solutions.
4. Use caution to avoid "speeding tickets"—in other words, if you shift the intervention between the individual to the family, the other members of the family may withdraw.
5. Add others to the intervention or see them in small sub-groups if there is an impasse.
6. Be less central by encouraging family members to talk to one another and not to or through you.

> **EXHIBIT 7.3**
>
> *Continued*
>
> 7. Using circular questioning, suggest that family members check assumptions with one another.
> 8. Be experiential by adding activities to the session (e.g., ecomaps or visual depictions of the family).
> 9. Reframe the problem as a relational issue (e.g., encourage family members to change "you never talk" to "I'd like us to talk more."
> 10. Hold process over content by focusing on the family's responsibility to challenges instead of the current problem situation.
> 11. Develop both family and individual goals to increase sense of investment in the process.
> 12. Integrate multigenerational information to provide insight into patterns and trends.
> 13. Expand the family system to explore interconnections with broader systems—an ecomap can be a helpful tool.
> 14. Check your own systems congruency (i.e., are you adhering to the tenets of the systems approach?).
> 15. Examine the potential for your own biases and values to influence the intervention.
>
> *Source:* Bohley & McGuire, 2022, pp. 266–267.

In addition to the model-specific behaviors already discussed, general skills and behaviors transcend the continuum of theoretical approaches presented here. The following strengths-based skills for intervening with families build on the behaviors social workers use in family engagement, assessment, and planning (Taibbi, 2018):

- Work with families to focus on problems in the present and their interactions with one another.
- Help families identify where the problems exist—they may be in the family structure (e.g., disagreements, power issues, or sibling conflict).
- Empower families to go beyond their comfort zones by addressing previously avoided topics and unexpressed emotions.
- Help families to move toward differentiation and problem-solving.
- Emphasize process, patterns, and their interconnectedness, while de-emphasizing facts and content, particularly in an era in which facts are often challenged.
- Maintain your role as the guide who offers options, not the expert.

When working with families, you will build on the practice knowledge and skills that you use in working with individuals with the expansion from one client to the family group. Exhibit 7.4 provides a summary of strategies for intervening with family groups.

EXHIBIT 7.4

Knowledge and Skills for Facilitating Family Interventions

1. Connecting contracting to intervention, goals, and evaluation—just as with individual practice (discussed in Chapter 5), a contract is developed in collaboration with the client to guide the work of the intervention. When developing contracts with families, it is essential that each family member can contribute to the plan and that the contract clarifies the expectations of and for each member of the family. The contract, which is developed during the planning stage, should reflect the family's agreed-upon goals and should be inclusive of evaluative strategies from the outset. The contract should become a working document that is regularly revisited throughout the intervention, termination, and evaluation stages so that changes can be made as needed, and a review of your work together can be assessed.

2. Session management—family meeting facilitation can be likened to group facilitation. Beginning the intervention by developing with the family guidelines for interactions can ease the challenging moments that will occur, including:

    a. Time and attention—with multiple clients, all of whom need to be able to speak in the time allotted for your meeting. Your role is to monitor the discussion, so each member has adequate time to share and be heard.

    b. Family behaviors—inevitably, there will be times when family members' behavior can be disruptive as they become emotional, monopolize the discussion, or talk over one another. If reminding the family of the pre-established meeting rules does not resolve the issue, you and the family can discuss other possible solutions (e.g., homework assignments to work on the issues or individual sessions).

3. Conflict—should conflict occur between family members or be directed toward you, the conflict must be addressed so it will not compromise the work of the intervention. If the conflict is between family members, it can be addressed within the meeting, using caution that it not become the primary focus of the intervention. If the conflict is directed toward you by one or more family members, this, too, should be discussed openly with the family to learn about the source of the conflict and strategize solutions. Addressing conflict within the intervention can serve to model healthy responses to dealing with conflict. You can also process in your supervision meetings to reflect on your learning.

4. Ethical issues—because the family includes multiple clients and possibly other professionals, be cognizant of potential ethical issues that can negatively impact the helping relationship, including:

    a. Confidentiality and informed consent—it is important to reach consensus with the family regarding parameters for sharing information outside the family meetings. Assure the family that the social work profession's ethical standards require you to obtain written informed consent from the family. This obligation extends to sharing information with other members of the family and professionals. It is also important to discuss with the family rules regarding sharing information with family members who are participating in the intervention outside of the meetings.

> **EXHIBIT 7.4**
>
> *Continued*
>
> b Documentation—share with the family the way in which you will document your work with them and their access to their records. Inform them if you will include information about individual members and how they can review their records, if desired.
> c Follow-up—inform the family of your agency's policies regarding ongoing contact with clients after the relationship has been terminated, disposition of their records, and your ability to share information following the termination.

Consider the strategies that you can employ when working through challenging emotional issues and crises with families. Families often seek help during times of crisis and the social worker can help them by eliciting stories that demonstrate past resilience which can be applied to the current situation (Walsh, 2022). Keeping in mind a strengths- and resiliency-focused perspective, the following skills and techniques can help to guide the family through the change process (Walsh, 2016a):

- Show interest in the family's journeys by encouraging them to share stories of crisis.
- Express compassion for their hardships and affirm their courage and efforts to cope.
- Help the family to:
  - Rebalance their problem focus by identifying resources, including their spirit (i.e., motivation, well-being).
  - Strengthen the transactions related to resilience and resourcefulness.
  - Find cohesion and restoration within the context of the crisis.
  - Encourage meaning, purpose, and connections within and outside the family.
  - Acknowledge their worst times and reflect on their best responses as crisis can prompt growth, healing, and new pathways.
  - Commit to not defining a person or the family by one event or behavior (e.g., divorce).
- Promote reminiscence by encouraging the family to share photographs and memories. From remembering the past, the family can gain wisdom from past hardships and their ability to be resilient.
- Acknowledge that crises and challenges are normal, but the way in which the family responds as a unit can be a defining point. (pp. 43–45)

Strategies like written homework assignments, task designation, and teaching can be helpful if they are appropriate to the family's situation, their investment in the process, and the framework you are using in the intervention. If these strategies are not appropriate for or welcomed by the family, consider alternatives with which the family feels comfortable (e.g., activities completed during your meeting with them, collaborative activities they can engage in together, asking them to teach you).

Return for a moment to the Murray family scenario and consider the previous list of practice skills. To mobilize the family toward crisis resolution, you can begin by asking each member their priorities for change. You will likely glean the pain, strengths, goals, and dreams each family member feels. You may engage the family in brainstorming strategies they can use to address each area of concern, or you might assign the family homework in which they develop ideas to address their concerns. An alternative may be to ask the family to have a family conference (a meeting of all family members in which they use a predetermined agenda to have a focused discussion on a matter relevant to the family) and to bring the resulting ideas to the next meeting with you. As the social worker is not present for the family conference, this is an important reminder that social work interventions are the "tip of the iceberg" in terms of the total work the family will engage in to address their issues. Once the family has developed ways to address their prioritized concerns, consider asking them to identify and assign specific tasks. Be sure to explore the possibility that the expertise for problem-solving resides within the family and that individual members can function as teachers and guides. In working with the Murray family, for example, you can ask each member to share their ideas for actions they can take to support the family, thus creating an opportunity for a family discussion and prioritization of tasks and activities.

In addition to individual and family skills, practice strategies with evidence-based efficacy, when used carefully in many family situations, include reframing, perspectival (or circular) questions, family group conferencing, motivational interviewing, and reenactments (i.e., role-playing or rehearsals), all of which we describe next.

Reframing

Reframing is a practice skill in which the social worker conceives of and describes a situation in different terms. Social workers use reframing to focus on strengths and positive alternatives. Reframing can be particularly helpful in family conversations in which one member makes a hurtful statement to or about another member. Careful reframing can help defuse a situation so that both members can listen to each other. To have a meaningful impact, reframing must be appropriately timed.

Suppose a 15-year-old, who sees their mother as an autocratic barrier to their freedom because she will not allow them to be driven anywhere by their friends, tells you, "There is no person on earth more controlling and overprotective than my mother. She's just like a prison warden! She keeps me locked up in jail." After acknowledging these strong feelings, you may suggest that the teen's mother cares for them so much that she fears they will be hurt in a car accident if their friends who just got their licenses drive them around.

When reframing, offer an alternative that does not resonate as a "gimmick" (e.g., a contrived, demeaning, or unrealistic interpretation) and that will be heard by the parties involved. Avoid interpreting the thoughts or feelings of another person without that person's input. In the example of the 15-year-old teen, you would not want to attempt a reframe such as "At least your mother doesn't insist on riding in the car with you." It is unlikely that the mother is intentionally attempting to torture her child (and likely that she worries about them being driven by friends), but they may not be able to "hear" this reframed interpretation as her being concerned. Reframing may be more effective depending on the relationship between the family members (and possibly the social worker and family) and the people involved. Effective reframing requires judgment and skill; reframe with caution and only when conditions are relatively straightforward.

> *How can a social worker reframe the Murray family's situation? Instead of focusing on the upheaval that Edna, Elle, and Elle's children moving into the house has created, consider emphasizing strong family commitments, caring environment, and flexibility, specifically the fact that the Murray family had a safe home for family members to take refuge when needed.*

Perspectival Questions

Perspectival questions can be effective in family social work. Seeking the perspective of another family member can help you clarify the feelings and meanings of one member's view of another. Consider the Williamson family:

Tori has announced that she is going to move out of the family home due to the stressful environment. You may ask Jocelyn, "What responses do you think your mother and Jamal will have if Tori moves out?" Or you may ask Jamal, "What do you think your mother would miss most about Tori?"

Responses to these questions can communicate thoughts and feelings that no one in the family previously recognized. Such communication assistance is vital when family members assume they know all they need to know about the thoughts and feelings of other family members because of long-term, "stuck" patterns of argument, difference, or "saving face." Use perspectival questioning carefully and only when you are confident you can respond appropriately to any statement. Jamal might respond with, "Mom will fall apart—she's always liked Tori better anyway," or he might say, "Mom will probably take it out on me." The same element of the unexpected that can create new ways of thinking for families can also catch the unprepared social worker off guard. Yet perspectival questions can elicit illuminating responses.

Suppose, for example, that you ask Edna Murray about the support her son and daughter-in-law have provided to Elle and her children. Edna responds that they should not have invited Elle and the children to move into their house. By expecting the unexpected and maintaining flexibility, you can effectively incorporate perspectival questions. We cannot assume how an individual family member perceives the situation.

Family Group Conferencing

Family group conferencing is an empowerment-focused intervention strategy that aims to create or strengthen a network of support for families experiencing a crisis or transition. Also known as Family Group Decision-Making, this strategy was originally developed in New Zealand (Child et al., n.d.) for work with families in which children were at risk of abuse or neglect but is now being used throughout the world in a range of settings and populations (de Jong et al., 2018). The family group conference is an empowerment-focused practice that places the client/family in the decision-making position from the beginning as they are asked to identify and include all family and social network members who may be able to contribute to the discussion (Ortega & Rodriguez-JenKins, 2021).

The goal of the conference is to gather family members and people who are connected to them to decide how to respond to the presenting challenge. The social worker confers with each potential participant individually prior to the conference to ensure that each agrees to be actively involved in decision-making and action steps. The impact of the family group conference is dependent on several factors, including (de Jong et al., 2018):

- Family's willingness to expand and invite members of the social network (e.g., professionals, extended family, and other support persons).

- Family's and network's willingness to share emotional and possibly negative feelings and grievances.
- Development of mutual trust between the facilitator-coordinator and the family.
- Professionals' encouragement for family to be self-directed and maintaining the focus on the family and not individual members.

The process for facilitation of a family group conference includes multiple, pre-planned steps, including (Mitchell, 2020; Ortega & JenKins, 2021):

1. A professional serving as the coordinator begins by describing the family group conference process, then invites all participants to describe and list the family's strengths and skills, challenges that may prevent a positive outcome, professionals and services involved with the family, and each person's potential contributions to the plan.
2. The coordinator and other professionals not involved in developing a plan leave the room, at which time the family and social network members create a plan for resolution of the situation/problem that also addresses barriers to the desired outcome.
3. The coordinator and other professionals return to the meeting and the family's proposed plan is discussed with the entire group. The plan is reviewed, including suggestions for monitoring and changes.

The group may reconvene after implementing the plan to discuss progress or renegotiate the plan if needed. Using a strengths perspective, you can point out to the family that their willingness to participate in a conference is a

strength in itself. Not all family conferences are successful on the first (or any) attempt.

Return for a moment to the Murray family. If you were to convene a family group conference with the Murrays, consider whom you would invite to participate and a rationale for that choice. What goals could provide an opportunity for the Murrays to mobilize their support network and strengthen their coping skills? What are the family's strengths? How might they benefit individually and collectively from participation in a family group conference? What is your role? While answers to these questions can only be speculative, you can use this exercise to begin to see yourself in the role of a family social work practitioner.

Motivational Interviewing

Recall from Chapter 5 that motivational interviewing (MI) can be used with a variety of clients (Paris & Martino, 2017). MI provides another opportunity for you to engage the client family in a collaborative partnership aimed at providing the opportunity for change. The four processes of MI—engaging, focusing, evoking, and planning—promote behavior change about which the family is motivated, making MI well suited to situations in which a client system is uncertain about making a change and in a variety of settings such as primary health care, addiction treatment, and programs that mandate participation (Salisbury et al., 2022).

MI is also useful in social work with families. Miller and Rollnick (2013) offer strategies for engaging in MI with families with adolescents. Using the FRAMES strategy, the social worker can conduct a family checkup that provides the social worker with the opportunity to perform the following actions (Miller & Rollnick, 2013, p. 375):

1 Provide **F**eedback regarding family members' personal status relative to family norms.
2 Designate **R**esponsibility for personal change to the family as individuals and a group.
3 **A**dvise family members regarding their situation and the benefits of change.
4 Provide the family with a **M**enu of change options to choose from.
5 Use an **E**mpathetic counseling style to validate family members' concerns.
6 Reinforce family members' **S**elf-efficacy.

Note the strategies described here do not necessarily occur in a linear sequence but are concepts that guide MI.

For example, using the FRAMES strategy with the Murray family, you may opt to check in with the family in this way:

1 Provide Feedback to each family member on strengths and areas for consideration related to their proposed solutions for the various crises they are experiencing. Encourage the family to provide feedback to one another.

2 *Designate Responsibility* for change, clarifying roles and tasks for each family member.
3 *Provide information* on the impact of ongoing stress for the family, dementia, risks of teen alcohol use, and the potential positive outcomes of collaborative change.
4 Provide family members with a *Menu of options* for behavior change, healthier interactions, services, and resources that may be mobilized in and outside the family.
5 *Empathetically validate* the concerns each family member expresses and acknowledge the pain they are experiencing. Reiterate that the family members are the experts about themselves and that it is within their power and responsibility to implement change. Try to create an environment in which the family is empowered to view themselves as having capacity to respond to their crises with resilience and efficacy.
6 Regularly reinforce each family member's *self-efficacy*, identifying their strengths, their commitment to change, and their progress toward goals.

While employing MI in social work practice with families can be an effective strategy for change, it can present challenges that do not exist in working with individuals. Given that families often come to social workers as the result of their inability to resolve relationship challenges on their own, it is critical that you ensure that each family member is given adequate opportunity to be heard (Miller & Rollnick, 2013). Moreover, you should balance the interactions to maintain a focus on positive change as opposed to continuing arguments and negative discussions. The support for the change process is delineated into four categories: (1) "Replanning" occurs to help the family modify plans as needed if earlier efforts are not working; (2) "Reminding" is returning to the original motivations for change; (3) "Refocusing" can be helpful if the original goals for change have lost focus or importance; and (4) "Reengaging" is used to address the disengagement of family member(s) from the change process or to check in with the family after the intervention is completed to monitor sustained change (Miller & Rollnick, 2013; Rosengren, 2018). MI strategies that may be helpful for families include:

1 *Scaling questions*—like solutions-focused interventions, scaling questions (discussed in Chapter 5), can separate importance of a change from confidence in ability to make the change and help the social worker assess their readiness (or lack of) for change (Teater, 2020).
2 Decisional *balance* can help to explore members' ambivalence and motivation to change through developing a "balance sheet: in response to these questions: (1) 'What are the good things about staying the same?'; (2) 'What are the not so good things about staying the same?' (3) 'What are the good things about changing?'; and (4) 'What are the not so good things about changing?'" (Teater, 2020, p. 136).
3 *Looking back and forward* questions can highlight hope and motivation from the past and current behaviors as positive or negative for moving forward. A looking back question might be "Do you remember a time

when things were going well? What has changed" while a looking forward question could be "How would you like things to be different?" (Teater, 2020; Rosengren, 2018).

Mapping as an Intervention

Mapping strategies are often discussed in the context of assessment. They do, however, have a place in the intervention process. While the genogram provides valuable assessment information, that information becomes the basis for the intervention in which family members can identify strengths, resiliencies, and vulnerabilities over time as seen in the genogram (McGoldrick, 2022). They may also be able to identify patterns of substance use/addictions, involvement with the criminal justice system, or other distressing patterns that can inform their collective and individual work. Using the identified patterns and unhealthy family issues to develop and facilitate change plans can be a liberating experience for family members. McGoldrick (2016) suggests that integrating the genogram throughout the intervention enables individuals to explore their cultural, spiritual, and psychological identities within the context of their connections to others and to understand their role in the family's history (p. 3). Being able to see historical patterns of loss, relationships (healthy and unhealthy), physical and mental health issues, substance use/addictions, responses to stress and crisis, and cultural traditions can make family members aware of the options they have for change. Creating and discussing genograms can also provide family members with an opportunity to engage in intergenerational dialogue and identify areas for change in their relationships with one another. Genograms can be helpful in interventions involving children. Best used with children 4 years and older, the Family Play Genogram can provide new insights and opportunities for creativity to help children be fully engaged in the intervention process (McGoldrick, 2016).

Similarly, ecomaps and culturagrams are also assessment tools that social workers can use in interventions, terminations, evaluations, and follow-up. Using a baseline ecomap or culturagram to monitor change throughout the intervention provides the family and social worker with a visual depiction of the work. The ecomap or culturagram can be updated to track and evaluate progress and to note any barriers preventing success. Social workers can work with families to construct new maps as a means of ritualizing a successful outcome. They can then reflect during the termination process on changes achieved or not achieved.

Family member resistance to bringing one of these assessment tools into the intervention is not uncommon and should be anticipated. Resistance to openly discussing family history can occur for various reasons and the social worker can redirect the discussion back to the current situation and help the family identify connections to their other experiences (McGoldrick, 2022).

Consider the Murray family. If the family members engage in dialogue with Edna, they might discover family history they have never heard before and have a meaningful experience with Edna before her memory fades away.

Documentation for Family Interventions

Documentation is a critical component of family interventions and should include assessment tools, intervention plans, case notes, and evaluation data. Documentation formats used with family interventions often use similar formats as those used for individual interventions. Summary, narrative, and structured formats (e.g., SOAP [subjective, objective, assessments, and plan]) are found in most family documentation styles. A summary is typically composed to document the termination of a family intervention and should include reason for services, beginning and ending dates, and overview of assessment and intervention activities with a plan for follow-up (Sidell, 2015). To aid in improving quality and continuity of services, family records should include contacts with all family members and others with connections to the intervention, and history of any critical incidents related to the family (e.g., crises, abuse, suicide attempts, etc.) (Reamer, 2020b). Exhibit 7.5 offers a sample family intervention plan template and Exhibit 7.6 provides an example of intervention plan documentation a social worker might develop with the Murray family.

EXHIBIT 7.5 *Family Intervention Plan Documentation*	**Intervention Plan**
	• Preliminary assessment
	• Preliminary plan for intervention and change (to be developed at first visit), including:
	    ◦ What will each family member do differently?
	    ◦ How does each family member think they will accomplish changes?
	    ◦ What support and services do family members need to accomplish change?
	    ◦ Who will provide support and services?
	    ◦ Who will arrange for support and services?
	• Interventions and plans for emergency/safety needs
	• Other interventions needed
	• Needs (include date, identified need, status [active, inactive, deferred, or referred], and reason for deferral or referral)
	• Strengths
	• Facilitating factors for intervention
	• Limitations
	• Barriers to intervention
	• Other care providers/referrals and purpose (including plan for service coordination)
	• Plan for involvement of individual family members, extended family members, significant others, and friends
	• Review and termination criteria
	• Planned frequency and duration of intervention
	
	Source: Adapted from St. Anthony's Medical Center (2010); Missouri Department of Social Services, n.d.

EXHIBIT 7.6

Documenting the Intervention Plan: The Murray Family

Preliminary Assessment

The Murray family has requested services from this agency to address multiple crises and concerns within the family. The family includes Robert, a 55-year-old high school teacher, Sharon, a 50-year-old occupational therapist, and their three children, Elle, Stephen, and Samantha. Elle is a 25-year-old divorced single mother of two young children, Stephen is a 21-year-old college student, and Samantha is a 16-year-old high school junior. Along with Robert's mother, 76-year-old Edna, all members of the family reside in the couple's now overcrowded home. Stephen and Samantha were displaced when Robert and Sharon gave their bedrooms to Edna and Elle and her children. Edna is experiencing cognitive impairment (Alzheimer's disease).

When Samantha was arrested for driving under the influence and suspended from school, the Murrays sought help. During the assessment, the family shared information that suggests that the family has been in crisis for some time and that Samantha's arrest and suspension brought that crisis to a climax.

Preliminary Plan for Intervention and Plan for Change

During the first meeting of the entire family, each member shared their concerns, needs, and potential solutions. Then, the social worker shared a summary of that information and collaborated with the family to create a list of priorities. Through this collaboration, the social worker and the family developed the following preliminary plan:

1. Sharon agreed to contact the local chapter of the Alzheimer's Association to obtain information on services available for families with members experiencing dementia. She will specifically inquire about programs that provide information on Alzheimer's disease and offer financial support for care needs (e.g., Family Caregiver Support Program).
2. All family members agreed (with varying degrees of enthusiasm) they would attend a presentation for families about the disease provided by the Alzheimer's Association.
3. Stephen will contact the campus housing department at his university to learn about applying for a resident advisor position, which would provide him with tuition support and free housing in exchange for living in one of the student residential facilities. While he waits to learn if his application is accepted, Robert and Sharon have agreed to work with Stephen to fix up the basement so he may have a private bedroom and workspace.
4. Sharon, Robert, and Samantha all agreed to attend the court-mandated program for teens arrested for driving under the influence.
5. Samantha agreed to attend the alternative school program for the duration of her one-month school suspension.

Interventions and Plans for Emergency/Safety Needs

The first meeting yielded two areas of immediate concern regarding the family's safety needs. All family members agreed upon the following plan:

EXHIBIT 7.6

Continued

1. Elle agreed to provide care for Edna during the day when Robert and Sharon are at work. This will reassure them that Edna is safe and that her supervision and transportation needs will be met. Elle will be able to remain home with her children and will not have to bear the expense of child care.
2. Samantha agreed not to drink and to be subjected to periodic alcohol tests if her parents are uncertain about her sobriety.

Other Interventions Needed

Longer-term interventions may include:

1. Exploration of all family members' feelings regarding their overcrowded living conditions and stressful relationships,
2. Discussion regarding Stephen's living arrangement if he is not accepted for a resident advisor position,
3. Decision-making regarding Edna's ongoing care needs as her disease progresses and to determine Edna's wishes regarding her advanced care planning,
4. Discussions regarding Elle's permanent employment and living situations, and
5. Re-establishing a trusting and healthy relationship between Samantha and her parents.

Needs

At this preliminary phase, the family's primary needs are to:

1. Ensure that Elle and her children are coping with their trauma and disruption.
2. Establish a safe environment for Edna.
3. Address Samantha's legal, school, and alcohol issues.
4. Provide adequate space for Stephen and Samantha.
5. Address family stressors.

Strengths

The Murray family has several important strengths on which to build, including:

1. Sharon and Robert's longstanding marital and employment history and commitment to each other and their family members as evidenced by their willingness to open their home to Edna and to Elle and her children.
2. Elle's commitment to her children.
3. Stephen's commitment to his education.
4. The family members' commitment to care for one another.

Facilitating Factors for Intervention

The family members' willingness to care for one another is the primary facilitating factor in this intervention. The family's resources, both internal (e.g., Elle's availability to care for Edna and her expertise in nursing care) and external (e.g., Alzheimer's Association, alternative school, or alcohol intervention) enable them to access needed services.

EXHIBIT 7.6

Continued

Limitations and Barriers to Intervention

1. While plans are under way to address the family's overcrowded situation, change may take time. Coping with the stress of the cramped living quarters in the interim presents a particular challenge.
2. While she agreed to attend the alternative school and to participate in family therapy, Samantha appears angry and may be reluctant to actively engage, particularly if the home continues to be a stressful environment and she feels she gets no attention or privacy.
3. The multitude of issues and tasks they are working to address may overwhelm the family, and this may render them less able to mobilize for change.

Other Care Providers/Referrals

1. School personnel at the alternative school and Samantha's regular school
2. Alzheimer's Association
3. Family Caregiver Support Program
4. Substance Use Disorder Treatment Program

Plan for Involvement of Individual Family Members, Extended Family Members, Significant Others, and Friends

Currently, there is no plan to include other family members. However, the family mentioned that Robert has two sisters who live out of town and who may be willing to help with Edna's care at some point or provide some financial resources to relieve the family's burden.

Review and Termination Criteria/Plan

All agreed that the goals will be achieved when the family members feel they are in better control of their lives, specifically when:

1. The overcrowded housing issue is resolved,
2. Plans for Edna's long-term care needs are determined,
3. Elle's employment and housing plans are clarified,
4. Samantha has successfully completed the court-mandated program and is once again a student in good standing at her school (one-year minimum of no school violations), and
5. Stephen has a permanent housing solution.

Planned Frequency and Duration of Intervention

The initial plan is for the social worker and family members to meet weekly. The social worker will be available by telephone in the interim. After the first four meetings, the social worker and family will discuss plans for ongoing contact. As issues resolve, meeting frequency will decrease to every other week and possibly to monthly. Final termination is scheduled to occur within one year of the intake.

Source: Adapted from St. Anthony's Medical Center (2010)

As with your work with individuals, interventions with families require social workers to complete comprehensive, ongoing assessments from which they can collaborate with families to create flexible, individualized interventions. The outcome of a successful intervention is, of course, the termination. We now direct our focus to the termination, evaluation, and follow-up phases of family interventions.

ENDING WORK WITH FAMILY CONSTELLATIONS

As in all terminations and evaluations, it is important to explore the meanings of and responses to endings for families. This discussion builds on prior discussions of terminations, evaluations, and follow-up (as appropriate) and applies those ideas as appropriate for interventions with families. The goals for termination are aimed at easing the transition to a future orientation and shifting to events, activities, and supports outside the helping relationship, including (Fortune, 2015):

- assessing progress and the helping process.
- generalizing gains to the family's life and their future.
- developing a plan for maintaining the knowledge and skills gained through the intervention.
- transitioning to discontinuation of all services or working with a new service or provider.
- addressing emotional responses to the intervention and the termination.

Ideally, when a family has sought services voluntarily, endings occur when the family is satisfied that they have achieved their goals or at a time predetermined by mutual agreement, or agency policy. If the family is mandated by an outside organization (e.g., court system, school, and/or insurance provider), the timeframe may be pre-determined or based on your recommendation. Recall from the earlier discussion on documentation that the contract with the Murray family proposed a period of three months for the social worker and the family to work together. The duration of the intervention was the agreed-upon timeframe to address each of the prioritized concerns voiced by the family. In some circumstances, the agency, court, or third-party insurer or **managed care** company may mandate an endpoint that occurs before goals can be achieved. In such situations, discussion regarding maintenance strategies that can be employed post-termination, continuing without reimbursement, sliding fee scale arrangements, or referral to another provider can occur. Time-limited interventions provide clarity from the outset and can seem easier to implement, while open-ended interventions can be ended through mutual agreement on a specific outcome (e.g., goals are met, improvements noted, or lack of success and unwillingness to continue) (Fortune, 2015).

Introduced from the first encounter, termination should be revisited over the course of the intervention to determine whether the intervention is on track, whether the timeline is realistic to achieve success in reaching goals, and/or to address new concerns that may arise. In circumstances in which the work is not completed but services must be terminated, plans can be made for referrals and/or follow-up contacts.

For the Murray family, termination plans are based on achieving the mutually agreed-upon goals and actions, some of which may be completed in less than one year, others which may be in process at one year, and others which may be determined to be unachievable.

Family work often focuses on the ways the family wants the dynamics of their relationships with each other or with outside entities to change and on the extent to which the family successfully achieves that change. The work also often focuses on preparing for future situations so that the family can anticipate how best to respond. For example, if a family is struggling with the decision to allow an adolescent more freedom when they have a history of legal altercations, it may help them to consider how they will manage that issue when the teen leaves for college. These positions are all consistent with the principles of review and exploration highlighted in Chapter 5.

Understanding the impact of termination on both the family and the social worker is an important part of the intervention process. Just as with terminations in practice with individuals, family interventions may end due to the family dropping out or individual members refusing to participate, the social worker leaving or being unable to continue, or the agency discontinuing the program (Fortune, 2015). Should an unplanned termination occur, one final session can help to process and gain closure on the intervention (Fortune, 2015). The reasons for termination are as varied as the responses to termination by the clients and the professional.

Endings can be perceived by family members in different ways. Some may view the termination as positive (e.g., pride in accomplishments and increased autonomy), with ambivalence (e.g., sadness or being unsure of success), or negatively (e.g., grief, anger, and/or regression) (Fortune, 2015). There may be disagreement among the members regarding the timing or need for termination—in such cases, your role is to help the family reach a compromise (Patterson et al., 2018). You can support the family by openly discussing the termination and members' feelings, build on the positive feelings, and (as appropriate) integrate ending rituals and celebrations (Fortune, 2015). As you help families transition through termination, be mindful of cultural influences about endings.

The following discussion will consider ending work with families from a strengths and empowerment perspective and through narrative-focused and solution-focused perspectives. These approaches strive to minimize the difficulty of endings. In general, they propose a comfortable, flexible process that gives clients control whenever possible.

Endings With Strength and Empowerment

The family as a whole and individually can benefit from openly discussing feelings and insights about the intervention, the strengths each individual and the family brought to the intervention, and the termination. Celebrating successes early and often is, in fact, a signal that termination is forthcoming; therefore, it is important to regularly discuss how and when the actual termination will occur within the context of clear and measurable outcomes (Simmons et al., 2022). The termination of the helping relationship is a process, not an event, that focuses on consolidating gains from the intervention, empowering the family to be confident they can sustain the change, and recognizing potential losses related to the ending (Patterson et al., 2018). In an evaluative spirit, these insights can reinforce what the family has accomplished in the intervention and enable members to acknowledge the ending. Keeping in mind the original goal, the social worker and the family can focus on the future and on how the family can sustain change. If the relationship is terminating even though the family did not achieve their desired goals, the termination and evaluation phases can focus on lessons learned that the family could use in the future. In terminating with the Murray family, for example, they acknowledge they were not able to fulfill their goal of locating an appropriate residential care facility for Edna. As they were moving toward this goal, the COVID-19 pandemic began, and they were fearful about having Edna live in a long-term care setting due to the high rates of residents being infected with and dying from coronavirus. They determined that they would continue on caring for her at home until it was safer for her to live in a group setting. While they did not achieve their goal, the family and you can use this time to reflect on other changes made, insights gained, reasons the goal was unmet, and strategies for the future if they want to continue to work on a goal.

A strengths- and empowerment-oriented social worker can focus the termination and evaluation around the strengths identified in the assessment

process and those identified or created during the intervention phase. Existing and new strengths can become the basis for the family to sustain the changes they have made. Together, you and the family can review the family's strengths. You can then ask the family to consider how they can apply these strengths to future situations. The family can also use these strengths as coping skills when and if they encounter new challenges. In the case of the Williamson family who were unable to achieve their goal of eating dinner together three times a week, you can ask if they feel they gained insights and motivation from setting and working on that goal. You can also ask family members to speculate on their motivation and ability to continue working on their goals even after the formal intervention has ended.

Endings in Narrative-Focused Work

Narrative social workers often punctuate endings by working with families to develop rituals or ceremonies in which the family invites an audience to witness the changes the family has made and to celebrate their achievements in the company of their support network. Such rituals serve to reinforce changes and provide opportunities to spread the news of their new realizations (Nichols & Davis, 2020; Smith, 2022). Known as definitional ceremonies aimed at validating the experiences, these gatherings may include siblings, other professionals who have worked with the family, and/or extended family. These ceremonies provide the opportunity for the individual family members to tell their future life story and for the "witnesses" to reflect on the stories from their perspectives (Suddeath et al., 2017). Using such strategies as certificates and celebratory (definitional) activities, these ceremonies highlight a family's successes and can affirm and inspire continuation of change (Van Hook, 2019). This focus, like solution-focused work, represents a departure from traditional views of endings while acknowledging the same concerns about maintaining gains. In revisiting the termination with the Williamson family, consider a scenario in which they not only achieved the goal of dining together three times a week but were able to increase that to five times a week. A celebratory termination activity to commemorate their progress may be to bring food that is special to the family (e.g., dessert) and share as a group.

Endings in Solution-Focused Work

Solution-focused work emphasizes endings almost from the beginning. As a short-term intervention approach, a solution-focused approach stresses that clients have abilities to competently manage their lives. Goal achievements, even small ones, can also prompt discussion of the upcoming termination (Corcoran, 2022a). Because this approach is built on the premise that change can occur within a brief, time-limited period, you can use scaling early in the process, perhaps asking, "What [number] do you need to get to in order for us to end our work together?" (De Jong, 2015). This question refers to the number from 1 to 10 that reflects the degree of well-being or change the client reports. This approach honors a family's concerns about needing further work, and the family determines the number and content of further sessions. Termination-related discussions can also serve to prepare for potential setbacks. The social worker can help the family by asking how they think they will identify and respond to a setback and continue to build on the changes they have made (Corcoran, 2022a). The approach places little emphasis on the relationship between the social worker and the family; it views "not needing to come to talk to me anymore" as the preferred reality and a natural and comfortable conclusion to a problem for which the family likely already has a solution (which the social worker may help bring to light). In this approach the ending is, by definition, a success. In situations in which family members disagree, the social worker can facilitate discussion in hopes of reaching a compromise on family members' perspective on goal achievement.

In summary, all terminations and follow-up processes (e.g., checking in with the family, inviting the family for a follow-up session, or making referrals) are as important to the planned change process as any other stage of the relationship. Bringing the intervention to a close can serve as an opportunity for the social worker and family to: (1) reflect on accomplishments; (2) anticipate upcoming challenges; (3) discuss possible responses should a setback occur and let the family know that it is not uncommon for families to experience distress with setbacks; and (4) plan for post-intervention follow-up contact (e.g., letter/email, phone call, and/or a brief in-person session) (Nichols & Davis, 2020).

Termination of the social worker–family relationship can be a time of mutual reflection and an opportunity for final declarations of hope for the future. You can remind the family that they should recognize that they fully own their enhanced ability to cope with the challenges in their lives (Van Hook, 2019, p. 387). This can be a final time in which you and the family can review the new or remobilized resources within (e.g., beliefs) and outside (e.g., extended family, friends, and community) the family; abilities; and strategies that have been integrated into their interactional patterns so that they can readily access them when challenges arise in the future (Van Hook, 2019). Engaging in these reflective activities during the ending phase of family work leads naturally into the process of formally and informally evaluating the work you have done together.

As we transition into a discussion of evaluation of family interventions, reflect on the following questions related to the ending of your work with families (Nichols & Davis, 2020):

1. Has the presenting problem improved?
2. Is the family satisfied that they have achieved what they came for and are they interested in continuing to learn about themselves and improve their relationships?
3. Does the family have an understanding of what they were doing that wasn't working and how to avoid the recurrence of similar problems in the future?
4. Do minor recurrences of problems reflect lack of resolution of some underlying dynamic or merely that the family must readjust to function without a professional?
5. Have family members developed and improved relationships outside the immediate family context as well as within it? (p. 28)

Evaluation of Social Work Practice With Families

As part of the termination process, evaluation provides the social worker and the family a chance to review and recognize progress made (Friedman & Olivera, 2022). Evaluating outcomes of the intervention serves multiple purposes, to include: (1) determining if your intervention enhanced the family's well-being and functioning (Thyer, 2021); (2) examining the effect of approaches and interventions (Corcoran, 2022b); (3) determining if you and your organization are meeting the needs of the community being served which can promote higher quality, trust, and satisfaction (Friedman & Olivera, 2022); and (4) highlighting gaps in the various models' and methods' appropriateness for use with all populations (Marsiglia et al., 2021).

As noted in the assessment and intervention phases of work, ensuring that the evaluation is culturally appropriate is essential. The evaluation process, including measurement tools, should capture the needs of all families being served and normed on that population (Friedman & Olivera, 2022). As with evaluation interventions with individuals, you may begin the evaluation process with families by asking similar questions (Sellon & Lassman, 2022):

1. How well did the intervention work for the client system?
2. Does the intervention perpetuate the inclusion of privileged groups and/or exclusion of oppressed groups?
3. What knowledge and skills did the clients gain?
4. How well did you check your own biases? Where did you struggle? (p. 308)

Evaluation is an essential component of the social work intervention. First and foremost, determining efficacy of interventions is critical for the development of evidence-based practice approaches, which ensure the quality of services being provided to families. Second, when family service organizations receive funding from grants and contracts, funders routinely require outcomes evaluations to determine if the services they invested in are, in fact, effective (Friedman & Olivera, 2022). Last, families' health care coverage expects to have evidence that your services are helping the family in the most cost-effective way (Friedman & Olivera, 2022). Funding sources require providers of health, mental health, and social services to identify, monitor, and be accountable for the outcomes they propose to achieve. Ongoing evaluation of interventions with families can not only enable you to monitor and assess treatment outcomes but can also directly impact the resources your organization is able to access.

Considerable evaluative research is available for family-focused behavioral and mental health interventions, which can make it challenging to determine which approaches are most effective. While your agency's mission may determine the approaches used, it is important to recognize that the connection you make with families and the closeness that is experienced through engagement in a helping relationship are of the utmost importance to family outcomes (Dallos & Draper, 2015). In addition, knowing that client satisfaction has been linked to the professional's commitment and skills in culturally responsive practice can prompt the social worker to re-examine their own and agency cultural competence (Olcoń, 2019).

Despite the availability of evaluation research findings linking the intervention to outcomes, we can also gather qualitative data from the client system, including (Dudley, 2020):

- Are my interventions helping you? In what ways?

- Are my interventions helping you in the areas in which you are seeking help (e.g., related to the presenting problems, identified needs, solutions desired, expressed hopes)?

- Are my interventions helping you meet your goals identified in our initial work together?

- How would you describe your progress so far in achieving your goals? How have my interventions played a part in helping you or in hindering you? (p. 237)

While these questions will yield subjective information that is potentially related to clients' satisfaction with your work together, they are nonetheless a helpful component of determining if the intervention was perceived to be effective (Dudley, 2020). Ideally, the evaluation will include both objective and subjective data to create a fuller picture of the experience and outcomes (Dudley, 2020).

If your intervention is an evidence-based practice approach, your evaluation can provide insights and contributions to your practice or your agency's practice. While evaluating your interventions with individuals can yield similar information about your practice, the same evaluative strategies are not always applicable to family interventions. Just as families are unique, so, too, are evaluations of family interventions.

The context and goals of the original contact often determine how a social worker conducts ongoing evaluation of work with a particular family. For example, if you are working with a family in child protective services, the priority may be the continued safety of the child. There may be other goals, such as improving the parents' family management skills or meeting the child's health needs. In most cases, you will document these goals in writing and refer to them throughout the work.

When evaluating interventions with families, social workers focus on the family unit itself and not on the individuals within the family. For example, if you and the family determine that power has shifted in a positive way among and between family members, this could indicate that the intervention has been effective. Alternatively, family members might deem the intervention successful because they agree that the stress level within the family has decreased, or the quality of their interactions has improved. Family evaluations may focus on the outcomes of the goals established during the assessment and planning phases and satisfaction with the relationship with the social worker and agency.

Strengths- and Resiliency-Based Family Evaluation Measures

While family-focused intervention evaluations differ from evaluations of individual and group practice, the same evaluative strategies described in Chapter 5 provide a basis for developing plans for evaluation of family interventions. To promote a family (versus the individual) focus for the evaluation, strategies such as single-system design, goal attainment scaling, and case studies can be effective evaluation tools. A mixed methodology approach can be used to evaluate family outcomes. Standardized empirical (quantitative) measures can be administered before, during, and after the intervention to assess, monitor, and evaluate change. Qualitative data can be gathered through individual, couple, and family interviews. Focus groups conducted with family members who have received services can yield informational trends in responses to the intervention delivered. Regardless of the type of evaluation used, the focus must be directed on the family as a unit.

An array of evaluation measurements has been developed specifically for use with families. While the scope of this book can only highlight a small sample, the following discussion will briefly explore the selection of measures grounded in a strengths-based perspective. Several instruments designed for use in strengths-based practice with families allow social workers to document their service effectiveness. Standardized evaluative tools are increasingly important as funders, agency boards of directors, client advocacy organizations, and the social work profession itself hold agencies and practitioners accountable for measuring client outcomes. Practice evaluation instruments can be helpful in maintaining the social worker's and family's focus on the work being done. Some of the instruments that have emerged as strengths-based, family-centered emphases were introduced in the 1980s and 1990s and remain useful today because they measure family perceptions and assets. The use of standardized tools allows for evaluation of the relationships between family-centered interventions and child, parent, and family outcomes (Dunst & Espe-Sherwindt, 2016, p. 40). Thyer (2021) emphasizes the importance of using valid outcome measurements that are available, practical, reliable, and inexpensive to administer and that are linked to the earlier assessments (thus, administered multiple times). Consider the following factors as you plan for using standardized measures (Corcoran, 2022b):

1 Timing, location, and participants—when and where will the administration occur and who will participate (including the social worker)?
2 Purpose of the tool—explain the rationale, provide specific instructions (best if read by the person administering it), and describe how the findings will be recorded and used. Obtaining informed consent for family member participation is required.
3 Feedback—provide the scoring and interpretation of the measures to the family and feedback regarding their meaning.

You and/or your agency will select the evaluative strategy that is most appropriate to your setting and to the families you serve. Before using any measure, prepare yourself by reading research and guidelines related to the tool, particularly related to adapting or altering the measure (which can compromise the instrument's psychometric validity). The following is a small representative list of reliable strengths and empowerment-focused evaluation measures that may be of help to you as you consider evaluating your practice with families:

- *The Rapid Caregiver Well-Being Scale (R-CWBS)* (Berg-Weger et al., 2000; Tebb, 1995; Tebb et al., 2013): A strengths-based clinical measure to help family caregivers of adults and/or children identify the strengths and areas for change in their caregiving experience. The R-CWBS is a rapid assessment tool adapted from two earlier versions (CWBS and Shortened CWBS). All three versions are grounded in the concept that caregivers' basic needs and activities of living must be adequately met for the caregiver to maintain their well-being. The self-report tool can be self-administered or incorporated into individual or family interventions with caregivers. Responses serve as conversation starters to promote more in-depth exploration of caregiver needs. See Quick Guide 18 for an example.

QUICK GUIDE 18 Caregiver Well-Being Scale

I ACTIVITIES

The list below includes activities that each of us do or that someone does for us. Thinking over the past three months, indicate by circling the appropriate number on the scale provided to what extent you think each activity has been accomplished in a timely way. You do not have to be the one who did the activity.

1 = Rarely   2 = Occasionally   3 = Sometimes   4 = Frequently   5 = Almost Always

1. Buying food — 1 2 3 4 5
2. Taking care of personal daily activities (meals, hygiene, laundry) — 1 2 3 4 5
3. Attending to medical needs — 1 2 3 4 5
4. Keeping up with home maintenance activities (lawn, cleaning, house repairs, etc.) — 1 2 3 4 5
5. Participating in events at church and/or in the community — 1 2 3 4 5
6. Taking time to have fun with friends and/or family — 1 2 3 4 5
7. Treating or rewarding yourself — 1 2 3 4 5
8. Making plans for your financial future — 1 2 3 4 5

II NEEDS

The list below includes a number of needs we all have. For each need listed, think about your life over the past three months. During this period of time, indicate to what extent you think each need has been met by circling the appropriate number on the scale provided below.

1 = Rarely   2 = Occasionally   3 = Sometimes   4 = Frequently   5 = Almost Always

1. Eating a well-balanced diet — 1 2 3 4 5
2. Getting enough sleep — 1 2 3 4 5
3. Receiving appropriate health care — 1 2 3 4 5
4. Having adequate shelter — 1 2 3 4 5
5. Expressing love — 1 2 3 4 5
6. Expressing anger — 1 2 3 4 5
7. Feeling good about yourself — 1 2 3 4 5
8. Feeling secure about your financial future — 1 2 3 4 5

Source: Berg-Weger et al., 2000; Tebb et al., 2013.

- *Walsh Family Resilience Questionnaire (WFRQ)* (Walsh, 2016a): A 12-item resiliency-focused self-report questionnaire that operationalizes the processes of Walsh's resiliency framework. Families are asked to rate perceptions of how they respond to crises and persistent stress. Their responses serve as a conversation starter to further explore the issues identified. The WFRQ is useful for pre- and post-assessment to monitor change over time and to determine effectiveness of the intervention. Walsh recommends adaptations for cultural, socioeconomic status, language, population, and type of adversity (Walsh, 2016c). See Quick Guide 19 for an example.

QUICK GUIDE 19 Walsh Family Resilience Questionnaire

	RARELY/ NEVER	INFREQUENT	SOMETIMES	OFTEN	ALMOST ALWAYS
1. Our family faces difficulties together as a team, rather than individually.	1	2	3	4	5
2. We view distress with our situation as common, understandable.	1	2	3	4	5
3. We approach a crisis as a challenge we can manage and master with shared efforts.	1	2	3	4	5
4. We try to make sense of stressful situations and focus on our options.	1	2	3	4	5
5. We keep hopeful and confident that we will overcome difficulties.	1	2	3	4	5
6. We encourage each other and build our strengths.	1	2	3	4	5
7. We seize opportunities, take action, and persist in our efforts.	1	2	3	4	5
8. We focus on our possibilities and try to accept what we can't change.	1	2	3	4	5
9. We share important values and life purpose that help us rise above difficulties.	1	2	3	4	5
10. We draw on spiritual resources (religious and non-religious) to help us cope well.	1	2	3	4	5
11. Our challenges inspire creativity, more meaningful priorities, and stronger bonds.	1	2	3	4	5
12. Our hardship has increased our compassion and desire to help others.	1	2	3	4	5

Source: Copyright 2015 by Froma Walsh (2015). Reprinted by permission.

- *Strengths-Based Practices Inventory (SBPI)* (Green et al., 2004): While most evaluative tools are aimed at families themselves, the SBPI is a valid and reliable 16-item measure designed to assess the agency's strengths-based delivery of services in the areas of empowerment, cultural competency, staff sensitivity/knowledge, and relationship-based/support approach. Quick Guide 20 provides an example.

QUICK GUIDE 20 Strengths-Based Practices Inventory (SBPI)

Family Name _____

The following questions ask you about your experience with (program name). Please circle the number that best describes your feelings about the program and its staff. Response categories:

1 = Strong Disagree	2 = Mostly Disagree	3 = Disagree a Little	
4 = Neither Agree or Disagree	5 = Agree a Little	6 = Mostly Agree	7 = Strongly Agree

To score, sum all items and divide by 16.

THE PROGRAM STAFF:	SD	MD	DL	N	AL	MA	SA
1. help me to see strengths in myself I didn't know I had.	1	2	3	4	5	6	7
2. encourage me to get involved to help improve my community.	1	2	3	4	5	6	7
3. work together with me to meet my needs.	1	2	3	4	5	6	7
4. know about other programs I can use if I need them.	1	2	3	4	5	6	7
5. encourage me to think about my own personal goals or dreams.	1	2	3	4	5	6	7
6. understand when something is difficult for me.	1	2	3	4	5	6	7
7. respect my family's cultural and/or religious beliefs.	1	2	3	4	5	6	7
8. encourage me to go to friends and family when I need help or support.	1	2	3	4	5	6	7
9. help me see that I am a good parent.	1	2	3	4	5	6	7
10. give me good information about where to go for other services I need.	1	2	3	4	5	6	7
11. have materials for my child/family that positively reflect our cultural background.	1	2	3	4	5	6	7
12. encourage me to share my knowledge with other parents.	1	2	3	4	5	6	7
13. encourage me to learn about my culture and history.	1	2	3	4	5	6	7
14. help me to use my own skills and resources to solve problems.	1	2	3	4	5	6	7
15. provide opportunities for me to get to know other parents in the community.	1	2	3	4	5	6	7
16. support me in the decisions I make about myself and my family.	1	2	3	4	5	6	7

Source: Green et al., 2004. SBPI is in the public domain.

- *The Three-Item Brief Assessment of Family Functioning Scale (BAFFS)* (Mansfield et al., 2018). Practitioners often look for standardized rapid/ultra-brief assessment tools that require less administration time. A psychometrically validated shortened version of the General Functioning Scale of the Family Assessment Device (Epstein et al., 1983), the BAFFS is a three-item proxy scale that provides the family's perception of satisfaction with overall family functioning (Mansfield et al., 2018). Quick Guide 21 provides an example.

In strengths- and empowerment-oriented measurements, self-reporting is an asset. Self-reporting can complement traditional, scientific measurements in which the goal of objectivity conflicts with the biases in self-reporting. Bias is inherent in self-reported information because it is difficult to be objective about yourself. However, the strengths perspective supports the expertise of individuals and families about their own lives, experience, and aspirations, thereby making self-report a natural and theoretically consistent method of data collection.

The evaluation tools and procedures mentioned here are just a few among many. Some are flexible and, with creativity, you can apply them to a variety of situations. However, you should be careful to confirm the tool has been validated with the same population you are evaluating. Using both quantitative (e.g., closed-ended questions, often multiple choice, or numeric ratings) and qualitative (e.g., narrative comments) evaluative strategies can provide the social worker and the profession with a comprehensive picture of the outcomes related to the intervention. The findings of the evaluation should be interpreted alongside the family, so that they are participating in the meaning-making of their own evaluations. Remember that all evaluative measures have their limitations.

Let us return for a last time to the Murray family. Through the commitment of the family and the social worker, several of the goals have successfully been

---

QUICK GUIDE 21 The Three-Item Brief Assessment of Family Functioning Scale (BAFFS)

Instructions: Circle the response that reflects your experience of family life. Try not to spend too much time thinking about each statement but respond as quickly and honestly as you can.

Summed totals < 6 indicate family satisfaction and scores > 6 indicate family distress.

	STRONGLY AGREE	AGREE	DISAGREE	STRONGLY DISAGREE
1. We can express feelings to each other.	1	2	3	4
2. We don't get along well together.	1	2	3	4
3. We confide in each other.	1	2	3	4

Source: Mansfield et al., 2018 with permission

achieved. After caring for her grandmother for a period, the Murray's daughter, Elle, is offered a better-paying job and can move to her own apartment, which makes the family's home less crowded. Stephen was once again able to have his own room so he did not have to seek alternative housing; this eased his financial burdens. Sadly, Edna's dementia continued to progress. While the family had hoped to be able to care for her in their home through the remainder of her life, her dementia caused her to begin to wander, often leaving the house. Despite a delay in her admission to a continuum of care facility due to the COVID-19 pandemic, they were able to re-locate her to a nearby facility that would enable her to be moved into a higher level of care should she require that. Samantha did successfully complete the mandated requirements that resulted from her alcohol and driving offense but continued to struggle emotionally. After completion of the family sessions, Samantha and her parents agreed that she would continue working individually with the social worker.

Positive or meaningful change may occur independent of the intervention or even if the family is unable to achieve the goals of the intervention.

In those situations in which the family does not reach identified goals by the time the intervention must end (i.e., as in the case of managed care, court- or school-mandated treatment, or inability to pay) or when the family terminates the relationship prior to the agreed-upon ending point, the social worker must process this experience. Talking with a supervisor or colleagues regarding the possible reasons for this unanticipated outcome can be a valuable professional development opportunity. While practice evaluations can be helpful tools, they must be viewed within a context for family, yourself as a practitioner, and your agency.

Practitioner Reflection The evaluation phase also provides you with the opportunity to evaluate your own practice, including selection of theoretical approaches and strategies. In addition to asking the family how they felt about the experience, you can reflect on your own knowledge and how to improve your skills (Sellon & Lassman, 2022). A second area for self-reflection is to consider if you were able to maintain distance between the family's interpretations of the process and their experience and your own (Ballan & Freyer, 2021).

Consider your role with the family and reflect on the quality or competency of your work. Reflection with families is typically an introspective and interactive process. Some questions you can ask family members as well as yourself include:

- Does each family member feel that their contribution to the work is valued?
- Are there issues regarding the family's culture that you did not address in a culturally responsive manner?
- Does the family still agree with the direction of the work?
- How is the work changing their experience?

At all levels of practice, it is important to check in with clients to make sure they feel heard, understood, and are invested in the work you are doing with them. Attend to unarticulated feedback from family members. Lack of follow-through on assignments or commitments are indicators that you and the family should have candid discussions about the intervention process and expectations so that the plan (or expectations) can be adjusted (Becvar & Becvar, 2018).

CRITICAL CONSIDERATIONS ABOUT FAMILY INTERVENTION, TERMINATION, EVALUATION, AND FOLLOW-UP

Practice with families is a complex enterprise, and the intervention, termination, evaluation, and follow-up processes can include the unexpected. Family members have individual relationships, networks, and influences outside the family, and those external persons or groups can positively or negatively affect the work the family accomplishes within the intervention. Family members may establish internal alliances that strengthen or, in some cases, undermine the work. Staying attuned to family members' descriptions of their activities, relationships, and pressures may help you accept that the unexpected is inevitable.

Like terminations with individuals, ending work with families can be emotional, particularly if family members have developed positive relationships with the social worker. The family may even view the social worker as a member of the family; therefore, termination can elicit powerful reactions. The process of terminating and evaluating the social work intervention can elicit negative responses from some family members, some of whom may refuse to participate or may display anger, denial, anxiety, or even regression as the termination approaches (Fortune, 2015). As a social worker, you may find yourself juggling a variety of different responses from family members to the ending of the intervention. Addressing individual and collective reactions to termination and evaluation, while building on the family's strengths and gains of the intervention, can serve as an intervention in and of itself. Empowering the family to handle a change (one they may perceive to be another loss) can be a meaningful new experience for the family; they can support each other, model new behaviors, and mobilize the strengths and resources they developed during the intervention.

Evaluations of family interventions may also yield unexpected results. If you opted (as described in Chapter 6) to complete a pre-intervention assessment, you can compare those data with a post-intervention evaluation. You may be surprised at the family members' perceptions. You can explore these unexpected responses with the family to gain insight into their interpretations.

Due to agency policy or family preference or availability, having contact with the family after the formal termination and evaluation processes are completed may not always be possible or advisable. For example, if you were working with a parent and children staying in your agency's domestic violence shelter and they return to their home with the perpetrator of violence, having contact with you may not be safe for them. In those situations in which you can communicate with the family, you can utilize this contact to receive an update on the family's status and continued progress on maintaining the goals and outcomes from the intervention. If you learn that the family has struggled to sustain or achieve the desired level of change, you can take the opportunity to reflect with them on the barriers that prevented the change from being maintained, and you can (with their consent) brainstorm with them about ways in which they can return to their planned strategies.

GRAND CHALLENGE

Build Healthy Relationships to End Violence

The American Academy of Social Work and Social Welfare Grand Challenges for Social Work Initiative identifies that one of the areas the profession should address is to end gender-based violence, both within and outside of families. The authors of Grand Challenge Working Paper No. 15, *Ending Gender-Based Violence: A Grand Challenge for Social Work* (Edleson et al., 2015, p. 4) provide the following basis for this challenge:

> Efforts to protect and support survivors of violence while also holding perpetrators accountable and working to rehabilitate them abound at the international, national, and local levels. Existing initiatives to prevent GBV [gender-based violence] and promote violence-free intimate relationships include building healthy teen and parenting relationships, providing emergency shelter, screening to identify those at highest risk of lethal violence and coordinated community responses to address system-level barriers. Culturally responsive interventions for survivors and perpetrators are less prominent but are emerging worldwide.

> **GRAND CHALLENGE**
>
> *Continued*
>
> Decades of research have provided evidence for the prevalence and long-lasting effects of an individual's experience of gender-based violence (GBV), including intimate partner violence (IPV), sexual violence, and exposure to violence as a child. While there is no one intervention or best practice that can be used to end GBV, the social work profession is being challenged to focus on the development and mobilization of interventions at the research, practice, and policy levels within the criminal justice and social service systems. Within the coming decade, the social work profession can address GBV through initiatives that: measure progress toward ending GBV, produce practice innovations, and transform perceptions and changing norms related to GBV (Edleson et al., 2015, p. 8).
>
> To familiarize yourself with the issues related to ending gender-based violence, visit the Grand Challenges website and read Working Paper No. 15, *Ending Gender-Based Violence: A Grand Challenge for Social Work* (Edleson et al., 2015) at: https://aaswsw.org. To learn about the progress on achieving this Grand Challenge, review the "Building Healthy Relationships to End Violence" by Barth and colleagues (2022). (See Exercise #1 for additional exploration of this Grand Challenge.)

CONCLUSION

Working with a family from engagement through termination and evaluation can be an immensely rewarding professional accomplishment for you and transformative for the family. Intervening with families requires you to develop a repertoire of theory- and evidence-based behaviors and skills to optimize family strengths and to create and mobilize needed resources. This chapter explored the integration of several theoretical approaches into social work practice with families and provided examples of ways the approaches can be applied to family situations. While refining your theoretically driven social work practice is a lifelong process, identifying the theoretical approaches that are most consistent with your professional and personal values is an important early commitment toward your development as a social worker. Clarifying your own views on families and your role as a family social worker can be helpful along your journey. This chapter highlighted approaches for working with families that you can use in a range of settings and with diverse types of families.

MAIN POINTS

- Social workers can choose from and blend an array of theoretical perspectives to guide interventions with families. Social workers' training, philosophical and value systems, available empirically supported evidence, and agency orientation influence which perspectives they select.

- This chapter highlights approaches for developing intervention plans with families including strengths, empowerment, solution-focused, and narrative perspectives. While these perspectives share some similarities, each has characteristics that make it unique.

- While different models of family intervention require certain specific skills and behaviors, collaborating, using strengths, and supporting the voice of each family member are common to most models.

- Your experience with your own family can influence your work with client families. Ongoing evaluation includes not only documenting the achievement of externally imposed goals (e.g., school or court system) but also determining if your role and relationship with the family are working.

- Each family social work intervention is multifaceted, and the termination and evaluation process should include candid discussion of potential internal and external influences. When ending work with families, consider how the professional–client relationships that formed may have affected the work; the effectiveness of chosen theoretical perspectives; and the practical, contextual dimensions of the work.

- The evaluation of the social work intervention with families may emphasize an empirical process and/or a qualitative one. Standardized tools may be helpful in the process of evaluating family social work.

- Some situations allow for following up with the family. In such situations, the social worker can focus on the degree to which the changes have been maintained and support the family in making appropriate adjustments.

EXERCISES

1 To apply your learning of the Grand Challenge for Social Work, "Ending Gender-Based Violence," which was highlighted in this chapter, visit the Grand Challenges website, and read Working Paper No. 15, *Ending Gender-Based Violence: A Grand Challenge for Social Work* (Edleson et al., 2015) at: https://aaswsw.org/. To examine GBV-related issues, review the information about Hector and Celia's daughter, Gloria, and her spouse, Leo, at www.routledgesw.com/interactive-cases/ (Sanchez case). After reading Working Paper No. 15 and reviewing the information on Gloria and Leo complete the following:
   a Select one of the family intervention approaches discussed in this chapter. Using assessment strategies identified in Chapter 6 (including mapping), complete an assessment for Gloria and Leo.
   b Building on the assessment that you completed for Gloria and Leo, develop an intervention plan that includes existing and needed resources and services.

c Develop a plan for the way in which you would complete the termination and evaluation processes.
2. Go to www.routledgesw.com/interactive-cases/ and review the case file for Carmen Sanchez (in Engage and Discover). Address Critical Thinking Questions #1, #2, and #3. For Critical Thinking Question #2, identify at least one peer-reviewed scholarly article in each of the two areas that concern Carmen: the impact on families of children with special health needs and outcomes of children in different types of families.

   Gather into groups with 4–5 of your classmates and develop a potential work plan for the family based on your answers to the Critical Thinking Questions. In your plan, focus on the following:
   a Identify areas of potential challenge.
   b Develop strategies for working with the entire Sanchez family around these challenges.
   c Develop a plan to insure Carmen's maximum participation in the process.
3. Go to www.routledgesw.com/interactive-cases/ and review the case file for Carla Washburn in Engage and Discover). While Carla does not have a traditional family network, she is connected to a support system. Strategize about ways in which you might integrate each of the members of her support network into your intervention with Carla, identifying the strengths and potential contributions each member of her chosen family can make. You may wish to review the case files and ecomap to develop your plan.
4. Go to www.routledgesw.com/interactive-cases/ and review the case for Brickville, focusing on Virginia Stone and her family. Based on the initial assessment and planning process you conducted in collaboration with Virginia (you may want to consider Exercise #4 in Chapter 6), the two of you have determined that a family group conference will help address the multiple concerns related to her mother's care, home ownership, and response to the proposed plans for neighborhood development. Using the information available to you (including the ecomap and genogram), develop two separate written plans for a family group conference from two perspectives (narrative and solution-focused), including your responses to the following questions:
   - Whom should you invite to participate in the family conference?
   - What location is optimal for the conference?
   - In preparation for your collaborative planning with Virginia, brainstorm a list of:
     ○ potential agenda items,
     ○ individual and family strengths and areas of concern, and
     ○ available and needed resources (within the family and community).
   - What is your anticipated role?
   - How might the family genogram and/or ecomap be incorporated into the family conference to develop a collaborative intervention, particularly as it relates to providing care for family members?

Upon completing your plans for a family group conference, reflect in writing on three areas:

- Differences and similarities of a narrative or solution-focused approach.
- Ways in which you can integrate a strengths-based perspective into the conference.
- Possible motivational interviewing strategies you can employ during the family conference.

5 As a social work practitioner at a community mental health center, you serve primarily individuals and families. Later today, you will conduct an intake appointment with the James family, who recently called you. You have the following information about the family:
- The father makes the appointments. He self-identifies his as a blended family. The family includes the mother, father, his spouse's two adolescent sons, and the father's parents who live with the family. He is a person of color, and his spouse is Latinx.
- The eldest son, age 18, is of most concern to the family. He has expressed suicidal thoughts and has recently been withdrawing from school, family, and community life. Last year, this son was a well-known school athlete, and this year he is not active in any school or athletic activities.
- The parents suspect that their sons are using alcohol or other drugs.
- Both sons are reluctant to attend the appointment, but they will do so because their stepfather has indicated they must.
- The mother will "go along" because she wants to avoid conflict.

In your preparation for this appointment, you consider several dimensions of the work, including the fact that you have only the father's perspective of the situation. With fellow students, discuss these dimensions and explore the questions. Share your discussion with the class.
   a There are differences between your culture and this family's culture, but you believe you can bridge those to some extent. What might you need to consider about your own assumptions?
   b What theoretical approach to family social work (among those discussed in this chapter) do you believe will provide the most useful base for work with this family? Discuss your reasons for this selection.
   c What specific information will you want to clarify from the start?
   d What specific approaches will be most important with this family?
   e How will you begin your intervention with this family? What skills and behaviors will you use? What might you say? (Give an example.)

6 Using the strengths-based strategies highlighted in this chapter, review the following list, and describe in detail the way in which you would incorporate each item into an intervention with the James family (from Exercise #5):
- Identify the issues and concerns, use active listening to enable family members to tell their stories, and reflect on the information they share.
- Acknowledge their pain.
- Look for and point out strengths.
- Ask questions about survival, support, periods of time that were positive for the family, interests, dreams, goals, and pride.

- Encourage the family to recognize that resilience begins with what one believes, and all people have the capacity for resilience.
- Link strengths to the goals and dreams of family members (both as a group and as individuals).
- Find opportunities for family members to contribute to the intervention by helping to educate other members and to serve as helping agents in achieving the family's agreed-upon goals.
- Brainstorm solutions to help the family view the situation and themselves differently.

7 Using a solution-focused approach, identify the techniques reviewed in this chapter that you believe will be appropriate for use with the James family described in Exercise #5. Describe the specific way you would implement the strategies.

8 Go to www.routledgesw.com/static-cases/ and review Downloadable Case #3: River's Family. After reviewing the information, develop responses to Questions #5–9.

9 Termination and evaluation are critical aspects of the social work intervention. Conduct a review of the peer-reviewed research to identify literature describing evidence-based practice skills and practices that address effective termination and evaluation with a family. Share your findings with your class and compare the results of your literature review.

CHAPTER 8

Social Work Practice With Groups: Engagement, Assessment, and Planning

WE ALL NEED SOCIAL CONNECTIONS IN OUR LIVES. Regardless of the ways in which we experience connections and whether we perceive them as positive or negative, virtually everyone has relationships to small collectives of other people or groups. In this context, **groups** refer to the natural or planned associations that evolve through common interest (e.g., supporting the local Little League), state of being (e.g., having a child with a disability), or task (e.g., working together at a particular agency). Connectedness to groups depends not only on an individual's needs for affiliation but also on cultural norms; social arrangements (e.g., marital/relationship status and personal affiliations); and social location (e.g., children's school or neighborhood of residence). Within social work, **group work** is "the active use of group process to bring a collection of individuals towards a common belonging and, usually but not always, a common purpose" (Doel, 2018, p. 193). Contemporary social work practice with groups is a broad and diverse field of practice that encompasses purposes, populations, practice settings, practitioners' roles, and practice approaches (Garvin & Galinsky, 2020, p. 2). Regardless of the specific group approach used, this area of social work practice is unique and important to the profession as it brings people together to provide mutual aid and support through sharing common issues, life experiences, and challenges and enabling creativity and problem-solving (Garvin & Galinsky, 2020).

Strengths of group work can be viewed from the worker-agency and member perspectives. Benefits for the participants include that: (1) group members provide more resources and support; (2) feelings of safety, belonging, and commitment are encouraged; (3) the group can be a replication of members' everyday world so learning and feedback is safe and able to be applied in their lives; and (4) power is derived from having peers and giving and receiving help (Erford & Bardhoshi, 2018, p. 15). From the agency perspective, group practice enables workers to use their time more efficiently by seeing multiple patients in one session and the cost-of-service delivery per person is reduced (Erford & Bardhoshi, 2018).

This chapter addresses the nature of groups, briefly reviews the history of group work in social work practice and explores the dimensions of group work that relate to types and purposes of groups. This chapter also explores the purpose of groups, the relationship of groups to other areas of social work practice, and engagement and assessment skills. We start with a case we will revisit throughout the chapter:

The residents of the Riverton community (see www.routledgesw.com/interactive-cases/) are becoming increasingly concerned about alcohol consumption and its negative impact on the community's residents and businesses, particularly on the children and youth who live in the neighborhood. As this chapter highlights, there are multiple strategies and formats for intervening in this problem at the group level. Riverton community members have proposed three potential group interventions to address their concerns about alcohol use in their neighborhoods:

- *Riverton Against Youth Drinking (RAYD)—a voluntary group of residents and professionals whose goal is to create activities and options for the community's youth as alternatives to substance use.*
- *Riverton Children's Grief Support Group—a group facilitated by the Community Service Agency for children who have lost a family member to drug- or alcohol-related death in Riverton or elsewhere; and*
- *Riverton Mental Health Center Groups for Persons with Co-occurring Diagnoses—a therapeutic treatment group for persons experiencing substance use and mental health challenges.*

Key Questions for Chapter 8

1. What competencies do I need to engage with and assess clients in social work group practice?
2. How can evidence-based and practice-informed research guide engagement and assessment with groups?
3. What potential ethical issues may arise in social work practice with groups?
4. What knowledge and skills do I need for culturally competent group-level engagement and assessment practice?

GROUPS: THE SOURCE OF COMMUNITY

The social dimension of social work implies that people need and want to relate to others within the context of a "community." Yet the ways to meet this need are not always clear to social work professionals or to the clients they serve. A brief online search using the term "support groups" provides evidence of our need to connect with others. The number of announcements for therapy groups, mutual aid groups, community groups, and educational groups suggests that people seek out groups to form community. Such groups can provide a safe environment that embodies the concepts of anti-oppressive practice (Teater, 2020).

By implication, social work practice with groups enables people to participate in meaningful experiences that the contexts of their personal and/or professional lives do not provide. Family, friends, and co-workers may be empathetic to and supportive of our challenges and form one type of group that provides community, but it might not be enough. We may find a stronger connection with nonfriends or family who share lived experiences, issues, or perspectives more than our natural groups. While the human need for social connection is universal, the way in which people experience and define these connections is often culturally bound. Groups can allow people who have felt isolated to feel a sense of belonging and liberation at being heard, sometimes for the first time in their lives (Doel, 2018, p. 192). Social workers facilitating groups can help to normalize and universalize the members' experience and concerns through helping them to share both mutual support and mutual demands (Knight & Gitterman, 2022, p. 459).

Implications of Global and Cultural Connections for Social Work Group Practice

An increasingly global and cultural anti-oppressive perspective on social work practice underscores the need for sensitivity to global awareness in social work group practice. The NASW *Code of Ethics* (2021a) includes the following statement: "Social workers should promote conditions that encourage respect for cultural and social diversity within the United States and globally. Social workers should promote policies and practices that demonstrate respect for difference, support the expansion of cultural knowledge and resources, advocate for programs and institutions that demonstrate cultural competence, and promote policies that safeguard the rights of and confirm equity and social justice for all people" (Standard 6.04c). This addition to the *Code of Ethics* (NASW, 2021a) called on the social work profession to embrace a more global consciousness, a perspective that has become well integrated into social work practice in general, and with groups, in particular. Due to the increased globalization of our society, social workers engaged in group work need heightened awareness of the expectations and needs of group members of diverse cultures.

As a helping professional, you will benefit from exploring the degree to which your own orientation to achievement, independence, and competition might be incompatible with the cooperation and collaboration that clients from other cultures may value more highly. Regardless of your own cultural heritage, be careful to avoid valuing your orientation to the ideals in your culture or privileging your cultural values as "normal" just because they are familiar. Suppose, for example, that you encounter a child, Jared, in a school-based social skills group. He was referred to the group by his teacher who describes him as lacking an eager, competitive spirit; seldom raising his hand when they ask a question; and always deferring to others. You attribute these behaviors to a personal deficit. You may find him slow, shy, or lethargic, and you may see him as dependent, or even as depressed or developmentally delayed. Rather than correlating with some deficit, however, Jared's behaviors may simply reflect a cultural orientation to cooperate, to prioritize the communications of others, and to maintain modesty in the company of people who are older and have authority.

While all people need and seek social connections, their cultural expectations related to family and community, customs, propriety, loyalty, authority, individualism, and the way in which these factors fit together can temper and shape this phenomenon. Although Western values of competitiveness and individualism have been responsible for many of the accomplishments and much of the power today, these values have the potential to create disconnection, isolation, and detachment. While individual self-determination is an important hallmark of social work practice, a group social worker must also understand that it could be perceived as oppressive to clients whose cultural orientation is more collective in nature. Group social workers should be able to adjust group work processes and expectations to account for the range of cultural orientations about collective versus individualistic orientations of group members.

On behalf of the Association for Specialists in Group Work (ASGW), Guth and colleagues (2018) compiled ten strategies to promote cultural humility and anti-oppressive practice in groups. Highlights of the strategies are provided in Exhibit 8.1.

EXHIBIT 8.1

Strategies to Intentionally Use Group Work to Transform Hate, Facilitate Courageous Conversations, and Enhance Community Building

I	*Acknowledge that culture and power are always present*—starting early in the planning phase of group work, social workers reflect on the impact of their own culture and positions of power on the group.
II	*Develop multicultural and social justice competencies*—by learning the history of these areas and integrating that knowledge into helping the group to engage, share, and benefit from the group experience.
III	*Create brave, affirming, and humanizing spaces*—from the outset of the group, social workers can establish and model language that embraces the importance of having space that is humanizing and establishes boundaries.
IV	*Process group experience with purpose*—differences should be transparently discussed as they relate to understanding the meaning of significant events and experiences in the members' lives, including acts of microaggression that occur within the group.
V	*Cultivate cultural humility skills* including: • strive for an accurate understanding of themselves and their limitations. • maintain an other-oriented stance that includes respect, openness, and humility. • show openness toward the cultural identity and experiences of the group members.

EXHIBIT 8.1

Continued

- demonstrate empathy and explore if group member(s) perceive them to be practicing cultural humility.
- demonstrate skills in welcoming diversity of thought and expression in groups.
- maintain an open mind and heart.
- allow group members to teach them.
- frame the possibilities for group members to gain useful perspectives and experiences from other members.
- acknowledge explicitly that relationships and interactions resemble the differences between privilege and oppression.
- recognize explicit and implicit mistakes and harm to others.
- use mistakes as teachable moments.
- appreciate difficult, enlightening, and inspiring moments shared with group members.
- understand that practicing cultural humility is a lifelong process.

VI *Engage in intentional unity building*—through discussion and activities, group members can come to understand others' perspectives and develop a shared meaning (if not agreement).

VII *Practice mindful and reflexive group facilitation*—group activities can be used to delve into difficult topics, emotions, and beliefs in a safe space (e.g., mindfulness and meditation).

VIII *Lean in and keep going*—using open-ended questions to elicit members' perspectives, pausing for reflection, and identifying discomfort are strategies for helping members grow through challenging discussions.

IX *Consider possibilities of action*—to move discussion/awareness to action, ask the members to reflect on their experiences in the group and transform their awareness into action steps.

X *Assess the impact*—evaluating members' experiences through informal and formal strategies can help members examine if/how the group was helpful in their own and others' growth.

Source: Adapted from Guth et al., 2018

Group Orientation as a Cultural Dimension

Culture has an important impact on the amount and type of connections people seek. While groups whose members represent diverse cultures, identities, and life experiences can enrich the group experience, social workers must ensure all members feel safe to share experiences and ideas, particularly for those with less privilege (Sellon et al., 2022). Groups that integrate culturally related issues, discussion, and activities can empower the members to increase their motivation to engage and thus, benefit from the group experience (Marsiglia et al., 2021).

The social worker facilitating any group must be culturally astute, aware of group participants' cultural backgrounds, and attuned to the cultural influences that affect group dynamics. Brown (2018) offers the following strategies for culturally responsive group facilitation:

- Ask if members have a preferred honorific (Mr., Mrs., etc.) or pronoun (he, she, they).
- Ask if there are nonverbal actions that may be viewed offensively (e.g., direct eye contact, not shaking hands, etc.).
- In working with immigrants and refugee groups, do not assume acculturation or assimilation—start where your group members are in adapting to their new country.
- Do not group members based on assumptions (i.e., all Latinx share the same culture) but do work to establish meaningful similarities among members.
- Clarify the meaning of confidentiality and problem-solving and decision-making processes.
- To prevent microaggressions:
  - recognize that differences can be a form of self-protection and should be challenged only when the group has matured and bonded.
  - learn about members' culture, religion/spirituality, socioeconomic status, geographic origins, race/ethnicity, and so on.
  - redirect/reframe members' intrusive culturally focused questions. (pp. 158–159)

Intercultural communication skills are key to culturally competent group facilitation. Gain insight into how the impact that your own experiences and cultural influences have can shape your leadership and communication style—will your style create a safe, open space or a restrictive, oppressive space (Teater, 2020). Exhibit 8.2 provides additional suggestions for developing culturally responsive group practice skills.

EXHIBIT 8.2

Cultural Competence and Humility in Group Work

While general roles of group work engagement and assessment apply across all populations, social workers practicing with groups can benefit from incorporating culturally responsive strategies, like those listed here, that build on culturally grounded and humble practice with individuals and families. These practice guidelines do not apply to all members of these populations, and they should be used in conjunction with, and not in place of, person-centered skills that focus on individual members of a group. The social worker should attend to individuals' needs within the group and not over-generalize about members of any particular group. One should maintain cultural humility by being open to learning from group members. The guidelines presented here are representative of three groups: immigrants and refugees, Latinx, and Blacks.

EXHIBIT 8.2

Continued

Immigrants and refugees: To practice with an anti-oppressive lens in working with immigrants (those who choose to leave their home country) and refugees (those who flee their home country due to war, political oppression, persecution, and/or violence), you must first understand their journey and view the group experience as like their transition to living in a new country. Both are new cultures, rules, and structures. Strategies for working with immigrants include these:

- Explore the benefits of participation in a group experience, including opportunities for social networking and support, decreased social isolation, building on strengths that enabled them to relocate to a new country, and increased interpersonal learning and knowledge of resources and opportunities.
- Complete a cultural assessment to learn about the individual's immigration experience, reasons for leaving their home country, conditions of the migration, level of acculturations, cultural identity, and ongoing connections to their home country.
- Invite group members to share stories of their experiences to promote mutual respect, acceptance, and cohesion.
- Embrace the many differences among immigrants and refugees and use that diversity as a strengths-based, problem-solving strategy to highlight their resiliencies.
- View the group as a microcosm of the community and society—skills and knowledge learned within the group can be applied in members' lives outside the group.

Source: López et al., 2017

Latinx: While the Latinx community is diverse and comprises the largest group of immigrants to the United States, its members often share a common language and cultural values. With a commitment to collectivism, family as the central unit, family traditions, harmonious interpersonal relationships, and respect, consider the following as you develop a group:

- Attend to issues of language, both written and oral, including ensuring that written materials are available in Spanish, having bilingual staff members, and using culturally appropriate strategies.
- Gain an understanding of the group members' (and/or their family's) experiences with immigration, adaptations, challenges, and resiliencies and connections to their family's country of origin.
- Use story circles/storytelling as a way for members to share their stories and listen to the stories of others, particularly in the areas of migrations, relationship building, collective problem-solving, and social action.
- Connecting with their ethnic heritages, engage group members in forms of artistic expression and share their thoughts and experiences with the group.

> - Involve trusted community leaders in the recruitment and promotion of the group intervention.
> - Consider the role of the members' children to determine if they will be present in the group and/or if child care is needed.
>
> *Source:* López et al., 2017
>
> *Blacks:* Recognizing that the Black community is diverse in the areas of social class, family structure, and environmental challenges, considerations for group practice include the following:
>
> - View the group members through a lens of the impacts they have experienced from an historical, cultural, social, economic, and political perspective environment.
> - Recognize that members can gain a sense of universality, hope, and strength in being part of a group.
> - Advocate focus on empowerment, particularly for Black men and boys.
> - Create a safe environment.
> - Advocate for and with members to address issues of discrimination.
> - Be aware of and attend to group members' racial and ethnic identity development and acknowledge it as possible that race and culture play a role in what brought them to seek help.
>
> *Source:* Greif & Morris-Compton, 2017; Sue et al., 2016

EXHIBIT 8.2

Continued

Historical and Contemporary Contexts for Group Work

Like other legacies in social work, social work group practice has roots in the settlement houses in England in the 19th century. The political and economic contexts of this time disrupted lives and broke down social connections within and among families. Such a sense of isolation led people to come together in groups around common interests and needs. Volunteers, often through charity organizations, brought groups together for socialization, recreation, advocacy, and social action. From the increased integration of group work in settlement houses, recreation, and adult education emerged differing philosophies regarding the scope of group work, primarily between case work and group work scholars as well as within the group work practice movement (Gitterman, 2017). Some viewed group work as a social movement, while others envisioned it as a field of practice within agencies, and yet others conceptualized it as a distinct process and method (Gitterman, 2017). The result was a perspective that defined group work boundaries and functions to include the linked concepts of: (1) growth and development of the individual; (2) development of the group; and (3) development of a democratic society (Gitterman, 2017, p. 115).

Group work developed in the United States in the late 19th and early 20th centuries at a time when many perceived a need for public, religious, or philanthropic organizations. Inspired by the work of religious and philanthropic organizations with individuals and families, the concept of bringing people together in small groups became a popular strategy for helping clients within community-based settings (e.g., YMCA/YWCA, Boy/Girl Scouts, and faith-based community centers). While one approach focused on individuals, another group of helping professionals focused group efforts on social reform with a humanitarian impulse, believing that social change was the critical ingredient in making a positive difference in people's lives. These reformers were more likely to see the group (rather than the individual) as the medium of intervention.

By the end of the 19th century, the Progressive Era promoted continued growth of group work. In response to the influx of immigrants and the needs of teeming urban environments, organizations began offering group work within settlement houses and community organizations. These organizations stressed group methods (e.g., language classes, cooking groups, recreation, the arts, and youth services) and aimed to address the social justice issues of inclusion and acculturation. Often led by settlement house workers and volunteers, the groups sought to increase access to society's assets for newly arrived residents to help them achieve their desired quality of life. Still, group work was not clearly identified with social work during this period.

Throughout the 1930s, many social work professionals tended to assign lesser status to group work than to social casework. This perception was due in part to the fact that recently developed curricula in schools of social work focused on individual casework, reflecting Freud's pervasive influence. With the Freudian focus, existing group work was strongly associated with recreational activities (e.g., sponsoring dances or creating arts and crafts with children) as well as inclusion and acculturation. Such activities were not held in as great esteem as more clinically focused casework. As professional attitudes toward group work changed and approaches became more developed, the profession slowly began to accept group work as equal with casework. Practitioners declared it a part of social work, but as a discrete unit with distinctive methods.

In the 1950s, group work expanded from the community into hospitals and psychiatric facilities, and social workers introduced **therapeutic group work or treatment groups**. For example, to complement individual therapy, patients in a psychiatric facility who were diagnosed with mental illness began to also participate in group therapy. These groups were designed to heal or help people change. This shift took a more professional stance than the former community-based model. Through the process, the distinctions between group work and casework began to blur.

Three classic models for group practice—the **social goals model**, the **reciprocal model**, and the **remedial model**—emerged between the late 1950s and the 1970s. As social workers still use these perspectives in contemporary social work practice with groups, we will discuss them in detail later in this chapter and the next. See Exhibit 8.3 for a brief description of the origins and aims of these three classic models.

EXHIBIT 8.3

Classic Models for Social Group Work, 1950s to 1970s

MODEL TYPE	MAJOR FOCUS	SOCIAL WORKER ROLE	EXAMPLE	ORIGINAL AUTHORS
Social Goals	Democratic values, social conscience, responsibility, and action; uses strengths of members.	Fosters social consciousness and serves as a model for democratic values.	School groups that promote student affiliation and contributions to student governance.	Papell & Rothman, 1962
Reciprocal	Interaction to pursue mutual affiliation goals; mutual aid.	Serves as mediator between each member and the group as a whole; finds common ground.	Adolescent children of incarcerated parents developing coping skills.	Schwartz, 1961
Remedial	Prevention and rehabilitation aimed at behavior change and reinforcing individual behaviors.	Works both inside and outside the group to ameliorate conditions in environments; acts as motivator.	Discharge group in mental health settings to increase patient capacity to navigate community.	Vinter, 1974

By the 1970s, the Council on Social Work Education (CSWE), the accrediting body for social work education in the United States, required all schools of social work to adopt a generalist focus throughout undergraduate programs and for the first half of master's programs. With an aim toward integrating all practice methods across levels, the generalist focus requirement served to de-emphasize the role of group work as a method and, many believe, to lessen its importance. Most school curricula already emphasized individual and family casework. With the CSWE mandate, there was little incentive to develop more group work courses. As a result, many social work students did not complete coursework that focused on groups.

Nevertheless, a strong core of social workers committed to the power of social work with groups founded the Association for the Advancement of Social Work with Groups, Inc. (AASWG, 2013) in 1979 (later renamed the **International Association for Social Work with Groups**, or **IASWG**). The IASWG first issued *Standards for Social Work Practice with Groups*, a guide for effective practice with groups that is widely used in contemporary social work practice, in 1999. The second edition of the *Standards*, issued in 2006 and updated in 2015, provides practitioners with guidelines and practice perspectives for gaining the knowledge, tasks, and skills needed in group work. These guidelines include core values and knowledge, phases of the group process (i.e., pregroup planning, beginning, middle, and ending), and ethical considerations. The Standards are derived from practice wisdom, theories of group work practice, and empirical evidence (IASWG, 2015, p. 1).

Social work practice today offers practitioners the opportunity to work with groups to help individuals meet their needs for genuine connection and social action. A group-focused orientation is one of the characteristics that distinguish social work group practice from psychology or mental health counseling groups. In group work, the social worker's efforts focus on the development of the group as a whole. Individual well-being is promoted through interactions and group structures. While social work and psychologist-led groups may work with the same population (e.g., patients receiving psychiatric treatment in an acute care hospital setting), social workers will use strengths-based, systemic approaches with a focus on support for the patients as they interact with their environments.

DIMENSIONS OF SOCIAL WORK PRACTICE WITH GROUPS

For this discussion of the dimensions of type, form, and function and the logistics of social work group practice, we define a social work group intervention as a small, face-to-face, virtual (videoconferencing, chat, text, or email), or telephonic gathering of people who come together for a particular purpose, which can be focused on the individual, organization, or community. The major feature of a group experience is the interdependence among person, group, and social environment for such purposes as individual or community growth and social advocacy/policy change.

Types, Forms, and Functions of Groups

At the most basic level, social work groups are either natural groups or formed groups. **Natural groups** occur in the context of socialization and are not organized from the outside. These may be based on spontaneous friendships, common interests, or common social location, such as living in a college dorm. Families are the original natural group. Although natural groups usually do not have formal sponsorship or agency affiliation, social workers may have occasion to work with them (e.g., members of a neighborhood). Social workers and their agencies can also provide support to these naturally formed groups in a variety of ways (e.g., offer meeting space, access to office equipment, or staff consultation).

Social workers are more likely to engage with or facilitate **formed groups**, which are organized by an institution or organization, such as a school or hospital, an agency, or a community center. Groups can be offered in face-to-face format or, increasingly, via technology-mediated strategies, primarily using videoconferences, text-based, and online discussion forums. Exhibit 8.4 provides information and guidelines for the use of technology in group work.

EXHIBIT 8.4

Technology-Mediated Group Practice

Prior to the COVID-19 pandemic, social workers were using technology to deliver a range of services, including facilitating groups as technology-mediated practice enables those who could not attend in-person sessions. The restrictions and lockdowns of the pandemic sparked a surge in the use of technology to deliver health and social services through videoconferencing, telephone, text, email, and chat rooms. While technology has become a common strategy for service delivery, social workers must be cognizant of the ethical and practice implications. The NASW *Code of Ethics* (2021a) now includes guidance for using technology in practice. Highlights of the standards for practice include:

1.03 Informed Consent

(1) Social workers should discuss with clients the social workers' policies concerning the use of technology in the provision of professional services.
(2) Social workers who use technology to provide social work services should obtain informed consent from the individuals using these services during the initial screening or interview and prior to initiating services. Social workers should assess clients' capacity to provide informed consent and, when using technology to communicate, verify the identity and location of clients.
(3) Social workers who use technology to provide social work services should assess the clients' suitability and capacity for electronic and remote services. Social workers should consider the clients' intellectual, emotional, and physical ability to use technology to receive services and the clients' ability to understand the potential benefits, risks, and limitations of such services. If clients do not wish to use services provided through technology, social workers should help them identify alternate methods of service.

EXHIBIT 8.4

Continued

1.04 Competence

(1) Social workers who use technology in the provision of social work services should ensure that they have the necessary knowledge and skills to provide such services in a competent manner. This includes an understanding of the special communication challenges when using technology and the ability to implement strategies to address these challenges.

(2) Social workers who use technology in providing social work services should comply with the laws governing technology and social work practice in the jurisdiction in which they are regulated and located and, as applicable, in the jurisdiction in which the client is located.

1.05 Cultural Competence

(1) Social workers who provide electronic social work services should be aware of cultural and socioeconomic differences among clients' use of and access to electronic technology and seek to prevent such potential barriers. Social workers should assess cultural, environmental, economic, mental or physical ability, linguistic, and other issues that may affect the delivery or use of these services.

1.06 Conflicts of Interest

(1) Social workers should avoid communication with clients using technology (such as social networking sites, online chat, email, text messages, telephone, and video) for personal or non-work-related purposes.

(2) Social workers should be aware that posting personal information on professional Web sites or other media might cause boundary confusion, inappropriate dual relationships, or harm to clients.

(3) Social workers should be aware that personal affiliations may increase the likelihood that clients may discover the social worker's presence on Web sites, social media, and other forms of technology. Social workers should be aware that involvement in electronic communication with groups based on race, ethnicity, language, sexual orientation, gender identity or expression, mental or physical ability, religion, immigration status, and other personal affiliations may affect their ability to work effectively with particular clients.

1.07 Privacy and Confidentiality

(1) Social workers should develop and inform clients about their policies, consistent with prevailing social work ethical standards, on the use of electronic technology, including Internet-based search engines, to gather information about clients.

1.08 Access to Records

(1) Social workers should develop and inform clients about their policies, consistent with prevailing social work ethical standards, on the use of technology to provide clients with access to their records.

> **EXHIBIT 8.4**
>
> *Continued*

(2) When providing clients with access to their records, social workers should take steps to protect the confidentiality of other individuals identified or discussed in such records.

1.09 Sexual Relationships

(1) Social workers should under no circumstances engage in sexual activities, inappropriate sexual communications through the use of technology or in person, or sexual contact with current clients, whether such contact is consensual or forced.

2.10 Unethical Conduct of Colleagues

(1) Social workers should take adequate measures to discourage, prevent, expose, and correct the unethical conduct of colleagues, including unethical conduct using technology.

5.02 Evaluation and Research

(1) When using electronic technology to facilitate evaluation or research, social workers should ensure that participants provide informed consent for the use of such technology. Social workers should assess whether participants are able to use the technology and, when appropriate, offer reasonable alternatives to participate in the evaluation or research.

There are three primary models of formed groups that accomplish different functions: *task groups, social action or goals groups,* and *client groups.*

Task Groups **Task groups** are designed to accomplish a specific purpose and include task forces, committees and commissions, legislative bodies, staff meetings, interprofessional teams, and case conferences and staffing. Like individual change groups, task groups are framed within the model of engagement and include assessment, intervention, termination, and evaluation. Task groups differ from individual change groups in that they typically have a specific agenda that requires decisions/action, group membership is based on the needs/purpose of the groups, and formal processes guide the work of the group (Ortega & Garvin, 2019).

The purpose of a task group or "working group" is to address the needs in one or more of the following areas (Zastrow & Hessenauer, 2019):

(1) Clients—professionals may come together to discuss/review cases and/or services.
(2) Organizations—committees including staff, service users, community professionals, and other service committees, task forces, and advisory groups meet to review, evaluate, and conduct planning regarding service delivery.
(3) Communities—coalitions of professionals and community members collaborate in areas of oversight, advocacy, and planning.

Task groups embody concepts of mutual aid by bringing together people who become connected through a common goal (Knight, 2017b). While the goal to achieve individual and group goals typically brings members to a task-oriented group, the major focus is on problem-solving and decision-making. The group specifically engages in a process in which the members: (1) identify and define the problem; (2) assess the size and cause of the issues; (3) develop alternative strategies to address the problem; (4) assess the strengths and barriers related to the alternatives; (5) select and implement the most viable strategies; and (6) evaluate the outcomes (Zastrow & Hessenauer, 2019, p. 183). The social worker can function as a convener, member, chair/leader, facilitator, or a combination of these roles. The roles of the social worker in a leadership role can include facilitation, mediation, and empowerment (Toseland & Rivas, 2017).

A task group may be formed for the purpose of assessing and developing a plan for improving the safety of the Alvadora neighborhood in Riverton. We explore task groups in more detail in Chapters 9 and 10.

Social Action or Goals Groups **Social action or goals groups** are task groups that advocate for change in a power structure, resource allocation, and/or social injustice-related issue for groups who are marginalized or oppressed (Zastrow & Hessenauer, 2019). A social action group is typically a small group of community members who serve as organizing, issue, or lobbying committees or negotiating teams (Staples, 2017). The social worker can engage in a variety of roles in working with a social action group, including advocate, agitator, activist, broker, and negotiator (Zastrow & Hessenauer, 2019).

The strengths of a social action approach center on the collective effort of a group. Social action is a cornerstone of the social work profession as it emphasizes social justice, and is consistent with social work values and ethics related to promoting empowerment through working with groups on their goals (Knight & Gitterman, 2018). As with task groups overall, the social worker can function in a variety of roles.

> *For example, as described at the beginning of this chapter, a group of residents of the Riverton community came together with professionals who work in the community to address their concerns about alcohol abuse among the youth in their neighborhoods by forming a social action group, Riverton Against Youth Drinking (RAYD). With in-kind support of the Riverton Association of Neighborhoods, RAYD has established the goal of developing organized activities and programs to deter the youth from engaging in drinking behaviors and worse and advocating for the city government to provide financial and law enforcement support. To reach their goals, the group plans to apply for grants, hold fundraising events in the community, and partner with family service organizations.*

Client Groups **Client groups** are geared toward personal change and may be aimed at support, education, growth, therapy, socialization, empowerment, and remediation. With a focus on mutual aid, client groups provide the opportunity for members to have an experience working with others which promotes empowerment and enhances feelings of self-efficacy (Knight & Gitterman, 2022, p. 455). The social worker's role may involve sole or co-leadership but has a dual focus on both the individual members as well as the entire group (Knight & Gitterman, 2022). Client groups can be formed for two purposes: reciprocal groups and remedial groups.

Reciprocal groups, also referred to as *support, self-help, mutual aid or sharing,* and *stabilization groups,* form to enable members who share a common experience to provide mutual aid to one another. With an emphasis on self-help and not specifically on therapeutic intervention, reciprocal groups can range from informal to highly structured to psychoeducational (blending mutual support and educational focus). Reciprocal groups provide members who "share a common characteristic, trait, or experience, to share their experiences, receive mutual aid, and foster individual, but more importantly, collective change" (Teater, 2020, p. 216). Finding others who share similar life experiences can be validating and affirming for group members and can provide them with opportunities to share insights and coping strategies. As well as mutual sharing and supporting, members can form a group identity, assume responsibility for the group for individual and collective growth and change and, lastly, have a safe space in which to test new behaviors and skills (Teater, 2020).

This model for group work intervention has wide applicability, particularly among adults who face a new or unanticipated struggle and can benefit from education and group support. Psychoeducational groups focus on educating group members regarding a psychological or health condition, life experience, or transition. One approach has been especially helpful to parents of young adult children experiencing mental illness. These individuals frequently develop new symptoms in their early 20s, and their parents may not have been touched by mental illness before. Local community mental health agencies often offer reciprocal group sessions to these families to help them learn more about mental illnesses, what to expect in terms of their children's behavior and symptoms, how they can best provide support, and how they can cope with their own grief. The National Alliance for the Mentally Ill (NAMI) first established these groups, and they have been particularly effective in helping persons with mental illness and their families enhance functioning and coping strategies. Psychoeducational groups usually incorporate information, but they also rely on the supportive and accepting attitudes of worker/facilitators and other group members. Groups can be structured, with a curriculum and lessons in sequence, or they can be freer in form. In some locations, parents who originally attended these groups have become group facilitators themselves, generally with training and technical support from the local agency.

Social work involvement in reciprocal groups can range from initiator to facilitator to "silent" support person. The social worker role will be related primarily to the origins of the group (i.e., a larger role if agency or social worker-initiated and a lesser role if member-initiated). The social worker can serve the groups in different ways, including (1) group leader/facilitator for the duration of the group; (2) group leader/facilitator for the initial formation of the group with a transition of leadership being passed on to the group at an agreed upon point; or (3) providing support for the group (e.g., arranging location, providing resources, etc.) (Teater, 2020). In the case of psychoeducationally focused groups, the social worker may play a more formal role based on possession of specific knowledge or skill expertise.

A grief support group for children living in the Riverton community who have lost a family member to alcohol or drug use is one example of a psychoeducational group. As described at the beginning of this chapter, the Riverton Children's Grief Support Group is offered by the Community Service Agency and facilitated by a social worker. The group relies primarily on community professionals from the school, the Community Service Agency, and Alvadora Community Mental Health for referrals.

Groups for persons who are in the early stages of dementia are one example of contemporary reciprocal or support groups. Social workers frequently work with persons who have dementia. The stigma and isolation some of those living with dementia experience can be devastating. This makes support a critical component of work with these individuals, and the support group can offer a chance to share feelings, combat loneliness, gain information, exchange resources, and normalize the experience. Similar issues arise for families and other loved ones of someone with dementia, and social workers may facilitate groups for them as well. To be effective facilitators of these groups, social workers need to understand the effects, symptoms, and issues that people with or affected by dementia experience.

The focus of **remedial groups** (also referred to as treatment, clinical, or therapy groups) is to facilitate change in persons experiencing emotional, behavioral, and/or interpersonal challenges (Zastrow & Hessenauer, 2019). While acknowledging the expertise people bring about their own struggles and recovery process, the social worker's role in these groups is typically that of facilitator or leader because they bring the clinical knowledge and skills needed to direct the group.

Returning to the Riverton community as an example, a remedial group may be formed at a mental health center or hospital to provide therapy for persons struggling with co-occurring illnesses (i.e., substance use/addiction and mental illness). The Riverton Mental Health Center Groups for Persons with Co-Occurring Diagnoses is co-facilitated by two clinical social workers with training in addictions and mental health treatment.

Roles and Phases of Group Interventions

Groups may also be distinguished by the role the social worker plays. In treatment or therapy groups, the social worker may use methods consistent with counseling and interpretation, while educational groups may focus on teaching and processing. Task groups are likely to direct the social worker's focus on facilitation and outcomes management, as they assist the group in taking action to address an issue. Exhibits 8.5–8.7 depict phases of group interventions, including social worker and member roles. Using the descriptions of the four groups in the Riverton case, these exhibits give examples of the beginning phases of group processes:

- Pregroup planning includes assessing the need for a group by clients and/or community being served; identifying evidence-based approaches to the group intervention; determining criteria for participation, promotion, and recruitment; developing assessment strategies and roles for agency and group facilitator; and finalizing group logistics (e.g., time, location, supplies, and agenda). Leadership (i.e., a single leader or co-leaders) is determined by the group purpose and workload and group membership—clinical groups and groups with children often benefit from co-leadership to manage group sessions.

- Engagement begins when you meet with and invite members to participate and continues with introductions and rapport-building during the first session.

- Assessment also begins when you interact during the engagement process. Identifying group member motivations to join the group, analyzing data to set the agenda and priorities for the group, and revisiting assessment throughout the intervention to revise as needed are components of the ongoing assessment process.

EXHIBIT 8.5

Riverton Against Youth Drinking ("RAYD"): An Example of a Social Goals Group

PHASE I: BEGINNING

Background: Concerned about the use of alcohol among their adolescent children, a group of parents, residents, and professionals in the Riverton community approaches a local community service agency to ask for help addressing this problem. Chapter 9 will highlight later phases of the group's work.

Note: The stages of group practice are not linear and may, in fact, overlap and appear to circle back to the beginning. The following depicts a possible approach to responding to the identified need.

PREGROUP PLANNING AND ENGAGEMENT	ASSESSMENT
Meet with parent groups to gather information	Determine individual and group members' "agendas"
Identify current and potential stakeholders who are/may be invested in the issue	Conduct community assessment, including needs, assets, and resources (see Chapter 10 for further information on community assessment)
Identify interests of group members	
Research evidence on approaches for facilitating social goals groups on this topic	Gather and analyze data from assessment; identify and prioritize options for intervention
Determine general focus/goal of launching an intervention	Re-determine/confirm focus of intervention
Identify roles for agency and social worker	Finalize plan for intervention, including objectives, tasks, activities, persons/groups responsible, time frame, and plans for evaluation and sustainability
Arrange first meeting and logistics, including time, location, refreshments, etc.	Re-clarify agency and social worker roles and responsibilities
Develop agenda for first meeting, building in ample time for introductions and rapport-building to promote trust and solidarity	Revisit needs
	Make plans for continued assessment

EXHIBIT 8.6

Riverton Grief Support Group: An Example of a Reciprocal Children's Group

PHASE I: BEGINNING

Background: A social worker in a local community service agency has become aware of several children in Riverton who have lost a parent to alcohol and substance-related deaths. The social worker takes steps toward offering a psychoeducational support group in the community. Chapter 9 will highlight later phases of the group's work.

Note: While the stages of group interventions are not linear and may, in fact, overlap, the following depicts a possible approach to responding to the identified need.

PREGROUP PLANNING AND ENGAGEMENT

- Gather information to support the need for and appropriateness of this group intervention/approach for the population
- Analyze data and confirm plans to move forward with forming a group
- Research evidence supporting approaches to facilitating reciprocal groups with children

Determine group components:

- Composition of group (number, age range, and gender)
- Recruitment strategies
- Format (open or closed)
- Time frame (time-limited or ongoing)
- Determine and implement appropriate recruitment strategies
- Conduct screening interviews with potential members
- Invite group members (for minors, written permission from legal guardians is required)
- Determine roles of agency, social work facilitator, children, and legal guardians

ENGAGEMENT AND ASSESSMENT

Pregroup
Prior to first meeting, meet individually with parents/guardians and separately with children to assess interest in and appropriateness (i.e., "fit") for a psychoeducational support group

First Session
- Lead introductions
- Orient members to the group; review purpose, goals, rules, norms, format, time frame, intervention plan, termination, evaluation, and confidentiality
- Assess individual member goals, functions, and interactions with other members
- Assess group cohesiveness
- Continue to assess individual and group needs (for support and education), interests, strengths, and "agendas"
- Monitor and assess social worker role
- Administer pregroup measurements to be used in the evaluation process

EXHIBIT 8.7

Riverton Mental Health Center Group for Persons With Co-Occurring Diagnoses: An Example of a Remedial Group

PHASE I: BEGINNING

Background: A new social worker at the Riverton Mental Health Center has recently assumed co-leadership with another social worker for a clinical intervention group for persons with co-occurring diagnoses (i.e., substance use disorder and mental illness) who receive outpatient services at the agency. The group is diverse; members represent a mix of gender identity, racial/ethnic group, and age. Some are mandated and some are voluntary participants. Membership turnover depends on members' "graduation" from the treatment program; therefore, group membership is fluid. Two new members have been referred to the group. This will be the first time new members have been referred since the social worker took over co-leadership of the group. Chapter 9 will highlight later phases of the group's work.

Note: While the stages of group interventions are not linear and may, in fact, overlap, the following depicts a possible approach to responding to the identified need.

PREGROUP PLANNING AND ENGAGEMENT	ENGAGEMENT AND ASSESSMENT
• Obtain information on potential new members from referral sources and agency records, as appropriate—this will be an ongoing process • Research evidence on incorporating new members into an existing group • Determine structure for admission, including criteria and process • Meet with potential new members to screen for potential "fit" with group purpose, goals, and other members • Mandated members should be assessed to determine if they will benefit from the group • Invite new members to first session, introduce self, and provide orientation (e.g., composition, goals, expectations, norms, and rules)	*First Session* • Facilitate introduction of new members to group and review group expectations, norms, and rules • Assess individual member goals, interests, and "fit" with group • Assess member reactions to new group members • Assess initial group cohesion • Monitor/assess progress of other members

During the group planning process, you must determine whether a group experience will meet the needs you have identified. A group approach is more suited to some situations than it is to others. Moreover, group modalities may be prescribed due to agency policies or practices and/or reimbursement requirements.

In addition to bringing together people who have a common life experience, concern, or need, a group effort can promote creativity and problem-solving, influence individual thoughts and behaviors, and provide a strategy for delivery of services to a large group of clients with similar issues that may not have materialized without a group effort (Garvin & Galinsky, 2020). While group interventions have a multiplying factor of serving more individuals at one time, their value can far exceed efficiency. Individuals can benefit from interacting with others in similar life situations, using new knowledge and skills in a safe environment, or mobilizing with others to achieve a larger goal they could not have achieved alone. While these can all be valid reasons for launching a group intervention, consider whether the potential gains for the group, both as individuals and as a collective, are optimally efficacious or whether another type of intervention would be better. For example, having multiple male and female clients of all ages who share a life experience (e.g., childhood sexual assault) does not ensure that developing a group intervention is the most appropriate intervention as practice wisdom has shown that engaging different ages and genders and gender identities around an issue as sensitive and personal as childhood sexual assault is not the most effective approach. Individual interventions or same-gender/same-age groups may be more helpful to clients.

Recognizing that the individual's own work is completed within the context of the group's fluid, interactive, and sometimes conflictual dynamic, ask yourself if your desire to establish a group meets the client's needs or your needs to efficiently serve a larger group of clients. Would group work primarily meet your agency's revenue goals, or would it mount an advocacy effort, or some combination of the two? Quick Guide 22 provides a set of questions to consider when determining the merits of forming a group.

Group Work Logistics

Social work groups may form and meet online or in person in community agencies, schools, community mental health centers, medical practices, public assistance offices, job training centers, residential care settings, church or faith organizations, or any other setting in which participants come together. The virtual location will likely utilize the agency technology resources and should be determined to be accessible and secure to potential members. The physical location may be a setting that group members already use (such as a school), or it may be a local community facility that makes itself available to group activities (a community hospital that houses a grief and loss group, for example). Many residential settings that host social work groups, like criminal justice centers or mental health facilities, restrict their use to residents and their significant others.

Social work groups may differ in other ways, such as the number of group meetings or the way in which they are organized. A group may meet for a fixed number of sessions, or it may be ongoing, with changing membership over time. Some groups are structured as **closed groups** in which group membership and the number of sessions is fixed. Others are **open groups**, which allow new members to join at any time (or occasionally only at fixed times, such as after the third and sixth sessions).

> ### QUICK GUIDE 22   The Pros and Cons of Creating a Group: Questions to Consider
>
> As you weigh options for intervening with client, organization, and community systems, first determine whether a group intervention is the most effective approach. To clarify your goals, consider the following:
>
> - What are my reasons for choosing a group intervention over an individual or family intervention? Specifically, what needs have I identified within my clients, my agency, or the community?
> - What type of group intervention am I considering—social goals, task, reciprocal, or remedial? What are my reasons for selecting this format? Should the group be offered face-to-face or with the use of technology?
> - What would the goal(s) of the group be? For the group members? For me? For the agency or community?
> - Should it be an open or closed group (i.e., a continuous group of members or open to members entering and leaving as needed)?
> - Will the needs of members best be met in a time-limited or open-ended group?
> - Who and what will determine the eligibility criteria for group membership?
> - Do I have the requisite competence to facilitate a group intervention in this modality and with the population and issue being addressed?
> - Should I be the sole facilitator, or would having a co-facilitator better serve the group? Does the agency or do I determine leadership?
> - Do I have the support of my supervisor and agency administration? If not, am I aware of the process for gaining approval?
> - What resources do I need to offer the group? Possibilities include meeting space and/or technology, supplies, and funds for recruitment, refreshments, transportation, and child or adult care.
> - What options exist for gaining the resources needed for the group?
> - Will there be a charge for participation?
> - What is the optimal group size? Will group membership be limited to that number?
> - Is there an adequate pool of potential group members within those my agency serves or the larger community?
> - If I am uncertain about the pool of candidates for the group, how would I recruit members? What marketing strategies would be appropriate?
> - What are the appropriate meeting dates, times, frequency, and longevity for the group?
> - When will group meetings begin?
> - How much time do I need to prepare to lead the group?
> - Should I obtain member (or legal guardian) informed consent for participation?
> - How will group activities be recorded and evaluated?

    Group interventions are often intentionally time-limited because of the nature of the work (e.g., mandated groups or psychoeducationally focused groups), financial or agency resources, or characteristics of the group members (e.g., children or adolescents). In developing plans for a group intervention, consider which of these formats will best meet the needs of the target population. Open groups may offer flexibility for the facilitator and group members and economic advantages for the organization due to ongoing recruitment bringing in new members, but this format may lack the cohesiveness and continuity of a closed group format.

Also consider the similarities and differences in the skill sets required to facilitate each type of group. For example, to effectively lead an open group in which the members can change with each session, the social worker will need to be flexible, review norms and highlights at the beginning of each session and include rapport-building into sessions with new members (Sakamoto & Couto, 2017).

Whether group participation is voluntary or mandated is another important distinction. In mandated situations, the social worker may not realize they have lower expectations of member investment, and the influence of the mandating institution (e.g., court) is likely to be greater than it is in voluntary groups. Many involuntary treatment scenarios employ groups, and we should not assume that being mandated means that members will be hostile or less invested. Traditional models use involuntary groups for work with clients who experience intimate partner violence, parenting issues, and substance use disorders/addictions. Group work focuses particularly on interrelatedness and extension to the "outside" world, thus creating opportunities to engage involuntary clients in a process from which they can benefit long after completing treatment.

During the engagement, assessment, and planning phases of group work with members who are mandated to participate, the social worker should be thoughtful about working with those who do not choose to participate in the group. Strategies to consider can include (Zastrow & Hessenauer, 2019):

- Interacting with and modeling respect can serve to de-escalate resistance to participation.

- Be open to and even invite members to voice their feelings about being required to participate and validate their right to feel as they do. Hearing individuals' concerns can provide insight into potential goals and topics for discussion.

- While it can be helpful to highlight truth and validity in expressions of displeasure about forced participation, the social worker must introduce limits to descriptions that become inappropriate and abusive. If limit-setting is not effective, the social worker can talk with the individual outside of the group about their behavior and continued participation in the group. (pp. 367–368)

Consider your approach if you are facilitating a group for adolescents who have been convicted of nonviolent criminal offenses in which the members are mandated by the court system to participate and are unhappy to be there. Rather than attempting to create an illusion of willingness or complacency about their situations, you may opt to address the involuntary aspect at the outset of the group with a statement such as:

I know that you are each required to participate in this group as a condition of your legal situation and that you may prefer not to be here. I also know that you have a choice in how you want to handle your time in this group, and I want to let you know that I will respect your right to participate at the level you feel comfortable. I am committed to facilitating our time together in a way that we can learn from one another and grow together. It is my hope that the group will be valuable for you, not just satisfy the requirements set out by the court system.

THEORETICAL APPROACHES TO ENGAGEMENT AND ASSESSMENT WITH GROUPS

Developing competencies for engaging, assessing, and planning in group practice begins with identifying a theoretical stance from which you will work. Just as in social work practice with individuals, families, and communities, social workers are ethically obligated to utilize a theoretically evidence-based intervention that incorporates empirically supported group interventions and process, evidence-supported guidelines, and practice evaluation (Macgowan & Hanbidge, 2022b). Regardless of the theoretical perspective you select, you should maintain a commitment to the strengths-based perspective. The following discussion is grounded in the premise that all members in a social work group have strengths on which the goals and objectives can be built. As Kurland (2007), "the very act of forming a group is a statement of our belief that every member of the group has something to offer the others, something to give to others, not just to get from them" (p. 12).

Systemic Perspective

Since all groups are created and function as a system, most theoretical frameworks for group practice derive from the systemic perspective (Garvin & Galinsky, 2020). You can apply your knowledge of systems theory as it relates to work with individuals and families to your work with groups. You may begin by viewing groups as fluid, dynamic interactions between a set of individuals who become interdependent (e.g., a change in group composition [member joins or exits] changes group dynamics and interpersonal interactions). A systemic approach views the group as an entity with a past, present, and future and an "evolution greater than and different from those of current members" (Tropman, 2017, p. 29). Tropman (2017) offers the "Seven C's" as a conceptualization for social workers to understand the influence, impact, structure, and culture of the group on the group process:

- *Character:* member demographics (e.g., race, ethnicity, age, etc.), culture, focus, and temperament. Social workers' influence on group composition can influence the group process.
- *Collaborations:* connections established among and outside the group. Social workers need to be aware of and work with the collaborations to support group functioning.

- *Crucibles:* transition or change in the group (e.g., membership, goals) and signature group experience that is significant for the group. Social workers must address these situations when they occur to gauge the impact on the group.
- *Competencies:* knowledge and skills to address issues. Social workers can assess competencies and provide education to support the learning.
- *Conditions:* group structure (organization) and culture (norms and values). Social workers and group members should contribute to the development of both areas.
- *Change:* group development over time and goals. Social workers can assess and monitor the group's growth and progress toward goals and share those observations with the group.
- *Context:* group as it relates to other groups, organizations, communities, and society. Social workers must be aware of the interactions and influences and share with the group.

Group work can be highly effective when approached from a strengths-based perspective. Building on the conceptualization that systemic and strengths-based frameworks guide social work group practice, the following discussion looks at narrative and solution-focused perspectives within group work. Visualize a group intervention like the building of a house—strengths-based and systems frameworks serve as the foundation, with the theoretical approaches and modalities you employ representing the multiple rooms built on top of the foundation.

Narrative Approach in Group Engagement and Assessment

Incorporating a narrative approach with groups begins with viewing the clients as collaborators with one another and the social worker. With a group, there are more potential collaborations than in individual work, which both enriches and complicates the interactions. Having a group of individuals who share common experiences can further aid in the process of engaging the individual group member to elicit their story, then challenging the client's perspective and partnering to reconstruct a new story/reality. Members can benefit not only from sharing and reconstructing their own narrative, but also from listening to other group members and contributing as they reconstruct their own stories. Metcalf (2017) offers assumptions for using a solutions-focused narrative approach with groups, including:

1 People are competent and are experts on their own lives.
2 Change is inevitable—watch for it in the session and outside.
3 Exceptions to problems always exist.
4 Specific goals are always better attainable. (p. 199)

Pointing out that solution-focused narrative groups emphasize processing current issues affecting the members, Metcalf (2017) suggests facilitators begin by asking each person to share their best hopes and move into discussions of the effects of problems, group goals, and exceptions. Within the context of assessment in group practice, group members can work with one another and with the social worker to identify members' strengths. The assessment process can also help members externalize or separate themselves from their problems in planning for change.

Solution-Focused Approach in Group Engagement and Assessment

Recall from earlier discussions that a solution-focused approach emphasizes brief, targeted interventions. With its grounding in a strengths-based perspective and its emphasis on solutions, this approach can quickly focus group members on the issues that brought them to the group, aid them in collaborating on the development of a plan for change, and activate the planned change—all with the input and support of other group members and the social work facilitator. Building on members' strengths, a solution-focused approach to group work promotes members to (Molina, 2022):

- ask one another questions and listen to the responses.
- display empathy.
- focus on present and future but not the past.
- move away from problem-saturated stories to those focused on solutions.

In engaging potential group members, the social worker can emphasize the time-limited, targeted, future-oriented nature of a solution-focused group. This orientation sets the stage that the work together will be purposeful, will occur within a specified time (ideally 6–12 meetings), and will emphasize concrete, achievable outcomes. Such an approach is likely to appeal to potential group members who may be reticent about joining a group either due to ambivalence about change or who have not joined the group voluntarily. Solution-focused strategies are helpful in school settings and mental health and health care clinical settings (Kim et al., 2019). The use of the "miracle question" enables both individuals and the group as a whole to establish small and manageable goals (de Shazer et al., 2021).

Because of the pragmatic, outcome-oriented nature of the solution-focused approach, the assessment phase of solution-focused group work can promote a range of helpful techniques. For example, creating individualized therapeutic goals and using scaling questions to gauge members' concerns enable group members to monitor their progress. Using a standard series of solution-focused questions to introduce assessment highlights previous successes, strengths, and resources while focusing the individual (and the group) on viable solutions.

> *For example, as a social worker working with the group of Riverton residents experiencing co-occurring disorders involving substance use disorder and mental illness, you could begin the assessment phase by asking individual members the "miracle" question: "How would your life be if you were no longer using opioids and other drugs?" You could then ask group members to recall a time when they successfully coped with a challenge or crisis without the use of drugs or alcohol. Recognizing that addiction is not easy to treat, you can guide group members to consider strategies for coping with stressors, including mental illness. The benefit of such a pragmatic, time-limited nature of the group process is that members can share ideas and strategies, identify strengths in themselves and others, and support and nurture one another.*

Social workers can effectively use a solution-focused approach alone or integrate solution-focused approaches with other intervention approaches. For example, incorporating strategies from other empowerment-focused approaches (e.g., strengths- and narrative-based) can serve to enhance the impact of the intervention with those who prefer solutions over problems (Corcoran, 2022a). These approaches all emphasize engagement, assessments, and planning focused on the resources of each person with the goal to empower and change. Specifically, the interactional nature of the group experience can encourage group members to articulate their stories as well as enable them to support one another as they explore and strategize potential solutions.

Regardless of the orientation(s) you choose, your client in group work is, in fact, the group itself, and the group experience can be powerful both for you and for group members. While the group is comprised of individuals and the group experience is aimed at impacting them individually, the focus of the intervention is on the group's process of members interacting with one another.

CONTEMPORARY TRENDS AND SKILLS FOR THE BEGINNING PHASES OF GROUP WORK: ENGAGEMENT AND ASSESSMENT

As with practice with individuals and families, the areas of group practice include: (1) engagement including preplanning and planning for the group experience; (2) assessment and planning for the group process planning; (3) intervention, focused primarily on the middle phase of group work; and (4) termination, evaluation, and follow-up encompassing the ending phase. Group practice skills build on the skills and knowledge needed in work with individuals and families, including rapport-building and developing trust, active listening, clarifying roles and expectations, and introducing termination. Here we will discuss new skills for pregroup formation planning (i.e., screening, engaging and assessment, group logistics, and process) (Macgowan & Hanbidge, 2022b).

Pregroup Planning

A successful social work group intervention requires careful planning prior to the first meeting. As a practitioner planning a group intervention, you should think about your planning efforts within the context of the agency, your supervisor's input or direction, and the larger social environment. These areas are interrelated and actions/decisions in one area may influence other areas. The considerations here do not presuppose certain answers. They are simply areas to keep in mind to avoid challenges later. Exhibit 8.8 presents a preplanning model and Exhibit 8.9 presents an example that applies this process to a social worker's intervention with a group.

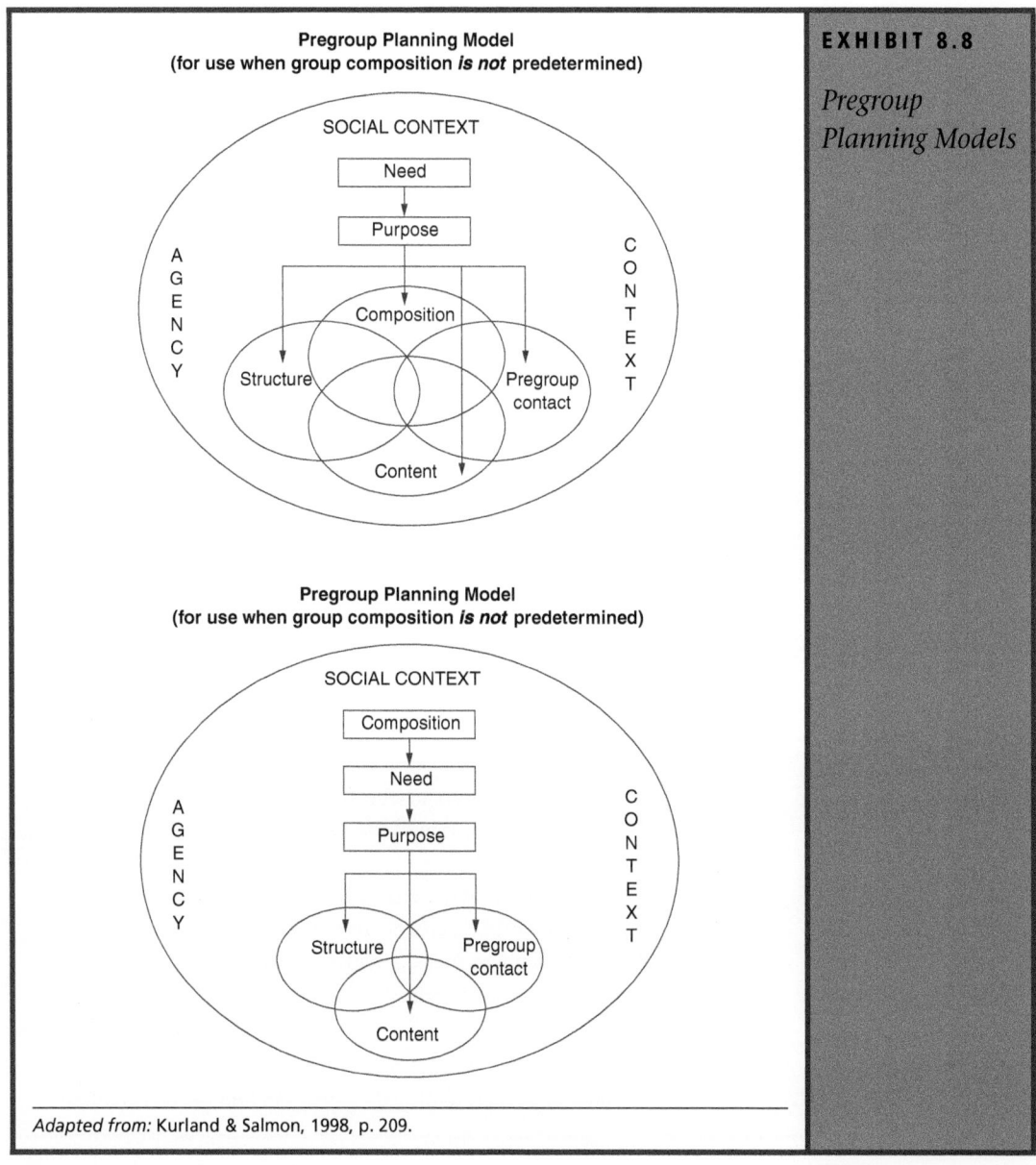

EXHIBIT 8.8

Pregroup Planning Models

Adapted from: Kurland & Salmon, 1998, p. 209.

EXHIBIT 8.9

Preplanning for a Group Intervention: Parents of Teens Support Group

Your agency has experienced an increase in the number of parents of teens seeking services out of concern for their relationships with their adolescent children. Together with your supervisor and colleagues you decide to form a support group for this population. You have been asked to lead this effort. Building on Kurland and Salmon's (1998) classic list of preplanning tasks, consider the following:

PREPLANNING ISSUE/TASK	CONSIDERATION FOR PARENTS OF TEENS SUPPORT GROUP
Client need	62 percent increase in the past six months of parents of teens seeking services out of concern for their relationships with their teenage children.
Purpose	After discussion at a staff meeting, family service staff agree that parents can benefit from a reciprocal, psychoeducationally focused group intervention.
Composition, eligibility, and appropriateness	*Composition:* The group will target parents of adolescents aged 12 to 19 and will not have a minimum or maximum number of participants. Recruitment will focus on a diverse group of parents who can learn from one another's experiences. *Eligibility:* Based on the changing needs of the target population, the group will be open to any interested parents of teens. Participants need not currently receive services from the agency. *Appropriateness:* Due to the psychoeducational/support orientation of the group, any parents who feel they need support will be appropriate for the group. This type of group is consistent with other services your agency offers.
Structure	The group will meet monthly for 90 minutes one evening a week in the agency's multipurpose room. You will serve as primary facilitator while the social work student completing practicum with you will serve as co-facilitator. The agency will provide refreshments and will offer child care. It will invite the teens to participate in a group experience facilitated by a co-worker. Service-learning students from a nearby university will oversee the child care area.
Content	As the group intervention focuses on the provision of mutual aid and education, each session will begin with a brief presentation by one of the facilitators or another professional. On an ongoing basis, parents will collaborate with co-facilitators to determine topics of interest. Following the presentation and discussion, members will be given the opportunity to check in with one another, raise issues, and ask for input from the group regarding their concerns.
Agency context	With support from your supervisor, agency administration, and co-workers, this group intervention helps promote the agency mission to provide services to families and children.

EXHIBIT 8.9

Continued

PREPLANNING ISSUE/TASK	CONSIDERATION FOR PARENTS OF TEENS SUPPORT GROUP
Social context	A psychoeducational, reciprocal support group meets a need within the community that no other agency or institution is currently meeting. Should members need additional support, your agency provides individual and family services. You will reach out to area schools to gather input and promote the program.
Pregroup contact	Together with your social work student, you will develop a program flyer to circulate among agency staff and post on the agency's website and bulletin boards. You will also promote the program to other social service agencies that serve this population, school social workers, a community service website, and elsewhere as appropriate.
Contacting prospective group members	Social service professionals may refer prospective group members or prospective members may contact the agency directly. You and your social work student will conduct a brief intake interview with each potential member to determine their appropriateness for the group. If you determine that the individual is a good fit, you will invite them to the first meeting.

Client Need To determine if a group approach would be most appropriate for clients, you may begin by identifying the relevant issues that confront the client population. To establish a vital, functioning group, you must understand members' lives and struggles and be able to focus on some aspect of their lives that is important to them. Social workers need specific knowledge about the unique characteristics and needs of the target group so that the group interventions can be culturally inclusive and meet the group's needs and goals (Association for Specialists in Group Work, 2021). For example, in working with a parents of teens group, consider the decisions you will make regarding the scheduling and location of meetings and the parents' schedules, transportation, and child care needs. Keep in mind the challenges these parents face in balancing parenting situations with work, the needs of other family members, and their own well-being, and focus on an issue relevant to their lives rather than on something they may deem irrelevant (e.g., retirement planning). On the other hand, self-care strategies (e.g., exercise or social activities) may be appealing to parents feeling stressed and concerned about their teenage children. The point is to know your clients' needs and respond to them in a way that is consistent with your agency's purpose. Community needs assessments, agency service statistics, and interviews with staff and clients can provide data that can help you make these decisions.

Purpose   Consider both collective and individual objectives:

- What hopes will the group as a whole have?
- What expectations will individuals have?
- Ask yourself, what is the group's function and what will your role be?

For example, the group may focus on counseling, education, or facilitating social action. Consider ways in which member interaction will contribute to the group's purpose. A group intervention should emphasize the benefits for the members which may include: (1) being part of a supportive community in which shared experiences promote empowerments; (2) increased coping skills and lessening challenges; and (3) opportunities to engage with others who experience barriers to receiving help (Goelitz, 2021). Returning to the parents of teens group, the group as a whole may hope to normalize the experience of parenting their children during the often turbulent years of adolescence. Individual goals may be to gain strategies and wisdom for responding to the challenges of parenting an adolescent that can be gained through group member sharing and psychoeducational content. Whether the group focus will be task- or social-action-centered, reciprocal, or remedial, your role is to provide accurate information, dispel misinformation, and approach the group with a lens of identifying commonalities, sharing, and problem-solving (Knight & Gitterman, 2022).

Composition, Eligibility, and Appropriateness   Group composition refers to the number of group members and their characteristics, such as their gender identity, age, experiences, skills, beliefs, and values. The major concern in determining the composition of a group is the degree of homogeneity or heterogeneity that is most conducive to achieving desired outcomes. In general, groups that are homogeneous (i.e., share commonalties) can provide a "safer," more successful group experience (Marsiglia et al., 2021). However, the group should also include enough member diversity to sustain members' interest and the potential for growth through exposure to different ideas. Frequently, a particular condition, such as caregiving for a family member with a chronic illness, can bridge differences on other dimensions, such as age or ethnic background, but these aspects should be evaluated carefully. Use caution in assuming that persons who seemingly have nothing in common cannot connect. In the case of the parents of teens group, parents share the experience of finding challenges in helping their children through adolescence, which can be a shared similarity, but each will bring different experiences, attitudes, and beliefs about their situations, which can show diversity of perspectives.

In addition to individual descriptive variables, behavioral characteristics are also important. The group has the potential to be more successful if members have compatible interpersonal styles, language and communication, and understandings of the potential for groups. Different types of groups will vary on the balance of these components—for example, similar ages in children's groups would probably be more important than in most adult groups. In thinking about the parents of teens group, the parents will likely be a range of ages with varying degrees of parenting experience, both of which can be an asset in the group's ability to support and guide one another.

Equally as important, consider the impact of race, ethnicity, culture, experiences with discrimination and oppression, and socioeconomic class on group dynamics, cohesion, and functioning. As you are engaged in the preplanning phase of the group, culturally related issues are critical to consider as one's lived experiences can influence the way in which they will engage and benefit from the group (Marsiglia et al., 2021). The social worker and group are well served by the social worker having knowledge of the cultures of the potential members in such areas as historical traditions, behaviors and norms, verbal and non-verbal communications, and responses to conflict (Marsiglia et al., 2021.

The need and purpose of the group interventions help determine the eligibility criteria and type of members appropriate for the group. As you explore the possibility of forming a group, consider the focus of the group and members' ability to connect to one another. For example, consider these questions: Will caregivers of spouses with Alzheimer's disease have issues that are similar to or different from caregivers of adult children with a developmental disability? Will people in recovery from opioid addiction be eligible to remain in the group if they are found to have relapsed? Will members of a grief support group whose family member died of an overdose relate to others who lost someone to cancer? Focusing on the goals of the group intervention will help you answer these questions and create a group that will be able to help one another. As you are determining group composition, ensure that the make-up of the group members is consistent with group purpose and type along with compatibility with members' developmental stages (Knight & Gitterman, 2022).

Structure Determine if the group will be open or closed and the pros and cons of your choice—will you exclude people who can benefit if the group is closed? What is the agency's position on this question? What challenges might you face in an open-ended or closed-ended group? What type of group will best address the short- and long-term needs of members?

Group leadership is another area to address as you develop a group intervention. Will the group have a sole facilitator, or will co-facilitators better meet the group's needs? While a single facilitator may be more economical in terms of time and financial resources, there may be compelling reasons for co-facilitation, including increased opportunity to capture member interchanges, support and encouragement for one another, continuity for the group, and modeling of appropriate conflict resolution and behaviors for the group (Offerman et al., 2017).

Structure also refers to the logistical arrangements of the group—location, frequency of sessions, time of meetings, and duration. Other practical questions include:

- What type or size of room will work best?
- Will group members require transportation or care for a loved one?

- Will there be a fee for participation in the group?
- How will members maintain confidentiality?
- Should informed consent be obtained for participation?
- What level of agency coordination will be required?
- Does the proposed meeting time conflict with faith/religious holidays or present challenges for the specific group?
- Are there implications for scheduling at the same/different time as other activities in the agency (e.g., holding a group for family members of persons with early-stage dementia to coincide with their loved one's participation in a group for persons with early-stage dementia)?

Using the parents of teens group as an example, taking into consideration the parents' work and family obligations and schedules will be critical to the parents' ability to join the group. Similarly, knowing that the information that each one shares will be maintained inside the group will enable the group to share more openly and without fear of their family issues becoming public knowledge.

Content You should determine the process for selecting the content the group will cover by analyzing the purpose of the group, its members' needs, and agency and personnel resources. Will you develop the content, will the group determine areas to address, or will it be a collaborative effort? The activities or other means used to accomplish the group's purpose may require special training, equipment, or materials. Consider the agenda and content of the meetings. Who will be responsible for planning for the group, establishing timelines, creating an agenda, and developing a group purpose? If the group will use discussion, will the content facilitate interaction among members? For the parents of the teen group, providing the members with an opportunity to establish their own rules, agendas, and areas to be discussed can serve to more accurately meet the parents' needs and to empower them as individuals and parents.

Agency Context Consider how the agency will affect the group and how the group will affect the agency. Composition and structure may be pre-determined by the agency (Knight & Gitterman, 2022). Specifically, do agency administration and personnel endorse group work for the population served, and is group work consistent with the agency's mission and emphasis? Do not assume you have the agency's support without confirming it. Your group is likely to have repercussions for others. For example, a children's group that meets at the agency is often noisy and may be disruptive to others. The addition of group work to the agency's suite of services may increase the support staff's administrative responsibilities (e.g., scheduling, room arrangements, managing participation records). Individual social workers may feel possessive of their clients and may be reticent to refer clients to a group. Co-workers may feel that groups cannot offer more than individual treatment or that the individual treatment process may be negatively affected. It is to your advantage to address these and other concerns as directly as possible prior to creating the group.

Social Context   Consider social and cultural influences that may influence the group's bonding and functioning. Will the group complement other community services? Are there appropriate supports and resources for members after the group to help them maintain changes? Do members' cultural contexts support group participation? For example, if you want to facilitate a group for adolescent girls, consider whether their families will approve of and provide support for the group and their daughters' participation.

Pregroup Contact   Prior to a first meeting, consider the following questions that will help you determine appropriate and effective strategies for pregroup interactions:

- How will members be recruited or referred?
- Will you conduct individual pregroup screening interviews to determine whether individuals are appropriate for the group?
- How will members prepare themselves for the group experience?
- How will you facilitate members' orientation to the group process so they can experience maximum participation and benefit?
- Does each member have access to the group (e.g., transportation, resources for care if they are a caregiver, and/or technology)? For instance, if the group is being delivered virtually, consider having a "session 0" with each person to ensure technology access and literacy.

While each group and potential member is unique, developing a plan to address these questions can enable you to assemble a group with which you are familiar and whose members are oriented to the purpose, structure, and format of the group.

In general, meeting with each potential group member is an appropriate strategy for providing relevant group information to the person. A "session zero" can include introducing yourself to the potential/new members and providing information about the purpose of the pre-group contact and the group, ways in which members can help one another, and group norms, expectations, and content (Steinberg, 2019). The social worker and potential/new member can then determine if they can benefit from a group experience and if there is a fit between the individual and other group members. This practice can be resource-intensive, particularly for open groups but can be worth the investment of time.

Pregroup contact can also be an opportunity for you and the client to discuss the client's participation in and balance with other services. The client may be receiving individual and/or family services, so strategizing about ways to maximize benefits from both types of services can be helpful. For client groups, the social worker can also let the potential group member know that, during the group experience, it is not unusual for the social worker to suggest individual or family services. The social worker can help the client who receives multiple services process and make use of the information gleaned from each intervention approach.

Contacting Prospective Group Members   There are many ways to build up the membership of a prospective group and to connect with potential group work clients. Outreach is a method for contacting people to inform them of services and information about which they may not have been aware (Barker, 2014). You may reach out to potential group members through connections with other professionals in the community (e.g., school social workers). Other times, outreach may require a more concerted coordination campaign (e.g., advertising, posting to agency website or social media, and individual contacts), particularly if potential clients fear discrimination or barriers to eligibility. For example, a potential participant in the parents of teens group may be concerned about participation because she is involved in a legal case regarding custody of her children and fears something she shares will get back to her ex-spouse. It may be helpful for current group members to recruit prospective group members. Having firsthand knowledge of the group's purpose and focus can be an effective strategy for recruitment of new members.

On-site service referral is often a useful way to connect with potential members. You may, for example, recruit members from your caseload of individual clients, or you might ask your colleagues for referrals after they give you their support. Postings and announcements are helpful, but they must be paired with personal contact, such as another staff member's enthusiastic recommendation, to be effective.

In nearly all scenarios, a pregroup interview is ideal. First, it allows you to get a sense of the potential member to determine their "fit" with the goals and purpose of the group. A pregroup meeting also provides an opportunity to assess any potential concerns about the person's interaction with other group members and for the prospective group member to express any anxieties, ask questions, and make a more educated choice about joining the group. A pregroup meeting is also the time to raise questions or concerns regarding time commitment, fees, or costs associated with joining the group. Finally, this contact is a form of engagement, assessment, planning, and introducing the issue of termination by letting the person know the expected length of their participation. Through this contact, you may learn that a potential member is ambivalent, and you may respond with "prepatory empathy" to increase their entry into the group (Knight & Gitterman, 2022). As such, it requires the same level of knowledge and skills as individual engagement and assessment and planning.

You can ease a potential or new group member's entry into the group by providing information regarding the group experience. Such a discussion and/or document may contain information on (Brown, 2018):

- the nature of and expectations for participating in the group (i.e., purpose and goals and how they will be established).

- confidentiality in the areas of mandatory reporting of child abuse, illegal activity, parental notifications, and/or potential for harm to self or others.

- members' rights related to participation and leaving the group and any consequences for non-participation or termination from the group.

- expectations that no member will be subjected to coercion and pressure and all members will be treated equitably by others.

- clarifying which, if any, dual relationships are acceptable within the group.

- techniques that will be used in the group experience (and that you have training in their use). (pp. 164–170)

Engagement

Overlapping with the important pregroup planning phase, engagement is the beginning phase of the group intervention. Exhibit 8.10 provides practice guidelines for working in the engagement or beginning phases of group work intervention.

The first session ideally begins with you and group members sharing your expectations for the group. Be transparent about what you (you alone or with a co-facilitator) hope to accomplish. Likewise, encourage members to talk about their perceptions of their roles. Confidentiality is often one of the first dimensions you will discuss; unless all members feel safe in revealing their struggles and feelings, it is not likely that many will participate fully.

Establishing norms, or expected rules of conduct, creates a productive group climate, and requires members to actively participate so the social worker is not in the position of dictating group regulations. The norms will depend on the type of group. For example, the major expectation for a socialization group for 7-year-old boys in residential treatment may be "no hitting." "No shouting" might be applicable to an anger management group but consider a more affirmatively framed expectation such as "Use your inside voice." Some groups also discourage members from contacting each other outside the group because it may impact the group if members form alliances that conflict with the group process, and others encourage it because it fosters translation of group benefits into the "real world."

The primary purpose of norms should be to facilitate group members' involvement through a relatively clear set of behavioral expectations that will increase their comfort in the group and encourage their participation. If, for

> **EXHIBIT 8.10**
>
> *Guidelines for Engagement and Beginning Phases of Group Work*
>
> - Identifying member aspirations and needs as perceived by the member, agency, and yourself.
> - Confirming organizational support for offering a group.
> - Determining the group type, structure, processes, and size that will complement group purpose and goals.
> - Developing strategy for and recruiting potential group members.
> - Completing organizational requirements for admission to the group.
> - Clarifying member goals and expectations along with the person's feelings about joining the group.
> - Establishing meeting time and location to ensure comfort, safety, and access.
> - Developing a group purpose (finalized during the first group meeting).
> - Planning group content, activities, and documentation format and obtaining needed resources.
>
> Following the pregroup phase of work, skills and behaviors needed for continuing the engagement and assessment of group members include:
>
> - developing contracts for explication of individual and group goals, tasks, and activities for the duration of the group and beyond.
> - introducing and clarifying your role in the group.
> - inviting members to introduce themselves and to share their reasons for joining and their hopes for the group.
> - in collaboration with group members, developing a statement of purpose, rules and norms, and roles that incorporate the individual, group, and agency goals, needs, and perceptions.
> - developing content, activities, and resources relevant to the group's purpose.
> - highlighting common interests and goals, direct interactions, and potential linkages to promote group cohesion among members and between the members and you.
> - in partnership with group members, establishing the plan for the group's planned time together (or for the individual's time in the group if the group is open-ended and not time-limited).
> - building awareness and recognition of the unique characteristics of each group member, including but not limited to cultural and ethnic heritage, age, gender, sexual identity, presenting concerns, and note that each person brings strengths to the group process.
>
> Source: *The Standards for Social Work Practice with Groups* (IASWG, 2015, pp. 6–9).

example, group members have differing cultural heritages, and some members interpret lateness as disrespectful while others view it as simply flexible, the social worker may opt to explore timeliness as an area for negotiation. Knowing the membership can help you anticipate issues that may affect group process. Group members may also develop informally and formally their own norms, so anticipating this can aid you in directly establishing the norms by which the group will function. These early negotiations with group members serve as opportunities for engagement and ongoing assessment.

The engagement phase can be challenging for the social worker and group members. The social worker is trying to engage with each member and the group as a whole to promote cohesion among members, establish the group structure and format, *and* keep the group on task and on target for its goals. The group is going through the same process—connecting to you and to one another. A key factor in the engagement process for the members is to feel the physical and social space of the group is a safe and supportive environment (IASWG, 2015). While the sense of safety is necessary for all groups, it is critically important for those members who have experienced trauma (Goelitz, 2021). Creating a safe environment in technology-delivered groups is different from in-person groups but is important, nonetheless. Addressing technology-related "net" etiquette during the pregroup and engagement stages should be considered a routine aspect of beginning a group.

When a group is engaged, group members become empowered to begin sharing with and supporting one another, alleviating the need for the social worker to take full responsibility for leading the group. Group cohesion also relates to members' engagement as well as attendance, commitment to the group, satisfaction, and goal attainment (Toseland, 2017).

Engaging new members or facilitators who join an established group can be challenging. The facilitator is responsible for engaging new members and for encouraging the group to do the same. If the social worker is new to the agency and/or group, they are responsible for reaching out to members to introduce themselves and begin to build rapport. If members do not feel engaged in the first meeting, attrition may occur. Members who join a group voluntarily but who do not feel connected to the group or to the facilitator may feel reticent about returning.

The beginning phases of group work can present challenges for group members as well. Whether group members are voluntarily or involuntarily participating in the group, they may be reticent to engage with the facilitator, fearing that the facilitator does not understand the member's situation or is judging the member for life choices or circumstances. It is important to recognize there are situations in which you will have some level of actual power over group members. For example, in involuntary groups, your assessment will determine members' trajectories. Regardless of the reasons for the member's hesitancy, the social worker can use **"tuning in"** to convey empathy, acknowledge the reasons the member may be reluctant to engage with the social worker or group members, and invite feedback (Shulman, 2022). Being attentive to individual reactions and responses will ensure that individuals are not "lost" or deterred from investing in the group experience. "Tuning in" to group members can also help to create a **therapeutic alliance**—a trusting working relationship—with members of the group as individuals, which can then allow individual members to create alliances with other group members (Shulman, 2022).

Assessment and Planning

As with social work practice with individuals and families, the transition from one phase of work to another is rarely linear or clearly defined. Just as engagement can be an ongoing process, you can revisit assessment and planning throughout the duration of the group experience. Both assessment and planning occur as you recruit and screen potential members and again as the group forms and collaborates on the development of individual and group contracts. You may find that you need to assess and plan at different points throughout the life of the group as individual and group goals change and evolve, as members arrive and depart, and as unanticipated events (e.g., conflict, change of facilitator, or termination) influence group interactions. Ongoing assessments must be conducted to establish the individual members' goals and desired outcomes, the group's outcomes, and the group processes (e.g., group cohesion and productivity) (Macgowan & Hanbidge, 2022b).

Regardless of the timing and frequency of assessment, bringing a biopsychosocial-spiritual and cultural lens to the information is essential for the group intervention. Within the context of group practice, the biopsychosocial-spiritual and cultural assessments are a strategy for determining the context of the individual member's situation as well as that of the group and whether the issues and characteristics a group member presents are consistent with those of other members, and for monitoring individual and group progress toward goals.

> *Recall the earlier example of the group for Riverton children who had lost a family member to substance use or addiction. As the facilitator of this group, you may initiate a group discussion about the biopsychosocial-spiritual aspects of addiction and grief, helping children understand that both experiences are complex and have components of the biopsychosocial-spiritual processes and how these processes can be used in the healing process.*

Group interventions can be an empowering and meaningful experience for individuals and groups that have experienced marginalization and oppression. Regardless of whether addressing issues of social injustice is the specific focus of a group intervention, the social worker should be vigilant to keep the potential cultural impact at the forefront of the assessment and planning process. Exhibit 8.11 outlines four principles of social justice when conducting a group assessment.

An issue that is important for the group process is the bonding (cohesiveness) experienced by the group. While individuals can experience growth and change without feeling close to other members, cohesiveness can be empowering. A range of factors impact group cohesiveness, including interpersonal attraction (connection to others), proximity, acceptance and approval, similar expectations, recognition and value, security, access to resources, and working on issues they feel they can influence (Toseland, 2017). Group cohesion also relates to issues such as ongoing attendance, commitment to the group,

> EXHIBIT 8.11
>
> *Principles for Group Practice Assessment in a Social Justice Model*
>
> - Group members engage fully in the decision-making related to assessment, including the selection of instruments, administration process (i.e., who, when, and how), and the way in which the data collected will be used and those with access to the data.
> - Identify social injustices, specifically in terms of:
>   - the extent of the social injustice.
>   - members' awareness of the injustice and its impact on the members.
>   - members' knowledge and skills for facilitating change.
>   - the extent to which change has and can be achieved.
> - Assessment tools/measures must be psychometrically validated on age, culture, language, gender, gender identity, and other relevant demographic characteristics.
> - With a lens on the impact of social injustice, tools/measures include assessment of outcomes and processes each time they are administered.
> - Ensure outcomes and processes will be meaningful and empowering for participants beyond the life of the life of the group.
>
>
>
> *Source:* Ortega & Garvin, 2019.

satisfaction, and goal attainment (Toseland, 2017). One standardized measure of group cohesion and engagement is the Group Engagement Measure (Macgowan, 2006) which assesses attendance, contributions, relationships, contracting, and focus on own and others' problems. Upon determining what you want to assess, you can opt to use standardized measures, observation, group member self-reports, or feedback from an external source (e.g., in person or through videos or audio recordings).

As with any area of social work practice, group leaders must be cognizant of the ethical obligations associated with engaging and assessing members of a new group. Similar to work with individuals and families, ethical challenges in group work often center around dual relationships, informed consent to share information, mandated participants, confidentiality, and boundaries; however, with multiple individuals being your client, the issues are often complex and multi-faceted (Banach & Pillay, 2019). While these challenges can be complex, social work ethical guidelines dictate the following of our principles, including (Brown, 2018):

- adherence to the principles of doing no harm, having a duty to protect, and being responsible to the general public.
- clarifying the content of information that will be shared with others, including supervisors and agency staff.
- practicing within one's area of competence and obtaining relevant training for group interventions.

Planning within the assessment phase of group work often requires attentiveness and flexibility. While most group facilitators spend considerable time and effort on pregroup planning and developing an agenda or plan for each session, experienced group practitioners can attest to the need to be willing and able to shift plans quickly and creatively. Regardless of the type of group you facilitate, it is likely that at any meeting a member or members will have an issue, crisis, request, or behavior that will take precedence over your plans for that session. While you will want to be responsive to each individual's needs, you must try to balance the needs of the entire group. You may be able to set aside your plans for that session to devote time to one or more specific individuals but use caution to ensure you do not sacrifice the needs of other members or agenda items in the process.

Participating in a group can trigger emotions for the members. To respond to this likelihood, the social worker can help members address and manage feelings by (Macgowan & Hanbidge, 2022a):

- encouraging the expression of feelings whether positive or negative—this strategy can create a sense of openness on your part.
- addressing non-productive norms—in the event that expressions of feelings uncover behaviors or language that is inappropriate or unhelpful, you can link the discussion to the purpose and norms of the group.

CRITICAL CONSIDERATIONS ABOUT GROUP ENGAGEMENT AND ASSESSMENT

Engagement

The engagement phase of group work is a time to not only discuss the "business" of the group (e.g., facilitator and member roles, purpose, goals, expectations, confidentiality, and communication) but also a time to ensure that members know they are welcome to share as much or as little as they choose so that they are empowered to be in control of their own narrative (Knight & Gitterman, 2022). While inviting members to have the freedom to share their thoughts, feelings, and lived experiences, you are communicating that you share power with them. It is tempting to want to be in control of the group; however, the group and you will realize greater benefits if you learn to share the helping role and some control of relationship(s) with group members and to allow the group to forge its own path. For many students and new social workers, however, learning to trust the group process and to maintain a stance of facilitator (not necessarily "leader" and certainly not "runner of" or "member") can be challenging. A willingness to relinquish control will serve you well. That said, despite your best efforts to refrain from controlling the group and to strive for empowering the group to assume increasing levels of power, it is important to recognize that you may be perceived as having more power than the group members. To clarify issues related to power, invite members directly to express differences in perceptions and opinions (Gitterman et al., 2021). Fortunately, early anxieties regarding control and its management usually abate with experience.

> Consider the RAYD group who is working on developing activities for youth as alternatives to using alcohol and drugs. Group members may have preconceived expectations about outcomes that differ from those of others, resulting in potentially adversarial discussions. As facilitator, you can remind the group of the ground rules regarding civility and respect, their mutual commitment to the well-being of the community's youth, and your role as moving the process toward a productive outcome.

When embarking on a facilitator role, it is important to think about the experience in the context of the members' participation. Group members essentially have two roles: (1) self-disclosure and sharing with other group members and facilitator and (2) providing feedback to other members (Salazar & Leddick, 2018). With that in mind, consider the following member-focused strategies to engage the members so they can have a meaningful experience (Milsom, 2018):

- By questioning, providing feedback, empathizing, and summarizing, you can help members share information and process the experiences that brought them to the group and attribute meaning to those experiences.
- Create a safe environment to promote the members' comfort in expressing their emotions.
- By maintaining the focus on the present (as opposed to the past), group members can feel freed to test new attitudes and behaviors in an honest manner. (pp. 102–103)

The engagement phase is a time to welcome, orient, and most importantly, to listen. By listening to members' introductions and reasons for attending, you can gather information to bond the group and set the stage for an effective and meaningful group experience. From listening, you can begin to connect group members to one another by (Gitterman et al., 2021):

1. *scanning* the entire whole, not just the person speaking.
2. *directing members' transactions* toward one another, not just to you.
3. *inviting members* to build on one another's contributions to promote commonalities.
4. *encouraging and reinforcing* cooperation and mutual support.
5. *describing members' reactions* to one another.
6. *encouraging members' participation* in discussion and activities.
7. *identifying and focusing* on common themes in members' discussion.
8. *connecting* the individual to the group and the group to the individual.
9. *using activities and programs* to facilitate connections among the members. (pp. 440–442)

Listening also enables you to gain insight about your own biases, unresolved personal concerns, or conflicted values that may prevent you from objectively and empathetically serving the group.

> *For example, in your role as facilitator of the RAYD group, "tune in" to your own experiences and feelings related to substance use and adolescence and to the origins and meanings of what the Riverton residents have to say about the problem in their community. "Tuning in" can enable you to understand the influence your own attitudes, feelings, and experiences may have on a client situation. For example, if you grew up with a parent who is an alcoholic, you may not be completely objective when a group member in a substance use treatment group talks about their inadequacies as a parent.*

Assessment and Planning

In addition to determining if potential members meet the pre-established criteria for inclusion in the group and if the group has the potential to be productive based on the individuals selected to participate, the assessment phase includes gathering demographic and needs-related information about potential members of client groups. Integrating biopsychosocial-spiritual information into the assessment process can aid in understanding the whole person and their needs and potential contributions.

Exhibit 8.12 provides samples of documentation that you might include for assessing potential members of a client-oriented group. Notice similarities to information gathered in individual and family assessments. Assessment for group work emphasizes previous experience with groups and feelings/motivation about joining the group. Depending on your agency's practices, you may be able to collect information that relates specifically to group participation—we want to be cautious about asking for information that is not relevant to services requested. Exhibit 8.13 provides a list of questions a social worker can ask individual clients to assess and document whether they are appropriate for membership in the group.

EXHIBIT 8.12

Intervention Plan Information to Include in a Group Assessment

AGENCY/ORGANIZATION NAME

GROUP NAME

Demographic Data

- Name
- Contact information
- Legal status and needs
- Group participation needs (e.g., child/adult care needs, transportation, etc.)
- Presenting concerns as they relate to the group purpose or focus
- Current living situation (level of stability, support, safety)
- Social environment (level of activity, satisfaction, relationships with others)
- Cultural environment (client satisfaction with and views on help-seeking and cultural views of help-seeking, particularly in the group environment)
- Religion/spirituality (statement of beliefs and levels of activity and satisfaction)
- Military experience (branch, time in service, discharge status, coping with experience, view of experience)
- Childhood (supportive of the client, strengths, and significant events—including trauma)
- Family (composition—parents, siblings, spouse/significant other(s), children, and others; level of support; family history of mental illness)
- Sexual history (activity level, orientation, satisfaction, concerns)
- Trauma history (physical, sexual, and/or emotional abuse or neglect and experience with perpetrator[s])
- Financial/employment circumstances (employment status, satisfaction, financial stability, areas of concern or change)
- Educational history (highest level achieved, performance, goals, challenges)
- Substance use/addictions (history of addictive behaviors, alcohol, drugs, gambling, sexual, other)

(For treatment groups only) History of Emotional/Behavioral Functioning: For each of the following areas, gather information regarding status (current, previous, or denies history), description of behavior, onset and duration, and frequency.

- Self-mutilation
- Hallucinations
- Delusions or paranoia
- Mood swings
- Recurrent or intrusive recollections of past events
- Lack of interest or pleasure
- Feelings of sadness, hopelessness, isolation, or withdrawal
- Decreased concentration, energy, or motivation
- Anxiety
- Crying spells
- Appetite changes
- Sleep changes
- Inability to function at school or work

EXHIBIT 8.12 *Continued*	• Inability to control thoughts or behaviors (impulses) • Irritability or agitation • Reckless behavior, fighting, or fire setting • Stealing, shoplifting, or lying • Cruelty to animals • Aggression (For treatment groups only) Past and Current Behavioral Health Treatment History (i.e., individual, family, and/or other group experiences): • Date(s) • Program or facility • Provider • Response to treatment Mental Status Exam (these items can determine functioning within the group, not diagnosis): • Attention (rate on scale of good, fair, easily distracted, or highly distractible, and describe behavior) • Affect (rate on scale of appropriate, changeable, expansive, constrictive, or blunted, and describe behavior) • Mood (rate on scale of normal, depressed, anxious, or euphoric, and describe behavior) • Appearance (rate on scale of well groomed, disheveled, or inappropriate, and describe behavior) • Motor activity (rate on scale of calm, hyperactive, agitated, tremors, tics, or muscle spasms, and describe behavior) • Thought process (rate on scale of intact, circumstantial, tangential, flight of ideas, or loose associations, and describe behavior) • Thought content (note normal, grandiose, phobic, reality, organization, worthless, obsessive, compulsion, guilt, delusional, paranoid, ideas of reference, and hallucinations, and describe behavior) • Memory (note normal, recent [good or impaired], past [good or impaired], and describe behavior) • Intellect (note normal, above, below, or poor abstraction, and describe behavior) • Orientation (note person, place, situation, and time, and describe behavior) • Judgment and insight (rate on scale of good, fair, or poor, and describe behavior) • Current providers (including psychiatrist, primary care physician, therapist, caseworker, etc.) • Community resources being used (including support groups, religious, spiritual, other) • Client goal(s) for treatment • Summary, including social worker's assessment of client "fit" with the group (see Exhibit 8.13 for assessment questions). *Source:* Adapted from St. Anthony's Medical Center (2010); Safe Connections, n.d.

> **EXHIBIT 8.13**
>
> *Screening Questions for Client Group Assessment*
>
> When you determine a client's appropriateness for membership in the group, you also seek to ensure the emotional and physical safety of all group members. Recognizing that you may not be able to ascertain this information during the assessment process, you can continue to assess throughout the group experience. The following is a list of general areas to consider as you assess clients for possible group membership:
>
> - How does the client respond to opinions, thoughts, and insights that differ from their own?
> - When the client becomes angry or upset, what is their reaction and thought process?
> - Is the client able to express their emotions in an appropriate way? Does the client assume responsibility for the emotion?
> - What triggers the client's emotional responses?
> - What is the client's developmental age? Is the client able to cope with negative emotions and thoughts at a level appropriate to the developmental level of other group members?
> - Does the client demonstrate:
>   - Impulse control challenges?
>   - Appropriate boundaries?
>   - Self-awareness?
>   - Self-destructive behaviors?
>   - Potential to monopolize or disrupt the group?
>   - Ability to respond to social cues?
>   - Sensitivity toward others?
>   - Potential for personal growth?
>   - Appropriate group interaction behaviors?
>   - Difficulty making decisions?
> - Might the client's behavior limit group participation or benefit?
> - If the client is currently experiencing a crisis, will the benefits of participating in the group outweigh risks for the client?
>
> *Source:* Adapted from Safe Connections (n.d.)

The early phases of a group experience can present unique and unexpected challenges for the social worker, particularly related to the ongoing assessment and planning activities. Your assessments may have found that group members have conflicting agendas and roles. Members may join the group with mixed emotions about themselves and others (Macgowan & Hanbidge, 2022a). You may encounter situations in which your goals for the group differ from those of group members or your role as a provider of individual and family services conflicts with your role as a group facilitator. Or you may find that some group members are not able to productively engage with other group members or are not interested in doing so. Challenges that can occur within any group experience include norms and patterns of nonproductivity being established by group members and conflict between group members and one or more members and the social worker (Macgowan & Hanbidge, 2022a).

Each of these situations relates to group member expectations and dynamics. Group members who struggle to see how the group process benefits them, particularly when compared to an individual helping relationship or in an immediate time frame, may leave the group. Group members often find that their common experiences extend beyond the group; this can lead to alliances within the group session and/or socializing outside the group. While not necessarily a problem, such relationships can be disruptive to the group process. Consider the scenario in which two members of the group for co-occurring disorders who met during the group begin an intimate relationship. While two members dating does not ensure disruption of the group, it is important for the group to be able to process the potential meaning for the group process.

As in practice with individuals and families, assessments serve to inform the planning process and ultimately the intervention itself. The group's launching and development is tied to the planning activities, particularly enlisting support from the agency to offer a group (Gitterman et al., 2021). Developing a proposal to outline your plans for the group can be a useful strategy for ensuring you are prepared for the first meeting, to include (Gitterman et al., 2021):

- Identify overall group goal and purpose—gains and benefits for members.
- Select the type of group model that meets members' needs and goals.
- Determine composition of the group.
- Arrange the physical (or virtual) space.
- Determine leadership, including sole or co-leadership, preparation, and expertise.
- Create a responsive organizational climate.
- Work with and within organizational realities and constraints. (p. 210)

As assessment and planning continue throughout the entirety of the group social work intervention, it is critical to have skills that will enable you to engage in continuously evaluating the individual members' concerns and issues. For example, consider the following reasons for ongoing assessment and re-planning:

- *Individual or group goals have changed*—members' life situations or their experience in the group may change their goals or ability to engage with the group.
- *Interactions between members of the group*—a conflict between two or more members may be impacting the group.

- *Physical or mental health issue*—the resolution or onset of a health-related issue may have a positive or negative impact on the member's participation.

If the group member does not share a change, you may not become aware of the member's absence or change of behavior or affect unless you ask. The group is essentially a microcosm of the larger world and members and facilitators can be impacted by their experiences outside the group; therefore, assessing and sometimes re-planning are to be expected throughout the lifetime of the group.

Documentation

While documenting the process of the group experience presents unique challenges, it need not be an overwhelming or complex task. Documenting any group experience serves a range of purposes, including (1) pre- and post-group individual and group assessments for planning and evaluation purposes; (2) contracts for the individual and group that include group purpose, norms, and roles/expectations; (3) group sessions, including interactions, process, progress, observations and monitoring, and revisions to the goals and/or intervention; (4) monitoring leadership skills and group process; and (5) accountability to the agency (IASWG, 2015).

Typically, the facilitator maintains records of both group and individual experiences. The group's record includes information on attendance, general themes, cohesion, interactions, and plans, while documentation in the individual group members' records includes only information regarding that client and their goals, needs, and so on. To protect individual client confidentiality, the names of other group members should not be included in an individual client's documentation as individuals have only the right to see their own individual record without information on other members. It is important to remember that both individual and group records are considered legal documents (Sidell, 2015). These records are not co-mingled in the same paper or electronic record except if they are subpoenaed by the court. At that point, the social worker would need to clarify for the court record that the information contained in the group document on any members not related to the court action should be redacted to protect their confidentiality.

Group practice documentation encompasses issues for ethical consideration, including confidentiality and informed consent, both of which relate to the group members' right to self-determination and our ethical obligation to honor the dignity of the individual. Two issues relate to confidentiality: (1) the type of group determines the level of confidentiality, including technology-delivered groups (i.e., minimal expectations for confidentiality occur in education-focused groups, while therapy groups have greater expectations); (2) confidentiality is not considered an absolute right in the social work relationship—exceptions include the social worker's concern that a client is of potential harm to self or others and receiving a subpoena to testify in court

(Barsky & Northen, 2017). The social worker should openly discuss with the group the levels of confidentiality, specifically the information that members can share outside the group and information included in client records (Barsky & Northen, 2017). These discussions determine the type of member informed consent needed.

While the documentation of the work of social goals and task groups may include some of the same basic information you would record with a client group (e.g., attendance, themes, and plans), the focus is more typically directed toward recording actions and decisions. Often compiled in the form of minutes or notes, the documentation of group process and outcomes for social action/goals or task groups emphasizes the work being completed as opposed to the interactions among group members. See Quick Guides 23 and 24 for templates to record the work of social goals and task groups. Quick Guide 23 provides a template for a matrix-style record depicting a sample from a RAYD group subcommittee tasked with planning a community event. If the group has opted to use a traditional meeting format as shown in the template, the facilitator will call the meeting to order, ask for review/approval of the minutes, and make and invite others to make announcements. Unfinished items from previous meetings are revisited before new items are introduced. Future meetings are scheduled, and the meeting is adjourned. For consistency and reference, decisions, next steps, and responsible person(s) are documented. Quick Guide 24 provides an outline for a narrative-style document of the same group. A notes form can make completing minutes an easier task.

QUICK GUIDE 23   Social Goals and Task Group Notes Template

AGENCY/ORGANIZATION NAME
GROUP NAME

Date _____ *Date group met*

Present: _____ *List all attendees with affiliation and guests*

Absent: _____ *List all absent members with affiliation*

Minutes submitted by: _____ *Name of recorder*

ISSUE	DISCUSSION	FOLLOW-UP/RECOMMENDATIONS	PERSON(S) RESPONSIBLE
Call to Order			
Minutes			
Announcements			
Old Business			
New Business			
Adjournment			
Future Meetings			

> **QUICK GUIDE 24   Task Group Minutes Template**
>
> Agency/Organization Name
>
> Group Name
>
> Date
>
> In attendance:
> Absent
>
> 1 Call meeting to order
> 2 Review meeting agenda
> 3 Review minutes from previous meeting
> 4 Announcements
> 5 Old business
> 6 New business
> 7 Adjournment and next steps
>
> Respectfully submitted,
> [Note taker's name and title]

Regardless of the challenges you may encounter as a group facilitator or leader, maintaining a transparent, open, and equitable style will best serve you and the group. As the group develops its own identity, norms, roles, and communication patterns, the social worker's role is continuously recognizing the group as the client (Knight, 2017a). Gaining as much *group* experience as possible throughout your social work education, particularly as facilitator or leader, can prepare you for being a capable leader throughout your social work career. As we continue to explore social work practice with groups in Chapter 9, consider the valuable lessons you can learn from experiencing different roles within a group, including member, facilitator, and observer.

> **GRAND CHALLENGE**
>
> *End Homelessness*
>
> The American Academy of Social Work and Social Welfare Grand Challenges for Social Work Initiative identifies one of the areas the profession should address as being to end homelessness. The authors of Grand Challenge Working Paper No. 9, *The Grand Challenge of Ending Homelessness* (Henwood et al., 2015, p. 4), emphasize that philosophy regarding homelessness has shifted from management and reduction to elimination:
>
> > To eradicate all forms of homelessness in 10 years, interdisciplinary and cross-sector collaboration will be necessary for accurately assessing the scope of the problem; improving data; establishing innovative and clear solutions to family, youth, and other subpopulation homelessness; and disseminating existing effective solutions. Ending homelessness cannot be accomplished simply by focusing on how best to respond to individuals who experience homelessness; it will require ongoing effort to address the structural, macro-level factors of poverty and income inequality.

> **GRAND CHALLENGE**
>
> *Continued*
>
> With the profession's expertise in working across all levels of social work practice, social work can and should have a significant role in the effort to end homelessness. However, new strategies are needed to provide housing and access to adequate health care and educational opportunities. The authors of the Grand Challenge charge the social work profession to engage in such innovative activities as gathering evidence to accurately measure the number of persons who are homeless, particularly those who are transient or hidden, and evaluating the efficacy of interventions; better utilizing community resources and services; promoting evidence-based intervention practices; and identifying and leveraging funding to support interventions (p. 14). These activities could involve the use of social goals and task groups among a wide variety of professionals, including social workers, working in an array of settings, such as government agencies, nonprofit social service agencies, and for-profits (e.g., banks and other lenders).
>
> To familiarize yourself with the issues related to ending homelessness, visit the Grand Challenges website and read Working Paper No. 9, *The Grand Challenge of Ending Homelessness* (Henwood et al., 2015) at http://grandchallengesforsocialwork.org/. To learn about the progress on achieving this Grand Challenge, review the "Ending Homelessness" by Henwood and colleagues (2022). (See Exercise #1 for additional exploration of this Grand Challenge within the context of the Riverton community.)

CONCLUSION

This chapter advocates for social work practitioners to recognize the values of groups within social work practice. We have explored group work using contemporary theoretical perspectives. Chapter 9 will turn to the next phases of social work practice with groups. Building on preplanning, engagement, and assessment work, the social worker–facilitated group moves first into the intervention or middle phase of work and then to the termination, evaluation (or ending), and follow-up phases of the group experience.

MAIN POINTS

- All people are members of groups that provide meaning to their lives and critical human connections.
- Group work in the social work profession remains a vital part of practice that lends itself especially to social justice, diversity, and human rights perspectives.
- Organizing a group requires careful planning and continuous consideration of the value of the work to the group as a whole and to its individual members.
- Traditional theoretical models for group work include the task group, social action or goals model, the reciprocal model, and the remedial model.

- Social work group practice employs a variety of theoretical frameworks. This chapter highlighted strengths, empowerment, systems, narrative-focused, and solution-focused perspectives.

- Engaging and assessing group members individually and collectively from a biopsychosocial-spiritual perspective is the first step in group formation.

- While primarily completed during the beginning phases of group work, engagement and assessment can be ongoing aspects of the group experience.

- The fluid and evolving nature of group work can result in changing membership and leadership, new and unexpected issues, and interpersonal dynamics and conflicts that can influence the course of the group intervention.

EXERCISES

1 To apply the Grand Challenge to end homelessness that was highlighted in this chapter, visit the Grand Challenges website, and read Working Paper No. 9, *The Grand Challenge of Ending Homelessness* (Henwood et al., 2015), at: http://grandchallengesforsocialwork.org/. To examine the issue of homelessness in the Riverton community, review the case information at www.routledgesw.com/cases. After reading Working Paper No. 9 and reviewing the Riverton information, complete the following:
   a Using the town map, sociogram, and interaction matrix (matching the homeless community icon with each of the other community entities), prepare an analysis of the homelessness situation in Riverton.
   b Develop a plan for engaging members and organizations in Riverton in group work using task groups and assessing homelessness in Riverton, including but not limited to identifying potential partners, strengths, barriers, and resources needed.
2 Go to www.routledgesw.com/interactive-cases/, review Carla Washburn's video vignette (in Engage and Discover), and complete the following:
   a Summarize the group's activities as depicted in the vignettes.
   b Document the group practice behaviors that the social worker, Shannon, uses.
   c Identify any potential challenges that may occur in a group intervention with the members of this group.
   d Brainstorm the next steps you would take as a social worker facilitating this group.
3 Review the Carla Washburn video vignette (in Engage and Discover) and explore options for facilitating this group using a range of approaches, then complete the following tasks:
   a Psychoeducational group—develop potential topics related to grief for inclusion.
   b Reciprocal group—develop a flyer to promote the grief and loss support group to potential members.

c Remedial group—identify potential goals for Carla Washburn participating in a treatment group for persons experiencing grief and loss.

Now respond to the following questions:

a How does the focus of each group differ?
b How does the social worker's role differ in each group?
c What engagement skills did the social worker use?

4 Go to www.routledgesw.com/interactive-cases/ and review the case for Brickville, focusing on Virginia Stone and her family. In the Intervention Create a Plan section, click on Family and Group interventions. Review Vignette #3, which describes the use of a social action group intervention focused on Virginia's efforts to save the park memorializing her family members who were lost in a fire 20 years earlier. Using the information, develop a written plan to:

a Determine the need for this group.
b Identify the purpose a task group would serve in this situation.
c Propose appropriate group composition and each member's potential contributions.
d Develop your thoughts regarding group structure (e.g., meeting time and place, documenting group activity, and leadership) and content.
e Reflect on the meaning of forming this group in the context of the agency and community.
f Describe your plans for initiating pregroup contact, engaging group members, and assessing members' potential commitment and contributions.
g Assess available and needed resources and potential barriers to success.

5 Go to www.routledgesw.com/interactive-cases/ and review the case for Hudson City. Recall that the Patel family experienced significant impact from Hurricane Diane. Several weeks after the hurricane, Sheetal Patel confides in you that she is concerned that her 12-year-old daughter, Aarti, is not coping well with life following the hurricane and the family's displacement from their home and restaurant. They have returned to their home and are working on reopening the restaurant. Aarti has returned to her school, but she continues to have nightmares about the storm, is uncomfortable being away from her parents, and seems to have less of an appetite. Other parents whose families were affected by the storm are expressing similar concerns, both to you and to your co-workers. Describe in writing your plan for developing a group intervention to address the needs of children who survived the hurricane, including:

- Type of group approach (include format and structure).
- Plans for member eligibility, recruitment, and parent involvement.
- Strategies for engaging group members in a culturally responsive manner, keeping in mind the diversity of the community and its large immigrant population.
- Strategies for assessing group members' appropriateness for the group.

6 Go to www.routledgesw.com/interactive-cases/ and review the case for Riverton, then, referring to the discussion of the Riverton community's

concerns about alcohol consumption throughout this chapter and Exhibits 8.5–8.7, conduct a search of the literature on group-level practice to find evidence to support developing the following group interventions:
  a Riverton Against Youth Drinking (RAYD): evidence-based practices for facilitating social action groups on prevention of teen drinking.
  b Riverton Children's Grief Support Group: evidence-based practices for facilitating reciprocal groups with children related to grief and loss.
  c Riverton Mental Health Center Groups for Persons with Co-Occurring Diagnoses: evidence-based practices for facilitating a treatment group for this population and for incorporating new members into an existing group.
7 Go to www.routledgesw.com/static-cases/ and review all the Downloadable Cases. Upon reviewing the cases, select one of the cases and develop a proposal to submit to your agency requesting approval to form a group (refer to the discussion in this chapter regarding the content to include in the proposal).
8 As a skilled individual and group practice social worker at a local community health center, you have several young clients who have been diagnosed with attention deficit hyperactivity disorder (ADHD). The clients are Latinx children between 6 and 8 years of age. When the children are picked up, you notice that some of their parents appear sad about their children, while others appear anxious, frustrated, or angry. The children themselves seem somewhat isolated and experience social, academic, and behavioral problems in school. Choose one of the following interventions that you think will be the most helpful:
  a A play/social skills group for the children
  b A support group for the parents
  c A psychoeducational group for the parents
  d An empowerment group for the children
  Develop a rationale and plan for offering the group to be submitted to your agency administration, who are skeptical of adding new programs at this time.
9 You work for a child welfare organization and facilitate a support group for adolescents who have recently given birth and are preparing to return to school. In some cases, the teens care for their own babies; in others, grandparents help with care, and some babies have been adopted through the agency. Some group members have concerns about returning to school while others are eager to get back into a "normal" social life. Most group members are participating well, although one member, Janine, has said almost nothing in the first three meetings. At the beginning of the first meeting, the mood of the group seems contentious. After you share brief pleasantries and restate the agenda for this session, you realize that Janine is quietly crying in the corner. At the same time, two other members start calling your name angrily, competing for your attention. They tell you they are annoyed at the group, at the plan for today, at the agency, and at Janine, who is sitting there acting like a "baby."

Respond to the following:
- a What additional information do you need to better understand the situation?
- b Identify two skills from the chapter that you would use in this situation and give an example of the way in which you would use these skills.
- c Provide a rationale for your selection of these skills. What results do you expect from their use?

10 Attend a mutual aid group in the community and write a reflection about your experience.
- a Describe the group type, purpose, and structure.
- b Identify the group leader and member roles.
- c Reflect on your previous experiences as a group member, if any. What role do you often play? Why? Do you want to do things differently?

11 In small groups of three or four, create your own social goals group and:
- a Identify an issue of mutual interest to group members.
- b Determine the roles for each member.
- c Develop a plan of action for the group. Prepare a presentation for the class.

12 Your field instructor at your aging service practicum has invited you to help in offering an online psychoeducational support group for persons who serve as caregivers for a family member with Parkinson's disease. Most group members are spouses and adult daughters. The group will be delivered via a live videoconference forum. Each session will begin with a presentation on a topic related to Parkinson's disease followed by discussion. Your field instructor has suggested that you assume responsibility for presenting on a topic of your choice relevant for this group. This is your first online group work experience. To accomplish your task:
- a Review the literature to learn more about Parkinson's disease.
- b Develop a plan for the session that you will present at, including identifying a relevant topic and strategies for engaging the group members in the discussion.

CHAPTER 9

Social Work Practice With Groups: Intervention, Termination, and Evaluation

THE EFFICACY OF SOCIAL WORK PRACTICE INTERVENTIONS, terminations, evaluations, and follow-up with groups stems from effective engagement and assessment. The middle and ending phases of group practice—the interventions, terminations, and evaluations—are viewed as the stages in which the work is done (Toseland & Horton, 2013). Terminations and evaluations are complex because of the dual focus on both the individual and the group.

To complete our exploration of social work practice with groups, this chapter follows the group experience from the intervention process through the termination, evaluation, and follow-up phases. We will focus on theoretical frameworks and models for group interventions and look at the social work behaviors you need to intervene effectively with groups. In Chapter 8, we followed three vignettes involving residents of the Riverton community through the engagement, assessment, and planning process. The exploration will continue in this chapter with a focus on intervention, termination, and evaluation.

Residents of the Riverton community (see case at www.routledgesw.com/static-cases/) have concerns about the impact of alcohol consumption on the community's residents and businesses, particularly on the children and youth who live in the neighborhood. The following groups have been formed to address residents' concerns:

- *Riverton Against Youth Drinking (RAYD)—a voluntary task group of residents and professionals who are developing activities and options for the community's youth as alternatives to substance use.*
- *Riverton Children's Grief Support Group—a support group facilitated by the Community Service Agency for children who have lost a family member to drug- or alcohol-related death in Riverton or elsewhere; and*
- *Riverton Mental Health Center Groups for Persons with Co-occurring Diagnoses—a therapeutic treatment group for persons who are experiencing substance abuse and mental health challenges.*

DOI: 10.4324/9781003301264-9

Key Questions for Chapter 9

1. What practice competencies do I need to intervene, terminate, and evaluate with each of the groups?
2. How can I use evidence to practice research-informed practice and practice-informed research to guide the evaluation of a group I am facilitating?
3. What is the appropriate response for a social worker leading a group if one group member violates the confidentiality of another member of the group?
4. What is the distinction between the appropriate social worker role in facilitating a self-help support group intervention and a clinical or treatment group?

INTERFACE: SOCIAL JUSTICE, DIVERSITY, AND HUMAN RIGHTS

Social work with groups is consistent with the profession's commitment to social justice, diversity, equity, and inclusion, anti-oppressive practice, and human rights concerns. As discussed elsewhere in this book, much of social injustice is rooted in exclusion—from resources, opportunities, respect, and supports. Ortega and Garvin (2019) offer a set of core practice principles to guide social workers working with groups (Ortega & Garvin, 2019):

1. The group's goals and purpose must be inclusive of social justice goals of the participants and host context in which they develop and perform.
2. Member relevance including unique intersectional social identities, needs, and experiences of each of its members both within and outside the group are recognized, appreciated, and valued.
3. The group's norms must support socially just participation.
4. Conflict regarding social differences should be resolved in the group.
5. The group worker facilitates and supports each member's contribution.
6. Group processes must consider whether issues are conceptualized and understood within a social justice framework through how language is being used, and the ways people are interacting and supporting each other; also, power, authority, and conflict resolution in a group must consider each member's intersectional social identities and their impact on participation.
7. Practice dimensions, as a whole, must consistently demonstrate and adhere to socially just knowledge and skills. (p. 6)

Diverse groups reflect the world in which most people live, but not all individuals feel comfortable or safe taking personal risks around others who are different from them in some way meaningful to them, or with others whose reasons for joining the group are different from their own. In addition to using research on group diversity to inform and guide interventions,

social workers must commit to the goal of facilitating a culturally responsive group. To achieve this goal, the social worker can regularly consider their own assumptions and beliefs and engage in critical self-reflection and be willing to be open and develop new perspectives (Ortega & Garvin, 2019). Social workers must also factor in their prior life and professional experience and the preferences of the group's members without allowing those personal considerations to drive group formation decisions.

Group work practice brings people together in meaningful ways that can serve as a forum for increasing understanding, appreciation, and respect for others. In short, whether group membership is homogeneous or heterogeneous, the experience can reduce the effects of exclusion and the injustices associated with feelings of marginalization. When working with groups, you can identify, establish, articulate, and mediate the rights and needs of group members. Viewing group intervention as reinforcing human rights can further integrate human rights practice into the profession.

Approaching group work with a focus on social justice requires a commitment to learning about and embracing conceptual foundations. As the social worker's role will involve helping group members navigate between their various, intersecting worlds, the facilitator must creatively and respectfully support the group by integrating culturally responsive content and resources (Marsiglia et al., 2021).

Consider the potential social justice issues that a social worker might encounter with the RAYD group. While most persons in the group and the community likely support activities to decrease youths' use of alcohol and drugs, there may be conflict regarding the source of funding of the activities. One perspective is that the funds should be raised from the community by RAYD, while another perspective is that the funds should be donated by local government, and yet a third perspective is that funds should be jointly provided from public and private funds. As Riverton is not a wealthy community, fundraising from either source will be challenging and create potential inequities between the youth of Riverton and other, more affluent, communities. The leader's role is to work with the group to achieve goals that are consistent with the realities of the external environment, recognize and integrate cultural issues into the discussions, and ensure that all members have an equal voice while honoring the group members' right to self-determination. In a group intervention, the leader's role is to balance potential tensions between the individual and the group's right to self-determination (Barsky & Northen, 2017). Once goals are established, the social worker can also advocate with and for the group to secure funding and support for the projects.

THEORETICAL APPROACHES TO INTERVENING WITH GROUPS

Just as there are many theoretical models for social work intervention with individuals and families, there are well-developed theoretical approaches related to group interventions, processes, skills, and ending points. Whether social workers subscribe to a specific theoretical perspective or a combination of frameworks, selecting those that are evidence-based is critical to having confidence that the approach can guide the development of the intervention (Macgowan & Hanbidge, 2022b).

In this section, we will continue our examination of theory-driven approaches to group practice. Following an overview of theoretical applications to group interventions, we will explore several classic, contemporary, and developmental models. Later, we will look at intervention skills, examples of current groups, and, finally, contemporary innovations in group work.

Strengths and Empowerment Perspectives on Group Intervention

This book is grounded in the premise that social workers should approach practice with groups from a strengths orientation. A strengths approach can affirm and motivate the individual's change process through a focus on "possibilities versus problems." The strengths perspective helps identify and integrate individual members' strengths into strengths for the whole group. For example, within the intervention itself, the social worker can build on individual members' strengths to develop both individual and group goals. Individual strengths can serve as models when group members share ideas and resources.

From the perspective of social work practice with groups, there are multiple opportunities to work with the Stone family of the Brickville neighborhood (www.routledgesw.com/interactive-cases/), including: (1) Virginia Stone, who is a caregiver for her mother and who may benefit from participation in a support group for caregivers of older adults; (2) Virginia's son, David, a participant in the Brickville Community Development Corporation's Youth Leadership Program (YLP) who is developing his leadership skills by serving as the Chair of the youth-led Committee for Healthy Teens; (3) Virginia's two granddaughters, Tiffany and Suzanna, who are the children of an incarcerated parent and are having behavioral and academic challenges in school that might be addressed in group work; and (4) the trauma of the tragic fire 20 years ago and the way that the family's sense of racial bias by the fire and police departments has been reignited by incidents that have occurred across the United States from which such groups as Black Lives Matter have emerged. For example, group members who have experienced multiple losses in their lives (Virginia Stone from Brickville, for instance) and continue to remain strong can serve as role models for other group members. In applying strengths-based group practice principles to potential group interventions with members of the Stone family, consider the following (Malekof, 2017):

- *Form groups based on members' felt needs and wants.* If Virginia Stone is in a caregiver support group you facilitate, it is critical that each member identify and explore their caregiving-related needs and wants, with the group providing support and suggestions—needs and wants may be common but also unique.

- *Structure groups to welcome the whole person (not just the troubled parts).* While all areas of one's life intersect, Virginia is more than a caregiver and deserves the opportunity to discuss and seek support for other areas of her life.

- *Integrate verbal and nonverbal activities.* Caregivers of older adults can benefit from sharing experiences, resources, and caregiving strategies, but can also enhance their well-being from self-reflection (e.g., journaling), social events with other caregivers, and respite care for their family member.

- *Decentralize authority and turn over control to group members.* Virginia and the other caregivers should identify issues and topics to be addressed.

- *Develop alliances with relevant other people in group members' lives.* A focus of the support group discussions may help caregivers to identify additional support resources inside and outside their families and communities.

- *Maintain a dual focus on individual change and social reform.* Because caregivers know firsthand the impact of policy decisions on their lives, many support groups choose to engage in advocacy work to inform and influence policy decisions.

- *Understand and respect group development as a key to promoting change.* As caregivers will be at different phases of the caregiving process, bring different life experiences and resources to the experience, and have different needs, the facilitator must balance individual and group development needs. (pp. 258–267)

A strengths-based perspective integrates easily with other theoretically driven intervention approaches, such as the empowerment perspective. Arising from an ecological perspective, empowerment-focused group interventions build on the tenets of the strengths-based perspective as the social worker emphasizes the members' capacity to feel empowered to make choices and advocate for their situation (Zastrow & Hessenauer, 2019). In practicing from a strengths-based, empowerment perspective, the social worker helps to establish an environment in which they support the members, and the members support one another while also making requests of others for their support (Gitterman et al., 2021).

In empowerment groups, joining a group can itself support the personal and interpersonal dimensions as well as the empowerment felt from helping and receiving help from other members. Critical analysis of the policy environment and individuals' participation in change efforts is also a way for group members to experience empowerment. Regardless of the type of group or focus of a group, empowerment is achieved when the group members share a vision for the process and decision-making process as collaborative through the life of the group (Ortega & Garvin, 2019).

With empowerment viewed as both a goal and a process in which individuals are valued by their peers through commonality, the social worker's role is to work with group members, know resources and sources of power, and support the group toward a sense of empowerment (Lee & Hudson, 2017). The social worker is a "co-activist," working with the group to achieve their goals. Such an approach works with many types of group interventions, including social goals and reciprocal mutual aid groups. Empowerment is aimed at enhancing members' sense of autonomy, mastery, and self-efficacy (Gitterman et al., 2021); however, the members need to have trust in the group process, the social worker, and the other members (Ortega & Garvin, 2019).

Recall Lakeisha's situation from Chapter 1: Lakeisha experienced intimate partner violence, and, after working with a social worker individually, she joined an empowerment group with other women who had been in violent relationships. This group and the social worker supported Lakeisha's needs for esteem and dignity to replace her perceived lack of power and worth; offered her the opportunity to identify her strengths (e.g., seeking help and protecting her children), options which provided hope, and action steps that enabled her to develop a plan for the next chapter of her life (Gitterman et al., 2021). An empowerment-focused group experience like Lakeisha's emphasizes and builds on the members' resilience. To promote member resilience, you can point out their commonalities and that positive change can emerge from crisis and that growth can come from their support of one another (Gitterman & Knight, 2016).

Narrative Theory and Group Interventions

Building on strengths- and empowerment-focused engagement and assessment processes, a narrative approach to intervening with groups emphasizes not only collaboration between the client and social worker, but also collaboration among group members. A narrative-oriented group intervention requires the social worker and group members to listen to each member's voice and to aid in the deconstruction and subsequent reconstruction of the individual or group "story" (i.e., their experience through their own perspective). Stories can be those of the individual member and the group. Reshaping individual or group perceptions can provide a basis for setting a plan in motion for members to achieve the outcome the group members desire. Group members can then work together to brainstorm and process members' motivations, options, and behaviors.

One of the hallmarks of the narrative approach is the use of witness groups and community supports. The social worker calls people together into **witness groups** to "witness" discussions between the social worker and the client and/or among group members. In the case of a group intervention, group members serve as witnesses to their own discussions. As group members share their best hopes for themselves and the group, discuss exceptions to problems, and set specific goals, they are also listening to other group members engage in the same process and providing feedback at the same time—these interactions help to shift the focus from the problems that interfered with their lives to their competencies (Metcalf, 2017). Such feedback can include questions, observations, and interpretations. The individual receiving feedback may then ask questions and respond. This process can help clients develop an alternative approach to their current dilemma or concern.

Using "insider" knowledge (i.e., hearing from others with similar life experiences) is a staple of the narrative approach. Group interventions are an opportunity to use this practice strategy, particularly if group members share similar life experiences and are at different phases of those experiences. For example, Metcalf (2017) describes how a facilitator used a narrative approach with clients in a residential treatment program. Using narrative strategies, the facilitator worked with staff and group members to shift focus away from pathology to viewing the residents as being competent experts on their lives who have experienced an interruption in their lives due to a problem. Group members were involved in all planning and encouraged to develop an "exceptions" focus (i.e., when the problem did not control their lives) (Metcalf, 2017). Understanding the beliefs that underpin behavior promotes assuming responsibility for one's choices. While understanding beliefs is important, narrative-focused group interventions do not emphasize dwelling on past situations themselves, but instead emphasize constructing a future with the help of the group (Metcalf, 2017). As noted in Chapter 8, narrative approaches are also well suited to many other theoretical frameworks.

Solution-Focused Group Interventions

Solution-focused interventions with groups are similar to family interventions in that they require the same knowledge and skills. A solution-focused group intervention positions the social worker in a not knowing stance which enables them to collaborate with the group members so the focus can be on member strengths and resiliency (Franklin et al., 2022a). During the beginning phases of solution-focused group work (discussed in Chapter 8), the facilitator asks each group member to articulate preferred realities (i.e., miracle questions), and the steps they believe are needed to reach the desired state (de Shazer et al., 2021). When you develop a solution-focused intervention plan, you can ask clients to reconsider the "miracle," "exceptions," and "scaling" questions to solidify the plan for change. While you pose these questions to individual group members, the entire group can contribute to the development, implementation, and evaluation of individual change plans, and they can continue to be a resource throughout the change process, presenting their own questions, observations, and experiences. Once the plan is developed and under way, you can monitor members' progress by asking group members to describe the changes they experience (i.e., "What's better?").

Solution-focused approaches can be used in conjunction with other approaches (e.g., empowerment and narrative approaches) to enhance the effectiveness and accountability of interventions. The solution-focused group intervention is well suited for a variety of client populations and settings. With its emphasis on positive changes in the client's life and client-developed individualized treatment plans, this intervention has reaped promising outcomes with groups across the life span (Bolton et al., 2017). The integration of solution-focused group interventions with adolescents and children in school settings shows promise. Serving in roles such as coach, facilitator, and/or mental health therapist, the social worker works with students to build solutions based on the students' strengths (Franklin et al., 2022a). Solution-focused approaches are well suited for the school setting as they show positive outcomes when addressing internalizing, interpersonal, and academic issues, particularly in the area of drop-out prevention challenges (Franklin et al., 2022a).

Developmental Models

One of the classic theoretical perspectives on group work, the developmental model assumes that group members (individually and collectively) grow and change in semi-predictable ways as the group process unfolds. This assumption does not mean groups go through rigid progressions but rather that group relationships ripen. Members are perhaps ambivalent about joining the group at the beginning. They then jockey for position within the group, grow closer through the work of the group, establish differences from one another, and separate at the group's ending. This perspective reflects the idea of stages (or phases) and has been influential in contemporary group work.

Developmental models are still the norm in many practice contexts. They are frequently useful in alerting the social worker to possible dynamics, gauging what is happening, and thinking about how to intervene. We now examine one type of developmental model: the Boston Model.

Boston Model First developed in the 1960s at Boston University's School of Social Work, the Boston Model outlines five stages of group development that are still applicable in contemporary group practice (Garland et al., 1965):

- During *preaffiliation*, members may feel ambivalence or reservations about joining the group, but also excitement and eagerness. For example, someone joining a support group for persons diagnosed with an illness may be eager to connect with others who have a similar experience. The thought of joining a group may evoke ambivalence as the group is unfamiliar to them. In those instances, the social worker can emphasize supportiveness, trust, and exploration (Zastrow & Hessenauer, 2019).

- In the *power and control* stage, members engage in establishing norms for themselves and the group which can sometimes result in efforts to seek control of the group which can create a sense of dissatisfaction which leads to dropouts (highest during this phase of the group) Zastrow and Hessenauer (2019). For example, in the beginning stage of a support group for individuals who share a diagnosis, members who are further along in their illness, treatment, or recovery may perceive themselves as having more status and influence than those who are recently diagnosed, leaving the newcomers questioning whether the group will be helpful to them. Should a power and control struggle evolve, the social worker can: (1) help members understand the events that are occurring; (2) provide support during discomfort and uncertainty; and (3) establish/re-establish norms that can move the group through this phase (Zastrow & Hessenauer, 2019, p. 19).

- *Intimacy* occurs when group members, having worked through their power issues, become closely connected; they may seem more homogeneous at this stage than at any other time in the group. Having processed the issues of power and control, they can begin to support each other around their common life experiences. Members often share coping strategies and develop relationships outside of the group sessions to help each other through crises. This third stage of work is the time when members feel safe and supported enough to begin the change process they hoped the group could offer (Zastrow & Hessenauer, 2019).

- During the continued "work" phase (*differentiation*), members feel they are safe enough to express and value the differences among themselves and the social worker; the homogeneity of the former phase matures into a respect for difference. In this phase, members of an illness support group may become comfortable enough to confront one another on differences of opinion, coping behaviors, or lack of compliance with group norms. Such confrontations can occur successfully only when members have reached a point of mutual respect, intimacy, and cohesion.

- In *separation*, members begin to withdraw from the group in anticipation of its ending. Members of an illness support group may separate as they finish treatment, recover, or learn that their illness is terminal. In situations in which separations are not positive, the social worker can discuss response strategies with the group.

Although the creators of the Boston Model propose a general progression through these stages, they do not assume that progress occurs as a linear sequence. There are likely to be points in the life of a group at which one or more members seem to loop back to the behavior typical of a previous stage or jump ahead to another one.

> *Returning to the Riverton group for persons with co-occurring disorders, members may feel anxious about joining a group as well as confronting their substance use (preaffiliation), question that a group can actually help them as they struggle with two powerful illnesses (power and control), then begin to experience validation and connection to others when they learn that others share their experiences of self-medicating with substances to allay the symptoms of mental illness and fears that they cannot possibly ever feel better (intimacy). Following the intimacy phase, the members begin to see positive changes in relating to others inside and outside the group and to experience improved mood and self-esteem. When the ending of the group is drawing close, members may begin to withdraw out of fear of losing the newly formed support system.*

Many valid theories and perspectives can guide group interventions. Each social worker must determine the theoretical perspective that is most

compatible with their philosophy and professional and personal value systems, given agency structures, guidelines, and funding sources. Once a practitioner identifies one or more perspectives with which they are comfortable, that practitioner must develop competency in the chosen approach(es). Regardless of which theory you choose, it is essential that you demonstrate competent behaviors.

CONTEMPORARY TRENDS AND SKILLS FOR THE MIDDLE PHASE OF GROUP WORK: INTERVENTION

In the middle phase of the group experience, the social worker and the group move into a pattern of interaction that enhances cohesion and "oneness" (Zastrow & Hessenauer, 2019). The primary function of the intervention phase of group work is to carry out the goals established during the assessment phase. The *Standards for Social Work Practice with Groups* (IASWG, 2015) provides guidelines for organizing this phase and the leader's responsibilities:

1 *Support progress toward individual and group goals:* Having established individual and group goals in the assessment phase, members can develop and implement a plan to accomplish the goals. Social workers must be attentive to the potential need to renegotiate goals during this phase of work.
2 *Attend to group dynamics and processes:* Social workers must be vigilant in their observations of group dynamics and processes. As group members become familiar with one another, they may feel more confident confronting one another, which can create conflict within the group. Moreo-

ver, social workers must be mindful of alliances that form within the group and outside the group and of the impact of those relationships on individual and group functioning.

3   *Use evidence-based group practices and resources inside and outside the group:* As the work phase progresses, social workers should be aware of and have access to resources that may be helpful to group members.

Examining the literature for evidence-based group interventions can help your group practice and determine the approach that will best serve your clients' needs and goals. Group work that is informed by both quantitative and qualitative evidence can be used to guide your selection of group interventions. The primary sources of evidence for use in group interventions includes: (1) empirically supported group interventions, processes, and structures; (2) evidence-supported guidelines; and (3) practice evaluations (Macgowan & Hanbidge, 2022a).

Using specific criteria for determining the strength of the evidence, evidence-based group practice enhances accountability, enables social workers to improve practice competencies using empirically validated tools and research outcomes, and bolsters the efficacy of the group intervention. Exhibit 9.1 outlines four stages of an evidence-based approach to implementing and evaluating a group intervention.

With the recent and rapidly expanding use of technology in social work practice, the profession must look both to the evidence and to our ethical standards to determine the best practices for integrating technology into group interventions. As highlighted in the Grand Challenge for Social Work, *Practice Innovation Through Technology in the Digital Age: A Grand Challenge for Social Work* (Berzin et al., 2015), the profession is well positioned to develop evidence for effective use of technology in practice. Technology has many potential uses in working with groups. For example, a group intervention for persons experiencing loneliness and social isolation can include sharing of favorite music, virtual tours of museums, group exercise during the group itself. In using technology-mediated strategies, developing techniques to monitor group dynamics and individual group experiences is critical since there are no face-to-face interactions.

EXHIBIT 9.1

Considerations for Evidence-Based Group Work

When reviewing the research on approaches to group interventions, consider the following questions:

1   Develop answerable questions.
2   Search for evidence to support interventions with your target group.
3   Review evidence for rigor, impact, and applicability.
4   Apply the evidence to determine its relevance and appropriateness for your group, particularly the diverse aspects of your group. Conduct a practice evaluation to determine if outcomes were successful based on goals.

Source: Macgowan & Hanbidge, 2022b, p. 661

Examples of Social Work Group Interventions

As we discussed in Chapter 8, practitioners often work within four types of groups: task groups, social goals groups, reciprocal groups (including psycho-educational groups and support groups), and remedial groups. These groups often have overlapping outcomes. For example, consider the earlier example of Virginia Stone, who is a caregiver for her mother. She can join a caregiver support group that promotes mutual aid among members. She could join a psychoeducational group for caregivers that provides both mutual aid and education related to caring for an older adult. A therapy group might help Virginia to learn coping strategies to address the depression she is experiencing. If she joined a caregiver-formed social goals group, she would learn about policies that impact caregivers and those they care for and possibly become an advocate for legislative change. Each of these groups addresses some aspect of social justice, diversity, or human rights. Following are three examples of social work group interventions that have applicability in one or more of the four groups.

Motivational Interviewing Groups Chapters 5 and 7 discussed motivational interviewing (MI) in the context of working with individuals and families. MI is also useful in a group setting, where it is known as ***group motivational interviewing (GMI)***. Often used in substance use disorder treatment groups, GMI uses the same general principles in groups as with individuals and families (i.e., collaboration, acceptance, compassion, and evocation) (Lynch et al., 2017). MI with groups requires a dual focus on the group and the individuals but should not be sequential individual sessions within the group meeting (Lynch et al., 2017). MI scholars Miller and Rollnick (2013) support the use of MI with a range of group interventions, but they offer two cautionary notes: (1) the group leader should be competent in the facilitation of MI with individuals before attempting to incorporate it into a group experience, and (2) due to the larger number of participants, there will be fewer opportunities for change talk, which may result in less predictable outcomes. Facilitator roles and skills include (Lynch et al., 2017):

1. introducing the spirit of MI at the first meeting and periodically throughout the group, particularly if new members join.
2. anticipating and normalizing members' ambivalence about change.
3. engaging in and modeling listening and supportiveness, enabling members to decide the best course of action for themselves.
4. addressing behaviors that are not consistent with MI (e.g., advising and criticizing), instead offering reflective statements and summaries to highlight general themes, provide affirmations, invite the sharing of similar experiences, and maximize change talk.

With its emphasis on change, non-confrontational interactions, and a future orientation, MI in groups can be a strategy for inclusion in client groups as well as social goals groups.

Intergroup Dialogue (IGD) and Social Justice Developed as a small group intervention, ***intergroup dialogue (IDG)*** is a "sustained face-to-face contact between people from social identity groups with a history of tension between them (e.g., persons of color and White people) (Frantell et al., 2019, p. 655). Through multi-week, semi-structured sessions, IGD strives to cultivate relationships between an equal number of participants from each group while also promoting critical consciousness and enhancing capacities for promoting social justice (Frantell et al., 2019). The group sessions evolve through four stages of dialogue: (1) form and build relationships; (2) explore member commonalities and differences related to social identity; (3) practice dialoguing by addressing controversial topics; and (4) prepare for and take action (Varghese, 2020). Co-facilitators that represent the two groups assume the following roles ((Varghese, 2020):

- Reflect on your own social identities and locate yourself within them.
- Demonstrate dialoguing as opposed to debating.
- Ensure that all members have an opportunity to share their perspectives.
- Know your own triggers and be prepared to address them before and during the intervention.
- Step outside of yourself to facilitate the group, specifically, work to create an environment in which uncomfortable issues can be safely and authentically discussed.
- Monitor and respond to group needs, dynamics, and member roles as they relate to social identities.

IGD's focus on exploring difficult conversations related to multicultural and social justice issues makes it well suited for use in all four models presented here as it allows for self- and group exploration and evaluation.

Narrative-Focused Practice With Groups With its focus on reconstructing a new story and identity, a narrative approach is a strategy to consider for groups addressing past trauma, child sexual abuse in particular (Aponte & Patrick, 2017). The group can serve as a safe, supportive environment in which the members can retell their stories and author a new story and identity that is separate (externalized) from the member as a person (Aponte & Patrick, 2017). As reciprocal and remedial groups often address trauma, a narrative approach can enable the members to serve as the witness group for the individual members in which the new story is shared. When working with groups in which members have experienced oppression and marginalization, a narrative approach can be an approach to consider as it can address issues of social justice. Facilitators invite members to share their stories of injustices that have influenced their lives and with the support of other members, those narratives can be challenged and replaced with new stories (Ortega & Garvin, 2019). These new stories are viewed as changeable and action strategies to bring them to life are created (Ortega & Garvin, 2019).

The examples provided here present a small sampling of the types of group interventions available to social workers. Identifying the intervention approach, format, and structure that best fit your goals for working with groups is the key issue to consider whether you are developing a task, remedial, reciprocal, or social goals group.

Social Work Skills and Strategies for Group Interventions

Many of the generalist practice roles and skills that social workers use in individual and family interventions are applicable to and vital for group work interventions. As in working at all levels of social work practice, social workers must consider the social justice implications of their work with groups. Cultural humility is a key component of facilitating a group with an anti-oppressive approach as it enables both facilitators and members to learn new information to promote mutual support and can dispel myths regarding differences and similarities (Ortega & Garvin, 2019). Exhibit 9.2 highlights areas of social justice that that are included in the facilitator role.

As you work to maintain a group-centered focus during an intervention, you will find that listening, supporting, and empathizing are as important in group work as they are in work with individuals and families. All effective

EXHIBIT 9.2

Group Facilitation Through a Social Justice Lens

1. *Learner*: Being open to gaining new knowledge from the members, acknowledging limitations of your own knowledge, and demonstrating and promoting cultural humility.
2. *Teacher*: Sharing relevant information and knowledge.
3. *Collaborator:* Show members that you are inclusive, tolerant, and accepting of them in times of success as well as failure.
4. *Facilitator*: Encouraging interactive group dynamics, decision-making, focus, and mutual support.
5. *Animator*: Providing socioemotional support while maintaining awareness of the presence and influence of power and privilege.
6. *Mediator*: Reconciling differences through compromise and alliance building.
7. *Advocate*: Support members through words, behaviors, and activities to work toward awareness and change in discriminatory and oppressive situations.
8. *Negotiator*: Extending the mediator role to include negotiating solutions and outcomes with and for members.
9. *Researcher*: Promoting ongoing reflection, assessment, and evaluation to guide group process toward desired goals and outcomes.
10. *"Bricoleur"*: Empowering members to use adaptive and transformative strategies to address individual and group challenges.

Source: Adapted from Ortega & Garvin, 2019, p. 76.

social work interventions make use of the social worker's ability to interact competently with clients with strengths-based and biopsychosocial-spiritual perspectives. Within those interactions, the social worker and group members may fulfill an array of potential roles. This section will focus on the role of the social worker during the intervention, termination, and evaluation phases of group work along with group member roles.

Social Worker Roles While the social worker's primary role is to provide leadership for the group, the type, format, and goals of the group determine the specific role the social worker plays. While much of the focus for the social worker is to trust in the group process and help the group support and collaborate with one another, you must also be comfortable addressing discomfort and conflict (Greif et al., 2017). During the middle (work) phase of the intervention, social work roles focus on helping the group make progress on individual and group goals and attending to group dynamics. Specific roles may (IASWG, 2015) be to:

1. Reinforce connection between individual concerns/needs and group goals.
2. Assess progress toward individual and group goals.
3. Identify obstacles that interfere with the group and its members' abilities to reach their goals.
4. Assist members in problem-solving, making decisions, and evaluating potential outcomes.
5. Summarize sessions and plan next steps with the group.
6. Support members to develop a system of mutual aid.
7. Clarify and interpret communication patterns among members, between members and worker, and between group and outside systems, and help members perceive verbal and nonverbal communication.
8. Develop, model, and encourage honest communication and feedback among members and between members and worker.
9. Review group values and norms and help members make connections with other group members.
10. Assist members to identify and articulate feelings.
11. Help members mediate conflict within the group.
12. Use tools of empowerment to assist members to develop "ownership" of the group. (pp. 12–14)

With the multiple roles that social workers play in group practice, having a repertoire of skills is essential to meet the numerous and sometimes conflicting needs of the individuals and the group. Exhibit 9.3 provides a comprehensive list of general skills important for group interventions that are applicable in any group situation, while Exhibit 9.4 highlights skills specific for facilitating task groups and Exhibit 9.5 describes key skills for use in facilitating groups whose members are not voluntary participants in the group.

EXHIBIT 9.3

Knowledge and Skills for Group-Level Interventions

As a social worker, you will use a diverse array of skills when working with groups of any type, including the ability to:

1. Understand your relationship to your agency and the way in which you and your agency fit within the context of the larger community.
2. Understand the flow of group work from beginnings through endings, including the ongoing assessment of and attention to the group's level of cohesion.
3. Conduct group interactions with multicultural awareness and sensitivity.
4. Advocate for individual clients, the group, and your agency.
5. Practice within the ethical guidelines of the profession.
6. Help the group establish adaptive norms.
7. Ensure that self-disclosure is consistent with agency policy and meets the needs of the group (as opposed to your personal needs). Use of self (incorporating your own experiences) can help reflection and role modeling for the group but should be limited.
8. Engage group members in setting individual goals for themselves that are consistent with the group's purpose.
9. Seek feedback from the group.
10. Demonstrate sensitivity to members' perspectives on change.
11. Provide information to members that promotes growth and healing.
12. Admit a lack of knowledge or confusion about an issue.
13. Use activity to promote the group's work and members' goals.
14. Encourage discussion of feelings and experiences.
15. Show positive regard for the expression of feelings and thoughts.
16. Normalize members' feelings.
17. Reach for members' feelings.
18. Partialize presenting problems (i.e., examine and prioritize problems one at a time).
19. Demand work of the group.
20. Use programming effectively and in a timely and appropriate manner.
21. Focus on the here and now.
22. Assist members to resolve conflicts that emerge in the group.
23. Teach the importance of "I" messages.
24. Use national events to teach about human nature and social justice.
25. Monitor change in members.
26. Build and reinforce self-esteem and competence.
27. Remain comfortable with ambivalence and ambiguity.

Source: Adapted from Greif et al., 2017, pp. 37–43.

EXHIBIT 9.4

Effective Methods for Working With Task Groups

While the skills outlined in Exhibit 9.2 are applicable to facilitating a task group, additional skills specific to working with task groups include awareness that:

1. **Silence** can be a useful strategy to display acceptance and interest but also enables others to have a voice.
2. **Mirroring** and reflecting feelings provides an opportunity for reassessment or refocusing the discussion and addressing obstacles.

| EXHIBIT 9.4

Continued | 3 *Exploring, probing, and questioning* with open-ended questions can elicit additional and/or expanded perspectives and thoughts.
4 Providing direction can be useful if used in moderation. **Universalizing** and *connecting points of view* may be more effective strategies to move the discussion forward.
5 *Confrontation*, when used to share a perspective on potential future implications of group decisions, can be helpful to the group.
6 *Support* may be provided in the form of supporting a point of view, the right to express a point of view, a group member, or the way in which the group handled a situation.
7 *Modeling, coaching, and shaping* enables the facilitator to represent a behavior or alternative for the benefit of the group.
8 *Supposals* are using one's imagination to consider possible solutions.
9 *Summarizing, focusing, partializing, sequencing, pacing, and grading* strategies occur when the facilitator provides a recap and/or analysis of the group's discussions to invite clarification and progress toward a decision.
10 *Decentering* can help to re-engage uninvolved members, while *setting limits* can serve to remind members of the group norms and rules for interacting.
11 *Dividing into smaller subgroups* can promote brainstorming strategies and solutions.
12 *Knowledge of the concepts and techniques of parliamentary procedure* can be important.

Source: Ephross et al., 2017, pp. 519–521. |
|---|---|
| EXHIBIT 9.5

Guidelines for Social Workers With Involuntary Groups | Working with groups whose members have not chosen to participate brings challenges and rewards, but requires attention to unique issues, including:
1 Joining and inclusion:
  a Clarify nonnegotiable issues.
  b Support positive choices made to date.
  c Provide general support.
  d Acknowledge self-motivating statements.
  e Address concerns.
  f Link to the group process and to other members.
  g Support inclusion.
  h Stimulate nonthreatening attention to issues.
  i Reframe resistance as ambivalence.
2 Deciding to make a change by assessing with members the costs and benefits of change
3 Supporting planning
4 Emphasizing choice versus confrontation
5 Providing a clear ending to the group, plan for maintenance of change, and addressing of potential relapse responses.

Source: Rooney & Chovanec, 2017, p. 245. |

Group Dynamics Interactions between group members and with the leader are the essence of the group experience. Facilitators engage in ongoing assessment and monitoring of group dynamics (i.e., interactions, communication, and structure) to determine if their leadership is facilitative or debilitative (Ortega & Garvin, 2019). Toseland (2017) categorizes groups dynamics into five areas and offers recommendations for the leaders' role in each:

- *Communication and interaction:*
    - When members are talking with one another, ask for feedback from the recipient of a statement by another member to avoid miscommunication.
    - Observe interaction patterns, including the "maypole" (leader is the center of the group), "round robin" (people take turns speaking), "hot seat" (extended exchange between leader and a member), and "free-floating" (all freely communicate).
    - Help members to expand their personal honesty, and self-awareness, particularly in relation to persons who are different from them.
    - To promote participation by all members, you can point out patterns in member communications.
    - Use "round robins" to encourage quieter members to share.
    - Selectively praise and reinforce members on salient points.
    - Assign roles and tasks to engage members.
    - Direct questions away from group members who monopolize discussions.
- *Interpersonal attraction and cohesion:*
    - Capitalize on the factors that make a group experience appealing for members (e.g., acceptance, approval, consensus, and security).
- *Social integration and influence:*
    - Group norms, roles, and status should be inclusive and empowering for all members.
- *Power and control:*
    - Reflect on your own issues related to power and control so that you can respond appropriately to members' feelings, perceptions, and attitudes during the group.
- *Culture:*
    - While the culture (values, beliefs, customs, and traditions) may be implicit, you can lead the group in exploring these areas to address differences that may exist and promote cohesion.

Leadership Skills Across all group interventions led by social workers, leadership skills are essential and may include (adapted from Brown, 2018; IASWG, 2015):

- Maintaining a *"thinking group"* posture, in which you consider the group as a whole first and as individual members second. This concentration on the whole can require a paradigm shift. For example, you may avoid a prolonged exchange with a single member because that focus would hinder the group's communication.

In the Riverton Children's Grief Support Group, ensuring that you focus equally on each child will serve to keep the children engaged.

- Exhibiting *"balanced leadership,"* in which you encourage the group to have some control over the process and outcome. This leadership can challenge social workers who believe they must have control of the group, or it will become chaotic. If you allow the group to evolve without close attention to process, it *can* become chaotic. Your ability to facilitate depends on factors including group connection, group functioning, and the presence of internal or indigenous leadership (leadership that evolves within the membership). Generally, social workers are more directive in early stages of groups, in groups with members with functional limitations, and in task-oriented groups. As the group progresses, the social worker's role is to gradually retreat and encourage growth in group ownership. The key is to recognize group needs and be flexible with the degree of direct leadership.

While you may be more directive in a children's group such as the Riverton Children's Grief Support Group, it is critical for you to trust the group process and invite the members to provide input.

- *Scanning*, engaging in observation and engagement with all members of the group, is a strategy for maintaining visual observation of all members—the group version of the attending skill.

Children in the Children's Grief Support Group may struggle to remain attentive and engaged for the duration of the group, so your role will be to constantly scan the group to gauge engagement. Having a co-leader can enable one of you to engage, while the other scans the group.

- Maintaining *cohesiveness*, or connectedness, means sustaining a common bond by using "we" language, encouraging rituals (e.g., marking the beginning and end of each meeting in a specific way), and recording the group's progress. Having a healthy balance of cohesion can facilitate a sense of belonging. Development and recording (e.g., through a chart on the wall) of the group's agreed-upon norms or customs contributes to a sense of connection.

Rituals work well in children's groups like the Children's Grief Support Group as they provide a familiar structure and can be fun, particularly when the children select the rituals.

- *Facilitating change* means assisting group members in progressing toward goals through support, programmatic activities, addressing obstacles, assessing progress, and making new contracts for goal achievement, as needed.

For example, if a goal for the Children's Grief Support Group is to no longer be angry because their loved one died, you can support the members through open discussion of their feelings and asking for their ideas for things they can do to remember their loved one without anger.

- *Promoting the development of mutual aid* may involve a review of group norms, group values, and conflict resolution.

  To maintain consistency, group norms and rules can be reiterated at the beginning of each session of the Children's Group.

Communication Skills Social work practice with groups requires social workers to demonstrate specialized communication skills, including:

- Careful selection of *communication strategies* to be used in your group. If you respond only to members who speak up, you will marginalize or exclude members. On the other hand, if you always go around the group, member by member, some members may feel pressed to contribute, and all will feel a certain amount of routinization. Instead, encourage a respectful balance so that all members have an opportunity to speak without any one member dominating. Alternatively, you may choose to invite all members (especially those members who remain quiet) to participate and ask if others in the group share the speaker's thoughts or feelings.

  In the Children's Grief Support Group, using diverse strategies to ensure all members participate is essential as each child may be grieving differently. For example, you can periodically remind members that there are many ways to experience loss and the norms they agreed upon and emphasize the group's accomplishments and history when appropriate.

- *Responding empathetically.* This is a critical skill in the group intervention that requires you to focus on the person speaking, restrict questioning to only those areas that need clarification, allow the group member to finish speaking, and resist the temptation to provide answers to client situations.

  With children such as those in the Children's Group, enthusiasm to contribute may require you (and a co-leader) to remind them of the rules of the group.

- *Redirecting questions* and concerns away from you back to the group or to individual members, which can be challenging. Some members will continue to address you as the source of authority or others may complain about other members through a third party (often you). In both situations, you can redirect the message. Exhibit 9.6 provides an example of redirection within a group.

  With the Children's Group your goal is to facilitate direct, constructive communication within the group and its supporting environment.

- *Establishing consensus and difference* by inviting agreement and disagreement on issues. A group member who has been quiet may find it challenging to express dissent when a group approves something heartily. Early feelings of connectedness and strong group bonds can make that dissent even harder. Later, as the group matures, expressions of difference may be easier, but you should continue to support difference and encourage others' capacities to respond.

  Monitoring the members of the Children's Group who are quiet is an important area for your (or your co-leader's) focus as you can assess their feelings if they are not engaging.

- *Exercising silence.* If the facilitator is talking, members cannot, so it is important that the facilitator work on exercising silence. The social worker's well-placed silence encourages the group to engage in the interchange, allowing members' communication patterns to develop.

  Being more directive with a children's group such as the Children's Grief Support Group can be an easy pattern to slip into, but one that should be avoided as the group purpose is to support the children in their grieving process.

Problem-Solving Skills Social work practice with groups requires social workers to demonstrate a variety of leadership problem-solving skills over the lifetime of the group. Problem-solving does not, however, mean giving advice or "fixing" the problem. Instead, there are several strategies that can be useful:

- *Connecting progress to goals* by summarizing progress, identifying options, prioritizing decisions, mediating conflicts, confronting lack of progress, and weighing potential outcomes are skills and activities that a social worker employs in problem-solving during the intervention phase of group work. On occasion, the social worker may have to negotiate an amended contract with individual members or

---

EXHIBIT 9.6

When Redirection Is Needed in Group Work

As the facilitator, you can use the following to redirect a group session in which one member appears to be leading the group away from its goal.

A member asks if visitors can attend a group meeting. Because the group has not addressed the issue before, you submit the question to the full membership:

"How do others see this question?" or "How do you as a group want to handle this?"

You may invite quieter members to participate and attempt to soften the messages of louder voices.

A second scenario involves one member of the group complaining about another member. In this scenario, you may simply say:

"Why don't you tell Bernard that?" or "I don't think you need my help talking to Kate about that."

the entire group or revise the discussion topics for future meetings. In renegotiating with the group, address the issue in a timely way, be open and clear, and invite the group's input.

Continuing with the Children's Grief Support Group, connecting the children's progress individually and as a group to their goals can be achieved by summarizing for each member the progress that you have observed. For the group, you might comment, for instance, on the increased mutual supportiveness that you have noticed them providing to one another.

- In problem-solving with groups, it is important that the social worker participate in *locating resources to benefit group members*. This involves working with members to identify resources, including natural assets (e.g., friends, family, or neighbors) into the helping network, and emphasizing the connections between the group and community. Engaging in a discussion among members early in the process conveys the expectation that the group has the ability and responsibility to deal with its own issues. Identifying resources outside the group expands the network for all members and supports the interdependence between members, groups, and the environment. Another potential resource for group members can be to incorporate activities in which the members can engage, including outside speakers, videos, group exercises, or journaling.

Within the Children's Grief Support Group, you may point out that the group members have become a resource for one another. You can ask the members to highlight for the group those resources in and outside the group that have been helpful to them. Should resources outside the group be needed, this discussion can become a focus of future sessions in which you and the group can brainstorm possibilities.

- *Reframing* is a problem-solving strategy that can be helpful to address challenging group member behaviors (e.g., scapegoating of one member by the others) and can be facilitated by: (1) asking members to clarify the meaning of their words and inviting members' feedback; (2) observing the inconsistency between verbal and nonverbal communication; and (3) clarifying your own communication and asking for feedback (Knight, 2017b, p. 30).

At the check-in which occurs at the beginning of each group, one member consistently states that they have no feelings about the loss that brought them to the Grief Group. You note, however, that this child does not make eye contact with the other members or you, often appears bored or angry, and you are certain you have noticed them tearing up on a few occasions. You might point out these inconsistencies and invite the child to share their thoughts.

- While *responding to conflict* within the group can be challenging, it is normal within group practice and should not be ignored. Addressing conflict is an ethical obligation and it can be addressed by reframing, de-emphasizing blame, identifying commonalities, and helping members to listen and validate (Barsky, 2017). If conflict occurs between group members or with the facilitator, members expect that you will resolve the situation (Toseland, 2017). You can stop the discussion and help the members process what they believe may be happening as a strategy for modeling appropriate conflict resolution that does not resort to aggression, violence, or unresolved negative feelings (Greif et al., 2017).

When a disagreement breaks out in the Children's Grief Support Group, you learn that some members feel that a sub-group that has formed within the group is being judgmental of those not in the "clique." You may respond by being open to hearing all perspectives, inviting all members of the group to share their thoughts, and mediating cooperative, rather than competitive solutions, being sure to explore if there are issues below the surface that may be fueling the conflict (Ortega & Garvin, 2019).

- The social worker can *make use of the unique characteristics of the group in problem-solving*. A social worker's goal in working with groups is to negotiate the tension between individual members and whole group needs, coming to a compromise that encourages creative enrichment that benefits both the individual and the group. The group must establish an acceptable expression and appreciation for difference.

Part of the group's traditions were to celebrate birthdays. On the eighth meeting, the members were bustling around preparing streamers and searching for birthday candles, giggling about how old Lily was really going to be. Some said she was probably going to be 60, not 12, judging by how glum she had seemed last week about the party they were planning. Lily was late, and when she finally showed up, she looked more miserable than ever. Finally, she blurted out, "I HATE BIRTHDAYS!" in a voice unlike her usual somber tones. The other children were horrified and silent for a moment—almost unheard of in this group. Lily started to cry. Finally, she choked out the story: Her mother had died the night before her birthday two years ago, and she didn't know how to tell the group that before. The very word "birthday" was a terrible reminder. She didn't want to celebrate.

The members seemed to feel sorry and unsure what to do, they liked Lily, but they also wanted to celebrate birthdays in this group. It was an important ritual for them. After a moment, Bettina, whose grandmother came from France, cheerfully volunteered, "Well, let's be trés francais in this group and say we're celebrating our anniversaries! That's what the French call them, the anniversary of birth!" The others responded loudly, hoping their ritual was rescued from certain demise. Lily was silent. She looked up. Finally, she almost smiled and said, "I think that would work." And that was that.

Group Member Roles

Group members bring their unique characteristics and traits to the group experience regardless of the type of group or its purpose, often serving as both learner and teacher. The social worker may experience these qualities as both strengths and challenges. While even strengths can be challenging, the associated behaviors can be reframed and used for positive individual and group outcomes. Group members' personalities and lived experiences shape their behaviors but group norms also influence group roles and interactions (Gitterman et al., 2021). When the roles that members adopt become disruptive or distracting, they can be labelled as resistance, when, in fact, they may be important signals that the group is not meeting their needs. Social workers can encourage appropriate group member interactions by setting expectations from the outset, but individual members' idiosyncrasies may still lead to challenging interactions within the group process. Quick Guide 25 presents a list of behaviors that can have a negative impact on group process with strategies for social workers to use in responding. As a facilitator, you can initiate discussion focused on the interactional and communication styles members possess and the functions those styles serve in their lives.

Individual personalities influence and interact with group dynamics. Competent group practitioners can anticipate these roles and behaviors and be

---

QUICK GUIDE 25 Group Member Roles and Potential Strategies to Address Them

Consider the member(s) who . . .:

a *does not contribute*—members who are silent can be perceived as having power since they are not sharing, but the uncertainty and discomfort that is created can be detrimental to the group. The social worker can explore with the individual and group the reasons for the silence and help the member to view the group as safe and potentially helpful.

b *dominates group sessions*—members who monopolize sessions may be seeking attention and/or feeling anxious about the group. Such behavior may be welcomed by others as they do not have to speak; however, most will eventually become annoyed with the behavior. The social worker can ask the individual and group to explore its meaning and acceptance.

c *is scapegoated by others in the group*—while having a group focus on one person can serve a function, the attention given and received is negative. The social worker asks others to consider how their behaviors undermine the group and helps the group re-focus on a common goal that does not include selecting one person to treat inappropriately.

d *is the indigenous leader*—having a "spokesperson" for the group can be a help and a hindrance as this person provides information but the role may be a source of conflict or burden and mean that others' voices are not heard. The social worker can help the group understand that a leader is not necessary for the success of the group.

e *form subgroups or alliances*—"cliques" can provide identity and safety for those who are involved but are not helpful for the group process. The social worker can supportively focus on the common bonds that join (versus divide) the group.

Source: Adapted from Gitterman et al., 2021.

prepared with an appropriate response. You must exercise caution, however, to ensure that you do not generalize or stereotype group member behaviors, but instead respond to each person as unique. Regardless of the label assigned to a role or behavior, it is important to recognize that the group member is simply aiming to gain self-orientation to the group, in order to find their place within the group, or to a challenge that stems from fear of self-disclosure, feedback, and/or personal responsibility—the behavior becomes a problem only when it disrupts the work (Salazar & Leddick, 2018). Strategies that focus on the behaviors that the members *should* be engaged in can enable you to address the challenging roles and behaviors, including (Salazar & Leddick, 2018):

1 exploring and processing the behaviors with the group to better understand the meaning and origins of the behavior.
2 focusing on the group member's intended roles by encouraging self-disclosure and feedback.
3 engaging the member displaying the challenging behavior by drawing them out, cutting them off, reframing their statements, and giving them permission to engage in the behavior to decrease the resistance to change.
4 helping members to identify the behaviors to one another to promote awareness of the behavior's underlying meanings.

The intervention phase of group practice can be complex and overwhelming for members and facilitators. To maintain forward movement, the social worker continues to promote mutual support, remind (and possibly renegotiate) expectations for participation, and challenge those who are avoiding the issues that brought them to the group (Knight & Gitterman, 2022). This stage is also an important time to monitor the group's cohesiveness, be aware of events in and outside the group that may impact their functioning

> **QUICK GUIDE 26 Summary of Intervention Skills for Social Work Group Practice**
>
> The social worker engaged in the intervention phase of social work practice with groups should:
>
> - be knowledgeable and skilled in group leadership (e.g., logistics and time management).
> - facilitate group communication and group dynamics.
> - be competent with individual and group problem-solving.
> - focus on promoting progress toward group and individual goals.

and progress (e.g., crises, conflicts), while also reminding members of their strengths, particularly those that are improved because of their group experience (Ortega & Garvin, 2019). See Quick Guide 26 for a recap of the skills needed to competently intervene with groups.

CONTEMPORARY TRENDS AND SKILLS FOR THE ENDING PHASES OF GROUP WORK: TERMINATION AND EVALUATION

The social worker's role in termination is to "help members examine their accomplishments, review their experience together, and prepare for the future . . . and express and integrate positive and negative emotion" (Garvin & Galinsky, 2020, p. 8). While the concepts we explored in our discussions of terminating, evaluating, and following up with individuals and families can be applied to work with most clients, there are some additional considerations in social work practice with groups. The intensity of the phases of ending a group and evaluating the work will depend on the group type and purpose.

Group Endings

Social work practice with individual members and/or the group can end in many ways. Essentially, groups end for the entire group either successfully because the time limit and/or goals have been reached or unsuccessfully because goals have not been met or the group is disbanded, or they may continue but end for certain individuals if a member or leader leaves (Zastrow & Hessenauer, 2019). Regardless of the reason for the group's termination, endings evoke a range of responses. Group members may experience positive feelings (e.g., joy), negative feelings (e.g., sadness), or a combination of the two. At termination, the leader may notice that members experience regression, withdrawal, conflicted feelings, sadness, anxiety, denial, and/or avoidance (Chang & Erford, 2018). Responses often depend on the group purpose and length. For example, members of an educational or task group are likely to experience fewer emotional responses than those of a support or treatment group. A group that has met only six times will probably not be as invested as a group that has met for three years. A member's developmental stage and investment in the group can also determine their response.

Negotiating endings with groups is an often-complex endeavor in which the social worker deals with endings on three levels:

- The relationship between group members and the social worker.
- Relationships among group members.
- The structure of the group itself.

The theoretical framework a practitioner uses should guide the termination phase. We now consider endings from each theoretical perspective discussed earlier.

Using the Strengths and Empowerment Approach in Group Endings Integrating strengths and empowerment concepts into the termination phase can enable individual members and the whole group to review progress toward goals and to develop strategies for sustaining change. The social worker can invite each member to review their individual experience in the group, including the strengths they brought to the group process; their status in the beginning, middle, and ending phases; the changes they experienced; and their plans to maintain the change(s). Having individual members engaged in review and reflection provides an opportunity for the social worker and other members to contribute to that individual's experience of the group process. Group members can take advantage of fellow members' reflections for their own review, reflection, and evaluation.

A strengths-based perspective can enable the social worker and group members to reflect on how the group's strengths have evolved. For example, a group strength may be the respectful and supportive way in which members interact. Social workers can provide feedback on the changes they have observed in the group, and group members can reflect on taking part in a strengths-focused experience. Such reflection can empower group members and social workers to integrate this enhanced sense of confidence and competence into the group process.

In situations in which individual or group goals are not realized, the formal ending of a group can still be oriented toward a strengths perspective. One strategy is to have members review the strengths the group had from the outset, the strengths they gained or mobilized during the group, and the strengths members can carry into the future. While group members (and the social worker) may be dismayed at the group's failure to achieve its goals, planning ways in which members can continue to work toward achieving those goals can be empowering.

For example, consider a scenario in which the RAYD group's application to the city was not selected to receive funding. From a strengths-based perspective, how might the group process this setback? As the facilitator, you can ask the group if they see options such as: (1) asking the city agency for feedback to strengthen the proposal; (2) noting that the group collaborated and completed a proposal, which could be re-submitted to the same agency during the next call for proposals or another potential funding organization; or (3) building on the work completed and strategizing about other ways to raise the funds.

Narrative-Focused Group Endings Ritual or ceremonial activities and public acknowledgment of growth and change work well in narrative-focused group terminations that emphasize strengths. Group members and the social worker can collaboratively plan a celebration to recognize the formal ending of the group's work together. Ceremonies enable the members to enrich and solidify their stories by having others external to the process witness and share their thoughts (Baker & Freund, 2018).

Group member feedback on individual testimonials can reinforce members' changes and solidify plans for maintaining change beyond the formal group experience. Social workers can use a process like one they might use with individuals, with group members serving as outsider-witnesses. The definitional ceremony begins with the social worker and group members listening as an individual group member re-authors their work in the group. The witnesses then reflect that re-authored story back to the individual, the individual member responds to the feedback, and the entire group engages in a discussion about the process. This activity can be helpful both as a tool for recognizing individual and group strengths and goal attainment and as a means of evaluating the change process.

Solution-Focused Group Endings Termination of the solution-focused group intervention can be viewed by the social worker and group members as the achievement of the initial and overall goals for the group even if not all members' individual goals were realized. Solution-focused group interventions identify issues and plan and implement a change effort. In group interventions, group members provide opportunities for individual members to process their issues and potential solutions. Recall that solution-focused interventions are grounded in the ongoing use of a series of questions to elicit strengths, thoughts, and feelings regarding change and to develop plans for change. During the termination phase, you can ask members about their individual progress as well as the group progress via scaling progress questions (e.g., "On a scale of 1 to 10, where were you when you joined this group? Where are you now? Where do you need to be to maintain this change when you leave the group?" "How will you know when it is time to leave the group?" "What will be different?") (De Jong, 2015). Group members can provide their own observations of an individual member's change process. Shifting the emphasis from the present to the future can help members perceive themselves as separate from the group and social worker, thus enabling them to view themselves as able to implement and maintain desired changes.

Skills for Social Work Group Endings

Whether endings are planned or unplanned, they can be complex and intense. Social workers need skills that reflect the unique features of ending a group intervention. During the termination phase, social workers emphasize bringing together the different phases of the work to achieve closure for individual group members, the group itself, and for themselves (IASWG, 2015). Endings evoke a range of emotional responses for group members and facilitators. An ending is a transition to the next phase and a focus of this last phase of work can emphasize each person setting and achieving new goals (Zastrow & Hessenauer, 2019). Individual and group reflection during termination is particularly powerful. Group members and social workers need time for closing this chapter of their lives which can include highlighting individual and group work and accomplishments, reflecting on those accomplishments and the group experience, and looking to the future (Teater, 2020).

Ending the Relationship Between Group Members and the Social Worker The end of the relationship between group members and the social worker places particular demands on the social worker. As with social work practice with individuals and families, ending a group should be introduced first session and transparently discussed through the life of the group as it is intended to signify the achievement of goals. Social work skills can be grouped into three distinct areas: (1) preparing for termination—easing the transition and promoting sustained change; (2) discussing the impact of the group experience on the individual, the group, and the group facilitator and reflecting on gains—reflecting on gains made/not made and strategies for sustaining; and (3) preserving group information—verbally and in writing, document group goals, processes, achievements, and referrals/connections in individual and group records (IASWG, 2015). Despite the number of times the social worker discusses the ending of the group, it is not uncommon for some members to say they were never told the group would end—this denial may be their way of communicating a fear of the group no longer existing (Steinberg, 2019). Exhibit 9.7 provides an overview of social work skills used in the termination phase of group interventions.

The social worker's tasks are to help the group end positively and to help members translate their achievements into the "real world" outside the group. Reminiscing about the work of the group, individual/group/worker experiences and feelings can help to elicit feelings about the ending of the group and can help members begin to see themselves outside of the group (Steinberg, 2019).

Social workers also monitor their own responses; after all, they have invested a great deal of effort in facilitating an effective experience, and groups in which significant personal and group changes have occurred can experience more difficult endings as they have developed strong bonds. Recalling the purpose of the group and focusing on the specifics of the process can help social workers balance their response between task and emotion.

EXHIBIT 9.7

Social Worker Skills for Ending Phase of Group Interventions

1. Prepare members for the group's ending in advance.
2. In client groups, help members identify gains and changes that have resulted from their participation in the group. In a task group, ask members what they learned that will be useful to them in other groups.
3. Discuss the impact of the group on external systems (e.g., family, organization, community).
4. Discuss the movement the group has made over time.
5. Identify and discuss direct and indirect signs of members' reactions to ending.
6. Share your feelings about ending with the group.
7. Help members share their feelings about ending with one another and you.
8. Systematically evaluate the achievement of individual and group goals. Routine and systematic evaluation of the group experience can/should occur over time rather than in the ending stage alone.
9. Help members make connections with other agencies and programs as appropriate.
10. Assist members in applying new knowledge and skills to their daily lives.
11. Encourage members to give feedback to you on your role and actions in the group.
12. Help members apply new knowledge and skills to their activities outside the group.
13. Document the group experience for the agency, individual members, and for referrals as needed.

Source: Adapted from IASWG, 2015, pp. 15–16.

Most group members generally accept the ending of their group experience. There may be those, however, who struggle with the pending termination. In addition to the denial response noted previously, other responses can include: (1) regression in which members appear to have lost the new knowledge and skills gained; (2) a mixture of emotions, including anger, rage, sadness, and/or depression; (3) bargaining to continue the group to discuss additional issues; (4) guilt over their words, actions, or perceived lack of success; and (5) "flight"—attendance ceases or becomes erratic (Steinberg, 2019; Zastrow & Hessenauer, 2019).

The responses to ending in groups are like those that occur in individuals and families. The fact that the number of people in the group may multiply those responses can make them feel momentous to you as the social worker. For example, when an entire collective of teens makes it clear, through sudden and orchestrated hostility toward you, that they do not want the experience to end, you can feel the power of the group. In this case, you can view the group's reaction as a function of the process (and perhaps of the group's success), rather than as a focused personal attack.

Ending Relationships Among Group Members Social workers should be prepared for responses that range from denial or flight behaviors to gratification to actual celebration. Some members may not attend meetings specifically dedicated to ending activities. Others may attend but refuse to interact, or they may simply resign themselves to feeling they have been rejected by other members or the social worker. Individuals may become increasingly short-tempered and impatient with other members, as if to negate the importance of their relationship and to render the ending insignificant or even a relief. This behavior may occur among members who have worked the hardest to connect with one other.

In other situations, individual members may question their ability to maintain change without the assistance of the group and social worker. These members sometimes lobby for individual sessions with the worker, a reconstituted "mini group" in which only a few members attend, or that the group meet on their own without the social worker. Some individuals may initiate more intense relationships with other members outside the confines of group meetings, as if to pretend the group is not ending or negate the need for the group.

To anticipate the range of strong responses to the group ending, you can engage in the following preparations (Knight & Gitterman, 2022):

- Routinely reflect on your own feelings about the ending.
- Monitor group members for indirect feelings (e.g., missing sessions or returning to previous discussions).
- Plan for ample time for all to express feelings (including avoidance) and provide regular reminders of the pending end date.

- Validate feelings about endings and the reasons for those feelings.
- Be ready to address and accept the negative feelings with such strategies as:
    - ensuring that you do not offer premature reassurances that can result in power struggles about ending the group.
    - connecting individual and group behaviors and action to the unexpressed feelings.
    - reinforcing your faith in the group members and the group process.
    - encouraging and supporting feelings of anger and sadness by sharing your own feelings about the termination.
    - using celebratory activities to escape the emotionally laden conversations about endings.

One of the most helpful things you can do is to articulate your observations regarding group dynamics, reflecting on your perceptions of their individual and group starting places, work completed, changes made, and goals achieved. Such a reflection can help members examine their own experiences through the lens of another person. On a cautionary note, social workers must be mindful of several potential pitfalls: (1) offering false promises of future contacts is counter to an effective group ending; (2) promoting a "big bash syndrome"—while a celebration of the ending of the group is appropriate, ensure it is not an event that suggests the group will continue; and (3) finding positives and strengths of the group experience is appropriate, but not overstating these if you do not feel your statements are fully truthful (Steinberg, 2019, pp. 219–220).

Staying focused on the group, rather than on individuals, can be challenging, but it is part of negotiating a successful ending.

Recall the Riverton Mental Health Center Group for Persons with Co-occurring Diagnoses. The group was formed as a time-limited group and the ending has arrived. With a heightened emotional impact, which is likely for such a group, endings may elicit an array of responses; therefore, it is critical for the social worker to integrate discussion of endings well in advance of the final meeting to enable the members to process their feelings, celebrate their gains, and gain confidence in their ability to maintain the changes. For those members who wish to or could benefit from additional resources and treatment, you may want to be prepared with suggestions and referrals.

Ending the Group Itself The ending of the group is at once philosophical and technical. On the philosophical level, it requires you to reflect on your feelings about ending this unit of work and this group. How will the experience contribute to your professional growth? What could you have done differently? How will group members benefit from it? If the group has been difficult, you may struggle with feelings of inadequacy or a sense of work left undone. When there is an overall sense that the group went well, you may feel exhilarated by a sense of accomplishment, of having crossed a hurdle, or of entering the realm of the skilled.

On a more practical side, when the group ends, you need to close out records of participation, complete the evaluation process, and terminate logistical arrangements such as space and place. Finally, you need to honor follow-up commitments and make referrals or transfers.

Consider the issues that arise in the following group termination scenario:

A community-based agency that serves new immigrants offers a group for high school students focused on the students' transitions from their country of origin to their new country. The group also has a secondary purpose: it provides an opportunity for the students to practice their English in a safe environment. The group is composed of a multiple of genders, gender identities, and racial and ethnic groups. The social worker facilitating the group has developed their cultural competency through a commitment to learn as much as they can about the students' heritage and traditions, language, cultural rules and norms for gender interactions, and faith traditions as well as committing to practice cultural humility. They interview each student referred to the group and the students' parents/family/guardians so they can be familiar with the student's needs and goals for joining the group.

The social worker has become aware of a potential dilemma. The current members have developed into a cohesive group, particularly around becoming "Americanized" as they adopt the customs of teens in their new country. The time-limited group is scheduled to come to an end, but several parents who are distressed that their children are abandoning their heritages have approached the social worker and have asked them to continue the group for reconnecting the teens to their ethnic and cultural roots. The teens have already planned their "graduation" celebration and appear ready to move on with life outside the group. The social worker is conflicted—they empathize with the parents but believes the group should terminate as planned, in part, because a continued or new group would not fulfill the same purpose as the current group.

Being culturally responsive during the termination is equally as important in the termination stage as it is throughout the engagement, assessment, and intervention processes (Marsiglia et al., 2021). How would you address the cultural issues raised in this situation? What options or alternatives might the social worker in this scenario consider for meeting the needs of both groups?

Endings can and should be a time for reflection and celebration. It is important that all social workers in group practice, particularly those in the early stages of their careers, review the group process as it has impacted their personal and professional growth.

Evaluating Social Work Practice With Groups

Evaluating practice with groups serves the same purposes as evaluating practice with individuals and families, to assess (Macgowan & Hanbidge, 2022b):

1 participant outcomes focused on the individual's reason for participation.
2 group outcomes related to the individual's and leader's experience with the group.
3 process and structure of the group experience from the perspective of cohesion and engagement related to positive outcomes.

Unlike family intervention evaluations that focus exclusively on the unit and individual intervention evaluations that focus solely on the individual, the evaluation of a group intervention encompasses both the individual and the group, thus elevating group evaluations to a higher level of complexity. While reminiscence is an effective strategy for closure, it can also be a form of group evaluation as it provides an opportunity to discuss achievements and transitions (Steinberg, 2019).

As noted, individuals arrive at the group with distinct goals, personalities, needs, and expectations. Often, social workers must consider evaluative strategies within the context of a large, diverse group of individuals who perceive their experiences differently from one another. Social workers must frame an evaluation of any group intervention within the context of the purpose, type, structure, and format of the group. Further complicating group evaluations, social workers must work within the agency or organizational structure in which the group is conducted. Having to address multiple needs with a group of individuals requires practitioners to have a clear and thoughtful approach to evaluation of the group intervention *prior* to the group's first meeting. Regardless of the method(s) used to evaluate the group intervention, it is important for everyone involved to participate in the evaluative process (Garvin & Galinsky, 2020).

To effectively evaluate the group intervention, it is essential to introduce the concept of assessment and evaluation from the preplanning stages and monitor progress throughout the duration of the group. With an aim toward determining if the group intervention was effective and efficient, two models of group evaluation are typically used (Zastrow & Hessenauer, 2019):

- *Process evaluations*: Also known as formative evaluation, this form of evaluation occurs throughout the life of the group with a goal toward improving the group experience. Member input is received regarding the helpfulness of the group, specific techniques/activities used, and the facilitator's group practice skills. Process data can be gathered through discussions that occur during the group sessions or through the use of a brief questionnaire in which members are asked to: (1) summarize the strengths of the group and leader skills and techniques; (2) summarize areas that did not meet their needs for both the group and leader; and (3) provide suggestions for change. Having a co-worker observe one or more group sessions and provide feedback to the facilitator is an alternative form of process evaluation.

- *Outcome evaluations* target specific changes made by group members and the degree to which the goals were achieved. Three evaluative approaches are commonplace in determining individual and group outcomes (Zastrow & Hessenauer, 2019):

    1 *single-system design evaluation*—As discussed in Chapters 5 and 7, this method of evaluation identifies a specific outcome and measure, collecting pre- and post-intervention data, and determining intervention impact. When used in group practice, this approach can be used with the individual members or the entire group.
    2 *task achievement scaling*—This evaluation protocol involves rating results for each task identified in the assessment and planning process on a numeric 1–4 scale. This approach is easily administered and is a straightforward mechanism for evaluating change but does not include effort or motivations related to change.
    3 *satisfaction questionnaires*—As noted in previous chapters, client satisfaction provides an opportunity to obtain feedback from group members about their experience but does not yield objective findings that lend insight into the effectiveness of the intervention.

Agencies and funders are increasingly requiring analysis of outcome data to determine ongoing investment in supporting the intervention. Specific areas to include in an analysis of your group intervention may include (Gant, 2017, pp. 531–532):

1 background and significance for the group.
2 procedures and methodologies used and the evidence to support their use.
3 measures used to gather evaluative data and the evidence indicating their psychometric reliability and validity.
4 descriptions of recruitment and screening processes.
5 operationalization of organizational processes.
6 detailed methodological procedures.
7 qualitative and quantitative data collected, analyzed, and presented.
8 clear connections between findings, analyses, and evaluation questions.

Facilitator self-evaluation is an important, but often overlooked focus for evaluation. Reflecting on your own experience with the group intervention can help you process the experience as well as your own facilitation skills. Additionally, asking the group members to provide feedback can give the group facilitator information for their own professional growth and development as well as input for improving future group experiences. Quick Guide 27 provides two examples of evaluation strategies to help you engage in self-evaluation.

QUICK GUIDE 27 Group Facilitator Self-Evaluation: Group Member Perspectives

EXAMPLE #1

When reflecting on your experience leading a group, ask group members to respond to the following questions:

1. What are some of my actions that you found helpful? Unhelpful?
2. What things might you have liked me to do that I didn't do?
3. Are there personal qualities of mine you found helpful or unhelpful (e.g., ways of speaking, timing of remarks, sense of humor, ways of expressing myself)?
4. How well do you think I understood what you were thinking and feeling? How did I communicate that?
5. How honest (or transparent) did you believe I was with you?
6. Did you experience me as supportive and caring?
7. How appropriately did you think I responded to members of different genders, ethnic cultures, or other identities?

Source: Ortega & Garvin, 2019, pp. 256–257.

EXAMPLE #2: GROUP COUNSELOR RATING SCALE

Instructions: Rate your group counselor's functioning in your group.

Respect: Shows respect for group members by attentiveness, warmth, efforts to understand, and supports freedom of personal expression.

5.0	4.5	4.0	3.5	3.0	2.5	2.0	1.5	1.0
Very high		high		moderate		low		very low

Empathy: Communicates an accurate understanding of group members' feelings and experiences. Group members know the counselor understands how they feel.

5.0	4.5	4.0	3.5	3.0	2.5	2.0	1.5	1.0
Very high		high		moderate		low		very low

Genuineness: Realness. Everything the group counselor does seems to be sincere. That's the way the person really is. This person doesn't put up a front.

5.0	4.5	4.0	3.5	3.0	2.5	2.0	1.5	1.0
Very high		high		moderate		low		very low

Concreteness: "Tunes in" and responds to specific feelings or experiences of group members. Avoids responding in generalities.

5.0	4.5	4.0	3.5	3.0	2.5	2.0	1.5	1.0
Very high		high		moderate		low		very low

Self-Disclosure: Lets group know about relevant immediate personal feelings. Open rather than guarded.

5.0	4.5	4.0	3.5	3.0	2.5	2.0	1.5	1.0
Very high		high		moderate		low		very low

QUICK GUIDE 27 Continued

Spontaneity: Can respond without consistently having to "stop and think." Words and actions seem to flow easily.

5.0	4.5	4.0	3.5	3.0	2.5	2.0	1.5	1.0
Very high		high		moderate		low		very low

Flexibility: Adapts to a wide range of conditions without losing composure. Can adapt to meet the needs of the moment.

5.0	4.5	4.0	3.5	3.0	2.5	2.0	1.5	1.0
Very high		high		moderate		low		very low

Confidence: Trusts their own abilities. Acts with directness and self-assurance.

5.0	4.5	4.0	3.5	3.0	2.5	2.0	1.5	1.0
Very high		high		moderate		low		very low

Open-ended questions like the following may also yield insightful group perceptions about the facilitator:

1. What changes have you become aware of in your attitudes, feelings about yourself, and relationships with other people since your group experience began?
2. How did the group experience help these changes come about?
3. What did the group leader do that was most helpful and least helpful to you?
4. Was the group experience hurtful to you in any way, or did it have any negative effect on you?
5. Briefly identify any group exercises you especially liked or disliked.
6. In what ways do you wish *you* had been different in the group?
7. How are you most different because of the group experience?

Source: Berg et al., 2013, pp. 143–144.

While each group experience is unique, aspects of each phase of the group process are often replicated. Recall from Chapter 8 the examination of the engagement and assessment phases of three group models (social goals, reciprocal, and remedial models) used within groups of parents from the Riverton community. Returning to the Riverton example, Exhibits 9.8, 9.9, and 9.10 depict the intervention, termination, and evaluation phases from the perspectives of the three models. In addition to the type(s) of evaluative strategies for examining group interventions discussed, consider using the data you gather and analyze to develop evaluation tools to use with future groups (Garvin & Galinsky, 2020). For example, you and other group facilitators may find it helpful to have a menu of strategies for monitoring group progress or a manual for conducting a group intervention.

EXHIBIT 9.8

Riverton Against Youth Drinking ("RAYD"): An Example of a Social Goals Group

PHASES II AND III: MIDDLE AND ENDING WORK

Background: A group of parents in the Riverton community, concerned about the use of alcohol among their adolescent children, approaches a local community service agency to ask for its help.

Work thus far: Stakeholders and their interests and goals have been identified. The social worker's role has been agreed upon. A community needs assessment has been conducted, including strengths, resources, needs, and priorities. A plan for intervention, termination, and evaluation has been established; it will focus on developing and mounting a public education campaign to raise awareness about the issue of teen drinking.

Note: While the stages of group interventions are not linear and may, in fact, overlap, the following depicts a possible approach to responding to the identified need.

INTERVENTION	TERMINATION	EVALUATION
Identify community partners who will support and help to disseminate the education campaign.	Conclude campaign.	Conduct evaluation.
		Analyze data gathered from evaluation effort.
Confirm the plan, time frame, and resources for intervention, termination, and evaluation continue to be viable.		Implement plan for sustainability.
		Document findings.
Launch the intervention.		
Monitor progress, particularly dissemination and relationships with community partners.		
Adapt the intervention, as needed.		
Revisit plan for evaluation and sustainability.		

EXHIBIT 9.9

Riverton Children's Grief Support Group: An Example of a Reciprocal Group

PHASES II AND III: MIDDLE AND ENDING WORK

Background: A social worker in a community service agency has become aware of several Riverton children who have lost a parent to alcohol- and substance-related deaths. The social worker takes steps toward offering an educationally focused support group.

Work thus far: Based on the social worker's assessment of need and interest, group members were recruited, screened, and invited to join the group. A first session was

EXHIBIT 9.9

Continued

held, at which the social worker and group members determined group rules and norms. Individual and group goals and needs were shared. The social worker's role as a facilitator/educator was established.

Note: While the stages of group interventions are not linear and may overlap, the following depicts a possible approach to responding to the identified need.

INTERVENTION	TERMINATION	EVALUATION
Begin each session by reviewing group rules and norms and conducting member check-in.	Begin termination as planned.	*Individual*
	Check in with each group member regarding feelings about the termination of the group and the process.	Determine if goals (informal or formal) were met.
Engage in ongoing assessment of individual member needs, group interactions, and group cohesiveness.		Administer post-group collection of data.
		Group
Develop a repertoire of agency and community resources to suggest as needed.	Invite each member to talk about individual gains and continuing needs.	Determine if group goals (informal or formal) were met.
Revisit group needs and adapt intervention and educational programming plans as appropriate.	Discuss plans for sustaining change and any perceived obstacles to maintaining desired changes.	Ask members to provide feedback regarding satisfaction with the group process.
Share information, as agreed upon prior to group initiation, with legal guardian consent.	Provide resources as needed to help members sustain change.	*Document findings.*
Monitor individual and group progress and adapt as needed.	Conduct termination ritual or celebration.	
Regularly revisit time frame and plans for termination and evaluation.		
Invite suggestions from group members regarding plans for recognizing group termination.		

EXHIBIT 9.10

Riverton Mental Health Center Group for Persons With Dual Diagnoses: An Example of a Remedial Group

PHASES II AND III: MIDDLE AND ENDING WORK

Background: A new social worker at the Riverton Mental Health Center recently assumed leadership for a clinical intervention group for persons with dual diagnoses (i.e., substance use disorder and mental illness) who receive outpatient services at the agency. Group membership is diverse and includes a mix of genders, ages, and mandated and voluntary members. Membership turnover depends on members' "graduation" from the treatment program; therefore, members are often entering and exiting the group. Two new members have been referred to the group. This will be the first time new members have been referred since the new social worker took over responsibility for the group.

Work thus far: The social worker has gathered information from different sources on eligibility criteria for group membership (agency) and integrating new members into an ongoing group (literature). The social worker has met with the two persons who have been referred and determined they would be appropriate for inclusion. The two members have been oriented and attended their first meeting. During this session, the social worker introduced the new members to the group, revisited group rules and norms, and assessed the individual goals and needs and group cohesion.

Note: While the stages of group interventions are not linear and may overlap, the following depicts a possible approach to responding to the identified need.

INTERVENTION	TERMINATION	EVALUATION
At the beginning of each session, remind members of group rules and norms.	Ongoing, as membership is open.	Complete formal evaluation as required by agency.
Conduct check-ins by asking members to share events/actions since the last session.	Determine termination ritual appropriate to an open-ended group.	Obtain information from existing members regarding achievement of goals and experiences with group format and process (e.g., open vs. closed and time-limited format) and social worker leadership.
Assess individual member needs and goals and monitor progress toward goals (critical as each person may be at a different point in their progress).	Prepare existing and remaining members for termination.	
Assess group cohesion.	Check in with members regarding their feelings about termination.	
When appropriate, members with longer membership can serve as guides/mentors for newer members.		

CRITICAL CONSIDERATIONS ABOUT GROUP INTERVENTION, TERMINATION, AND EVALUATION

The social worker's role and purpose is to encourage and mobilize the group's strengths. The social worker's concern for individual well-being and growth is augmented by the individual relationships within the group, one member to another. Consistent with trusting the group process, social workers should strive to avoid overinvestment in the centrality or power of their role. The goal, after all, is for the group to gain its voice and develop its strengths, even as individual members continue to grow. You will not be able to take credit, even in your own mind, for all the potential successes in your group. In exchange, you will have the privilege of experiencing the power of group connection and the autonomy the group can exercise as it liberates the power of its members.

The emphasis on the group does not mean that your role is any less important. You are responsible for the structure of the group, the emotional and physical safety of members, and ensuring group members maintain focus on their goals. Accordingly, your role is to evaluate group process and functioning on an ongoing basis. This evaluation will vary based on the nature of your group. For example, if you work in a task group, the intervention and evaluation processes will focus on monitoring progress in completing the group's project. If you facilitate a group for school-aged children, you must make sure to use an appropriate developmental level. Other forms of evaluation that are especially useful come from members: Is the group meeting its members' social and affiliation needs? Do members feel safe in the group? Is it a helpful forum to address the issues they want to deal with? As always, consider the work of evaluation as an ongoing process.

GRAND CHALLENGE

Harness Technology for Social Good

The American Academy of Social Work and Social Welfare Grand Challenges for Social Work Initiative identifies one of the areas the profession should address as being to use technological innovations in social work practice, including group practice. The authors of Grand Challenge Working Paper No. 12, *Practice Innovation Through Technology in the Digital Age: A Grand Challenge for Social Work* (Berzin et al., 2015, p. 13), charge the social work profession with investing in resources to leverage information and communication technology (ICT) to enable the profession to better prepare students and practitioners and serve consumers.

Technology shifts at a rapid pace and social work is poised to be part of these advances. Social workers can begin to play a more active role in guiding the development side with their content knowledge and exploiting technology created for other purpose by ensuring . . . meaningful progress.

While the profession must consider the ethical and practical implications of further integrating technological advances into individual, family, and group practice, there are a number of potential benefits, including increasing accessibility and flexibility in service delivery; using social media to reach more

> **GRAND CHALLENGE**
>
> *Continued*

people; using global positioning systems (GPS) and sensor systems to personalize treatment processes and gather evidence for practice innovations; and redefining social work roles and boundaries. The authors of the Grand Challenge advocate for the social work profession to promote evaluation of cutting-edge technologies to support practice interventions, develop training programs to encourage adoption of technologies, and advocate for regulations to support online service delivery (Berzin et al., 2015, pp. 13–14).

The 2017 NASW, ASWB, CSWE, & CSWA *Standards for Technology in Social Work Practice* provides the profession with guidelines for the use of technology in social work practice (for more information, visit www.socialworkers.org). To familiarize yourself with the issues related to the use of technology, visit the Grand Challenges website and read Working Paper No. 12, *Practice Innovation Through Technology in the Digital Age: A Grand Challenge for Social Work* (Berzin et al., 2015) at: http://grandchallengesforsocialwork.org/. To learn about the progress on achieving this Grand Challenge, review the "Harnessing Technology for Social Good" by Singer and colleagues (2022). (See Exercise #1 for additional exploration of this Grand Challenge.)

CONCLUSION

This chapter presented social work practice with groups as functioning to mediate a range of social and emotional issues, including isolation, oppression, and life crises. Group work harnesses the relationship component of humanity toward individual and group goals. Currently, there are many exciting adventures in social work practice with groups that build upon contemporary theoretical perspectives, social justice, and diversity. The scenarios presented in this chapter that emphasize first the "story over problem" and second "process over stages" all point to the empowering impact of social work group practice. Social work practice with groups offers significant potential for the future and is particularly relevant for the social justice, diversity, and human rights connections that give social work its meaning.

MAIN POINTS

- Effective social work practice interventions with groups provide a methodology to serve as a powerful tool for connecting people in the purpose of social justice, diversity, and human rights.

- Strengths and empowerment, narrative, and solution-focused approaches are useful middle-phase (intervention) and ending-phase (termination and evaluation) strategies in group practice, just as in practice with individuals and families.

- Developmental models, such as the Boston Model, are widely used in group work. Many applications of and departures from these models can be found in the contemporary practice environment.

- Social workers working with groups add to the skills they have honed for intervening with individuals and families, developing additional skills for group intervention in the areas of group dynamics and leadership, problem-solving, and management of group functioning.

- Contemporary examples of innovative, evidence-based group practice models, such as constructionist groups and narrative groups, help to provide vision and possibility for responding to current cultural and social issues.

- Termination occurs in three distinct areas of group practice interventions: between group members and the social worker, among group members, and of the group itself.

- While evaluation of group practice shares some commonalities with evaluation of individual and family interventions, evaluating group interventions is more complex as it requires examinations both of the individual members of the group and of the group itself.

EXERCISES

1 To apply your learning of the Grand Challenge to use technology for social good that was highlighted in this chapter, visit the Grand Challenges website and read Working Paper No. 12, *Practice Innovation Through Technology in the Digital Age: A Grand Challenge for Social Work* (Berzin et al., 2015) at: http://grandchallengesforsocialwork.org/. To examine the potential use of technology in the aftermath of the hurricane in the Hudson City area, review the case information at www.routledgesw.com/static-cases/. After reading Working Paper No. 12 and reviewing the information on Hudson City, complete the following items:
   a Using the town map, sociogram, and interaction matrix, identify potential group interventions in each of the four areas of social work group practice discussed in this chapter.
   b For each of the proposed group interventions, research existing technological models and resources that could be utilized to provide or enhance the social worker's ability to develop and conduct the group intervention.
   c Reflect on the potential strengths, weaknesses, and ethical dilemmas associated with each of the proposed technological strategies.
2 Go to www.routledgesw.com/interactive-cases/, review Carla Washburn's video vignette in Engage and Discover, and consider the roles each member

plays. Then, complete the following activities and answer the following questions:

a *Gather into groups:* Start with the group session from the conclusion of the video vignette and role-play the next session. What happens next? Process the group session with the class.

b *Round robin:* Each student takes the opportunity to role-play the social worker. Change roles when the "social worker" is not sure how to proceed with the group. Debrief about the experiences and practice behaviors demonstrated for each role-play. What were strengths and areas for growth for each student as a facilitator?

c Select a member of the group and discuss their role in the group process.

d Identify the social worker's strengths as a group facilitator along with those practice behaviors that they may be able to improve.

3 Terminating a group intervention can be challenging. Returning to the grief support group depicted in the Carla Washburn video vignette, role-play the final session. Consider the following:

a What is the most important role the social worker plays at this stage of the group process?

b What practice behaviors are critical for the termination phase of a group intervention?

c Brainstorm strategies for responding to the array of possible member reactions to the ending of the group experience.

4 At the end of a group intervention, the evaluation of the intervention's effectiveness is critical. Research evaluation tools and complete the following for the grief support group in which Carla Washburn is a member:

a Create a satisfaction survey.

b Create or locate a standardized pre-test/post-test.

c Create a six-month evaluation tool.

5 Go to www.routledgesw.com/interactive-cases/ and view the Riverton video vignette (in Engage and Discover) that depicts a group meeting of the Riverton Neighborhood Association or the Carla Washburn video vignette (in Engage and Discover) that depicts a grief support group. Using one of the two Group Facilitator evaluation tools (Quick Guide 27), evaluate the group leader. Write a reflection identifying the group leader's strengths and areas for growth and change.

6 Go to www.routledgesw.com/interactive-cases/ and review the case for Brickville (in Engage and Discover), particularly Virginia Stone and her family. In Chapter 8, Virginia was involved in the creation of a social goals group targeted at saving the park that was built in memory of her family members who were lost in a fire 20 years earlier. The exercise in Chapter 8 focused on determining the need, purpose, composition, structure, and content for such a group. Using the information available to you, develop a written plan that includes the following:

a Development of the social action plan—areas to address may include: (1) needs assessment information and data; (2) group goal; (3) existing partners; and (4) timeframe.
b Strategies for implementing the plan.
c Resources needed to implement the plan, including individuals, groups, organizations, and funding, as appropriate.
d Plan for determining the success or failure of the social goals effort.
e Your reflection on the process of implementing a social goals plan at the community level.

7 Go to www.routledgesw.com/interactive-cases/ and review the case for Hudson City (in Engage and Discover). Recall from Chapters 6, 7, and 8 that the Patel family experienced significant impact from Hurricane Diane. Because of her response to the experience, you refer the 12-year-old daughter, Aarti, to a group to help her process the experience and develop her coping skills. While Aarti was a regular and active participant in the support group, there is mounting concern that she continues to struggle with the challenges that resulted in her being referred to the group (e.g., nightmares, discomfort when required to be away from her parents for activities other than school and group, and decreased appetite). Describe in writing your thoughts about the concerns her parents and the leader of the support group express and a plan for addressing the ongoing challenges that Aarti and her family are experiencing, including:
- Gaining Aarti's perspective and wishes
- Continuation in the support group
- Alternative intervention strategies
- Resources needed for a revised intervention plan

8 Go to www.routledgesw.com/interactive-cases/ and review the case for Brickville, then, referring to the discussion of the Stone family's potential participation in group interventions at the beginning of this chapter, conduct a search of the literature on group-level interventions to find social work skills needed to conduct and evaluate the following group interventions:
a Through a community needs assessment of services for older adults, the Bethany Catholic Church has additionally identified community members who are caring for older family members and determined that offering a group for family caregivers would be of service to the caregivers and their older family members.
b The Brickville Community Development Corporation Youth Leadership Program (YLP) uses evidence-based practices for facilitating a task group focused on helping teens to make healthy life choices.
c The Catholic Charities Community Center offers a group for children experiencing behavioral concerns.
d A group of residents in the Brickville area have banded together to form a group to bring attention to issues of police and fire department lack of/slow responses to their community.

9 Go to www.routledgesw.com/static-cases/ and review all the Downloadable Cases. Upon reviewing the cases, select one of the cases, and provide a rationale for the type of group you will plan to facilitate. Develop an intervention and evaluation plan for the group. If you completed Exercise #9 in Chapter 8, you may choose to build on your work.
10 To relate the information in this chapter to your own group experience, reflect on a specific experience you have had as a member of a group by responding to the following items:
  a Describe in detail a formed group (e.g., support group, committee) to which you belong or have belonged. Include the following:
   - Type of group (use one of the types described in Chapter 8)
   - Purpose of group
   - Structure of group (e.g., open or closed membership, time-limited or open-ended, number of members, eligibility for membership)
   - Your role within the group
  b Consider the quality of your involvement by reflecting on:
   - How did you feel about being a member of the group? Your role? Your contributions?
   - Did the group fulfill stated expectations? Your expectations? If not, explain the reasons.
   - What were the strengths of the group?
   - What were areas for the group's growth or change?
   - Was group leadership formally determined or did it evolve naturally?
   - What was the style of the leader(s)?
  c Based on your experience and your new knowledge of the group process, reflect on the following:
   - Would you engage with the group differently? If yes, how would your involvement change? Explain your reasons.
   - Was the group formally or informally evaluated? What were the outcomes?
11 Develop a plan for the way in which you, as a group leader of a support group, will respond to each of the following behaviors that may emerge during your experience in group work—consider your responses to a member who:
  a does not contribute
  b dominates group sessions
  c does not appear to want to receive help
  d appears to want to take care of and/or coordinate the group
  e responds to others with anger and criticism
  f wants everyone to get along with one another
  g uses humor to interact and sometimes deflect
  h attempts to elicit others' sympathy for their situation
   After developing your response plan for each behavior, reflect in writing on the challenges you anticipate facing and strategies for learning and growing as a group facilitator.

12 Recall from Chapter 8 that you, as a practicum student, were invited to serve as a co-facilitator for an online psychoeducational support group for family caregivers of persons experiencing Parkinson's disease. In the previous exercise, you focused on familiarizing yourself with Parkinson's disease and developing a plan for the session that you facilitate. In preparing for the intervention, termination, and evaluation phases of group work, respond to the following items:
   a Identify potential needs for ongoing psychoeducational support that caregivers of persons with Parkinson's disease will likely experience.
   b Develop a plan for evaluating the online group with a specific emphasis on strategies you will use to gather feedback from group members.

CHAPTER 10

Social Work Practice With Communities: Engagement, Assessment, and Planning

IT IS IN COMMUNITIES THAT PEOPLE FIND identity and meaning for their lives in their various roles as individuals, parents, children, partners, friends, and professionals. Community provides the structure that supports social interaction and connectedness among people over time. The characteristics of the community in which people grow, live, and develop can have important implications for the resources and opportunities available to them. For example, growing up in communities that offer a safe environment and strong schools helps children grow into secure and well-educated adults with strong prospects for the future. As such, it is clear that community practice is an important aspect of social work practice. Many issues that arise in individual and family practice can also be addressed in community practice. For example, the Sanchez family members (see www.routledgesw.com/interactive-cases/) have a range of challenges that could be the focus of community practice. Celia struggles with low English proficiency, and the family has financial struggles and does not access health care often due to barriers. These struggles may be shared by other families in their community. Beyond just being referred to existing services for their challenges, the family may also ultimately benefit from a community engagement and needs assessment process to uncover how common these issues are in the community, and whether there are other issues that need to be addressed community-wide.

This chapter examines the concept of community and your relationship to it as a social work practitioner. It explores the types of communities and the functions that give community meaning. We consider methods of inquiry into the study of community, including community analysis, community needs assessment, and community asset mapping. We begin the chapter with a case on homelessness and affordable housing that serves as a foundation for this chapter.

Victoria is a social worker in a small city in the Midwest that is in the center of a large agricultural region. Because of the small size of her agency's service area, Victoria works with a variety of clients and communities using a professional tool kit that is full of generalist social work practice skills and abilities. One of the families that Victoria is currently helping consists of a single father, Nate, and his 7-year-old son. Like many of the agency's clients, Nate and his son have been evicted from their most recent apartment for past-due rent. They have been staying with one friend after another. Nate has been able to keep working his construction job when the company has work for him, and his son has continued to attend school.

Affordable housing in the city has been declining for a number of years, as older units have been left vacant by landlords who can no longer afford the expensive maintenance. Landlords who still own homes and apartments have been increasingly able to raise rents as a result of the declining number of rental units. What social work skills and abilities can Victoria use to help Nate and his son find housing in such circumstances?

Key Questions for Chapter 10

1. What competencies do I need to engage with, assess needs in, and plan with communities?
2. What are the social work practice behaviors that enable me to effectively engage, assess, and plan with different kinds of communities?
3. How can I use evidence to guide engagement, assessment, and planning with communities?
4. How can I apply social work values and ethics to engagement, assessment of needs, and planning with communities?

COMMUNITY AS A CONTEXT FOR SOCIAL WORK PRACTICE

Education, housing, health, recreational opportunities, local businesses, religious/faith communities, and employment opportunities are important to the quality of life for members of a community. Community members often invest time, energy, and resources to create community resources and opportunities that will enhance their well-being. Challenges and issues also compel residents to take action on behalf of their communities. For example, residents and business owners of a neighborhood may work to maintain and increase property values and to decrease crime in their neighborhoods. During the early days of the COVID-19 pandemic, Asian American residents and business owners, throughout the United States, faced increased acts of violence and hate crimes. These acts were the result of individuals accusing and blaming the Chinese government for the creation and spread of the novel coronavirus throughout the world. In response to the violence, neighborhood residents and volunteers organized to provide protection for business owners, workers, and shoppers in Chinatown communities. In other communities, residents may strive to keep landfills out of their neighborhoods and to garner resources to increase the quality of public education in their communities. Encouraging individuals, families, and groups to work to improve their communities is a critical component of social work practice.

Community Practice and Generalist Practice

Social workers in community practice focus on communities defined either by geography, identity, or shared social issues. They work with residents and/or members of the community, as well as organizational partners, to mobilize resources in order to better meet community needs, develop new services to enhance the well-being of the community, and build community capacity. The Council on Social Work Education (CSWE) (2018) notes that "Community practitioners work in a range of settings, including community and neighborhood-based organizations, faith-based organizations, community development corporations, public development agencies, and broader human services agencies in public, private nonprofit or for-profit sectors, and coalitions, collaborations, and other alliances" (p. xxix).

Promoting and facilitating community involvement is important for social workers working with clients at every level. Communities are critical because it is within communities that individuals live their lives, and communities are the formal conduits through which resources, formal and informal systems, and political, social, environmental, and economic forces shape individuals, families, and neighborhoods. Communities therefore influence the ability of social workers to affect outcomes for the people with whom they work.

Even when social workers primarily work with individuals and families, the success of their efforts depends, in large part, on the nature and responsiveness of the clients' communities. For example, a community's overall capacity to provide decent, affordable housing for single parents who receive public assistance will impact a young, low-income client with two children who is seeking shelter. If a client in this situation asks for your help finding housing, you need to know about the resources for shelter, transitional housing, and low-income housing available in the community, as well as resources to combat discrimination if the client suspects that they are being denied housing illegally. For example, this situation arises when landlords have a long history of not renting to single mothers who receive public assistance. Other factors to consider surrounding the client's housing choices may include employment, schools, child care, the quality and quantity of after-school programs, public parks, and the existence of a community center. The client may be interested in information about the safety of the community, including the crime rate, the proximity of a former partner who may pose safety concerns, and the presence of gangs in the area.

To practice competently, social workers need both professional skills and knowledge of community resources to address challenges related to those resources; the entities that make decisions about resources; and ways to secure resources for people in need. Social workers also need to know about the various dimensions of a community in order to be effective catalysts for community change. Skills honed working with individuals, families, groups, and organizations are vital to community practice, and skills honed working with communities are likewise important in every other type of social work practice.

> *As an example, return to Victoria, the social worker introduced at the beginning of this chapter who is helping Nate and his son find affordable housing. As it turns out, another community that Victoria serves is seasonal agricultural workers who live and work in the area from spring through early fall each year. Three years ago, she worked with a team of colleagues from her agency and other community organizations to write federal, state, and foundation proposals to build affordable housing units for these seasonal agricultural workers and their families. The successful proposal to the state U.S. Department of Agriculture was granted with the expected condition that the housing be used for farm workers. However, once the housing was built, it had to be boarded up during the winter months each year when it was not occupied. Advocates noted that winter is when it is most dangerous for families like Nate and his son to be homeless. How might Victoria use her social work values, skills, and abilities with other community members to better use the affordable housing year-round?*

Working with communities requires mastery of many social work competencies and behaviors (CSWE, 2022). For example, social workers must be able to respond to the contexts that shape practice by being proactive and engaging in community work that seeks to prevent problems and unnecessary challenges from occurring in the first place or recurring over time. As in work with individuals, families, and groups, social workers in community practice must employ ethical principles and have cultural humility. Community practice uses research-informed and evidence-based practice to advance human rights and economic justice. Lastly, as in practice at all levels, community practitioners use the same phases of the change process—engagement, assessment, intervention, and evaluation—as they facilitate changes that will enhance the well-being of people and their communities.

Challenges in Community Engagement

In the United States, focusing on individualism and individual responsibility for family well-being has a long history. The individualistic character of US society has provided less social reinforcement of responsibility for community well-being. While volunteerism and private-sector involvement in community well-being have been important features of our collective welfare in the United States, the strongly held belief in the responsibility of individuals to take care of themselves and their families continues to create challenges for social workers in community engagement. Increasing residential mobility can also make it more difficult to aid the development of strong place-based community connections, as workers move to find optimal employment opportunities. New technologies allow people to maintain contact with family and long-time friends, and to build new bonds with those who share their interests or identify with social groups near and far. Since much of this communication can take place virtually, this can lead to people feeling less engaged with their neighbors and local groups, unless the community intentionally captures their functionality and promise as resources for building community ties.

Last but not least, the human service system also reinforces society's focus on individualism through its emphasis on individual and family counseling. Social work is different from other helping professions because of our focus on both individuals and their social environments, but we still have much work to do to balance the emphasis between helping facilitate individual change and social change.

TYPES OF COMMUNITY

In social work, different types of communities are emerging in practice, policy, and research all the time. Keeping up with new studies in your area of practice will help you stay current with developing communities that are most important for the populations you serve. This section describes three types of community that are of importance to all social workers: spatial, social, and political.

Spatial Communities

One type of community is a geographic entity, such as a town, city, small neighborhood, or college dormitory. These **spatial communities** are structures of connectedness based on a physical location. In some cases, these communities have clear, physical boundaries, such as a river, mountain, gate, wall, or a legally defined boundary. In other cases, **stakeholders**—those who have an interest in community affairs, such as county or city officials or neighborhood leaders—agree on their boundaries. People also construct cognitive maps, or mental images, of their communities that inform their relationship to their physical space, movement within their spatial communities, and social interactions. These boundaries may provide a sense of familiarity, safety, and security for community members, but they may also be a means of excluding others.

The degree to which community residents perceive themselves as community members depends on many dimensions, but access to the community's benefits is among the most influential. Those residents of a community who do not have affordable or convenient access to community benefits such as community centers, public libraries, and other resources may not feel personally affiliated with the communities in which they live, which can be an environmental justice issue. You can see this at work in cities that have been divided by the built environment, such as major interstates that have changed walkability and public transportation routes to community institutions on the "other" side of all of the concrete and steel.

Spatial communities of all sizes can be diverse. Many people think of large spatial communities when they consider diverse areas. For example, in

Queens, one of the five boroughs of New York City, 44 percent of more than 2.2 million residents speak English as their primary language (Suburban Stats, Inc., 2019). However, at least 631 other languages are spoken in Queens. In fact, Queens has more languages than anywhere in the world (Endangered Language Alliance, 2019).

As the United States becomes more diverse, social workers in small towns and rural areas are working with many people that speak non-English languages from a variety of places. In Garden City, Kansas, for example, the population count is only about 26,000 and the total area of the town is 8.5 square miles. However, almost 24 percent of the town's residents were born outside of the United States in a number of countries across the world. In fact, compared with the national average of 21.5 percent of people speaking a non-English language, 44 percent of Garden City residents speak a Southeast Asian language, Spanish, or another non-English language. As this example points out, social workers need to be increasingly ready to work with diverse communities whether they work in urban or rural areas. Spatial communities can be quite diverse regardless of size (World Population Review, 2022).

Social Communities

Groups that share common interests, concerns, norms, identity, or interactions and share a similar sense of belonging are **social communities**. Student communities, Asian communities, gay, bisexual, transgender, queer, intersex, asexual, and persons whose sexual orientation or gender identity is not included in the acronym (LGBTQIA+) communities, veterans' communities, graduates of Historically Black Colleges and Universities, and skateboard communities are all examples of social communities. As in spatial communities, members attach different meanings to their communities and affiliate with those communities to varying extents over time. For example, a religious community

may play a significant lifelong role for some but have less significance for others, or a community of skateboarders may play an important role in members' lives for several years but fade in importance as they reach adulthood.

People are usually part of more than one type of social community. For example, a person may be affiliated with a professional community, an online community of gamers, a community of yoga teachers, and a community of graduates from the same college. Social communities often serve to provide meaning to one's identity. While social communities have the potential to function as exclusionary associations, they can also offer members a powerful sense of connection and commitment.

Some social workers focus their careers on specific social communities, such as women who experience intimate partner violence or those who have lost a partner to dementia or suicide. Social workers may develop an interest in a particular social community based on their personal experiences or early professional experiences. Social workers are also interested in people's social communities because these communities provide socialization and resources, such as formal or informal helping networks that may be useful when facing crises or challenges.

Political Communities

Political communities serve as venues through which people demonstrate their civic engagement, participate in democratic governance, and promote social change through voting, community organizing, and political mobilization. The spatial community, as a formal political unit, and the social community, through which people interact, are both incorporated in a political community since they can both serve political functions. Efforts to promote democracy using political communities focus on increasing the capacities of both spatial and social communities to practice self-determination and be involved in governing. Social workers may facilitate civic engagement by encouraging people to attend neighborhood meetings, support candidates for office, meet with elected officials to share ideas about local needs, vote, and become involved in grassroots community organizing efforts. Residents in marginalized communities are less likely than residents of middle- and high-income neighborhoods to vote in local or national elections (Hall & Yoder, 2019; Rome, 2022). Importantly, marginalized communities are also less likely to receive legislative attention and government resources than middle- and high-income communities with higher percentages of registered voters who are more likely to vote (Martin & Claibourn, 2013). People who have not been involved in helping change policies may need to be introduced to civic engagement over time, but such engagement can lead to a sense of personal empowerment and community belonging and improved community outcomes.

FUNCTIONS OF COMMUNITIES

Often communities are where social work practice and macro practice, in particular, take place. It is in communities where residents and individuals learn a shared history, cultural values, and traditions, including the following (Netting et al., 2017):

- *The production, distribution, and consumption of goods and services:* This may include basic needs like food, clothing, shelter, health care, and employment. Organizations that produce and distribute goods and services provide jobs so that people can get the things they need to take care of their families.

- *The transmission of knowledge, social values, customs, and behavior patterns:* This socialization process guides how community members view themselves, others, and their rights and responsibilities. Both formal institutions, such as schools and faith communities, and informal institutions, such as friends and peer groups, can be involved in this function.

- *The maintenance of conformity to community norms through social control:* Formal governmental entities, such as law enforcement and court systems, enforce laws, rules, and regulations. Informal systems of enforcement, such as schools, families, peers, and organized neighborhood watches, reinforce community standards. Eligibility guidelines for public assistance and private services regulate access to resources and thereby also serve as mechanisms of social control.

- *Social participation through formal and informal groups:* Interaction with others through groups, associations, and organizations provides social outlets and helps build natural helping and support networks. People engage in social participation when they join sports leagues, attend religious services, volunteer, vote, and attend Parent–Teacher Association (PTA) meetings.

- *The provision of mutual support:* Families, friends, neighbors, and volunteers provide aid, support one another, and assist individuals and families to solve problems independent of professional help. Due to the complexities of modern society, the work of human service professionals, such as social workers, often supplements mutual support.

UNDERSTANDING COMMUNITIES

Given their complex nature, understanding the many ways that communities can be conceptualized is imperative before moving into the process of engagement, assessment, intervention, and evaluation. Here we examine communities as viewed from different theories and perspectives.

Systems Theory on Community

Systems theory offers a helpful framework for understanding communities. From this framework, a community is a system of dynamic and interrelated components such that when one component changes, all other components of the system change to reestablish the status quo. Some components of a system perform specialized functions for the larger system—the community as a whole. One example of a specialized function is public transportation in a larger community in that a change in public transportation can result in changes in many other parts of the community, such as employment, education, access to food, and strength of the retail and overall business community.

Social workers in community practice use their critical thinking skills to anticipate how changes in one component of the community may result in changes in other parts of the community, especially those changes that may have disproportionate effects on marginalized groups. Being able to anticipate proposed changes in this way makes it possible for social workers to advocate for making changes in ways that will minimize negative impacts and maximize positive impacts for disadvantaged people and their immediate neighborhoods (Netting et al., 2017).

Ecosystems Perspective on Community

The ecosystems perspective focuses on the interdependence of people and their environments in our understanding of communities. **Interdependence** in this context refers to the ways in which individuals and the physical and social environment are linked in complex ways, and therefore dependent on one another. The ecosystems perspective facilitates thinking about both natural and built components of the physical environment. Using this framework, social workers consider the spatial organization of community resources, the relationship of these resources to one another and to groups of people, and the corresponding social and economic consequences.

For example, a major road or highway bisecting a community can have implications for the social organization, the environment, and economics of the community. Specifically, in the 1950s and 1960s, the Federal Aid Highway Act of 1956 routed some highway systems through Black communities. In some instances, the federal government took properties through the eminent domain laws. Highways were built in Greenwich Village, New York, Washington, DC, New Orleans, Louisiana, and St. Paul, Minnesota to name a few. The result for Black communities was a loss of cohesive communities, homes, churches, and businesses. Many of these communities remain underdeveloped, lacking necessary resources and opportunities (Archer, 2021). The social organization implications of the highway include the possibilities that individuals and groups may interact more or less with one another. Moreover, the highway may separate extended family members, including those who help provide informal caregiving to both younger and older generations. Economically, the new road may bring in more customers for some businesses and shut down others, leading to changes in employment patterns within the community.

Social workers can use an ecosystems perspective to help build leadership among community members who can, in turn, organize their friends, family members, and neighbors to advocate for an environmentally safe way such as a pedestrian bridge, over or under the new road—for pedestrians to continue to travel to all parts of the community. Such advocacy can also help establish local policies so that future road and highway construction projects include pedestrian access to affected communities.

Power and Conflict Within Communities

Political, economic, and social dominance of some groups over others within a community often results in decreased access to resources for certain groups. Power dynamics among different groups in a community, especially when those groups tend to live in different neighborhoods, can lead to differential access to high-quality public education, employment opportunities, health care facilities, and police and fire protection. As mentioned previously, this is an environmental justice issue for marginalized communities because inequities in public education lead to inequities in higher education rates, employment opportunities, and income levels.

A number of factors are related to power and control of some groups over others within communities, including:

- Segregation: the geographical division of groups, often on the basis of race, ethnicity, and/or socioeconomic status.

- Centralization: the concentration of resources in one part of a community.

- History: patterns of influence and dominance over time in the community.

- Succession: the movement of different groups of people into and out of various areas of a community.

Together, these factors help explain the ways in which populations move and settle in various neighborhoods and why resources differ from one neighborhood to another. Social workers use such factors to analyze communities in which they work as they plan how best to help clients and community members (Netting et al., 2017; Streeter, 2013).

Theories Regarding Power and Conflict Theories can also assist in our understanding of the community as a setting for power and conflict.

In the context of community practice, **power dependency theory** addresses the ways in which communities can be shaped by their relationships with entities that provide resources. The effects of these dynamics between powerful resources and communities can be dramatic. For example, a community's dependence on a funding source with close ties to a large retail chain may influence its decisions about promoting small, locally owned businesses. Without advocacy on behalf of small, locally owned businesses, they may falter due to the community's dependence on the interests of the retail chain as its funding source. Social workers in community practice are often in the best position to use their engagement and assessment skills and abilities to help balance competing interests and make sure that all voices are heard as decisions affecting the entire community are discussed.

Conflict theory views the community as divided into influential groups ("haves") and groups without influence ("have-nots") that compete for limited resources. This theory assumes that the influential group has power over groups without influence and that dimensions of diversity play a central role in oppression. For example, people with greater income and political connections may have more influence over decisions that affect the community than those who have lower income and fewer connections. Once again, social workers can be advocates for marginalized populations and help build the influence of lower-income people as a group by thinking and acting strategically. For example, if a community forum about how resources are to be used and distributed historically take place in the evenings at the city government building, social workers may work with community members to bring decision-makers to various neighborhood centers for those meetings, and to arrange for transportation and child care to be provided.

Resource mobilization theory similarly focuses on the conditions needed to promote change through community practice. Large-scale community change occurs more easily when groups that have been historically excluded from the decision-making process come together to learn how to organize themselves into a group that can speak with one voice on a critical matter. With social workers to support and facilitate, such groups can develop a message that appeals to other stakeholders in the community who are sympathetic to the cause. For example, groups can reach out to faith communities who have shown support to families who are homeless, or they can reach out to teachers in the community, especially if the issue affects school-age children. Including natural advocates is one way to mobilize resources to work with historically excluded community members.

Taken together, these theories inform the social work profession's thinking about the community as a setting in which power and control play crucial roles. Groups within a community vie for power and control to implement change that will benefit their interests. Balancing these competing interests and facilitating change requires the skill sets of social workers in the community. Such change efforts can occur through rational planning and collaboration that assure the inclusion of diverse groups within the community. Because dimensions of diversity, such as race, socioeconomic status, and ethnicity, can be driving factors in community conflicts, the need for cultural humility among social workers in community practice cannot be overstated. When rational planning and collaboration do not work initially, negotiation and confrontation may be necessary in some community change efforts.

Viewing the community as a center for power and conflict can help social workers assess the community power structure and understand the process of community decision-making, the reasons behind it, and their own roles in community processes. Social workers may also use this lens to learn how best to work with marginalized groups in communities to reclaim some power in the process of getting their needs met. We can see an example of this kind of community practice in Victoria's work with Nate, the single father facing homelessness with his son.

> *After Victoria helped Nate and his son find emergency housing through a local association of faith communities that provide housing and meals for up to 30 days, she worked with him on his permanent housing needs. Victoria also approached the leaders of the emergency housing program about the affordable housing units for seasonal agricultural workers that stood empty during the winter months.*
>
> *In collaboration with emergency housing clients, Victoria's agency and the faith communities co-sponsored a listening session on homelessness and near homelessness to which they invited elected officials and representatives from the original funders of the seasonal agricultural housing. Nate spoke at the listening session, sharing his gratitude for emergency housing and his need for a longer transitional period to save money so that he could afford the deposit and first month's rent for a permanent apartment for he and his son. Other clients shared similar experiences, with specific dollar amounts that were necessary to rent housing in the local housing market.*
>
> *The original funders of the seasonal agricultural housing were certain that their investment in and commitment to the affordable housing complex would not change if transitional housing for individuals and families who were homeless was introduced as a secondary purpose. However, the representative from the State Department of Agriculture indicated that their funding was granted with the understanding that the housing units would be used for farm workers, not only in their community but in other communities across the state. At the end of the listening session, everyone agreed to keep the discussion going by planning a community forum on the issue the following month.*

Strengths, Empowerment, and Resilience in Communities

Let us now turn to a discussion of strengths, empowerment, and resiliency perspectives on communities and community practice. These perspectives move us toward a deeper understanding of community and toward assessing community needs.

The strengths perspective, as detailed by Saleebey (2013), focuses on identifying possibilities and strengths of individuals, groups, and communities, rather than on their deficits and problems. It may seem challenging to apply the strengths perspective in communities that have few resources. It is important to remember that a community's strengths include intangible resources such as the skills and talents of its residents. As in all communities, identifying strengths in these communities can help community members empower themselves. Assisting them to recognize both the intangible and tangible resources they possess can also increase resiliency and the potential for successful problem-solving.

For example, using a strengths perspective can lead social workers to encourage leaders in communities with large plots of vacant land and boarded-up homes to think about the land and homes as valuable assets rather than as problems. Perhaps the vacant land could be used for community gardens or for greenhouses for small businesses such as farm-to-table urban agricultural concerns or flowers for florists.

ENGAGING COMMUNITIES

In their work in communities, social workers can approach engagement, the first step in the change process, in many ways. Engagement with communities involves working with individuals and institutions on behalf of entire communities. Many of the engagement and assessment skills we discussed in previous chapters are helpful in practice with communities. Active listening skills, for example, are as useful in community practice as they are in work with individuals and families.

Social work practice with communities begins with a focus on challenges and opportunities. For example, a social worker working for a community-based education program attached to a local public school may discover that community residents lack adequate employment opportunities. This may lead to the formation of a small-business development task force with the goal of helping with training and capital for residents with a desire to be self-employed. Another example would be social workers who are employed by a local or state correctional system and learn about an opportunity to apply for funding to prevent juvenile crime and engage community members. In collaboration with community residents, they may plan and write a grant with prevention as its goal to benefit the local community.

Social workers may also engage in community practice through their work with a particular population. A social worker in a health care setting may learn about a lack of respite services available for the family caregivers of older adults with dementia. The social worker may help the caregivers organize themselves to approach a potential funder—such as decision-makers at local, state, and federal levels and in both public and private sectors—to advocate funding for respite care.

Social workers also become engaged with communities based primarily on setting. For example, a social worker in a community may learn that illegal trash dumping is becoming a problem in a nearby neighborhood, endangering the health of the residents as the trash attracts rodents and creating an eyesore which may bring down property values. The social worker may work to engage local community leaders to conduct community-wide meetings and/or communicate with decision-makers and work to address the issue. In this case, interorganizational efforts may be possible with social workers, city officials, and public health professionals collaborating with families to develop a plan to eradicate the problem. In a school setting, social workers can be imagined in helping the Sanchez family if a school-based group of parents is formed to try to engage parents and families about improvements needed in the school for children with disabilities.

One aspect of community engagement is interacting with institutions and professionals that provide resources or potential resources for, make decisions for, or have influence in a community. Engaging institutions and professionals that specialize in health, public health, mental health, counseling, psychology, urban planning, religious institutions, education, business, and/or law is common in community practice. Professionals with these backgrounds work in a variety of roles, such as business leader, politician, community planner, program manager, faith leader, and others.

Interprofessional collaboration skills, including such interpersonal skills as active listening and building trust, are needed to effectively engage these professionals and their institutions. Social workers also need a strong understanding of social work values and ethics to guide them in collaboration. Other professions often have different values and ethics; therefore, interprofessional collaboration requires a curiosity about differences in the knowledge, skills, and values of various professions, as well as a strong social work identity. In the engagement process, the goal is to build relationships useful for working together on a shared vision within a climate that is trusting and capable of resolving conflicts productively and professionally (Hardina, 2013). For example, a social worker who is facilitating the school-based group of parents that includes the Sanchez family may work with other professionals, such as those with legal and educational degrees, along with the parents, to advocate with the school district to provide more resources for children with disabilities. Throughout the process, social workers should be mindful of the National Association of Social Workers (NASW) *Code of Ethics* (2021a) to guide them in their advocacy work and should be aware that those with legal and educational backgrounds may be guided by different professional values and ethics. One of the roles that social workers often play in community practice of this kind is to ensure it is understood that advocacy efforts often take an indeterminate length of time to result in success.

ASSESSING COMMUNITIES

In keeping with the earlier discussion on spatial, social, and political communities, community assessment can focus on geographically defined communities, communities based on identity or shared social circumstances, and/or community needs that can best be met by social change through policy practice. Historically, community assessment has been central to social work practice at all levels, from work with individuals and families to work to address social problems affecting large groups or entire populations. When social workers help individuals, we must understand the communities in which our clients and their families live, work, and go to school. Similarly, when we try to make our organizational practice more responsive to our clients' needs, the resources and dynamics of the surrounding community can help or hinder our efforts. Community organization is often a necessary precursor to successful policy practice endeavors.

While community assessment can follow a distinct phase of community engagement, as often happens in social work practice with individuals, families, and groups, it is more likely that the assessment process in community work occurs in tandem with the engagement process. In the case of simultaneous engagement and assessment, social workers must be especially careful to pay adequate attention to engagement and relationship building in order to secure trust for the complex assessment and planning work ahead.

The communication skills used in social work practice to build strong relationships and rapport, and develop a deep level of trust with individuals and groups within a community, are the same skills we use in practice at other levels and include active listening, warmth, empathy, genuineness, reflection of content and feeling, paraphrasing and summarizing, shared power and control over goal-setting as well as the direction and timing of the change effort, and other demonstrations of unconditional positive regard.

Along with ongoing relationship and trust building, community assessment often begins slowly and can involve several strategies. The following discussion begins with a consideration of community needs assessment and then explores two prominent assessment techniques and related tools: comprehensive community-based analysis and asset mapping.

Community Needs Assessment

A **community needs assessment** is a formal process for identifying unmet community needs, placing needs in order of priorities, and planning to target resources to solve problems. A needs assessment can be conducted to focus on the overall functioning of a community. Alternatively, many social workers begin to learn about a community through the focus on the predominant population they are serving, or because of a specific community challenge such as poor-quality housing, gang activity, or truancy. Focusing on a particular community or population and assessing the degree to which the social services system meets their needs is another way to do a needs assessment. The process concentrates on the gap between needs and resources.

The overall process of a community needs assessment can be compared to a research project. As with a research project, the goals of the study's sponsor may shape the purpose of the assessment. Social workers serving the community can add to the original goals of the assessment based on what they have learned through their community practice. For example, a social service organization may want more information about the needs of the older adult population in a community. Social workers involved in gathering such information can make sure that they include the needs of the growing LGBTQIA+ older adult population. The principles of evidence-based practice, as discussed in the next section, should guide the needs assessment process.

Using Evidence-Based Practice in Community Social Work Social workers using evidence-based practice begin with a review of relevant research literature about communities that are similar to their practice settings. They also review theories of change to guide the design of the needs assessment. The next step is to clarify the unit of analysis for the study, whether that is a specific population, a geographic area, individual residents, households, a particular challenge—such as homelessness—or a number of different units of analysis. Consultation with community members, the sponsor, and other interested parties about current evidence; local knowledge; assessment design; study methods; analysis; and the structure of a final report can help achieve the highest-quality needs assessment (Ohmer & Underwood, 2022).

Community Needs Assessment Process   Social workers are involved in community needs assessments for many reasons, including seeking new resources and support for a program, modifying a program to best meet community needs, or simply getting to know the community to better serve individuals, families, and groups. For example, when food pantries experience increased demand, as was the case during the COVID-19 pandemic, the program may consider changing its eligibility policy and can use data from a community assessment to determine which population has the highest unmet need. Funders considering a request to back a program will often ask the agency or institution making the request to justify the proposed program or services by demonstrating community need. Policymakers also can use the findings of a community assessment to modify policy.

Finally, social workers may become involved in a needs assessment to establish or strengthen partnerships. For instance, a unhoused shelter may increasingly encounter children who are medically fragile. The staff of the organization may conduct a community needs assessment to collect data about the health needs of children who are homeless and near-homeless so that they can present that information when they approach local health providers to develop a service partnership.

Sources of Data for Community Needs Assessments

There are many potential sources of data for a community needs assessment. Some of the most common sources are recent studies, service statistics, and census data. One of the most helpful sources of census data for community needs assessments is the U.S. Census Bureau's (2021a) American Community Survey (www.census.gov/programs-surveys/acs/). In addition, social workers gathering primary data often use observation, interviews, focus groups, and surveys. We discuss several of these types, as well as guidelines for making decisions about methods, in this section.

Observation In community needs assessments, the purpose of observation is to collect information about community processes and events as they occur. Observers can attend popular community events such as free concerts, plays, and/or political rallies to notice aspects of community life, including ethnic composition, geographical divisions, and apparent patterns. For example, an observer may detect the presence or absence of late-night street activity, the number of older adults visible in a community, the number of children playing outside during school hours, and the number of young adults hanging out on the streets during the day.

Other targets of observation in community needs assessment include interpersonal relationships, patterns and styles of how residents relate to one another, and residents' relationships to the community space. Observers may simply witness events, or they may actually participate in the community activities being observed.

Observers may walk around and/or attend events within the community in places like the city hall, coffee shops, community centers, busy parks, commercial strips, and fairs and markets. Using this method, observers can gather notes about observations as well as collect information from local newspapers, pamphlets that describe community resources, local maps, local directories, and historical markers.

Participant observation occurs when an observer joins in community events and interacts with local residents. For example, a participant observer could learn about a community by eating at local establishments and interacting with patrons and staff. During the interaction, a participant observer asks questions from the perspective of a respectful learner and avoids taking the stance of an expert or a change agent.

Previous Studies and Service Statistics Social workers often begin assessing community needs by reading recent studies about the history and development of community problems and community resources. These previous studies may have focused at the national level or may have been conducted by local public health departments or community organizations. Data from local human service organizations may be helpful for the needs assessment. Such data can include types of services provided, rates of service utilization, caseload data, and waiting list information. Data from other types of organizations, such as businesses, faith communities, neighborhood groups, and youth organizations, can also be helpful. This information may be available through a variety of sources, including annual reports, public data available on the Internet, a contact person at an organization, or an elected or appointed community official.

Census Data   The US Census Bureau conducts a national census every 10 years, gathering extensive demographic information about people living in the United States. The Census Bureau also conducts the American Community Survey (ACS) each year, collecting some data from a sample of residents. A variety of databases and websites, some of which are user-friendly, provide access to census data. These resources allow you to access data at small geographic levels within broader communities, so they can be very useful for needs assessments. Social workers should routinely visit the ACS website at www.census.gov/programs-surveys/acs/ to stay appraised of the data that policymakers and others are likely using in analysis of and planning for the communities in which they work.

Administrative Data   School districts, public assistance offices, child welfare offices, public health agencies, and law enforcement agencies make some administrative data available to the public. Such data is often only available after it has been aggregated or at least de-identified. This is important in protecting confidentiality of individuals. Administrative data can help illuminate a wide variety of community issues, including local academic performance, truancy, child abuse and neglect, rates and prevalence of sexually transmitted infections, teen pregnancy, and crime. These data may be available at the zip code level and can help social workers assess comparative needs across a larger community. The data may provide information about a topic directly or indirectly. For example, there may be limited data that focuses on choices between public, private schools, and Charter schools (private or publicly funded but operated by independent groups) in a community, but by comparing available enrollment numbers from first grade through twelfth grade over a consecutive number of years, you can demonstrate a pattern of public school students switching to Charter or private schools as they get older. Exhibit 10.1 lists a selection of census and administrative sources of data.

Interviews With Key Informants   Key informants are individuals who have expertise in a given area, such as the history of the community, recent growth in the business sector, political leadership, or groups who have formal or informal influence on community issues. These may be formal leaders (e.g., mayors, business association chairs, executive directors of organizations, religious leaders, or city council members) or informal leaders (e.g., long-time citizen advocates, volunteers for a community association, or gang leaders).

If you are seeking information for a community assessment involving systemic and political barriers to solving community problems, carefully select key informants who have extensive history with the community, population, or issue at hand. Choosing a key informant who is well informed about the

EXHIBIT 10.1

Sample of Sources for Census and Administrative Data

Centers for Disease Control and Prevention www.cdc.gov/	This site provides available health-related data, such as mortality, births, and sexually transmitted morbidity for specific locations.
KIDS COUNT Data Center https://datacenter.kidscount.org/	The KIDS COUNT Data Center from the Annie E. Casey Foundation provides access to hundreds of measures of child well-being on a national and state level.
FedStats www.usa.gov/statistics	This site includes a listing of many federal agencies (e.g., the National Center for Health Statistics) with links to information on statistics and other resources.
Microdata Access https://data.census.gov/mdat/#/	The Census Bureau's Microdata Access allows you to map census data for specific geographic locations.
National Neighborhood Indicators Partnership www.neighborhoodindicators.org/	This network of the Urban Institute and multiple partner cities supports the development and use of neighborhood indicators across many domains. Each partner city maintains neighborhood-level indicators across topic areas.
Statistical Abstract of the United States	This US Census site provides a summary of statistics on the social, political, and economic organization of the United States.
US Bureau of Justice Statistics www.census.gov/library/publications/time-series/statistical_abstracts.html	This site contains information on crime, criminal offenders, victims of crime, and the operation of justice systems at all levels of US government.
US Bureau of Labor Statistics www.bls.gov/	This site, updated by the Department of Labor, enables you to download raw data on local area unemployment statistics and geographical profiles.
US Census Bureau www.census.gov/	This site provides the most up-to-date information from the US Census Bureau. The QuickFacts feature allows you to search statistical information about a particular state.

individuals and institutions involved in shaping the community, population, and/or challenge is also helpful.

To locate key informants, begin by approaching leaders of community meetings and organizations and those quoted in local news sources. Your first key informants may direct you to other people you might contact for an interview. Quick Guide 28 provides a structure for a key informant interview and examples of questions to ask. The questions relate to informants' personal views and their sense of significant community facts, relationships, and dynamics.

QUICK GUIDE 28 Guide to Key Informant Interviews

General Guidelines
Based on your previous research about the community, prepare a few general questions prior to conducting the interview.
  The format should be flexible enough to allow for more depth on some questions, depending on the informant's answers.
  Prepare for a 30- to 40-minute interview, with the option for a longer interview if the key informant is amenable.
  Educate yourself ahead of time with available census and administrative data, prior needs assessments, observations, and/or other available information about the issue at hand.

Interview Format
Practice the interview skills discussed in Chapter 3, such as empathy, genuineness, and warmth.
  At the beginning of the interview, develop rapport by engaging the key informant, defining the purpose of the interview, and confirming the time allotted for the interview. Provide the key informant with the interview format such as the topics, number of questions, and confidentiality as well as what you will do with the information you collect. If you want to tape the interview, obtain the informant's consent to do so.
  At the end of the interview, consider asking the key informant to share any other pertinent information that may not have come up. You may also ask if others in the community may be willing to be interviewed as needed depending on the purposes and timing of your needs assessment.

Questions
Consider funneling the questions (i.e., moving from general questions to specific).
  Avoid using jargon.
  Avoid double-barreled, leading, long, and negative questions:

- double-barreled questions include more than one topic
- leading questions lead the key informant to an answer
- negative questions need to be simplified by asking in the affirmative

  Ask about the strengths of and challenges in the community.
  Ask about organizations and decision-makers both in and outside the community.

Sample Questions for Key Informants
- Tell me a little bit about your history in the community. Why have you chosen this community in which to live/work/volunteer?
- What are the advantages of living/working/volunteering in this community?
- What are the main challenges?
- What are some of the organized groups in this community?

Survey Data Surveys are a common method of collecting data for community practice and can gather information on attitudes, beliefs, opinions about an issue or proposal, and specific needs within a community or population that even census and administrative data cannot provide. Surveys can also provide information about the availability and accessibility of services, and they can identify unmet needs or gaps in services.

Surveys should be clear and easy to complete. To quickly survey a large number of people door-to-door, online, by phone, or face-to-face in public spaces, social workers should focus on closed-ended survey questions.

Depending on the resources available for data collection, you can create a survey on your own or partner with a researcher from a university. In many cases, you want to gather information from specific groups within the larger community and are not going to attempt to generalize your findings to a larger population. In these cases, you are not interested in distributing the survey to a large, random sample. Targeted surveys may be given to certain groups of residents, business owners, organizational members, and service providers. For example, you might collect data on the impacts of the use of methamphetamine in a community by surveying treatment providers, physicians, social workers, clergy, health providers, lawyers and judges, and others with firsthand information.

In other cases, you may need information from a broad and representative sample of community residents about their needs and their perceptions of community needs. In this case, you want to distribute the survey widely and make every effort to collect data from as many people as possible. Quick Guide 31 provides sample needs assessment survey questions.

QUICK GUIDE 31 Sample Needs Assessment Survey Questions

Circle any of the following that are needs for you or your family.

Medical Health Care	Job Transportation	Childcare
Dental Health Care	Medical Transportation	Care for Older Adults
Vision Health Care	Housing	Legal Services
Prescriptions	Disability Assistance	Utilities
Mental Health Care	Housing Loans	Counseling
Hospice	Housing Repairs	Domestic Violence Services
Clothing	Employment	Income Tax Preparation
Food	Education	Older Adult Services

What are your barriers to childcare services, if any? (Circle all that apply)

☐ None needed	☐ Location of childcare providers	☐ Not enough childcare providers
☐ No barriers		
☐ Cost	☐ No transportation	☐ Quality of childcare providers
☐ Hours not sufficient	☐ Children have special needs	

How many household members do NOT currently have health insurance? (Including insurance from Medicare, Medicaid, Children's Health Insurance Program (CHIP), Private Insurance) _____

QUICK GUIDE 31 Continued

Of those with NO health insurance, how many are: Under 18: _____ Over 65: _____

What are your barriers to health care? (Check all that apply)
- ☐ No barriers
- ☐ Cost
- ☐ No insurance
- ☐ Fear
- ☐ No doctor in my area
- ☐ No doctor will take my insurance
- ☐ No childcare during appointment
- ☐ No transportation to doctor

What are your barriers to employment? (Check all that apply)
- ☐ No barriers
- ☐ No jobs for my field
- ☐ No transportation
- ☐ Pay too low to support family
- ☐ No childcare during work
- ☐ Physical disability
- ☐ Lack of training or experience
- ☐ Mental Health Challenges

What are your barriers to reliable transportation? (Check all that apply)
- ☐ No barriers
- ☐ No car/Can't afford car
- ☐ No routes near home
- ☐ Price of gas
- ☐ No private transportation
- ☐ No routes near work
- ☐ No public transportation

What are your major housing concerns? (Check all that apply)
- ☐ Rent too high
- ☐ House needs major repairs
- ☐ Utility costs too high
- ☐ Can't afford house payments
- ☐ Can't find house in price range
- ☐ No concerns

Circle if you HAVE a:
Phone   Computer   Internet access

What do you feel is the primary cause of unemployment in this community? (Check only one)
- ☐ Lack of child care
- ☐ Not enough jobs
- ☐ Wages are too low
- ☐ Lack of encouragement to work
- ☐ Lack of education
- ☐ Not enough on-the-job training
- ☐ Lack of transportation
- ☐ Not enough help available to find a good paying job
- ☐ Other _____

What do you feel is the primary cause of transportation barriers in this community (Check only one)
- ☐ Suspended driver's license
- ☐ Lack of reliable / affordable vehicle Insurance prices
- ☐ Gasoline prices
- ☐ Bus service not available / reliable
- ☐ Other _____

What do you feel are the biggest problems facing youth (ages 5 to 17) in the community? (Check up to three)
- ☐ Not much to do away from school
- ☐ Lack of adult role models
- ☐ Adults not in touch with needs of youth
- ☐ Stress
- ☐ Depression
- ☐ Alcohol /drug abuse by youth
- ☐ Alcohol /drug abuse in family
- ☐ Other _____
- ☐ Lack of opportunities to develop skills needed as an adult
- ☐ Violence

What do you feel are the biggest problems facing adults in the community? (Check up to three)
- ☐ Inability to pay all bills and on Time
- ☐ Stress
- ☐ Bad credit
- ☐ Lack of education
- ☐ Lack of assets
- ☐ High rent/mortgage costs
- ☐ Alcohol / drug abuse
- ☐ Low wages
- ☐ Nowhere to turn for help in Crises
- ☐ Unemployment
- ☐ Other _____

Do you have and use a bank account (checking or savings)? Yes No

Do you presently use a prepaid card, check cashing, or cash advance services instead of banking services? Yes No

Source: University of Kansas Work Group for Community Health and Development, 2022.

Comprehensive Community-Based Analysis

Social workers in different settings and jobs need an understanding of the overall community in which they work as well as the populations they serve and the challenges clients and community members face. Understanding communities involves learning about their structures and how they function. When you learn about key aspects of a community, you discover its unique characteristics, including its strengths, challenges, and history as well as the concerns of its residents. One useful visual tool for understanding the connections among aspects of a community is the **sociogram**, as shown in Exhibit 10.2. A sociogram notes which parts of a community interact and the nature of these interactions. It also notes which parts of the community do not yet have interactions so that social workers can consider facilitating connections that are likely to enhance the well-being of the community.

EXHIBIT 10.2

Lakeshore Sociogram

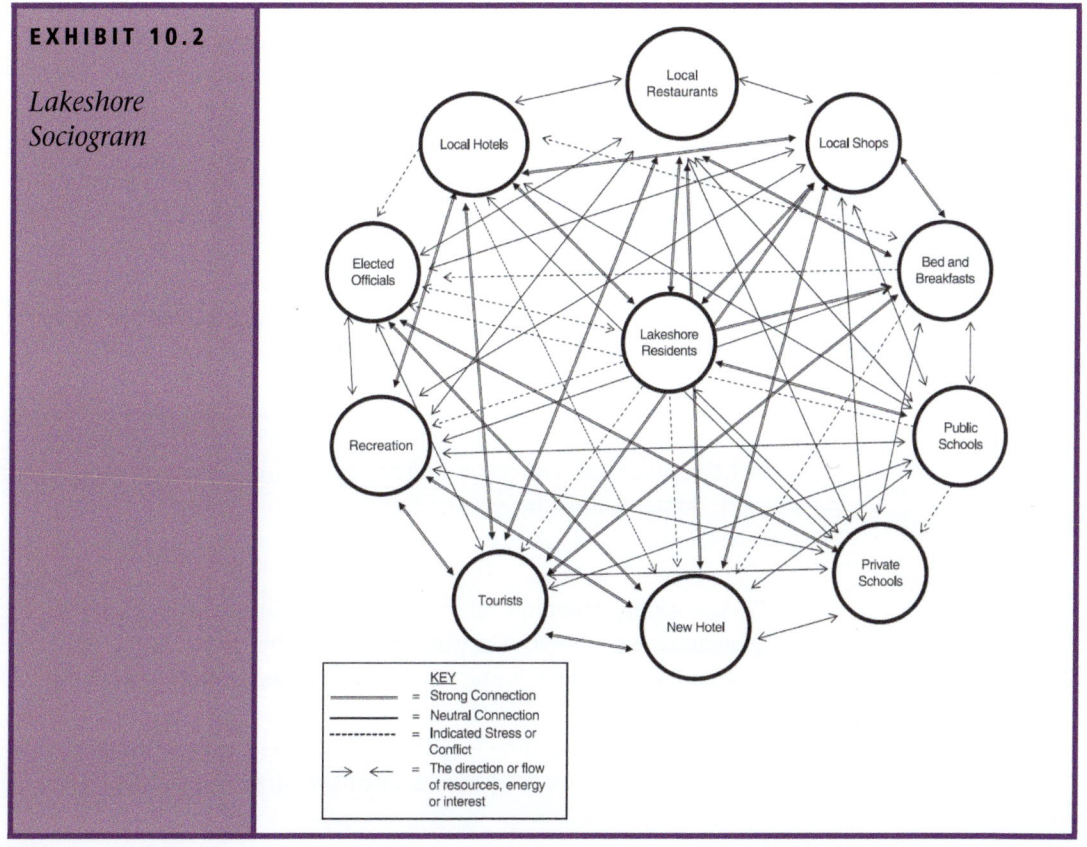

EXHIBIT 10.2

Continued

Lakeshore is a town in the northern part of the United States. It is a popular tourist destination in the warmer months because of the beautiful lake and beaches that surround it. Its many restaurants and shopping districts prosper in those warm months. As evident from the sociogram, the relationships among the various entities in the town vary. A few are described in the following list:

1. The restaurant owners have a strong positive relationship with the local shops because the shops recommend the restaurants to tourists. The residents also are supportive of local shops, and they enjoy a strong positive relationship.
2. There are many thriving small bed and breakfasts, vacation rentals, and locally owned hotels, but this year a large, high-rise hotel is scheduled to be built in the town. This will be the first hotel of its kind in Lakeshore, and there are mixed feelings about what this hotel will bring to the town. Therefore, the relationship between the hotel, the bed and breakfasts, residents wishing to rent their properties for short periods of time, and smaller local hotels is stressed/conflicted.
3. Due to the tourism industry at the lake, there are many recreational opportunities in the town, such as miniature golf courses and lake/water activities, but residents get upset in the tourist months when traffic is heavy, parking is difficult to find, and shops and restaurants increase their prices. Therefore, the relationships between the residents and the tourists, and between the residents and business owners, are stressed/conflicted.
4. There are both public and private schools in Lakeshore. The public school leadership believes that the private schools drain resources from the public schools, because the parents of the private school children are not as supportive of campaigns for additional public funds for schools. Further, fewer students in the public schools mean fewer state funds for the schools. Therefore, the relationship between the two is stressed/conflicted.
5. Elected officials voted on and passed plans for the addition of the new high-rise hotel in town. The owners of the new hotel therefore have a positive relationship with elected officials, while the local hotels, bed and breakfasts, and residents have a conflicted relationship with the elected officials. While some residents believe the hotel will benefit the town's small businesses and overall economy, most prefer to support locally owned vacation rentals, smaller hotels, and bed and breakfasts.

To achieve an overall understanding of a community, the following major community domains must be explored during a comprehensive community assessment (Netting et al., 2017):

- *Physical setting:* The physical setting of a community includes the geography (e.g., presence of water or flat or hilly land), main geographical boundaries and natural barriers such as mountain ranges and rivers, and the degree to which communities are integrated into or isolated from surrounding neighborhoods. Questions to consider include: Is the community near a downtown area, a vital entertainment or shopping district, or a medical complex? Do the streets dead-end or go through to other communities?

- *History:* The history of a community includes the identity of the population(s) that originally settled the community, when it was settled, and the major historical events that shaped the community. You might also consider the ways in which the architecture and layout of the community reflect early inhabitants and whether the community history impacts the current dynamics of community functioning. Consider asking the following: What is the history of different populations settling in the community? Have transitions occurred? If so, have these transitions been marked with conflict?

- *Demographics of the population:* Knowledge of the current populations of the community, as well as the well-defined and informal subpopulations with their own distinct cultures within the community, is very important. Questions to consider include: What are the largest population groups in the community? Can the community be characterized as homogeneous or heterogeneous?

- *Economic system:* The economic system includes employment for community residents; number and type of large businesses; the presence of small, locally owned businesses; the presence of stores that residents can use for their basic needs, such as grocery stores and co-ops, farmers' markets, clothing stores, and hardware stores; the rate of employment in the community; and the type of transportation available to community residents. You may ask: Who are the major employers? Where are the jobs located? Are the jobs conveniently located to the unemployed or underemployed? What are the relationships between employers and community residents? What are the needs of the employers? What are the needs of community members?

- *Political system:* An awareness of a community's political system provides helpful information about who makes key decisions affecting the community. To understand the community, it is important to learn about all types of elected officials who have the authority to make decisions for the community. It is also important to seek information about the level of political activity in the community (e.g., by looking at bumper stickers and yard signs and learning about recent voting rates). Information about the degree to which the business community is organized into a business association and involved in politics is also helpful. You might ask: To what degree are human service systems involved in the local political system? To what degree is the political system organized and connected to community residents? What is the level of activity of local politicians in the day-to-day life of the community?

- *Social characteristics:* Social characteristics include the demographics of the residents in terms of socioeconomics, race, ethnicity, age, and other dimensions of diversity, as well as places where people gather. Questions to consider include: Do new residents and visitors consider the community friendly or unfriendly? Are there many places of worship? What sizes are the congregations and which religions and denominations are present? Are there formal or informal meeting places besides places of worship (i.e., coffee shops, meeting halls, clubs, associations, or community centers)? What is the condition of the parks or recreational areas? What are housing conditions in terms of upkeep, quality, and the proportion of rental versus family owned? Does it vary by neighborhood? Is housing for sale? Is the for-sale housing dispersed or clustered? Is there evidence of home construction and/or repair? Are there strong institutions in the community related to social needs?

- *Human service system:* The human service system includes education, health, and social services of all types. Questions to consider include: What kinds of public, charter, and private schools are located in the community? What are their funding sources, educational quality, and physical condition? What kinds of voluntary agencies are located in the community? How available are services to residents? How well funded are the organizations within the community? Are professional networks in the community strong or weak?

- *Values, beliefs, and traditions:* While observing and building relationships to learn about values, beliefs, and traditions, consider what community residents value. Questions to consider include: Are differences based on race, ethnicity, and sections of the community, or on another dimension of diversity? Do members of the community celebrate specific traditions that may be unique to that community or to a subpopulation of the community?

- *Evidence of oppression and discrimination:* A social justice perspective requires social workers to look for oppression and discrimination within the community. Questions to consider include: Is there a history of oppression and discrimination in the community (such as housing patterns that suggest discrimination, and/or school enrollment and quality patterns that suggest discrimination)? Are there current patterns of discrimination and oppression?

Mapped Data, Asset Mapping, and Asset Building in Community Practice

In the community practice literature, the terms "mapping" and "asset" are used in similar ways but with somewhat different meanings. It is important for social workers to be able to identify the distinct manner in which this terminology is being used by different groups and people in the community, especially in work that is interprofessional in nature. Even so, all of the meanings of these terms can help in engaging and assessing communities.

Mapped Data Turning first to information that is already available to us in many cases, mapped data can help us visually demonstrate both resources and challenges to community members and leaders. Geographic information systems (GISs) are enhancing the usefulness of available data in specific geographic locations such as neighborhoods or entire communities. GIS technology uses the geocoding of spatially mapped data and allows us to include data from different sources on one map (Hillier & Culhane, 2013).

For example, as Exhibit 10.3 demonstrates, plotting both marginalized populations and home mortgage loans on the same map can provide useful data for community needs analysis and present them in a visual manner. This map illustrates the possible relationship between neighborhoods with large marginalized populations and home mortgage loans in the St. Louis, Missouri area. It was used to inform a local task force working to encourage home ownership among people of color. GIS technology also offers the possibility of adding more layers of data, such as income, to a map like this to enable advocates to study possible relationships among income, race and ethnicity, and home mortgage loans.

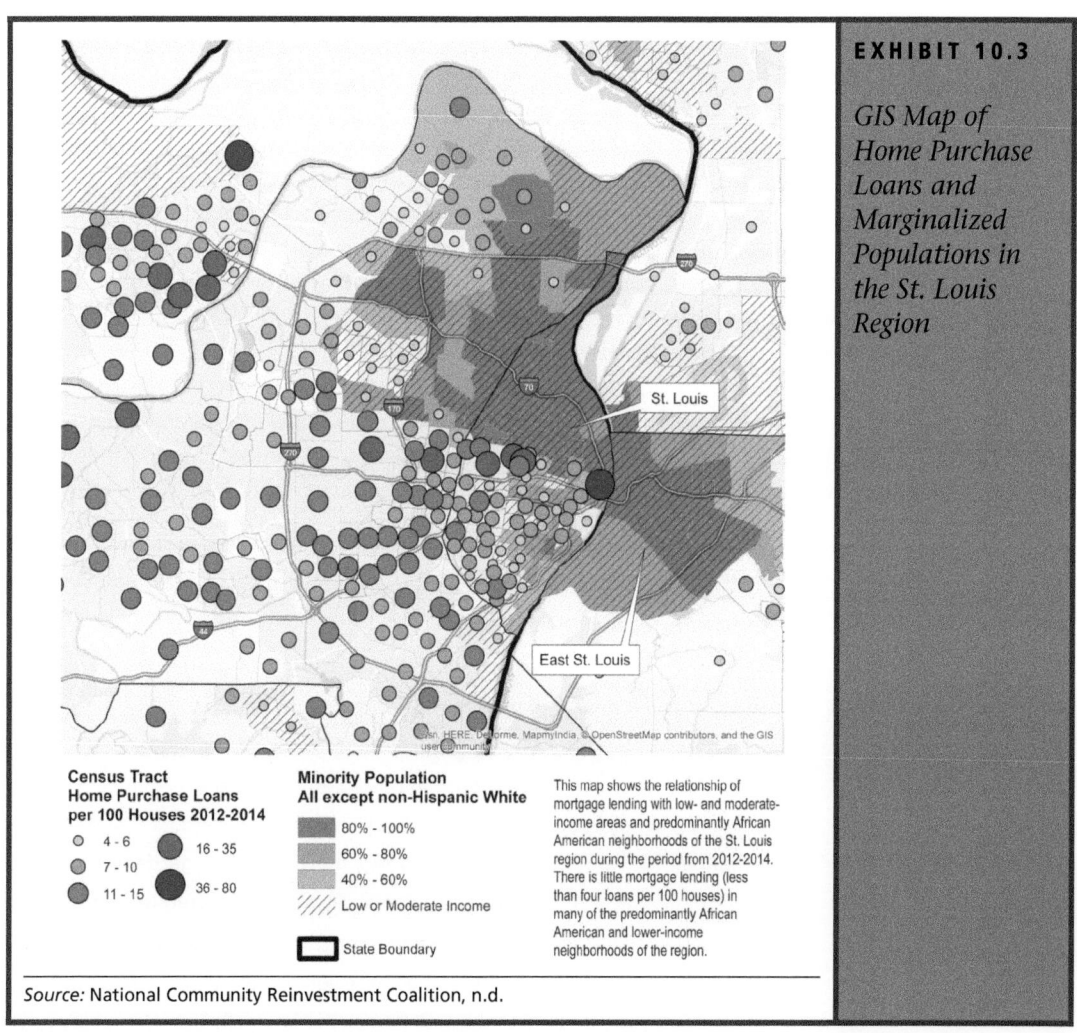

EXHIBIT 10.3

GIS Map of Home Purchase Loans and Marginalized Populations in the St. Louis Region

Source: National Community Reinvestment Coalition, n.d.

Asset mapping is a technique to systematically learn about a variety of different types of assets that may be helpful in community practice. Such mapping can lay the foundation for interventions that focus attention on the ways in which people and organizations are interdependent, and empower people by identifying ways that they can contribute to a community change effort (Hillier & Culhane, 2013).

The community mapping process is the first stage of asset-based community development first described by McKnight and Kretzmann (1996). In this approach, the term "asset" can include tangible resources in a community but usually refers to skills and abilities of individuals, and the capacities of organizations and institutions, to contribute to the community. "Mapping," according to this approach, means creating an inventory of these assets in the community. A geographical map visualizing these assets can be created, but lists of skills, abilities, and capacities are often the "maps" referred to in asset mapping.

The first activity of community practice is to inventory—to "map"—the assets of a community. For example, an inventory of the assets of individual people lists the abilities, talents, gifts, and capacities of community members. Such inventories can be used to identify underused home repair skills, child care or older adult care experience, household financial skills, home-based business ventures, or artistic abilities.

Social workers using an asset mapping process would also inventory formal and informal organizations, associations, and institutions that exist within the community, including economic, education, political, religious, and extended kinship groups. Associations can include many types of formal and informal organizations and groups, such as self-help groups that assist with addictions, youth groups, environmental groups, and charitable groups. Institutions can include parks, libraries, schools, law enforcement agencies, hospitals, and other health care resources.

Exhibit 10.4 provides examples of community asset mapping tools for individuals, organizations, and institutions. In addition, several helpful asset mapping tools are available on the Internet, including one at Americorps/VISTA (2019) at www.vistacampus.gov/what-asset-mapping.

EXHIBIT 10.4

Asset Mapping

CATEGORY	EXAMPLES
Asset Mapping Examples: Individuals	
Childcare	Caring for children, assisting with field trips
Construction and Repair	Painting, roof repair, demolition
Food	Catering, bartending, baking, washing dishes
Health	Caring for an older adult or person with a mental illness
Maintenance	Washing windows, mowing lawns, gardening
Music	Singing, playing an instrument, giving lessons
Office	Typing, writing letters, telephone skills
Transportation	Driving a ride-share vehicle, trucking, or hauling

EXHIBIT 10.4

Continued

Asset Mapping Examples: Organizations and Associations	
Business	Chamber of Commerce
Civic	Lions and Rotary Clubs
Community Centers	Senior centers
Ethnic Associations	League of Americans of Ukrainian Descent
Health and Fitness	Basketball league
Mutual Support	La Leche League, Alcoholics Anonymous
Neighborhood	Block group, neighborhood associations
School	Parent–teacher association
Service/Nonprofits	Habitat for Humanity, United Way
Asset Mapping Examples: Institutions	
Hospitals and Public Health	Prevention and treatment, population trends
Libraries	Available data, space/facilities
Local Government	Ordinances, public revenue and expenditures
Parks	Space/facilities, equipment
Police, Fire Departments	Trends in public safety, speakers
Public Transportation	Access, safety, trends in public transportation
Universities	Recent studies, research expertise

Adapted from: Asset-Based Community Development Institute. (2001–2019). *ABCD institute toolkit*.

The process of mapping assets will vary depending on your needs, sponsor, and resources. While some circumstances may lend themselves to a thorough mapping process in a relatively short period of time, in other circumstances, the mapping process may take a year or longer. Like a community needs assessment, asset mapping provides a foundation for a community intervention, yet it is also a process that may continue while an intervention is under way.

Asset Building Aside from the use of the term *assets* to mean resources that exist within residents, organizations, and institutions within a community, another increasingly important use of the term *assets* in community practice involves efforts to help people, especially people with low and moderate incomes, build tangible financial and property assets with which to achieve long-term developmental goals. This is known as ***asset building***.

Many higher-income people receive help in building financial and property assets through the US income tax code through tax benefits such as exclusions for retirement savings and deductions for home mortgage interest. Social workers help many clients and community members who do not earn enough income to have federal tax liability and, thus, do not benefit from tax breaks. For example, there are now many asset-building policies and programs throughout the United States and in a number of other countries designed to help lower-income individuals and families access post-secondary education, buy a first home, or capitalize a small business (Sherraden et al., 2021).

The asset-building movement began with an innovative idea for Child Development Accounts (CDAs) that would be universal, meaning that every child born in the United States would have an account, and it would be progressive, meaning that children living in lower-income families would receive larger deposits into their accounts. Since Sherraden (1990, 1991) introduced his theory of well-being based on assets, and CDAs as a mechanism for building assets, there have been many local, state, national, and international pilot programs, demonstrations, and new policies to establish CDAs, test their feasibility, and study outcomes associated with asset-building accounts for children and families.

The most rigorous research on CDAs is from a current randomized controlled trial involving the general population of children born in Oklahoma. Half of the randomly selected children had a $1,000 college savings account opened in their names at birth by the state, while the other half of the children and their parents served as the control group. Research findings demonstrate that the children with CDAs had significantly higher socioemotional scores at age 4 to 5 than children in the control group. In addition, mothers of children with CDAs reported higher educational expectations for their children, more positive parenting practices, and fewer symptoms of maternal depression than mothers in the control group. Many of these outcomes have been most significant for lower-income families and have held steady across racial and ethnic groups (Beverly et al., 2016). For more on these studies and updates from future research, see "Seed for Oklahoma Kids (SEED OK)." International research is also continuing and suggesting promising outcomes consistent with the theory that asset building empowers children and families and strengthens communities (Huang et al., 2019). Findings suggest that there are greater impacts for children with CDAs and who are from low-income families than those with more advantaged circumstances. In addition, CDA policies are an essential aspect of the Grand Challenge for Social Work "Financial Capability and Asset Building for All" discussed near the end of this chapter.

PLANNING

A needs assessment process will bring many issues, challenges, and ideas to the forefront. The planning phase involves sorting through and prioritizing them to be able to move forward with an intervention. To make these choices, a set of criteria must be developed to provide the structure needed to select the most important issues and ideas in a fair manner. The criteria can include any one or any combination of the following:

- Seriousness or frequency of an issue.
- Cost of the issue or resources needed to address the issue.
- Feasibility of affecting the issue.

- Readiness of the community to recognize and address the issue.
- The long-term impact or benefit of addressing an issue or implementing an idea.

Ideally, the criteria are developed in a collaborative, democratic manner with community members. The community analysis and needs assessment process offers valuable opportunities to engage in community-based participatory methods. Often used in community research, these methods involve engaging a wide group of people who are stakeholders in the issues at the center of the assessment. Involving community members, representatives of organizations, elected officials, and other stakeholders in the assessment makes it more likely to be responsive to the community's needs.

The following key principles guide participatory action methods (Barnett, 2019):

- Seek to identify and work with communities as a whole and to strengthen the social bonds of community by engaging community members.
- Use a strengths-based approach. Identify, build on, and promote strengths and assets as well as processes that promote community involvement in decision-making.
- Seek to collaborate with community partners in all phases of the research. In particular, use community members' knowledge, share information and resources among all involved, and maintain an equitable decision-making process.
- Structure the process so members of the community and community groups have the power and ability to act on findings of the assessment.
- Seek to promote and develop the capacity of local people and organizations to create and sustain any change that may occur as a result of the assessment process and outcomes.

Participatory action assessment methods can be used to gather information in conjunction with many other tools and techniques. The participatory action process itself is a mechanism by which to enhance the well-being of communities through the inclusion of community members and organizations in all phases of the assessment process, including the development of research questions. Using participatory action methods to promote collaboration increases the likelihood that the assessment will accurately reflect needs and that community residents will engage in action to assure that those needs are met. Participatory action methods can be empowering for community members. Exhibit 10.5 provides an example.

EXHIBIT 10.5	The Floating Hospital (TFH), located in New York City, provides primary health care for families and children in homeless shelters. Academic researchers partnered with TFH to engage in a community-based approach to advocate for health care for children who are homeless. They used the strengths-based approach by identifying TFH's strengths through gathering internal agency data and client case summaries. They also used empowerment by engaging in "photovoice," using pictures taken by clients to record the barriers to accessing education faced by children who are homeless. TFH enhanced its capacity by collaborating with other community agencies for data sharing. They also created advocacy briefs to provide the facts and tell client stories to be used in their advocacy. Ultimately, they were able to create the resources needed to advocate with the New York General Assembly for medical resources for children who are homeless so that they meet the health requirements for public education such as vaccinations. They found that as they worked closely with the community, their capacity to advocate for the needs of children who are homeless was enhanced.
Community-Based Participatory Research to Advocate for Homeless Children	

Source: Fetherman & Burke, 2015.

In addition to including community residents and members in planning community practice interventions, you will need to include people with technical expertise, in areas such as public health and community development, who can provide information that will be important in the planning process.

Because the needs assessment process results in the emergence of a number of different issues, challenges, and proposals, social workers in community practice must assure that the planning phase allows the group to carefully evaluate and prioritize them before moving forward to the intervention phase of helping. It is vital to empower the group to establish a fair process for selecting the most important issues, taking frequency, severity, costs, feasibility of making a difference, as well as short-term and long-term benefits of addressing the issues into account.

Steps toward selecting the issues to be addressed by the community can occur at any point in the process, from the beginning to the end of the needs assessment, participatory action, or planning processes. After setting the criteria that will be used to determine priority issues and assuring that all voices are heard, a systematic, democratic process can be used to apply the criteria to the issues generated through the community needs assessment process to plan the intervention (University of Kansas Work Group for Community Health and Development, 2022).

CONTEMPORARY TRENDS IN COMMUNITY PRACTICE

The COVID-19 pandemic effectively illustrates that 21st century community social work practice comes with many opportunities and challenges. Social workers often intervene in marginalized communities that face unique challenges with political, economic, environmental, and social changes in recent decades, such as the following (Cain, 2022; Mariscal et al., 2022; Wehrmann, 2022; Wilson, 2020):

- *Human migration and related issues of refugees, those seeking asylum, and migrants:* Increased conflict regarding policies and programs on human migration has been a common experience in the United States as well as in Europe in recent years. Social workers in community practice have historically welcomed new immigrants and helped them become established in their new countries. We have also worked extensively with refugees and people who are applying for asylum. Social workers will likely continue to be at the forefront of issues related to human migration and will therefore be able to provide much needed leadership in decreasing partisanship and increasing understanding regarding the needs of individuals and families who have been displaced by wars, poverty, violence, and strife in their home countries (Wilson, 2020; Wroe et al., 2019).

- *The devolution, or decentralization, of control of many federally funded programs and policies, including those that support community practice:* The term *devolution* in social welfare policy refers to the transfer of responsibilities for citizen well-being from the federal to state and local governments. In turn, state and local governments rely on nonprofit and for-profit organizations to deliver social services. This decentralization, along with cuts in funding, has increased the importance of involving communities and neighborhoods in informing, designing, and delivering services, and in raising local funds to pay for them. For example, some federal block grants for child welfare give state and local governments the power to allocate funds, which offers opportunities for community participation. Moreover, during the stay-at-home mandate phase of the COVID-19 pandemic, the federal government allocated rental aid funds to the states to stave off evictions of renters who were unemployed and could no longer pay the rental rates. Social workers are frequently in a position to contribute to the local-level discussions about how public funding will be used through their work with state and local agencies, public hearings on regulations, and legislative testimony. In these ways, social workers have helped raise private funding and maintain public funding to pay for resources to meet human and social needs in their communities.

- *The increasingly multicultural composition of society:* With each successive generation, the US population becomes more diverse by race and ethnicity (Jensen et al., 2021). The increase in marginalized populations in communities offers social workers the opportunity to advocate for greater inclusion, reduced conflict between races and ethnicities, participation, decreases in disparities in income and wealth, and social justice through increased attention to community issues that impact these populations such as immigration, bilingual education, and health care.

- *High childhood poverty rates and increasing economic inequality:* Childhood poverty has remained stubbornly high in recent decades. Despite decreasing unemployment, wages have not risen, so poverty and near poverty continue to plague working families (Kneebone & Holmes, 2016). Income and wealth inequalities are the most extreme they have been since prior to the Great Depression in the late 1920s and 1930s due to factors such as the decline in unions, outsourcing of employment, stagnation of wages, and changes in tax policy (Saez & Zucman, 2016). Another factor is differential access to technology and the Internet, which continues to be a significant barrier for many individuals and communities, particularly those that are rural and low income, in their educational and employment efforts. The COVID-19 pandemic brought into sharper relief the inequities in broadband access across the country. For example, the COVID-19 pandemic's social distancing restrictions resulted in social workers having to shift to only providing social services and counseling, through the use of online video conferencing platforms and telecommunications for individuals who lacked broadband access or acumen (Mishna et al., 2021; Walter-McCabe, 2020). Many marginalized individuals in rural and disadvantaged communities were unable to access services and information due to their not being able to access the information online. Social workers will continue to play a central role in working with and advocating for more inclusive and responsive economic policies at federal, state, and local levels for all citizens.

- *The widening venues and locations for community practice:* Social workers have increased opportunities to work with different types of communities, including those based on identity or shared experiences, geography, and faith. For example, social workers may work with an online community of people with a similar medical diagnosis, a planning group for HIV/AIDS prevention, people living in a specific neighborhood, or people in various faith communities. Social workers may also work in communities experiencing poverty for the first time, such as inner-ring and outer suburbs.

- *Distrust of political institutions:* Hyper-partisanship among political candidates and in national and state legislatures has created an intense atmosphere of estrangement and distrust among the American public. Social workers can engage with politicians, political groups, and community members to encourage respectful dialogue and bipartisan collaboration on social issues.

- *The decline of democratic participation and civic engagement:* The decline of social capital, including the networks, norms, and trust that facilitate collective action, is a growing concern among community practitioners. The degree to which citizens engage in public life can reflect shared values and thereby affects community practice. Not all participation and engagement has positive effects but much of it does, and social workers can work to energize and mobilize a diverse array of individuals and groups to be engaged in public life within their communities.

- *The increasing integration of community-based strategies with other types of social work practice:* Newer services for children, families, and older adults increasingly use community-based practice methods. For example, social workers are increasingly using Assertive Community Treatment, a community-based, intensive, wrap-around case management program for individuals with severe mental illness and their families (Kondrat & Early, 2022; Slade et al., 2013).

We see this integration of community practice and practice with individuals and families in the work of Victoria to help Nate and his son find housing.

Following their 30-day stay in the faith-based emergency housing program, Nate got an offer from Henry and Gladys Bullard, who were volunteers in the program, to use the basement apartment in their home in exchange for regular yard work, snow removal, and household repairs as well as the installation of their new backyard fence. Nate was grateful and agreed to the arrangement under the condition that he and his son would move into their own apartment as soon as he saved enough money for a deposit and first month's rent. Nate also stayed active in the effort to get a waiver from the State Department of Agriculture so that winter transitional housing would be available in the future for other families facing homelessness during the winter months. When the waiver was granted, Nate was hired on a part-time basis to teach home maintenance and repair skills to adults who moved into the housing units when they were not being used by seasonal agricultural workers.

CRITICAL CONSIDERATIONS IN COMMUNITY PRACTICE

In addition to the other 21st-century challenges for social workers discussed previously, several recent Supreme Court decisions may create additional challenges for marginalized cities, women, and social workers who provide them with services. For example, following a 2013 amendment to the Voting Rights Act (VRA) of 1965, which removed key voter protections, states with Republican-majority legislatures began adopting new and more restrictive voting policies. Specifically, the Section 5 of the VRA ensured that states could no longer enact Jim Crow-type voting restrictions, requiring states with a history of discriminatory voting practices to have any new voting laws preapproved by the United States Attorney General or the US District Court for the District of Columbia before being enacted into law. This requirement was known as Preclearance (U.S. Commission on Civil Rights, 2018). However, in 2013, the US Supreme Court determined that Preclearance was no longer needed because minorities had reached near voter parity with White voters, effectively removing the tool used to preapprove any changes to voting rights. Almost immediately, several states with Republican-majority legislatures began enacting more restrictive voter initiatives, such as requiring new voter identification requirements, closing polling locations, reducing early voting options, purging voters, and increasing voter registration training requirements. Researchers soon found that these newly enacted policies resulted in a decrease in ballots cast by low-income and racial minorities (Morris, 2019). In addition, in 2022, the US Supreme Court declared Roe v Wade to be unconstitutional and left the decision to each state to determine if women in their states were allowed to have an abortion. These two Supreme Court decisions may have far reaching consequences for marginalized communities, women, and the nation. Social workers have and will continue to work with and advocate for marginalized women and girls, who will face the health, economic, mental, and social consequences of these decisions.

The changing US economy has rapidly moved from a basis in manufacturing to a foundation of information and technology. The loss of well-paying manufacturing jobs with benefits and the increase in lower-wage, hourly work in the service industry has resulted in economic insecurity for people in many vulnerable communities, sometimes weakening local institutions such as places of worship, schools, and businesses. Areas of concentrated poverty have left increasing numbers of low-income communities isolated from economic development, making it difficult for families in those communities to take advantage of mainstream social and economic opportunities. For example, it may be more difficult for people in low-income communities to access available living-wage job opportunities if the jobs are located far from the community and if transportation options are limited.

A related trend is the gentrification of metropolitan areas with rapidly growing populations. Gentrification occurs when people with resources who want to live in the cities where they work move to low-income communities to renovate older properties. These patterns often result in increased property values and decreased affordability for long-term residents and people who have similar demographic characteristics to those residents. Groups of people who have lived in neighborhoods for generations can suddenly be displaced as their housing costs and property taxes increase. These issues reflect many of the challenges that social workers face today, but also present unique and exciting opportunities to create new tools and techniques for community practice, including efforts to renew neighborhoods without displacing long-term residents.

In rural regions, the loss of the working age population is a trend with myriad implications for social workers in community practice. Generalist social work is of special value in rural communities because the needs are broad, with few people experiencing the same set of needs. Given the trend of younger generations relocating to urban areas, some of the most pressing needs in rural areas are those of older adults and families experiencing health and/or mental health issues in the face of limited community resources. Generalist social workers are well positioned to work at multiple levels to help individuals, families, groups, organizations, and communities in rural regions.

GRAND CHALLENGE

Financial Capability and Asset Building for All

One of the Grand Challenges for Social Work is "financial capability and asset building for all." Lack of financial capability and assets contributes to poverty and inequality, two key concerns for the social work profession. Social workers have been involved in this work since the founding of the profession and are today involved in related policy, practice, and research efforts. For example, social workers not only help families obtain resources to take care of basic needs, such as public benefits, and affordable food and housing, but also work to economically empower families through financial education and access to mainstream financial services. In fact, the term *financial capability* has a unique meaning for social workers that includes financial knowledge and abilities as well as structural changes to ensure access to safe, secure, and affordable places to save money and build assets.

Sherraden and colleagues (2015) lay out the professional obligation to help people achieve financial security in a number of ways:

1. *Gain financial capability:* Social workers must help people gain financial knowledge and skills, as well as access to sound financial products and services. This involves helping people strengthen their financial behavior as well as changing institutions that provide financial services. In this way, lower-income people have an alternative to the high-cost financial services available in their neighborhoods such as pawn shops, check-cashing services, and pay-day lenders.
2. *Build assets:* Financial stability is also increased when people have some wealth in the form of personal savings, retirement plans, home equity, and small-business ownership. Asset building is especially important for low-income families. Social workers must be involved in helping families gain a financial foothold through building assets. In addition to financial stability in the current generation, assets can have positive intergenerational effects in low-income families just as they do in high-income families.

How might the mandate to work toward financial capability and asset building for all be applied to community engagement and assessment? To familiarize yourself with financial capability and asset building, visit the Grand Challenges. In addition, you can learn more about financial capability and asset building within the context of the Brickville community by completing Exercise #1 later.

CONCLUSION

This chapter introduced the concept of community as an arena that impacts all areas of practice. For this reason, all social workers benefit from a working knowledge of community practice. Community is the structure that supports interaction and connectedness among people over time, and it can be understood using various theories and perspectives. The characteristics of the community in which people live and grow have important implications for the resources and opportunities available to community residents. Having considered community engagement, assessment, and planning, we move on to examine community intervention and evaluation in the next chapter.

MAIN POINTS

- Communities play a critical role in the lives of clients and community members and are critical components of social work practice with individuals, families, and groups.

- Community engagement, assessment, and planning involves many skills and practice behaviors, including community analysis, needs assessment, asset mapping, asset building, and community-based participatory research.

- Various factors, including your available resources, help in determining the assessment approach.

- Social and economic trends are changing the nature of community social work practice.

- Skills of engagement, assessment, and planning in community practice build on basic communications and engagement abilities in social work practice with individuals, families, and groups. In addition, you will find skills such as data mapping, facilitating focus groups, organizing listening sessions and community forums, key informant interviewing, and conducting surveys useful as you advance in your career.

EXERCISES

1. Go to www.routledgesw.com/interactive-cases/ and click on the Brickville case (click on "Start This Case"). To familiarize yourself with the case, under the "Engage" tab, review the Introduction, "You, the Social Worker," and Critical Thinking Question #1. Consider the following: Your employer, the Brickville Community Development Corporation (CDC), wants to engage and assess the community about their financial capability and tangible assets such as savings, home equity, and business ownership. You will start by approaching and engaging with other community institutions about this topic before engaging and assessing individual community residents. What kind of institutions would be involved in the financial capability and assets of community residents? What kind of information might you want from the other institutions to learn about the residents' financial capability and their assets?

2. Go to www.routledgesw.com/interactive-cases/ and click on the Riverton case (click on "Start This Case"). Familiarize yourself with the Riverton Town Map (under "Explore the Town" case study tool), the sociogram

(case study tool), and the interaction matrix (case study tool). Answer the Critical Thinking Questions on the Riverton case. What other players would you add to the interaction matrix?

3 After completing Exercise #2, consider the following case. In your position as social worker at the Alvadora Community Mental Health Center, you have observed that there are some strained connections between the center's staff and the Latinx community it serves. You would like to learn more about the Latinx community, both to become more culturally competent and to learn more about the needs of the community. You decide to explore the idea of a community analysis.
   a Define the type of community you would study.
   b Discuss the approach you might take to conduct a community analysis. What type of information would you seek? Who would you involve? With whom might you talk?

4 After completing Exercises #2 and #3, you decide to conduct a community needs assessment. Using the content covered in Chapter 10, create a plan for a community needs assessment of the Latinx population in Riverton. Include the sources of data and the assessment approach that you plan to use.

5 Go to www.routledgesw.com/interactive-cases/ and become familiar with the Brickville case. Using the Brickville community redevelopment scenario, create a 10-question survey that could be used in a community needs assessment.

6 Select a community of which you are a member. Reflect on an issue that your community faces. What is the issue? How might you conduct a community analysis of your community? How might you conduct a needs assessment of your community? Create a concise overview of your plan in a 1- to 2-page paper.

7 Go to www.routledgesw.com/static-cases/ and (click on "Case 2: The Community Reacts to Mr. Richardson's Killing"). After reading the case, answer the following questions:
   a What micro social work practice tasks do you confront? What skills will you need in order to tackle these tasks effectively? Who is your "client"? How should you engage with these focal interests?
   b What ethical dilemmas could you encounter in your work around the killing of Mr. Richardson? What should you consider as you decide how to approach these potential conflicts?

8 Using the chapter opening case involving Victoria and Nate as an example, create a scenario that begins with an individual case and leads to the obvious need for community practice skills. Then discuss the methods you would use in engaging, assessing, and planning for intervention in a 1- to 2-page paper.

9 Revisit Exhibit 10.5 and notice the reference to advocacy briefs. Search media sources for a real-life situation in which there is a threat to an established community resource. Create a one-page advocacy brief that could be useful in reducing the threat. Be sure to include brief stories that illustrate, in a confidential manner, the potential impact of the threat to the community resource for residents.

CHAPTER 11

Social Work Practice With Communities: Intervention, Termination, and Evaluation

LIKE SOCIAL WORK PRACTICE WITH INDIVIDUALS, FAMILIES, AND GROUPS, the middle and ending phases of work with communities are intervention, termination, evaluation, and follow-up. As noted in Chapter 10, *community practice* is a broad term that includes grassroots community organizing, community development, human service program development, planning and coordination, and advocacy (Weil et al., 2013). There are many types of community interventions, all of which are based on the data gathered and process used for community assessment. The aim of many community practice interventions is to build community capacity and shape institutional arrangements that meet the needs of community members.

In this chapter, we discuss theoretical traditions and practice models that can help guide social work intervention with communities. Our focus is on the most recognized models of community intervention, as well as the ways in which they can be mixed in practice. After providing an overview of social work interventions with communities, the chapter continues with a look at the termination, evaluation, and follow-up processes. We start the chapter with a case that focuses on an intergenerational community gardening intervention.

> *Taylor is a social worker who works with youth in an urban school district. During the academic year, they helped school district administrators raise money for a summer program designed to give students at the high school an introduction to youth entrepreneurship while providing hands-on work experience. Taylor gets together frequently with another social worker, Mateo, whom they know from local meetings of the Association for Community Organization and Social Action (ACOSA). Mateo is the activities director at a senior center near the high school. When Taylor tells Mateo about the summer youth entrepreneurship program, he mentions that many older adults who come to the senior center are interested in helping youth in the city but are reluctant to reach out to high school students they do not know. Taylor and Mateo plan a "meet-and-greet" to bring the youth and older adults together for a barbeque and to share ideas for small enterprises that would help build skills for the youth and meet needs in their community.*

Key Questions for Chapter 11

1. How can I use theoretical traditions to help guide the development of intervention, termination, and evaluation with communities?
2. What models can I use to intervene in communities?
3. How do I use evidence to guide research-informed practice and practice-informed research in intervention, termination, and evaluation with communities?
4. How can I apply social work values and ethics to community intervention, termination, and evaluation?

THEORETICAL TRADITIONS AND MODELS FOR COMMUNITY INTERVENTION

As we discussed in Chapter 10, conceptual and theoretical traditions in social work provide a lens through which to understand and analyze communities. For example, you can apply the strengths approach to communities by identifying assets and resources of individuals, groups, and institutions in that community. You can utilize the empowerment approach by helping community members realize their capacity to build on the community's strengths (Netting et al., 2017).

Community practice models, which are primarily based in the concepts and language of systems, ecological, power, change, and politics theories, guide community interventions (Netting et al., 2017). As Exhibit 11.1 notes, systems theory helps to demonstrate that planned community change reverberates throughout a community and affects units within and outside of a community. Therefore, when you choose a community intervention, you should consider the possibility that community change may affect more people than you intend.

EXHIBIT 11.1

Understanding Community Practice: Theoretical Contributions

THEORETICAL TRADITIONS	CONTRIBUTIONS TO UNDERSTANDING COMMUNITY PRACTICE
Social Systems	Reveals that changes in one community unit impact other units
	Indicates that changes in subunits influence the larger community
	Allows comparisons of the functioning of different communities
Ecological	Sheds light on relationships among community units
	Recognizes that community groups compete for limited resources
	Recognizes that groups without power must adapt to community norms
	Acknowledges the interconnections and mutual shaping of physical and social structures
Power, Change, and Politics	Reveals the influence of external sources of resources on communities
	Views the community as divided into "haves" and "have-nots"
	Focuses heavily on "isms" such as racism
	Acknowledges the role of power in all interpersonal transactions

Source: Netting et al., 2017.

Ecological theory's focus on competition for limited resources, which can affect the relationships among different parts of a community or between communities, informs community interventions. Theoretical traditions that focus on power, change, and politics emphasize the ways in which external forces influence local communities and the ways in which some members of a community possess social or political power while other members do not. Social workers in community practice can help members of a community critically examine both external and internal power and the influence of the various types of power. Without examining power dynamics, community members cannot have honest and open discussions about what is best for the community as a whole, and how to establish priorities for their community's future.

As highlighted in Chapter 10, data from the community-assessment process provides the basis for community change efforts, which often use a variety of approaches. The models most common in the literature are Rothman's (2008) three models of community practice: planning/policy, community capacity development, and social advocacy. These three models have the goal of improving social, economic, and/or environmental well-being and share several common elements, including the following:

- the formulation of a change goal,
- roles for staff,
- leaders and members,
- a process for selecting issues to work on,
- a target of the change effort,
- assessment of resources needed to produce change, and
- an understanding of the role of organizations in the change process.

The Planning/Policy Model

The **planning/policy model** of community intervention focuses on data and logic to achieve community change, using experts to assist in the process of studying problems and applying rational planning techniques. Social workers using social planning consider political realities and the usefulness of advocacy in the intervention process, but the primary emphasis is on rational planning.

The planning/policy model can be implemented in a range of practice situations. Social workers engage in social planning when they participate in efforts to envision, develop, coordinate, deliver, and improve human services. Planning is needed for all types of human services (i.e., child welfare, health, aging) and topics (i.e., gang violence, neighborhood development), and in all types of host organizations, including local, state, or federal governments, faith-based organizations, and community councils (Sager & Weil, 2013). As one example, social workers prioritize data when they are involved in comprehensive planning, such as working with city officials to create a plan for homeless shelters or a community garden on an abandoned corner lot in the community. In these situations, data from local nonprofit organizations, local and state governments, and the US Census Bureau can be of great use in shaping decisions.

The Community Capacity Development Model

The **community capacity development model** focuses on fostering the community's ability to accomplish change by building relationships and skills that help solve local problems in a cooperative manner. Participant consensus is the optimal decision-making process for this model. This model emphasizes building competency of community members, groups, and the community as a whole through self-help and local problem-solving. Building community capacity often focuses on empowerment of members, solidarity among members, participation in civic action within a democratic process, and the development of leadership from the community. For example, neighborhood associations may work to educate themselves on ways to address a trash dumping problem. The work of the US Peace Corps, in which international volunteers work with local communities to create a project or increase capacity in an ongoing community effort, is another example of the community capacity development model.

> *For another example of the community capacity development model, we return to Taylor and Mateo, the social workers planning a barbeque for youth from a high school and older adults from a senior center. Taylor spoke with two students who had excellent communication skills and asked them to help serve food. Mateo similarly lined up two senior center members to help. This seemed to smooth the initial moments of the "meet-and-greet" and gave the two age groups a chance to get to know one another. Soon after people finished their meals, Taylor and Mateo started the discussion by explaining how "brainstorming" worked and asking everyone to share ideas for small enterprises that would help build skills for the youth while also meeting needs in the community.*
>
> *A number of people shared ideas for small businesses that seemed feasible. One of the older adults said that he would love to have salads and vegetables with the senior center congregate meals that many participants brought as side dishes to accompany the barbeque. While he contributed the idea as a compliment to the cooks, one of the students said that he would grow vegetables for the senior center if he knew anything about gardening. Another student said she would be happy to help cook if she knew anything about cooking. These comments had the group laughing but also led to the older adults sharing stories about learning how to garden and cook.*
>
> *By the end of the meet-and-greet, an idea for a community garden had begun to form. Many of the youth seemed interested in learning how to grow vegetables for older adults to add to their congregate meals, and in being able to sell the leftover vegetables to neighbors for a reasonable price.*

Several older adults offered to help plan the community garden and teach the youth how to cultivate and harvest vegetables. Others said they would teach students how to prepare and cook vegetable dishes. One of the youths suggested creating a digital cookbook featuring vegetables from the community garden and selling e-copies to earn money for the garden. The group agreed to meet again the following week to develop a list of what each person could do to contribute. Taylor and Mateo had used a community capacity development model to form an intergenerational team to improve the neighborhood.

The Social Advocacy Model

The **social advocacy model** is based in theoretical traditions that focus on conflict, power dependency, and resource mobilization. This model is both process- and task-oriented and focuses on shifting power relationships and redistributing resources to facilitate change in community structures or institutions to resolve problems affecting many residents. Through this model, community members often experience empowerment when they feel a sense of achievement in helping to influence decisions and policies that affect the entire community.

A helpful example of the social advocacy model is the work of Greenpeace. To seek solutions to environmental dilemmas such as climate change, Greenpeace nonviolently confronts decision-makers and those who may influence decision-makers. The goal of their work is to promote public dialog about climate change and other environmental issues and to advocate for policies that protect the earth.

As listed in Quick Guide 32, there are a wide variety of social advocacy activities, including, but not limited to, protesting, registering new voters, walking on picket lines, online advocacy using social media platforms, and testifying (Ritter, 2022; Rothman, 2008; Weil & Gamble, 2009).

QUICK GUIDE 32 Activities to Promote Social Change

Coalition building
Conduct petition drives
Conduct public hearings
Develop relationships with decision-makers
Educational outreach
Lobby decision-makers
Online advocacy/social media
Organize boycotts
Organize public demonstrations
Provide testimony
Recruit and develop leaders
Register voters
Use legal action
Write letters or emails to legislators and/or the media

Source: Bobo et al., 2010; University of Kansas Work Group for Community Health and Development, 2022; Ritter, 2022.

Applying Community Practice Models to a Case Example

Exhibit 11.2 provides a case example and applies each type of model to the example.

EXHIBIT 11.2

Applying Community Practice Models to the Brickville Redevelopment Example

The Brickville community is in a quandary. Although the community needs redevelopment, the current proposal to completely overhaul the physical structures in the community, including razing some buildings, has stirred major controversy among community residents, neighborhood social service providers, and sympathetic outsiders. The community has had little input into the plan, and some residents fear that they would no longer be able to afford to live in the neighborhood after the redevelopment. After similar redevelopment efforts in other parts of the city, both rents and property taxes increased, leading to long-term residents needing to move to other, more affordable neighborhoods. Other people do not like the plan itself, believing that the planned changes in community real estate will alter the look and character of the area. Some residents think that the community will benefit from redevelopment despite the possible negative effects. Still others do not trust the developer proposing the redevelopment. Over the past half-century, real estate developers have made several half-hearted efforts to redevelop the residential and commercial parts of the community, with little success. However, several real estate developers are working to redevelop different areas of the community, and all are requesting public funding in addition to applying for loans from area banks for their development efforts. While some developers are working with residents, most have not asked community groups or local political leaders for their input or feedback on the redevelopment plans.

EXHIBIT 11.2

Continued

The Planning/Policy Model: Using the planning/policy model, the community group or local political leader would request that city planners generate data or use previously existing data to create a redevelopment plan for the community to which all developers would have to adhere.

The Community Capacity Development Model: Using the community capacity development model, one or more community groups from the affected area would begin a process of developing their ability to create a comprehensive community redevelopment plan that they could present to real estate developers and/or city officials.

The Social Advocacy Model: Using the social advocacy model, one or more leaders from the affected area would organize community residents and groups to communicate with specific decision-makers, and sometimes bring pressure to bear as needed, to affect outcomes of interest such as zoning ordinances, public funding, and the availability and structure of tax breaks for redevelopers. Advocacy efforts including messaging workshops, sign-making parties for public protests, and strategic timing and locations for community outreach and educational events would likely be involved using this model.

One of the ways that social workers facilitate social change in community practice is to provide testimony to decision-making bodies such as neighborhood associations, city councils, departments at the local or state level, and state legislatures. Preparing and providing testimony is a strategy that can be used in conjunction with any of the community intervention models. Quick Guide 33 provides details on preparing and presenting testimony.

QUICK GUIDE 33 Providing Testimony

Social workers often provide testimony to legislative and planning committees at the local, state, regional, and national levels. The main purpose of testimony is to share information and advocate for evidence-based solutions. The following steps are helpful when preparing to provide testimony to a legislative body:

1. Learn about how legislative proposals (bills) work their way through the legislature. Who sponsored or co-sponsored the bill? To what committee(s) has the bill been assigned? What are the possible outcomes of committee work on the bill? Where will the bill go next if the committee approves it? Has a similar bill been introduced in the other chamber?
2. Learn about the history of the topic and bill. Has this bill been proposed before? Who sponsored it? What happened to the bill? Did the general public already vote on the topic through a referendum? Has this bill already been amended?
3. Engage in research about the topic. Research existing statutes that the bill seeks to amend, revise, supplement, or delete. If possible, research the cost of the bill, if enacted. A "fiscal note" is often prepared by staff members of the legislative body to estimate the potential costs in some detail.
4. Engage in research about the politics of the bill. Which individuals or what groups are working for the bill? Against the bill? What are their perspectives?

> **QUICK GUIDE 33 Continued**
>
> 5. Research the committee membership. Who is the chair? What is the chair's perspective on the topic of your bill? Who else is on the committee? What are their interests and those of their constituents? How have they voted on this topic before?
> 6. Determine how long your testimony should be, and, depending on time, draft a written statement that: (1) provides factual data, including cost estimates, needed to support the desired policy changes; (2) analyzes the proposed changes/additions to present law; (3) discusses how the desired policy changes would alleviate community problems and any possible new problems that various attempts to do so may create; and/or (4) provides suggestions for needed amendments to changes that have been previously suggested.
>
> *When delivering your testimony, consider the following:*
> 7. Dress professionally, make eye contact, and display a calm and confident demeanor. Use effective nonverbal communication.
> 8. Start your testimony by introducing yourself and the organization you represent. Use full titles to address committee members. Thank the committee chair and decision-makers for allowing you to speak. Provide background information (e.g., where you live, your credentials, or your connection to the topic). Describe your involvement with the topic, including any helpful context or background. If the testimony is related to your employment, provide your employer's name and interest in the topic. Clearly state your request for the outcome of the decision-making process. Convey passion for the topic you are addressing, balanced with professionalism.
> 9. End by thanking the committee again, and offer to be of further assistance. Offer to leave a copy of your written statement with the committee.
> 10. If you are asked questions, maintain your professionalism. Do not take questions personally, but rather state facts and your position on the bill. Offer to get facts or call on someone else to help, if needed.
>
> Remember that a vote can be the result of a particular amendment to the bill, budget projections, position of party leadership, or complex interrelationships between procedural and substantive issues—not necessarily the subject of the bill. This means that it is important not to assume that votes against the community's interest are the result of lack of support for the community at other times or on other issues.
>
> *Source:* Kleinkauf, 1981; Oregon Legislature, n.d.; University of Kansas Work Group for Community Health and Development, 2022.

Blending Models

While we present models here in a "pure" form, in practice, strategies from various models are often used together in community practice. For this reason, it is important for social workers to know about and plan to use parts of all of the models as needed (Rothman, 2008; Weil & Gamble, 2009). We present examples of using strategies from different models, or blending the models, in this section.

Blending the Planning/Policy and Community Capacity Development Models

It is possible to blend the planning/policy model and the community capacity development model with the use of citizen input and a data-driven planning process. For example, the State Boards of Mental Health periodically completes a needs assessment of local mental health services to identify unmet needs. The Board then creates a multiyear plan to allocate funding to best meet those needs. Throughout the process, the Board receives feedback from mental health providers and citizens, including those who receive mental health services. In this way, the Board uses strategies from two models through the strong reliance on data (planning/policy) and the use of citizen and provider input into the planning process (community capacity development) (Rothman, 2008).

Another example of using strategies from different models can be seen in social work practice within **community development corporations (CDCs)**, which are resident-driven organizations that exist to provide assistance to the community. This assistance can include facilitating housing improvements throughout the community, supporting businesses and commercial real estate efforts, and improving child care availability, community centers, and other community resources. Boards of residents, business owners, and local government officials generally govern CDCs. They often use data-informed approaches in creating small-business assistance programs, helping to establish **cooperatives**, which are member-owned and -operated businesses, or rehabilitating affordable housing in the community (Fairfax, 2022; Soifer et al., 2014).

Blending the Social Advocacy and Planning/Policy Models This is done by emphasizing the use of data and logic in policy advocacy efforts. For instance, social workers in community practice often work with residents in using data from needs assessments and funding allocation plans to advocate for policy changes at the local or state levels in educating decision-makers and engaging in citizen lobbying efforts as needed. In this manner, community practice efforts can involve both the use of data (planning/policy) and advocacy efforts (social advocacy) to facilitate community change (Rothman, 2008).

This blend can best describe the efforts of many prominent social justice pioneers in history, such as Jane Addams, John Dewey, Margaret Sanger, and Ida B. Wells-Barnett. These pioneers based their arguments about social ills such as child labor, lynching, inadequate housing codes, laws against birth control, and many other issues on data and logical arguments. Using tactics associated with different models that bring pressure to bear on decision-makers (social advocacy) with data and logic (planning/policy) most closely aligns with the roots of the profession (Rothman, 2008). Today, think-tanks such as the Urban Institute and the New America Foundation provide well-researched factual reports that social advocacy groups use to work for change.

Blending the Social Advocacy and Community Capacity Development Models By blending these models, networks of community stakeholders are encouraged to advocate with leaders, elected officials, and other decision-makers to improve the community. For example, a neighborhood group may learn about plans to build a drug rehabilitation facility in their community and decide to fight it by lobbying key decision-makers, delivering petitions, and/or picketing the local government. A group of parents of children who are lesbian, gay, bisexual, transgender, queer, intersex, asexual, and persons whose sexual orientation or gender identity is not included in the acronym (LGBTQIA+) may decide to engage in an online effort to advocate for civil rights for transgender people in a local public school district. If their elected officials and key decision-makers in public offices responsible for civil rights protections are not responsive, the parent group may plan a more public action such as a sit-in at a strategic location to advocate for the support they need. This approach emphasizes building community capacity with social advocacy techniques in situations where this mix will maximize the possibility for community change (Rothman, 2008). The use of strategies associated with community capacity development and social advocacy together is common in long-term social change efforts such as the LGBTQIA+ rights, environmental rights, women's rights, and women's reproductive rights movements. Strategically using social advocacy techniques while building the capacities of community members helps create an aptitude for long-term involvement in community intervention (Rothman, 2008).

SKILLS FOR COMMUNITY INTERVENTION

Community intervention involves social work practice to improve community conditions and quality of life for neighborhood residents or community members. We discuss community social and economic development, asset building and asset mapping, and community organizing. We also cover the skills of conducting meetings and facilitating decision-making in community practice.

Community Social and Economic Development

Community social and economic development (hereafter referred to as "community development"), also called "locality development" and "community building," is an ambiguous term with a variety of definitions. In this text, it is a community intervention method that seeks to maximize human potential by focusing on social relationships and the environment to improve the physical and social fabric of communities (Rubin & Rubin, 2008). Community development emphasizes social development through relationship building, education, motivation for self-help, and leadership development. It encourages local participation in community efforts toward the goal of strengthening democracy at the local community level and can include efforts to revitalize institutions. Community development that is focused on economics includes economic development, affordable housing, employment services, and other activities. Often community social development and community economic development efforts are simultaneous and interdependent, and they can be viewed as a continuum.

Community development may include professions from many fields in addition to social work, including business, sociology, anthropology, psychology, public health, and others (Austin, 2018; Wehrmann, 2022). Community development work most closely aligns with the community capacity development model discussed earlier, because its goal is to mobilize communities to solve problems and effectively work with institutions rather than to engage in social advocacy or planning/policy work. However, community development work also can use a mix of models, depending on the needs at the time.

The following assumptions drive community development (Cnaan & Rothman, 2008, pp. 247–248):

- People may need to become aware of a common problem and create a desire to act in order to solve problems.

- A diverse group of people across various dimensions of diversity (i.e., race, ethnicity, socioeconomic status, etc.) adds value and authenticity to the efforts and ensures that they serve the interests of more than one group of people.

- Democratic decision-making and participatory democracy values and fosters local self-determination.

- Empowerment, or the capacity to solve problems by working with the authorities and institutions that affect the lives of community members, is a central goal of community development.

- The primary constituents of the community development social worker are community members and community organizations, rather than those who hold more power.

- Planned change is preferred to inaction that allows current conditions to continue.

Community Development Skills The most commonly used practice skills are group work skills. Group work, covered extensively in Chapters 8 and 9, is a major part of community development work, as this type of work is often conducted in meetings. To ensure success, community development social workers must employ task group work skills including leadership; communication; problem-solving; and managing group function and processes such as educating, forming groups, seeking consensus, encouraging group discussion, and focusing to solve concerns and problems common to the group. Other skills include analyzing community issues and facilitating the increase of communication among community members (Cnaan & Rothman, 2008).

As discussed in Chapter 9, promoting leadership from within the community in social work directed at community development requires the ability to distribute leadership as widely as possible. Facilitation of effective task meetings is one example of a leadership skill that social workers may use or teach to community leaders. Quick Guide 34 provides an overview of the tasks involved in effective meeting facilitation. These tasks can be distributed among individuals during meetings or handled by a small group in preparation for a larger meeting as a way to learn and exercise leadership skills.

QUICK GUIDE 34 Elements of Effective Meetings

STAGE	ELEMENT	NOTES
Preparation	Goals	Develop goal(s) for each meeting.
	Site	Establish a meeting site that is familiar, accessible, safe, and has parking.
	Date/Timing	Set a date and time that is convenient for the majority of prospective participants.
	Facilitator	Involve the facilitator in setting the agenda.
	Agenda	Include information about each item, the name of the person introducing the item, and a time limit. Discuss easy items first, followed by hard and then moderate decisions.
	Food	Offer food and drinks in ways that are least disruptive.
	Recruitment/Turnout	Use word-of-mouth, written meeting announcements, social media outreach, and remind people a few days prior to the meeting.
	Meeting Roles	Assign roles ahead of time, including facilitator, note taker, timekeeper, presenter, and greeter.
	Room Logistics	Set up chairs, AV equipment, flipchart, sign-in table, food/drink, and microphone early enough to check the equipment.
	Background Materials	Prepare background materials about pending decisions and preliminary proposals to discuss.
Meeting	Timeliness	Begin and end the meeting on time.
	Welcome, Introductions	Begin with a warm welcome and introductions to set a positive tone, regardless of the turnout.
	Agenda	Review the agenda with the group and make changes as needed.
	Meeting Rules Discussion	Explain any rules, including decision-making rules. Encourage discussion of various viewpoints; encourage all to speak by drawing out quieter people, limiting those who dominate, and encouraging respect for viewpoints; summarize; and bring closure to discussion.
	Focus	Bring the group back to the agenda if the discussion wanders.
	Ending	Summarize meeting results, decisions, and needed follow-up. Thank people for attending.
Follow-up	Thank People	Contact people, especially new people, to thank them for their contribution to the meeting, to encourage follow-up on commitments for action, and to encourage them to attend the next meeting.

Source: Adapted from Bobo et al., 2010; Minieri & Getsos, 2007.

In task groups, using decision-making processes that promote full participation is important. Decision-making for groups can be handled in many ways, including the **parliamentary procedures**, sometimes known as **Robert's Rules of Order** (Robert et al., 2020), and **consensus decision-making**. Quick Guide 35 provides an overview of Robert's Rules of Order, and Quick Guide 36 provides an overview of consensus decision-making. Both types of decision-making processes are common in task groups, depending on the context of the work. Social workers need to be familiar with decision-making processes to fully participate as individuals and to help others participate.

QUICK GUIDE 35   Utilizing Robert's Rules of Order

Many formal groups, such as boards of directors, committees, and policy-making groups, often use some form of a formal decision-making process. *Parliamentary procedures*, or *Robert's Rules of Order*, are often used because they are well known, help to maintain order, and allow actions to be taken in an expedient and consistent manner. Although the process can be quite complex, some groups utilize the general rules without learning the minutiae. Understanding the major concepts of parliamentary procedure is a critical social work skill for facilitating and participating in a meeting.

Robert's Rules of Order provide a structured, democratic (majority rules) mechanism whereby formal groups can engage in efficient and fair decision-making. The following are major elements of the process:

- The use of a *motion* to introduce a proposal. Any idea for the group's consideration must be introduced as a motion (i.e., "I move that . . ."). Only one motion can be considered at a time.
- The *seconding* of a motion to move a proposal forward for discussion. A motion cannot move forward in the process unless someone other than the person who made the motion "seconds" the motion (i.e., "I second the motion"). Without a second, a motion dies and is not discussed.
- The use of *open discussion* to enable participants to present perspectives and ask questions about a motion. After a motion is made and seconded, the facilitator can open discussion about the motion, and group members can ask questions of the people who made and seconded the motion.
- *Amendments* to reflect revisions to an original motion based on the debate/discussion. During the discussion, one or more participants may offer an amendment to clarify or narrow the motion. This amendment must be voted on before the original motion is voted on. A majority vote is required to pass an amendment.
- *Majority rules* (i.e., a minimum of 51 percent of members agreeing) to establish a motion as a decision.

Source: Adapted from Robert et al., 2020.

> ### QUICK GUIDE 36   Utilizing Consensus for Decision-Making
>
> Real change, at the individual, family, group, community, or organizational level, comes from individuals who are highly committed to a decision or direction in which they fully participated. *Consensus decision-making*, or a cooperative process in which all members develop and agree to support a decision that is in the best interests of the whole group, can be effective in situations in which the following conditions are present:
>
> - Participants feel a genuine stake in the decision.
> - Participants share a common purpose and values.
> - Participants trust each other.
> - Participants are willing to put the best interests of the group over personal preferences.
> - Participants can share their ideas and opinions freely, without fear of ridicule.
> - Enough time is available for the process.
> - Participants can engage in active listening and consider different points of view.
>
> After preparing for the meeting, the process helps meeting participants:
>
> - Explore the issue toward the goal of developing an informed, shared understanding of the facts and the issue.
> - Establish decision criteria, including such factors as interests/needs that must be met, resource constraints, and possible ramifications of decisions.
> - Develop and discuss a written preliminary proposal.
> - Test for consensus, asking participants whether they can live with the proposal (original or amended), whether it meets the decision criteria, and whether it is the best decision possible.
> - Reach agreement by restating the proposed decision and ensuring that participants can support the implementation of the proposal.
>
> *Source:* Adapted from Dressler, 2006.

Recruitment of new participants is an ongoing and important community development skill. Participants involved in community development work are often volunteers, and recruiting, training, monitoring, and rewarding volunteers is important to the success of long-term goals. The most effective ways to recruit participants include focusing on people who are most likely to join, using a well-formed recruiting message, using multiple recruitment methods, providing orientation for new participants, and making it easy to join activities. Volunteer activities have to be calibrated to fit the skills, time, and interests of volunteers and be meaningful to them (Cnaan & Rothman, 2008).

Community Development Programs   Community economic development (CED) approaches use economic approaches to develop the capacities of low-income people and neighborhoods (Fairfax, 2022; Soifer et al., 2014). Policies and programs that facilitate community development include the following

(Gutiérrez & Gant, 2018: McKnight & Russell, 2022; Robinson & Green, 2011; Rubin & Rubin, 2008):

- *Asset-building policies and programs:* Examples of this approach include Individual Development Accounts (IDAs) and Child Development Accounts (CDAs), which are savings accounts for dedicated purposes such as post-secondary education, home ownership, starting a small business, or income security in retirement. IDAs for adults are sometimes matched by public and/or private funds for lower-income individuals and can include financial education and case management. CDAs are often "seeded" with an initial deposit from public and/or private sources and are most often established under a state's post-secondary education authority in the form of so-called "529" accounts. The proposal for IDAs and CDAs was originally made by a social work scholar, and social workers have been involved in developing, administering, and advocating for universal and progressive asset-building policies and programs (Sherraden et al., 2021).

- *Employment training and placement:* Job training programs prepare people for employment opportunities and assist participants in securing and maintaining their employment. Social workers work to recruit and serve community members who need employment training and job placement, as well as businesses and organizations who need trained workers, in communities across the United States.

- *Support of small and home-based businesses:* Programs are available to assist people to start and expand small business, including training, technical assistance, support, and access to small-business loans. Social workers have been key members of interdisciplinary teams to establish and administer microenterprise and other business development programs.

- *Financial education and credit building:* Nonprofit and for-profit organizations provide financial education to build financial knowledge and also help people increase their credit scores. In addition to helping individuals build financial knowledge and household financial management skills, social workers work on the community and policy levels to assure access to mainstream financial services for low- and moderate-income families (Friedline et al., 2018).

- *Services to help low-income families purchase a home:* Home ownership services, heavily staffed by social workers, are available to assist families to build their credit, obtain affordable financing, locate and secure a home, avoid foreclosure, and maintain their home ownership.

- *Tax assistance for low-income households:* Assistance for families is available to file their federal and state taxes and receive the Earned Income Tax Credit (EITC), which is a refundable tax credit for working, low-income families. Social workers in many family service agencies and other community practitioner venues work with the Volunteer Income Tax Association (VITA) in cities and towns across the United States to arrange for free tax preparation services for clients and community members who may be eligible for EITC refunds (Internal Revenue Service [IRS], 2022).

- *Human rights work:* Social workers are involved in advocacy for human rights and social justice for community groups, including fair housing laws and regulations, civil rights, environmental justice, women's rights, disability rights, and LGBTQIA+ rights.

There are many examples of community social and economic development programs. Youth development often involves leadership development and relationship skills as well as job training and employment placement services (Chaskin, 2010; Soifer et al., 2014; Wheeler & Thomas, 2011). Domestic violence services can include education, financial education, credit building, IDAs and CDAs, employment training, and other types of economic advocacy (Family Forward, 2022).

Building community partnerships for school-based services, such as physical and mental health services, counseling, mentoring, and other programs, is an example of community social and economic development (Poole & Iachini, 2015). Work with immigrants and refugees can include community development, including language learning opportunities; financial literacy; assistance for small-business owners to start, expand, and strengthen their businesses; and lending for small businesses that often include mentoring and case management, translation and interpretation, and other services (International Institute of Saint Louis, 2022). Some community development focuses solely on improving the physical environments of communities through efforts such as building affordable housing, the development of commercial space in low-income communities, and/or the redevelopment of entire streets and neighborhoods. Community development efforts are also called into play when low-income and marginalized communities experience the detrimental effects of environmental changes and damages to their homes, buildings, and businesses from tornados, hurricanes, and/or floods. For example, southern and midwestern communities throughout the United States are experiencing increased flooding following heavy rains and hurricanes. In the Midwest, tornados have caused severe damage to homes, businesses, and entire communities and towns. Meanwhilehile, warmer winters, less snow, and less snow runoff have led to decreased water availability in southwestern states. Social workers can help affected individuals and communities apply for government grants to repair or to help them locate to other areas of the community, state, or country. For more information on environmental changes and marginalized communities see the Grand Challenge, Creating social response to a changing environment, at https://grandchallengesforsocialwork.org.

We can see an example of social and economic development by returning to the intergenerational effort to create and maintain a community garden.

At the second meeting of student participants in the summer youth entrepreneurship program and members of the senior center, the group put a list together of tasks that needed to be accomplished to create a community garden. For example, a subgroup of students and older adults assigned themselves the task of planning the garden and procuring donated gardening tools from nearby hardware stores. Mateo, the social worker who directed activities at the senior center, said that he would make copies of the not-for-profit or 501(c)(3) documentation and create donation receipts for the hardware stores.

The chairperson of the senior center advisory board had earlier agreed to approach the Executive Director about using the large yard surrounding the center for the gardening initiative. Taylor, the social worker in the school district, volunteered to contact the extension service at the state university to have the soil tested for safety and quality. A student who had suggested a digital cookbook worked with older adults who had agreed to teach the students about preparing and cooking vegetables to plan for classes and recipe compilation. One of the older adults who had retail experience suggested that the remaining participants begin planning for how to advertise, display, price, and sell vegetables to neighbors. The small task groups agreed to work before the next meeting and to report back to the larger group on successes and challenges. Taylor and Mateo noted that it was never too early to plan for how to sustain the garden effort over time, and the group added this discussion to the agenda for their third meeting.

Asset-Based Community Development

We discussed community asset mapping as an assessment strategy in Chapter 10. You can use the community data you gather as part of the assessment process in community interventions. After collecting the data, the next step is to group the data into categories, such as capabilities of individuals, including those marginalized within the community; associations; local institutions; physical assets; and (potential) leaders. Exhibit 11.3 provides examples of the types of information you can group in each category.

As a social worker, building relationships with and among these types of assets is key in a community change effort. Building strong networks among these assets strengthens the social fabric of the community and builds capacity as a whole community. For example, social workers may be involved in establishing a network of social service providers, representatives of educational institutions, and business leaders in communities to work on local challenges. Social workers may need to identify the self-interest of various groups when recruiting them to become involved, such as mentioning to local businesses that strengthening their ties to organizations serving local youth also involves the possibility of expanding their pool of future labor.

EXHIBIT 11.3

Community Assets

Associations:	Physical Space:	Individuals:
Animal Care Groups	Bike Paths	Gifts, Skills, Capacities
Anti-Crime Groups	Bird Watching Sites	Knowledge of:
Business Organizations	Campsites	Activists
Charitable Groups	Fishing Spots	Artists
Civic Event Groups	Forests/Forest Preserves	Educators
Cultural Groups	Gardens	Entrepreneurs
Disability/Special Needs Groups	Housing Complexes	Ex-Offenders
Education Groups	Natural Habitats	Older Adults
Environmental Groups	Parking Lots	Parents
Health Advocacy and Fitness	Playgrounds	People With Disabilities
Hobby and Collectors Groups	Ponds and Lakes	Students and Youth
Local Unions	Streets	Veterans
Men's Groups	Transit Stops and Facilities	
Mentoring Groups	Vacant Land and Buildings	**Institutions:**
Mutual Support Groups	Walking Paths	Community Colleges
Neighborhood Groups	Wildlife Center	Fire Departments
Older Adult Groups	Zoos	Foundations
Political Organizations		Hospitals
Recreation Groups		Libraries
Religious Groups		Media
Service Clubs		Museums
Social Groups		Nonprofit Organizations
Veteran's Groups		Police Departments
Women's Groups		Schools
Youth Groups		Social Service Agencies
		Universities
Local Economy:		Urgent Care Clinics
Banks		
Barter and Exchange		
Business Associations		
Chamber of Commerce		
Corporations and Branches		
Credit Unions		
Merchants and Businesses		

Source: Kretzmann et al., 2005.

As relationships are built, the ability of the community to solve problems locally increases. Social workers prompt associations and institutions to increase their contributions to community efforts. For example, social workers can facilitate and support organizations to develop websites, and they can contact local newspapers, television, and radio stations to aid the flow of useful information. To make sure that information flows to younger members of the community, it is important to build and maintain a social media presence.

Social workers can also use social media networks to gather input as well as to spread information about plans and strategies.

The process of community development may also involve community meetings to develop a local vision and the strategies to implement this vision. Faith communities (such as churches, mosques, and synagogues), faith networks (such as ministerial alliances), associations (such as clubs or groups), or institutions (such as a local school district or large employer) can sponsor community planning meetings, which can be recorded or livestreamed to reach members of the community who cannot attend in person.

After residents complete a planning process, social workers can help the group seek outside resources, if needed, to help carry out the community plan. Bringing in outside resources, such as foundations that show interest in funding the plan; representatives from local, county, or state government who can advise on regulations and ordinances that may impact the plan; and other interested parties *after* creating a plan ensures that community plans are truly resident- or member-driven. If the group brings in outside resources during the planning process, careful participatory planning must occur to ensure that citizens' knowledge and views about what is good for the community are heard and considered. The outcomes of a participatory, community-driven planning process reflect the desires of residents and members (Ohmer, 2022).

Community Organizing and Related Skills

In addition to community development work, community social work practice interventions also include community organizing. **Community organizing** is the process that social workers use to mobilize people and their resources in order to identify problems and advocate for change to improve the quality of life in marginalized communities (Ohmer, 2022). Community organizing skills can be used within any of the three models of community practice (planning/policy, community capacity development, and social advocacy). Community organizing efforts can involve organizing efforts to advocate for change with local, state, and federal government officials, legislators, private landlords, faith leaders, school administrators, business owners, and corporate CEOs. For example, in the Brickville case, the supporting and opposing groups both target public officials who have control over the public resources needed for the budget of the redevelopment effort.

While community organizing typically focuses on a particular change effort, such as passing a local ballot issue about sales tax, the form that community organizing takes can vary widely. Community organization can include accepting and working with the existing power relationships, or **consensus organizing**, and challenging the existing power relationship, or **direct action organizing**.

Exhibit 11.4 describes the continuum of forms of community organizing by the degree to which people accept the existing power relationships within a community. The left side of the exhibit depicts consensus organizing. Consensus organizing involves developing strong relationships and partnerships among and between community members and stakeholders. This form of

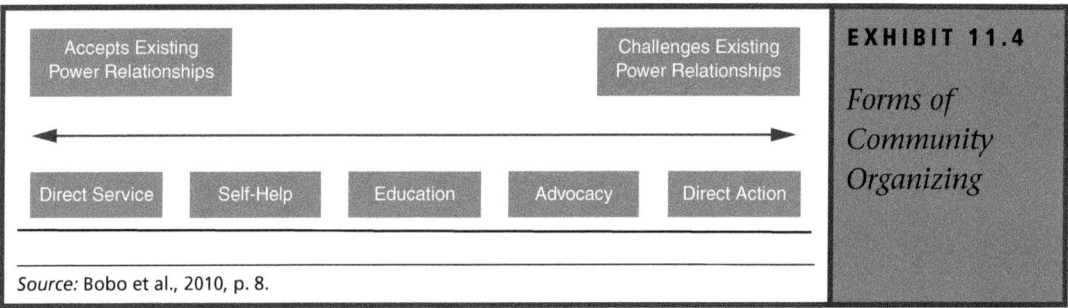

EXHIBIT 11.4

Forms of Community Organizing

Source: Bobo et al., 2010, p. 8.

EXHIBIT 11.5
Assumptions of the Consensus Organizing Approach

- Ordinary people can and should be involved in creating sustainable community change.
- It is important to identify and build on community strengths and capabilities rather than deficits.
- Potential leaders are everywhere and often need recognition and support to thrive.
- The organizer must be a selfless promoter of others.
- The organizer must seek to achieve self-interest for residents and external partners.
- Powerful people and institutions want to assist with community change.

Source: Adapted from Ohmer & DeMasi, 2009.

community organizing can also involve and create support from people and institutions that are external to the community and hold power that can facilitate community change.

External powers can include government officials, people who own rental property in the community, and/or private business owners. Engaging in consensus community organizing brings together community participants and uses the existing power structure to help make change in the community. Exhibit 11.5 shows the assumptions of the consensus organizing approach.

The right side of Exhibit 11.4 represents direct action community organizing, sometimes called *conflict organizing*. This form of community organizing assumes that a marginalized population must be organized to make demands for equal treatment/resources, with the larger goal of gaining power and changing the structure of power. With **conflict organizing**, the power structure is not seen as a partner but more as a target of action (Ohmer & DeMasi, 2009). The targets of direct-action organizing are those with power to make change, such as landlords and government officials—the same people and institutions with which consensus organizers seek to create partnerships.

In the Brickville example, both sides could use consensus or conflict organizing. Using conflict organizing, both groups could organize their supporters to press public officials and the developer to demand more power in the decision-making process about the redevelopment plan. In contrast, both sides could use consensus organizing by attempting to partner with the developer and/or the public officials and gain input through a collaborative process.

Community Organizing Skills Regardless of which form of community organizing social workers use, three essential elements in the work are (1) empowering individuals, (2) building and strengthening community bonds, and (3) building organizations that are committed to progressivity (Rubin & Rubin, 2008).

Organizers can empower individuals by (1) encouraging participation, (2) arranging tasks so individuals experience success and build their confidence to engage in community affairs, (3) organizing tasks so individuals' involvement is meaningful and builds leadership skills, and (4) recognizing and supporting their efforts (Minieri & Getsos, 2007). People build bonds by developing a shared sense of community. When individuals work together to identify and analyze community issues that need to be addressed, prioritize and select changes to be made, and develop and implement strategies toward a common goal, they create bonds and social networks in the process (Rubin & Rubin, 2008). A commitment to progressivity involves a mission to promote social equity and participatory democratic processes (Rubin & Rubin, 2008). In this sense of the word, progressivity refers to policies, programs, and processes that help redistribute tangible and intangible resources, leading to more social and economic equity.

In community organizing, social workers and members of the community can use many strategies to take steps toward desired outcomes. For example, at the conflict end of the organizing continuum, the desired outcome is to alter the balance of power so that resources are more equitably distributed. At the consensus building end of the continuum, the desired outcomes are strong partnerships between community residents and external power sources that result in tangible resources (Ohmer & DeMasi, 2009). For example, in the Brickville case, using conflict organizing, the groups supporting and opposing redevelopment could seek to change the balance of power between themselves and the developer and public officials. Using consensus organizing, the groups would seek strong and enduring partnerships among all players and build relationships with powerful decision-makers that could endure beyond the current redevelopment effort (Ohmer & DeMasi, 2009).

A Generalist Approach to Community Intervention

Depending on the context of the community intervention, generalist social workers often integrate aspects of community organizing and community development activities into their practice. For example, social workers can help community members develop a shared identity, interpersonal bonds, skills for public discourse, the ability to determine priorities and work on common challenges together, as well as leadership skills. All of these must be developed for community change efforts to be possible. Further, social workers who work primarily with individuals, families, and groups can support the development of these skills and encourage people to participate in community efforts.

Social workers can help build the capacity of individuals to engage in community interventions in many ways. At the interpersonal level, social workers emphasize collaboration with both clients and community members to optimize rights, strengths, and capabilities. Social workers discuss power and control with clients and community members to increase awareness of these dynamics in everyday life and in community activities. As first suggested by Paulo Freire (1973), educating people about social conditions, patterns of resource distribution, oppression, and other social and environmental realities, and using respectful discussion and questioning, can help and support people to engage in collective action.

Social workers strive to provide evidence-based interventions in community practice. Creating a body of research to inform evidence-based practice has proven challenging due to the complexity of community interventions, the difficulties of community research, and many organizations' lack of capacity to engage in research. Yet social workers must conduct or locate research before intervening. Quick Guide 37 lists sample resources for locating evidence on community practice interventions. Exhibit 11.6 provides research findings about the most effective community intervention activities that social workers undertake (Ohmer & Korr, 2006).

QUICK GUIDE 37 Examples of Efforts to Promote Evidence-Based Community Practice

Children, Families, and Communities

- Harvard Family Research Project, Harvard Graduate School of Education. The Education Resources Information Center (ERIC) contains new studies on programs and policies, particularly those focused on children, families, and communities. Available at https://eric.ed.gov.
- Society for Child and Family Policy and Practice, Division 37 of the American Psychological Association (APA). The Society provides information about services and service structures for children and youth. See www.apa.org/about/division/div37.

Community Change

- The Aspen Institute. The report *Building Knowledge About Community Change* summarizes key learning about how to evaluate community change initiatives and how to identify strategies for enhancing the evidence base for improving conditions in low-income communities.
- Society for Community Research and Action, Division 27 of the American Psychological Association (APA). The Society provides access to research on community interventions. See www.apa.org/about/division/div27.

Early Childhood, Health Care, and Housing

- The Centers for Disease Control and Prevention. The CDC's *Guide to Community Preventive Services* includes systematic reviews of interventions in early childhood development programs, culturally competent health care, and housing. Available at www.thecommunityguide.org.

General Evidence-Based Resources for Community Practice

- The Campbell Collaboration. This organization promotes positive social change through the production and use of systematic reviews and other evidence synthesis for evidence-based policy and practice. Available at campbellcollaboration.org.
- Laura and John Arnold Foundation Evidence-Based Policy and Innovation. This nonprofit organization is committed to evidence-based social policies and programs. See www.arnoldventures.org/work/evidence-based-policy.

QUICK GUIDE 37 Continued

Housing

- US Department of Housing and Urban Development (HUD). HUD has done much research on housing issues, and reports are available at www.huduser.gov/portal/reports/home.html.

NAMI: National Alliance on Mental Illness

- The National Alliance on Mental Illness (NAMI) is a nationwide, grassroots mental health organization. NAMI offers educational programs, advocates for individuals and families affected by mental illness, and operates a toll-free helpline.

Violence Prevention

- The Center for the Study and Prevention of Violence (CSPV), University of Colorado at Boulder provides research on effective violence prevention. Available at https://cspv.colorado.edu.

Sources: Updated from Ohmer, 2008; Thyer, 2008.

EXHIBIT 11.6

Effectiveness of Community Practice

Community practice interventions are often complex, with multiple community locations, goals, and activities that make them difficult to evaluate. However, scholars suggest that community practice interventions:

- have a positive impact on facilitating citizen participation, including increasing collective action and community involvement;
- facilitate personal and collective competencies among participants, including increasing self-esteem, personal and community empowerment, leadership and political skills, and community pride and belonging;
- have a positive impact on improving the physical, social, and economic conditions of communities (i.e., creating and improving affordable housing; increasing home ownership, improving infrastructure and physical appearance; increasing income, investment, and employment; improving high school education; and reducing the sale of alcohol to and its use among young people);
- are often unable to find statistically significant effects (many studies indicate that interventions do not affect the physical and economic attributes of the communities); and
- increase the likelihood of involving the community organizing efforts of older female residents, Blacks, and Latinx.

Other factors that help to explain and predict citizen participation include interest in the problems the intervention was attempting to solve, neighborhood perceptions and relationships, and length of residency.

Community practice interventions more easily improve citizen participation and associated benefits (i.e., improving collective action and personal and political skills of participants) than they improve complex physical, social, and economic problems in low-income communities. Therefore, social work strategies should simultaneously focus on developing ways to strengthen citizen participation and on building the capacity of individuals.

Source: Ohmer & Korr, 2006.

Social workers also engage in social planning efforts when they participate in proposing that elected officials or human service planning councils take action. They engage by writing letters, testifying to committees, becoming members of planning committees, and/or organizing others to lobby planning councils.

As part of that process, social workers can carefully create opportunities for community members to participate so that their participation is meaningful and effective, rather than a token effort to "involve" residents. For example, social workers can invite community residents to testify at public hearings about proposals to close schools in their neighborhoods and help prepare them to testify. Social workers can also seek resident involvement in neighborhood committees and work to ensure that residents can voice their opinions, participate fully in decision-making, and assist to implement decisions.

Social workers can also make connections between people in disparate situations, so that the needs of individuals are connected to broader efforts and wider structures. For example, if a social worker encounters a resident whose child has lead poisoning, the social worker may be able to link this "case" to a broader "cause" of a community problem with lead poisoning due to the old housing stock in the neighborhood and the reluctance of landlords to remediate the lead in their units. Social workers can also invite residents to participate in community-wide efforts to alleviate and prevent the problem, such as lead screenings in schools and programs to help tenants test for lead paint in their apartments.

SKILLS FOR TERMINATION, EVALUATION, AND FOLLOW-UP IN COMMUNITY PRACTICE

Community social work practitioners join the community in change efforts and facilitate the community leadership of the tasks required. Often, community practice accomplishments are the result of months and even years (or decades) of work and consist of many smaller change efforts. Using the prior example, social workers may engage in community development efforts to rid the community of lead poisoning over time. This overarching change effort can involve tasks to change local policy regarding rental housing, work with landlords to remediate lead paint, promote local school screening for lead poisoning, and work with the local public health department to create an outreach program to prevent lead poisoning and reach persons potentially affected. Each of these may involve lengthy efforts.

Achieving the goals of community change efforts, whether smaller goals achieved in the process of working toward a larger goal or the larger goal itself, leads us to the next phases of the change effort: termination and evaluation.

Community Social Work Practice Termination

Termination in community social work practice can be more complex than termination with individuals, families, and groups. Community practice can involve long-term, complex change efforts such as Brickville's redevelopment efforts that would likely evolve over many years and have the potential involvement of many players and institutions. The termination phase in community practice often involves planning ahead for the continuation of community change efforts in the absence of the social workers who helped in the beginning, their sponsoring agencies or organizations, and the residents who helped initiate and plan the effort. Termination of one change effort can also occur when the community has prioritized other needs. For example, a social worker may terminate with a community prevention and remediation effort to eradicate lead poisoning if the rates of such poisoning drop dramatically and/or if local leadership is effectively working on the issue and no longer needs the social worker's assistance.

As in all terminations in social work practice, endings can be emotional, particularly if the intervention has been longstanding. Building relationships is a key element to all types of community practice; therefore, the social worker's role in termination is to help participants examine their accomplishments, review the experience, and prepare for the future (Garvin & Galinsky, 2020). Social workers may also help community members express emotions regarding community change efforts, which can include feelings such as joy about successes achieved as well as disappointment, rejection, abandonment, or anger, depending on the circumstances of the termination. Once all emotions have been expressed and affirmed, social workers and community participants can celebrate milestones and successes along the way toward larger goals, even if those currently involved do not see an intervention through to the final, hoped-for result.

Termination and Follow-Up in Community Practice Social workers facilitate the community process of reviewing progress toward identified goals and developing strategies for sustaining changes. In community practice, social workers can invite participants to review and reflect on their experiences in change efforts, including strengths brought to the process, changes they personally experienced, and plans for contributing to the maintenance of the changes. Engaging community members in this process can provide closure for all involved. Like group work practice, participants can also use other participants' reflections to examine their own growth processes.

The termination process can employ a strengths perspective even when community goals are not realized. Participants can review the community and group strengths that existed at the outset of their efforts, those abilities they gained or mobilized during the process, and the positive changes they will carry with them after the change effort has ended. While both social workers and community members may be dismayed at not fully achieving goals, strategizing about ways in which participants can continue to work toward their goals can be empowering.

As in terminations with individuals, families, and groups, a key element of the termination process with communities is a focus on sustaining the gains achieved, such as community bonding, leadership skills, civic engagement, and/or the continuation and growth of community networks and programs.

Regardless of the circumstances of the termination, a focus on community strengths and the positive outcomes of the intervention can motivate community members and institutions to continue their efforts. If the termination occurs because the community intervention achieves its goal, the community can build on its successes and begin the assessment, intervention, and evaluation process anew.

Following up after a community intervention involves helping to sustain gains from the effort, and often requires contact with many people and institutions. For example, social workers in community practice need to provide an update and thank sponsors and those who contributed in any way to the intervention.

Follow-up also involves honoring any commitments made during the intervention and termination process and welcoming any new actors into the change process. New actors, such as new community participants or institutions, may need to become involved to continue the community change efforts if professional social work resources will not be available. For example, consider the social worker involved in the change efforts related to lead paint discussed earlier. When social workers who are involved in such interventions move to different positions, they need to transfer responsibilities to another person, such as a co-worker, parent, or a group of professionals involved in the effort, so that the change effort can continue. Following up involves ensuring that the new leaders have the resources they need to continue the work.

The intergenerational community garden provides an example of planning for termination and evaluation in community practice.

With task groups working between meetings, the students in the youth entrepreneur group and the senior center participants made enough progress that they were able to build raised garden beds and plant vegetables. Their yield provided fresh vegetables for the senior center lunches on a regular basis. They also had enough excess vegetables to earn money to support continuation of the garden. This was important because the money from the school district was guaranteed for only three years.

  Termination: Because the gardening team had discussed how to sustain the project early in the process of starting the garden, they were prepared for the job of recruiting and training future participants. The group decided to use an "each one, reach one" strategy whereby each student entrepreneur would recruit a younger student to join the effort and each older adult would recruit a new adult at the senior center.

  Taylor and Mateo also began requesting student interns from local social work programs who were interested in community practice or intergenerational issues. Because of the nature of the gardening project, the cooperating social work programs were thrilled that Taylor and Mateo could offer supervision for summer "block" practicum placements, which are generally few and far between. Mateo also offered to supervise a social work student specializing in administrative practice to establish budgeting and fiscal management policies and procedures for the garden, and teach the young entrepreneurs about resource management for financial sustainability.

Evaluation: Evaluation of the project was ongoing as a requirement of the school district and the funding entities. Taylor and Mateo helped the team get into the practice of ending all meetings with a brief period of reflection so that the group could identify their individual and joint strengths from the beginning of the project through planning and implementation. These reflections and feedback from the participants for the following growing and selling season were documented as a component of the evaluation of the garden. The documentation of the process included information about the program's impact on community cohesiveness, leadership skills for the students and older adults, knowledge of and engagement with community neighbors and civic leaders, the self-efficacy of youth as they gained skills, and tolerance of and appreciation for other generations.

Another important aspect of ongoing evaluation of the project was documentation of growth in youth knowledge, skills, and abilities; community garden yield across growing seasons; time spent by Taylor, Mateo, interns, youth, and older adults on the project; and expenses and revenues. The documentation provided valuable information for new members of the team and helped in the transition of leadership when Taylor ended her official involvement after three years of school district funding. Mateo continued to follow up with new cohorts of community garden participants, and the project continued to provide community residents with activities that regularly brought them into the senior center.

Evaluation of Social Work Practice With Communities

Similar to evaluation with individuals, families, and groups, evaluation of social work community practice interventions can assess the process along the way (i.e., **process evaluation**); the extent to which goals were achieved (i.e., **outcome evaluation**); and the social worker's skills in the intervention phase. Evaluation seeks to determine the value of the intervention and differs from simply monitoring one's practice (Netting et al., 2017). Just as the community change effort is a collaborative process, so too is the evaluation. Community participation is important throughout the change effort to empower participants. Similarly, community members who are able to collaborate as equal partners in evaluation are likely to feel a deserved sense of ownership in the process.

The evaluation process begins as an element of the intervention design and may be predetermined by an organization, a funder, or a public entity. It requires social workers and community members first to determine: (1) whether both the process and outcomes will be evaluated, (2) the ways in which the process and outcomes will be evaluated, and (3) the means by which data will be collected as the basis for the evaluation. Evaluation of community change efforts may include documentation of individual, interpersonal, and community processes and outcomes. Preferably, the evaluation process will include both qualitative and quantitative data to provide information about the process of community change and progress on the desired outcomes at the individual, interpersonal, and community levels.

CRITICAL CONSIDERATIONS IN COMMUNITY INTERVENTION, TERMINATION, EVALUATION, AND FOLLOW-UP

Community social work practice, including the intervention, termination, evaluation, and follow-up phases, offers many rewards and challenges. One challenging aspect of some types of community social work practice is long hours. For example, community social work practice can involve working during the day with professionals in organizations and institutions and in the evenings and on weekends with community participants. Efforts to change institutions, policies, and practices can take a long time, and there may be many setbacks along the way. Tangible rewards and successes for the work may be few and far between, which can lead to burnout unless social workers have a solid understanding of practice at the community level (Rubin & Rubin, 2008).

Rewards include the satisfaction of working to change environments to better meet the needs of, and to provide empowerment opportunities for, individuals and communities. Many community practitioners appreciate the ability to partner with individuals, families, and groups to better their lives, while avoiding the view of persons as clients, which can involve diagnostic labels, treatment plans, and a primarily individualistic perspective. In community practice, community members are involved in making decisions that affect their lives, sometimes for the first time. Helping people gain their voices and work toward large-scale social change is work toward social justice. The variety of tasks completed, the joy of successes, and the autonomy and flexibility are other factors that attract social workers to community practice (Rubin & Rubin, 2008).

Community practitioners must have the energy for long-term work and must be able to see value in the process and effort involved, rather than just in the outcomes. The occasional victories, even short-term or small, along with the benefits of working with and on behalf of entire communities, must be enough to sustain community practitioners. Community practitioners must celebrate small gains. They must often work diligently on short-term or immediate goals, while keeping the larger, systemic, institutional change in focus.

GRAND CHALLENGE

Reduce Extreme Economic Inequality

A Grand Challenge for Social Work identified by the American Academy of Social Work and Social Welfare is reducing extreme economic inequality in the United States. Although the economy is producing more wealth than ever before, those who own and manage large corporations are getting most of the growing profits, while workers are earning a shrinking share. In fact, most workers in the United States have not seen increases in their real wages since 1979 (Desilver, 2018). Heads of companies often earn hundreds of times as much as the ordinary worker. This trend has led to increasing hardship and concentrated income poverty.

> **GRAND CHALLENGE**
>
> *Continued*
>
> The racial wealth gap is even wider than the income gap. For example, the median net wealth of White households was $142,500 in 2019 compared to $24,100 for Black households (Bhutta et al., 2020). Lein et al. (2015) call for social work involvement in public policy to reduce extreme inequality. Community organizing has been successful across the country, especially at the city level, in increasing earnings from low-skill jobs by raising the minimum wage. Expansion of the Earned Income Tax Credit (EITC), a refundable tax credit for working, low-income taxpayers, would result in some reduction of poverty and inequality. Expanding child and dependent care to enable stable employment would help working families trying to achieve a stable income and some savings for the future. To familiarize yourself with the topic of reducing extreme economic inequality, visit the Grand Challenges website and read the fact sheet *Reduce Extreme Economic Inequality* at https://grandchallengesforsocialwork.org.

CONCLUSION

Engaging in community practice offers social workers the opportunity to influence their environments to help shape communities that are truly responsive to the needs of all members. Community practice involves developing leaders, strengthening bonds among residents, and facilitating the work that results in community change. Such complexity requires the social worker to possess a vast array of practice skills in order to help lead community interventions from initiation through evaluation.

MAIN POINTS

- Many community interventions are guided by community practice models based on systems, ecological, and power theories.

- The three most common models of community practice are Rothman's (2008): planning/policy, community capacity development, and social advocacy. These models can be blended to best match the context of the community change effort.

- Social workers must be competent at facilitating meetings using a variety of tools, including parliamentary procedure and models of consensus decision-making.

- The intervention strategies of community social and economic development, community organizing, and community asset mapping aim to improve community conditions and the quality of life for community members.

- Termination in community practice can be more complex than termination with individuals, families, and groups because of the potential involvement of many players and institutions in the change process.

- Social work community practice evaluations can assess the process along the way as well as the extent to which goals are achieved by the end of the intervention.

EXERCISES

1 To apply your learning of the Grand Challenge to reduce extreme inequality that was highlighted in this chapter, visit the Grand Challenges website at https://grandchallengesforsocialwork.org. Research whether there are any community interventions in your community that might reduce extreme income inequality. For example, is there an organization or coalition working to do any of the following:
   a Raise the minimum wage in your community?
   b Create or expand a state Earned Income Tax Credit (EITC)?
   c Pressure employers or local or state policymakers to require more predictability of income for low-wage workers?

2 Go to www.routledgesw.com/interactive-cases/ in the Engage Discover tab, click "video" and review the video of the Alvadora neighborhood association meeting within the Riverton case. In groups, begin a role-play where the video ends and continue the discussion. Does the chair of the committee vote? If not, what may have occurred? If the committee delays their vote, what additional information might be helpful to the decision-making process? Summarize the points of view. Which arguments are most persuasive? How might you vote if you were on the committee? What result would you prefer? Compare your preferences with classmates.

3 After completing Exercise #2, discuss the following questions with your classmates. What other information would you need to make a decision? If you were the chair, what might you have done differently? What elements of Robert's Rules of Order were used in the Alvadora video? What elements were not used? How might other elements have been used? How might that have changed the course of actions in the video?

4 Go to www.routledgesw.com/interactive-cases/ and become familiar with the Riverton case file. Choose either the planning/policy, community capacity development, or social advocacy models of community intervention described in Chapter 11 and describe a possible community intervention for Riverton to address the concerns about the coal-fired power plant. Describe a community intervention using a second model and compare and contrast the intervention with the first intervention. What are some key differences?

5 Go to www.routledgesw.com/interactive-cases/ and become familiar with the Riverton case file. You would like to begin to address community concerns and issues using a community social and economic development approach. What issues could you address? How would you address the issues using a community social and economic development approach?

6 Go to www.routledgesw.com/interactive-cases/ and become familiar with the Riverton case file. With many types of community interventions, recruiting allies from diverse groups adds to the strength of the intervention. Describe how you would recruit from various populations within Riverton to participate in a community intervention.

7 Go to www.routledgesw.com/interactive-cases/ and become familiar with the Brickville case. An evaluation of the youth group community empowerment effort could entail many different types of activities. Create a 5- to 7-question key informant interview guide that the youth group could use for evaluation purposes to gather feedback about the level of involvement and empowerment of neighborhood residents. The interviews would include faith leaders, neighborhood leaders, politicians, and professionals who serve the community through area nonprofits.

8 Review the categories and examples of assets in Exhibit 11.3. List all of the types of assets present in your community (i.e., campus or neighborhood) within each of the categories.

9 Go to www.routledgesw.com/static-cases/ and click on the Riverton case (click on "Case 2: The Community Reacts to Mr. Richardson's Killing"). After reading the case, answer the following questions:

   a Given what you know about human development and traumatic experiences, what challenges would you expect for this community moving forward? How might different individuals experience his killing differently?

   b What are the group-level social work practice challenges you face as a representative of your organization and a part of this evolving community response?

   c How does your understanding of the policy change process inform how you engage the community around the different options for action around Mr. Richardson's funeral? How could you work collaboratively with the community to determine a course of action?

   d What should you consider in terms of the effective use of self, particularly given your identification with the Black community and your traumatic reaction to the killing? What should you look for in terms of secondary trauma, and how might you incorporate self-care into your practice?

CHAPTER 12

Social Work Practice With Organizations: Engagement, Assessment, and Planning

SOCIAL WORKERS WORK in many types and sizes of organizations, using their knowledge of organizations to promote the best interests of their clients and communities. This chapter focuses on the nature of organizations and social work agencies, particularly as experienced by social work practitioners. It explores theoretical perspectives on and dimensions of organizations as well as the engagement, assessment, and planning processes with organizations. The discussion emphasizes the social worker's interface with organizations and the ways in which organizational functions shape professional practice. The chapter also examines the skills social workers need for organizational engagement, assessment, and planning and discusses types of organizations most often used for social service delivery. We start the chapter with a case involving collaborative practice among social workers whose agencies are members of a state-wide coalition of shelters and intimate partner violence (IPV) prevention programs.

Tyra is a social worker who is the director of a small shelter serving a four-county rural area for women who have survived intimate partner violence (IPV) and their children. One day, Tyra gets an email from another social worker, Michelle, who is the director of a shelter in a large city in the state. Michelle has worked tirelessly to convince her state legislators to increase state funding for efforts to prevent IPV in the upcoming legislative session. Michelle's email suggests that state legislators from rural areas may be able to help support the effort and asks Tyra if she and members of her Board of Directors with legislative contacts would help by talking with their state-level elected officials.

Considering Michelle's request strategically, Tyra responded that she was encouraged to hear about the possibility of increased state funding and wanted to consult with her staff and Board members about the best way to proceed. In the past, both staff and Board members had voiced concerns that IPV programs serving urban areas appeared to be better funded than those in the rural parts of the state. Tyra agreed but also encouraged everyone to consider the differences in population density, diversity of survivors, and cost of living between urban and rural shelters. After taking these considerations into account, the Board encouraged Tyra to work in partnership with Michelle and other IPV programs that were willing to make a commitment to find an equitable way to proceed with the work to increase state funding.

Tyra talked with Michelle and offered her organization's support as well as shared the concerns about funding equity. Because both the urban and rural programs were members of a state coalition of IPV programs, Tyra suggested that they begin by talking with other directors of IPV programs across the state at the monthly videoconference meeting of the coalition. Michelle agreed, and they sent a joint message to the coalition chairperson to ask that this discussion be placed on the agenda.

Key Questions for Chapter 12

1 What competencies do I need for engagement, assessment, and planning with organizations?
2 In engaging and assessing organizations, what questions do I need to ask about purpose, structure, and internal power relations?
3 What are some important internal and external elements to assess in an organization?
4 What tools can I use to assess the internal and external factors shaping an organization?
5 How can I assess the extent of cultural humility embodied within an organization?

UNDERSTANDING ORGANIZATIONS

Social workers address individual, family, group, and community needs through organizations. We can use theories, models, and perspectives to help us better understand social service agencies and social justice organizations. In fact, a theoretical understanding of organizations can assist social workers in the process of engagement, assessment, and planning, ultimately leading to successful intervention, termination, evaluation, and follow-up. In this section, we examine organizations as social systems and discuss the purposes and structure of organizations.

Organizations as Social Systems

General systems theory posits that an organization is a system that is composed of intersecting components that are part of larger systems, such as communities and societies at large. Organizations, therefore, acquire resources from their environments and return products or services to their environment. In the engagement, assessment, and planning processes, social workers can examine the extent to which subsystems, such as funders, divisions or departments, or referring agencies, meet the needs of the organization. The organization can use this information to advocate for a higher level of functioning of a subsystem, which ultimately benefits the organization and those being served.

In learning to understand organizations, it is important to pay attention to several factors including

- the role of culture in helping to understand how organizations define and pursue collective goals;

- the idea of quality as the benchmark in organizational structures, processes, and evaluation;

- respect for how tasks are accomplished as a factor as important as the outcomes of programs and services; and

- recognition that there is no one correct approach to structuring organizations.

Many aspects of an organization, including size, mission, clients, and staff qualifications, are important to consider when structuring an organization and developing a management style (Netting et al., 2017).

The characteristics and qualities that exist within social service organizations affect both service delivery to clients and the employee experience. The three most important dimensions of these differences are (1) the purpose of the organization, (2) the structures of governance, and (3) the internal power relations.

Purpose of the Organization

The stated purpose of an organization is the rationale for the organization's existence. While organizational objectives state the ways in which organizations work toward their goals, the purpose describes the concerns of the organization in broad terms. The three types of purposes are: (1) filling a public mandate, (2) providing a particular service, and (3) fostering social change related to an ideological concern to which the organization is committed.

For social workers in the United States, it is important to understand the differences between public and private-sector organizations that fill public mandates, provide social services, and foster social change. All three purposes of organizations and agencies can be seen in both the public and private sectors. Public agencies and organizations fund and/or deliver services and employ many social workers. Examples include federal Veteran's Administration facilities, state child protection services, and shelters for the unhoused funded by city or county governments.

Private-sector nonprofit organizations and agencies may provide similar services, hire many social workers, and receive grants from local, county, state, and federal sources in addition to raising funds from private donors including individuals, foundations, and corporations. Finally, there are private for-profit organizations that provide social services and hire social workers. These organizations are businesses and operate to make a profit for owners and/or

investors, though a secondary goal may involve providing quality services to help meet human needs. Examples are national chains that provide child care, long-term care facilities, and health care systems.

Organizations Sanctioned by Law The law sanctions organizations in several ways. First, organizations sanctioned by federal and state law ("public organizations") provide mandated social services widely recognized by the public. For example, adult protection services, available in all 50 states, are usually housed within a large and visible state organization. Social workers representing these organizations are expected to act in the best interests of adults who cannot protect themselves against abuse, neglect, or exploitation; independently carry out the activities of daily living; or manage their own affairs. Public organizations are directly accountable to the community, as they derive the vast majority of their funding through tax revenue (i.e., federal, state, county, or local government funds).

Second, most social services are offered through nonprofit organizations designated as **501(c)3** organizations by the US Internal Revenue Service (IRS). As 501(c)3 organizations, nonprofit organizations are sanctioned by law to meet specified public needs. Designated nonprofit organizations are exempt from paying taxes on organizational income, and donors are allowed to deduct contributions from their taxes. Nonprofit organizations are accountable to the community through their volunteer boards of directors, which are required by the tax code to include members who represent the larger community.

Legal sanctions for private for-profit organizations include the state-by-state requirements for business licenses and registrations. Further, the state and/or federal governments have regulatory requirements for providers of child care, long-term care, and health care that must be met, and they are "audited" for compliance on a regular basis. Generally, such regulatory

> **EXHIBIT 12.1**
>
> *Examples of Public, Nonprofit, and For-Profit Organizations in Aging*
>
> The Area Agencies on Aging (AAA) is a network of *public* agencies across the country that provides a comprehensive and coordinated system of community-based services for older adults. Services include congregate and home-delivered nutrition programs, case management, abuse prevention programs, legal assistance, personal assistance, and other programs. The AAAs are public organizations because they are funded through tax dollars and overseen by the US Department of Health and Human Services.
>
> The Alzheimer's Association (AA) is the leading global nonprofit (also referred to as voluntary) health organization in Alzheimer's and dementia care and support, and the largest private, nonprofit funder of Alzheimer's research. Through over 70 agencies across the country, the AA provides services such as referrals for resources, family education, support, and respite care to families impacted by Alzheimer's disease as well as advocacy at the local, state, and national levels. The AA is a *private* organization because it is not exclusively supported through tax dollars, though some AA agencies may receive public funding through grants for specific programs. As a private nonprofit, the AA receives financial resources from individuals, foundations, and corporations that support its work. Agencies are also overseen by volunteer members of a Board of Directors that represent the local community.
>
> Assisted living facilities most often operate in the private, for-profit sector and provide housing for older adults seeking independent living with options for increased monitoring and care as needed. Most skilled care (nursing homes) facilities and similar long-term care facilities operate as private, for-profit organizations as well. While nursing homes have to meet regulatory requirements as health care providers, many states do not have required standards of care for independent and assisted living facilities. Oversight of these facilities is the responsibility of owners, major investors, and/or corporate boards of directors, who attempt to provide high-quality living environments in response to the growing need for low-maintenance housing for older adults and the related competition for market share.

requirements are designed to assure consumer protection and public safety, and they apply to public and for-profit and nonprofit service providers. Exhibit 12.1 provides an example of public and private organizations that provide services for older adults.

Organizations With Service Goals Organizations with service goals develop as a result of an agreed-upon need or concern and are often started by and operated by professionals. Service goals define the work of the organization and the social need addressed by the organization. For example, for those who leave before graduating, high school dropouts are a high-risk population for poverty, health concerns, and criminal activity. Organizations providing youth services offer prevention services to help youth avoid dropping out, assist adolescents who leave school to acquire resources, and provide legal assistance and referrals to addiction treatment. Such organizations can be funded through public grants at local, county, state, and federal levels;

individuals, foundations, and corporations in the private sector; or a combination of public and private sources.

Organizations Arising From Social Movements Some grassroots organizations, which are often organizations started by citizens rather than professionals, arise in response to ideological positions on particular social problems. Frequently, the founders and volunteers of such organizations are indigenous to the movement, which means they have personally experienced the oppression that is the focus of the organization.

Examples of social movements include the Suffrage movement for voting rights for women and the Civil Rights movement for equality and voting rights for Blacks. Contemporary examples are the Earth Day, Me Too, and Black Lives Matter. Earth Day events are designed to bring awareness and governmental resources to combat climate change. The "Me Too" movement came together in response to and to bring awareness to the sexual harassment and sexual abuse of women in the workplace. The Black Lives Matter movement that seeks to bring awareness to and elimination of racism, discrimination, and inequality experienced by Black people in the United States is also a social movement (Kendi, 2019; McCammon et al., 2017; Rome, 2022). As organizations are created and mature, professionals, such as social workers, are often employed to do the ongoing work of the organizations. The early development of shelters for women experiencing intimate partner violence is another example of a **social movement**, a political effort designed to change some aspect of society. A social movement is led by citizens whose commitments and energies are channeled into a political movement, and organizations are created to implement the long-term work of the social movement (Ballentine et al., 2018; Kendi, 2019; Pittman et al., 2022; Woodly, 2021). Professionals and volunteers often have extraordinary commitment to the mission of such organizations. We can see an example of such commitment by returning to the case involving a statewide coalition of IPV programs from the beginning of the chapter.

> *One of the values embodied in Michelle and Tyra's IPV programs is that people and organizations must work together to end violence against women. The social movement from which such programs emerged started decades ago, with the first shelters opening in the United States in the early 1970s. State coalitions of IPV programs began to form not long after and have been pivotal as alliances for social change. Michelle and Tyra referenced this history as they began a discussion about a potential increase in state funding with their colleagues at the videoconference meeting of the state coalition of IPV programs.*
>
> *Several meeting participants voiced concerns that any increases in state funding may not be distributed equitably between programs working to prevent IPV across the state. One shelter director noted that state legislators who served on appropriations committees or represented certain parts of the state may have more power than others in determining details of any legislative effort to increase or allocate IPV funding. Further, the group knew that most legislators wanted to benefit their own constituents whenever possible. Given the historical values of the group, how could the coalition help assure that both urban and rural IPV prevention efforts equitably benefited from increased state funding?*

Structures of Governance

Organizational structure, much like family structure, refers to the ways in which members, tasks, and units relate to one another. The structure shapes the rules, or norms, of the organization. Some of the rules are explicit, such as personnel policies, and others are implicit, such as the best ways to influence the decision of an administrator. These rules, governed by organizational culture, may be communicated openly to employees and volunteers, while others may be communicated nonverbally or through interpretation of decisions. In this section, we explore three kinds of organizational structures as representative of those found in many contemporary agencies: bureaucracies, project teams, and functional structures.

Bureaucracies Many human service organizations, including state and local government organizations and nonprofits, are structured as a bureaucracy; therefore, social workers benefit from knowledge about the structure of their employing organizations.

German sociologist Max Weber invented the term *bureaucracy* as an ideal conceptual type, rather than a reality, of organizational structure. The following points describe the characteristics of a bureaucracy (Netting et al., 2017):

- Each position in the organization has a limited area of authority and responsibility.
- Control and responsibility are concentrated at the top of a clear hierarchy.
- The activities of the organization are documented in a central system of records.
- The organization employs highly specialized workers based on expert training.
- Staff demands require full-time commitment, and each position represents a career.
- Activities are coordinated through clearly outlined rules and procedures.
- The relationships among workers are characterized by impersonality.
- Recruitment is based on ability and relevant technical knowledge.
- The private and public lives of the organization's members are distinct.
- Promotions in the organization are made by seniority and/or achievement.

Several aspects of bureaucracy have been incorporated into the organizational experiences of many professionals, even those in smaller organizations. For example, the notion that recruitment of staff is based on ability, rather than a relationship with other staff members, is a widely accepted idea of fairness in employment practices. On the other hand, the top-down, hierarchical authority or the impersonality of relationships among employees is often an aspect of bureaucracies that challenges social workers in agency settings because it may make it difficult to make needed or necessary change. The organizations that most often display the characteristics of bureaucracies are those embedded in large systems, such as local, state, or federal government; therefore, child and adult protection, public health, mental health, and corrections are fields in which bureaucratic approaches are most common.

Project Teams In sharp contrast with bureaucracy, project teams consist of a group of people who collectively work on organizational challenges or opportunities through committee or task force structures. Project teams are a flexible way to accomplish work tasks because the committees may exercise their best collective judgment in decision-making, and the group has minimal hierarchy. Often, such groups find maintaining this structure challenging for many reasons, such as growth of the group and limitations imposed by a higher authority. Sometimes organizations structured as bureaucracies create project teams within them to accomplish certain tasks.

For example, a group of people concerned about adult survivors of child sexual abuse may use a project team approach to develop and operate an organization that provides services to survivors and adult family members. The intended services include support group services, individual counseling, community awareness, and child sexual abuse prevention efforts. Team members may decide to structure the organization so that everyone shares the tasks of managing the agency's physical space, and identical salaries are paid to everyone. The project team structure has many positive aspects. However, the structure may be challenged by those with concerns relating to the appropriateness

of some duties for those staff members with higher educational degrees. For example, social workers who interview for new positions at the agency may question the appropriateness of a person with a master's degree answering phones or vacuuming the agency offices. The project team approach can be challenged as organizations experience staff turnover as their budget grows or as new members join the board of directors.

Functional Structures When an agency becomes too large for a single person to administer, a layer of personnel will be added. These administrative additions are usually divided by function or area of responsibility—thus the name functional structures. In a community agency, for example, the executive director may appoint an experienced social worker as the program director of the youth services department and appoint another as the program director of the affordable housing development unit. In this situation, the two mid-level administrative leaders would be equals and may form a management team that works directly with the executive director in larger administrative functions and decisions. Frequently, these administrative roles are added to existing service delivery roles, particularly in smaller organizations. For example, the program director of the youth services programs would retain responsibility for actually implementing one of the programs. As the agency grows, the program directors may not provide actual services due to the heavy demands of the supervisory and administrative activities.

Internal Power Relations

While organizations have overt arrangements of power, such as hierarchical arrangements of personnel, they also have various types of authority structures that can be subtle and unique to the organization. In this section, we discuss traditional authority, charismatic authority, and rational authority.

Traditional Authority Traditional authority is authority attributed by title or ancestry, such as someone with powerful family ties. In the United States, this type of authority is most often seen as being based on profession, family relationships, and history or inheritance of money. For example, CEOs of large corporations are often related to other powerful people, such as former presidents or other CEOs, and are frequently members of the original family who started the business. Social workers may see traditional authority work in this way if they are employed by large for-profit companies that provide human services. In nonprofit agencies, traditional authority structures are sometimes seen when a founding executive director grooms a long-term associate director to assume the executive position in the future.

Charismatic Authority Charismatic authority suggests that a captivating personality is the variable required to gain power. This form of authority is often displayed in state and national elections when, for example, entertainers and celebrities run for and win public office without previous political experience.

Such authority is often present with founders of human service agencies who are successful at the necessary startup tasks of garnering supporters, raising funds, recruiting an initial board of directors, and other tasks that involve persuasion. However, charismatic authority often introduces a leadership approach that is not able to last in the long run because it is based on a single person with a unique personality type, who may eventually leave the agency or organization.

Rational Authority Rational authority is based on the ability to achieve outcomes. In one way it is similar to charismatic authority because it is persuasive rather than coercive. An example of a person with rational authority is an agency staff member who is an expert in program development. A staff member with a particular expertise and a track record of accomplishments in successfully starting new services is likely to be persuasive in appeals to initiate new programs. Large human service agencies, particularly bureaucracies, often contain staff members with rational authority because the staff is able to specialize and develop areas of expertise. Staff in smaller organizations can also develop rational authority depending on their backgrounds, interests, opportunities, and agency needs, especially if they have a generalist social work practice background and have used it to learn multi-level skills.

In social work practice, these forms of authority can exist on a continuum and/or commingle. For example, human service organizations may have an executive director who was the founder and began the position with a great deal of charismatic authority and who developed rational authority while in the position by developing expertise as an administrator. An associate director may have initially had mainly traditional authority due to a connection with an influential family member in human services and then developed rational authority by demonstrating solid success in supervision and human resource management.

Intersections Among Dimensions of Organizations

Thus far, the discussion has focused on dimensions of organizations that influence practice and the social worker's experience. These dimensions, purpose, structures of governance, and internal power relations often intersect in practice, and some dimensions are likely to be intertwined. For example, domestic violence shelters are part of a social movement to end violence against women. With this ideological position, such organizations are more likely to adopt a project team rather than a bureaucratic structure. With feminist organizational roots, a domestic violence shelter is also more likely to be subject to charismatic or rational authority, as social workers with strong interpersonal skills may tend to take on leadership roles even without a formal position of authority.

Understanding interconnections among these dimensions aids in understanding the nature of organizations and developing a framework for examining their distinctions and impact on social workers. Ultimately, understanding possible interconnections can assist in discerning the combination of dimensions that best fits the talents and work styles of workers. For example, some social workers learn that an organization structure characterized by a project team approach and rational authority is the best fit for them because they would prefer to work within a more flexible organization. Gaining knowledge about agency dimensions also helps social workers recognize how agencies can most effectively help clients reach their goals.

Social Work Practice in Host Settings

Many social workers practice in **host settings**, such as hospitals, long-term care facilities, schools, libraries, and correctional facilities. Host settings are organizations in which social workers provide social services as a support to the organization's primary focus. For example, the primary service in a school is education, yet social workers provide services to augment and support the educational goals; likewise, various programs maintained by the court system include social workers, while housing programs employ social workers to support the main goal of the organization. Next, we discuss two situations with opportunities and challenges: being a guest in a host setting and being a member of an interprofessional team.

Guest Status Expectations and privilege accompany guest status for a social worker practicing within a host setting. Professionals of other disciplines in the setting may not understand the scope of the social work role and may have inaccurate expectations—too high or too low—of the social worker. For example, social workers in a hospital setting may find that other professionals assume they are only qualified to give referrals to clients rather than engage in the many activities for which they are qualified. At the same time, social workers may experience the privilege of working with other professionals on a team that is able to accomplish more than a social worker could independently. The experience of social worker Meera can illustrate the point:

Meera is a recent Bachelor's in Social Work (BSW) graduate hired to facilitate discharges in a residential psychiatric treatment center that has a positive reputation in the community. A staff psychiatrist serves as medical director, and the executive director has a graduate degree in public health. Meera is the first social worker ever employed by the center. The nursing staff had responsibility for discharge work until the number and pace of discharges outgrew their capacity to conduct discharge planning along with their other duties.

Meera is warmly welcomed by staff, who hope that she will fill an acute organizational need. Meera is hopeful that she will gain competencies and behaviors because she will be exposed to different perspectives and practices for treatment strategies, medication, and ethics. She knows that she will have the opportunity to observe firsthand the work of the psychiatrist, the public health administrator, nurses, and others and learn about how different professional perspectives can assist clients.

While many of these hopes are realized, Meera also discovers that she does not have a role in decision-making about discharges; rather, the other staff expect her to simply carry out instructions she is given. The exclusion from the decision-making process occurs because she is viewed as extraneous to the medical discharge decisions. Because she is excluded from decision-making, Meera feels undervalued, and more as a guest than a valued team member.

While she understands that the center is primarily a medical facility and medical issues take priority over other concerns, she also understands the potential value of her involvement in decision-making about discharge planning activities. She knows she has much more to contribute than she is currently allowed and wishes to articulate her possible contributions in a way that will facilitate the staff's appreciation and growth rather than engendering their resistance and resentment. Specifically, she knows that she needs to educate the staff about the complexities of discharge planning and about the possible contributions she could make to addressing these complexities within the decision-making process about the timing of discharge and the appropriate placement for patients.

Clearly, one's status within a host setting can pose unique challenges for social workers. Some professionals with this status function as part of interprofessional teams while others work side by side with other professionals in multiprofessional settings. Social workers in host settings should exhibit effective professional behaviors concerning the education of other professions about the roles and responsibilities of social workers. Building credibility and networks of support within host organizations, employing a keen sense of timing, and displaying diplomacy are key skills in this process. On the other hand, social workers in host settings must also advocate for themselves and their professional obligations to clients and communities.

Interprofessional Teams   Projects and programs that include members of several professions (e.g., health professions, public health, public administration, and social work) create interprofessional teams. These teams can provide an enriching and exciting atmosphere in which to practice social work. Although the social work profession emphasizes a holistic view of clients and communities, social workers join many helping professionals in delivering services in a fragmented fashion. Many families seeking the assistance of social workers are also involved with other helping professionals, such as vocational counselors, psychologists, income maintenance specialists, physicians—including psychiatrists—and community support workers.

In an interprofessional setting, all professions ideally carry equal power and share decision-making responsibilities. To be effective, each profession must value the contribution of others. Social workers need competent collaborative skills when working with other professionals, including conflict mediation skills. However, a truly interprofessional setting is challenging to implement in practice. For example, in many medically oriented interprofessional teams, physicians are dominant and appear to have a privileged standpoint, while in others, a social worker may be the leader/facilitator of the team. The socialization of many professions can encourage narrow views that bias the perspective of the chosen profession over other perspectives. Nevertheless, interprofessional settings offer opportunities to wrestle with the challenges of providing an integrated, highly skilled approach in the best interests of clients and community members, as well as to explore the internal dynamics of teams through the lens of multiple perspectives.

ORGANIZATIONAL ENGAGEMENT, ASSESSMENT, AND PLANNING

This section spotlights the process of organizational engagement, assessment, and planning, including sources of data and information for the assessment. These phases are important to ensure that organizations implement their mission and serve community needs effectively. For example, the RAINN organization (see www.routledgesw.com/interactive-cases/) engages, assesses, and plans prior to implementing an intervention and then evaluates the intervention. These phases set the stage for the organizational change process of intervention, termination, evaluation, and follow-up.

Engaging the Organization

Engagement of an organization first involves the perception of the organization as a client system. An organization is comprised of many individuals and systems, yet social workers must view the entire organization as a client system to facilitate a change process with an organization. This first step in the change process uses many of the skills needed for engagement with individuals, families, groups, and communities—namely, active listening, reflection of feeling, summarization of process, research, evaluation, and analytical skills.

Social workers can engage organizations as an employee, volunteer, interested citizen, or as a consultant, although most often social workers facilitate change within employing organizations. Social workers often see the need for organizational change, so the organization can operate more effectively. For example, social workers who work for a school system may identify the need to make a change in the schools and begin to engage other social workers, teachers, principals, administrators, committees, and task groups across the school district and even across districts to address a specific organizational need.

Social workers may also engage organizations as part of advocacy efforts. For example, a social worker might engage with a public agency that serves children living in foster care to advocate for better handling of the transition when these young adults age out of the foster care system. Many of these young adults need assistance to begin living on their own. For example, they often need housing assistance, and assistance applying to college and applying for federal college grants and loans. Social workers may also engage with a community of organizations, such as a network of homeless shelters, to work for changes across many organizations, such as to coordinate data management systems to better meet the needs of individuals and families who are homeless.

In all these cases, engagement skills common across social work settings are necessary. Returning to the case at the beginning of the chapter, we can explore an example of social workers Tyra and Michelle using their engagement skills in communicating with other organizational members of the state coalition of IPV programs.

As the discussion regarding the possibility of increased state funding for IPV prevention continued in the coalition's monthly videoconference, a number of approaches to supporting legislative efforts for funding and its equitable distribution emerged. Using their preferred consensus decision-making (wherein all members reach an agreement style), the group eventually came to consensus around a plan to work collaboratively on taking two courses of action simultaneously. Everyone on the call agreed to ask their state elected officials to sign on to the legislation that Michelle's state legislators had agreed to introduce for increased state funding for IPV prevention. Tyra emphasized the importance of letting both legislators and legislative staff members know that the need for increased funding was a statewide need.

Participants in the meeting also agreed to host five town hall meetings, three in rural parts of the state and two in urban areas, with the support of local state legislators and their legislative staff members, before the proposed legislation came up for a vote. Michelle reminded the group that two messages needed to be delivered at each town hall gathering. The first message was that IPV prevention funds are needed statewide. The second message was to vary depending on town hall location, so that those attending rural town hall meetings would hear how much urban IPV programs needed state funds and participants at urban town halls would hear of the needs in rural parts of the state.

Project teams began to form before the end of the discussion to work on preparations for the town hall meetings, with members choosing the strategically selected locations of the town halls geographically closest to their IPV programs. The state coalition chairperson volunteered to talk with members of the coalition who were not represented on the call about the plan, explaining the two-fold strategy of working to increase state funding and assure equitable distribution between urban and rural IPV programs, and asking them to join project teams.

Assessment of Organizations

The overall assessment of organizations involves research into both the internal environment of the organization, or the internal mechanisms within organizations, and the external environment with which the organization receives and provides resources, such as funders, accreditation organizations, suppliers of goods and services, clients, other organizations, and others. Exhibit 12.2

> **EXHIBIT 12.2**
>
> *Assessment Framework*
>
> **Internal Assessment**
> - Legal basis, mission, bylaws, and history
> - Administrative structure and management style
> - Program structure, programs, and services
> - Organizational culture (i.e., physical surroundings, public relations, language, procedures, social justice/diversity)
> - Personnel policies and procedures
> - Resources (i.e., financial, technological, personnel)
>
> **External Assessment**
> - Relationship with funders and potential funders
> - Relationship with clients
> - Relationship with organizations in network (i.e., referrals and coalitions)
> - Relationships with political figures
> - Relationships with others (i.e., regulatory bodies, professional associations, etc.)

presents an assessment framework that is an integration of previous frameworks and that may be helpful in the assessment task (Gitterman et al., 2021; Netting et al., 2017).

Assessment of an organization involves gathering data. Like community assessment, data can be gathered through observation, written documents, key informant interviews, publicly available sources, service statistics, previous organizational assessment, administrative sources, and focus groups. Depending on the size of the organization to be assessed, a public forum and survey may also be appropriate ways to gather data (Gitterman et al., 2021; Netting et al., 2017).

Organizations often create documents that may be helpful in the assessment process. These include organizational charts, policy and procedure manuals, personnel manuals, job descriptions, meeting minutes, and annual reports. Information from media sources and reports from other organizations can also be useful.

Elements of an Internal Assessment

The internal structures and dynamics of an organization affect many aspects of its service delivery, as well as the experiences of executives, staff members, and members of the board of directors (Tebbe, 2019). This section discusses the elements of an organization that can be part of an organizational assessment.

Legal Basis Organizations must be recognized by the law to legitimately operate. The legal basis for public organizations is a statute or executive order, while a private organization has a legal basis in the articles of incorporation. These documents authorize an organization to officially exist and define the parameters for their operations.

Mission Statement Most organizations create a mission statement, which is a concise, broad statement of the purpose of the organization. While the

> **EXHIBIT 12.3**
>
> *Mission Statement, Longview Community Center*
>
> Our mission is to enhance the quality of life of older adults, children, and families in the regional area by providing:
>
> 1. Access to education, counseling, and health services;
> 2. Recreation and social programs; and
> 3. Daily nutritional meals.

statement is too broad for details, the statement identifies the client needs the organization meets, the population served, and the intended client outcomes. The details about programs, services, organizational structure, and other specifics are outlined in other documents, such as annual reports, an organizational chart, and program descriptions. The mission statement states why the organization exists and is less changeable than programs and services. Revising a mission statement is needed if an organization perceives a mismatch between the mission statement and current client needs and organization activities. For example, many child welfare agencies were founded in the early 20th century as orphanages and needed to revisit their mission statements in light of the focus in child welfare on home-based placements. Exhibit 12.3 provides an example of a mission statement.

Bylaws The way in which a nonprofit organization governs itself is described in the bylaws. Bylaws are legal documents that describe the structure and abilities of the board of directors, such as the composition of the board, terms of the members, permanent committees, voting rights, and other matters that concern governance. Bylaws are typically brief, and rules about them vary from state to state.

History Organizations develop their own histories that help to define them over time. Organizational histories shape both the agencies themselves and the communities they serve. Important aspects of history include the founding of the organization, major funders, influential staff members and administrators, accomplishments, and challenging periods. Following challenging periods, executive directors and members of the board of directors often work together to reframe any difficulties in a way that addresses the survival and strengthening of the organization.

Administrative Structure and Management Style Organizations often depict their administrative structure on an organizational chart that shows the units of the organization and their relationship to one another. The management style of the organization can be seen in the way work is allocated, decisions are made, employees are supervised, and conflict is handled. Some elements of management style are included in written documents, while others are less formal and can be learned through experience or from other staff members.

Structure of Programs, Services, and Activities Human service organizations provide programs and services and/or carry out activities to meet overall organizational goals and objectives. An assessment process would include a review of official documents where these are described and the extent to which the programs, services, and activities are consistent with the overall mission, goals, and objectives of the organization and with evidence-based practices.

Organizational Culture Organizational culture consists of many factors, including history, philosophy, styles of communication, patterns of decision-making, expectations, personal styles of staff members, myths, typical behaviors, and formal and informal rules. Culture is also shaped by the organization's purpose, structure of governance, and internal power relations.

While not reflected in the mission statement or any one official document, the organizational culture is, nevertheless, an important element that shapes aspects of the agency's work and employees' experiences. For example, the extent to which social workers are expected to work overtime, earned time off, and how much autonomy practicum students experience represent the types of issues shaped by organizational culture. Exhibit 12.4 discusses the dimensions of organizational culture. Exhibit 12.5 helps you review your own

EXHIBIT 12.4

Dimensions of Organizational Culture

Observed behavioral regularities when people interact, including their language, customs, traditions, and rituals

Group norms that evolve as standards and values for working together

Espoused values that the organization is trying to achieve

Formal philosophy—the broad policies and ideologies that direct the work

Rules of the game, informal behavioral expectations—often referred to as "knowing the ropes"

Climate—the physical layout and how it feels

Embedded skills—abilities that can easily be passed along to the next generation of social workers and other staff members because they have been institutionalized by the organization

Habits of thinking, mental models, and/or linguistic paradigms—things taught to new members as they are socialized to the organization

Shared meanings—group understandings that develop as people work together

Root metaphors or integrating symbols—the ideas, feelings, images, and even physical layout that represent the group's artifacts, as well as how people describe them

Formal rituals and celebrations—ways that a group celebrates key events that reflect important values or events

Source: O'Connor & Netting, 2009; Schein & Schein, 2016.

EXHIBIT 12.5

Rate Your Organizational Style

Using the following list and the key at the bottom, rate yourself on these items to review your organizational style. Add other items you think are important. Be prepared to discuss this survey in class and to apply it to your field placement. What obstacles do you encounter in fulfilling these points?

☐ I offer positive feedback to my colleagues for behaviors that contribute to effective services.

☐ I involve my colleagues in seeking changes in policies and programs to improve the quality of services.

☐ I value learning about my colleagues' points of view. For example, I seek feedback that will help me enhance my competencies, behaviors, and cultural responsiveness. When I have a complaint, I discuss it with the person directly involved.

☐ I involve others in arranging opportunities to discuss practice/policy issues/topics.

☐ I communicate congratulations to others regarding professional or personal events/accomplishments.

☐ I come prepared for all types of meetings.

☐ I make positive contributions at meetings.

☐ I refrain from idle gossip at work.

☐ I make more positive than negative comments at work.

Key: 0 (not at all) 1 (a little) 2 (a fair amount) 3 (a great deal) 4 (best that could be)

Source: Adapted from Gambrill, 2013.

organizational style. While the concept of organizational culture is intangible and imprecise, culture is an important dynamic of any organization.

Physical Surroundings If organizations have a physical presence that clients and community members see, the location and interior of an organization can provide information about its culture. An organization with dark, messy physical surroundings and/or little privacy for personal interactions could be an organization with a culture that places a lower priority on the potential impact of physical surroundings on outcomes than a clean organization with bright lighting and plenty of space for private interviews. To best serve clients and communities, many human service agencies are located in or near residential areas, often in low- and moderate-income areas. While many social workers are not employed by organizations that are housed in luxurious surroundings and/or in upscale locations, the physical atmosphere and location of an organization reflects and impacts aspects of organizational culture and affects employee well-being (Shier, 2012).

Public Relations Organizations reflect their culture in their public relations activities and products. Public relations is the practice of managing communication between an organization and the public. Organizations can use a variety of media to manage their public information and image, such as websites, social media, blogs, printed materials, radio and television, public service announcements and appearances, and face-to-face encounters.

Language The language used in agency settings includes the tone and degree of empathy and respect expressed. Language both reflects and shapes the thoughts and feelings expressed. Therefore, the language used in organizations reflects and shapes the self-perceptions of the social workers, their work, and their clients and communities. For example, social workers' use of disrespectful language toward and about clients violates the *Code of Ethics* (NASW, 2021a), displays a violation of the core commitment to respect people and treat them with dignity, and can affect other social workers through a culture of disrespect. While some organizations may attempt to justify pejorative language patterns by stating that staff members need to "blow off steam," the lack of respectful, strengths-based language can have a powerful, detrimental impact on organizational culture.

Procedures A simple agency procedure, such as greeting a new client, asking them to sit down, inviting them to an office from the waiting room, or giving them paperwork impacts the quality of the client experience. Social workers must be respectful and sensitive about the explanation of the procedures concerning such matters as confidentiality, fees, appointment times, and negotiations in scheduling appointments. These aspects are relevant as a social worker's expression of respect for clients but also as clearly understood agency policy. Quick Guide 38 provides an opportunity to assess client and employee treatment regarding procedures at an organization familiar to you.

QUICK GUIDE 38 Dignity Assessment and Human Services Guide

1. Persons seeking services from my agency are more likely to experience:

    ____ a poorly maintained waiting room   ____ a warm and well-furnished waiting room

    ____ a place to sign in   ____ a courteous and personal greeting

    ____ having their name called out and being led to the office   ____ being personally met and invited to "follow me" to the office

    ____ nonverbal cues from the staff that they are a bother   ____ nonverbal cues that suggest we are glad they are here

    ____ treatment that says "you are another case"   ____ treatment that says "you are a person"

2. Persons seeking services in my agency are more likely to be:

    ____ treated as problems that need to be solved   ____ treated as partners in a mutual process of deciding how to proceed

    ____ given treatment based on the medical model   ____ provided treatment based on a competency model

    ____ seen as problems   ____ seen as people with issues and needs

    ____ seen as needing an expert   ____ seen as the expert

3. Employees within my setting are more likely to experience:

    ____ getting written memos about new changes   ____ being asked for input about new changes

    ____ an expectation of independent work without much support   ____ being supported in their roles

    ____ wishing for another job   ____ joy in coming to work

    ____ feeling like their consumers are not important to the agency   ____ feeling their consumers are important to the agency

    ____ feeling like they are a drain to the community   ____ feeling like they are a resource to the community

    ____ feeling unimportant to the agency   ____ feeling important to the agency

    ____ lack of respect for other employees   ____ respect for other employees

4. My experience with the organizational culture is that:

    ____ respect for human diversity is ignored   ____ respect for human diversity is valued

    ____ membership in the community is blocked to those who are different   ____ membership in the community is open to all

    ____ social services are at best tolerated   ____ social services are willingly supported

Source: Adapted from Locke et al., 1998, pp. 278–279.

Social Justice/Diversity Factors Aspects of social work practice that affirm social justice and support diversity can be nurtured and sustained in organizations. Unless organizations promote social justice through anti-oppressive policies and practices, clients and community members may find their social workers to be "nice people" but feel victimized by unjust organizational practices.

To fully promote social justice, organizations may arrange the internal administrative practices of the agency to reflect diversity, cultural humility, cultural responsiveness, and social justice and anti-oppression concerns. For example, posters, magazines, and signs in the waiting area can reflect multiple languages and cultures to convey a welcoming atmosphere for people from diverse backgrounds. Activities and services that clearly take into account cultural values, such as food at events that reflect ethnic food traditions and restrictions, and materials available in multiple languages, send an inclusive message. Activities and services can also honor the history of groups and/or reflect histories of oppression for specific populations.

Just as ethnically dominant White middle-class social workers struggle to become culturally responsive in working with other cultures, so must organizations assess their cultural responsiveness and the extent to which the organization works toward social justice goals. Exhibit 12.6 addresses some of the assumptions that underlie organizational inclusive practices and approaches.

EXHIBIT 12.6

Characteristics of Organizations That Demonstrate Cultural Humility

Organizations that embody cultural humility display the following characteristics:

- Respect the unique, culturally defined needs of various client populations
- Acknowledge culture as a predominant force in shaping behaviors, values, and institutions
- View natural systems (i.e., family, community, faith communities, healers) as the primary mechanism of support for marginalized communities and populations
- Start with the "family," as defined by each culture, as the primary and preferred point of intervention
- Acknowledge that people who have low incomes and who live in marginalized communities are served in varying degrees by the natural system
- Recognize that the concepts of "family," "community," etc., are different for various cultures and even for subgroups within cultures
- Believe that diversity within cultures is as important as diversity between cultures
- Function with the awareness that the dignity of the person is not guaranteed unless the dignity of their people is preserved
- Display understanding that clients are usually best served by persons who are part of or have knowledge about their culture

EXHIBIT 12.6 *Continued*	• Acknowledge and accept that cultural differences exist and have an impact on service delivery • Advocate for effective services on the basis that the absence of cultural humility in any part of the organization compromises the cultural responsiveness of the entire organization • Respect the family as indispensable to understanding the individual, because the family provides the context within which the person functions and is the primary support network of its members • Recognize that the thought patterns of non-Western peoples, though different, are equally valid and influence the ways in which clients view problems and solutions • Respect cultural preferences that value process rather than product and harmony or balance within one's life rather than achievement • Acknowledge that when working with clients who are from marginalized populations, process is as important as product • Recognize that taking the best of the Western and non-Western worlds enhances the capacity of all • Recognize that People of Color have to at least be bicultural, which in turn creates its own set of mental health issues such as identity conflicts resulting from assimilation • Function with the knowledge that some behaviors are the expression of adjustments to being different • Understand when values of marginalized groups are in conflict with dominant society values *Source:* Adapted from Sue et al., 2016.

Personnel Policies and Procedures The size and legal basis of an organization are important factors in the creation of staff policies and procedures; small, newly created nonprofit organizations have relatively simple and concise policies and procedures. Having fewer policies and procedures lends itself to flexibility and creativity but also more uncertainty about responsibilities, processes, and scope of work. Larger, public organizations often have highly formal, complex policies and procedures, which creates a more constricted work environment yet also provides a structure to better navigate a more multifaceted set of activities and responsibilities. Nevertheless, the development of written policies and procedures, including a plan for staff recruitment, selection, development, evaluation, and termination, is important. Some organizations also develop plans to address personnel changes and issues, such as increasing staff diversity or developing career pathways for employees within the organization.

Resources Other types of resources are also important to organizations. For example, the adequacy of the financial resources of organizations can be assessed through annual and monthly budgets, where income and liabilities are documented. Technical resources include the facilities and equipment of the organization, such as the office space, computers, software, and cell phones. Personnel resources include the number and capacity of current staff, including their knowledge, skills, and expertise.

Elements of an External Assessment

The external environment of organizations consists of many players. The assessment process focuses on the external environment and includes individuals, groups, organizations, and policies that impact operations. The external environment can offer opportunities and challenges for organizations, and maintaining a focus on relationships with external players is important. This section discusses those elements external to an organization that can be considered as part of an organizational assessment.

Relationship With Funders and Potential Funders An assessment process should uncover the sources of agency funding, as well as the nature of the relationship between the organization and each funding source. For example, the assessment process would uncover the amount and percentage of the overall budget received from each funding source. The funding sources could include government appropriations and contracts, donations, investment income, fees, fundraising events and activities, and related profit-making ventures. A source of funding that constitutes nearly half or more of the organization's overall budget indicates a strong relationship. Organizations that rely on a diverse source of funds often have increased program and staff flexibility compared to those that rely on fewer sources.

> *An example from this chapter's case involving IPV can be seen through an analysis of the budgets of the IPV programs. This analysis revealed a pattern of urban shelters having a greater number of sources of funding on average than rural shelters. Further, the rural shelters were operating on smaller overall budgets than the urban shelters, even after taking into account the differences in number of women and children served. One key factor that emerged from budget analysis was that urban IPV programs were able to attract and maintain more donations from private individuals and family foundations than rural IPV programs, making them less dependent on public funding from city, state, and federal sources.*
>
> *In monthly videoconferences as they prepared for the town hall meetings, the directors of both urban and rural programs discussed the importance of including some information about the urban/rural disparity in the town halls and also in their ongoing communications with funders, potential funders, and members of their boards of directors. In the absence of this information, it would be all too likely that people whose primary concern was for "their" IPV program would focus on resources for that organization alone, instead of valuing the principle of working together to end IPV for women throughout the state.*

Serving Clients and Communities With Limited Resources Human service organizations rarely have the resources to serve all individuals, families, groups, and communities in their service area; therefore, organizations create eligibility requirements for programs and services. An assessment in this area may include examining how people are deemed eligible, the manner in which people are treated who are not eligible for services, the extent to which some clients and communities have mandates to receive services, and the network of organizations that are sources of referrals.

Relationships With Organizations in Service Network Constructive, professional relationships with other organizations are imperative to a positive community perception and to the ability of the organization to function effectively. Organizations that deliver similar services often work together to meet community needs yet may also compete for funding from similar sources. As we have seen by exploring the case of the IPV coalition in this chapter, strong relationships between similar organizations benefit the community through stronger service delivery and collective advocacy efforts. However, forming these relationships can be challenging due to competition for resources. An assessment of this aspect of agencies would uncover the nature of relationships with similar and referring organizations. Quick Guide 39 provides guidance on various types of organizational partnerships.

QUICK GUIDE 39 Guide to Nonprofit Organizational Partnerships

A local nonprofit organization, Citizens Against Climate Change (CACC), would like to expand its influence without necessarily expanding its organization. It is exploring the idea of partnering with other organizations locally, statewide, regionally, nationally, or internationally. The forms of partnership from which it could choose are:

A Task Force
Task forces are temporary, flexible structures to address a community challenge to be resolved in a relatively short period of time. Membership includes representatives of all types of organizations focused on similar challenges. Advantages include pooling of resources, ease of short-term commitment, and flexibility in structure; disadvantages include lack of organizational engagement and commitment, resources, and general trust due to the short-term nature of the arrangement.

- *For example, CACC could decide to create a task force with organizations to promote the creation of bike lanes on local roads as one way to help to combat climate change.*

A Collaborative Partnership
Collaborative partnerships can be relatively long term and involve sharing of resources, such as staff and funds, to engage in sustained service delivery among member organizations. Each member organization provides a unique contribution to the work. Collaborative organizations can work closely over time and are often motivated to reduce costs, receive funding that otherwise would not be available, or fulfill unmet, complex needs. Advantages include resource sharing and expansion and improvement of services, while challenges include potential competition for similar funding opportunities and creating consensus among diverse partners.

- *For example, CACC could decide to create a collaborative partnership to develop a bike share program for community members.*

A Coalition
Coalitions are groups of organizations that take collective action, such as lobbying elected officials. While most coalitions have informal structures and fluid membership, some are formal organizations. Member organizations pool resources and devote staff and members to take action. The loose structure and fluid membership is both a strength (i.e., it is reasonably easy to recruit like-minded organizations) and a challenge (i.e., it is difficult to create consensus with organizations that are diverse and do not work together regularly).

- *For example, CACC could form or join a coalition to advocate for additional state transportation dollars to be devoted to walkable/bikeable community projects, such as sidewalks, bike lanes, bike corridors, and traffic-calming infrastructure improvements on side roads.*

An Interfaith Alliance
These organizational partnerships involve faith communities and other nonprofits, local groups, and institutions (e.g., public health departments or child welfare departments). Advantages of interfaith alliances include (1) faith communities offer a place of recruitment of active individuals motivated by their faith to take action on issues; (2) faith communities are able to add credibility to efforts to address societal needs; and (3) faith communities are able to offer many types of resources. As with other partnerships, challenges include developing consensus among diverse groups and individuals.

- *For example, CACC could join an interfaith alliance at the local or national level to engage in advocacy about emissions standards for autos or to fund complete composting systems for food waste at local public schools.*

An Affiliation With a National/International Organization
National and international organizations sponsor local chapters to work at a smaller (e.g., state) level to carry out their agenda. Local chapters benefit from affiliation by increased political influence, access to funding, and networks with similar-sized organizations across the country or world. Challenges include reaching agreement among diverse groups with varying agendas, and/or forfeiting some decision-making powers at the local level to the national/international organization.

- *For example, CACC could join with other, similar groups to create a chapter of Greenpeace, an international organization focused on climate change.*

A Social Movement
Organizations can participate in social movements by joining with broad-based coalitions and national organizations dedicated to the same cause. Social movements are often the mechanism for marginalized and oppressed groups to obtain access to resources and political rights, as well as for allies to support them in their advocacy through organizational resources. Rather than a single organization, the work of a movement is carried out through partnerships of multiple organizations and coalitions to generate public support and links to decision-makers and funders.

- *For example, CACC could join with organizations such as the Global Campaign for Climate Action and other similar networks working with organizations and groups around the world to create political pressure for action on climate change.*

Source: Adapted from Hardina, 2013; Netting et al., 2017.

Relationships With Political Figures Elected and appointed officials often carry considerable influence over public opinion about, and resources for, public and private organizations. An assessment would investigate the key political figures that may have influence on an organization and describe the organization's relationship with them.

Social workers in organizations need to know their elected and appointed political representatives and regularly communicate with them. Attending community meetings and functions at which politicians routinely appear or are scheduled to speak often benefits your organization. Michelle and Tyra, the social workers from this chapter's case, saw such benefits for their IPV programs and other programs in the state coalition because they had developed solid working relationships with their state legislators.

> In preparing for the five town hall meetings on IPV prevention, the shelter project teams sent early email invitations to all state legislators. A week later, they contacted legislative staff members to follow up on the invitations and provide detailed information about the town hall closest to each legislator's district. When they received a confirmation of attendance from a legislator's office, they reserved 5 minutes on the town hall agenda to allow the officials or their appointed representatives to introduce themselves and deliver brief comments.
>
> The project teams also began to reach out to staff, volunteers, and former clients of IPV programs across the state. They encouraged everyone they talked with to attend the town hall meetings and to invite friends, family members, co-workers, members of faith communities, and neighbors to join them. Project teams also prepared people who were committed to attending to speak during the town halls about the need for increased state funding for IPV prevention and equitable distribution of the funds to urban and rural programs.
>
> One component of the preparation involved providing some brief specific examples of need via text message to people who had committed to attending the meetings. For example, those who were going to attend town halls in cities received text messages about the lack of resources available to IPV programs serving rural areas, distance between IPV survivors and the nearest shelter, and lack of public transportation. People who were planning to attend rural town halls received text messages with information on the waiting lists for IPV services in urban areas and the difficulties involved in finding and maintaining affordable shelter space, given the high cost of living in the cities.
>
> Coalition members were successful in meeting their community awareness and resource development goals through the town hall strategy. At least one state legislator attended each town hall, along with a number of legislative staff members. In feedback from attendees collected in writing before the meetings ended, there was some surprise at the appeals for funding of IPV programs in other parts of the state, but generally the reactions were positive.
>
> Elected and appointed officials who attended went on to call and email both the IPV coalition and member programs in the days following the town hall meetings to get more information on the need for increased state funding for IPV prevention throughout the state. In addition to responding to specific questions, IPV coalition members asked those in policy-making positions to be in

touch with legislators representing the districts that included the IPV programs that Tyra and Michelle directed. By the time legislation was introduced to increase state funding for IPV prevention, a number of legislators from different political parties and various parts of the state had signed on to sponsor the bill, which included provisions for equitable distribution to urban and rural programs.

An organizational assessment tool is available in Quick Guide 40 that allows you to practice your assessment skills. The Quick Guide covers all of the internal and external organizational elements discussed in this chapter. Further, the kind of policy advocacy that Michelle, Tyra, and their colleagues in the IPV coalition engaged in is the focus of Quick Guide 41, which affords an opportunity to learn about other organizational practice in the policy arena.

QUICK GUIDE 40   Nonprofit Organizational Assessment

Using an organization with which you are familiar, complete the following assessment:

Internal Assessment

- *Legal basis, mission, bylaws, and history*
  - ____ The legal basis is clearly stated in appropriate documents.
  - ____ The mission statement is current and accurate and specifies the reason for existence and expected outcomes.
  - ____ The bylaws are relevant, current, and accurately portray the needs of the organization.

- *Administrative structure and management style*
  - ____ The administrative structure and management style fit the mission and services of the organization.
  - ____ Transparent and structured lines/systems for decision-making exist.
  - ____ Roles are clearly defined.
  - ____ Decision-making involves broad participation as practical and appropriate.
  - ____ Clear communication lines exist for dissemination of decisions.
  - ____ A comprehensive, integrated system is used for measuring the organization's performance and progress on a continual basis.

  - *Program structure, programs, and services*
    - ____ Continual monitoring and assessment of the structure, processes, and programs occurs.
    - ____ Program evaluation data is collected, used, and linked to systematic improvements.
    - ____ Programs and services reflect evidence-based practice.
    - ____ The need for programs and services is well documented.
    - ____ Programs and services are well-defined and fully aligned with the mission.
    - ____ A system is in place to collect data about gaps in the ability of existing programs to meet recipient and community-wide needs.
    - ____ New ideas are continually offered to meet service gaps.
    - ____ Programs and services are efficient, effective, and high quality.

QUICK GUIDE 40 Continued

- *Organizational culture (i.e., physical surroundings, public relations, language, procedures, social justice/diversity)*
  - ____ Physical infrastructure is well suited to current and anticipated needs.
  - ____ Physical infrastructure enhances effectiveness.
  - ____ Informal expectations are clearly articulated and supported by staff.
  - ____ A communications plan and strategy is in place and is updated frequently.
  - ____ Marketing materials are professional, used consistently, and current.
  - ____ Materials are provided in multiple languages as needed and reflect diversity.
  - ____ Communications carry a consistent and powerful message.

- *Personnel policies and procedures*
  - ____ Recruitment, selection, orientation, supervision, training and development, performance appraisal, termination, and grievance processes are identified.
  - ____ Relationships between and among positions and position qualifications are identified.
  - ____ Diversity is characterized as an asset.
  - ____ Organizational resources devoted to staff continuing education are sufficient.
  - ____ Policies and procedures reflect systems that are culturally competent.

- *Resources (i.e., financial, technological, personnel)*
  - ____ Funding is sufficient, comes from diverse sources, fits the mission, and provides insulation from market instabilities.
  - ____ Board members embrace fundraising as a core role.
  - ____ Board fundraising plans are in place.
  - ____ Electronic data systems sufficiently gather and report appropriate data regarding clients, staff, volunteers, program outcomes, and financial information.
  - ____ The website and social media pages are sophisticated, comprehensive, interactive, and regularly maintained.
  - ____ Positions are adequately and appropriately staffed and vacancies are quickly filled.
  - ____ Staff are capable, committed, and bring complementary skills and momentum for improvement.
  - ____ Technology needs (e.g., computers, phones, etc.) are adequately met.

External Assessment
- *Relationship with funders and potential funders*
  - ____ Fundraising skills and expertise are adequate for funding needs.
  - ____ Sustainable revenue-generating activities are used.
  - ____ A system for regular communication and reporting with current funders is used.
  - ____ Feedback from current funders is sought and considered.

____ A system to cultivate potential funders is used and continually updated.

____ Ideas for revenue diversification are continually considered.

- *Relationship with clients*

____ A system to actively recruit and involve clients in offering feedback is used.

____ A system to actively involve clients in making decisions is used.

____ When possible, clients work collaboratively with staff in important roles, such as volunteer positions of leadership.

- *Relationship with organizations in network (i.e., referrals and partnerships)*

____ Strong, positive relationships with similar and related organizations exist.

____ Presence on relevant partnerships is evident, and leadership roles are appropriately taken.

____ Reciprocity is sought with relevant organizations.

- *Relationships with political figures*

____ Strong, high-impact relationships using regular communication with a variety of political entities (i.e., local, state, and federal government) and community leaders exist.

____ Participates in substantive policy discussions with opinion and political leaders.

____ Proactively and effectively influences policy-making at the local, state, and/or national level.

Source: Adapted from: Netting et al., 2017; Marguerite Casey Foundation, 2012.

QUICK GUIDE 41   Organizational Policy Advocacy Activities

Complete the following tool about organizational policy advocacy activities using an organization with which you are familiar. Completing this assessment can shed light on the degree to which organizations use opportunities to engage in policy activities for the benefit of their clients and organization. Organizations that engage in few of these could consider expanding their policy advocacy activities to more opportunities, such as those listed here.

In the past, our agency has:

(Organizational Activities)

____ Testified at public hearings held by the city council, state legislature, or other decision-making body.

____ Participated in legislative or policy working groups with government officials.

____ Engaged in nonviolent civil disobedience (i.e., deliberately broke a law to draw attention to unjust government policies, programs, or actions).

____ Sent unique letters, emails, or texts to the city council, the mayor, local government agency directors, or senior staff members regarding legislation, government policies, government programs, or other issues that affect our clients.

____ Participated in rallies, protests, vigils, and/or demonstrations to draw attention to an issue that affects our clients.

QUICK GUIDE 41   Continued

____ Attempted to engage television, radio, print, or web-based/social media reporters to give attention to legislation, government policies, government programs, or other issues that affect our clients.

____ Submitted letters to the editor or op-ed pieces to the local media regarding legislation, government policies, government programs, or other issues related to our client population.

____ Helped draft legislation.

____ Sponsored or co-sponsored forums or other community events to educate the general public about legislation, government policies, government programs, or a social issue.

____ Submitted formal comments on rules, regulations, strategic plans, or other administrative governmental documents.

____ Met with the city council members, the mayor, and/or local government agency directors or senior staff to discuss legislation, government policies, government programs, or other issues that affect our clients.

____ Contacted city council members, the mayor, and/or local government agency directors or senior staff to discuss legislation, government policies, government programs, or other issues that affect our client populations.

____ Participated in letter-writing campaigns, "sign-on" letters, "call-in days," postcard drives, petition drives, text message drives, or email drives to contact public officials about legislation, government policies, government programs, or other issues that affect our clients.

____ Submitted articles in our newsletter about legislation, government policies, government programs, or other issues that affect our clients.

____ Posted fact sheets, issue briefs, articles, and/or testimony about legislation, government policies, government programs, or other issues that affect our client population on our website.

____ Invited council members and/or the mayor to visit our program(s) to educate them about the issues that affect our clients.

____ Actively participated in coalitions related to our area of service or issue of concern. (*Actively participated means attended and gave input at coalition meetings, joined and actively participated in coalition committees, attended coalition events, etc.*)

(Activities with Clients and Community Members)

____ Met with and/or distributed written information to clients and community members to educate/inform them about legislation, government policies, government programs, or upcoming public policy activities, (e.g., meetings, public hearings).

____ Solicited input from clients and community members to inform our agency's advocacy priorities.

____ Included clients and community members when making visits to the city council, state representatives, or other decision-makers.

____ Provided skill-building workshops to clients and community members to encourage their public policy participation. (*Skill building may include how to write and how to give testimony, writing letters, making phone calls, meeting with decision-makers, and other tactics.*)

____ Met with clients and community members to help them formulate direct action strategies around issues of their choice.

____ Conducted voter registration drives.

____ Facilitated transportation for clients and community members to encourage their participation in public policy activities and/or to vote at the polls.

Source: Adapted from Plitt & Shields, 2009.

ORGANIZATIONAL ENGAGEMENT, ASSESSMENT, AND PLANNING IN GENERALIST PRACTICE

While administrators have official roles and responsibilities, and therefore are naturally involved in the organizational change process, social workers who practice with individuals, families, groups, and communities, including generalist practitioners, must also be involved with the organizational change process. Both social work practitioners and administrators are bound by the *Code of Ethics* (NASW, 2021a) to work to improve services, to carry out their ethical obligations even if employment structures are challenging, and to act to eliminate anti-oppressive practices in organizations.

What does the ethical obligation to participate in organizational change mean for social workers who are not administrators? Social workers must learn about as many aspects of their affiliated organization as possible. Many organizational problems emerge through the experiences of clients or members of the community, and defining and documenting client or community member problems is a powerful way to make a strong case for organizational change. Social workers can engage others in identifying and documenting client and community problems to which the organization contributes (Gitterman et al., 2021). Successful organizational change efforts often involve many individuals and groups.

Organizational engagement and assessment involve many of the same competencies and behaviors used in practice with individuals, families, groups, and communities. The next section discusses skills needed to effectively begin the organizational change process.

SKILLS FOR ENGAGEMENT, ASSESSMENT, AND PLANNING WITH ORGANIZATIONS

Social work skills in engagement, assessment, and planning include gathering and analyzing data to provide direction to the next helping phases such as intervention, termination, evaluation, and follow-up. One tool for assessment and planning is called **SWOT analysis**. SWOT stands for strengths, weaknesses, opportunities, and threats. In a SWOT analysis, organizational staff identify and assess both internal and external factors that impact the organization and can be the basis for developing a plan for intervention and change. Exhibit 12.7 presents a sample SWOT analysis.

Another tool for organizational assessment is a **force field analysis (FFA),** a conceptual representation of the changes proposed and achieved (Gitterman et al., 2021; Houston & Swords, 2021). To begin an FFA, a social worker identifies forces that could impact the outcomes of change efforts, including constraints that work to prevent a change and advantages that will help overcome resistance to change. The forces could include influential individuals who could shape the opinion of others or who are decision-makers; organizations, committees, and task forces; and organized groups of people. These individuals and groups may be internal or external to the organization. FFA enables a

EXHIBIT 12.7

SWOT Analysis

The Latinx Community Development Center (LCDC), a 3-year-old nonprofit organization, wanted to increase its capacity to provide additional services to a growing Latinx population in the community. While LCDC had been providing food, rent, utility assistance, and English as a Second Language (ESL) classes for three years with one paid staff member, the Board wanted to increase its capacity to provide health services to the population in response to high rates of teen pregnancy, low access to health care, and poor oral health.

In its planning process, LCDC used a SWOT analysis to analyze the strengths and weaknesses inside the organization and the opportunities and threats outside of it. The SWOT analysis was conducted to help decide between two options: (1) raising funds to deliver health services itself or (2) partnering with another organization(s) for service delivery at LCDC.

	Strengths	**Weaknesses**
Internal	• Reputation among Latinx • History in community • Reputation among non-Latinx • Only Latinx-serving nonprofit • Evidence of need for health services • Diverse board with community connections	• Lack of capacity to deliver health services • Lack of enough paid staff • Little experience in raising money • Little experience in partnering
	Opportunities	**Threats**
External	• Potential partnership with local institutions (i.e., public health department, free health clinic, university) • Potential coalition building with other human service organizations • Create LCDC capacity to meet growing needs	• Other institutions may deliver services without LCDC involvement • Increased financial and liability risk with more services • Partner institutions may require proof of documentation status of clients • If effort fails, damage to reputation

Ultimately, the organization decided to attempt to raise money and deliver the health services itself rather than partner with another organization. The primary reasons for this decision were to avoid the requirement that LCDC clients show proof of documentation status and to preserve the organization's reputation among the Latinx community. Instead of formally partnering, the LCDC Board decided to request training from other organizations that provided health services in the larger community.

Source: Adapted from Larson & McGuiston, 2012.

social worker to make a decision about whether to move forward with a change process and/or to create a plan based on knowledge of the forces working for and against a proposed change (Gitterman et al., 2021; Hardina, 2013).

SUPPORTING FORCES	NEUTRAL FORCES	OPPOSING FORCES
Student leaders	Principal Association	Four influential teachers
Student government	School counselors	Parent Association members
All high school principals	Local TV and radio station	Two student groups/clubs
American Civil Liberties Union	Chair of the School Board	Three School Board members
Three School Board members	Two School Board members	All middle school principals

EXHIBIT 12.8

Force Field Analysis, Assessment of Forces Impacting LGBTQIA+ Initiative

For example, say a school social worker has studied the research demonstrating that LGBTQIA+ students experience a higher number of social and academic problems in middle and high school than other students. The social worker has completed an organizational assessment, documented the same pattern in her school district, and would like to move forward to plan an intervention. Working with a group of students who self-identify as LGBTQIA+, the social worker conducts an FFA with the goal of systematically identifying sources of support and potential barriers to providing more comprehensive services for this population across the school district.

As seen in Exhibit 12.8, there are many forces that support an initiative to provide more comprehensive services to LGBTQIA+ teens, including student leaders, student government, and high school principals. Neutral forces, including the association of principals and school counselors, could support or oppose a change process, and the social worker does not yet have information about the association's position. Through engagement and education, the association could become a supporting force. The forces opposed to providing support services, including several influential teachers and members of the parent association, are likely to work against comprehensive programming for LGBTQIA+ students. The FFA is one tool that can assist the social worker and LGBTQIA+ work group in making a decision regarding whether to proceed with their efforts. An FFA can also help to make an intervention plan if the group decides to proceed.

The advantages of an FFA are numerous—the individuals, groups, and coalitions relevant to the issue are identified, as are the driving and restraining forces most likely to affect the change effort. The strength of each force is assessed and ranked, and the amenability to change of each force is ranked as high, low, or uncertain. A plan for change is then created based on the information contained in the FFA. The FFA is a simple tool that can be used with groups of all sizes that fosters creativity and critical thinking. The social worker must demonstrate keen group facilitation skills to help the group identify forces for and against change, to avoid the domination of a marginalized group, and to encourage the group to be specific and detailed in the analysis (Gitterman et al., 2021).

Moving from assessment to planning for an intervention happens in many ways in organizational practice. Sometimes an organizational assessment process is focused on one aspect of an organization, and a decision-making person such as the executive director or a group such as the board of directors can review the assessment data and analysis to make a decision regarding planning for an intervention.

At other times, an assessment process brings many organizational issues, challenges, and ideas to the forefront. In that case, as in community assessment, the planning phase for organizations involves sorting through and prioritizing the issues in order to be able to move forward with an intervention.

A set of criteria is needed to provide structure and transparency to the decision-making process. The criteria can include any combination of the following:

- seriousness or frequency of an issue;
- cost of the issue, or resources needed to address the issue;
- feasibility of affecting the issue;
- readiness of the community to recognize and address the issue; and
- the long-term impact or benefit of addressing an issue or in implementing a program.

Criteria may be established at any point in the process. Organizations may choose to have some combination of administrators, staff, and/or board members set the criteria and then decide whether and how to move forward with an intervention by applying the criteria. After setting the criteria, a democratic process can also be used to apply the criteria to the issues/ideas generated in the assessment process before moving on to planning an intervention (University of Kansas Work Group for Community Health and Development, 2022).

CRITICAL CONSIDERATIONS IN PRACTICE WITH ORGANIZATIONS

Different types of organizations offer distinct professional rewards, opportunities, and challenges. Expectations and experiences differ from one organizational setting to another, and work style preferences that fit one type of organization may not be a match at another organization or type of organization.

Although working for public organizations brings challenges, there are advantages unique to employment with public agencies. Compared to working in the private sector, needed services can be offered to clients and communities with less consideration given to ability to pay, especially for services required to be provided by law. In stable economic times, social workers in public agencies enjoy relative predictability and job security, with highly structured job and salary levels, especially in the military and in state and federal government positions. Many clients and community members who have served in public organizations are those without private alternatives; therefore, social workers within these agencies are implementing the historical preference of social work for working on behalf of those with low incomes. Lastly, social workers in public organizations gain invaluable experience with a wide range of client and community issues.

Because of demographic changes in the United States and peer nations, and especially the expected growth in the proportion of the population living in retirement, the number of social workers that will be needed in health care and long-term care settings is likely to increase. The growth in these sectors will result in a demand for social workers in the private sector, with increasing job opportunities in nonprofit and for-profit organizations.

GRAND CHALLENGE

Promote Smart Decarceration

The United States has the world's largest proportion of people in prison. The expansion of the criminal justice system, or mass incarceration, is a social justice issue. This challenge has been identified by the American Academy of Social Work and Social Welfare as one of the Grand Challenges for Social Work. In addition to the overwhelming financial cost, Epperson and Pettus-Davis (2015, p. 4; Charles et al., 2022) provide an overview of this problem from a social justice perspective:

> The exponential growth of incarceration in the United States is a compelling problem not only because of sheer numbers, but also because of who is most affected. The majority of the imprisoned population is made up of people of color and people suffering from poverty or behavioral health disorders. For these reasons, social workers and the American public increasingly understand mass incarceration as unaffordable.

Smart decarceration interventions build on structural and behavioral interventions that have been shown to reduce incarcerated populations. They include (1) diverting criminal offenders from prison by first implementing alternatives to incarceration, (2) reducing recidivism and thereby reducing prison populations, and (3) reinvesting criminal justice resources into treatment and prevention.

With its long history of reform efforts and focus on social justice, the social work profession is well suited to provide leadership toward promoting decarceration. Society needs to explore and evaluate a range of alternatives to transform the criminal justice system of incarceration, including multidisciplinary approaches to policy and practice intervention. Social work can promote cross-sector and transdisciplinary collaboration to encourage evidence-based practice toward smart decarceration. Consider the dimensions of organizations discussed in this chapter. How can organizations be structured to promote cross-sector and transdisciplinary collaborative work? To familiarize yourself with smart decarceration, visit the Grand Challenges website at https://grandchallengesforsocialwork.org.

Depending on the type of services provided, social workers in for-profit organizations may enjoy a more comfortable physical setting and the more varied and abundant resources for intervention and evaluation of outcomes that come with private insurance to help cover many health and mental health services. Other social workers will prefer the opportunity to work in nonprofit organizations and advocate for low- and moderate-income clients and community members who depend on public insurance such as Medicaid.

A final note for consideration in terms of social work employment options is the growing interest in social enterprises, or organizations that seek to enhance the well-being of individuals and communities while making a profit, or at least generating enough revenue to break even financially (Bruneel et al., 2016). For more information about the relationship between social work and social entrepreneurship, one resource is the Social Entrepreneurship Committee at the School of Social Work at Wayne State University (https://socialwork.wayne.edu/socialentrepreneurship).

CONCLUSION

This chapter has introduced organizations as an important arena for social work practice. Social workers in practice with individuals, families, and groups have expertise on the impact of organizational operations on clients. Social workers may best be able to identify unmet client and community needs and initiate a change process designed to meet the best interests of the people receiving help from social workers. Social workers, therefore, have a mandate to engage people in and external to the organization and learn about the internal and external environments of organizations to competently lead and participate in organizational change processes. In addition to engagement, this chapter focused on the assessment process to provide the foundation needed to initiate the change process, as well as the planning process. Chapter 13 focuses on organizational intervention strategies, termination, evaluation, and follow-up.

MAIN POINTS

- Social workers work in many types of organizations and use their knowledge to promote the best interests of their clients and communities.

- Organizations can be understood using various perspectives, including systems theory, and by studying structures and dynamics in contemporary social service organizations and agencies.

- Three main dimensions of difference between organizations are: (1) the purpose of the organization, (2) the structure of governance, and (3) internal power relations.

- Social workers also practice in host settings, which are organizations in which social workers provide social services that are beyond the primary activity of the host organization.

- Social workers can help change organizations to provide a higher quality of services to clients and communities.

- The overall assessment of organizations involves a review of the internal and external environments of the organization.

- The NASW *Code of Ethics* (2021a) provides direction to both generalist and specialist social workers to improve services, to carry out their ethical obligations in the workplace, and to act to eliminate racism and anti-oppressive practices in organizations.

- Helpful tools for organizational assessment include SWOT analysis and FFA. These tools can help gather and sort data and aid in the intervention planning process.

- The type of organization in which a social worker is employed offers different rewards, opportunities, and challenges. Common types of social service organizations include public, private nonprofit, and private for-profit.

EXERCISES

1 To apply your learning of the Grand Challenge to achieve equal opportunity and justice that is highlighted in this chapter, visit the Grand Challenges website at https://grandchallengesforsocialwork.org and read the five concept papers that address issues faced by low-income individuals and marginalized groups in the United States. Research whether there are any community organizations in your community that are working to achieve equal opportunity for marginalized groups. Write a one-paragraph summary of each organization. For example, is there an organization or coalition working to do any of the following:
   a Integrating immigrants and refugees into American society?
   b Developing programs to promote the success of Black children and youth in schools and in employment?
   c Working to address and alleviate housing discrimination experienced by marginalized groups and African Americas, in particular, in the United States.
   d Working to achieve equal opportunity and justice in the juvenile justice system.
   e Working to educate individuals on how to write letters to the newspaper editor or to their state legislature to address an issue such as Intimate Partner Violence (IPV) and the need to increase funding for domestic abuse shelters throughout the state.
2 Log onto www.routledgesw.com/interactive-cases/ and read about RAINN's service components. Draft a short mission statement for RAINN.
3 Imagine you were hired as a social worker three months ago at a community center that provides recreational and well-being programs for residents of a multiracial, multiethnic neighborhood. As you have settled

into your job, you notice tensions within the agency. Several social workers grumble at "the way things are around here." As you consider the reasons for your unsettled feelings about this situation, you decide to gather information about the organization to gain a better understanding of the dynamics. Referring back to the chapter, discuss ways in which you might obtain knowledge about the organization's purpose, structure, and internal power relations, and how each of these factors could influence the experience of staff members (one paragraph for each).

4 After you have completed Exercise #3, you still are unsure about the dynamics that have led you to feel unsettled and co-workers to grumble. You decide to learn more about the agency but are not ready to undertake a full organizational assessment. You decide to start your mini-assessment by focusing on culture. Using the concepts described in the chapter, describe the elements of culture that exist in the center and how you would go about understanding them. Include the types of individuals you might interview, the documents you would seek, the groups you would approach for information, and any other source of information you might use. Include a brief justification for your choices.

5 Log onto www.routledgesw.com/static-cases/. Review Case 1: Willow's Transition. Answer the following questions.
   a What about at the macro level? What changes at the state and federal level—particularly related to policy—would help students like Willow to have a safe and inclusive learning environment?
   b What can you learn about efforts to pursue these changes, and how might you get involved in this work?

6 Log onto www.routledgesw.com/interactive-cases/. Review the Riverton case file. View the community sociogram "located under the case study tools tab." Note all of the organizations and their relationships to one another. Develop a sociogram for an organization with which you are familiar.

7 Using the Riverton case (www.routledgesw.com/interactive-cases/), answer Critical Thinking Question #2.

8 Go to www.routledgesw.com/interactive-cases/ and become familiar with the Brickville case. Several events have occurred that prompt the Brickville Community Development Corporation (CDC) to conduct an organizational assessment. First, the Brickville CDC has been asked to join the coalition working for the redevelopment plan. Second, as part of the needs assessment, the youth development organization encouraged the Brickville CDC to become more politically engaged for the benefit of the neighborhood. The CDC director has stated that the organization has never taken a stance on an issue like this before. Olivia, the social worker, and her colleagues have decided to work toward organizational change by creating a process through which the Brickville CDC can take a stance on neighborhood issues. In a 1-page paper, discuss the elements of an internal assessment that Olivia and her colleagues would need to complete in preparation for developing an intervention plan to create change in the organization.

9. Choose an organization with which you are familiar. Familiarize yourself with the elements of an organizational assessment, as discussed in this chapter. Interview a person familiar with the organization to gather as much information as possible related to the internal and external elements of an organizational assessment. As part of the interview, ask whether the organization has completed an organizational assessment in the past and whether there are any documents that describe the assessment that you could review.
10. Using the SWOT diagram in Exhibit 12.7 as an example, complete a SWOT diagram for an organization with which you are familiar. Briefly explain the contents of your SWOT analysis.
11. Using the examples of forms of partnership in Quick Guide 39, describe the forms of partnerships that a nonprofit, "Men Against Sexual Assault," could take if they wanted to expand its influence without expanding its organization.

CHAPTER 13

Social Work Practice With Organizations: Intervention, Termination, and Evaluation

THERE ARE MANY SITUATIONS THAT PROMPT ORGANIZATIONAL CHANGE. Such change can range in scale from large to small and from short-term to long-term. Some examples of social service organizational change include:

- changing the decision-making process within an organization,
- changing eligibility for a program,
- implementing flexible work shifts for staff members, and
- creating new programs and finding a way to fund them.

Large-scale change, such as a merger with another organization, can alter the very mission and nature of an organization. However, smaller-scale change can also make a difference to clients and the community. One example would be offering a new approach to programming that allows people who are unhoused and have substance use problems to move into supportive housing first and then begin the work to eliminate substances from their lives. Organizational change, like all types of social work practice, involves engagement, assessment, planning, intervention, termination, and evaluation.

This chapter examines strategies social workers can use to change policies, programs, projects, and practices within organizations. Based on the engagement, assessment, and planning phases of the change process, the next steps—intervention, termination, and evaluation and follow-up—can help organizations become more responsive to those they serve. First, we discuss approaches, perspectives, and models for interventions with organizations. The next section provides a framework for organizational change. We explore challenges and methods for implementing organizational change, followed by a discussion of termination and evaluation in organizational practice. The chapter ends with an overview of the challenge of maintaining a hopeful stance with clients and communities regarding organizational change. We start this chapter with a case on organizational change in a school setting.

Marquis is a school social worker whose practice is with middle and high school students. Toby, a tenth-grader, told Marquis that he wished other kids would just "leave him alone" and that things would be better if he had friends that were like him at school. Toby, who shared with Marquis that he is gay, was the third student that week to say similar things to Marquis. Marquis supported Toby, as he does all his students, and he is eager to get more services for marginalized students in the school.

The small group of social work staff members serving the school district have been meeting to develop a plan to better address the needs of lesbian, gay, bisexual, transgender, and queer, intersex, asexual, and persons whose sexual orientation or gender identity is not included in the acronym (LGBTQIA+) students. Marquis has taken an active role in these meetings, sharing his experiences with LGBTQIA+ students who have been bullied and feel socially isolated at school. In these circumstances, academic challenges often begin to emerge or worsen. As a group, the social workers have decided that it is not enough just to make sure that they have the skills to help students one by one. They believe it is important for school board members and the superintendent to make district-wide changes to help marginalized students in all the middle and high schools.

Marquis and the other social workers in the group realize that the work they must do involves intervening with the entire school district as an organization. They also understand that implementing changes of this nature will likely take time. How can the social workers proceed so that they address immediate student needs while they continue to work at the organizational level for long-term changes?

Key Questions for Chapter 13

1. What are some approaches, perspectives, and models that I can use to guide intervention, termination, and evaluation with organizations?
2. How can I help create a working group to promote organizational change within my agency?
3. What social work practice skills do I need in order to research and select strategies for organizational change to better serve clients and communities?
4. What tools can I use to implement and evaluate change in my agency?
5. How do I identify and respond to challenges to the implementation of organizational changes?
6. What are the most important considerations in termination, evaluation, and follow-up in social work practice involving organizational change?

APPROACHES, PERSPECTIVES, AND MODELS FOR INTERVENTIONS WITH ORGANIZATIONS

When social workers practice with organizations, they rarely use only one approach or model to facilitate organizational change. By considering multiple perspectives on why and how complex organizations change in response to internal and external factors, we can be guided by those models that are particularly relevant to the situation at hand. In this section, we discuss three useful approaches that, together, suggest a variety of skills that social workers may use when they practice with organizations. These approaches reflect views of organizational change happening in response to self-learning, the nature of social systems, and/or power dynamics.

Self-Learning Approaches to Organizational Change

One approach to understanding organizational change rests on the notion that organizations can "learn" as they evolve, even to the point of learning to self-correct when needed (Gambrill, 2019). Self-learning organizations regularly seek and use evaluative feedback from internal and external sources. For example, such organizations conduct ongoing monitoring and continuously solicit feedback from clients and community members about their experiences with services. Self-learning organizations also change in response to feedback from others who provide information about the external environment of the organization.

A self-learning model of organizational change assumes a rational process in which all members of an organization agree on the mission, goals, and objectives of the organization and work collaboratively to achieve them. Although no organization perfectly implements its mission, goals, and objectives, those with clear goals and values that are committed to quality improvement are well-situated to be able to self-correct as they evolve. An organization that seeks feedback from many sources—clients, funders, referral sources, political leaders, and other community members—and then considers this feedback when deciding whether to make change is using a self-learning approach to organizational change.

The Systems Model and Organizational Change

The systems model, with a basis in systems theory, recognizes an organization as a system composed of individuals, subsystems, rules, roles, and processes operating within a wider environment. Using a systems approach, change in one part of the organization creates change in other parts of the organization. For example, changing a program's eligibility requirements may result in other programs having fewer, more, or different types of prospective clients and communities with which to work. It could also result in changes to other organizations, such as referral sources having more or less work to do with clients and community members. A change in eligibility requirements could also affect the number of staff members employed, program budgets, and the outcomes of the larger organization.

In another example, low morale among social workers and their colleagues in an underfunded agency attempting to serve an ever-increasing number of clients may require changes that will, in turn, change the larger organization. When stress among workers in an organization reaches the point of constant disagreement between staff members, or between staff members and administration, change within the organization may be necessary to rebuild morale, reestablish equilibrium, and refocus energy on services to clients and communities. Working from a systems model to achieve organizational change in this situation may involve a series of staff meetings, in-service training sessions, or retreats designed to improve morale, clarify goals and roles, and practice communication skills.

Social workers who use a systems model in their practice with organizations know that a change in one area will lead to changes in other areas, and they are ready to facilitate such changes. Using this approach also allows for a focus on the work lives of social workers. As work lives improve for those on the front lines, a systems approach would suggest that the organization as a whole will regain a sense of status quo rather than remain in chaos.

Perspectives on Power in Organizational Change

People with good intentions can have different perspectives on the need for organizational change. Even when there is fairly wide agreement on the need for change, people will have different ideas regarding what changes to pursue and how to go about making them. In addition, when working with organizations to make meaningful change, you have to have a champion who has respect and power to move change forward, specifically facilitating buy-in from those who are key to the change effort. Organizational change efforts may start smoothly when coworkers operate under the assumption that everyone involved shares some beliefs, such as that:

- change is possible,
- there are likely to be many ways to work through the change process,
- the best outcome of the change process will involve listening to all voices,
- negotiation in good faith will be required of all organizational members, and
- power is best shared in efforts to assure positive organizational changes.

This final point may be the most difficult to achieve as a shared belief because people have different perspectives on the role of power in organizations.

The most common situation for social service agencies and social justice organizations facing change is one of limited resources relative to the needs of clients and communities. Operating in a resource-constrained environment can lead some people to believe that competition for power will result in being able to control more of the limited resources available. Other people may be motivated to try to operate from a position of power in times of organizational change in an attempt to achieve personal advancement through the change process. Rather than a belief in shared power, some people believe that having strategic access to, or influence over, decision-makers who hold much power assures that their ideas will have the best chance of being heard and adopted as plans for organizational change are developed.

There is nothing inevitable about the structures and processes that shape and guide institutions or practice—people have created them and have the ability to change them. When social workers want to help make changes in organizations and agencies, analyzing power and power dynamics is essential in the early stages of the intervention. It is necessary to consider power issues that may emerge, and the role that power may play, in the midst of change efforts.

One common strategy is to identify ways that a needed organizational change is in the best interests of clients and communities, staff members, and decision-makers. Aligning interests in this way depends on remembering that there are many different perspectives of the organization and the services the organization offers, and that all these views are "accurate" in the minds of those who hold them. Exploring the perceptions, values, ideologies, ideas of reality, and assumptions of administrators, staff members, clients, and community members is an important step in planning and implementing an organizational change intervention.

In addition, the language we use can shape how people understand the proposed change, which in turn can help or hurt the change effort. For example, in the case involving support services for LGBTQIA+ students, framing the unmet need as part of a larger problem with bullying may help begin discussions about the need for all students to develop tolerance for, and appreciation of, differences. Such discussions at all organizational levels can be an effective tool in building support for a change proposal. Using this approach during an organizational change process means paying particular attention to the way in which we approach dialogue and how discussions can shape people's perceptions. Dialogue that is continuous, patient, and respectful can positively impact the views of decision-makers and others about the change proposal, which can break down barriers to organizational change.

The approaches and models discussed previously offer perspectives on organizational change efforts as well as ideas for social workers involved in such efforts. Components of these approaches and models are often used together in organizational practice depending on the organization and needed changes.

FRAMEWORK FOR ORGANIZATIONAL CHANGE

Promoting change within organizations can be challenging. Sometimes change is needed because there is an issue, but other times, it is due to an opportunity, such as a new source of funding. In this section, we explore origins of organizational change and introduce a framework for intervention with organizations. We discuss recruiting allies into a group to work on making needed organizational change by choosing feasible solutions, selecting a change strategy, intervening or implementing the change strategy, terminating the change effort, and evaluating the change effort and resulting program or project.

Origins of Organizational Change

The impetus for organizational change can come from many sources, both internal and external to the organization. Social workers who are staff members or administrators may be the first people who articulate issues that they believe need to be addressed at the organizational level. Social workers often see problems with services being provided firsthand and may be the first staff members to suggest changes in programs or development of new programs. Social workers who practice with individuals, families, and groups are often the first to notice when clients experience difficulty with organizational policies and procedures; they have a responsibility to voice their concerns in a way that will lead to positive change.

The members of the board of directors may also charge administrators and staff members with the responsibility of making specific organizational changes. People external to the organization such as those in positions with funding sources, agencies that provide similar social services or social justice goals, or advocates for the communities that need help may also bring needed changes to light.

Consider the following examples:

Avery works for the Santa Clara County Social Service Agency (SSA). Years ago, she noticed that the client population was increasingly diverse, with growing numbers of Asian, Latinx, Hawaiian/Pacific Islander, Black, and multiracial clients. At a staff meeting, she initiated a discussion about culturally responsive practices, and most of the staff agreed they needed to know more about it. Avery's supervisor agreed that this issue needed to be studied, with the possibility of educating staff and making changes to the organization. A committee was authorized, chaired by Avery, and the supervisor asked her to recruit other staff members to work on the committee.

Over many years, major organizational changes occurred as a result of committee efforts. Various subcommittees composed of staff at various levels, including administrative leaders, now meet on a regular basis to discuss cultural issues and promote agency-wide change. One subcommittee is responsible for monitoring the progress being made regarding culturally responsive policies, procedures, and training programs related to improving client services in each department. All subcommittees contribute to increased collaboration, the direct involvement of administrators, increased capacity for employees on all levels to be heard, and increased focus on shaping policy for cultural responsiveness (Chun-Chow & Austin, 2008).

Ethan works for The Island, an agency that helps adolescents and their families who are disadvantaged. Even though Ethan loves his job, he felt that he was working solely toward the goal of helping teens and their families adjust to challenging community conditions, rather than also trying to improve those conditions. The community struggled with high unemployment, poor housing, and underperforming schools. Many residents believed that the community needed more responsive local politicians. In talking with co-workers, Ethan realized that many felt similarly about their agency and the community. He invited his co-workers to join him at lunch to discuss possibilities, including evidence-based programs that sought to involve clients and community members with change efforts.

Eventually, the group organized itself into a committee to engage in making change through three teams. One team analyzed a recent local assessment of youth and family involvement in their community; another team engaged in an organizational assessment of the agency that included speaking informally to other staff members, administrators, and community leaders; while a third team researched evidence-based community programming for youth. The Island administrators eventually agreed to appoint a formal committee to develop new resources for additional youth programs in the community. These efforts were successful over time, and youth civic action teams now work out of local community centers, in partnership with The Island staff, to address community issues of concern to teen participants and their friends and families. The ultimate goal is to assist youth to be agents of change in activities with the potential to transform the community conditions that create problems in their lives (Evans et al., 2007).

It can be helpful to have a framework—a rough map—to guide such efforts. This section discusses the need to (1) create a group to work on the needed organizational change, (2) develop feasible solutions, and (3) select a strategy and tactics for the intervention.

Gathering Allies and Creating a Group to Work on Organizational Change

Organizational change usually requires the resources of more than one person. A group, informal or formal, adds credibility and power to a change effort and also allows members to share work. Even if the engagement and assessment process began with one person, social workers will want to identify supporters and allies while assisting with the change process. Volunteers will vary from passively supportive to highly active. Those who are supportive may change their involvement level throughout the process, becoming more or less active in the effort to make change over time. The key is to continually recruit allies through both formal methods, including regular announcements of when and where the group is meeting, and informal methods, such as word-of-mouth. By recruiting allies throughout the change process, even if membership of the group changes, a work group is in place to support the effort. While some change processes are short-term, many are long-term and require a large number of allies and a great deal of energy (Packard, 2021).

In the ally recruitment process, social workers must raise concerns discovered in the assessment process in staff and committee meetings and in discussions with their colleagues. When trying to garner support for a change proposal from other colleagues, social workers will want to be as explicit as possible and use real-world client examples, when applicable. Statements about problems that are in clear, behavioral, and values-oriented terms are the most effective. In these discussions, problems must be translated into potential solutions in which the organization can participate.

> *For example, if Marquis and his allies think the problem is that LGBTQIA+ adolescents in a school district need additional social and administrative support, they must first consider solutions in which the organization can participate. Can each school in the district partner with a local health center to provide education about sexuality and gender to all students? Should the partnership provide in-school or in-home family services related to sexuality and adolescents to promote family acceptance and support? Should the partnership provide individual support sessions? Should the school district provide services without organizational partners, either in-school or in-home? Should the school district engage the parent–teacher association in their efforts? Should the school refer LGBTQIA+ students to support groups? Or should the school provide services more quietly, so as not to arouse opposition, by providing, but not widely marketing, support services through the social work department?*

Translating the problem into potential solutions will help others understand, propose other solutions, have input into decisions, and potentially contribute/access resources. After recruiting allies into a working group and establishing the group dynamics—leadership, decision-making, and other aspects—the group must generate possible solutions and select one or more changes to adequately address the problem.

Developing Feasible Solutions for Organizational Change

The social worker and other members of the working group must ultimately develop a potential solution to the identified problem that is acceptable to decision-makers and that addresses the identified problem to the best of the organization's ability, based on the information gathered and analyzed in the engagement and assessment process. The proposal for change may take the shape of an oral presentation for a small, easy-to-implement change or a formal, written document for larger, more complicated organizational changes.

Some proposals for change can be reviewed and accepted by social workers and other colleagues within the organization. These include proposals for change in practices completely under their purview, such as distribution of client or community cases, adopting helping practices that are evidence-based according to the most up-to-date research, and determining timing and locations for service provision to better meet the needs of clients and community members. Proposals for organizational change that require more complex solutions will often need to be approved by agency administrators, the board of directors, legislative bodies, or existing funders. Moreover, some proposals to address the issue may also need to take into account the current political climate of the community and the state.

Selecting Feasible Solutions There are several important considerations for selecting feasible solutions:

1 Depending on the scope of the problem, potential solutions, and the organization's size, the working group must account for *resistance to change* (Tolbert & Hall, 2016). According to systems theory, all organizations seek to maintain status quo, or stability. **Inertia** can impede change by preserving a stable state that works against change. Social workers and allies must expect opposition to change, regardless of the specifics, because making changes takes energy away from other pursuits (Gambrill, 2019) and people tend to prefer routine and stability (Tolbert & Hall, 2016). Organizations structured as bureaucracies tend to change more slowly because of their size and complexity. Organizations with a more open, flexible structure tend to make changes more easily.

2 Employee attitudes and behaviors impact the success of change efforts (Packard, 2021). Therefore, the amount of organizational *effort* and *risk* involved is an important consideration (Packard, 2021). Some changes require considerable time, energy, and/or risk to the organization. If, for example, an organization has spent significant resources on a program, the process for ending that program may take a long time. In another example, a change proposal that involves implementing activities that are new to the organization may be perceived as risky for the financial stability and reputation of the organization. Such a change process will require an effort to educate workers throughout the organization that the new activities are evidence based.

3 The change process may encounter *competition* for financial and other organizational resources. The assessment process should have uncovered any plans of the organization for future change efforts, as well as the timing of such plans. For example, organizations often create **strategic plans**, which are long-term, formal plans for the organization's future. These plans often involve incremental modifications to current operations projected to contribute to better organizational outcomes (Austin & Solomon, 2009). A change process occurring in a different part of an agency can be a barrier to consideration of another change if the organization does not have enough resources to make more than one change at a time.

4 The organization must possess the *ability* to implement the change, experience a *need* for change, and the change proposal must *match with the mission and values* of the organization (Packard, 2021). The engagement, assessment, and planning processes, depending on the methods used, may have made administrators and staff aware of a possible problem or opportunity, potential solutions or options, and the possibility of an organizational change effort. If not, staff members and administrators must become aware of the problem, become dissatisfied with the current situation, and perceive that a proposed solution will alleviate the problem. In sum, the organizational system that supports the current structure that creates or exacerbates the problem must become weakened.

5. You must consider *perceived advantages and disadvantages* to the organization and staff (Packard, 2021). For example, if potential solutions will result in more work for a particular staff member or group of staff, that person(s) or unit(s) should be consulted before choosing a solution. Others' input may shape the change proposal or strengthen the support for the proposed solution; their suggestions and concerns can be considered and possibly addressed in the solution and change strategy. Consulting with a person(s) or unit(s) may garner their support. If possible, implementing a solution should be shared widely.

6. Gathering *history* on the organization's policy-making efforts or program changes will provide helpful context to future change efforts. For example, did prior change efforts induce staff disgruntlement or staff support? Were changes perceived as coming from the top down (i.e., imposed from administrators) or from the bottom up (i.e., suggested by staff)? Long-term staff members may be helpful sources of historical information.

7. In discussions with other staff members about potential solutions, the working group should also gather an initial impression about change ideas and the degree to which they are *understandable* and will likely be met with support. The working group must also learn about formal and informal groupings of staff members and charismatic leaders within the organization and account for the sentiment of such "subgroups" and leaders regarding the change proposal.

8. Prior to developing a change proposal, the working group must engage in *evidence-based practice* by researching the identified problem and potential solutions using empirical evidence (Packard, 2021).

9. The *timing* of a proposed solution can significantly impact the proposal's reception. For example, the time in which one administrator is leaving an organization and a new administrator is arriving is a window of opportunity for certain change proposals. We can explore a situation like this by returning to the chapter case. If the outgoing administrator was not in favor of developing support services specifically for LGBTQIA+ students, Marquis and other group members working for change may want to be certain that they will be represented on the committee that screens and interviews candidates for the open position. The group may also want to proceed with developing plans to implement new support services for LGBTQIA+ services to avoid losing time during the administrative transition.

These considerations speak to the need for a comprehensive process to determine a solution or option. Some considerations may be more important than others, and there may be special considerations for certain organizations. Developing a change proposal involves thinking through such considerations. Your proposal may also be impacted by your chosen change strategy. Additionally, the proposal may evolve as you garner more information.

Structure of Change Proposals A change proposal may be in the form of a policy change, a program change, or a change of project, practice, personnel, or some combination (Netting et al., 2017). The policy approach involves a formal statement regarding the direction for a course of action. A policy change often involves the decision of people with a high level of decision-making authority, such as administrators, elected officials, or a board of directors, that involves large-scale change to create a new or amend an existing policy. For example, in the case at the beginning of the chapter, the social worker, Marquis, and other members of the working group that is striving to create improved services to LGBTQIA+ students in the school district may determine that the most effective change strategy is to work toward a harassment policy that would include harassment based on sexual orientation and gender identity.

A program approach involves the creation of or change to "structured activities, designed to achieve a set of goals and objectives" (Netting et al., 2017, p. 306). Programs are designed to provide services to clients and are long-term activities. These are often high-profile aspects of an organization because clients interact with, and know organizations for, their programs. For example, a program approach to the perceived unmet needs of LGBTQIA+ adolescents in the school system would be to create an education program about sexual orientation for all students.

Projects are similar to programs but are typically smaller and more flexible, can be adapted to changing needs relatively easily, and are not permanent. A demonstration project, a short-term test of an idea, can be a less controversial way of implementing change. For example, the education program described earlier could be implemented for a specific time period, such as a semester, with the possibility of extension of the program in the spring semester and the possibility of changing the program in the first semester, as needed.

A change in personnel can address different types of problems in programs and projects. Staff members within organizations may lack the specific competencies or practice behaviors to effectively work within programs or projects, and a personnel approach is needed. A personnel approach can include additional education, internships, change in responsibilities for staff, or complete change of staff. Changes that involve personnel must be undertaken carefully, with a thorough examination to determine whether such a change will better serve the client (rather than simply change office dynamics). Using the example of the unmet needs of the LGBTQIA+ adolescents, the proposed solution may be to educate teachers on how to become more supportive of LGBTQIA+ adolescents in the school. If this strategy is employed, the working group should first initiate a dialogue with teachers to understand their perspective of the needs for the group in question (LGBTQIA+ in this case). Teacher buy-in is essential and their views must be taken into consideration to lessen resistance.

Lastly, a change for an organization can involve a practice approach, or the way in which organizations implement basic functions, which may or may not be formally described in written documents. For example, a subset of social workers like Marquis and teachers may become the unofficial resource and support persons for LGBTQIA+ adolescents in each school, so LGBTQIA+ adolescents have supportive adults at school (Netting et al., 2017). Exhibit 13.1 provides a summary of these approaches. Exhibit 13.2 provides a case example of an organization that implemented these approaches to change.

APPROACH	DEFINTION
Policy	A formally adopted statement that reflects goals and strategies or agreements on a settled course of action.
Program	Prearranged sets of activities designed to achieve a set of goals and objectives.
Project	Similar to programs but have a time-limited existence and are more flexible so they can be adapted to the needs of a changing environment.
Personnel	Persons who interact within the change arena.
Practice	The way in which organizations or individuals do business. Practices are less formalized than policies and may be specific to persons or groups.

Source: Netting et al., 2017, p. 308.

EXHIBIT 13.1

Approaches to Organizational Change

A local mental health organization has a longstanding program for persons with serious mental illness who also have problems with substance use (i.e., clients with co-occurring disorders). In recent years, the social work case managers have noticed increasing difficulty locating affordable, safe, and habitable rental housing for clients in the program. The case managers have convened a working group to increase access to affordable housing, and they are considering a variety of change approaches, including the following:

- *A policy approach:* The working group may approach the administration and the board of directors to change organizational policy so the organization can move from only providing social services to an organization that also owns and manages affordable, supportive housing for clients.
- *A program approach:* The working group may propose that the organization partner with local landlords to provide the intensive, on-site case management and supportive services needed to maintain a stable living environment through a live-in care provider. The organization will guarantee that the rent and utilities will be paid on time and that the apartment will be kept clean. The live-in care provider will be the first responder for any problems in the building that involve the client.
- *A project approach:* This change will be the same as the program change but will involve a six-month trial period. During the trial period, the social worker overseeing the project will report weekly to the administrator, who will then report on the project monthly to the board of directors. Ongoing adjustments will be made to the project as needed. If the project is deemed successful, the board of directors may consider creating a long-term program.
- *A personnel approach:* Using this approach, social workers will be trained to become trainers to the family members of clients about being live-in case managers to their family member with chronic mental health challenges. The trained live-in family member approach will allow clients to live with their families, thus alleviating the need for rental housing.

EXHIBIT 13.2

A Dearth of Affordable Rental Housing: A Case Example of Approaches to Change

> **EXHIBIT 13.2**
>
> *Continued*
>
> - *A practice approach:* Using a practice approach, social workers will learn different approaches for assisting clients to live together in their current rental housing, so that at least two clients can live in each apartment. This will have the effect of housing more clients with the same number of rental units.

Selecting Organizational Change Strategies

Thus far, the social worker has completed the engagement, assessment, and planning process; gathered allies; and created a working group to implement change. Together with allies in the working group, the social worker has taken many factors into consideration when developing a proposed solution, including evidence-based practice, and made a decision about a specific change proposal or intervention to pursue that entails a change in the organization. The next step in the process is to determine the strategy for making a change. A **strategy** is an overall approach to a change effort. In contrast, a **tactic** refers to specific actions, or skills, taken to implement a strategy (Hardina, 2013). This section includes discussion of strategies, while the next section focuses on tactics, or specific skills, needed to implement strategies.

There are three basic strategies for organizational change: collaborative, campaign, or conflict (Brager et al., 1987).

Collaborative Strategy A collaborative change is one in which the working group and the decision-maker(s) agree that some type of change in the organization is required, and cooperation is needed to create change. The group that is working for change and the decision-makers communicate, plan, coordinate, and share tasks to implement a change. All parties involved agree that a change is needed; therefore, the group's decisions will determine the approach (i.e., whether policy, program, project, personnel, or practice); the ways in which the needed resources can be obtained; and other details of implementation. Choosing this strategy means there is little opposition to a change, and the change can best be carried out collaboratively.

> *For example, if the working group and the school principal and administrators agree that LGBTQIA+ adolescents need additional support and that the school should and can assume a supportive role, the working group and administrators could partner in a change effort to determine the form the support would take (e.g., further education of teachers, support groups, and/or education of the students) and to implement the change.*

Campaign Strategy A campaign strategy is used when communication can occur between the decision-makers and the working group, but there is no agreement that a change is needed. The key to this strategy is the willingness of decision-makers to listen to arguments on behalf of a change proposal. The decision-makers may need additional information or persuasion.

For example, if the working group and the school principal and administrators do not agree with Marquis and other members of the working group that LGBTQIA+ adolescents need additional support from the school, group members could choose a campaign strategy of providing additional information, developing persuasive arguments, and arranging regular communication about this topic with the principal and administrators.

Conflict Strategy A conflict strategy can be used when the decision-makers are opposed to a change and are unwilling to communicate with the working group. Due to the lack of communication, the group working for change is unable to educate or persuade the decision-makers through organizational processes and is only able to influence them through a public conversation. This strategy involves efforts to draw support from a wider group of supporters and often involves public conflict. The conflict strategy often involves heated and/or passionate discussion that includes negative reactions and is therefore not typically used as a first change option.

For example, if the school principal and administrators do not agree that the school can take a role in providing additional support for the LGBTQIA+ adolescents and are unwilling to communicate with the working group about the topic, members of the group could choose to try a conflict strategy. The group may decide to organize a public forum on the prevention of school bullying to apply additional pressure to school district decision-makers.

Exhibit 13.3 provides an overview of change strategies and tactics.

We can further explore approaches and strategies for creating change in organizations by returning to Marquis, who has formed a group of other social workers and allies to promote services and support for LGBTQIA+ students in the school and throughout the school district.

Understanding the length of time that it will likely take to create change throughout the school district, Marquis and other members of the working group begin identifying solutions to the problem of students needing services and support currently as well as in the long run. Listing possible solutions leads the group to consider each possibility from the standpoint of feasibility, and to eliminate those that appeared to be likely to generate high costs or resistance. Through the process of carefully considering various ways to move forward, the group working for LGBTQIA+ services and support eventually decides to first propose a pilot project at one school. If the principal of one school approves of the pilot project, the working group can proceed in a way that will address some immediate student needs while they continue to work for change in schools throughout the district. Marquis and other members of the group also realize that starting with a pilot project will allow them to use collaborative strategies, building capacity as they go, as a preferred next step. Further, as the pilot project is evaluated, they will have gained valuable information about whether the pilot project makes a positive difference for students and, if so, how.

> **EXHIBIT 13.3**
>
> *Rapid Assessment Tool*
>
> **RELATIONSHIP BETWEEN GROUP PROMOTING CHANGE AND DECISION-MAKERS**
>
> **Collaboration**
>
> Decision-makers and the working group agree (or are easily convinced to agree) that change is needed and that resources must be allocated for a change.
>
> 1 Implementation
> 2 Capacity Building
> a Participation
> b Empowerment
>
> **Campaign**
>
> Decision-makers are willing to communicate with the working group but do not agree that a change is needed or that resources are needed for a change.
>
> 1 Education
> 2 Persuasion
> a Co-optation
> b Lobbying
> 3 Mass Media Social Media Appeal
>
> **Contest**
>
> Decision-makers oppose change and/or allocation of resources and are unwilling to communicate with the group working for change.
>
> 1 Bargaining and Negotiation
> 2 Group Actions
>
> Adapted from Netting et al., 2017, p. 312.

Strategies and Skills for Interventions With Organizations

The skills needed for interventions with organizations are built on the skills for intervention covered in previous chapters. In addition to these basic relationship and intervention skills, social workers need specific skills for working with change processes in organizations. The following tactics, or skills, are organized by the strategy with which they are most commonly associated.

Social work skills for collaborative change include the following:

Implementation Skills Implementation skills are those that involve solving problems and making decisions about logistics. Examples include engaging in research about an issue, developing written materials relating to the change proposal (e.g., written proposals, fact sheets), creating and facilitating task groups and workshops, and communicating with interested parties and decision-makers (Dudley & Herman-Smith, 2020; Schneider & Lester, 2001).

Capacity Building Building the capacity of client systems has two components: (1) participation, or involving members of the client system in the change process, and (2) empowerment of clients through participation in the effort. These efforts, both a process and an outcome, can improve the ability of client systems to remove real or perceived barriers to participation in change processes and increase the likelihood of clients participating in future change processes.

To elaborate on the earlier example of the principal and administrators agreeing with Marquis and the working group that LGBTQIA+ adolescents in the school needed additional support and that the school could play a role in providing that support, these collaborative change skills could be used to create a new program. The group working for change can use supporters, parents, friends, and allies of LGBTQIA+ students and LGBTQIA+ students themselves to assist with every aspect of the program, including researching, analyzing, and creating program ideas; facilitating groups; educating other students and education personnel about their unmet needs; and carrying out other tasks. Involving LGBTQIA+ students and student supporters in this effort can increase their competence in these skills and potentially enable them to teach others in a manner appropriate to their stage of life development.

Social work skills for campaign change include the following:

Education Education involves communication skills, which may include in-person meetings with individuals and groups, formal and informal presentations, written materials, and education materials designed for persons and groups influential with decision-makers. The goal of such efforts is to present different types of information to impact the perception, knowledge, attitude, and opinions of decision-makers through information.

Persuasion Convincing others to accept and support a particular view of an issue is the goal of persuasion. Skillful communication that appeals to the reasoning of decision-makers is an essential part of persuasion. The group working

for change must discern the information or incentives that are important to decision-makers and appeal to these. Additionally, choosing people with credibility with the decision-makers to communicate with them also helps make a persuasive argument.

One form of persuasion is **co-optation**, defined as minimizing anticipated opposition by including in the change effort those who would be opposed to it (Netting et al., 2017). Including the opposition in the change effort can neutralize the opposition because the opposition was part of designing the change effort and may be able to advance an interest through it. Lobbying is the action used to persuade policy makers or other targeted decision-makers who are essential to approval for the proposed change effort (Segal, 2020). Quick Guide 42 outlines specific skills needed for persuasion.

QUICK GUIDE 42 Persuasion Skills

Persuasion skills involve doing the following:

1. *Target your case to the other person:* Find out as much as you can about the person or group you wish to persuade, including their roles in the organization as well as their individual characteristics. Learning about their values, priorities, goals, motivations, personality, and habits will help you shape a reasoned argument that appeals to them.
2. *Be clear about "who," "what," and "why":* Create a reasoned argument that includes the essentials and that appeals to the other person(s) (not necessarily yourself). The reasoned argument should not be constructed as a debate—there are no winners/losers.
3. *Highlight common ground:* Build your reasoned argument on interests that both sides can agree on, even if lofty (such as "freedom" or "justice").
4. *Keep it simple:* People tend to make decisions by generalizing from a limited amount of evidence. Using a few powerful arguments that provide evidence of a unifying theme, presented in simple and relevant terms, is the most effective.
5. *Appeal to "head" and "heart":* Persuasive arguments include both rational and emotional elements. Pairing case stories or anecdotes told with vivid language with compelling "hard" evidence is particularly effective.
6. *Focus on delivery:* Effective verbal delivery includes the use of "I" statements, taking responsibility for your statements, projecting a positive image and adopting an active tone, showing respect to others and giving them credit, telling the truth, and showing a willingness to learn from experience. Effective nonverbal behaviors include using a clear and concise tone of voice; being calm, relaxed, and confident; using carefully articulated statements; and being attentive to the nonverbal behaviors of the other person.
7. *Use dialogue rather than monologue:* Use active listening by asking for information, summarizing, and testing for understanding. Respond in a constructive way to comments made by the other party. Dissent and disagreement are natural and functional in that they acknowledge differences of roles, goals, values, and personal qualities out in the open.

8   *Work with challenges:* When differences arise in the conversation, one response is to ask more questions. After learning where the other party stands on the matter, ask questions to learn the basis for their position, whether they are interested in reassessing their position, and if they have any ideas for resolving the differences. If confronting the other party, it is helpful to first summarize the other party's concerns and priorities and discuss any areas of your proposal that would address any of their concerns (i.e., common ground). It can also be helpful to offer your ideas as suggestions rather than proposals. Above all, avoid hostile or aggressive responses.

Source: Adapted from Manning, 2012.

Mass Media and Social Media Appeals   This skill refers to the use of all types of media to influence public opinion, as well as the opinion of decision-makers, either directly or indirectly. Involved in this skill are the development and shaping of newsworthy stories that will affect viewer opinion in the hoped-for direction.

In the example of the unmet needs of LGBTQIA+ adolescents in the school setting, these campaign skills can be applied if Marquis and the group working for change and the school principal are able to communicate the need for additional support. However, if the principal does not agree that additional support is needed and/or that the school can provide additional support, Marquis and his allies in the working group may need to consider other strategies. The working group can be involved in education efforts with the principal by holding meetings or using school media, such as a school newspaper, to present factual information about LGBTQIA+ adolescents and the challenges they face. The group could also submit op-ed (opinion-editorial) articles and letters to the editor of the local newspaper. The working group can also engage in persuasive efforts. For example, the group can appeal to the interests of decision-makers by describing the potential for increased academic performance and tolerance for diversity throughout the school that would result from the program. The working group can also use co-optation by inviting the principal or another administrator to join their efforts by becoming a member of an advisory committee to the group. As part of the change effort the group can also use websites, blogs, social media, as well as print media, to influence the opinion of other students, staff, parents, community members, and district administrators about the unmet needs of LGBTQIA+ adolescents in the hope that these populations will be persuaded to attempt to influence the opinions of school district decision-makers.

Social work skills for contest change include the following:

Bargaining and Negotiation   Discussing a change proposal, with the possibility of both the decision-maker and the working group making compromises to their preferred change proposal, involves bargaining and negotiation skills. **Bargaining and negotiation skills** are used when both the decision-maker and the group working understand the position of one another and understand the change proposal and when there is a sense of urgency on both sides about settling the matter. Rather than confrontation, at the core of this skill is the assumption that both sides use persuasive arguments about their position and that both give and receive accommodation to their preferences in the final decision. This process may involve a third party acting in the role of a mediator (Gitterman & Knight, 2022; Pierce & Boys, 2022).

Group Actions Group actions include many activities designed to increase political pressure on decision-makers. These confrontational tactics cover a wide range of legal and illegal activities, including rallies, demonstrations, marches, picketing, sit-ins, vigils, blockages, strikes, slowdowns, boycotts, class action lawsuits, and civil disobedience. Several of these actions require the involvement of attorneys and other professionals, while others are possible with a skilled social worker, working group members, and/or a large group of supporters (Mizrahi, 2022; Rome, 2022).

Ethics and Change Strategies The choice of strategies utilized for a change effort is influenced by a number of factors, including the type of relationship between the decision-makers and the group promoting change, the degree to which they agree on a goal, the extent of the communication, as well as social work ethics. Actions taken, particularly group actions that can involve confrontation, should be undertaken after careful thought and consideration, as well as after preparing clients and community members involved for any possible negative consequences, such as negative publicity, missed work time, or even fines, arrests, or physical injuries if the change effort should involve public protests. As mentioned, when there is a moderate amount of agreement and communication between the parties, more cooperative strategies should be attempted prior to campaign and conflict-oriented strategies are often the last set of tactics used when nothing else has been effective (Netting et al., 2017). The National Association of Social Workers *Code of Ethics* (2021a) should always be used as a guide for ethical decision-making in planning for and promoting change.

The following example describes actions and practices that, in some employment situations, may jeopardize one's employment. Before undertaking conflict actions, be sure to understand what employees, at your agency, are not allowed to do and what actions are prohibited. For example, public schools and government agencies have clear policies on employee actions, social media usage, and public statements.

Returning to the example of the unmet needs of LGBTQIA+ students, if Marquis and the working group attempt strategies associated with collaborative and campaign strategies without success, the next set of tactics may be contest strategy tactics. We can imagine a situation in which the working group wants the principal to implement a new program, and the principal has

rejected the idea and is unwilling to communicate further about the change proposal. In response, the working group may consider several actions in terms of their perceived effectiveness, their best estimate of any negative consequences, and their comfort level with each. The group promoting change may decide to organize a rally to raise awareness of this unmet need. The rally can be on public property in front of the school and can occur before or after school hours, so no school or district rules will be violated. Social workers can play a role in helping their allies in the group research local ordinances to assure compliance with rules and regulations beyond the school district.

This choice of a tactic involves several social work skills, including the review of research-based evidence about social action in general and rallies in particular, as well as empowerment work with LGBTQIA+ adolescents in academic settings. Marquis may also seek to involve external organizations that specialize in advocacy and diversity issues. This, or any subsequent actions, may persuade the principal, other administrators, and school board members to begin formally communicating again with the working group. If so, bargaining and negotiation may produce a satisfactory outcome, such as a program to be piloted for one year, with evaluation occurring throughout and at the end of the year.

While social workers and allies working to promote change in organizations are often successful, such change can take a long time and some change efforts do not result in the changes promoted. Working groups may need to change strategies or tactics, and the result of the change process may differ from the original proposals. A proposed permanent program may end up being a short-term pilot, an organizational policy change may differ from the original vision for change, and the requirements of funders may become a barrier to the provision of new services.

When change efforts are not successful at all, the status quo is maintained. At this point, the social worker and allies in the working group must reassess the situation to determine next steps. The change effort may benefit from starting over at the engagement and assessment phase to determine whether the identified unmet need is still as urgent as it was at the beginning of the action. Alternatively, the change effort may need to begin anew at the intervention stage, where the decision to pursue an intervention, the type of intervention, and/or the change strategy may need revisiting. An evaluation of the process so far will help determine whether different directions may yield more successful results toward the goal of better meeting the needs of clients or communities.

Overall, advocates for change benefit from persistence because many factors may be impacting the possibility of change, including external factors, such as a poor economy. Social workers who work with others to propose organizational change must be aware that many change efforts take much time and energy. Exhibit 13.4 provides a case example of the use of strategies and tactics.

EXHIBIT 13.4

A Dearth of Affordable Housing: Strategies and Tactics

The social work case managers of a local organization who work with clients with co-occurring disorders experiencing challenges in locating affordable rental housing have convened a group to work for change. The goal of the group is to pursue an organizational policy change so the agency can develop and manage affordable rental housing. The decision-makers are the board of directors, which includes the executive director. The group is considering a variety of change approaches, including the following:

- The group may first attempt collaborative change strategies with decision-makers. If all agree that a policy change is needed, the work will involve implementation skills. The social worker and other members of the working group may be involved in activities such as locating and presenting data regarding affordable housing development and management, creating written materials relating to the policy change, and communicating with other housing developers and managers, interested parties, and decision-makers. Another tactic used is capacity building. The social worker, with the other working group members, would ensure that clients and community members are represented at all levels in the change process. This involvement can be considered empowerment work with clients and community members in that the social workers involved can work to build skills related to organizational change such as committee work and public speaking.
- The group may decide to begin with campaign change strategies if collaborative change strategies are unsuccessful or if decision-makers will communicate with the group but do not agree that a policy change is needed. The group can utilize education skills, including conducting in-person meetings with individuals on the

> board of directors and others who can influence board members. The group can also provide formal presentations at board meetings and create educational materials for these meetings. In addition to education efforts using facts, the group must also utilize persuasion to convince the board to support a policy change. The group must attempt to appeal to the interests of board members to include better meeting client needs, as well as potentially raising revenue for the organization and raising the status of the organization among peer organizations. The group carefully chooses people with credibility, including clients, community members, and long-time employees, to communicate with board members and other decision-makers. Group members may also use co-optation if they invite a member of the board of directors to join the group in determining the exact direction and wording of the policy change proposal. Working group members may also lobby decision-makers about the policy change.
> - If the group promoting change is unsuccessful using campaign approaches, members may decide to embark on contest change strategies. After careful thought and deliberation, the group may use a group action to raise the pressure on the members of the board of directors and others in decision-making roles. For example, the group may decide to organize a public forum with other similar service providers and community members experiencing the same challenges with inadequate affordable housing. The forum can be organized to include information on the need for affordable rental housing for those with chronic mental illness. Such public events can encourage board members and other decision-makers to see the urgency in responding to the situation, making them more likely to engage in bargaining and negotiation with members of the group promoting change.

EXHIBIT 13.4

Continued

IMPLEMENTING ORGANIZATIONAL CHANGE

If the working group has been successful in creating organizational change, the next step is to implement the change. At this point, the change effort requires administrative work, such as writing a new or modified policy, designing a project or program, selecting personnel with the best skills and experience to implement the change, or training practitioners in the new practice. A change in one element of the organization, such as a new policy, can often impact change in another area, such as a new program, project, or even another policy change.

For example, a policy change that affects the members of a committee that screens and interviews candidates for administrative positions will result in practice changes: clients will now be recruited for the committee and educated about organizational personnel procedures, interviewing techniques, and written evaluation processes for interviews. Those changes that involve policies, programs, or projects most significantly impact organizations, and those that impact personnel and practices, while important, may not represent an in-depth change to the organization. The following discussion applies to implementing a new or modified program or project, including developing goals, objectives, and evaluation criteria, and possibly using a Gantt chart to guide the timeframe of activities.

Implementation Structure

Successful programs and projects need structure to guide implementation and for evaluation purposes, although the elements for a project may be less elaborate than those for a program due to the short-term nature of a project. The elements of a program include goals and objectives, timelines, eligibility criteria, rules and procedures, an evaluation plan, and a management information system (Hardina, 2013).

Goals are broad statements related to an ideal state for a target, such as a population or community, while objectives are steps toward reaching the goals. Objectives can relate to an outcome, a specific task, a process, or the means to completing a task. A timeline spells out in detail the activities that will carry out the goal and objectives, with specific deadlines in place. The eligibility criteria define the clients or community members who can participate in the program, while the rules and procedures provide the structure for the day-to-day functioning of the program, such as the roles that individuals will play, the decision-making process, the responsibilities for each person involved, and the process for delivering the program. The evaluation plan provides the details about the instruments and/or data to be collected on a timetable and the identity of those who will collect, analyze, and report on the program data. The management information system (MIS) is the systematic method of collecting program data and is often a type of software or Internet-based application.

> *For example, if Marquis and other members of the working group focused on the unmet needs of LGBTQIA+ adolescents are successful in starting a pilot within one high school in the district to better educate, support, and nurture LGBTQIA+ students, the next step is to create the elements of a program. Marquis and other members of the working group, and/or administrators, can create program goals and objectives, and corresponding evaluation criteria, such as the following (Hardina et al., 2007):*
>
> - *Program goal: To enhance the academic and social functioning of LGBTQIA+ students and allied students in the high school.*
> - *Outcome objective: By December 20XX, at least one support group and three sexual orientation educational sessions will be offered to students.*
> - *What were the students' perceptions of the education sessions offered?*
> - *Evaluation criteria: Number of support groups and educational sessions offered.*
> - *Process objective: By November 30, 20XX, recruit at least ten students for an LGBTQIA+ support group through one-to-one contact and advertising in the school.*

- *Evaluation criteria: Number of students recruited, number of in-person recruiting contacts made, and amount of school newspaper coverage.*
- *Process objective: By October 20XX, create outlines of two different curricula related to sexual orientation education for consideration by the administration.*
- *Evaluation criteria: Number of existing curricula reviewed and number of curricular outlines created.*

Using a Gantt Chart

An important component of planning the implementation of a new program is specifying activities and corresponding timeframes so that actions can be undertaken in a logical, sequential order. A **Gantt chart** provides a visual display of the activities that must be undertaken and the timeframe for the completion of each activity, which can be helpful in both implementing a program and evaluating the success of the implementation (Gertler et al., 2016; O'Connor & Netting, 2009). The Gantt chart in Exhibit 13.5 depicts a sample of the activities to be completed for implementation of an LGBTQIA+ support group and sexual orientation education sessions.

EXHIBIT 13.5

Rapid Assessment Tool

ACTIVITY	SEPT	OCT	NOV	DEC
Form working group with staff allies	x			
Locate and review sexuality and gender identity education materials in current use by school districts*	x			
Recruit interested students to join working group	x			
Produce recruitment materials and begin recruiting for support group	x			
Choose the sexuality and gender identity educational materials most appropriate to middle and high school students		x		
Recruit five students		x		
Recruit five additional students			x	
Recruit student facilitator and begin weekly support groups			x	x
Conduct one education session with student co-facilitator			x	
Conduct two education sessions with student co-facilitators				x

Source: Adapted from O'Connor & Netting, 2009.

In addition to the activities in the Gantt chart, participant eligibility criteria, program rules and procedures, and a management information system will be created to track program participants and evaluation criteria for the program.

> Returning to the social worker Marquis and his colleagues, we can further explore the implementation of the pilot project they decided to propose as a first step. The group reached out to middle and high school principals and found that several administrators were supportive of their pilot project. One principal offered to partner with them to write a grant proposal to fund "innovative school services for vulnerable student groups," which was a new resource at the school district level. The grant was awarded and, although modest, it would cover a pilot project at one school.
>
> Designing a pilot project and describing how it would be evaluated was helpful to the working group. The principal left the design of the project to the working group, who researched what other schools and districts around the country were doing to better serve LGBTQIA+ students. The group also created a Gantt chart as a visual plan for implementation that the principal included in the grant proposal. When the grant was awarded, feedback from the school district was that the careful planning and the partnership between the working group and the principal were key factors in making the decision to fund the pilot project.

Challenges to Implementation

Due to the complexity of organizations, implementation of a change effort can be fraught with difficulty. The organization may be facing challenges imposed by external constraints, such as a scarcity of available funding for the change proposal. The challenges faced by social workers attempting to implement a change can include the following (Winship & Lee, 2012).

Staff Member Resistance Although the change proposal has been successfully approved and authorized, staff members may be more or less committed to implementing the change. Change proposals often encounter resistance from staff members with a different perspective or philosophy. Staff members may oppose the change for many reasons, including a different worldview about the matter at hand, skepticism regarding the potential for change in people and organizations, a fear of conflict, or a high comfort level with the status quo. If staff members were opposed to the change initially, they may covertly express their opposition through inaction or subversion.

Generality of the Change Changes that are major in scope, such as policy changes, tend to be worded too generally; therefore, the implementation of the change may suffer from distortion because the staff member making the change may not understand or be suited to make the intended change. For example, some staff members may incorrectly implement the change due to a lack of understanding or skill, or may decide to implement the change using their unique styles such that the original intent is not realized. Specificity in explaining the change both in writing and training sessions is essential for effective organizational change.

Organizational Supports Change proposals may be adopted with low levels of commitment by the decision-makers, and the implementation consequently may suffer from inadequate financial, planning, implementation, and other types of resources. A partial implementation of a change proposal may mean that the change is unsuccessful, when a complete implementation may have resulted in a highly successful implementation. A decision-maker's perspective on change may be affected by relationships with other organizations because a change could create or exacerbate competition with other organizations or unnecessarily duplicate another organization's program. This could happen while the administrator is trying to create a stronger relationship with another organization. In short, support for the implementation by the organization's decision-makers can be affected by many factors other than the merits of the change proposal. Exhibit 13.6 provides an example of the ways in which staff resources impact change efforts.

EXHIBIT 13.6

Organizational Challenges in Implementing Change

The death of an infant under the supervision of the Human Services Agency (HSA) led to a decision to seek accreditation in all eligible agency services by the Council on Accreditation (COA). Accreditation by an outside body, such as the COA, provides an external, unbiased "stamp of approval" on an organization and is a confirmation of the highest level of professionalism of an organization. The process of seeking accreditation is a challenging, arduous, resource-laden process of organizational self-assessment toward meeting specific standards supported by documented evidence. Ultimately, it is to build capacity of the organization toward better organization and client outcomes.

The Quality Assurance and Accreditation Committee, which operated as a working group to promote change, consisted mostly of administrators, while subcommittees consisted of staff members. As the two-year process got under way, it was clear that some subcommittee members were passive or resistant to the work. In general, the staff were not highly motivated to respond to communication or meet deadlines. They lacked clarity about the importance of the work and questioned how seeking accreditation would help the clients and communities they served. They were also frustrated about being asked to work overtime for accreditation efforts. Some staff members felt that the process devalued their many years of practice experience and reflected judgment on the quality of service they provided.

In response to early problems, the value of the accreditation process to services and outcomes was clarified. Additionally, communication systems were clarified, administrators provided more encouragement to accomplish tasks and assistance in balancing work priorities, and "tip sheets" on relevant topics were delivered to each subcommittee. Yet, even after staff better understood the importance of the work, some staff members were resistant to solving the problems uncovered in the process, such as a lack of formal written procedures, documentation, and evaluation in all areas required by COA. Administrators reminded staff of the

| EXHIBIT 13.6

Continued | importance of the work and encouraged them to take some ownership of the process as a legacy of their work at the agency. Finally, a mock site visit by COA volunteers prior to the "real" site visit by COA evaluators was planned. The mock site visit led to clarification for the staff of the inadequacies of the accreditation documents produced thus far and an increased focus to complete the work. While challenged to finish the work by the deadline, staff members experienced a higher level of camaraderie with one another and administrators, who also worked overtime during this period. Ultimately, HSA received accreditation by COA.

Source: Winship & Lee, 2012. |
|---|---|

TERMINATION, EVALUATION, AND FOLLOW-UP IN PRACTICE WITH ORGANIZATIONS

The next phase in the organizational change process, termination, applies to the end of the work toward change within the agency. Social workers engaged in an organizational change effort often continue to participate in the work of the organization as employees and are engaged in follow-up activities after an intervention ends. In a sense, many organizations experience continual change processes, as the agency seeks to maintain programs and services that address the needs of clients and communities.

If the change process has been unsuccessful, the working group may decide to begin anew at the assessment phase to gather more information and consider different possible unmet needs as the basis for a new intervention effort. The group may also decide to pursue a change effort based on the same unmet need, but with a different change proposal or strategy for change. Alternatively, the working group may decide to abandon intervention efforts and disband. In this case, termination of the change process may occur until the next unmet need is identified, when the change process can begin anew, possibly with new members of a working group who will promote the change.

If the change process has been successful, the end of the change effort may occur when the change proposal has been approved by decision-makers, or after the policy, program, or project change has occurred and an evaluation has determined that the change has positively impacted the organization. The group promoting change may disband after either the approval, implementation, or evaluation. Follow-up efforts may involve continuing to monitor the effects of a change within an organization for a longer period of time than typical program evaluation processes. In certain cases, the working group may have been so effective that they decide to continue to work together on the next organizational change effort. An example can be seen in the case of the partnership between Marquis and the other social workers and allies with the school principal, who wrote a successful proposal for funding to support a pilot project. The working group carefully monitored and evaluated the project and immediately began planning a change effort to replicate services and support for LGBTQIA+ students in other middle and high schools in the district.

When a working group disbands, the termination may evoke an emotional response from participants, and group termination processes may be helpful. Just as in other groups, the role of the social worker in termination is to help group members examine and celebrate their experiences and accomplishments and discuss ways in which their shared experiences and skills may be useful to future participants (Gitterman et al., 2021). Termination processes may involve celebration, public announcements, debriefing meetings, and efforts to document the change process and lessons learned.

Evaluation of Social Work Practice With Organizations

Evaluation of social work practice with organizations is an important part of the change process. The evaluation process can focus on the change process itself as well as the result of the change process (i.e., a new or changed policy, program, or project). Evaluation of an advocacy effort or of a program or project begins with a decision about the measurable objectives, usually made at the beginning of a change effort. The evaluation process requires some decisions, including (1) whether both the process and outcomes will be evaluated, (2) the ways in which the process and/or outcomes will be evaluated, and (3) the means by which data will be collected as the basis for the evaluation.

Types of Evaluation For both the change process and the implementation of programs and projects, three types of evaluation can be used to assess the objectives:

- *Process Evaluation.* A process evaluation focuses on the *degree to which the change effort went well.* For example, did the group have a sufficient number of persons for the work involved? What methods were used to recruit members to the group? If evaluating a program, a process evaluation could focus on whether sufficient resources were available for the program, the ways in which decisions were made, or whether there was sufficient and timely communication between staff members implementing a program.

- *Outcome Evaluation.* An outcome evaluation focuses on *specific results* that the effort achieved. Questions to be answered may be: Did the group successfully arrange meetings with decision-makers? Create educational materials? Were there any policy changes? Were new programs or projects created as a result of policy changes? An outcome evaluation for a program focuses on the results of program efforts. For example, did support groups meet? Were educational trainings held? The objectives for the program should be reviewed, and success in their achievement should be noted.

- *Impact Evaluation.* An impact evaluation reviews the *impact of the efforts and seeks to determine the impact, if any, of a program on the outcome of interest* (Gertler et al., 2016).

For example, in relation to advocacy efforts, is there a new decision-making process in the organization that is more participatory? In relation to the new program we are discussing in this chapter, are LGBTQIA+ adolescents achieving at higher academic levels as a result? Have clients or community members experienced behavioral or social changes as a result of a new policy, program, or project? Have specific changes occurred in the community, such as decreased graffiti in public areas or increased involvement in community programs?

Structure of Evaluation The structure of evaluation involves four specific concepts: inputs, activities, outputs, and outcomes. Inputs are those resources necessary to implement a change effort or a program. Inputs can include funding, equipment, staff, time, expertise, and other resources needed for the effort or program. Activities are those actions that organizations take to produce change. Activities can include attending meetings, creating flyers, interviewing clients and community members, and conducting assessments. Outputs are products that emerge from the activities. Outputs are often measured by a number (e.g., number of clients served by a program, flyers produced, or hours worked). Outcomes are the benefits gained or changes that have occurred as a result of the activities. Outcomes may relate to behaviors, skills, knowledge, attitudes, values, conditions, or other attributes. In essence, the outcomes are the impact made by the change effort or program (Dudley, 2020).

Logic Model A **logic model** is a tool to analyze a program or practice intervention, which helps to highlight, graphically, how the stages and elements of an intervention may be logically linked to the organization as a whole (Dudley, 2020). They are created at the beginning of a change effort, such as when a program or project is being developed, to understand how all of the different parts will interact with one another. Exhibit 13.7 provides an example of a logic model used for a program of rental housing for people with dual diagnoses.

In this example, funding is needed to purchase and/or renovate an apartment building (*input*), so that clients can be housed with a trained, supportive roommate and provided with intensive case management (*activities*). These activities may result in clients being housed in a decent, affordable unit, leading a more stable life, and being compliant with their medication (*output*), so that fewer clients would be homeless and/or incarcerated (*outcome*).

This logic model can be useful in making a persuasive argument to decision-makers interested in decreasing the number of dual-diagnosed clients who are hospitalized or incarcerated. Other decision-makers may be interested in other outcomes, such as lowering levels of homelessness among persons who

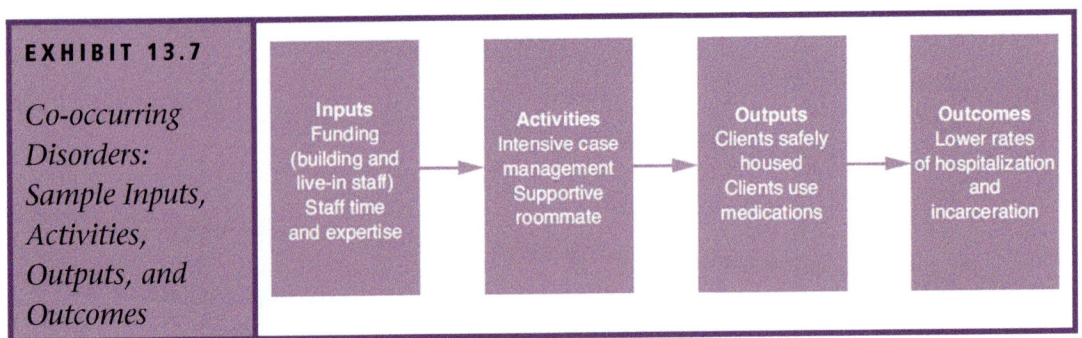

EXHIBIT 13.7

Co-occurring Disorders: Sample Inputs, Activities, Outputs, and Outcomes

have co-occurring disorders in the community or improving the relationship between the police force and the organization. Logic models provide a rational connection between inputs, activities, outputs, and outcomes and are often used in evaluating change efforts, programs, and projects (Hardina, 2013).

Information and Data Sources During the evaluation process, it is imperative to develop and maintain effective tracking systems to track information, data, change efforts, programs, and projects. Information that may be helpful includes the following:

- sign-in sheets, logs of activities, and meeting minutes;
- document time spent on activities, appointments, assessments, client and community progress, activities in need of completing, and accomplishments;
- evaluation materials, including standardized measures;
- mission and value statements, goals, objectives, strategic plans, and timelines;
- mass media and social media coverage;
- previous internal and external evaluations of advocacy efforts and programs/projects;
- records and reports about previous internal and external advocacy efforts;
- funding sources, dollar amounts, deliverables, and required timelines and communications;
- information about key individuals involved in change efforts or programs/projects; and
- government organizations related to the change effort and/or programs/projects.

As with evaluations of community change efforts, the evaluation process ideally includes qualitative and quantitative data to provide information about the process and outcomes of organizational change. Methods may include pre- and post-measures of organizational and/or community functioning, such as validated and standardized measures, direct observation, use of publicly available data (i.e., US Census data and others), and feedback from other professionals.

Roles in Evaluation Generalist social work practitioners commonly contribute in several ways to the evaluation efforts. Social workers can lead and/or assist with evaluation efforts by helping maintain organizational records, submitting data for analysis, participating in interviews and focus groups, or creating questions to be used in the evaluation process. Participation on evaluation teams and committees provides a way for social workers to learn about and shape evaluation efforts. Some social workers function as full-time researchers to collect, analyze, and report on quantitative and qualitative data. Organizations benefit from well-designed and executed evaluation efforts that are informed by social workers.

CRITICAL CONSIDERATIONS ON ORGANIZATIONAL LIFE

This chapter has highlighted both the challenging and the exhilarating aspects of social work practice in organizational settings. Social workers can be tempted to view the organization as a source of challenges in practice. Sometimes organizations can be perceived as posing barriers to the helping process due to policies, procedures, and practice requirements.

In much the same way that some people blame their families for their challenges, some social workers point to the organization as the source of the problem when work becomes challenging or proves more difficult than expected. Shifting responsibility for challenges to organizations relieves the burden of responsibility from social workers for their roles in organizational challenges. Social workers may not always fully understand the practice constraints inherent in organizations (such as constraints on practice by funders or regulators) and may find it easier to adopt a cynicism that eases their sense of responsibility.

A related problem can occur if social workers join with clients or community members to collude in identifying the problems of the organization as the source of challenges for clients and communities. In colluding with clients or community members, the social worker may feel temporarily relieved by sharing in their desperation with the organizational system. However, such collusion can convey a sense of hopelessness even though the social worker's goal may be to convey a sense of hopefulness about the possibility of change.

In its most extreme implication, a hopeless stance may promote a generalized, scornful distrust of all helping efforts. Clients and community members may generalize that all helping efforts are ineptly carried out by social workers who are helpless and caught in troubled organizational structures that fail to implement their mission statements. For social workers, an important element of empowerment practice is creating an alliance with clients and community members to undertake a joint effort that promotes more effective agency services. In this way, social workers can help convey an overall hopeful message to clients and communities about their interactions with an organization.

Social workers who facilitate organizational change efforts must be well informed and have completed the earlier phases of the change process, knowing that every change effort will encounter resistance. Further, social workers need to understand the dynamics of bureaucracies and the slow nature of change within them before engaging in a change effort. In addition to understanding the organization and the nature of change, social workers must also understand their own strengths and weaknesses and enlist allies to assist with the effort. Social workers who do not address any problematic organizational policies or practices due to fear of criticism or loss of employment are likely to have difficulties in social work careers. Social work practice requires principled, thoughtful, and respectful risks across all settings to fully implement the work of the profession.

CONCLUSION

Organizations are structures that shape and facilitate social work practice. The change process in organizations provides an opportunity to offer improved services to clients. While the change process can be lengthy and complex, the process is an opportunity to make changes that positively impact a large number of people, including entire communities. Most organizations undergo at least modest change on a regular basis due to changes in many factors, such as funding, relationships, personnel, accreditation, or accountability requirements. Social workers are in a unique position to implement the change process based on their knowledge and critical thinking about the needs of clients and communities they serve. While organizations can seem too mired in tradition and complexity to change, understanding and impacting organizations is important to social work practitioners because of the significant impact on clients and communities. Taking an active role in shaping organizations and agencies is a significant part of generalist social work practice.

GRAND CHALLENGE

Achieve Equal Opportunity and Justice

In the history of the United States, some groups of people have long endured prejudice, discrimination, oppression, and exclusion from success in education and employment. A challenge for social work, identified by the American Academy of Social Work and Social Welfare, is to end racial and social injustice, dismantle inequality, and end unfair practices.

The Grand Challenge of Promoting Equality by Addressing Social Stigma, by Goldbach et al. (2015), describes the problems associated with social stigma and opportunities for social workers to end these problems. They describe stigma as "negative labeling" based on characteristics that others perceive as undesirable and that distinguish people from the rest of society. Stigma results in social disadvantage and loss of opportunities throughout life because of inequality, and leads to less favorable outcomes regarding health, academic achievement, income, and wealth, among others. Stigma can be based on race and ethnicity, gender, sexual orientation, immigration status, age, ability status, health status, housing situation, and other characteristics.

The authors suggest a number of steps that social workers can take to reduce stigma, including examining social work's role in societies that have supported inequality and working to unearth unconscious biases of social workers. They also suggest engaging in employment-based training to reduce bias in service delivery, as well as active participation in public policy efforts to reduce inequality.

One effort that can be taken is at the organizational level. Organizations can make efforts to overcome stigma built into institutional arrangements. Stigma can result in biases built into organizations, even when they are unrecognized. Organizations can examine the assumptions built into their policies, practices, programs, and personnel to determine where biases may be present that reinforce social stigmas. For example, unexamined biases could exist in such policies as the length of time a participant is allowed to participate in a program, the process of developing and managing waiting lists for services, or sources of recruitment for programs.

To consider these questions further, familiarize yourself with Working Paper No. 18, *Promoting Equality by Addressing Social Stigma* (Goldbach et al., 2015).

MAIN POINTS

- The approach best used for an organizational change effort will be impacted by the results of the engagement and assessment process as well as the perspectives and models that guide the change process.

- The organizational change effort is facilitated by using a framework that addresses gathering supporters and allies into a working group to promote change, considering important factors when developing a change proposal, and selecting organizational change strategies and tactics.

- Social workers consider social work ethics when choosing specific tactics to use in the change process.

- The implementation of an organizational change is facilitated by a structure comprised of identifying goals, objectives, timeline, eligibility criteria, and evaluation plans, as well as consideration of challenges to implementation.

- Termination of a change effort can occur after a change proposal has been accepted or after the implementation of the change.

- The evaluation phase can include evaluation of the change effort as well as evaluation of the change, such as outcomes associated with a program or a project.

- Social workers should exercise caution about identifying organizational challenges with clients and community members, and only do so while maintaining a hopeful stance about the ability of the organization to change in order to provide better services.

EXERCISES

1 To apply your learning of the Grand Challenge to promote equality by addressing social stigma that was highlighted in this chapter, visit the Grand Challenges website (https://grandchallengesforsocialwork.org) and read Working Paper No. 18 under the "achieve equal opportunity and justice link" (Goldbach et al., 2015). Then, go to www.routledgesw.com/interactive-cases/ and become familiar with the RAINN case. Under the "Evaluate Your Results" tab, review both "Purpose of RAINN Evaluation Data" and "What Data CAN'T Tell Us" sections. Consider whether any collected data could provide hints about potential organizational bias in RAINN service delivery. Are there any evaluation questions that cannot be answered with the data collected? If additional data could be collected, could it shed light on bias in the organization?

2 Go to www.routledgesw.com/interactive-cases/ and become familiar with the Carla Washburn case, including reviewing her client history, concerns, and goals. Explore the town map and determine those organizations that may be able to assist Carla with her concerns and goals. Choose

one of the organizations and consider the way(s) in which the organization may be able to assist Carla with one or more of her concerns and/or goals. Imagine that you are employed by the organization, and the assistance needed for Carla is currently not offered by the organization. Using the material from Chapter 13, describe the following:
- The type of approach, perspective, or model with which you most closely identify
- The way in which you would go about creating a working group to promote organizational change
- Two to three possible solutions to Carla's concern or goal with which the organization could assist
- Two to three considerations that are important to consider in deciding on the change proposal

3 Go to www.routledgesw.com/interactive-cases/ and become familiar with the Riverton case, including the history, concerns, and goals, as well as the town map and the interaction matrix. Imagine that you decide to work to find a solution to the problem of public intoxication by working with the organizations in the community as a "nonemployee." Which organizations would you approach to develop a community-wide response to this problem? What kind of changes might be needed in those organizations to better meet the unmet needs of the clients and communities? What steps might you take to facilitate the development of a working group to promote change in these organizations? What might be some feasible solutions that organizations could implement through a partnership?

4 Go to www.routledgesw.com/interactive-cases/ and become familiar with the Brickville case. After an organizational assessment related to organizational engagement in political affairs, the Brickville CDC decided to move forward with a change proposal to engage more fully in local politics. The social worker, Olivia, and her colleagues formed a committee to work on the organizational change effort. For this change effort, create a goal, outcome objective, and evaluation criteria. In addition, create two to three process objectives and corresponding evaluation criteria for the change effort.

5 Using the Brickville case scenario described in Exercise #4, describe a policy, program, project, personnel, and practice approach to more fully engage in local politics as an organization.

6 Review Exhibit 13.2. Create a different policy, program, project, personnel, or practice approach to the case than those provided.

7 Review Exhibit 13.2. Create an approach to change that mixes these approaches.

8 You are a social worker at an organization that provides treatment for adolescents who have substance use issues. Yesterday, you suggested that the organization extend the service hours of the organization into the evenings and weekends so that client families would have greater access to meet with staff, participate in treatment planning, and provide additional face-to-face support for their children. The staff were enthusiastic

about the idea, and you agreed to the director's request that you compose a written proposal to be discussed at the next staff meeting.

In your weekly meeting with your supervisor, you learn that she is upset with you. In your discussion, she is curt and states that you may not have considered the increased amount of work that extended service hours would entail. She states that increased service hours will have a negative impact on her in terms of her social life and time with family members, and cost the agency additional funds. Considering the material discussed in this chapter, discuss the factors that may have led to this barrier to organizational change. Discuss possible next steps for this change process.

9 Using the case scenario in Exhibit 13.6, apply the key points in Quick Guide 42. What steps could have been taken to be more persuasive to those opposed?

NOTE

* See online resources for student-led Gay Straight Alliances and Gender and Sexuality Alliances at www.glsen.org/participate/student-action/gsa

References

Abramovitz, M., Sherraden, K. H., Hill, K., Rhodes Smith, T., Lewis, B., & Mizrahi, T. (2019). Voting is social work: Voices from the national social work voter mobilization campaign. *Journal of Social Work Education, 55*(4), 626–644.

Adler-Baeder, F., & Higginbotham, B. (2020). Efforts to design, implement, and evaluate community-based education for stepfamilies: Current knowledge and future directions. *Family Relations, 69,* 559–576.

Aguilar, J., Smith, C. F., & Tomczak, S. M. (2021). Appropriately uncomfortable: A conversation among three colleagues about structural oppression focusing on racism and the need for action. *Reflections: Narratives of Professional Helping, 27*(2). Retrieved from https://reflectionsnarrativesofprofessionalhelping.org/index.php/Reflections/article/view/1858/1678

Alexander Street (Producer). (2018). *Ethics and values in social work: Client-centered processes for managing ethical concerns.* Alexandria, VA: Microtraining Associates. [Streaming Video]. Retrieved from video.alexanderstreet.com/watch/ethics-and-values-in-social-work-client-centered-processes-for-managing-ethical-concerns database

American Academy of Social Work & Social Welfare. (2016). *Grand challenges: About.* Retrieved from http://aaswsw.org/grand-challenges-initiative/about/

American Academy of Social Work & Social Welfare. (2021). *Grand challenges: About.* Retrieved from https://grandchallengesforsocialwork.org/about/

American Federation of Government Employees. (2016). *Violence against health & social service workers.* Retrieved from www.afge.org/article/violence-against-health-care--social-service-workers-must-end/

American Psychological Association. (2017). Facing the divide: Psychology's conversations on race and health: an APA Committee on Ethnic Minority Affairs video series. *Instructor discussion guide.* https://www.apa.org/education-career/undergrad/diversity/facing-divide-instructor-guide.pdf

AmeriCorps/VISTA. (2019). *What is asset mapping?* Retrieved from www.vistacampus.gov/what-asset-mapping

Anderson, H. (2016). Postmodern/poststructural/social construction therapies: Collaborative, narrative, and solution-focused. In T. L. Sexton & J. Lebow (Eds.), *Handbook of family therapy* (pp. 184–203). New York, NY: Routledge.

Anderson, L. R., Hemez, P. F., & Kreider, R. M. (2022). *Living arrangements of children: 2019 current population reports* (pp. 70–174). Washington, DC: U.S. Census Bureau. Retrieved from www.census.gov/content/dam/Census/library/publications/2022/demo/p70-174.pdf

Anderson, W. L. (2018). Safety, ethics, and the elephant in the room. Webinar presented by *Social Work Today.* Retrieved from www.socialworktoday.com/marketing/webinars/2018/une/RecordedSlides.pdf

Anthony, W. L., Mills, D., & Nower, L. (2020). Internet gaming disorder and problematic technology use. In A. L. Begun & M. M. Murray (Eds.), *Routledge handbook of social work and addictive behaviors* (pp. 141–155). [E-version]. New York: Routledge Publishing.

Aponte, D. A., & Patrick, S. (2017). Narrative approaches to counseling survivors of child sexual abuse. *Wisdom in Education, 7*(2). Retrieved from http://scholarworkslib.csusb.edu/wie/vol.7/iss2/2

Archer, D. N. (2021). *Transportation policy and the underdevelopment of Black communities.* 106 Iowa Law Review 2125 (2021), NYU School of Law, Public Law Research Paper, No. 2125–2151.

Asay, T. P., & Lambert, M. J. (1999). The empirical case for the common factors in therapy: Quantitative findings. In M. A. Hubble, B. L.

Duncan, & S. D. Miller (Eds.), *The heart and soul of change: What works in therapy* (pp. 23–55). Washington, DC: American Psychological Association.

Asset-Based Community Development Institute. (2001–2019). *ABCD institute toolkit.* Chicago, IL: DePaul University. Retrieved from https://resources.depaul.edu/abcd-institute/resources/Pages/tool-kit.aspx

Association for the Advancement of Social Work with Groups, Inc. (2013). *Standards for social work practice with groups* (2nd ed.). Retrieved from www.aaswg.org/files/AASWG_Standards_for_Social_Work_Practice_with_Groups.pdf

Association for Specialists in Group Work. (2021). *Multicultural and social justice competence principles for group workers.* Retrieved from www.asgw.org/resources-1

Association of Social Work Boards. (2017). *2017 Analysis of the practice of social work.* Retrieved from https://www.aswb.org/wp-content/uploads/2020/11/2017-Tech-Report.pdf

Austin, M. J. (2018). Social work management practices, 1917–2017: A history to inform the future. *Social Service Review, 92*(4), 487–503.

Austin, M. J., & Solomon, J. R. (2009). Managing the planning process. In R. J. Patti (Ed.), *The handbook of human services management* (pp. 321–337). Thousand Oaks, CA: Sage Publications.

Bae, J., Jennings, P. F., Hardeman, C. P., Kim, E., Lee, M., Littleton, T., & Saasa, S. (2020). Compassion satisfaction among social work practitioners: The role of work: Life balance. *Journal of Social Service Research, 46*(3), 320–330. doi:10.1080/01488376.2019.1566195

Baker, A. Z., & Freund, R. R. (2018). Addressing spirituality themes with narrative therapy. In C. S. Gill & R. R. Freund (Eds.), *Spirituality and religion in counseling* (pp. 147–158). New York, NY: Routledge.

Ballan, M. S., & Freyer, M. (2021). Qualitative clinical assessment methods. In C. Jordan & C. Franklin (Eds.), *Clinical assessment for social workers: Quantitative and qualitative methods* (5th ed.) (pp. 139–174). New York: Oxford University Press.

Ballentine, J., Roberts, J., & Korgen, K. (2018). *Our social world: Introduction to sociology* (6th ed). Thousand Oaks, CA: Sage.

Banach, M., & Pillay, R. (2019). Ethical challenges in group work: Potential perils and preventive practices. In S. M. Marson & R. E. McKinney (Eds.), *The Routledge handbook of social work ethics and values* (pp. 191–197). New York, NY: Routledge.

Barker, R. L. (2014). *The social work dictionary* (6th ed.). Washington, DC: NASW Press.

Barnett, T. M. (2019). Community-based participatory research. In C. Franklin (Ed.), *Encyclopedia of social work* [E-reader version]. Washington, DC, and New York, NY: National Association of Social Workers and Oxford University Press. doi:10.1093/acrefore/9780199975839.013.69

Barsky, A. E. (2017). *Conflict resolution for the helping professions.* New York, NY: Oxford University Press.

Barsky, A. E. (2019). *Ethics and values in social work: An integrated approach for a comprehensive curriculum* (2nd ed.). Oxford: Oxford University Press.

Barsky, A. E., & Northen, H. (2017). Ethics and values in group work. In C. D. Garvin, L. M. Gutiérrez, & M. J. Galinsky (Eds.), *Handbook of social work with groups* (2nd ed.) (pp. 74–92). New York, NY: The Guilford Press.

Barth, R. P., Johnson-Motoyama, M., Jonson-Reid, M., Kulkarni, S. J., Herrenkohl, T. I., Holmes, M. R., Aymer, S. T., & Kohl, P. (2022). Building healthy relationships to end violence broadening the vision of the grand challenge to stop family violence. In R. P. Barth, J. T. Messing, T. R. Shanks, & J. H. Williams (Eds.), *Grand challenges for social work and society: Milestones achieved and opportunities ahead* (2nd ed.) (pp. 72–110). New York: Oxford University Press.

Bathgate, L. (2016). 5 practical points for social workers on interdisciplinary teams. *The New Social Worker, 23*(1), 14–15.

Beck, J. S. (2011). *Cognitive therapy for challenging problems: What to do when the basics don't work.* New York, NY: Guilford Press.

Beck, J. S., & Hindman, R. (2018). Cognitive therapy. In M. J. Dewan, B. N. Steenbarger, & R. P. Greenberg (Eds.), *The arts and sciences of brief psychotherapies: An illustrated guide* (3rd ed.) (pp. 97–133). [E-version]. Arlington, VA: APA Publishing.

Becvar, D. S., & Becvar, R. J. (2018). *Systems theory and family therapy: A primer* (3rd ed.). New York, NY: Hamilton Books.

Berg, R. D., Landreth, G. L., & Fall, K. A. (2013). *Group counseling concepts and procedures* (5th ed.). New York, NY: Routledge.

Berg-Weger, M., & Murugan, B. (2022). *Social work and social welfare: An invitation* (6th ed.). New York, NY: Routledge.

Berg-Weger, M., Rubio, D. M., & Tebb, S. (2000). The caregiver well-being scale revisited. *Health and Social Work, 25*(4), 255–263.

Berlin, R., & Cannon, H. (2013). *Mixed blessings: A guide to multicultural and multiethnic relationships*. Seattle, WA: Mixed Blessings, LLC.

Berzin, S. C., Singer, J., & Chan, C. (2015). *Practice innovation through technology in the digital age: A Grand Challenge for social work*. Working Paper No. 12, American Academy of Social Work and Social Welfare Grand Challenges for Social Work Initiative. Retrieved from http://aaswsw.org/grand-challenges-initiative/12-challenges/harness-technology-for-social-good/

Beverly, S. G., Clancy, M. M., & Sherraden, M. (2016, March). *Universal accounts at birth: Results from SEED for Oklahoma Kids (CSD Research Summary No. 16–07)*. St. Louis, MO: Washington University, Center for Social Development. doi:10.7936/K7QC030S

Bhutta, N., Chang, A. C., Dettling, L. J., & Hsu, J. W. (2020, September 28). *"Disparities in wealth by race and ethnicity in the 2019 survey of consumer finances," FEDS notes*. Washington: Board of Governors of the Federal Reserve System. https://doi.org/10.17016/2380-7172.2797

Bobo, K., Kendall, J., & Max, S. (2010). *Organizing for social change*. Santa Ana, CA: The Forum Press.

Bohley, T., & McGuire, M. E. (2022). Family systems. In L. Rapp-McCall, K. Corcoran & A. R. Roberts (Eds.), *Social workers' desk reference* (4th ed.) (pp. 263–270). New York, NY: Oxford University Press.

Boland-Prom, K., Johnson, J., & Gunaganti, G. S. (2015). Sanctioning patterns of social work licensing boards, 2000–2009. *Journal of Human Behavior in the Social Environment, 25*(2), 126–136.

Bolton, K. W., Hall, J. C., Blundo, R., & Lehmann, P. (2017). The role of resilience and resilience theory in solution-focused practice. *Journal of Systemic Therapies, 36*(3), 1–15.

Botha, M., Hanlon, J., & Williams, G. L. (2021). Does language matter? Identity-first versus person-first language use in autism research: A response to Vivanti. *Journal of Autism and Developmental Disorders*. https://doi.org/10.1007/s10803-020-04858-w

Bousseau, A., & Martell, D. (2021). Critical race theory and macro social work practice. In C. Franklin (Ed.), *Encyclopedia of social work* [E-reader version]. Washington, DC, and New York, NY: National Association of Social Workers and Oxford University Press.

Bowlby, J. (1982). *Attachment and loss: Vol. 1: Attachment* (2nd ed.). New York, NY: Basic Books.

Brager, G., Specht, H., & Torczyner, J. (1987). *Community organizing*. New York, NY: Columbia University Press.

Briar-Lawson, K., & Naccarato, T. (2021). Family services. In C. Franklin (Ed.), *Encyclopedia of social work* [E-reader version]. Washington, DC, and New York, NY: National Association of Social Workers and Oxford University Press. https://doi-org.ezp.slu.edu/10.1093/acrefore/9780199975839.013.145

Brimhall, A. S. (2020). Therapy with remarried and stepfamilies. In K. S. Wampler (Ed.), *The handbook of systemic family therapy* (Vol. 3) (pp. 317–341). Hoboken, NJ: John Wiley & Sons, Inc.

Brown, N. W. (2018). *Psychoeducational groups: Process and practice*. New York, NY: Routledge.

Brown, S., Sabbath, E. L., Cosby, R. L., Munson, J. K., Crewe, S. E., Tracy, E. M., & Lubben, J. E. (2022). Eradicating social isolation. In R. P. Barth, J. T. Messing, T. R. Shanks, & J. H. Williams (Eds.), *Grand challenges for social work and society: Milestones achieved and opportunities ahead* (2nd ed.) (pp. 145–180). New York, NY: Oxford University Press.

Bruneel, J., Moray, N., Stevens, R., & Fassin, Y. (2016). Balancing competing logic in for-profit enterprises: A need for hybrid governance. *Journal of Social Entrepreneurship, 7*(3), 263–288. doi:10.1080/19420676.2016.1166147

Buckner, F., & Firestone, M. (2000). Where the public peril begins: 25 years after Tarasoff. *The Journal of Legal Medicine, 21*(2), 187–222.

Budiman, A. (2020). Key findings about U.S. immigrants. *Pew Research Center*. Retrieved from www.pewresearch.org/fact-tank/2020/08/20/key-findings-about-u-s-immigrants/

Bureau of Labor Statistics, U.S. Department of Labor. (2022). *Occupational outlook handbook: Social workers*. Retrieved from www.bls.gov/ooh/community-and-social-service/social-workers.htm

Cain, D. S. (2022). Disasters in times of sheltering in place: Social work and the Covid-19 pandemic: In social work desk reference. In L. Rapp-McCall, K. Corcoran, & A. R. Roberts (Eds.), *Social workers' desk reference* (4th ed.) (pp. 61–68). New York, NY: Oxford University Press.

Canda, E. R., & Gomi, S. (2019). Zen philosophy of spiritual development: Insights about human development and spiritual diversity for social work education. *Journal of Religion & Spirituality in Social Work: Social Thought, 38*(1), 43–67. doi: 10.1080/15426432.2018.1520671

Caringi, J. C., Hardiman, E. R., Weldon, P., Fletcher, S., Devlin, M., & Stanick, C. (2017). Secondary traumatic stress and licensed clinical social workers. *Traumatology, 23*(2), 186–195.

Centers for Disease Control and Prevention/National Center for Health Statistics. (2021). *National marriage and divorce rate trends for 2000–2020.* Retrieved from www.cdc.gov/nchs/fastats/marriage-divorce.htm

Chan, K. L., Chen, M., Ming, K., Lo, C., Chen, Q., Kelley, S. J., & Ip, P. (2019). The effectiveness of interventions for grandparents raising grandchildren: A meta-analysis. *Research on Social Work Practice, 29*(6), 607–617.

Chang, C. Y., & Erford, B. T. (2018). Termination. In B. T. Erford (Ed.), *Group work: Processes and applications* (2nd ed.) (pp. 264–301). New York, NY: Routledge.

Charles, P., Epperson, P. C., & Pettus-Davis, C. (2022). *Promoting smart decarceration: In grand challenges for social work and society.* New York, NY: Oxford Press.

Chaskin, R. J. (2010). The Chicago school: A context for youth intervention, research and development. In R. J. Chaskin (Ed.), *Youth gangs and community intervention: Research, practice, and evidence* (pp. 3–23). New York, NY: Columbia University Press.

Chertoff, J. (2018). How to navigate challenges as a blended family. *Healthline.* Retrieved from www.healthline.com/health/parenting/blended-family-tips

Children's Defense Fund. (2021). *The state of America's children, 2021.* Washington, DC.

Child, Youth, and Family (n.d.). *The family group conference.* Retrieved from www.cyf.govt.nz/keeping-kids-safe/ways-we-work-with-families/family-group-conference-or-fgc.html

Chodnody, J. M., & Teater, B. (2018). Exploring how practicing social workers define evidence-based practice: Research note. *Advances in Social Work Practice, 18*(4), 1237–1249.

Choi, J. J. (2019). A microanalytic case study of the utilization of "solution-focused problem talk" in solution-focused brief therapy. *American Journal of Family Therapy, 47*(4), 244–260.

Chun-Chow, J., & Austin, M. J. (2008). The culturally responsive social service agency: The application of an evolving definition to a case study. *Administration in Social Work, 32*(4), 39–64.

Cnaan, R. A., & Rothman, J. (2008). Capacity development and the building of community. In J. Rothman, J. Erlich, & J. Tropman (Eds.), *Strategies of community intervention* (7th ed.) (pp. 243–262). Peosta, IA: Eddie Bowers Publishing.

Collins, D., Jordan, C., & Coleman, H. (2013). *An introduction to family social work* (4th ed.). Belmont, CA: Brooks/Cole.

Columbia Law School. (2017). *Kimberlé Crenshaw on intersectionality, more than two decades later.* Retrieved from www.law.columbia.edu/pt-br/news/2017/06/kimberle-crenshaw-intersectionality

Columbia Lighthouse Project. (n.d.). *Suicide risk assessment.* Retrieved from https://cssrs.columbia.edu/

Congress, E. P. (2015). The culturagram. In K. Corcoran & A. R. Roberts (Eds.), *Social workers' desk reference* (3rd ed.) (pp. 1011–1018). New York, NY: Oxford University Press.

Congress, E. P. (2022). Individual and family development theory. In K. W. Bolton, J. C. Hall, & P. Lehmann (Eds.), *Theoretical perspectives for direct social work practice* (4th ed.) (pp. 61–79). New York, NY: Springer Publishing.

Corcoran, J. (2022a). Solution-focused therapy. In K. W. Bolton, J. C. Hall, & P. Lehmann (Eds.), *Theoretical perspectives for direct social work practice* (4th ed.) (pp. 349–360). New York, NY: Springer Publishing.

Corcoran, J. (2022b). Using standardized tests and instruments in family assessment. In L. Rapp-McCall, K. Corcoran & A. R. Roberts (Eds.), *Social workers' desk reference* (4th ed.) (pp. 338–340). New York, NY: Oxford University Press.

Corley, N. A., & Young, S. M. (2018). Is social work still racist? A content analysis of recent literature. *Social Work, 63*(4), 317–326.

Council on Social Work Education. (2018). *Specialized practice curricular guide for macro social work practice.* Alexandria, VA: Author.

Council on Social Work Education. (2022). *Educational policy and accreditation standards.* Washington, DC: Author. Retrieved from www.cswe.org/accreditation/info/2022-epas/

Cross, T. L. (2013). Cultural competence. In C. Franklin (Ed.), *Encyclopedia of social work.* Washington, DC, and New York, NY: National Association of Social Workers and Oxford University Press.

Cuartero, M. E., & Campos-Vidal, J. F. (2019). Self-care behaviours and their relationship with satisfaction and compassion fatigue levels among social workers. *Social Workers in Health Care, 58*(3), 274–290.

Cummings, S. (2021). Social work tech notes: Beyond pushing buttons: Social workers and the need to anticipate the future of tech. *The New Social Worker*. Retrieved from www.socialworker.com/feature-articles/technology-articles/beyond-pushing-buttons-social-workers-future-tech/

Dallos, R., & Draper, R. (2015). *An introduction to family therapy: Systemic theory and practice* (4th ed.). New York, NY: McGraw-Hill Education.

Day, P. J., & Schiele, J. H. (2013). *A new history of social welfare* (7th ed.). Boston, MA: Pearson.

De Jong, G., Schout, G., & Abma, T. (2018). Understanding the process of family group conferencing in public mental health care: A multiple case study. *British Journal of Social Work, 48*, 353–370.

De Jong, P. (2015). Solution-focused therapy. In K. Corcoran & A. R. Roberts (Eds.), *Social workers' desk reference* (3rd ed.) (pp. 268–274). New York, NY: Oxford University Press.

De Jong, P., & Berg, I. K. (2013). *Interviewing for solutions* (4th ed.). Belmont, CA: Brooks/Cole.

DeMaria, R., Weeks, G. R., & Twist, M. L. C. (2017). *Focused genograms: Intergenerational assessment of individuals, couples, and families* (2nd ed.). New York: NY: Routledge.

de Shazer, S. (1984). The death of resistance. *Family Process, 23*, 11–21.

de Shazer, S., Dolan, Y., Korman, H., Trepper, T., McCollum, E., & Berg, I. K. (2021). *More than miracles: The state of the art of solution-focused therapy* (Classic ed.) [e-version]. New York, NY: Routledge.

Desilver, D. (2018). For most US workers, real wages have barely budged in decades. *Pew Research Center*. Retrieved from www.pewresearch.org/fact-tank/2018/08/07/for-most-us-workers-real-wages-have-barely-budged-for-decades/

Dessel, A. B., & Rodenborg, N. (2017). Social workers and LGBT policies: Attitude predictors and cultural competence course outcomes. *Sexuality Research and Social Policy, 14*(1), 17–31.

Detlaff, A., Weber, K., Pendelton, M., Boyd, R., Bettencourt, B., & Burton, L. (2020). It is not broken system, it is a system that needs to be broken: The upEnd movement to abolish the child welfare system. *Journal of Public Child Welfare, 14*(5), 500–517.

Dill, K. (2017). Field education literature: Volume 2: Emotional triggers to field experiences: Preparing students and field instructors. *Field Educator, 7*(2), 1–6.

Dodd, S. J., & Savage, A. (2016). Evidence-informed social work practice. In C. Franklin (Ed.), *Encyclopedia of social work* [E-reader version]. Washington, DC, and New York, NY: National Association of Social Workers and Oxford University Press. doi:10.1093/acrefore/9780199975839.013.915

Doel, M. (2018). Group work. In N. Thompson & P. Stepney (Eds.), *Social work theory and methods* (pp. 191–201). New York, NY: Routledge.

Dolbin-MacNab, M. L. (2020). Interventions to support grandparents raising grandchildren. In K. S. Wampler (Ed.), *The handbook of systemic family therapy* (Vol. 2) (pp. 479–501). Hoboken, NJ: John Wiley & Sons, Inc.

Dolgoff, R., Harrington, D., & Loewenberg, F. M. (2012). *Ethical decisions for social work practice*. Itasca, IL: F. E. Peacock.

Dolgoff, R., Loewenberg, F. M., & Harrington, D. (2012). *Ethical decisions for social work practice* (9th ed.). Washington, DC: Author.

Dombo, E. A. (2011). Rape: When professional values place vulnerable clients at risk. In J. C. Rothman (Ed.), *From the front lines: Student cases in social work ethics* (3rd ed.) (pp. 185–188). Boston, MA: Allyn & Bacon.

Donaldson, L. P., Hill, K., Ferguson, S., Fogel, S., & Erickson, C. (2014). Contemporary social work licensure: Implications for macro social work practice and education. *Social Work, 59*(1), 52–61.

Doran, G. T. (1981). There's a S.M.A.R.T. way to write management's goals and objectives. *Management Review, 70*(11), 35.

Dressler, L. (2006). *Consensus through conversation*. San Francisco, CA: Berrett-Koehler Publishers.

Drisko, J., & Grady, M. D. (2018). Teaching evidence-based practice using cases in social work education. *Families in Society, 99*(3), 269–282.

Dudley, J. R. (2020). *Social work evaluation: Enhancing what we do* (3rd ed.). New York, NY: Oxford University Press.

Dudley, J. R., & Herman-Smith, R. (2020). Chapter 8: Improving how programs and practice work. In Dudley, J. R. (Ed.), *Social work evaluation: Enhancing what we do* (3rd ed.) (pp. 171–212). New York, NY: Oxford University Press.

Dunn, B., & Wamsley, B. (2018). Grandfamilies: Characteristics and needs of grandparents raising grandchildren. *Journal of Extension, 56*(5). Retrieved from https://tigerprints.clemson.edu/joe/vol56/iss5/7

Dunst, C. J., & Espe-Sherwindt, M. (2016). Family-centered practices in early childhood intervention. In B. Reichow, B. A. Boyd, E. E. Barton, & S. L. Odom (Eds.), *Handbook of early childhood special education* (pp. 37–55). New York, NY: Springer Publishing.

Eaton-Shull, Y. (2022). Crisis intervention for social worker practice. In L. Rapp-McCall, K. Corcoran, & A. R. Roberts (Eds.), *Social workers' desk reference* (4th ed.) (pp. 242–248). New York, NY: Oxford University Press.

Edleson, J. L., Lindhorst, T., & Kanuha, V. K. (2015). *Ending gender-based violence: A Grand Challenge for social work*. Working Paper No. 15, American Academy of Social Work and Social Welfare Grand Challenges for Social Work Initiative. Retrieved from http://aaswsw.org/grand-challenges-initiative/12-challenges/stop-family-violence/

Edwards, T. M., Williams, L. M., Speice, J., & Patterson, J. E. (2020). Multilevel assessment. In K. S. Wampler (Ed.), *The handbook of systemic family therapy* (Vol. 1) (pp. 601–618). Hoboken, NJ: John Wiley & Sons, Inc.

Egan, R., Maidment, J., & Connolly, M. (2017). Trust, power, and safety in the social work supervisory relationship: Results from Australian research. *Journal of Social Work Practice, 31*(3), 307–321.

Endangered Language Alliance. (2019). *NYC language pap: 631 Languages at 970 sites*. Retrieved from elalliance.org

Ephross, P. H., Vassil, T. V., & Rose, S. R. (2017). Group work with working groups. In C. D. Garvin, L. M. Gutiérrez, & M. J. Galinsky (Eds.), *Handbook of social work with groups* (2nd ed.) (pp. 510–524). New York, NY: The Guilford Press.

Epperson, M. W., & Pettus-Davis, C. (2015). *Smart decarceration: Guiding concepts for an era of criminal justice transformation*. CSD Working Paper No. 15–53. St. Louis, MO: Washington University, Center for Social Development.

Epstein, N. B., Baldwin, L. M., & Bishop, D. S. (1983). The McMaster family assessment device. *Journal of Marital and Family Therapy, 9*(2), 171–180.

Erford, B. T., & Bardhoshi, G. (2018). Introduction to group work: Historical perspectives and functional group models. In B. T. Erford (Ed.), *Group work processes and applications* (2nd ed.) (pp. 3–31). New York, NY: Routledge.

Erickson, C. L. (2018). *Environmental justice as social work practice*. New York, NY: Oxford University Press.

Evans, S. D., Hanlin, C. E., & Prillehensky, I. (2007). Blending ameliorative and transformative approaches in human service organizations: A case study. *Journal of Community Psychology, 35*(3), 329–346.

Fairfax, C. N. (2022). Principles and practices in African American community development. In L. Rapp-McCall, K. Corcoran, & A. R. Roberts (Eds.), *Social workers' desk reference* (4th ed.) (pp. 827–833). New York, NY: Oxford University Press.

Family Forward. (2022). *Redevelopment opportunities for women*. Retrieved from https://familyforwardmo.org/how-we-help/redevelopment-opportunities-women/

Fetherman, D. L., & Burke, S. C. (2015). Using community-based participatory research to advocate for homeless children. *Social Work in Public Health, 30*(1), 30–37.

Fischer, J., Corcoran, K., & Springer, D. W. (2020). *Measures for clinical practice and research: A sourcebook* (6th ed.). New York: Oxford University Press.

Fluckiger, C., Del Re, A. C., Wampold, B. E., & Horvath, A. O. (2018). The alliance in adult psychotherapy: A meta-analytic synthesis. *Psychotherapy, 55*(4), 316–340.

Folkwein, L. (2022). Immigrant communities in the United States and macro practice. In C. Franklin (Ed.), *Encyclopedia of social work* [E-reader version]. Washington, DC, and New York, NY: National Association of Social Workers and Oxford University Press. https://doi-org.ezp.slu.edu/10.1093/acrefore/9780199975839.013.128

Fong, R., McRoy, R. G., Griffin, A., & LaBrenz, C. (2019). Adoption: Transracial and intercountry. In C. Franklin (Ed.), *Encyclopedia of social work* [E-reader Version]. Washington, DC, and New York, NY: National Association of Social Workers and Oxford University Press. doi:10.1093/acrefore/9780199975839.013.837

Fortune, A. E. (2015). Terminating with clients. In K. Corcoran & A. R. Roberts (Eds.), *Social workers' desk reference* (3rd ed.) (pp. 697–704). New York, NY: Oxford University Press.

Franklin, C., Ding, X., Kim, J. W., Kelly, M. S., & Tripodi, S. J. (2022a). Solution-focused brief therapy interventions for at-risk students in schools. In L. Rapp-McCall, K. Corcoran, & A. R. Roberts (Eds.), *Social workers' desk reference* (4th ed.) (pp. 1115–1129). New York, NY: Oxford University Press.

Franklin, C., Jordan, C., & Hopson, L. M. (2022b). Effective couple and family treatment for client populations. In L. Rapp-McCall, K. Corcoran, & A. R. Roberts (Eds.), *Social workers' desk reference* (4th ed.) (pp. 623–628). New York, NY: Oxford University Press.

Franklin, C., Streeter, C. L., Webb, L., & Guz, S. (2018). *Solution focused brief therapy in alternative schools: Ensuring student success and dropout prevention.* Abingdon, UK: Routledge.

Franklin, C., Zhang, A., Froerer, A., & Johnson, S. (2016). Solution focused brief therapy: A systematic review and meta-summary of process research. *Journal of Marital and Family Therapy, 43(1)*, 16–30.

Frantell, K. A., Miles, J. R., & Ruwe, A. M. (2019). Intergroup dialogue: A review of recent empirical research and its implications for research and practice. *Small Group Research, 50(5)*, 654–695.

Freedenthal, S. (2013). Suicide. In C. Franklin (Ed.), *Encyclopedia of social work* [E-reader version]. Washington, DC, and New York, NY: National Association of Social Workers and Oxford University Press. doi:10.1093/acrefore/9780199975839.013.137

Freire, P. (1973). *Education for critical consciousness.* New York, NY: Seabury Press.

Friedline, T., Despard, M. R., & Birkenmaier, J. (2018, May). *Policy recommendations for expanding access to banking and financial services.* Policy Brief No. 11-4, American Academy of Social Work and Social Welfare Grand Challenges for Social Work Initiative. Cleveland, OH: American Academy of Social Work & Social Welfare.

Friedman, B., & Olivera, R. (2022). Outcome measures in human services. In C. Franklin (Ed.), *Encyclopedia of social work* [E-reader version]. Washington, DC, and New York, NY: National Association of Social Workers and Oxford University Press. https://doi-org.ezp.slu.edu/10.1093/acrefore/9780199975839.013.995

Gambrill, E. (2013). *Social work practice: A critical thinker's guide.* New York, NY: Oxford University Press.

Gambrill, E. (2019). *Critical thinking and the process of evidence-based practice.* New York, NY: Oxford University Press.

Gant, L. (2017). Evaluation and research design. In C. D. Garvin, L. M. Gutiérrez, & M. J. Galinsky (Eds.), *Handbook of social work with groups* (2nd ed.) (pp. 527–534). New York, NY: The Guilford Press.

Garland, J., Jones, H., & Kolodny, R. (1965). A model for stages of development in social work groups. In S. Bernstein (Ed.), *Explorations in group work: Essays in theory and practice* (pp. 12–53). Boston, MA: Boston University School of Social Work.

Garvin, C. D. (2015). Developing goals. In K. Corcoran & A. R. Roberts (Eds.), *Social workers' desk reference* (3rd ed.) (pp. 560–565). New York, NY: Oxford University Press.

Garvin, C. D., & Galinsky, M. J. (2020). Groups. In C. Franklin (Ed.), *Encyclopedia of social work* [E-reader version]. Washington, DC, and New York: National Association of Social Workers and Oxford University Press. doi:10.1093/acrefore/9780199975839.013.167

Gazda, J. (2021). The art of practicing self-care. *The New Social Worker.* Retrieved from www.socialworker.com/feature-articles/self-care/art-practicing-self-care/

Gellis, Z. D., & Kenaley, B. (2022). Geriatric depression: Assessment and treatment. In L. Rapp-McCall, K. Corcoran & A. R. Roberts (Eds.), *Social workers' desk reference* (4th ed.) (pp. 438–446). New York, NY: Oxford University Press.

Gertler, P. J., Martinez, S., Premand, P., Rawlings, L. B., & Vermeersch, C. M. J. (2016). *Impact evaluation in practice* (2nd ed.). Washington, DC: Inter-American Development Band and World Bank.

Ghelani, A., Haywood, A., & English, M. (2021). Integrating anti-oppressive practice with cognitive behavior therapy. *Social Work Today, 21(2)*, 20.

Gibson, D. M. (2013). Ambiguous roles in a stepfamily: Using maps of narrative practices to develop a new family story with adolescents and parents. *Contemporary Family Therapy, 35,* 793–805.

Gilbert, D. J., & Olcón, K. (2021). Multicultural assessment. In C. Jordan & C. Franklin (Eds.), *Clinical assessment for social workers: Quantitative and qualitative methods* (5th ed.), (pp. 341–368). New York: Oxford University Press.

Gitterman, A. (2017). The mutual aid model. In C. D. Garvin, L. M. Gutiérrez, & M. J. Galinsky (Eds.), *Handbook of social work with groups* (2nd ed.) (pp. 113–132). New York, NY: The Guilford Press.

Gitterman, A., & Germain, C. B. (2013). Ecological framework. In C. Franklin (Ed.), *Encyclopedia of social work* [E-reader version]. Washington, DC, and New York, NY: National Association of Social Workers and Oxford University Press. doi:10.1093/acrefore/9780199975839.013.118

Gitterman, A., & Knight, C. (2016). Empowering clients to have an impact on their environment: Social work practice with groups. *Families in Society: The Journal of Contemporary Social Service, 97*(4), 278–285.

Gitterman, A., Knight, C., & Germain, C. B. (2021). *The life model of social work practice: Advances in theory and practice* (4th ed.). New York, NY: Columbia Press.

GLAAD. (2020). *Accelerating acceptance*. Retrieved from www.glaad.org/sites/default/files/Accelerating%20Acceptance%202020.pdf

Goelitz, A. (2021). *From trauma to healing*. New York: Routledge Publishing.

Goldbach, J., Amaro, H., Vega, W., & Walter, M. D. (2015). *The Grand Challenge of promoting equality by addressing social stigma*. Working Paper No. 18, American Academy of Social Work and Social Welfare Grand Challenges for Social Work Initiative. Retrieved from http://aaswsw.org/wp-content/uploads/2016/01/W16-The-Grand-Challenge-of-Promoting-Equality-by-Addressing-Social-Stigma1-1-2.pdf

Goldberg, A. E., & Allen, K. R. (2013). *LGBT-parent families: Innovations in research and implications for practice*. New York, NY: Springer Publishing.

Gonzales, E., Matz, C., Morrow-Howell, N., Lai, P. H. L., Whetung, C., Zingg, E., Keating, E., James, J. B., & Putnam, M. (2022). Advancing long and productive lives. In R. P. Barth, J. T. Messing, T. R. Shanks, & J. H. Williams (Eds.), *Grand challenges for social work and society: Milestones achieved and opportunities ahead* (2nd ed.) (pp. 111–144). New York: Oxford University Press.

Gottfried, R., & Bride, B. E. (2018). Trauma-secondary, vicarious, compassion fatigue. In C. Franklin (Ed.), *Encyclopedia of social work* [E-reader version]. Washington, DC, and New York, NY: National Association of Social Workers and Oxford University Press. https://doi-org.ezp.slu.edu/10.1093/acrefore/9780199975839.013.1085

Gottlieb, M. (2020). The case for a cultural humility framework in social work practice. *Journal of Ethnic & Cultural Diversity in Social Work, 30*(6), 463–481. doi:10.1080/15313204.2020.1753615

Grady, M. D., & Dombo, E. A. (2016). *Moving beyond assessment: A practical guide for beginning helping professionals*. New York, NY: Oxford University Press.

Grady, M. D., & Drisko, J. W. (2014). Thorough clinical assessment: The hidden foundation of evidence-based practice. *Families in Society: The Journal of Contemporary Social Service, 95*(1), 1–10. doi:10.1606/1044-3894.2014.95.2

Grady, M. D., & O'Toole, R. (2022). The biopsychosocial-spiritual perspective. In L. Rapp-McCall, K. Corcoran, & A. R. Roberts (Eds.), *Social workers' desk reference* (4th ed.) (pp. 179–186). New York, NY: Oxford University Press.

Green, B. L., McAllister, C. L., & Tarte, J. M. (2004). The strengths-based practices inventory: A tool for measuring strengths-based service delivery in early childhood and family support programs device. *Families in Society: The Journal of Contemporary Social Services, 85*(3), 326–334.

Greif, G. L., Ephross, P., & Knight, C. (2017). A summary: Skills for working in groups across populations at risk. In G. L. Greif, P. Ephross, & C. Knight (Eds.), *Group work with populations at risk* (4th ed.) (pp. 37–43). New York, NY: Oxford University Press.

Greif, G. L., & Morris-Compton, D. (2017). Group work with urban African American parents in their neighborhood schools. In G. Greif & C. Knight (Eds.), *Group work with populations at risk* (4th ed.) (pp. 375–389). New York, NY: Oxford University Press.

Gricus, M. (2019). Of all the social workers . . . I'm the bad one: Impact of disciplinary action on social workers. *Social Work Research, 43*(1), 5–16.

Griffin, G. (2022). Digital technology. In C. Franklin (Ed.), *Encyclopedia of social work* [E-reader version]. Washington, DC, and New York, NY: National Association of Social Workers and Oxford University Press. https://doi-org.ezp.slu.edu/10.1093/acrefore/9780199975839.013.1440

Grise-Owens, E. (2021). Follow your own self-care advice. *The New Social Worker*. Retrieved from www.socialworker.com/feature-articles/self-care/follow-your-own-self-care-advice/

Grise-Owens, E. (2022). Best self-care advice from social workers: From the experts. *The New Social Worker*. Retrieved from www.socialworker.com/feature-articles/self-care/best-self-care-advice-from-experts/

Grise-Owens, E., & Miller, J. (2022). Self-care for social workers. In L. Rapp-McCall, K. Corcoran, & A. R. Roberts (Eds.), *Social workers' desk reference* (4th ed.) (pp. 29–37). New York, NY: Oxford University Press.

Grise-Owens, E., Owens, L. W., & Miller, J. J. (2016). Recasting licensing in social work: Something more for professionalism. *Journal of Social Work Education, 52*(51), S126–S133.

Gutiérrez, L. M., & Gant, L. M. (2018). Community practice in social work: Reflections on its first century and directions for the future. *Social Service Review, 92*(4), 617–647.

Guth, L. J., Nitza, A., Pollard, B. L., Puig, A., Chan, C. D., Bailey, H., & Singh, A. A. (2018). *Ten strategies to intentionally use group work to transform hate, facilitate courageous conversations, and enhance community building*. Retrieved from Association for Specialists in Group Work: https://asgw.org/resources/

Hahn, S. A., & Scanlon, E. (2016). The integration of micro and macro practice: A qualitative study of clinical social workers' practice with domestic violence survivors. *Affilia: Journal of Women and Social Work, 31*(3), 331–343.

Hall, A. B., & Yoder, J. (2019). Does homeownership influence political behavior? Evidence from administrative data. *The Journal of Politics*. Retrieved from https://www.andrewbenjaminhall.com/homeowner.pdf

Hall, J. C. (2016). Narrative therapy. In C. Franklin (Ed.), *Encyclopedia of social work* [E-reader version]. Washington, DC, and New York, NY: National Association of Social Workers and Oxford University Press. doi:10.1093/acrefore/9780199975839.013.992

Hall, J. C. (2022). Narrative therapy. In K. W. Bolton, J. C. Hall, N. Coady, & P. Lehmann (Eds.), *Theoretical perspectives for direct social work practice* (4th ed.) (pp. 313–332). New York, NY: Springer Publishing.

Hall, J. C., Blundo, R., & Bolton, K. W. (2019). Strengths-based frameworks. In C. Franklin (Ed.), *Encyclopedia of social work* [E-reader version]. Washington, DC, and New York, NY: National Association of Social Workers and Oxford University Press. https://doi-org.ezp.slu.edu/10.1093/acrefore/9780199975839.013.381

Hammond, A. (2019). Pleading poverty in federal court. *Yale Law Journal, 128*(6), 1478–1488.

Hardina, D. (2013). *Interpersonal social work skills for community practice*. New York, NY: Springer Publishing.

Hardina, D., Middleton, J., Montana, S., & Simpson, R. A. (2007). *An empowering approach to managing social service organizations*. New York, NY: Springer Publishing Company.

Hargons, C., Benner, K., Hollan, J., & Bohmer, C. (2021). Striving, surviving, but not thriving: Mental health trainees adjusting during COVID-19. *Field Education, 11*(2).

Hawkins, J. D., Jenson, J. M., Catalano, R. F., Fraser, M. W., Botvin, G. J., Shapiro, V., Bender, K. A., . . . & the Coalition for Behavioral Health. (2015). *Unleashing the power of prevention*. Working Paper No. 10, American Academy of Social Work and Social Welfare Grand Challenges for Social Work Initiative. Retrieved from http://aaswsw.org/grand-challenges-initiative/12-challenges/ensure-healthy-development-for-all-youth/

Hayslip, B., Fruhauf, C. A., & Dolbin-MacNab, M. L. (2017). Grandparents raising grandchildren: What have we learned over the past decade? *The Gerontologist, 57*(6), 1196–1208.

Healy, L. M. (2016). International social work: An overview. In C. Franklin (Ed.), *Encyclopedia of social work* [E-reader version]. Washington, DC, and New York, NY: National Association of Social Workers and Oxford University Press. https://doi-org.ezp.slu.edu/10.1093/acrefore/9780199975839.013.561

Healy, L. M. (2017). No longer welcome: Migration policy and challenges for social work. *Affilia, 32*(2), 247–250.

Henwood, B. F., Tiderington, E., Aykanian, A., & Padgett, D. K. (2022). Ending homelessness. In R. P. Barth, J. T. Messing, T. R. Shanks, & J. H. Williams (Eds.), *Grand challenges for social work and society: Milestones achieved and opportunities ahead* (2nd ed.) (pp. 181–200). New York: Oxford University Press.

Henwood, B. F., Wenzel, S. L., Mangano, P. F., Hombs, M., Padgett, D. K., Byrne, T., Rice, E., Butts, S. C., & Uretsky, M. C. (2015). *The Grand*

Challenge of ending homelessness. Working Paper No. 9, American Academy of Social Work and Social Welfare Grand Challenges for Social Work Initiative. Retrieved from http://aaswsw.org/grand-challenges-initiative/12-challenges/end-homelessness/

Higham, P. (2020). *Communication and interviewing skills for practice in social work, counselling, and the health professions*. London: Routledge.

Hillier, A., & Culhane, D. (2013). GIS applications and administrative data to support community change. In M. Weil, M. Reisch, & M. L. Ohmer (Eds.), *The handbook of community practice* (2nd ed.) (pp. 827–844). Thousand Oaks, CA: Sage Publications.

Hodge, D. R. (2022). Spiritual assessment and intervention. In L. Rapp-McCall, K. Corcoran, & A. R. Roberts (Eds.), *Social workers' desk reference* (4th ed.) (pp. 1003–1008). New York, NY: Oxford University Press.

Hodgson, J. L., Lamson, A. L., & Kolobova, I. (2016). A biopsychosocial-spiritual assessment in brief or extended couple therapy formats. In G. R. Weeks, S. T. Fife, & C. M. Person (Eds.), *Techniques for the couple therapist: Essential interventions from the experts* (pp. 213–217). New York, NY: Routledge.

Holmes, C. (2021). Self-care can be needed most when you least expect it. *The New Social Worker*. Retrieved from www.socialworker.com/feature-articles/self-care/self-care-needed-most-when-least-expect-it/

Hölscher, D., & Chiumbu, S. (2020). Anti-oppressive community work practice and the decolonization debate: A contribution from the global South. In S. Todd & J. L. Drolet (Eds.), *Community practice and social development in social work* (pp. 223–242). Singapore: Springer.

Houston, S., & Swords, C. (2021). Analysing a parent's capacity to change: Towards a model for child protection social workers. *Journal of Social Work Practice, 35*(3), 231–244.

Huang, J., Zou, L., & Sherraden, M. (Eds.). (2019). Inclusive child development accounts: Toward universality and progressivity [Special issue]. *Asia Pacific Journal of Social Work and Development, 29*(1).

Hubble, M. A., Duncan, B. L., & Miller, S. D., & Wampold, B. E. (2010). *The heart and soul of change*. Edited by B. L. Duncan, B. E. Wampold, & M. A. Hubble (2nd ed.) (pp. 23–46). Washington, DC: American Psychological Association.

Huff, S. C., & Hartenstein, J. L. (2020). Helping children in divorced and single-parent families. In K. S. Wampler (Ed.), *The handbook of systemic family therapy* (Vol. 2) (pp. 521–529). Hoboken, NJ: John Wiley & Sons, Inc.

Institute for Healthcare Improvement. (2022). *Person- and family-centered care*. Retrieved from www.ihi.org/Topics/PFCC/Pages/Overview.aspx

Internal Revenue Service. (2022). *Free tax return preparation for qualified taxpayers*. Retrieved from www.irs.gov/individuals/free-tax-return-preparation-for-qualifying-taxpayers

International Association for Social Work with Groups, Inc. (2015). *Standards for social work practice with groups* (2nd ed.). New York, NY: IASWG, Inc. Retrieved from www.iaswg.org/standards

International Federation of Social Workers. (2018). *Global social work statement of ethical principles*. Retrieved from www.ifsw.org/global-social-work-statement-of-ethical-principles/

International Institute of Saint Louis. (2022). *Economic development*. Retrieved from www.iistl.org/economic-development/

Israeli, M. (2017). The reluctant storyteller. In A. Burack-Weiss, L. S. Lawrence, & L. B. Mijangos (Eds.), *Narratives in social work practice* (pp. 69–78). New York, NY: Columbia University Press.

Jensen, E., Jones, N., Rabe, M., Pratt, B., Medina, L., Orozco, K., & Spell, L. (2021). *The chance that two people chosen at random are of different race or ethnicity groups has increased since 2010*. Census.gov. America counts stories behind the numbers. Retrieved from https://www.census.gov/library/stories/2021/08/2020-united-states-population-more-racially-ethnically-diverse-than-2010.html

Jensen, T. M., Shafer, K., & Holmes, E. K. (2017). Transitioning to step family life: The influence of closeness with biological parents and step parents on children's stress. *Child and Family Social Work, 22*, 275–286.

Jenson, J. M., & Howard, M. O. (2013). Evidence-based practice. In C. Franklin (Ed.), *Encyclopedia of social work* [E-reader version]. Washington, DC, and New York, NY: National Association of Social Workers and Oxford University Press. doi:10.1093/acrefore/9780199975839.013.137

Jordan, C., & Franklin, C. (2013). Assessment. In C. Franklin (Ed.), *Encyclopedia of social work* [E-reader version]. Washington, DC, and New York, NY: National Association of Social Workers and Oxford University Press. https://doi-org.ezp.slu.edu/10.1093/acrefore/9780199975839.013.24

Jordan, C., & Franklin, C. (2021). Assessment process and methods. In C. Jordan & C. Franklin (Eds.), *Clinical assessment for social workers: Quantitative and qualitative methods* (5th ed.) (pp. 3–53). New York: Oxford University Press.

Joubert, J., & Guse, T. (2021). A solution-focused brief therapy (SFBT) intervention model to facilitate hope and subjective well-being among trauma survivors. *Journal of Contemporary Psychotherapy*, 51, 303–310.

Kaasbøll, J., Pedersen, S. A., & Paulsen, V. (2022). What is known about the LGBTQ perspective in child welfare services: A scoping review. *Child & Family Social Work*, 27, 358–369.

Kagle, J. D. (2013). Recording. In C. Franklin (Ed.), *Encyclopedia of social work* [E-reader version]. Washington, DC, and New York, NY: National Association of Social Workers and Oxford University Press. doi:10.1093/acrefore/9780199975839.013.33

Kaushik, A. (2017). Use of self: Rhetoric or reality. *Journal of Social Work Values & Ethics*, 14(1), 21–29.

Kemp, S. P., & Palinkas, L. A. (2016). *Strengthening the social response to the human impacts of environmental change*. Working Paper No. 5, American Academy of Social Work and Social Welfare Grand Challenges for Social Work Initiative. Retrieved from http://aaswsw.org/wp-content/uploads/2015/12/WP5-with-cover.pdf

Kendi, I. X. (2019). *How to be an antiracist*. New York, NY: One World.

Ketner, M., Cooper-Bolinsky, D., & Van Cleave, D. (2017). The meaning and value of supervision in social work field education. *Field Educator*, 7(2), 1–18.

Killian, M. O., & Springer, D. W. (2022). Use of rapid assessment instruments (RAIs) in clinical social work practice. In L. Rapp-McCall, K. Corcoran, & A. R. Roberts (Eds.), *Social workers' desk reference* (4th ed.) (pp. 307–319). New York, NY: Oxford University Press.

Kim, J. S., & Bolton, K. W. (2019). Strengths perspective. In C. Franklin (Ed.), *Encyclopedia of social work* [E-reader version]. Washington, DC, and New York, NY: National Association of Social Workers and Oxford University Press. doi:10.1093/acrefore/9780199975839.013.382

Kim, J. S., Jordan, S. S., Franklin, C., & Froerer, A. (2019). Is solution-focused brief therapy evidence-based? An update 10 years later. *Families in Society*, 100(2), 127–138.

Kleinkauf, C. (1981, July). A guide to giving legislative testimony. *Social Work*, 297–303.

Kneebone, E., & Holmes, N. (2016). *U.S. concentrated poverty in the wake of the Great Recession*. Washington, DC: Brookings Institution. Retrieved from www.brookings.edu/research/reports2/2016/03/31-concentrated-poverty-recession-kneebone-holmes

Knight, C. (2017a). Introduction: The context of contemporary group work practice and education. In G. L. Greif & C. Knight (Eds.), *Group work with populations at risk* (4th ed.) (pp. 3–16). New York, NY: Oxford University Press.

Knight, C. (2017b). Group work practice: Phases of work and associated skills and tasks. In G. L. Greif & C. Knight (Eds.), *Group work with populations at risk* (4th ed.) (pp. 17–36). New York, NY: Oxford University Press.

Knight, C., & Gitterman, A. (2018). Merging micro and macro intervention: Social work practice with groups in the community. *Journal of Social Work Education*, 54(1), 3–17. New York, NY: Oxford University Press.

Knight, C., & Gitterman, A. (2022). Developing and facilitating mutual aid groups. In L. Rapp-McCall, K. Corcoran, & A. R. Roberts (Eds.), *Social workers' desk reference* (4th ed.) (pp. 454–464). New York, NY: Oxford University Press.

Kohli, H. K., Huber, R., & Faul, A. C. (2010). Historical and theoretical development of culturally competent social work practice. *Journal of Teaching in Social Work*, 30, 252–271.

Kondrat, D. C., & Early, T. J. (2022). Case management with persons with severe mental illness. In L. Rapp-McCall, K. Corcoran, & A. R. Roberts (Eds.), *Social workers' desk reference* (4th ed.) (pp. 783–789). New York, NY: Oxford University Press.

Kondrat, D. C., & Miller, K. (2020). Solution-focused practice. In B. Teater (Ed.), *An introduction to applying social work theories and methods* (3rd ed.) (pp. 167–181). New York, NY: McGraw-Hill Education Open University Press.

Konrad, S. C. (2020). Interprofessional collaborative practice. In C. Franklin (Ed.), *Encyclopedia of social work* [E-reader version]. Washington, DC, and New York, NY: National Association of Social Workers and Oxford University Press. https://doi-org.ezp.slu.edu/10.1093/acrefore/9780199975839.013.1321

Koop, J. J. (2009). Solution-focused family interventions. In A. C. Kilpatrick & T. P. Holland (Eds.), *Working with families: An integrative model by level of need* (5th ed.) (pp. 147–169). Boston, MA: Pearson.

Kretzmann, J. P., McKnight, J., & Puntenney, D. (2005). *Discovering community power: A guide to mobilizing local assets and your organization's capacity.* Chicago, IL: Asset-Based Community Development Institute, School of Education and Social Policy, Northwestern University.

Kurland, R. (2007). Debunking the "blood theory" of social work with groups: Group workers are made and not born. *Social Work with Groups, 31(1)*, 11–24.

Kurland, R., & Salmon, R. (1998). *Teaching a methods course in social work with groups.* Alexandria, VA: Council on Social Work Education.

Kwon, G. (2017). Focusing. In P. Levounis, B. Arnaout, & C. Marienfeld, C. (Eds.), *Motivational interviewing for clinical practice* (pp. 53–64). Arlington, VA: American Psychological Association Publishing.

Larson, K., & McGuiston, C. (2012). Building capacity to improve Latino health in rural North Carolina: A case study in community-university engagement. *Journal of Community Engagement and Scholarship, 5(1)*, 14–23.

Laurio, A. (2016). A grand challenge for social work: Isolation seen as a critical social problem. *NASW News, 61(6)*, 7, 9.

LeCroy, S. M. (2022). Cognitive-behavioral therapy techniques for youth and adults. In L. Rapp-McCall, K. Corcoran, & A. R. Roberts (Eds.), *Social workers' desk reference* (4th ed.) (pp. 555–562). New York, NY: Oxford University Press.

Lee, J. B., & Hudson, R. E. (2017). Empowerment approach to social work treatment. In F. J. Turner (Ed.), *Social work treatment: Interlocking theoretical approaches* (6th ed.) (pp. 142–165). New York, NY: Oxford University Press.

Lee, M. Y., Eads, R., & Magier, E. (2022). The miracle question and scaling questions for building solutions. In L. Rapp-McCall, K. Corcoran, & A. R. Roberts (Eds.), *Social workers' desk reference* (4th ed.) (pp. 504–510). New York, NY: Oxford University Press.

Lee, M. Y., Ely, C. G., Eads, R., & Want, X. (2020). Collaborative and strengths-based intervening with students from single-parent families. In C. Franklin (Ed.), *Encyclopedia of social work* [E-reader version]. Washington, DC, and New York, NY: National Association of Social Workers and Oxford University Press. https://doi-org.ezp.slu.edu/10.1093/acrefore/9780199975839.013.1234

Lein, L., Romich, J. L., & Sherraden, M. (2015). *Reversing extreme inequality.* Working Paper No. 16. Washington, DC: American Academy of Social Work and Social Welfare Grand Challenges for Social Work Initiative. Retrieved from http://aaswsw.org/wp-content/uploads/2016/01/WP16-with-cover-2.pdf

Lewis, T. F., Larson, M. F., & Korcuska, J. S. (2017). Strengthening the planning process of motivational interviewing using goal attainment scaling. *Journal of Mental Health Counseling, 39(3)*, 195–210.

Libal, K. R., & Harding, S. (2015). *Human rights-based community practice in the United States: Springer briefs in rights-based approaches to social work.* New York, NY: Springer Publishing.

Lietz, C. A., & Geiger, J. M. (2017). Advancing a family-centered practice agency in child welfare. *Journal of Family Social Work, 20(4)*, 267–270.

Life Crisis Services. (n.d.). *Suicide assessment.* St. Louis, MO: Author.

Lindsey, J. (2019). Testimonial injustice and vulnerability: A qualitative analysis of participation in the Court of Protection. *Social & Legal Studies, 28(4)*, 450–469.

Lo, J., Rae, M., Krutika, A., Cox, C., Panchal, N., & Miller, B. F. (2022). *Telehealth has played an outsized role meeting mental health needs during the COVID-19 pandemic.* Kaiser Family Foundation. Retrieved from www.kff.org/coronavirus-covid-19/issue-brief/telehealth-has-played-an-outsized-role-meeting-mental-health-needs-during-the-covid-19-pandemic/#:~:text=Telehealth%20has%20played%20a%20particularly,for%20these%20services%20via%20telehealth

Locke, B., Garrison, R., & Winship, J. (1998). *Generalist social work practice: Context, story, and partnerships.* Pacific Grove, CA: Brooks/Cole.

López, L. M., Vargas, E. M., & Hermanto, J. (2017). Group work with immigrants and refugees. In G. Greif & C. Knight (Eds.), *Group work with populations at risk* (4th ed.) (pp. 201–220). New York, NY: Oxford University Press.

Lubben, J., Gironda, M., Sabbath, E., Kong, J., & Johnson, C. (2015). *Social isolation presents a Grand Challenge for social work*. Working Paper No. 7, American Academy of Social Work and Social Welfare Grand Challenges for Social Work Initiative. Retrieved from https://aaswsw.org/wp-content/uploads/2015/03/Social-Isolation-3.24.15.pdf

Luguet, W., & Muro, L. (2018). Imago relationship therapy alignment with marriage and family common factors. *The Family Journal, 26*(4), 405–410.

Lynch, M., Arnaout, B., & Rosenthal, R. N. (2017). Integrating motivational interviewing with other psychotherapies. In P. Levounis, B. Arnaout, & C. Marienfeld (Eds.), *Motivational interviewing for clinical practice* (pp. 107–130). Arlington, VA: American Psychological Association Publishing.

MacDonald, S.-A. (2016). Attempting to engage in "ethical" research with homeless youth. *Intersectionalities: A Global Journal of Social Work Analysis, Research, Policy and Practice, 5*(1), 126–150.

Macgowan, M. J. (2006). The group engagement measure: A review of its conceptual and empirical properties. *Journal of Groups in Addiction and Recovery, 1*(2), 33–52.

Macgowan, M. J., & Hanbidge, A. S. (2022a). Best practices in social work with groups: Beginnings to endings. In L. Rapp-McCall, K. Corcoran, & A. R. Roberts (Eds.), *Social workers' desk reference* (4th ed.) (pp. 670–675). New York, NY: Oxford University Press.

Macgowan, M. J., & Hanbidge, A. S. (2022b). Best practices in social work with groups: Foundations. In L. Rapp-McCall, K. Corcoran, & A. R. Roberts (Eds.), *Social workers' desk reference* (4th ed.) (pp. 661–669). New York, NY: Oxford University Press.

Mackelprang, R. W., Salsgiver, R. O., & Salsgiver, R. (2016). *Disability: A diversity model approach in human service practice*. New York, NY: Oxford University Press.

Madigan, S. (2019). *Narrative therapy* (2nd ed.). Washington, DC: The American Psychological Association.

Malekof, A. (2017). Strengths-based group work with children and adolescents. In C. D. Garvin, L. M. Gutiérrez, & M. J. Galinsky (Eds.), *Handbook of social work with groups* (2nd ed.) (pp. 255–270). New York, NY: The Guilford Press.

Malmstrom, T. K., & Morley, J. E. (2013). Frailty and cognition: Linking two common syndromes in older persons. *Journal of Nutrition, Health, & Aging, 17*, 723–725.

Manning, T. (2012). The art of successful persuasion: Seven skills you need to get your point across effectively. *Industrial and Commercial Training, 44*(3), 150–158.

Mansfield, A. K., Keitner, G. I., & Sheeran, T. (2018). The brief assessment of family functioning (BAFFS): A three-item version of the general functioning scale of the family assessment device. *Psychotherapy Research*. doi:10/1080/10503307.2017.1422213

Marguerite Casey Foundation. (2012). *Organizational capacity assessment tool*. Retrieved from caseygrants.org/resources/org-capacity-assessment/

Mariscal, S. E., Johnson-Motoyama, M., & Dettlaff, A. J. (2022). Social work practice with Latinas/Latinos/Latinx. In L. Rapp-McCall, K. Corcoran, & A. R. Roberts (Eds.), *Social workers' desk reference* (4th ed.) (pp. 923–931). New York, NY: Oxford University Press.

Marsiglia, F. F., Kulis, S. S., & Lechuga-Peña, S. (2021). *Diversity, oppression, and change: Culturally grounded social work* [E-version]. New York: Oxford University Press.

Marson, S. M., & McKinney, Jr., R. E. (Eds.). (2019). *The Routledge handbook of social work ethics and values*. New York, NY: Routledge.

Martin, P. S., & Claibourn, M. P. (2013). Citizen participation and congressional responsiveness: New evidence that participation matters. *Legislative Quarterly, 38*(1), 59–81.

Martin, J. A., Hamilton, B. E., & Osterman, M. J. K. (2021). *Births in the United States, 2020*. NCHS Data Brief No. 418. Centers for Disease Control and Prevention National Center for Health Statistics. Retrieved from https://dx.doi.org/10.15620/cdc:109213

Matthew, L., Barron, I., & Hodson, A. (2019). Participatory action research: Confidentiality and attitudes of victimized young people unknown to child protection agencies. *International Journal on Child Maltreatment, 2*(1–2), 79–97.

McCammon, V. T., Reger, J., & Einwohner, R. L. (Eds.). (2017). *The Oxford handbook of U.S. Women's social movement activism*. Oxford: Oxford University Press.

McCauley, H., & PettyJohn, M. E. (2020). Redefining "family." In K. S. Wampler (Ed.), *The handbook of systemic family therapy* (Vol. 1) (pp. 79–95). Hoboken, NJ: Wiley Blackwell.

McClintock, A. S., Perlman, M. R., McCarrick, S. M., Anderson, T., & Himawan, L. (2017). Enhancing psychotherapy process with common factors feedback: A randomized clinical trial. *Journal of Counseling Psychology, 64*(3), 247–260.

McCubbin, L. D., McCuban, H. I., & Sievers, J. A. (2012). *Family wellbeing: Stress, coping, resilience: Assessment measurements for research and practice.* Pullman, WA: Washington State University Press.

McGoldrick, M. (2016). *The genogram casebook: A clinical companion to genograms: Assessment and intervention.* New York, NY: W. W. Norton.

McGoldrick, M. (2022). Using genograms to map family patterns. In L. Rapp-McCall, K. Corcoran, & A. R. Roberts (Eds.), *Social workers' desk reference* (4th ed.) (pp. 341–350). New York, NY: Oxford University Press.

McKenzie, E. D. (2021). Self-care A-Z: Self-care cliches and how they became important life lessons. *The New Social Worker.* Retrieved from www.socialworker.com/feature-articles/self-care/self-care-cliches-important-life-lessons/

McKnight, J. L., & Kretzmann, J. P. (1996). *Mapping community capacity.* Evanston, IL: Institute for Policy Research. Retrieved from www.racialequity-tools.org/resourcefiles/mcknight.pdf

McKnight, J. L., & Russell, C. (2022). Asset-based community development. Social Work Desk Reference. In L. Rapp-McCall, K. Corcoran & A. R. Roberts (Eds.), *Social Worker's Desk Reference* (4th ed.) (pp. 849–855). New York, NY: Oxford University Press.

Mehrotra, G. R., Tecle, A. S., Ha, A. T., Ghneim, S., & Gringeri, C. (2018). Challenges to bridging field and classroom instruction: Exploring field instructors' perspectives on macro practice. *Journal of Social Work, 54*(1), 135–147.

Metcalf, L. (2017). *Solution focused narrative therapy.* New York, NY: Springer Publishing.

Meyer, C. (1993). *Assessment in social work practice.* New York, NY: Columbia University Press.

Miller, J. J. (2020). Nothing was the same: 3 reasons post-COVID-19 social work practice is never going back. *The New Social Worker.* Retrieved from www.socialworker.com/feature-articles/practice/nothing-was-the-same-3-reasons-post-covid-19-social-work-practice-is-never-going-back/

Miller, J. J., Lianekhammy, J., & Grise-Owens, E. (2018). Examining self-care among individuals employed in social work capacities: Implications for the profession. *Advances in Social Work, 18*(4), 1250–1266.

Miller, W. R., & Rollnick, S. (2013). *Motivational interviewing: Helping people change* (3rd ed.). New York, NY: The Guilford Press.

Millington, M. J., & Madden, R. H. (2018). Counseling in the context of family identity. In I. Marini & M. A. Stebnicki (Eds.), *The psychological and social impact of illness and disability* (7th ed.) (pp. 177–188). New York, NY: Springer Publishing.

Milsom, A. (2018). Leading groups. In B. T. Erford (Ed.), *Group work: Processes and applications* (2nd ed.) (pp. 86–111). New York, NY: Routledge.

Minieri, J., & Getsos, P. (2007). *Tools for radical democracy.* San Francisco, CA: Jossey Bass.

Minuchin, S. (1974). *Families & family therapy.* Cambridge, MA: Harvard University Press.

Mishna, F., Sanders, J. E., Sewell, K. M., & Milne, E. (2021). Teaching note-preparing social workers for the digital future of social work practice. *Journal of Social Work Education, 57*(S1), 19–26.

Missouri Department of Social Services. (n.d.). *Family intervention plan.* Jefferson City, MO: Author.

Mitchell, M. (2020). Reimagining child welfare outcomes: Learning from family group conferencing. *Child and Family Social Work, 25*, 211–220.

Mizrahi, T. (2022). Community organizing principles and practice guidelines. In L. Rapp-McCall, K. Corcoran, & A. R. Roberts (Eds.), *Social workers' desk reference* (4th ed.) (pp. 816–826). New York, NY: Oxford University Press.

Molina, O. (2022). Mutual aid groups. In L. Rapp-McCall, K. Corcoran, & A. R. Roberts (Eds.), *Social workers' desk reference* (4th ed.) (pp. 676–682). New York, NY: Oxford University Press.

Morris, A. (2019). *Voter purge rates remain high, analysis finds.* Brennan Center for Justice. Retrieved from https://www.brennancenter.org/our-work/analysis-opinion/voter-purge-rates-remain-high-analysis-finds

Morrow-Howell, N., Gonzales, E., Matz-Costa, C., & Greenfield, E. A. (2015). *Increasing productive engagement in later life.* Working Paper No. 8, American Academy of Social Work and Social Welfare Grand Challenges for Social Work Initiative. Retrieved from http://aaswsw.org/grand-challenges-initiative/12-challenges/advance-long-and-productive-lives/

Movement Advancement Project. (2022). *Equality maps: Foster and adoption laws*. Retrieved from www.lgbtmap.org/equality-maps/foster_and_adoption_laws

Moya, E. M., Chávez-Baray, S., Adcox, C., & Martínez, O. (2017). *Community-engaged scholarship outside of the social work classroom with the homeless*. London: Sage Research Methods Cases.

Nadan, Y. (2017). Rethinking "cultural competence" in international social work. *International Social Work, 60*(1), 74–83. doi:10.1177/0020872814539986

National Academies of Sciences, Engineering, and Medicine. (2020). *Understanding the well-being of LGBTQI+ populations*. Washington, DC: The National Academies Press. https://doi.org/10.17226/25877

National Association of Cognitive-Behavioral Therapists. (n.d.). *Cognitive behavioral therapy*. Retrieved from www.nacbt.org/whatiscbt-htm/

National Association of Social Workers. (2013a). *NASW guidelines for social worker safety in the workplace*. Washington, DC: NASW.

National Association of Social Workers. (2013b). *Standards for social work case management*. Washington, DC: NASW. Retrieved from www.socialworkers.org/LinkClick.aspx?fileticket=acrzqmEfhlo%3D&portalid=0

National Association of Social Workers. (2015). *Standards and indicators for cultural competence in social work practice*. Washington, DC: NASW. Retrieved from www.socialworkers.org/LinkClick.aspx?fileticket=7dVckZAYUmk%3d&portalid=0

National Association of Social Workers. (2021a). *Code of ethics*. Washington, DC: NASW. Retrieved from www.socialworkers.org/pubs/code/code.asp

National Association of Social Workers. (2021b). *Practice alert: New federal rule provides patients with access to records*. Retrieved from https://naswcanews.org/new-practice-alert-new-federal-rule-provides-patients-with-access-to-records/

National Association of Social Workers. (2021–2023a). *Confidentiality and information utilization: Social work speaks: National Association of Social Workers policy statements 2021–2023* (12th ed.). Washington, DC: NASW Press.

National Association of Social Workers. (2021–2023b). *Cultural and linguistic competence in the social work profession: Social work speaks: National Association of Social Workers policy statements 2021–2023* (12th ed.). Washington, DC: NASW Press.

National Association of Social Workers, Association of Social Work Boards, Council on Social Work Education, & Clinical Social Work Association. (2017). *NASW, ASWB, CSWE, & CSWA standards for technology in social work practice*. Washington, DC: NASW Press. Retrieved from www.socialworkers.org

National Center for Cultural Competence. (n.d.). *Definitions of cultural competence*. Retrieved from www.nccccurricula.info/culturalcompetence.html

National Community Reinvestment Coalition. (n.d.). *GIS map of home purchase loans and minority populations in the St. Louis region*. Washington, DC: NCRC.

Nesmith, A. (2018). Reaching young people through text-based crisis counseling: Process, benefits, and challenges. *Advances in Social Work, 18*(4), 1147–1164.

Netting, F. E., Kettner, P. M., McMurtry, S. L., & Thomas, L. (2017). *Social work macro practice*. Boston, MA: Pearson.

Nichols, M. P., & Davis, S. D. (2020). *The essentials of family therapy* (7th ed.). Boston, MA: Pearson.

O'Connor, M. K., & Netting, F. E. (2009). *Organization practice: A guide to understanding human service organizations*. Hoboken, NJ: Wiley.

Offerman, B., Beltran, M., Rollo, C., & Connors, K. M. (2017). Group work with children impacted by sexual abuse. In G. Greif & C. Knight (Eds.), *Group work with populations at risk* (4th ed.) (pp. 347–372). New York, NY: Oxford University Press.

Ohmer, M. L. (2008). Assessing and developing the evidence base of macro practice: Interventions with a community and neighborhood focus. *Journal of Evidence-Based Social Work, 5*(3/4), 519–547.

Ohmer, M. L. (2022). Consensus organizing: Facilitating community change. In L. Rapp-McCall, K. Corcoran, & A. R. Roberts (Eds.), *Social workers' desk reference* (4th ed.) (pp. 807–815). New York, NY: Oxford University Press.

Ohmer, M. L., & DeMasi, K. (2009). *Consensus organizing: A community development workbook*. Thousand Oaks, CA: Sage Publications.

Ohmer, M. L., & Korr, W. S. (2006). The effectiveness of community practice interventions: A review of the literature. *Research on Social Work Practice, 16*(2), 132–145.

Ohmer, M. L., & Underwood, E. (2022). Community needs assessment. In C. Franklin (Ed.), *Encyclopedia of social work* [E-reader version]. Washington, DC, and New York, NY: National Association of Social Workers and Oxford University Press. https://doi-org.ezp.slu.edu/10.1093/acrefore/9780199975839.013.128

Olcoń, K. (2019). State of the art in U.S. multicultural social work practice: Client expectations and provider challenges. *Journal of Ethnic & Cultural Diversity in Social Work, 28*(1), 7–30. doi:10.1080/15313204.2019.1570893

Oluo, I. (2018). *So you want to talk about race.* New York: Seal Press.

Oregon Legislature. (n.d.). *How to testify before a legislative committee.* Retrieved from www.leg.state.or.us/comm/testify.html/

Ortega, D., & Rodriguez-JenKins, J. (2021). Empowerment practices. In C. Franklin (Ed.), *Encyclopedia of social work* [E-reader version]. Washington, DC, and New York, NY: National Association of Social Workers and Oxford University Press. https://doi-org.ezp.slu.edu/10.1093/acrefore/9780199975839.013.128

Ortega, R. M., & Duntley-Matos, R. (2020). Cultural sensitivity in the context of cultural humility. In C. Franklin (Ed.), *Encyclopedia of social work* [E-reader version]. Washington, DC, and New York, NY: National Association of Social Workers and Oxford University Press. https://doi-org.ezp.slu.edu/10.1093/acrefore/9780199975839.013.128

Ortega, R. M., & Garvin, C. D. (2019). *Social just practice in groups: A social work perspective.* Thousand Oaks, CA: Sage.

Packard, T. (2021). Organizational change in human service organizations. In C. Franklin (Ed.), *Encyclopedia of social work* [E-reader version]. Washington, DC, and New York, NY: National Association of Social Workers and Oxford University Press. doi:10.1093/acrefore/9780199975839.013.272

Papell, C. P., & Rothman, B. (1962). Social group work models: Possession and heritage. *Journal of Education for Social Work, 2*(2), 66–77.

Paris, M., & Martino, S. (2017). Motivational interviewing. In M. J. Dewan, B. N. Steenbarger, & R. P. Greenberg (Eds.), *The arts and sciences of brief psychotherapies: An illustrated guide* (3rd ed.) (pp. 69–95) [E-version]. Arlington, VA: APA Publishing.

Paris, R., & DeVoe, E. R. (2013). Human needs: Family. In C. Franklin (Ed.), *Encyclopedia of social work* [E-reader version]. Washington, DC, and New York, NY: National Association of Social Workers and Oxford University Press. doi:10.1093/acrefore/9780199975839.013.555

Parker, K., Morin, R., & Horowitz, J. M. (2019). Views of demographic changes. *Pew Research Center Reports.* Retrieved from www.pewresearch.org/social-trends/2019/03/21/views-of-demographic-changes-in-america/

Patterson, J., Williams, L., Edwards, T. M., Chamow, L., & Grauf-Grounds, C. (2018). *Essential skills in family therapy* (3rd ed.). New York, NY: Guilford Publications.

Payne, M. (2020). *Modern social work theory* (5th ed.). New York: Oxford University Press.

Payne, M., & Reith-Hall, E. (Eds.). (2019). *The Routledge handbook of social work theory.* London: Routledge.

Pettus-Davis, C., & Epperson, M. W. (2015). *From mass incarceration to smart decarceration.* Grand Challenges for Social Work Initiative Working Paper No. 4. Cleveland, OH: American Academy of Social Work and Social Welfare.

Pierce, B., & Boys, S. (2022). Rural social work practice. In L. Rapp-McCall, K. Corcoran, & A. R. Roberts (Eds.), *Social workers' desk reference* (4th ed.) (pp. 979–985). New York, NY: Oxford University Press.

Pink, S., Ferguson, H., & Kelly, L. (2022). Digital social work: Conceptualising a hybrid anticipatory practice. *Qualitative Social Work, 21*(2), 1–18.

Pittman, M. E., Perryman, E., McDaniel, D., & Tirmazi, T. (2022). The legacy of racism for social work practice today and what to do about it. In L. Rapp-McCall, K. Corcoran, & A. R. Roberts (Eds.), *Social workers' desk reference* (4th ed.) (pp. 889–898). New York, NY: Oxford University Press.

Plitt, D. L., & Shields, J. (2009). Development of the policy advocacy behavior scale: Initial reliability and validity. *Research on Social Work Practice, 19*(1), 83–92.

Poole, D. L., & Iachini, A. (2015). Community partnerships to support youth success in school. In K. Corcoran & A. Roberts (Eds.), *Social workers' desk reference* (2nd ed.) (pp. 928–934). New York, NY: Oxford University Press.

Popple, P. R. (2018). *Social work practice and social welfare policy in the United States: A history.* New York, NY: Oxford University Press.

Potocky, M., & Naseh, M. (2019). Asylum-seekers, refugees, and immigrants in the United States. In C. Franklin (Ed.), *Encyclopedia of social work* [E-reader version]. Washington, DC, and New

York, NY: National Association of Social Workers and Oxford University Press. https://doi-org.ezp.slu.edu/10.1093/acrefore/9780199975839.013.193

Praetorius, R. T. (2021). Assessment for suicide risk. In C. Jordan & C. Franklin (Eds.), *Clinical assessment for social workers: Quantitative and qualitative methods* (5th ed.) (pp. 369–386). New York: Oxford University Press.

Prendergast, S., & MacPhee, D. (2018). Family resilience amid stigma and discrimination: A conceptual model for families headed by same-sex parents. *Family Relations, 67*, 26–40.

Quinn, A., Ji, P., & Nackerud, L. (2019). Predictors of secondary traumatic stress among social workers: Supervision, income, and caseload size. *Journal of Social Work, 19*(4), 504–528.

Ramisch, J. L., & Piland, N. (2020). Systemic approaches for children, adolescents, and families living with neurodevelopmental disorders. In K. S. Wampler (Ed.), *The handbook of systemic family therapy* (Vol. 2) (pp. 369–396). Hoboken, NJ: John Wiley & Sons, Inc.

Rasheed, M. N., & Rasheed, J. M. (2013). Family: Practice interventions. In C. Franklin (Ed.), *Encyclopedia of social work* [E-reader version]. Washington, DC, and New York, NY: National Association of Social Workers and Oxford University Press. doi:10.1093/acrefore/9780199975839.013.546

Reamer, F. (2001). *The social work ethics audit: A risk management tool*. Washington, DC: NASW Press.

Reamer, F. G. (2013a). Ethics and values. In C. Franklin (Ed.), *Encyclopedia of social work* [E-reader version]. Washington, DC, and New York, NY: National Association of Social Workers and Oxford University Press. doi:10.1093/acrefore/9780199975839.013.134

Reamer, F. G. (2013b). Social work malpractice, liability, and risk management. In C. Franklin (Ed.), *Encyclopedia of social work* [E-reader version]. Washington, DC, and New York, NY: National Association of Social Workers and Oxford University Press. doi:10.1093/acrefore/9780199975839.013.977

Reamer, F. G. (2015). *Risk management in social work: Preventing professional malpractice, liability, and disciplinary action*. New York, NY: Columbia University Press.

Reamer, F. G. (2018a). Ethical standards for social workers use of technology: Emerging concerns. *Journal of Social Work Values & Ethics, 15*(2), 71–80.

Reamer, F. G. (2018b). *Social work values and ethics* (5th ed.). New York, NY: Columbia University Press.

Reamer, F. G. (2018c). Ethical issues in integrated health care: Implications for social workers. *Health & Social Work, 43*(2), 118–124.

Reamer, F. G. (2018d). Evolving standards of care in the age of cybertechnology. *Behavioral Sciences & the Law, 36*(2), 257–269.

Reamer, F. G. (2019). Social work education in a digital world: Ethical standards or education and practice. *Social Work Education, 55*(3), 420–432.

Reamer, F. G. (2019b). The ethics of whistle blowing. *Journal of Ethics in Mental Health, 10*, 1–19.

Reamer, F. G. (2020a). Digital technology in social work. In C. Franklin (Ed. in Chief), *Encyclopedia of social work* [E-reader version]. Washington, DC and New York: National Association of Social Workers and Oxford University Press. https://doi-org.ezp.slu.edu/10.1093/acrefore/9780199975839.013.1160

Reamer, F. G. (2020b). Social work malpractice, liability, and risk management. In C. Franklin (Ed. in Chief), *Encyclopedia of social work* [E-reader version]. Washington, DC and New York: National Association of Social Workers and Oxford University Press. https://doi-org.ezp.slu.edu/10.1093/acrefore/9780199975839.013.977

Reamer, F. G. (2020c). Ethics and values. In C. Franklin (Ed.), *Encyclopedia of social work* [E-reader version]. Washington, DC, and New York, NY: National Association of Social Workers and Oxford University Press. doi:10.1093/acrefore/9780199975839.013.134

Richmond, A., Braughton, J., & Borden, L. M. (2018). Training youth program staff on the importance of cultural responsiveness and humility. *Children & Youth Services Review, 93*, 501–507.

Richmond, M. E. (1917). *Social diagnosis*. New York, NY: Russell Sage Foundation.

Ritter, J. A. (2022). *Social work policy practice: Changing our community, nation, and the world* (3rd ed.). Cognella: Academic Publishing.

Robert III, H., Honemann, D. H., & Balch, T. J. (2020). *Robert's rules of order newly revised* (12th ed.). Philadelphia, PA: Da Capo Press.

Roberts, A. R. (2013). Crisis interventions. In C. Franklin (Ed.), *Encyclopedia of social work* [E-reader version]. Washington, DC, and New York, NY: National Association of Social Workers and Oxford University Press. doi:10.1093/acrefore/9780199975839.013.137

Roberts-DeGennaro, M. (2013). Case management. In C. Franklin (Ed.), *Encyclopedia of social work* [E-reader version]. Washington, DC, and New York, NY: National Association of Social Workers and Oxford University Press. doi:10.1093/acrefore/9780199975839.013.42

Robinson, J. W., & Green, G. P. (2011). *Introduction to community development: Theory, practice, and service-learning.* Thousand Oaks, CA: Sage Publications.

Rogers, C. (1957). The necessary and sufficient conditions of therapeutic personality change. *Journal of Consulting Psychology, 22,* 95–103.

Rome, S. H. (2022). *Promote the vote: Positioning social workers for action.* Cham: Springer.

Rooney, R., & Chovanec, M. (2017). Involuntary groups. In C. D. Garvin, L. M. Gutiérrez, & M. J. Galinsky (Eds.), *Handbook of social work with groups* (2nd ed.) (pp. 237–254). New York, NY: The Guilford Press.

Rorai, V., & Perry, T. E. (2020). An innovative telephone outreach program to seniors in Detroit, a city facing dire consequences of Covid-19. *Journal of Gerontological Social Work, 63*(6–7), 713–716.

Rosengren, D. B. (2018). *Building motivational interviewing skills: A practitioner workbook* (2nd ed.). New York: The Guilford Press.

Rosenzweig, S. (1936). Some implicit common factors in diverse methods of psychotherapy. *American Journal of Orthopsychiatry, 6,* 412–415. doi:10.1111/j.1939-0025.1936.tb05248.x

Rothman, J. C. (2008). Multi modes of community intervention. In J. Rothman, J. Erlich, & J. Tropman (Eds.), *Strategies of community intervention* (7th ed.) (pp. 141–170). Peosta, IA: Eddie Bowers Publishing.

Rothman, J. C. (2015). Developing therapeutic contracts with clients. In K. Corcoran & A. R. Roberts (Eds.), *Social workers' desk reference* (3rd ed.) (pp. 553–559). New York, NY: Oxford University Press.

Rubin, H. J., & Rubin, I. S. (2008). *Community organizing and development.* Boston, MA: Pearson Allyn & Bacon.

Saez, E., & Zucman, G. (2016). Wealth inequality in the United States since 1913: Evidence from capitalized income tax data. *The Quarterly Journal of Economics, 131*(2), 519–578.

Safe Connections. (n.d.). *Group assessment screening.* St. Louis, MO: Author.

Sage, M., & Singer, J. B. (2022). Technology and social work practice. In L. Rapp-McCall, K. Corcoran, & A. R. Roberts (Eds.), *Social workers' desk reference* (4th ed.) (pp. 45–52). New York, NY: Oxford University Press.

Sager, J. S., & Weil, M. (2013). Larger-scale social planning: Planning for services and communities. In M. Weil (Ed.), *The handbook of community practice* (pp. 299–325). Thousand Oaks, CA: Sage Publications.

Sakamoto, I., & Couto, S. (2017). Group work with immigrants and refugees. In C. D. Garvin, L. M. Gutiérrez, & M. J. Galinsky (Eds.), *Handbook of social work with groups* (2nd ed.) (pp. 360–383). New York, NY: The Guilford Press.

Salazar, C. F., & Leddick, G. R. (2018). Distinguishing group member roles. In B. T. Erford (Ed.), *Group work: Processes and applications* (2nd ed.) (pp. 112–128). New York, NY: Routledge.

Saleebey, D. (2013). *The strengths perspective in social work practice* (6th ed.). Boston, MA: Allyn & Bacon.

Salisbury, A., Smith, D., & Campbell, C. (2022). Motivational interviewing. In K. W. Bolton, J. C. Hall, & P. Lehmann (Eds.), *Theoretical perspectives for direct social work practice* (4th ed.) (pp. 241–242). New York, NY: Springer Publishing.

Sanchez, B. (2020). Cultural humility: A tool for social workers when working with diverse populations. *Reflections: Narratives of Professional Helping, 26*(2). Retrieved from https://reflectionsnarrativesofprofessionalhelping.org/index.php/Reflections/article/view/1747

Schein, E. H., & Schein, P. A. (2016). *Organizational culture and leadership* (5th ed.). Hoboken, NJ: Wiley.

Schneider, R. L., & Lester, L. (2001). *Social work advocacy.* Belmont, CA: Brooks/Cole.

Schwartz, W. (1961). The social worker in the group. In *The social welfare forum* (pp. 146–177).

Segal, E. A. (2020). Social empathy. In C. Franklin (Ed.), *Encyclopedia of social work* [E-reader version]. Washington, DC, and New York, NY: National Association of Social Workers and Oxford University Press. https://doi-org.ezp.slu.edu/10.1093/acrefore/9780199975839.013.128

Sellon, A. M., & Lassman, H. (2022). Anti-oppressive theory and practice. In K. W. Bolton, J. C. Hall, & P. Lehmann (Eds.), *Theoretical perspectives for direct social work practice* (4th ed.) (pp. 299–312). New York, NY: Springer Publishing.

Senger, P., & Wiest, C. (2022). Professionalism in the field of social work. In L. Rapp-McCall, K. Corcoran, & A. R. Roberts (Eds.), *Social workers' desk reference* (4th ed.) (pp. 12–20). New York, NY: Oxford University Press.

Shapiro, V. B., Lippold, M. A., Bender, K., & Jenson, J. M. (2022). Ensuring health development in youth. In R. P. Barth, J. T. Messing, T. R. Shanks, & J. H. Williams (Eds.), *Grand challenges for social work and society: Milestones achieved and opportunities ahead* (2nd ed.) (pp. 19–46). New York: Oxford University Press.

Shebib, B. (2019). *Choices: Interviewing and counseling skills for Canadians* (7th ed.). New York, NY: Pearson Canada.

Sherraden, M. (1990). Stakeholding: Notes on a theory of welfare based on assets. *Social Service Review, 64*(4), 580–601.

Sherraden, M. (1991). *Assets and the poor*. Armonk, NY: ME Sharpe.

Sherraden, M. S., Huang, J., Jacobson Frey, J., Birkenmaier, J. M., Callahan, C., Clancy, M., & Sherraden, M. (2015). *Financial capability and asset building for all*. American Academy of Social Work and Social Welfare. Retrieved from http://aaswsw.org/wp-content/uploads/2016/01/WP13-with-cover.pdf

Sherraden, M. S., Johnson, L., Clancy, M. M., Beverly, S. G., Sherraden, S. S., Schreiner, M., Elliot III, W., . . . Han, C.-K. (2019). Asset building toward inclusive policy, Updated on 28 March 2018. In C. Franklin (Ed.), *Encyclopedia of social work*. Alexandria, VA: National Association of Social Workers and Oxford University Press. doi:10.1093/acrefore/9780199975839.013.25

Sherraden, M. S., Johnson, L., Clancy, M. M., Beverly, S. G., Sherraden, S. S., Schreiner, M., Elliot III, W., . . . Han, C.-K. (2021). Asset building toward inclusive policy. In C. Franklin (Ed.), *Encyclopedia of social work*. Alexandria, VA: National Association of Social Workers and Oxford University Press. doi:10.1093/acrefore/9780199975839.013.25

Shier, M. L. (2012). Work-related factors that impact social work practitioners' subjective well-being: Well-being in the workplace. *Journal of Social Work, 12*(6), 402–421.

Shier, M. L., Graham, J. R., & Nicholas, D. (2018). Interprofessional interactions, workplace violence, and occupational health outcomes among social workers. *Journal of Social Work, 18*(5), 525–547.

Shrider, E. A., Kollar, M., Chen, F., & Semega, J. (2021). *Income and poverty in the United States: 2020*. U.S. Census Bureau, Current Population Reports, P60–273, U.S. Government Publishing Office, Washington, DC.

Shulman, L. (2020). Supervision. In C. Franklin (Ed.), *Encyclopedia of social work* [E-reader version]. Washington, DC, and New York, NY: National Association of Social Workers and Oxford University Press. https://doi-org.ezp.slu.edu/10.1093/acrefore/9780199975839.013.385

Shulman, L. (2022). Developing successful relationships: The therapeutic and group alliances. In L. Rapp-McCall, K. Corcoran, & A. R. Roberts (Eds.), *Social workers' desk reference* (4th ed.) (pp. 520–626). New York, NY: Oxford University Press.

Sidell, N. L. (2015). *Social work documentation*. Washington, DC: NASW Press.

Simmons, C. A., Shapiro, V. B., Accomazzo, S., & Manthey, T. J. (2022). Strengths-based social work: A meta-theory to guide social work research and practice. In K. W. Bolton, J. C. Hall, & P. Lehmann (Eds.), *Theoretical perspectives for direct social work practice* (4th ed.) (pp. 99–115). New York, NY: Springer Publishing.

Simon, B. (1990). Re-thinking empowerment. *Journal of Progressive Human Services, 1*(1), 29.

Simonson, J. (2019). The place of "the people" in criminal procedure. *Columbia Law Review, 199*(1), 249–307.

Singh, R., Killian, K. D., Bhurgun, D., & Tseng, S. (2020). Clinical work with intercultural couples. In K. S. Wampler (Ed.), *The handbook of systemic family therapy* (Vol. 3) (pp. 155–183). Hoboken, NJ: John Wiley & Sons, Inc.

Singer, J. B., Sage, M., Berzin, S. C., & Coulton, C. J. (2022). Harnessing technology for social good. In R. P. Barth, J. T. Messing, T. R. Shanks, & J. H. Williams (Eds.), *Grand challenges for social work and society: Milestones achieved and opportunities ahead* (2nd ed.) (pp. 230–256). New York: Oxford University Press.

Slade, E. P., McCarthy, J. F., Valenstein, M., Visnic, S., & Dixon, L. B. (2013). Cost savings from assertive community treatment services in an era of declining psychiatric inpatient use. *Health Services Research, 48*(1), 195–217.

Slayter, E. M. (2021a). On being anti-racist as a white social worker. *The New Social Worker*. Retrieved from www.socialworker.com/feature-articles/practice/being-anti-racist-white-social-worker/

Slayter, E. M. (2021b). Want to be evidence-based? Here's a literature review hack that will help you get there. *The New Social Worker*. Retrieved from www.socialworker.com/feature-articles/practice/want-to-be-evidence-based-literature-review-hack/

Smith, M. (2022). Narrative therapy. In L. Rapp-McCall, K. Corcoran, & A. R. Roberts (Eds.), *Social workers' desk reference* (4th ed.) (pp. 249–256). New York, NY: Oxford University Press.

Soifer, S. D., McNeely, J. B., Costa, C. L., & Pickering-Bernheim, N. (2014). *Community development in social work*. New York: Columbia University Press.

Sormanti, M. (2012). Writing for and about clinical practice. In W. Green & B. L. Simon (Eds.), *The Columbia guide to social work writing* (pp. 114–132). New York, NY: Columbia University Press.

Specht, H., & Courtney, M. E. (1994). *Unfaithful angels: How social work has abandoned its mission*. New York, NY: The Free Press.

St. Anthony's Medical Center. (2010). *Family intervention and planning*. St. Louis, MO: Author.

Staples, L. H. (2017). Social action groups. In C. D. Garvin, L. M. Gutiérrez, & M. J. Galinsky (Eds.), *Handbook of social work with groups* (2nd ed.) (pp. 473–490). New York, NY: The Guilford Press.

Steenbarger, B. N. (2018). Solution-focused brief therapy: Building strengths, achieving goals. In M. J. Dewan, B. N. Steenbarger, & R. P. Greenberg (Eds.), *The arts and sciences of brief psychotherapies: An illustrated guide* (3rd ed.) (pp. 199–218) [E-version]. Arlington, VA: APA Publishing.

Steinberg, D. M. (2019). *Teaching group work content in social work education*. Alexandria, VA: CSWE Press.

Stewart, C. (2022). Spiritual assessment. In L. Rapp-McCall, K. Corcoran, & A. R. Roberts (Eds.), *Social workers' desk reference* (4th ed.) (pp. 358–363). New York, NY: Oxford University Press.

Stokes, M. N., Charity-Parker, B. M., & Hope, E. C. (2021). What does it mean to be Black and White? A meta-ethnographic review of racial socialization in multiracial families. *Journal of Family Theory & Review, 13*, 181–201.

Straus, S. E., Glasziou, P., Richardson, W. S., & Haynes, R. B. (2019). *Evidence-based medicine: How to practice and teach* (5th ed.). Philadelphia, PA: Elsevier.

Streeter, C. L. (2013). Community: Overview. In C. Franklin (Ed.), *Encyclopedia of social work* [E-reader version]. Washington, DC, and New York, NY: National Association of Social Workers and Oxford University Press. doi:10.1093/acrefore/9780199975839.013.531

Strom-Gottfried, K. J. (2008). *The ethics of practice with minors*. Chicago, IL: Lyceum Books, Inc.

Strom-Gottfried, K. J. (2015). *Straight talk about professional ethics* (2nd ed.). Chicago, IL: Lyceum Books.

Substance Abuse and Mental Health Services Administration (SAMHSA). (2017). *Setting goals and developing specific, measurable, achievable, relevant, and time-bound objectives*. Retrieved from www.samhsa.gov/sites/default/files/nc-smart-goals-fact-sheet.pdf

Suburban Stats, Inc. (2019). *Population information and statistics from every city, state, and county in the US*. Retrieved from suburbanstats.org

Suddeath, E. G., Kerwin, A. K., & Dugger, S. M. (2017). Narrative family therapy: Practice techniques for more effective work with couples and families. *Journal of Mental Health Counseling, 39*(2), 116–133.

Sue, D. W., Rasheed, M. N., & Rasheed, J. M. (2016). *Multicultural social work practice: A competency-based approach to diversity and social justice*. Hoboken, NJ: Wiley.

Sue, D. W., Sue, D., Neville, H. A., & Smith, L. (2019). *Counseling the culturally diverse* (8th ed.). Hoboken, NJ: Wiley.

Supreme Court of the United States. (2015). *Obergefel et al. v. Hodges, director, Ohio Department of Health, et al.* Retrieved from www.supremecourt.gov/opinions/14pdf/14-556_3204.pdf+&cd=2&hl=en&ct=clnk&gl=us

Taibbi, R. (2018). Family therapy. In N. Thompson & P. Stepney (Eds.), *Social work theory and methods: The essentials* (pp. 180–190). New York, NY: Routledge.

Tariq, S. H., Tumosa, N., Chibnall, J. T., Perry, M. H., & Morley, J. E. (2006). Comparison of the Saint Louis University mental status examination and the mini-mental state examination for detecting dementia and mild neurocognitive disorder: A pilot study. *American Journal of Geriatric Psychiatry, 14*, 900–910.

Teasley, M. L., McCarter, S., Woo, B., Conner, L. R., Spencer, M. S., & Green, T. (2021). *Eliminate racism*. Working Paper No. 26, American

Academy of Social Work and Social Welfare Grand Challenges for Social Work Initiative. Retrieved from https://grandchallengesforsocialwork.org/wp-content/uploads/2021/05/Eliminate-Racism-Concept-Paper.pdf

Teater, B. (2020). *An introduction to applying social work theories and methods* (3rd ed.). New York, NY: McGraw-Hill Education Open University Press.

Tebb, S. C. (1995). An aid to empowerment: A caregiver well-being scale. *Health and Social Work, 20*(2), 87–92.

Tebb, S. C., Berg-Weger, M., & Rubio, D. M. (2013). The caregiver well-being scale: Developing a shortform rapid assessment instrument. *Health and Social Work, 38*(4), 222–230. doi:10.1093/hsw/hlt019

Tebbe, D. (2019). *Chief executive transitions: How to hire and support a nonprofit CEO* (2nd ed.). Washington, DC: BoardSource.

Tervalon, M., & Murray-Garcia, J. (1998). Cultural humility versus cultural competence: A critical distinction in defining physician training outcomes in multicultural education. *Journal of Health Care for the Poor and Underserved, 9*(2), 117–125.

Thyer, B. A. (2008). Evidence-based macro practice: Addressing the challenges and opportunities. *Journal of Evidence-Based Social Work, 3/4*, 453–472.

Thyer, B. A. (2021). Linking assessment to outcome evaluation using single-system and group research designs. In C. Jordan & C. Franklin (Eds.), *Clinical assessment for social workers: Quantitative and qualitative methods* (5th ed.) (pp. 389–409). New York: Oxford University Press.

Tolbert, P. S., & Hall, R. J. (2016). *Organizations: Structures, processes, and outcomes*. New York, NY: Routledge.

Toseland, R. W. (2017). Group dynamics. In C. D. Garvin, L. M. Gutiérrez, & M. J. Galinsky (Eds.), *Handbook of social work with groups* (2nd ed.) (pp. 9–27). New York, NY: The Guilford Press.

Toseland, R. W., & Horton, H. (2013). Group work. In C. Franklin (Ed.), *Encyclopedia of social work* [E-reader version]. Washington, DC, and New York, NY: National Association of Social Workers and Oxford University Press. doi:10.1093/acrefore/9780199975839.013.168

Toseland, R. W., & Rivas, R. (2017). *Introduction to group work practice* (8th ed.). Boston, MA: Pearson.

Tropman, J. E. (2017). An ecological/systems/seven C's perspective on group practice. In C. D. Garvin, L. M. Gutiérrez, & M. J. Galinsky (Eds.), *Handbook of social work with groups* (2nd ed.) (pp. 28–42). New York, NY: The Guilford Press.

Twikirize, J. M. (2019). *Social work in Africa: Indigenous and innovative approaches*. Kampala, Uganda: Fountain Publishers.

United Nations High Commissioner for Refugees. (2020). *Global trends report: Forced displacement in 2019*.

University of Kansas Work Group for Community Health and Development. (2022). *Community toolbox*. Retrieved from https://ctb.ku.edu/en

U.S. Census Bureau. (2021a). *American community survey*. Retrieved from www.census.gov/programs-surveys/acs/

U.S. Census Bureau. (2021b). *Family group: 2021*. Table FG10. Current Population Survey, 2021 Annual Social and Economic Supplement, Table FG10, U.S. Census Bureau, Washington, DC. Retrieved from www.census.gov/data/tables/2021/demo/families/cps-2021.html

U.S. Commission on Civil Rights. (2018). *An assessment of minority voting rights access in the US: 2018 Statutory enforcement report*. Retrieved from https://www.usccr.gov/pubs/2018/Minority_Voting_Access_2018.pdf

Van Hook, M. P. (2019). *Social work practice with families: A resiliency-based approach* (3rd ed.). New York, NY: Oxford University Press.

Van Soest, D. (2013). Oppression. In C. Franklin (Ed.), *Encyclopedia of social work* [E-reader version]. Washington, DC, and New York, NY: National Association of Social Workers and Oxford University Press. doi:10.1093/acrefore/9780199975839.013.271

Van Treuren, R. R. (1993). Self-perception in family systems: A diagrammatic technique. In C. Meyer (Ed.), *Assessment in social work practice* (p. 119). New York, NY: Columbia University Press.

Varghese, R. (2020). Intergroup dialogue: Frequencies of social justice. *Social Work with Groups, 43*(1–2), 109–113.

Vinter, R. D. (1974). Program activities: An analysis of their effects on participant behavior. In P. Glassner, R. Sarri, & R. Vinter (Eds.), *Individual change through small groups* (pp. 233–243). New York, NY: The Free Press.

Voshel, E. H., & Wesala, A. (2015). Social media & social work ethics: Determining best practices in an ambiguous reality. *Journal of Social Work Values & Ethics, 12(1),* 67–76.

Wagaman, M. A., Geiger, J. M., Shockley, C., & Segal, E. A. (2015). The role of empathy in burnout, compassion satisfaction, and secondary traumatic stress among social workers. *Social Work, 60(3),* 201–209.

Walker, L., & Taylor, D. (2021). *Same-sex couple households: 2019.* Current Population Reports, ACSBR-005, U.S. Census Bureau, Washington, DC. Retrieved from www.census.gov/content/dam/Census/library/publications/2021/acs/acsbr-005.pdf

Walsh, F. (2015). *Walsh family resilience questionnaire.* Copyright 2015 from Froma Walsh.

Walsh, F. (2016a). A family developmental framework: Challenges and resilience across the life cycle. In T. L. Sexton & J. Lebow (Eds.), *Handbook of family therapy* (pp. 30–48). New York, NY: Routledge.

Walsh, F. (2016b). Applying a family resilience framework in training, practice, and research: Mastering the art of the possible. *Family Process, 55(4),* 616–632.

Walsh, F. (2016c). *Strengthening family resilience* (3rd ed.). New York, NY: The Guilford Press.

Walsh, F. (2022). A family resilience framework. In L. Rapp-McCall, K. Corcoran, & A. R. Roberts (Eds.), *Social workers' desk reference* (4th ed.) (pp. 257–262). New York, NY: Oxford University Press.

Walter-McCabe, H. A. (2020). Coronavirus pandemic calls for an immediate social work response. *Social Work in Public Health, 35(3),* 69–72.

Walters, K. L., Spencer, M. S., Smukler, M., Allen, H. L., Andrews, C., Browne, T., Maramaldi, P., Wheeler, D. P., Zebrack, B., & Uehara, E. (2016). *Health equity: Eradicating health inequalities for future generations.* Working Paper No. 19, American Academy of Social Work and Social Welfare Grand Challenges for Social Work Initiative. Retrieved from http://aaswsw.org/wp-content/uploads/2016/01/WP19-with-cover2.pdf

Warde, B. (2012). The cultural genogram: Enhancing the cultural competency of social work students. *Social Work Education, 31(5),* 570–586.

Wehmeyer, M. L. (2020). The importance of self-determination to the quality of life of people with intellectual disability: A perspective. *International Journal of Environmental Research and Public Health, 17(19),* 7121. https://doi.org/10.3390/ijerph17197121

Wehrmann, K. C. (2022). Emerging fields of practice in American social work. In L. Rapp-McCall, K. Corcoran, & A. R. Roberts (Eds.), *Social workers' desk reference* (4th ed.) (pp. 100–107). New York, NY: Oxford University Press.

Weil, M., & Gamble, D. N. (2009). Community practice model for the twenty-first century. In Roberts (Ed.), *Social workers' desk reference* (pp. 882–892). New York, NY: Oxford University Press.

Weil, M., Gamble, D. N., & Ohmer, M. L. (2013). Evolution, models, and the changing context of community practice. In M. Weil (Ed.), *The handbook of community practice* (pp. 167–193). Thousand Oaks, CA: Sage Publications.

Weisman, D., & Zornado, J. L. (2013). *Professional writing for social work practice.* New York, NY: Springer Publishing.

Weisman, D., & Zornado, J. L. (2018). *Professional writing for social work practice* (2nd ed.). New York, NY: Springer Publishing.

Wheeler, W., & Thomas, A. M. (2011). Engaging youth in community development. In J. W. Robinson Jr. & G. P. Green (Eds.), *Introduction to community development: Theory, practice and service-learning* (pp. 209–227). Los Angeles, CA: Sage Publications.

Wilson, M. (2020). Social justice brief: Implications of Coronavirus (Covid-19) for America's vulnerable and marginalized populations. *National Association of Social Workers.* Retrieved from www.socialworkers.org/LinkClick.aspx?fileticket=U7tEKlRldOU%3D&portalid=0

Winship, K., & Lee, S. T. (2012). Using evidence-based accreditation standards to promote continuous quality improvement: The experience of San Mateo County Human Services Agency. *Journal of Evidence-Based Social Work, 9(1–2),* 68–86.

Wolkenstein, A. S. (2021). One of the secrets of success in social work is to self-assess. *The New Social Worker.* Retrieved from www.socialworker.com/feature-articles/practice/one-secret-of-success-social-work-self-assessment/

Wood, J. (2018). The United States divorce rate is dropping, thanks to millennials. *World Economic Forum.* Retrieved from www.weforum.org/agenda/2018/10/divorce-united-states-dropping-because-millennials/

Woodly, D. R. (2021). *Reckoning: Black lives matter and the democratic necessity of social movements*

(Transgressing boundaries: Studies in black politics and black communities). New York: NY: Oxford University Press.

World population review: 2022 world population by county: Retrieved from https://worldpopulationreview.com/

Wroe, L., Larkin, R., & Maglajlic, R. A. (2019). *Social work with refugees, asylum seekers, and migrants: Theory and skills for practice*. Philadelphia, PA: Jessica Kingsley Publishers.

Xu, Y., Pace, S., McCarthy, L. P., Harrison, T. M., & Wang, Y. (2022). Interventions to improve outcomes of grandchildren raised by grandparents: A systematic review. *Research on Social Work Practice*, 1–16. doi:10.1177/10497315221079352

Yeager, K. R., & Roberts, A. R. (2015). *Crisis intervention handbook: Assessment, treatment, and research* (4th ed.) (pp. 183–213). New York, NY: Oxford University Press.

Young, N. A. E. (2021). *Childhood disability in the United States: 2019*. ACSBR-006, American Community Survey Briefs, U.S. Census Bureau, Washington, DC.

Zastrow, C. H., & Hessenauer, S. L. (2019). *Social work with groups* (10th ed.). Boston, MA: Cengage.

Zhang, A., & Franklin, C. (2021). Quantitative clinical assessment methods. In C. Jordan & C. Franklin (Eds.), *Clinical assessment for social workers: Quantitative and qualitative methods* (5th ed.) (pp. 57–88). New York: Oxford University Press.

Zhang, A., & Franklin, C. (2022). Solution-focused therapy. In L. Rapp-McCall, K. Corcoran, & A. R. Roberts (Eds.), *Social workers' desk reference* (4th ed.) (pp. 211–217). New York, NY: Oxford University Press.

Zhang, A., Franklin, C., & Hopson, L. (2021). Family systems. In C. Jordan & C. Franklin (Eds.), *Clinical assessment for social workers: Quantitative and qualitative methods* (5th ed) (pp. 265–306). New York: Oxford University Press.

Zweban, A., & West, B. S. (2020). Intervening around addictive behaviors. In A. L. Begun & M. M. Murray (Eds.), *Routledge handbook of social work and addictive behaviors* (pp. 297–320). [E-version]. New York: Routledge Publishing.

Index

acceptance 22
acting in context 181–182
activities: organizational policy advocacy 567–568; to promote social change 513; structure of 555
administrative data 482
administrative structure 554
administrative tasks 145–147
advocacy: case advocacy 205; cause advocacy 205; client advocate role 204–206; legislative advocacy 206; power and 206
affective processes 11
agencies: critical considerations about assessment and planning 144–148; and group work 394; and involuntary clients 157
anger: skills for working with clients who display anger 157
agreement for work 225
allies 584
anti-racism 5, 63–64, 172
anti-racist/anti-oppressive practice xxv–xxvi, xxviii, 7, 156–157, 244; behaviors 120–121; and cultural humility 191–192; in culturally-responsive assessment 117–119
appropriateness, group 392
assessment 16, 100–103; assessing resources 143; Brief Assessment of Family Functioning Scale (BAFFS) 353; clinical considerations 144–148; with communities 478–483; contemporary trends 283–297, 400–401; critical considerations 404–408; developing a shared vision of 130; dignity 558; diversity and culture in 115–122; documenting 303; external 561–562; with families 283–297, 303, 353–354; generalist practice skills guidelines for 293–297; with groups 386–387, 400–401, 404–408; with individuals 100–103, 117–119, 123–133, 142–148; internal 552–557; mapping 295–297; narrative theory in 283–287, 386; nonprofit 565–566; oppressive practice in 117–119; with organizations 552–557, 561–562, 565–566, 569–571; questions for discovering strengths 125–133; skills for 123–124, 142–143, 283–297; solution-focused approach 289–290, 387; theoretical perspectives 104–107, 385–387

assets: asset-based community development 524–525; building 494, 497, 505; mapping 494
attachment theory 106
authority: charismatic 547; rational 548; traditional 547
available resources 143

bargaining 595
behaviors: anti-racist and anti-oppressive 120; interpreting client behavior 195
bisexual couples and families *see* lesbian, gay, bisexual, transgender, and queer couples and families
blended families 277–278
blending models 515–516
Boston Model 425–426
boundaries 261–262
Brief Assessment of Family Functioning Scale (BAFFS) 353–354
brokering: broker role 200–201; building and maintaining networks for 200; functions and context 200; making the match in 201
building relationships: critical considerations 90–93; *see also* relationship skills
bureaucracies 545
bylaws 554

campaign strategy 590
capacity building 592
Caregiver Well-Being Scale 350
case advocacy 205
case management: case manager role 197–198; common components of 197; purposes and practice of 198
case summary 240–244
cause advocacy 205
census data 482
change 22; plans for maintenance of 226; strategies for 596–598; *see also* organizational change
charismatic 547
classic theories 105–106
client advocate role 204–206

clients 11–15; client groups 376–377; *see also* families, practice with; groups, practice with; individuals, practice with; organizations, practice with; relationship skills
clinical writing 239
cognitive behavioral-focused interventions 189–190
cognitive processes 11
cognitive theory 106
collaborative strategy 590
collaborator role 207–208
common ground 201
communication skills 76–78, 437; *see also* relationship skills
communities 11–15; assessing 478–483; engaging 477; functions of 471; types of 469–470; understanding 472–476
communities, practice with 465; activities to promote social change 513; assessing communities 478–483; community forums 487–489; consensus 521–528; contemporary trends 500–502; context 466–468; critical considerations 503–504; economic inequality 535; effective meetings 519; engaging communities 477; evaluation 534–535; evidence-based 529–530; financial capability and asset building for all 505; focus groups 485–486; follow-up 535; functions of communities 471; key informant interviews 484–485; needs assessment survey questions 489–497; planning 498–499; providing testimony 514–516; Robert's Rules of Order 520; skills for 517–518; termination 531–533, 535; theoretical and traditional models 509–512; types of community 469–471; understanding communities 472–476
community capacity development model 511, 515, 516
community development: asset-based 524–525; programs 521–523; skills 518; social and economic 517–518
community forums 486–489
community members, talking with 76–77; *see also* relationship skills
community needs assessment 479–480; sources of data for 481–483
community organizing 526–527; skills 528
community practice 13–15; *see also* communities, practice with
community social and economic development 517–518
competencies 5–11
competent practice 169, 309; phases of 16–18
composition, group 392
comprehensive community-based analysis 491–493
conferencing: family group conferencing 333–334
confidentiality 91

conflict: within communities 474–475; organizational change strategy 591
confrontation 136–137, 194
consensus 521–528
constructionist approaches 291–292
contemporary theoretical perspectives 107
content, group 394
context: acting in context 181–182; community as a context for social work practice 466–468
contracting 133; sample contract 134–141
counselor role 199
countertransference *see* transference and countertransference
COVID-19 pandemic xxv, 12–15, 25, 31, 39; and communities, practice with 466, 480, 500–502; and families, practice with 344, 354; and groups, practice with 373; and individuals, practice with 103, 124, 167–169, 172, 212, 221; and relationship skills 75, 93
crisis intervention 157–159
critical considerations 30–31; with communities 503–504, 535; with families 301–302, 355; with groups 402–409, 458; with individuals 144–148, 216–221, 229–230, 245–246; with organizations 572, 608; relationship skills 90–92; values and ethics 61–63
critical thinking 45–46
cultural competence xxv, 6, 117–119, 122, 367–368, 374
cultural connections 364–365
cultural considerations 78
cultural heritage 123; families of multiple cultural heritages 272–273
cultural humility xxiv–xxv, 7, 10–11; and groups, practice with 365–367, 431; and individuals, practice with 117–118, 191–192, 229; and organizations, practice with 559–560; and relationship skills 78–79, 90
culturally-responsive practice xxiv–xxv, 7, 120, 273, 367, 419, 583; assessment 117–119
culture: group orientation as a cultural dimension 36–368; implications in assessment 115–122; organizational 555–556

data: administrative 482; census 482; mapped 494–496; sources 481–483, 607; survey 489–497
decarceration 573
decision-making: consensus for 521–528
developmental models 424–426
dialogue: using mapping skills to enhance 139–141
dignity assessment 558
disabilities, persons with: families that include 274–276

diversity 418–419, 559; implications in assessment 115–122
diversity, equity, inclusion, and belonging (DEIB) xxv, xxviii, 5, 115–116, 171, 418–419
documentation 148; families 302–303, 338–341; group engagement and assessment 409; recommendations for 149–152
dreams *see* goals and dreams
dual relationships 56–58
dynamics, group 435

ecomaps 141
economic development, community 517–518
economic inequality 535
economic justice 63
ecosystems perspective 27; on community 473
education 593; educator role 203–204
eligibility, group 392
empathy 72–73
empirical processes 232–235
empowerment: in communities 476; and different strategies 213; endings with 344; and group endings 444; and group intervention 420–421; practice 209–211, 213; and roles 212
endings 222–230; *see also* termination
engagement 16, 69; challenges 468; with communities 468, 477; constructionist and social justice approaches 291–292; contemporary trends and skills 283–297, 388–401; critical considerations 90–93, 402–409; with families 283–297; generalist practice skills guidelines for 293–297; with groups 385–409; narrative theory in 283–287; with organizations 551, 569–571; pregroup planning 389–396; solution-focused family work 288–291; theoretical approaches 385–387; *see also* relationship skills
environmental justice 63
environment-focused processes and skills 191–196, 291
Educational Policy and Accreditation Standards (EPAS) xxvi–xxvii, 5, 21, 24, 569
equal opportunity 609
equity 93, 528; *see also* diversity, equity, inclusion, and belonging
errors, communication 86–87
ethical principles screen 54–60
ethics 36–37; brief history 38; create social responses to a changing environment 63; critical considerations 61–63; elements of the ethical principles screen 54–60; identifying and resolving ethical dilemmas 53–54; and the law 47–53; and organizational change 596–598; professional code of 39–47; sustaining ethical practice in the face of challenges 171

ethnic heritage: families of multiple ethnic heritages 272–273
evaluation 16, 231–235, 245–246; communities 534, 535; critical considerations on 245–246, 355, 458, 535; group facilitator self-evaluation 453–457; group work 443–452; ongoing 93; with organizations 604–607; of practice with families 347; strengths- and resiliency-based family evaluation measures 348–349; roles in 607; supporting clients' strengths in 222
evidence/evidence-based practice: with communities 479, 529–530; with individuals 112–114, 232–235
excessive questioning 87
exercises: communities, practice with 506, 537; families, practice with 306, 358; groups, practice with 413, 460; individuals, practice with 175, 249; organizations, practice with 575, 610; relationship skills 95; understanding social work practice 34; values and ethics 65
experts 23–24
external assessment 561–562

families, practice with 12, 20–21, 253–254, 311; blended families 277–278; Brief Assessment of Family Functioning Scale (BAFFS) 353–354; caregiver well-being scale 350; constructionist and social justice approaches to 291–292; contemporary context for 266–282; contemporary trends and skills for engagement and assessment with families 283–297; critical considerations 301–302, 355; documenting 303, 338–341; endings 342–347; evaluation 347–348, 355; familiar perspectives 255–257; families that include persons with disabilities 274–276; families of multiple racial, ethnic, and cultural heritages 272–273; family group conferencing 333–334; follow-up 355; gender-based violence 356; generalist practice skills guidelines for family engagement and assessment 293–297; grandparents rearing grandchildren 267–268; healthy development for youth 304–305; historical antecedents 258–263; immigrant and refugee families 279–281; lesbian, gay, bisexual, transgender, and queer couples and families 269–270; mapping 298–301, 337; motivational interviewing 335–336; narrative theory 283–287, 317–319; perspectival questions 332; reframing 332; single-parent families 271; solution-focused 288–291, 320–325; Strengths-Based Practices Inventory (SBPI) 352; strengths and empowerment perspectives 315–316; systems theory for 264–265; termination 355; theoretical approaches 312–325; trends and skills for intervening with 326–341; Walsh Family Resilience Questionnaire (WFRQ) 351

feasible solutions for organizational change 585–589
feelings, reflection of 80
financial capability 505
focus groups 485–486
follow-up: communities 532–533, 535; critical considerations 355, 535; with organizations 604; supporting clients' strengths in 222
formal resources 143
forms of groups 373–377
forums *see* community forums
functional structures 547
functions of communities 471
functions of groups 373–377
funders 561

Gantt chart 601
gay couples and families *see* lesbian, gay, bisexual, transgender, and queer couples and families
gender-based violence 356
generalist practice 467; and community practice 467, 528; organizational engagement, assessment, and planning in 569; skills guidelines 293–294; and systems theory 264–265
generality of change 602
genograms 139–140
genuineness 74
global connections 25, 121–122, 364–365
goals and dreams 131–133; aligning goals with possibilities 138; goal attainment scaling 234–238; organizations with service goals 543; social goals 410
governance, structures of 545–547
grandparents rearing grandchildren 267–268
group actions 596
groups, practice with 12, 20–21, 362, 417; assessment and planning 400–401; contemporary trends and skills 388–401, 427–441; critical considerations 402–409, 458; dimensions of 372–382; end homelessness 411; ending phases 443–452; engagement 397–399; facilitator self-evaluation 453–457; harness technology for social good 458; middle phase 427–441; intervention 427–439, 443; pregroup planning 389–396; pros and cons 383–384; roles 441–442; social goals and task group notes template 410; social justice, diversity, and human rights 418–419; source of community 363–371; task group minutes template 411; theoretical approaches 385–387, 420–426
guest status 549

health gap 93
healthy development: for youth 304–305
helping alliance 75; power imbalances within 88–89
helping relationships: common factors in 72–75
heritage: families of multiple racial, ethnic, and cultural heritages 272–273
history 554
homelessness 411
honest responding 136–138
host settings 549–550
human rights 418–419
human services 558
humility 117–119

identifying ethical dilemmas 53–54
immigrant families 279–281
implementation of organizational change: challenges to 602–603; implementation skills 592; structure 600
individuals, practice with 12, 20–21, 99, 179, 209–213; assessment and planning 100–103; case summaries 240–244; clinical writing 239; critical considerations 144–148, 216–221; cultural heritage 123; documentation 149–152; eliminating racism 172; evaluations 231–235, 245–246; goal attainment scaling (GAS) 236–238; implications of diversity and culture in assessment 115–122; implications of theoretical perspectives 104–107; interventions that support client strengths 180–196; involuntary clients 153–171; motivational interviewing 214; sample contract 134–141; skills for assessing resources 142–143; skills for assessment and planning 123–124; social work roles in social work practice 196–208; strengths-based supportive questions 108–114, 125–133; termination and endings 222–230; where does the client want to go 104
informal resources 143
informants *see* key informants
information 193, 607
integrated social work practice 21
intergenerational patterns 265
intergroup dialogue (IGD) 430
internal assessment 553–557
internal power relations 547–548
interpreting client behavior 195
interprofessional teams 550
intersectionality 117–119
intervention 16, 179, 209–213, 311; case summaries 240–244; clinical writing 239; communities 509–512, 517–518; critical considerations 216–221, 355, 458, 535; documenting 303, 338–341; evaluations 231–235, 245–246; examples 429–430; family group conferencing 333–334; generalist approach 528; goal attainment scaling 236–238; group work

427–441, 443; interventions that support client strengths 180–196; mapping 196, 337; motivational interviewing 214, 335–336; with organizations 579–581; perspectival questions 332; reframing 332; roles and phases of group interventions 378–382, 441; skills and strategies 431–440, 517–518, 592–593; social work roles in social work practice 196–208; termination and endings 222–230; theoretical approaches 312–325, 420–426; trends and skills for 326–341

interviewing 79–85; and community needs assessment 482–483; family interview 298–300; guide to 484–485; motivational 214–215, 335–336; *see also* relationship skills

involuntary clients 151, 153–160; challenges in working with 152; social worker perspective 166–171

irrelevant questions 87

jargon 86
justice 609; *see also* social justice

key informants 482–485
knowledge 6; critical considerations on 245–246

language 557
larger environment, work in 20–21
Latinx: and communities, practice with 507, 530; and families, practice with 256, 360; and groups, practice with 367–369, 415; and individuals, practice with 119, 180; and organizations, practice with 570
law: and ethics 47–52; and internal assessment 553; organizations sanctioned by 542
leadership skills 435–436
leading questions 86
legal basis of internal assessment 553
legislative advocacy 206
lesbian, gay, bisexual, transgender, and queer couples and families 269–270
listening: avoiding communication errors 86–87; common factors in helping relationships 72–75; communication skills 76–78; interviewing abilities 79–85; listening to and engaging with clients and community members 69–89; minimizing power imbalances within the helping alliance 88–89
local practice 25
logic model 606

main points: communities, practice with 506, 536; families, practice with 306, 357; groups, practice with 412, 459; individuals, practice with 174, 248; organizations, practice with 574, 610; relationship skills 94; understanding social work practice 33; values and ethics 64

management style 554
mandated clients 151
mapping 139–141; family work 295–301, 337; as an intervention strategy 196; needs assessment 494–496
marginalized communities 17, 30, 47; and communities, practice with 471–475, 495, 500–504, 523–524, 527; and families, practice with 256–257, 292, 314; and groups, practice with 376, 400, 419, 430, 437; and individuals, practice with 193, 239; and organizations, practice with 559–560, 563, 571, 575
mass media 595
mediator role 201–202
meetings 519
middle phase of group work 427–441; examples 429–430; group member roles 441; intervention 427–440; skills and strategies 431–440
mission statement 553
motivational interviewing 214–215, 335–336; groups 429

narrative theory and narrative-focused work 29, 108–109, 125–127, 183; and endings 345; in family engagement and assessment 283–287; and family interventions 317–319; groups 386, 422, 430, 445
need: client need 391; needs assessment 489–497
negotiation 595
nonprofit organizations: assessment 565–566; relationships with political figures 564; *see also* organizations, practice with
nonvoluntary clients *see* involuntary clients
norms, family 263

observation 481
organizing, community 526–527; skills 528
organizational change: creating a group 584; developing feasible solutions for 585–589; framework for 582–598; gathering allies 584; implementing 599–603; origins of 583; perspectives on power in 581; selecting strategies 590–591; self-learning approaches to 580; and the systems model 580
organizational culture 555–556
organizational life 608
organizational practice 13–15
organizational supports 603
organizations, practice with 539, 578–581; assessment 552–557, 565–566, 569–571; critical considerations 572, 608; dignity assessment and human services guide 558–562; engagement 551, 569–571; equal opportunity and justice 609; evaluation 604–607; follow-up 604; framework for organizational change 582–593;

governance, structures of 545–546; in host settings 549–550; implementing organizational change 599–603; internal power relations 547–548; intersections among dimensions of organizations 548; nonprofit organizational assessment 565–566; nonprofit organizational partnerships 562–564; persuasion skills 594–598; planning 569–571; policy advocacy activities 567–568; and power 581; promote smart decarceration 573; purpose of the organization 541–544; self-learning approaches 580; skills 569–571; social systems, organizations as 540; systems model 580; termination 604; understanding organizations 540–550

painful events 166
paraphrasing 82
parenthood 270
paternalism 60
personnel policies and procedures 560
perspectival questions 332
persuasion 593; skills 594–598
phases of competent practice 16–18
physical surroundings 557
planning 16; with communities 498–499, 510; critical considerations 144–148, 404–408; documenting 303; endings and termination 223–228; with families 295–297, 301, 303; with groups 389–396, 400–401, 404–408; with individuals 100–103, 123–124, 130, 132, 144–148; mapping 295–297, 301; with organizations 569–571; planning/policy model 510, 515–516; skills for, 123–124, 389–396, 400–401
policy: organizational policy advocacy activities 567–568; personnel 560; planning/policy model 510, 515–516; practice 13–15
political communities 471
political figures 564
possibilities, aligning goals with 138
postmodern views of evaluation 237
power: and advocacy 206; within communities 474–475; imbalances 88–89; in organizations 547–548, 581; shared 23–24
practice: clients and communities in 11–15; integrated 21; phases of competent practice 16–18; *see also* communities, practice with; families, practice with; groups, practice with; individuals, practice with; organizations, practice with
practicing social work 2–3
pregroup contact 395
pregroup planning 389–396
privacy 92
problem-solving skills 438–440
procedures 557

professional codes of ethics 39–47
professionalism 219
professional tensions 19–25
programs, structure of 555
project teams 546
psychoanalytic theory 105
public relations 557
purpose: of the organization 541–544; pregroup planning 392; of social work 2

qualitative processes 238
quantitative processes 232–235
queer couples and families *see* lesbian, gay, bisexual, transgender, and queer couples and families
questions: asking clarifying questions 83; assessment questions for discovering strengths 125–133; balancing open-ended and closed-ended questions 84–85; excessive 87; irrelevant 87; leading 86; needs assessment 489–497; strengths-based supportive questions 108–114

racial heritage: families of multiple racial heritages 272–273
racism 172; *see also* anti-racism; anti-racist/anti-oppressive practice
rational authority 548
reflective processes 238
refocusing 194
reframing 332
refugee families 279–281
relationship quality 244
relationship skills 68; avoiding communication errors 86–87; close the health gap 93; common factors in helping relationships 72–75; communication skills 76–78; critical considerations 90–92; interviewing abilities 79–85; listening to and engaging with clients and community members 69–89; minimizing power imbalances within the helping alliance 88–89
resilience/resiliency-based approach: in communities 476; family evaluation measures 348–349
resistance to change 602
resolving ethical dilemmas 53–54
resources 560; serving clients and communities with limited resources 561; skills for assessing 142–143
responsibility 59
risk management 61–62
Robert's Rules of Order 520
roles 4, 196; broker 200–201; case manager 197–198; client advocate 204–206; collaborator 207–208; counselor 199; educator 203–204; and empowerment 212; in evaluation 607; group interventions 432–434; group member 441–442; mediator 201–202

self, therapeutic use of 218
self-care 168–170, 220; families 302
self-determination 60
self-evaluation 453–457
self-knowledge 7
self-learning approaches 580
service goals, organizations with 543
service network 562
services, structure of 555
service statistics 481
shared power 23–24
shared vision of assessment and planning 130
shortcomings 225
silence 81
single-parent families 271
single-subject design 233
skills 10; for assessment 123–124, 142–143, 293–297, 400–401, 569–571; communication 437; with communities 517–518, 526–528, 531–534; community development 518; community organizing 528; conferencing 333–334; developing client skills 203; documentation 338–341; for endings 446–450; for engagement 293–297, 397–399, 569–571; environment-focused 191–196; for evaluation 534; with families 293–297, 326–341; for follow-up 532–533; with groups 388–401, 431–441, 443, 446–450; implementation 592; with individuals 123–124, 139–143, 157, 191–196, 203, 215; leadership 435–436; mapping 139–141, 337; for motivational interviewing 215, 335–336; perspectival questions 332; persuasion 594–598; for planning 123–124, 400–401, 569–571; pregroup planning 389–396; problem-solving 438–440; reframing 332; for termination 531–533; for working with clients who display anger 157; *see also* relationship skills
social action or goals groups 376
social advocacy model 512, 516
social and economic development, community 517–518
social change 22; activities to promote 513
social communities 470–471
social context 394
social control 22
social goals 410
social good 458
social justice 27, 63, 418–419, 559; approaches to family social work 291–292; and intergroup dialogue (IGD) 430
social media 595
social movements, organizations arising from 544
social responses to a changing environment 63
social systems, organizations as 540
social work 1; clients and communities 11–15; competencies 5–11; critical considerations 30–31;
perspectives for 29; phases of competent practice 16–18; practicing of 2–4; professional tensions in 19–25; purpose of 2; roles 4; theoretical perspectives for 26–29; *see also* communities, practice with; families, practice with; groups, practice with; individuals, practice with; organizations, practice with; relationship skills
social worker: critical considerations about assessment and planning 144–148; as a whole person 166–171; *see also* roles
society, responsibility to 59
solution-focused approach 29, 110–111, 128–129, 288–290; endings in 345; family work 288–291, 320–325, 345; groups 387, 423, 445; interventions 184–188
spatial communities 469
spiritual aspects of the client 121
staff member resistance 602
strengths/strengths-based perspective 28, 107; assessment questions 125–133; in communities 476; evaluation 348–349; examples of questions 108–114; family interventions 315–316; group endings 444; group intervention 420–421; interventions that support client strengths 180–196; skills for assessment and planning 124; Strengths-Based Practices Inventory (SBPI) 352; in termination, evaluation, and follow-up 222, 344
structure: administrative structure 554; of change proposals 587–589; of evaluation 606; family structure 265; functional structures 547; of governance 545–547; group structure 393; implementation structure 600; of programs, services, and activities 555
studies 481
subsystems 261–262
successes, processing 225
suicide 160–165
summarizing 83
supports, organizational 603
survey data 489–497
systems/systems theory: on community 472; family as 260–263; groups 385; implications for generalist practice with 264–265; and organizational change 580

talking with clients and community members 76–77
task groups 375; minutes template 411; notes template 410
technology 220–221; and social good 458
telehealth 124, 221
termination 16, 222–230, 311; communities 531–533, 535; critical considerations 355, 458, 535; with family constellations 342–347; group work 443–452; with organizations 604

testimony 514–516
theoretical perspectives 26–29; communities 509–512; compatibility with 243; engagement and assessment with groups 385–387; groups 420–426; implications of 104–107; power and conflict 474–475; *see also* systems/systems theory
timing: termination 223–224
traditional authority 547
transference and countertransference 219
transgender couples and families *see* lesbian, gay, bisexual, transgender, and queer couples and families
trends, contemporary: assessment and planning 400–401; with communities 500–502; communication skills 437; conferencing 333–334; constructionist and social justice approaches 291–292; documentation 338–341; engagement 397–399; with families 283–297, 326–341; generalist practice skills guidelines 293–297; group dynamics 435; group member roles 441; with groups 388–401, 427–441; intergroup dialogue (IGD) and social justice 430; leadership skills 435–436; mapping 337; motivational interviewing 335–336, 429; narrative theory 283–287, 430; perspectival questions 332; pregroup planning 389–396; problem-solving skills 438–440; reframing 332; social worker roles 432–434; solution-focused 288–291
triggers 167
types of groups 373–377

unavailable resources 143
unconditioned positive regard 74
unexpected events 217

values 8–9, 36–37; value conflicts 53
violence 156; gender-based 356; workplace violence in social work practice 156

Walsh Family Resilience Questionnaire (WFRQ) 351
warmth 72
well-being: Caregiver Well-Being Scale 350; responsibility to 59
workplace violence 156
writing *see* clinical writing

youth 304–305